LEARNSMART ADVANTAGE WORKS

A	B	C	D	
30.5%	33.5%	22.6%	8.7%	4.7%

A	B	C	D	
19.3%	38.6%	28.0%	9.6%	4.5%

Without LearnSmart

More C students earn B's

*Study: 690 students / 6 institutions

Over 20%
more students
pass the class
with LearnSmart

*A&P Research Study

LEARNSMART™ Pass Rate - 70%

Without LearnSmart Pass Rate - 57%

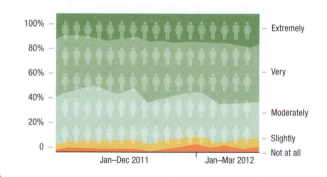

100% — Extremely
80%
60% — Very
40%
20% — Moderately
0 — Slightly
    — Not at all

Jan–Dec 2011   Jan–Mar 2012

More than 60%
of all students agreed
LearnSmart was a
very or extremely
helpful learning tool

*Based on 750,000 student survey responses

> *AVAILABLE*
ON-THE-GO

http://bit.ly/LS4Apple

http://bit.ly/LS4Droid

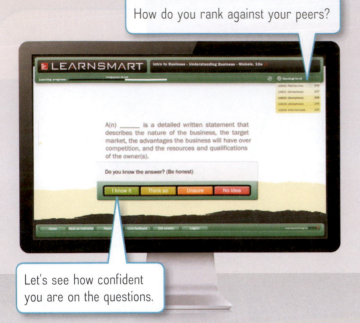

How do you rank against your peers?

Let's see how confident you are on the questions.

What you know (green) and what you still need to review (yellow), based on your answer

COMPARE AND CHOOSE WHAT'S RIGHT FOR YOU

	BOOK	LEARNSMART	ASSIGNMENTS	
connect plus+	✓	✓	✓	LearnSmart, assignments, and SmartBook—all in one digital product for maximum savings!
connect plus+ Looseleaf	✓	✓	✓	Pop the pages into your own binder or carry just the pages you need.
connect plus+ Bound Book	✓	✓	✓	The #1 Student Choice!
SMARTBOOK™ Access Code	✓	✓		The first and only book that adapts to you!
LEARNSMART™ ADVANTAGE Access Code		✓		The smartest way to get from a B to an A.
CourseSmart eBook	✓			Save some green and some tr
create™	✓	✓	✓	Check with your instructor abo custom option for your course

> Buy directly from the source at www.ShopMcGraw-Hill.com.

Essentials of
Contemporary
Management

Sixth Edition

Gareth R. Jones

Jennifer M. George
Rice University

Mc
Graw
Hill
Education

ESSENTIALS OF CONTEMPORARY MANAGEMENT, SIXTH EDITION

Published by McGraw-Hill Education, 2 Penn Plaza, New York, NY 10121. Copyright © 2015 by McGraw-Hill Education. All rights reserved. Printed in the United States of America. Previous editions © 2013, 2011, and 2009. No part of this publication may be reproduced or distributed in any form or by any means, or stored in a database or retrieval system, without the prior written consent of McGraw-Hill Education, including, but not limited to, in any network or other electronic storage or transmission, or broadcast for distance learning.

Some ancillaries, including electronic and print components, may not be available to customers outside the United States.

This book is printed on acid-free paper.

2 3 4 5 6 7 8 9 0 DOW/DOW 1 0 9 8 7 6 5 4

ISBN   978-0-07-786253-4
MHID   0-07-786253-8

Senior Vice President, Products & Markets: *Kurt L. Strand*
Vice President, Content Production & Technology Services: *Kimberly Meriwether David*
Managing Director: *Paul Ducham*
Executive Brand Manager: *Michael Ablassmeir*
Executive Director of Development: *Ann Torbert*
Senior Development Editor: *Trina Hauger*
Marketing Manager : *Elizabeth Trepkowski*
Director, Content Production: *Terri Schiesl*
Content Project Manager: *Harvey Yep*
Senior Buyer: *Michael R. McCormick*
Design: *Matt Diamond*
Cover Image: *Veer Images*
Lead Content Licensing Specialist: *Keri Johnson*
Typeface: *10.5/12 Baskerville*
Compositor: *Laserwords Private Limited*
Printer: *R. R. Donnelley*

All credits appearing on page or at the end of the book are considered to be an extension of the copyright page.

Library of Congress Cataloging-in-Publication Data

Jones, Gareth R.
    Essentials of contemporary management/Gareth R. Jones, Jennifer M. George.—Sixth edition.
        pages cm
    Includes index.
    ISBN 978-0-07-786253-4 (alk. paper)—ISBN 0-07-786253-8 (alk. paper)
    1. Management. I. George, Jennifer M. II. Title.
HD31.J5974 2015
658–dc23

                                                                                    2013042410

The Internet addresses listed in the text were accurate at the time of publication. The inclusion of a website does not indicate an endorsement by the authors or McGraw-Hill Education, and McGraw-Hill Education does not guarantee the accuracy of the information presented at these sites.

Brief Contents

Contents

Management in Action

Management in Action

Contents

Contents

Management in Action

Management in Action

Contents

Contents

Management in Action

Management in Action

Contents

Contents

Management in Action

Management in Action

Preface

In this sixth edition of *Essentials of Contemporary Management,* we continue to focus on providing the most up-to-date account of the changes taking place in the world of management and management practices while maintaining our emphasis on making our text relevant and interesting to students. And we know from feedback from instructors and students that the text does engage them. Our increased focus on the challenges and opportunities facing businesses large and small and integrated timely examples bring management issues to life for students.

The number and complexity of the strategic, organizational, and human resource challenges facing managers and all employees have continued to increase throughout the 2000s. In most companies, managers at all levels are playing catch-up as they work toward meeting these challenges by implementing new and improved management techniques and practices. Today, relatively small differences in performance between companies, such as in the speed at which they bring new products or services to market or in the ways they motivate their employees to find ways to reduce costs or improve performance, can combine to give a company a significant competitive advantage. Managers and companies that utilize proven management techniques and practices in their decision making and actions increase their effectiveness over time. Companies and managers that are slower to implement new management techniques and practices find themselves at a growing competitive disadvantage that makes it even more difficult to catch up. Thus, in many industries there is a widening gap between the most successful companies whose performance reaches new heights and their weaker competitors, because their managers have made better decisions about how to use company resources in the most efficient and effective ways.

The challenges facing managers continue to mount as changes in the global environment, such as increasing global outsourcing and rising commodity prices, impact organizations large and small. Moreover, the revolution in information technology (IT) has transformed how managers make decisions across all levels of a company's hierarchy and across all its functions and global divisions. This sixth edition addresses these emerging challenges. For example, we extend our treatment of global outsourcing, examine its pros and cons, and examine the new management problems that emerge when millions of functional jobs in IT, customer service, and manufacturing are performed in countries overseas. Similarly, increasing globalization means that managers must respond to major differences in the legal rules and regulations and ethical values and norms that prevail in countries around the globe.

Other major challenges we continue to expand on in this edition include the impact of the steadily increasing diversity of the workforce on companies and how this increasing diversity makes it imperative for managers to understand how and why people differ so that they can effectively manage and reap the performance benefits of diversity. Similarly, across all functions and levels, managers and employees must continually seek ways to "work smarter" and increase performance. Using new IT to improve all aspects of an organization's operations to enhance efficiency and customer responsiveness is a vital part of this process. So too is the continuing need to innovate and improve the quality of goods and services, and the ways they are produced, to allow an organization to compete effectively. We significantly revised this edition of *Essentials of Contemporary Management* to address these challenges to managers and their organizations.

Major Content Changes

Once again, encouraged by the increasing number of instructors and students who use each new edition of our book, and based on the reactions and suggestions of both users and reviewers, we revised and updated our book in many ways. However, the organization and sequence of chapters remain the same in this new edition. Instructors tell us that they like the way the chapters flow, and the way they build up a picture of management part by part, to provide an excellent learning experience and a comprehensive coverage of management. The way we link and integrate topics, such as our inclusion of entrepreneurship in Chapter 5, "Decision Making, Learning, Creativity, and Entrepreneurship," allows students to make connections among these important topics. As examples of the many changes we made, this new edition expands the coverage of ways to encourage high motivation, creativity, and innovation in organizations and the importance of managers' and organizations' taking steps to protect the natural environment and promote sustainability. Our three-chapter sequence on strategy, structure, and control systems to improve competitive advantage is also updated in many ways. And, in this new edition, throughout the chapters we offer increased coverage of new approaches to leadership and the design of reward systems, new uses of advanced IT at all levels in the organization and across all functions to improve job design and employee motivation, and expanded coverage of the pros and cons associated with global outsourcing.

CHAPTER-BY-CHAPTER CHANGES We made the following specific changes to this edition.

Chapter 1

- New "Management Snapshot" on Tim Cook as CEO of Apple.
- New "Manager as a Person" box on Joe Coulombe of Trader Joe's.
- New "Managing Globally" box on outsourcing and insourcing.
- New 2013 "*Bloomberg Businessweek* Case in the News."

Chapter 2

- New "Management Snapshot" on "Kevin Plank's Determination at Under Armour."

- New "Ethics in Action" on "Protecting the Environment and Jobs at Subaru of Indiana Automotive."
- New discussion of how sometimes emotions can be triggers for change in organizations.
- New "Management Insight" on "Emotions as Triggers for Changes in Organizations."
- Updated example of IBM.
- New 2013 "*The Wall Street Journal* Case in the News."

Chapter 3

- New "Management Snapshot" on how "Whole Foods Market Practices What It Preaches."
- Updated section on age.
- Updated and revised section on gender.
- Updated and revised section on race and ethnicity.
- New "Ethics in Action" on how "Disabled Employees Make Valuable Contributions."
- Updated and revised section on socioeconomic background.
- Updated and revised section on sexual orientation.
- Updated "Focus on Diversity" box on "Preventing Discrimination Based on Sexual Orientation."
- Updated discussion of women's earnings in comparison to men's earnings.
- Updated sexual harassment section.
- New 2013 "*The Wall Street Journal* Case in the News."

Chapter 4

- New "Management Snapshot" on Nokia and managing the global environment.
- New "Managing Globally" box on Microsoft and Nokia.
- New "Manager as a Person" box on Kazuo Hirai as CEO of Sony.
- New 2013 "*Bloomberg Businessweek* Case in the News."

Chapter 5

- Updated "Management Snapshot" on "Decision Making and Learning at Garage Tek."
- Updated examples.
- New "Manager as a Person" on "Curbing Overconfidence."
- New discussion of the position of chief sustainability officer.
- New "Ethics in Action" box on "Helping to Ensure Decisions Contribute to Sustainability."
- New 2013 "*Fast Company*" Case in the News."

Chapter 6

- New "Management Insight" box on Krispy Kreme.
- New "Management Insight" box on VF Corp and Timberland.
- New 2013 "*Bloomberg Businessweek* Case in the News."

Chapter 7

- New "Management Snapshot" on Avon.
- New "Management Insight" box on Dick's Drive-In Restaurants.
- New 2013 "*Bloomberg Businessweek* Case in the News."

Chapter 8

- New "Management Snapshot" on Alan Mulally and Ford.
- New "Management Insight" box on eBay.
- New "Manager as a Person" box on UPS and Walmart.
- New "Management Insight" box on Google.
- New 2013 "*Bloomberg Businessweek* Case in the News."

Chapter 9

- New "Management Snapshot" on "High Motivation at Enterprise Rent-A-Car."
- New "Managing Globally" box on "Seeking Intrinsic Motivation in Far Flung Places."

- New "Management Insight" on how "Training Spurs Learning at Stella & Dot."
- New discussion of how managers can recognize top performers when they are unable to use merit pay due to tough economic times.
- Revised discussion of how advances in IT dramatically simplify the administration of piece-rate pay.
- New 2013 "*The New York Times* Case in the News."

Chapter 10

- New "Management Snapshot" on how "Lorenzo Effectively Leads Frog Design."
- New examples of women CEOs.
- Updated "Ethics in Action" box on "Servant Leadership at Zingerman's."
- New discussion of how managers with expert power need to recognize that they are not always right.
- New "Manager as a Person" box on "Gregory Maffei and Expert Power."
- Updated statistics on the underrepresentation of women in corporate officer and top-earner positions.
- New 2013 "*The Wall Street Journal* Case in the News."

Chapter 11

- New "Management Snapshot" on "Using Teams to Innovate at Boeing."
- New "Information Technology Byte" on how "Pizza Teams Innovate at Amazon."
- New "Management Insight" box on "Self-Managed Teams at Louis Vuitton and Nucor Corporation."
- New 2013 "*The Wall Street Journal* Case in the News."

Chapter 12

- Updated "Management Snapshot" on "Effectively Managing Human Resources at Zappos."
- New "Managing Globally" box on "Recent Trends in Outsourcing."

- New "Information Technology Byte" on "Fog Creek Software's Approach to Recruiting."
- Updated discussion of the use of background checks by employers.
- Updated discussion of concerns about excessive CEO pay and pay comparisons between CEOs and average workers.
- Updated statistics on union membership in the U.S.
- New 2013 "*The Wall Street Journal* Case in the News."

Chapter 13

- New "Management Snapshot" on Salesforce. com.
- New "Management Insight" box on cloud computing, bricks-and-mortar, and mobile container data center storage solutions.
- New 2013 "*Bloomberg Businessweek* Case in the News."

Chapter 14

- New "Management Snapshot" on Zynga Inc.
- New 2013 "*Bloomberg Businessweek* Case in the News."

UPDATED RESEARCH CONCEPTS Just as we included pertinent new research concepts in each chapter, so we were careful to eliminate outdated or marginal management concepts. As usual, our goal is to streamline our presentation and keep the focus on recent changes that have the most impact on managers and organizations. In today's world of video downloading, streaming media, and text messaging and tweeting, less is often more—especially when students are often burdened by time pressures stemming from the need to work long hours at paying jobs. New chapter opening "Management Snapshot" cases, the many boxed illustrations inside each chapter, and new (2013) "Case in the News" closing cases reinforce updated content critically but succinctly.

We feel confident that the changes to the sixth edition of *Essentials of Contemporary Management* will stimulate and challenge students to think about their future in the world of organizations.

Emphasis on Applied Management

We went to great lengths to bring the manager back into the subject matter of management. That is, we wrote our chapters from the perspective of current or future managers to illustrate, in a hands-on way, the problems and opportunities they face and how they can effectively meet them. For example, in Chapter 3 we provide an integrated treatment of ethics and diversity that clearly explains their significance to practicing managers. In Chapter 6, we provide an integrated treatment of planning, strategy, and competitive advantage, highlighting the crucial choices managers face as they go about performing the planning role. Throughout the text, we emphasize important issues managers face and how management theory, research, and practice can help them and their organizations be effective.

The last two chapters cover the topics of managing information systems, technology, and operations management, topics that tend to be difficult to teach to new management students in an interesting and novel way. Our chapters provide a student-friendly, behavioral approach to understanding the management processes entailed in information systems and operations management. As our reviewers noted, while most books' treatment of these issues is dry and quantitative, ours comes alive with its focus on how managers can manage the people and processes necessary to give an organization a competitive advantage.

Flexible Organization

We designed the grouping of chapters to allow instructors to teach the chapter material in the order that best suits their needs. Instructors are not tied to the planning, organizing, leading, controlling framework, even though our presentation remains consistent with this approach.

Acknowledgments

Finding a way to integrate and present the rapidly growing literature on contemporary management and make it interesting and meaningful for students is not an easy task. In writing and revising the several editions of *Essentials of Contemporary Management,* we have been fortunate to have had the assistance of several people who have contributed greatly to the book's final form. First, we are grateful to Michael Ablassmeir, our executive brand manager, for his support and commitment to our project, and for always finding ways to provide the resources that we needed to continually improve and refine our book. Second, we are grateful to Trina Hauger, our senior development editor, for so ably coordinating the book's progress, and to her and Elizabeth Trepkowski, our marketing manager, for providing us with concise and timely feedback and information from professors and reviewers that have allowed us to shape the book to the needs of its intended market. We also thank Matt Diamond for executing an awe-inspiring design and Harvey Yep for coordinating the production process. We are also grateful to the many colleagues and reviewers who provided us with useful and detailed feedback, perceptive comments, and valuable suggestions for improving the manuscript.

Producing any competitive work is a challenge. Producing a truly market-driven textbook requires tremendous effort beyond simply obtaining reviews on a draft manuscript. Our goal behind the development of *Essentials of Contemporary Management* has been clear-cut: to be the most customer-driven essentials of management text and supplement package ever published! The favorable reception that our book has received from its users suggests that our thorough product development plan did lead to a book that has met the expectations of both faculty and students. For the new edition, we have continued to add new reviewers to the over 200 faculty who originally took part in developmental activities ranging from regional focus groups to manuscript reviews and surveys. Consequently, we're confident that the changes we have made to our book and its excellent support package will even more closely meet your expectations and needs.

Our thanks to these faculty who have contributed greatly to *Essentials of Contemporary Management:*

Garry Adams, *Auburn University*
M. Ruhul Amin, *Bloomsburg University of Pennsylvania*
Fred Anderson, *Indiana University of Pennsylvania*
Jacquelyn Appeldorn, *Dutchess Community College*
Barry Armandi, *SUNY–Old Westbury*
Dave Arnott, *Dallas Baptist University*
Debra Arvanites, *Villanova University*
Douglas E. Ashby, *Lewis & Clark Community College*
Joe Atallah, *Devry University*
Kenneth E. Aupperle, *The University of Akron*
Barry S. Axe, *Florida Atlantic University*
Andrea D. Bailey, *Moraine Valley Community College*
Jeff Bailey, *University of Idaho*
Robert M. Ballinger, *Siena College*
Moshe Banai, *Bernard M. Baruch College*
Frank Barber, *Cuyahoga Community College*
Reuel Barksdale, *Columbus State Community College*
Sandy Jeanquart Barone, *Murray State University*
Lorraine P. Bassette, *Prince George's Community College*
Gene Baten, *Central Connecticut State University*
Myra Jo Bates, *Bellevue University*
Josephine Bazan, *Holyoke Community College*
Hrach Bedrosian, *New York University*
Omar Belkhodja, *Virginia State University*
James Bell, *Texas State University–San Marcos*
Ellen A. Benowitz, *Mercer County Community College*
Stephen Betts, *William Paterson University*
Jack C. Blanton, *University of Kentucky*
David E. Blevins, *University of Arkansas at Little Rock*
Mary Jo Boehms, *Jackson State Community College*
Karen Boroff, *Seton Hall University*
Jennifer Bowers, *Florida State University*
Barbara Boyington, *Brookdale Community College*
Dan Bragg, *Bowling Green State University*
Charles Braun, *Marshall University*

Dennis Brode, *Sinclair Community College*

Gil Brookins, *Siena College*

Murray Brunton, *Central Ohio Technical College*

Patricia M. Buhler, *Goldey-Beacom College*

Judith G. Bulin, *Monroe Community College*

David Cadden, *Quinnipiac College*

Thomas Campbell, *University of Texas–Austin*

Thomas Carey, *Western Michigan University*

Barbara Carlin, *University of Houston*

Daniel P. Chamberlin, *Regents University–CRB*

Larry Chasteen, *Stephen F. Austin State University*

Raul Chavez, *Eastern Mennonite University*

Nicolette De Ville Christensen, *Guilford College*

Anthony A. Cioffi, *Lorain County Community College*

Sharon F. Clark, *Lebanon Valley College*

Sharon Clinebell, *University of Northern Colorado*

Dianne Coleman, *Wichita State University*

Elizabeth Cooper, *University of Rhode Island*

Anne Cowden, *California State University–Sacramento*

Thomas D. Craven, *York College of Pennsylvania*

Kent Curran, *University of North Carolina*

Arthur L. Darrow, *Bowling Green State University*

Tom Deckelman, *Walsh College*

D. Anthony DeStadio, *Pittsburgh Technical Institute*

Ron DiBattista, *Bryant College*

Thomas Duening, *University of Houston*

Charles P. Duffy, *Iona College*

Steve Dunphy, *The University of Akron*

Subhash Durlabhji, *Northwestern State University*

Robert A. Eberle, *Iona College*

Karen Eboch, *Bowling Green State University*

Robert R. Edwards, *Arkansas Tech University*

Susan Eisner, *Ramapo College of New Jersey*

William Eldridge, *Kean College*

Pat Ellsberg, *Lower Columbia College*

Stan Elsea, *Kansas State University*

Scott Elston, *Iowa State University*

Judson Faurer, *Metro State College of Denver*

Dale Finn, *University of New Haven*

Charles Flaherty, *University of Minnesota*

Alisa Fleming, *University of Phoenix*

Lucinda Fleming, *Orange County Community College*

Robert Flemming, *Delta State University*

Jeanie M. Forray, *Eastern Connecticut State University*

Marilyn L. Fox, *Minnesota State University*

Mankato Ellen Frank, *Southern Connecticut State University*

Joseph A. Gemma, *Providence College*

Neal Gersony, *University of New Haven*

Donna H. Giertz, *Parkland College*

Leo Giglio, *Dowling College*

David Glew, *Texas A&M University*

Carol R. Graham, *Western Kentucky University*

Matthew Gross, *Moraine Valley Community College*

John Hall, *University of Florida*

Eric L. Hansen, *California State University–Long Beach*

Justin U. Harris, *Strayer College*

Allison Harrison, *Mississippi State University*

Sandra Hartman, *University of New Orleans*

Brad D. Hays, *North Central State College*

Gary Hensel, *McHenry Community College*

Robert A. Herring III, *Winston-Salem State University*

Eileen Bartels Hewitt, *University of Scranton*

Stephen R. Hiatt, *Catawba College*

Tammy Bunn Hiller, *Bucknell University*

Adrienne Hinds, *Northern Virginia Community College*

Anne Kelly Hoel, *University of Wisconsin–Stout*

Eileen Hogan, *Kutztown University*

Jerry Horgesheiner, *Southern Utah State*

Gordon K. Huddleston, *South Carolina State University*

John Hughes, *Texas Tech University*

Larry W. Hughes, *University of Nebraska at Kearney*

Tammy Hunt, *University of North Carolina–Wilmington*

Gary S. Insch, *West Virginia University*

Charleen Jaeb, *Cuyahoga Community College*

Velma Jesser, *Lane Community College*

Richard E. Johe, *Salem College*

Gwendolyn Jones, *The University of Akron*

Kathy Jones, *University of North Dakota*

Marybeth Kardatzke, *North Harris Montgomery Community College District*

Jim Katzenstein, *California State University–Dominguez Hills*

Jehan G. Kavoosi, *Clarion University of Pennsylvania*

Robert J. Keating, *University of North Carolina at Wilmington*

Frank Khoury, *Berkeley College*

Peggi Koenecke, *California State University–Sacramento*

Donald Kopka, *Towson University*

Dennis Lee Kovach, *Community College of Allegheny County–North Campus*

Mark Kunze, *Virginia State University*

Ken Lehmenn, *Forsyth Technical Community College*

Lianlian Lin, *California State Polytechnic University*

Grand Lindstrom, *University of Wyoming*

John Lipinski, *Robert Morris University*

Mary Lou Lockerby, *College of DuPage*

Esther Long, *University of Florida*

E. Geoffrey Love, *University of Illinois*

George S. Lowry, *Randolph–Macon College*

George E. Macdonald Jr., *Laredo Community College*

Bryan Malcolm, *University of Wisconsin*

Z. A. Malik, *Governors State University*

Mary J. Mallott, *George Washington University*

Christine Marchese, *Nassau Community College*

Jennifer Martin, *York College of Pennsylvania*

Lisa McCormick, *Community College of Allegheny County*

Reuben McDaniel, *University of Texas*

Robert L. McKeage, *The University of Scranton*

John A. Miller, *Bucknell University*

Richard R. J. Morin, *James Madison University*

Don Moseley, *University of South Alabama–Mobile*

Behnam Nakhai, *Millersville University of Pennsylvania*

Robert D. Nale, *Coastal Carolina University*

Daniel F. Nehring, *Morehead State University*

Thomas C. Neil, *Clark Atlanta University*

Brian Niehoff, *Kansas State University*

Judy Nixon, *University of Tennessee*

Cliff Olson, *Southern Adventists University*

Karen Overton, *HCC–Northeast College*

Ralph W. Parrish, *University of Central Oklahoma*

Dane Partridge, *University of Southern Indiana*

Sheila J. Pechinski, *University of Maine*

Marc Pendel, *Ball State University*

Fred Pierce, *Northwood University*

Mary Pisnar, *Baldwin Wallace College*

Laynie Pizzolatto, *Nicholls State University*

Eleanor Polster, *Florida International University*

Paul Preston, *University of Texas–San Antonio*

Samuel Rabinowitz, *Rutgers University–Camden*

Gerald Ramsey, *Indiana University Southeast*

Charles Rarick, *Transylvania University*

Deana K. Ray, *Forsyth Technical Community College*

Robert A. Reber, *Western Kentucky University*

Bob Redick, *Lincoln Land Community College*

Douglas Richardon, *Eastfield College*

Tina L. Robbins, *Clemson University*

Deborah Britt Roebuck, *Kennesaw State University*

Harvey Rothenberg, *Regis University*

Catherine Ruggieri, *St. John's University*

George Ruggiero, *Community College of Rhode Island*

Kathleen Rust, *Elmhurst College*

Robert Rustic, *University of Findlay*

Cyndy Ruszkowski, *Illinois State University*

Nestor St. Charles, *Dutchess Community College*

Lynda St. Clair, *Bryant College*

Michael Santoro, *Rutgers University*

John L. Schmidt Jr., *George Mason University*

Gerald Schoenfeld Jr., *James Madison University*

Don Schreiber, *Baylor University*

Robert Schwartz, *University of Toledo*

Amit Shah, *Frostburg State University*

Michael Shapiro, *Dowling College*

Raymond Shea, *Monroe Community College*

Richard Ray Shreve, *Indiana University Northwest*

Sidney Siegel, *Drexel University*

Thomas D. Sigerstad, *Frostburg State University*

Roy L. Simerly, *East Carolina University*

Randi L. Sims, *Nova Southeastern University*

Sharon Sloan, *Northwood University*

Erika E. Small, *Coastal Carolina University*

Brien Smith, *Ball State University*

Marjorie Smith, *Mountain State University*

Raymond D. Smith, *Towson State University*

William A. Sodeman, *University of Southern Indiana*

Carl J. Sonntag, *Pikes Peak Community College*

Robert W. Sosna, *Menlo College*

William Soukup, *University of San Diego*

Rieann Spence-Gale, *Northern Virginia Community College–Alexandria Campus*

H. T. Stanton Jr., *Barton College*

Jerry Stevens, *Texas Tech University*

William A. Stoever, *Seton Hall University*

Charles I. Stubbart, *Southern Illinois University at Carbondale*

James K. Swenson, *Moorhead State University*

Karen Ann Tarnoff, *East Tennessee State University*

Jerry L. Thomas, *Arapahoe Community College*

Joe Thomas, *Middle Tennessee State University*

Kenneth Thompson, *DePaul University*

John Todd, *University of Arkansas*

Thomas Turk, *Chapman University*

Isaiah Ugboro, *North Carolina A & T University*

Linn Van Dyne, *Michigan State University*

Jaen Vanhoegaerden, *Ashridge Management College*

Barry L. Van Hook, *Arizona State University*

Gloria Walker, *Florida Community College*

Stuart H. Warnock, *University of Southern Colorado*

Toomy Lee Waterson, *Northwood University*

Philip A. Weatherford, *Embry-Riddle Aeronautical University*

Ben Weeks, *St. Xavier University*

Emilia S. Westney, *Texas Tech University*

Donita Whitney-Bammerlin, *Kansas State University*

Robert Williams, *University of North Alabama*

W. J. Williams, *Chicago State University*

Shirley A. Wilson, *Bryant College*

Robert H. Woodhouse, *University of St. Thomas*

Michael A. Yahr, *Robert Morris College*

D. Kent Zimmerman, *James Madison University*

Finally, we are grateful to two incredibly wonderful children, Nicholas and Julia, for being all that they are and for the joy they bring to all who know them.

Gareth R. Jones

Jennifer M. George
Jesse H. Jones Graduate School of Business,
Rice University

Authors

Gareth Jones currently offers pro bono advice on solving management problems to nonprofit organizations in Houston, Texas. He received his BA in Economics Psychology and his PhD in Management from the University of Lancaster, U.K. He was formerly Professor of Management in the Graduate School of Business at Texas A&M University and earlier held teaching and research appointments at Michigan State University, the University of Illinois at Urbana–Champaign, and the University of Warwick, U.K.

He continues to pursue his research interests in strategic management and organizational theory and his well-known research that applies transaction cost analysis to explain many forms of strategic and organizational behavior. He also studies the complex and changing relationships between competitive advantage and information technology in the 2010s.

He has published many articles in leading journals of the field and his research has appeared in the *Academy of Management Review*, the *Journal of International Business Studies*, and *Human Relations*. He published an article about the role of information technology in many aspects of organizational functioning in the *Journal of Management*. One of his articles won the *Academy of Management Journal*'s Best Paper Award, and he is one of the most cited authors in the *Academy of Management Review*. He is, or has served, on the editorial boards of the *Academy of Management Review*, the *Journal of Management*, and *Management Inquiry*.

Gareth Jones has used his academic knowledge to craft leading textbooks in management and three other major areas in the management discipline: organizational behavior, organizational theory, and strategic management. His books are widely recognized for their innovative, contemporary content and for the clarity with which they communicate complex, real-world issues to students.

Jennifer George is the Mary Gibbs Jones Professor of Management and Professor of Psychology in the Jesse H. Jones Graduate School of Business at Rice University. She received her BA in Psychology/Sociology from Wesleyan University, her MBA in Finance from New York University, and her PhD in Management and Organizational Behavior from New York University. Prior to joining the faculty at Rice University, she was a professor in the Department of Management at Texas A&M University.

Professor George specializes in organizational behavior and is well known for her research on mood and emotion in the workplace, their determinants, and their effects on various individual and group-level work outcomes. She is the author of many articles in leading peer-reviewed journals such as the *Academy of Management Journal*, the *Academy of Management Review*, the *Journal of Applied Psychology*, *Organizational Behavior and Human Decision Processes*, *Journal of Personality and Social Psychology*, and *Psychological Bulletin*. One of her papers won the Academy of Management's Organizational Behavior Division Outstanding Competitive Paper Award, and another paper won the *Human Relations* Best Paper Award. She is, or has been, on the editorial review boards of the *Journal of Applied Psychology*, *Academy of Management Journal*, *Academy of Management Review*, *Administrative Science Quarterly*, *Journal of Management*, *Organizational Behavior and Human Decision Processes*, *Organization Science*, *International Journal of Selection and Assessment*, and *Journal of Managerial Issues*; was a consulting editor for the *Journal of Organizational Behavior*; was a member of the SIOP *Organizational Frontiers Series* editorial board; and was an associate editor of the *Journal of Applied Psychology*. She is a fellow in the Academy of Management, the American Psychological Association, the American Psychological Society, and the Society for Industrial and Organizational Psychology and a member of the Society for Organizational Behavior. She also has coauthored a textbook titled *Understanding and Managing Organizational Behavior*.

Guided Tour

RICH AND RELEVANT EXAMPLES

An important feature of our book is the way we use real-world examples and stories about managers and companies to drive home the applied lessons to students. Our reviewers were unanimous in their praise of the sheer range and depth of the rich, interesting examples we use to illustrate the chapter material and make it come alive. Moreover, unlike boxed material in other books, our boxes are seamlessly integrated into the text; they are an integral part of the learning experience, and not tacked on to or isolated from the text itself. This is central to our pedagogical approach.

A Management Snapshot opens each chapter, posing a chapter-related challenge and then discussing how managers in one or more organizations responded to that challenge. These vignettes help demonstrate the uncertainty and excitement surrounding the management process.

Our box features are not traditional boxes; that is, they are not disembodied from the chapter narrative. These thematic applications are fully integrated into the reading. Students will no longer be forced to decide whether to read boxed material. These features are interesting and engaging for

MANAGEMENT SNAPSHOT

Tim Cook Succeeds Steve Jobs as CEO of Apple

What is High-Performance Management?

In 2011 Tim Cook took full management control of Apple as its CEO six weeks after Steve Jobs stepped down as its CEO before his untimely death. Cook had been Apple's longtime chief operating officer and had been responsible for organizing and controlling its global supply chain to bring its innovative products to market as quickly and efficiently as possible.[1] One of Apple's major strengths is to continuously introduce new and improved products such as its iPhones and iPads, often at six-month and yearly intervals, to offer customers more options and to stay ahead of the competition. Cook was acknowledged as the leader who controlled Apple's purchasing and manufacturing operations and of ensures he had intimate knowledge of Apple's new product design and engineering. However, Steve Jobs had been the manager who ultimately decided what kinds of new products Apple would develop and the design of their hardware and software.

Starting with Apple's founding in 1977, Jobs saw his main task as leading the planning process to develop new and improved PCs. Although this was a good strategy, his management style was often arbitrary and overbearing. For example, Jobs often played favorites among the many project teams he created. His approach caused many conflicts and led to fierce competition, many misunderstandings, and growing distrust among members of the different teams.

Jobs's abrasive management style also brought him into conflict with John Sculley, Apple's CEO. Employees became unsure whether Jobs (the chairman) or Sculley was leading the company. Both managers were so busy competing for control over Apple that the task of ensuring its resources were being used efficiently was neglected. Apple's costs soared, and its performance and profits fell. Apple's directors became convinced Jobs's management style was the heart of the problem and asked him to resign.

After he left Apple, Jobs started new ventures such as PC maker NEXT to develop powerful new PCs and Pixar, the computer animation company which became a huge success after it made blockbuster movies such as *Toy Story* and *Finding Nemo*, both distributed by Walt Disney. In both these companies Jobs developed a clear vision for managers to follow, and he built strong management teams to lead the project teams developing the new PCs and movies. Jobs saw his main task as planning the companies' future product development strategy. However, he left the actual tasks of leading and organizing to managers below him. He gave them the autonomy to put his vision into practice. In 1997 Jobs convinced Apple to buy NEXT and use its powerful operating system in new Apple PCs. Jobs began working inside Apple to lead its turnaround and was so successful that in 1997 he was asked to become its CEO. Jobs agreed and continued to

INFORMATION TECHNOLOGY BYTE

Fog Creek Software's Approach to Recruiting

Fog Creek Software is a small, privately owned software company founded in 2000 by Joel Spolsky and Michael Pryor in a renovated loft in the Fashion District of New York City.[59] Fog Creek has earned a profit each year since its founding.[60] Hiring great computer software developers is essential for a company like Fog Creek; according to Spolsky, the top 1% of software developers outperform average developers by a ratio of around 10:1. And the top 1% are the inventive types who can successfully develop new products while also being highly efficient.[61]

Finding, never mind recruiting, the top 1% is a real challenge for a small company like Fog Creek because many of these people already have great jobs and are not looking to switch employers. Realizing that the top 1% of developers might rarely apply for positions with Fog Creek (or any other company), Fog Creek uses paid summer internships to recruit over 50% of its developers while they are still in college; they are hired full-time after graduation.[62]

In the fall of every year, Fog Creek sends personalized letters to computer science majors across the country who have the potential to be top developers in the future, contacts professors

Fog Creek Software uses paid summer internships to help identify and attract promising software developers

their website.[63] The best of whom are candidates describe the process of solving a software... thing they want at the...

Those who do... expense paid visit to... a hip hotel, receive... Fog Creek, and the... themselves) to get... recruits who has a...

Interns perform... of four interns de... Creek Copilot.[66] T... interns they would... paid, they receive f... in New York City. A... which interns are gr... graduation with gr... Although Fog Cree... more than pays for... indicates, "An inter... long pipeline, so yo...

emotions and moods signal that things are going well and thus can lead to expansive, and even playful, thinking. Negative emotions and moods... there are problems in need of attention and areas for improvement... people are in negative moods, they tend to be more detail-oriented and... on the facts at hand.[74] Some studies suggest that critical thinking and efficacy may be promoted by a negative mood, and sometimes especially... judgments may be made by managers in negative moods.[75]

As indicated in the following "Management Insight," emotions can be the impetus for important changes in an organization.

MANAGEMENT INSIGHT

Emotions as Triggers for Changes in Organizations

In our personal lives, intense emotional experiences can often be triggers for changes for the better. For example, the fear that accompanies a near miss auto accident may prompt a driver to slow down and leave more time to get to destinations. Embarrassment resulting from being underprepared for a major presentation might prompt a person to be more prepared in the future. Anger over being treated poorly can sometimes help people get out of bad personal relationships.

Interestingly enough, some managers and organizations are using emotions to prompt needed changes. For example, the CEO of North American Tool, Curt Lansbery, was dismayed that employees weren't contributing as much as they could to their 401(k) retirement plans, even though the company had a matched contribution plan whereby the company contributed a percentage of an employee's contributions. North American Tool makes industrial cutting tools, and each year has an annual 401(k) enrollment meeting. Lansbery decided to bring a bag full of money to one such meeting that equaled the amount of money employees did not receive the prior year because they did not contribute the maximum to their 401(k) plans. He dumped the money on a table and told the employees that this money should be ours but is not—prompted managers to maximize their 401(k) contributions for the next year and reap the benefits of the matched contribution.

Dr. Leon Bender and other colleagues at Cedars-Sinai Medical Center were concerned that doctors and nurses weren't washing their hands as often as they should. Repeated hand-washing by medical staff is a key contributor to keeping patients free of secondary bacterial infections and avoiding these kinds of preventable bacterial

Need to change your culture? Try a tug at the heartstrings—or the gut. A screen saver image of how quickly and how thoroughly medical personnel hands get dirty was the impetus for a turnaround at a hospital with low hand-washing stats.

students while bringing the chapter contents to life.

In-depth examples appear in boxes throughout each chapter. Management Insight boxes illustrate the topics of the chapter, while the Ethics in Action, Managing Globally, Focus on Diversity, and Information Technology Byte boxes examine the chapter topics from each of these perspectives.

Further emphasizing the unique content covered in Chapter 2, "Values, Attitudes, Emotions, and Culture: The Manager as a Person," the Manager as a Person boxes focus on how real managers brought about change within their organizations. These examples allow us to reflect on how individual managers dealt with real-life, on-the-job challenges related to various chapter concepts.

NEW! EXPANDED USE OF SMALL BUSINESS EXAMPLES

To ensure that students see the clear connections between the concepts taught in their Principles of Management course and the application in their future jobs in a medium or small business, Jones and George have expanded the number of examples of the opportunities and challenges facing founders, managers, and employees in small businesses.

EXPERIENTIAL LEARNING FEATURES

We have given considerable time and effort to developing state-of-the-art experiential end-of-chapter learning exercises that drive home the meaning of management to students. These exercises are grouped together at the end of each chapter in a section called "Management in Action." The following activities are included at the end of every chapter:

TOPICS FOR DISCUSSION AND ACTION are a set of chapter-related questions and points for reflection. Some ask students to research actual management issues and learn firsthand from practicing managers.

BUILDING MANAGEMENT SKILLS is a self-developed exercise that asks students to apply what they have learned from their own experience in organizations and from managers or from the experiences of others.

MANAGING ETHICALLY is an exercise that presents students with an ethical scenario or dilemma and asks them to think about the issue from an ethical perspective to better understand the issues facing practicing managers.

SMALL GROUP BREAKOUT EXERCISE is designed to allow instructors in large classes to utilize interactive experiential exercises.

BE THE MANAGER presents a realistic scenario where a manager or organization faces some kind of challenge, problem, or opportunity.

Management *in Action*

TOPICS FOR DISCUSSION AND ACTION

Discussion

1. Would a flexible or a more formal structure be appropriate for these organizations: (a) a large department store, (b) a Big Five accountancy firm, (c) a biotechnology company? Explain your reasoning. **[LO 7-1, 7-2]**

2. Using the job characteristics model as a guide, discuss how a manager can enrich or enlarge subordinates' jobs. **[LO 7-2]**

3. How might a salesperson's job or a secretary's job be enlarged or enriched to make it more motivating? **[LO 7-2, 7-3]**

4. When and under what conditions might managers change from a functional to (a) a product, (b) a geographic, or (c) a market structure?

5. How do matrix structures and product team structures differ? Why is the product team structure more widely used? **[LO 7-1, 7-3, 7-4]**

Action

6. Find and interview a manager, and identify the kind of organizational structure that his or her organization uses to coordinate its people and resources. Why is the organization using that structure? Do you think a different structure would be more appropriate? If so which one? **[LO 7-1, 7-3, 7-4]**

7. With the same or another manager, discuss the distribution of authority in the organization. Does the manager think that decentralizing authority and empowering employees are appropriate? **[LO 7-1, 7-3]**

8. Interview some employees of an organization, and ask them about the organization's values and norms, the typical characteristics of employees, and the organization's ethical values and socialization practices. Using this information, try to describe the organization's culture and the way it affects the way people and groups behave. **[LO 7-1, 7-3]**

BUILDING MANAGEMENT SKILLS
Understanding Organizing **[LO 7-1, 7-2, 7-3]**

Think of an organization with which you are familiar, perhaps one you have worked for—such as a store, restaurant, office, church, or school. Then answer the following questions.

1. Which contingencies are most important in explaining how the organization is organized? Do you think it is organized in the best way?

2. Using the job characteristics model, how motivating do you think the job of a typical

3. Can you think of any ways in which a typical job could be enlarged or enriched?

4. What kind of organizational structure does the organization use? If it is part of a chain, what kind of structure does the entire organization use? What

organization to operate more effectively? For example, would the move to a product team structure lead to greater efficiency or effectiveness? Why or why not?

5. How many levels are there in the organization's hierarchy?

MANAGING ETHICALLY **[LO 4-4, 4-5]**

In recent years the number of U.S. companies that buy their inputs from low-cost overseas suppliers has been growing, and concern about the ethics associated with employing young children in factories has been increasing. In Pakistan and India, children as young as six years old work long hours to make rugs and carpets for export to Western countries or clay bricks for local use. In countries like Malaysia and in Central America, children and teenagers routinely work long hours in factories and sweatshops to produce the clothing that is found in most U.S. discount and department stores.

Questions

1. Either by yourself or in a group, discuss whether it is ethical to employ children in factories and whether U.S. companies should buy and sell products made by these children. What are some arguments for and against child labor?

2. If child labor is an economic necessity, what methods could be employed to make it as ethical a practice as possible? Or is it simply unethical?

SMALL GROUP BREAKOUT EXERCISE **[LO 4-1, 4-2]**
How to Enter the Copying Business

Form groups of three to five people, and appoint one group member as the spokesperson who will communicate your findings to the whole class when called on by the instructor. Then discuss the following scenario:

You and your partners have decided to open a small printing and copying business in a college town of 100,000 people. Your business will compete with companies like FedEx Kinko's. You know that over 50% of small businesses fail in their first year, so to increase your chances of success, you have decided to perform a detailed analysis of the task environment of the copying business to discover what opportunities and threats you will encounter.

1. Decide what you must know about (a) your future customers, (b) your future competitors, and (c) other critical forces in the task environment if you are to be successful.

2. Evaluate the main barriers to entry into the copying business.

3. Based on this analysis, list some steps you would take to help your new copying business succeed.

BE THE MANAGER **[LO 4-1, 4-2]**
The Changing Environment of Retailing

You are the new manager of a major clothing store that is facing a crisis. This clothing store has been the leader in its market for the last 15 years. In the last three years, however, two other major clothing store chains have opened, and they have steadily been attracting customers away from your store—your sales are down 30%. To find out why, your store surveyed former customers and learned that they perceive your store as not keeping up with changing fashion trends and new forms of customer service. In examining how the store operates, you found out that the 10 purchasing managers who buy the clothing and accessories for the store have been buying from the same clothing suppliers and have become reluctant to try new ones. Moreover, salespeople rarely, if ever, make suggestions for changing how the store operates, and

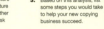

THE WALL STREET JOURNAL CASE IN THE NEWS [LO 3-1, 3-3]

Legislators Step Up Push for Paid Sick Leave

Amid the worst flu season in recent years, lawmakers in at least a half-dozen cities and states are intensifying a push for laws requiring paid time off when workers take sick days.

Some 39% of private-sector workers aren't entitled to paid time off when they fall ill, according to the Bureau of Labor Statistics, and 11% of state and local government workers lack the benefit. Low-wage and part-time workers, particularly those at small firms or who work in restaurants, are among the least likely to get paid sick time.

To change that, Democratic lawmakers and their allies in Maryland, Washington, and Massachusetts, and in cities including New York, Philadelphia, and Portland, Ore., are trying to advance measures that would make paid sick time a legal requirement for most firms. In Congress, Sen. Tom Harkin (D., Iowa) plans to reintroduce a federal paid-sick-leave bill this spring.

Such efforts started before this year, but a vicious flu season that sidelined many workers has given them new urgency. Former President Bill Clinton chimed in this month, calling for the first federal paid-sick-leave law. The White House also supports a federal paid-sick-leave law.

Opponents of codifying paid sick leave say such laws weigh on businesses and ultimately hurt workers. In Connecticut, which last year became the first state to mandate paid sick leave, some employers contend the measure has raised costs and harmed workers

by prompting cuts in wages or increases. Most firms there with 50 or more workers must provide five paid sick days a year, which employees accrue at a rate of one hour of leave for every 40 worked.

A canvassing of Connecticut businesses from the right-leaning Employment Policies Institute found that, of 156 respondents, more than half had begun complying with the law and most of those said it wasn't good for business. Many said they had offset expected expenses ahead of the law, including by raising prices, cutting workers' hours, and limiting their expansion in the state.

Dan Shackford, owner of Great Beginnings day care in Plainville, Conn., said that before the law, his 50 employees were welcome to call in sick without pay and earn a day off for three months of perfect attendance. Now when someone calls in sick, he has to pay a substitute and the worker. "The law is hurting me," he said.

To cope, he and his wife have lowered the annual raises they selectively give, to 3% from 5%. Mr. Shackford estimates it would cost up to $30,000 annually if his workers used all their sick time. The BLS says that, on average, full-time private-sector workers with a fixed number of days don't use them all.

Proponents contend the benefits outweigh the costs. Connecticut Gov. Dannel Malloy, a Democrat who signed the law, said it has been good for the state as people "aren't going to work and therefore making other people sick." He said he has talked with

a variety of employers statewide who "now admit it really wasn't that big of a deal."

Cities with such laws include Seattle, Washington, D.C., and San Francisco, whose policy was enacted in 2007. Research by the left-leaning Institute for Women's Policy Research found that San Francisco's paid-sick ordinance is rarely misused by workers, supported by most employers now, and isn't hurting profits for the vast majority.

The federal Bureau of Labor Statistics also said the benefits of paid sick leave have been shown to help productivity and reduce the spread of workplace disease, but it wasn't specific about the extent.

It is "not only the right thing to do for families, but good for businesses and the economy," said Sen. Harkin, who is chairman of a Senate labor committee. His Healthy Families Act would let workers accrue up to seven paid sick days a year through hours worked to care for themselves or family, including doctor visits.

Tennessee Sen. Lamar Alexander, the top Republican on the labor committee, contends such a requirement "would only make a bad unemployment problem worse" by increasing hiring costs.

The majority of workers who already have paid sick time receive it from employers that provide it voluntarily, usually through a fixed number of days or, less frequently, as needed.

Karen Barnes, a single mother and part-time director of a Philadelphia day care, wants options like that. She is advocating for a paid-sick bill that

These exercises provide students with a hands-on way of solving "real" problems by applying what they've just learned in the chapter.

CASE IN THE NEWS Each chapter has one Case in the News that is an actual or shortened version of a current article. The concluding questions encourage students to think about how real managers deal with problems in the business world.

ASSURANCE OF LEARNING READY

Many educational institutions today are focused on the notion of assurance of learning, an important element of some accreditation standards. *Essentials of Contemporary Management, Sixth Edition,* is designed specifically to support your assurance of learning initiatives with a simple, yet powerful solution.

Each test bank question for *Essentials of Contemporary Management* maps to a specific chapter learning outcome/objective listed in the text. You can use our test bank software, EZ Test and EZ Test Online, or **Connect Management** to easily query for learning outcomes/objectives that directly relate to the learning objectives for your course. You can then use the reporting features of EZ Test to aggregate student results in similar fashion, making the collection and presentation of assurance of learning data simple and easy.

AACSB STATEMENT

The McGraw-Hill Companies are a proud corporate member of AACSB International. To support the importance and value of AACSB accreditation, *Essentials of Contemporary Management, Sixth Edition,* recognizes the curricula guidelines detailed in the AACSB standards for business accreditation by connecting selected questions in the text and/or the test bank to the six general knowledge and skill guidelines in the AACSB standards.

The statements contained in *Essentials of Contemporary Management, Sixth Edition,* are provided only as a guide for the users of this textbook. The AACSB leaves content coverage and assessment within the purview of individual schools, the mission of the school, and the faculty. While *Essentials of Contemporary Management* and the teaching package make no claim of any specific AACSB qualification or evaluation, we have within *Essentials of Contemporary Management* labeled selected questions according to the six general knowledge and skill areas.

INTEGRATED LEARNING SYSTEM

Great care was used in the creation of the supplementary material to accompany *Essentials of Contemporary Management.* Whether you are a seasoned faculty member or a newly minted instructor, you'll find our support materials to be the most thorough and thoughtful ever created.

Instructor's Manual (IM) The IM supporting this text has been completely updated in order to save instructors' time and support them in delivering the most effective course to their students. For each chapter, this manual provides a chapter overview and lecture outline with integrated PowerPoint® slides, lecture enhancers, notes for end-of-chapter materials, video cases and teaching notes, and more.

PowerPoint® Presentation Forty slides per chapter feature reproductions of key tables and figures from the text as well as original content. Lecture-enhancing additions such as quick polling questions and company or video examples from outside the text can be used to generate discussion and illustrate management concepts.

Test Bank and EZ Test The test bank has been thoroughly reviewed, revised, and improved. There are approximately 100 questions per chapter, including true/false, multiple-choice, and essay. Each question is tagged with learning objective, level of difficulty (corresponding to Bloom's taxonomy of educational objectives), AACSB standards, the correct answer, and page references. The new AACSB tags allow instructors to sort questions by the various standards and create reports to help give assurance that they are including recommended learning experiences in their curricula.

McGraw-Hill's flexible and easy-to-use electronic testing program **EZ Test** allows instructors to create tests from book-specific items. It accommodates a wide range of question types, and instructors may add their own questions. Multiple versions of the test can be created, and any test can be exported for use with course management systems such as WebCT or BlackBoard. And now **EZ Test Online** (**www.eztestonline.com**) allows you to access the test bank virtually anywhere at any time, without installation, and it's even easier to use. Additionally, it allows you to administer EZ Test–created exams and quizzes online, providing instant feedback for students.

MCGRAW-HILL CONNECT MANAGEMENT

Less Managing. More Teaching. Greater Learning.   McGraw-Hill *Connect Management* is an online assignment and assessment solution that connects students with the tools and resources they'll need to achieve success.

McGraw-Hill *Connect Management* helps prepare students for their future by enabling faster learning, more efficient studying, and higher retention of knowledge.

MCGRAW-HILL *CONNECT MANAGEMENT* FEATURES

Connect Management offers a number of powerful tools and features to make managing assignments easier, so faculty can spend more time teaching. With *Connect Management,* students can engage with their coursework anytime and anywhere, making the learning process more accessible and efficient. *Connect Management* offers you the features described below.

Diagnostic and Adaptive Learning of Concepts: LearnSmart

Students want to make the best use of their study time. The LearnSmart adaptive self-study technology within *Connect Management* provides students with a seamless combination of practice, assessment, and remediation for every concept in the textbook. LearnSmart's intelligent software adapts to every student response and automatically delivers concepts that advance the student's understanding while reducing time devoted to the concepts already mastered. The result for every student is the fastest path to mastery of the chapter concepts. LearnSmart

- Applies an intelligent concept engine to identify the relationships between concepts and to serve new concepts to each student only when he or she is ready.
- Adapts automatically to each student, so students spend less time on the topics they understand and practice more those they have yet to master.
- Provides continual reinforcement and remediation, but gives only as much guidance as students need.

- Integrates diagnostics as part of the learning experience.
- Enables you to assess which concepts students have efficiently learned on their own, thus freeing class time for more applications and discussion.

Online Interactives

Online Interactives are engaging tools that teach students to apply key concepts in practice. These Interactives provide them with immersive, experiential learning opportunities. Students will engage in a variety of interactive scenarios to deepen critical knowledge of key course topics. They receive immediate feedback at intermediate steps throughout each exercise, as well as comprehensive feedback at the end of the assignment. All Interactives are automatically scored and entered into the instructor gradebook.

Student Progress Tracking

Connect Management keeps instructors informed about how each student, section, and class is performing, allowing for more productive use of lecture and office hours. The progress-tracking function enables you to

- View scored work immediately and track individual or group performance with assignment and grade reports.
- Access an instant view of student or class performance relative to learning objectives.
- Collect data and generate reports required by many accreditation organizations, such as AACSB.

Smart Grading

When it comes to studying, time is precious. **Connect Management** helps students learn more efficiently by providing feedback and practice material when they need it, where they need it. When it comes to teaching, your time also is precious. The grading function enables you to

- Have assignments scored automatically, giving students immediate feedback on their work and side-by-side comparisons with correct answers.
- Access and review each response; manually change grades or leave comments for students to review.
- Reinforce classroom concepts with practice tests and instant quizzes.

Simple Assignment Management

With *Connect Management,* creating assignments is easier than ever, so you can spend more time teaching and less time managing. The assignment management function enables you to

- Create and deliver assignments easily with selectable end-of-chapter questions and test bank items.
- Streamline lesson planning, student progress reporting, and assignment grading to make classroom management more efficient than ever.
- Go paperless with the eBook and online submission and grading of student assignments.

Instructor Library

The *Connect Management* Instructor Library is your repository for additional resources to improve student engagement in and out of class. You can select and use any asset that enhances your lecture. The *Connect Management* Instructor Library includes

- Instructor Manual.
- PowerPoint® files.
- TestBank.
- Management Asset Gallery.
- eBook.

Student Study Center

The *Connect Management* Student Study Center is the place for students to access additional resources. The Student Study Center

- Offers students quick access to lectures, practice materials, eBooks, and more.
- Provides instant practice material and study questions, easily accessible on the go.
- Give students access to self-assessments, video materials, Manager's Hot Seat, and more.

Lecture Capture Via Tegrity Campus

Increase the attention paid to lecture discussion by decreasing the attention paid to note taking. For an additional charge, Lecture Capture offers new ways for students to focus on the in-class discussion, knowing they can revisit important topics later. See page xxxviii for further information.

McGraw-Hill *Connect Plus Management*

McGraw-Hill reinvents the textbook-learning experience for the modern student with *Connect Plus Management*. A seamless integration of an eBook and *Connect Management, Connect Plus Management* provides all of the *Connect Management* features plus the following:

- An integrated eBook, allowing for anytime, anywhere access to the textbook.
- Dynamic links between the problems or questions you assign to your students and the location in the eBook where that problem or question is covered.
- A powerful search function to pinpoint and connect key concepts in a snap.

In short, *Connect Management* offers you and your students powerful tools and features that optimize your time and energies, enabling you to focus on course content, teaching, and student learning. *Connect Management* also offers a wealth of content resources for both instructors and students. This state-of-the-art, thoroughly tested system supports you in preparing students for the world that awaits.

For more information about *Connect,* go to **www.mcgrawhillconnect.com,** or contact your local McGraw-Hill sales representative.

TEGRITY CAMPUS: LECTURES 24/7

Tegrity Campus is a service that makes class time available 24/7 by automatically capturing every lecture in a searchable format for students to review when they study and complete assignments. With a simple one-click start-and-stop process, you capture all computer screens and corresponding audio. Students can replay any part of any class with easy-to-use browser-based viewing on a PC or Mac.

Educators know that the more students can see, hear, and experience class resources, the better they learn. In fact, studies prove it. With Tegrity Campus, students quickly recall key moments by using Tegrity Campus's unique search feature. This search helps students efficiently find what they need, when they need it, across an entire semester of class recordings. Help turn all your students' study time into learning moments immediately supported by your lecture.

Lecture Capture enables you to

- Record and distribute your lecture with a click of a button.
- Record and index PowerPoint® presentations and anything shown on your computer so it is easily searchable, frame by frame.
- Offer access to lectures anytime and anywhere by computer, iPod, or mobile device.
- Increase intent listening and class participation by easing students' concerns about note taking. Lecture Capture will make it more likely you will see students' faces, not the tops of their heads.

To learn more about Tegrity, watch a two-minute Flash demo at **http://tegritycampus.mhhe.com**.

MCGRAW-HILL CUSTOMER CARE CONTACT INFORMATION

At McGraw-Hill, we understand that getting the most from new technology can be challenging. That's why our services don't stop after you purchase our products. You can e-mail our product specialists 24 hours a day to get product training online. Or you can search our knowledge bank of Frequently Asked Questions on our support website. For customer support, call **800-331-5094**, e-mail **hmsupport@mcgraw-hill.com**, or visit **www.mhhe. com/support**. One of our technical support analysts will be able to assist you in a timely fashion.

Support Materials

MCGRAW-HILL'S MANAGEMENT ASSET GALLERY!

McGraw-Hill/Irwin Management is excited to now provide a one-stop shop for our wealth of assets, making it super quick and easy for instructors to locate specific materials to enhance their courses.

All of the following can be accessed within the Management Asset Gallery:

MANAGER'S HOT SEAT

This interactive, video-based application puts students in the manager's hot seat and builds critical thinking and decision-making skills and allows students to apply concepts to real managerial challenges. Students watch as 15 real managers apply their years of experience when confronting unscripted issues such as bullying in the workplace, cyber loafing, globalization, intergenerational work conflicts, workplace violence, and leadership versus management.

Self-Assessment Gallery   Unique among publisher-provided self-assessments, our 23 self-assessments provide students with background information to ensure that they understand the purpose of the assessment. Students test their values, beliefs, skills, and interests in a wide variety of areas, allowing them to personally apply chapter content to their own lives and careers.

Every self-assessment is supported with PowerPoint® slides and an instructor manual in the Management Asset Gallery, making it easy for

SUPPORT MATERIALS

the instructor to create an engaging classroom discussion surrounding the assessments.

Test Your Knowledge   To help reinforce students' understanding of key management concepts, Test Your Knowledge activities give students a review of the conceptual materials followed by application-based questions to work through. Students can choose practice mode, which provides them with detailed feedback after each question, or test mode, which provides feedback after the entire test has been completed. Every Test Your Knowledge activity is supported by instructor notes in the Management Asset Gallery to make it easy for the instructor to create engaging classroom discussions surrounding the materials the students have completed.

Management History Timeline   This Web application allows instructors to present and students to learn the history of management in an engaging and interactive way. Management history is presented along an intuitive timeline that can be traveled through sequentially or by selected decade. With the click of a mouse, students learn the important dates, see the people who influenced the field, and understand the general management theories that have molded and shaped management as we know it today.

Video Library DVDs   McGraw-Hill/Irwin offers the most comprehensive video support for the Principles of Management classroom through course library video DVDs. This discipline has volume library DVDs tailored to integrate and visually reinforce chapter concepts. The library volume DVDs contain more than 80 clips! The rich video material, organized by topic, comes from sources such as *Bloomberg Businessweek* TV, PBS, NBC, BBC, SHRM, and McGraw-Hill. Video cases and video guides are provided for some clips.

Destination CEO Videos   *Bloomberg Businessweek* produced video clips featuring CEOs on a variety of topics. Accompanying each clip are multiple-choice questions and discussion questions to use in the classroom or assign as a quiz.

ONLINE LEARNING CENTER (OLC)

www.mhhe.com/jonesecm6e

Find a variety of online teaching and learning tools that are designed to reinforce and build on the text content. Students will have direct access to the learning tools while instructor materials are password protected.

eBOOK OPTIONS

eBooks are an innovative way for students to save money and to "go green." McGraw-Hill's eBooks are typically 55 percent off the bookstore price. Students have the choice between an online and a downloadable CourseSmart eBook.

Through CourseSmart, students have the flexibility to access an exact replica of their textbook from any computer that has Internet service without plug-ins or special software via the online version, or to create a library of books on their hard drive via the downloadable version. Access to the CourseSmart eBooks is one year.

Features CourseSmart eBooks allow students to highlight, take notes, organize notes, and share the notes with other CourseSmart users. Students can also search for terms across all eBooks in their purchased CourseSmart library. CourseSmart eBooks can be printed (five pages at a time).

More Info and Purchase Please visit www.coursesmart.com for more information and to purchase access to our eBooks. CourseSmart allows students to try one chapter of the eBook, free of charge, before purchase.

Create Craft your teaching resources to match the way you teach! With McGraw-Hill Create, www.mcgrawhill-create.com, you can easily rearrange chapters, combine material from other content sources, and quickly upload content you have written, like your course syllabus or teaching notes. Find the content you need in Create by searching through thousands of leading McGraw-Hill textbooks. Arrange your book to fit your teaching style. Create even allows you to personalize your book's appearance by selecting the cover and adding your name, school, and course information. Order a Create book and you'll receive a complimentary print review copy in three to five business days or a complimentary electronic review copy (eComp) via e-mail in about one hour. Go to www.mcgrawhillcreate.com today and register. Experience how McGraw-Hill Create empowers you to teach *your* students *your* way.

Essentials of

Contemporary Management

1 The Management Process Today

LEARNING OBJECTIVES

After studying this chapter, you should be able to:

1 Describe what management is, why management is important, what managers do, and how managers use organizational resources efficiently and effectively to achieve organizational goals. **[LO 1-1]**

2 Distinguish among planning, organizing, leading, and controlling (the four principal managerial tasks), and explain how managers' ability to handle each one affects organizational performance. **[LO 1-2]**

3 Differentiate among three levels of management, and understand the tasks and responsibilities of managers at different levels in the organizational hierarchy. **[LO 1-3]**

4 Distinguish among three kinds of managerial skill, and explain why managers are divided into different departments to perform their tasks more efficiently and effectively. **[LO 1-4]**

5 Discuss some major changes in management practices today that have occurred as a result of globalization and the use of advanced information technology (IT). **[LO 1-5]**

6 Discuss the principal challenges managers face in today's increasingly competitive global environment. **[LO 1-6]**

Tim Cook Succeeds Steve Jobs as CEO of Apple

What is High-Performance Management?

In 2011 Tim Cook took full management control of Apple as its CEO six weeks after Steve Jobs stepped down as its CEO before his untimely death. Cook had been Apple's longtime chief operating officer and had been responsible for organizing and controlling its global supply chain to bring its innovative products to market as quickly and efficiently as possible.[1] One of Apple's major strengths is to continuously introduce new and improved products such as its iPhones and iPads, often at six-month and yearly intervals, to offer customers more options and to stay ahead of the competition. Cook was acknowledged as the leader who controlled Apple's purchasing and manufacturing operations, and of course he had intimate knowledge of Apple's new product design and engineering. However, Steve Jobs had been the manager who ultimately decided what kinds of new products Apple would develop and the design of their hardware and software.

Starting with Apple's founding in 1977, Jobs saw his main task as leading the planning process to develop new and improved PCs. Although this was a good strategy, his management style was often arbitrary and overbearing. For example, Jobs often played favorites among the many project teams he created. His approach caused many conflicts and led to fierce competition, many misunderstandings, and growing distrust among members of the different teams.

Jobs's abrasive management style also brought him into conflict with John Sculley, Apple's CEO. Employees became unsure whether Jobs (the chairman) or Sculley was leading the company. Both managers were so busy competing for control of Apple that the task of ensuring its resources were being used efficiently was neglected. Apple's costs soared, and its performance and profits fell. Apple's directors became convinced Jobs's management style was the heart of the problem and asked him to resign.

After he left Apple, Jobs started new ventures such as PC maker NEXT to develop powerful new PCs and Pixar, the computer animation company, which become a huge success after it made blockbuster movies such as *Toy Story* and *Finding Nemo*, both distributed by Walt Disney. In both these companies Jobs developed a clear vision for managers to follow, and he built strong management teams to lead the project teams developing the new PCs and movies. Jobs saw his main task as planning the companies' future product development strategies. However, he left the actual tasks of leading and organizing to managers below him. He gave them the autonomy to put his vision into practice. In 1996 Jobs convinced Apple to buy NEXT and use its powerful operating system in new Apple PCs. Jobs began working inside Apple to lead its turnaround and was so successful that in 1997 he was asked to become its CEO. Jobs agreed and continued to put the new management skills he had developed over time to good use.

The first thing he did was create a clear vision and goals to energize and motivate Apple employees. Jobs decided that, to survive, Apple had to introduce state-of-the-art, stylish PCs and related digital equipment. He delegated considerable authority to teams of employees to develop all the many different hardware and software components necessary to build the new products, but he also established strict timetables and challenging "stretch" goals, such as bringing new products to market as quickly as possible, for these teams. Moreover, he was careful to keep the different teams' activities separate; only he and his chief designers knew what the new products would actually look like and their capabilities—and his demand for secrecy increased over time.[2]

In 2003 Jobs announced that Apple was starting a new service called iTunes, an online music store from which people could download songs for 99 cents. At the same time Apple introduced its iPod music player, which can store thousands of downloaded songs, and it quickly became a runaway success. By 2006 Apple had gained control of 70% of the digital music player market and 80% of the online music download business, and its stock price soared to a new record level. The next milestone in Jobs's product strategy came in 2007 when he announced that Apple would introduce the iPhone.

Once again he assembled different teams of engineers not only to develop the new phone's hardware and software but also to create an online iPhone applications platform where users could download applications to make their iPhones more valuable. In 2010 Jobs announced that Apple planned to introduce a new iPad tablet computer.

Since Cook assumed leadership of Apple, it has become apparent to its employees and shareholders that he brings a new, more open, and participative approach to managing the company. While Jobs was respected as a guru, magician, and ruler—someone to be revered as well as feared—Cook makes himself available to employees in Apple's cafeteria and talks directly to shareholders and analysts, something that Jobs had no time for. Cook has also worked to integrate Apple's global supply chain and project management functions with its engineering functions to break down the barriers between teams in the company and increase the flow of information between product units as the company grows and becomes more complex. Following Jobs, Cook's goal is for Apple to focus on introducing innovative new products and not to lose its commitment to being the leader in every market in which it competes. However, while Cook is a demanding boss, he is down to earth, approachable, and well respected, as opposed to Jobs who became increasingly isolated, forbidding, and secretive as time went on.

Overview

The story of Steve Jobs's and Tim Cook's rise to the top of Apple illustrates many challenges facing people who become managers: Managing a company is a complex activity, and effective managers must possess many kinds of skills, knowledge, and abilities. Management is an unpredictable process. Making the right decision is difficult; even effective managers often make mistakes, but the most effective managers, like Jobs and Cook, learn from their mistakes and continually strive to find ways to increase their companies' performance. In 2013 Cook was facing a host of new competitive challenges.

In this chapter we look at what managers do and what skills and abilities they must develop to manage their organizations successfully. We also identify the different kinds of managers that organizations need and the skills and abilities they must develop to succeed. Finally, we identify some challenges managers must address if their organizations are to grow and prosper.

What Is Management?

When you think of a manager, what kind of person comes to mind? Do you see someone who, like Tim Cook, can determine the future prosperity of a large for-profit company? Or do you see the administrator of a not-for-profit organization, such as a community college, library, or charity, or the person in charge of your local Walmart store or McDonald's restaurant, or the person you answer to if you have a part-time job? What do all these people have in common? First, they all work in organizations. Organizations are collections of people who work together and coordinate their actions to achieve a wide variety of goals or desired future outcomes.[3] Second, as managers, they are the people responsible for supervising and making the most of an organization's human and other resources to achieve its goals.

Management, then, is the planning, organizing, leading, and controlling of human and other resources to achieve organizational goals efficiently and effectively. An organization's *resources* include assets such as people and their skills, know-how, and experience; machinery; raw materials; computers and information technology; and patents, financial capital, and loyal customers and employees.

Achieving High Performance: A Manager's Goal

One of the most important goals that organizations and their members try to achieve is to provide some kind of good or service that customers value or desire. The principal goal of CEO Tim Cook is to manage Apple so it creates a continuous stream of new and improved goods and services—such as more powerful phones and tablets and to provide excellent quality customer service and support versatility that customers are willing to buy. In 2013 Apple still led the field in many of these areas but competitors like Samsung and Google were quickly catching up. Apple managers are currently working to make its hardware, software, and support service the most competitive in its industry. Similarly, the principal goal of doctors, nurses, and hospital administrators is to increase their hospital's ability to make sick people well—and to do so cost-effectively. Likewise, the principal goal of each McDonald's restaurant manager is to produce burgers, salads, fries, coffees, and drinks that people want to pay for and enjoy so they become loyal return customers.

Organizational performance is a measure of how efficiently and effectively managers use available resources to satisfy customers and achieve organizational goals. Organizational performance increases in direct proportion to increases in efficiency and effectiveness (see Figure 1.1). What are efficiency and effectiveness?

Efficiency is a measure of how productively resources are used to achieve a goal.[4] Organizations are efficient when managers minimize the amount of input resources (such as labor, raw materials, and component parts) or the amount of time needed to produce a given output of goods or services. For example, McDonald's develops ever more efficient fat fryers that not only reduce the amount of oil used in cooking, but also speed up the cooking of french fries. UPS develops new work routines to reduce delivery time, such as instructing drivers to leave their truck doors open when going short distances. Tim Cook instructed Apple's engineers not only to develop ever more compact, powerful, and multipurpose mobile devices but also to find cost-effective ways to do so. A manager's responsibility is to ensure that an organization and its members perform as efficiently as possible all the work activities needed to provide goods and services to customers.

---

organizations Collections of people who work together and coordinate their actions to achieve a wide variety of goals or desired future outcomes.

management The planning, organizing, leading, and controlling of human and other resources to achieve organizational goals efficiently and effectively.

LO 1-1 Describe what management is, why management is important, what managers do, and how managers utilize organizational resources efficiently and effectively to achieve organizational goals.

organizational performance A measure of how efficiently and effectively a manager uses resources to satisfy customers and achieve organizational goals.

efficiency A measure of how well or how productively resources are used to achieve a goal.

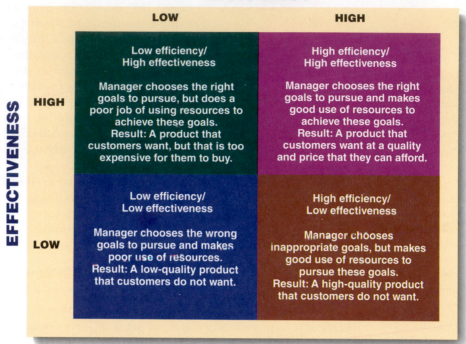

EFFICIENCY

LOW	HIGH

EFFECTIVENESS

HIGH

Low efficiency/
High effectiveness

Manager chooses the right
goals to pursue, but does a
poor job of using resources to
achieve these goals.
Result: A product that
customers want, but that is too
expensive for them to buy.

High efficiency/
High effectiveness

Manager chooses the right
goals to pursue and makes
good use of resources to
achieve these goals.
Result: A product that
customers want at a quality
and price that they can afford.

LOW

Low efficiency/
Low effectiveness

Manager chooses the wrong
goals to pursue and makes
poor use of resources.
Result: A low-quality product
that customers do not want.

High efficiency/
Low effectiveness

Manager chooses
inappropriate goals, but makes
good use of resources to
pursue these goals.
Result: A high-quality product
that customers do not want.

High-performing organizations are efficient *and* effective.

effectiveness

A measure of the
appropriateness of the
goals an organization is
pursuing and the degree
to which the organization
achieves those goals.

Effectiveness is a measure of the *appropriateness* of the goals that managers have selected for the organization to pursue and the degree to which the organization achieves those goals. Organizations are effective when managers choose appropriate goals and then achieve them. Some years ago, for example, managers at McDonald's decided on the goal of providing breakfast service to attract more customers. The choice of this goal has proved smart: Sales of breakfast food now account for more than 30% of McDonald's revenues and are still increasing because sales of its new lines of coffees and fruit drinks have risen sharply. Cook's goal is to create a continuous flow of innovative PC and digital entertainment products. High-performing organizations, such as Apple, McDonald's, Walmart, Intel, Home Depot, Accenture, and Habitat for Humanity are simultaneously efficient and effective. Effective managers are those who choose the right organizational goals to pursue and have the skills to utilize resources efficiently.

Why Study Management?

Today more students are competing for places in business courses than ever before; the number of people wishing to pursue Master of Business Administration (MBA) degrees—today's passport to an advanced management position—either on campus or from online universities and colleges is at an all-time high. Why is the study of management currently so popular?[5]

First, in any society or culture resources are valuable and scarce; so the more efficient and effective use that organizations can make of those resources, the greater the relative well-being and prosperity of people in that society. Because managers decide how to use many of a society's most valuable resources—its skilled employees, raw materials like oil and land, computers and information systems, and financial assets—they directly impact the well-being of a society and the people in it. Understanding what managers do and how they do it is of central importance to understanding how a society creates wealth and affluence for its citizens.

Second, although most people are not managers, and many may never intend to become managers, almost all of us encounter managers because most people have jobs and bosses. Moreover, many people today work in groups and teams and have to deal with coworkers. Studying management helps people deal with their bosses and their coworkers. It reveals how to understand other people at work and make decisions and take actions that win the attention and support of the boss and coworkers. Management teaches people not yet in positions of authority how to lead coworkers, solve conflicts between them, achieve team goals, and thus increase performance.

Third, in any society, people are in competition for a very important resource—a job that pays well and provides an interesting and satisfying career; and understanding management is one important path toward obtaining this objective. In general, jobs become more interesting the more complex or responsible they are. Any person who desires a motivating job that changes over time might therefore do well to develop management skills and become promotable. A person who has been working for several years and then returns to school for an MBA can usually, after earning the degree, find a more interesting, satisfying job that pays significantly more than the previous job. Moreover, salaries increase rapidly as people move up the organizational hierarchy, whether it is a school system, a large for-profit business organization, or a not-for-profit charitable or medical institution.

Indeed, the salaries paid to top managers are enormous. For example, the CEOs and other top executives or managers of companies such as Apple, Walt Disney, GE, and McDonald's receive millions in actual salary each year. However, even more staggering is the fact that many top executives also receive bonuses in the form of valuable stock or shares in the company they manage, as well as stock options that give them the right to sell these shares at a certain time in the future.[6] If the value of the stock goes up, the managers keep the difference between the option price at which they obtained the stock (say, $10) and what it is worth later (say, $33). For example, when Steve Jobs became CEO of Apple again in 1997, he accepted a salary of only $1 a year. However, he was also awarded stock options that, with the fast rise in Apple's stock price throughout the 2000s, are worth billions of dollars today (he was also given the free use of a $90 million jet).[7] In 2010 Goldman Sachs paid its top managers stock bonuses worth $16.2 billion, and its CEO Lloyd Blankfein received Goldman Sachs stock worth over $8 billion—but this was only half the value of the stock that JPMorgan Chase CEO Jamie Dimon received from his company![8] These incredible amounts of money provide some indication of both the responsibilities and the rewards that accompany the achievement of high management positions in major companies—and go to any entrepreneur who successfully creates and manages a small business that dominates its market. What is it that managers actually do to receive such rewards?[9]

Essential Managerial Tasks

The job of management is to help an organization make the best use of its resources to achieve its goals. How do managers accomplish this objective? They do so by performing four essential managerial tasks: *planning, organizing, leading,* and *controlling*. The arrows linking these tasks in Figure 1.2 suggest the sequence in which managers typically perform them. French manager Henri Fayol first outlined the nature of these managerial activities around the turn of the 20th

LO 1-2 Distinguish among planning, organizing, leading, and controlling (the four principal managerial tasks), and explain how managers' ability to handle each one affects organizational performance.

planning Identifying and selecting appropriate goals; one of the four principal tasks of management.

century in *General and Industrial Management,* a book that remains the classic statement of what managers must do to create a high-performing organization.[10]

Managers at all levels and in all departments—whether in small or large companies, for-profit or not-for-profit organizations, or organizations that operate in one country or throughout the world—are responsible for performing these four tasks, which we look at next. How well managers perform these tasks determines how efficient and effective their organizations are.

Planning

To perform the planning task, managers identify and select appropriate organizational goals and courses of action; they develop *strategies* for how to achieve high performance. The three steps involved in planning are (1) deciding which goals the organization will pursue, (2) deciding what strategies to adopt to attain those goals, and (3) deciding how to allocate organizational resources to pursue the strategies that attain those goals. How well managers plan and develop strategies determines how effective and efficient the organization is—its performance level.[11]

As an example of planning in action, consider the situation confronting Michael Dell, founder and CEO of Dell Computer, who in 2013 was struggling to increase the PC sales of his company given competition from HP, Apple, and Acer. In 1984 the 19-year-old Dell saw an opportunity to enter the PC market by assembling PCs and selling them directly to customers. Dell began to plan how to put his idea into practice. First, he decided that his goal was to sell an inexpensive PC, to undercut the prices charged by companies like Apple, Compaq, and HP. Second, he had to choose a course of action to achieve this goal. He decided to sell PCs directly to customers by telephone and so bypass expensive computer stores that sold Compaq and Apple PCs. He also had to decide how to obtain low-cost components and how to tell potential customers about his products. Third, he had to decide how to allocate his limited funds (he had only $5,000) to buy labor and other resources. He hired three people and worked with them around a table to assemble his PCs.

Figure 1.2

Four Tasks of Management

Michael Dell sits in the dorm room at the University of Texas–Austin, where he launched his personal computer company as a college freshman. When he visited, the room was occupied by freshmen Russell Smith (left) and Jacob Frith, both from Plano, Texas.

Thus to achieve his goal of making and selling low-price PCs, Dell had to plan, and as his organization grew, his plans changed and became progressively more complex. After setbacks during the 2000s that saw HP, Apple, and a new Taiwanese company, Acer, achieve competitive advantage over Dell in performance, styling, or pricing, Dell and his managers actively searched for new strategies to better compete against agile rivals and help the company regain its position as the highest-performing PC maker. In 2013 Dell was still locked in a major battle with its competitors, and its performance had not recovered despite attempts to introduce innovative new models of laptops and digital devices. Dell needed a new approach to planning to compete more effectively; and new strategies Dell has followed in the 2010s include more powerful customized lines of new laptops, and a major focus on providing computer hardware, software, and consulting geared to the need of corporate customers.

As the battle between Dell, HP, Acer, and Apple suggests, the outcome of planning is a strategy, a cluster of decisions concerning what organizational goals to pursue, what actions to take, and how to use resources to achieve these goals. The decisions that were the outcome of Michael Dell's original planning formed a *low-cost strategy*. A low-cost strategy is a way of obtaining customers by making decisions that allow an organization to produce goods or services more cheaply than its competitors so it can charge lower prices than they do. Throughout its history, Dell has continuously refined this strategy and explored new ways to reduce costs. Dell became the most profitable PC maker as a result of its low-cost strategy, but when HP and Acer also lowered their costs, it lost its competitive advantage and its profits fell. By contrast, since its founding Apple's strategy has been to deliver to customers new, exciting, and unique computer and digital products, such as its iPods, iPhones, and its new iPads—a strategy known as *differentiation*.[12] Although this strategy almost ruined Apple in the 1990s when customers bought inexpensive Dell PCs rather its premium-priced PCs, today Apple's sales have boomed as customers turn to its unique PCs and digital products. To fight back, Dell has been forced to offer more exciting, stylish products—hence its decision to introduce powerful customized PCs.

Planning strategy is complex and difficult, especially because planning is done under uncertainty when the result is unknown so that either success or failure is a possible outcome of the planning process. Managers take major risks when they commit organizational resources to pursue a particular strategy. Dell enjoyed great success in the past with its low-cost strategy; but presently Apple is performing spectacularly with its differentiation strategy and hurting competitors such as HP, Sony, Nokia, and Blackberry. In Chapter 6 we focus on the planning process and on the strategies organizations can select to respond to opportunities or threats in an industry. The story of the way Joe Coulombe, the founder of Trader Joe's, used his abilities to plan and make the right decisions to create the strategies necessary for his and his new organization's success is discussed in the following "Manager as a Person" box.

strategy A cluster of decisions about what goals to pursue, what actions to take, and how to use resources to achieve goals.

MANAGER AS A PERSON

Joe Coulombe Knows How to Make an Organization Work

Trader Joe's, an upscale specialty supermarket chain, was started in 1967 by Joe Coulombe, who owned a few convenience stores that were fighting an uphill battle against the growing 7-11 chain. 7-11 offered customers a wider selection of lower-priced products, and Coulombe had to find a new way to manage his small business if it was going to survive. As he began planning new strategies to help his small business grow, he was struck by the fact that there might be a niche for supplying specialty products, such as wine, drinks, and gourmet foods, which were more profitable to sell; moreover, he would no longer be competing against giant 7-11. Coulombe changed the name of his stores to Trader Joe's and stocked them with every variety and brand of California wine produced at the time. He also began to offer fine foods like bread, crackers, cheese, fruits, and vegetables to complement and encourage wine sales.

Pictured is Trader Joe's first New York City store that opened in 2006. Founder Joe Coulombe's approach to motivating and rewarding his employees to provide excellent customer service paid off in a city where the prices of food and drink are so high that customers were delighted to shop in stores with a great ambiance and friendly customer service.

From the beginning Coulombe realized that good planning was only the first step in successfully managing his small, growing company. He knew that to encourage customers to visit his stores and buy high-priced gourmet products, he needed to give them excellent customer service. So he had to motivate his salespeople to perform at a high level. His approach was to decentralize authority, empowering salespeople to take responsibility for meeting customer needs. Rather than forcing employees to follow strict operating rules and to obtain the consent of their superiors in the hierarchy of authority, employees were given autonomy to make decisions and provide personalized customer service. Coulombe's approach led employees to feel they "owned" their supermarkets, and he worked to develop a store culture based on values and norms about providing excellent customer service and developing personalized relationships with customers. Today many employees and customers are on first-name terms.

Coulombe led by example and created a store environment in which employees are treated as individuals and feel valued as people. For example, the theme behind the design of his stores was to create the feeling of a Hawaiian resort: He and his employees wear loud Hawaiian shirts, store managers are called captains, and the store decor uses lots of wood and contains tiki huts where employees give customers food and drink samples and interact with them. Once again, this helped create strong values and norms that emphasize personalized customer service.

Finally, Joe Coulombe's approach from the beginning was to create a policy of promotion from within the company so that the highest-performing salespeople could rise to become store captains and beyond in the organization. He had always recognized the need to treat employees (people) in a fair and equitable way to encourage them to develop the customer-oriented values and norms needed to provide personalized customer service. He decided that full-time employees should earn at least the median household income for their communities, which averaged $7,000 a year in the 1960s and is $48,000 today—an astonishingly high amount compared to the pay of employees of regular supermarkets such as Kroger's and Safeway. Moreover, store captains, who are vital in helping create and reinforce Trader Joe's store culture, are rewarded with salaries and bonuses that can exceed $100,000 a year. And all salespeople know that as the store chain expands, they may also be promoted to this level. In 2014 Trader Joe's had over 400 stores in 33 states and was still expanding because Coulombe's approach to managing his small business created the right foundation for an upscale specialty supermarket to grow and prosper.

Organizing

organizing
Structuring working relationships in a way that allows organizational members to work together to achieve organizational goals; one of the four principal tasks of management.

organizational structure A formal system of task and reporting relationships that coordinates and motivates organizational members so they work together to achieve organizational goals.

Organizing is structuring working relationships so organizational members interact and cooperate to achieve organizational goals. Organizing people into departments according to the kinds of job-specific tasks they perform lays out the lines of authority and responsibility between different individuals and groups. Managers must decide how best to organize resources, particularly human resources.

The outcome of organizing is the creation of an organizational structure, a formal system of task and reporting relationships that coordinates and motivates members so they work together to achieve organizational goals. Organizational structure determines how an organization's resources can be best used to create goods and services. As his company grew, for example, Michael Dell faced the issue of how to structure his organization. Early on he was hiring 100 new employees a week and deciding how to design his managerial hierarchy to best motivate and coordinate managers' activities. As his organization grew to become one of the largest global PC makers, he and his managers created progressively more complex forms of organizational structure to help it achieve its goals. We examine the organizing process in detail in Chapter 9.

Leading

leading Articulating a clear vision and energizing and enabling organizational members so they understand the part they play in achieving organizational goals; one of the four principal tasks of management.

An organization's *vision* is a short, succinct, and inspiring statement of what the organization intends to become and the goals it is seeking to achieve—its desired future state. In leading, managers articulate a clear organizational vision for the organization's members to accomplish, and they energize and enable employees so everyone understands the part he or she plays in achieving organizational goals. Leadership involves managers using their power, personality, influence, persuasion, and communication skills to coordinate people and groups so their activities and efforts are in harmony. Leadership revolves around encouraging all employees to perform at a high level to help the organization achieve its vision and goals. Another outcome of leadership is a highly motivated and committed workforce. Employees responded well to Michael Dell's hands-on leadership style, which has resulted in a hardworking, committed workforce. Managers at Apple appreciate the way Steve Jobs, and now Tim Cook, have adopted a leadership style based on a willingness to delegate authority to project teams and to help

controlling

Evaluating how well an organization is achieving its goals and taking action to maintain or improve performance; one of the four principal tasks of management.

managers resolve differences that could easily lead to bitter disputes and power struggles. We discuss the issues involved in managing and leading individuals and groups in Chapters 9 through 12.

Controlling

In controlling, the task of managers is to evaluate how well an organization has achieved its goals and to take any corrective actions needed to maintain or improve performance. For example, managers monitor the performance of individuals, departments, and the organization as a whole to see whether they are meeting desired performance standards. Michael Dell learned early in his career how important this is; if standards are not being met, managers seek ways to improve performance.

Ken Chenault, pictured here, is the president and CEO of American Express Company. Promoted in 1997, he climbed the ranks from its Travel Related Services Company thanks to his even temper and unrelenting drive. Respected by colleagues for his personality, most will say they can't remember him losing his temper or raising his voice. His open-door policy for subordinates allows him to mentor AmEx managers and encourages all to enter and speak their minds.

The outcome of the control process is the ability to measure performance accurately and regulate organizational efficiency and effectiveness. To exercise control, managers must decide which goals to measure—perhaps goals pertaining to productivity, quality, or responsiveness to customers—and then they must design control systems that will provide the information necessary to assess performance—that is, determine to what degree the goals have been met. The controlling task also helps managers evaluate how well they themselves are performing the other three tasks of management— planning, organizing, and leading—and take corrective action.

Michael Dell had difficulty establishing effective control systems because his company was growing so rapidly and he lacked experienced managers. In the 1990s Dell's costs suddenly soared because no systems were in place to control inventory, and in 1994 poor quality control resulted in a defective line of new laptop computers—some of which caught fire. To solve these and other control problems, Dell hired hundreds of experienced managers from other companies to put the right control systems in place. As a result, by 2000 Dell was able to make computers for over 10% less than its competitors, which created a major source of competitive advantage. At its peak, Dell drove competitors out of the market because it had achieved a 20% cost advantage over them.[13] However, we noted earlier that through the 2000s rivals such as HP and Acer also learned how to reduce their operating costs, and this shattered Dell's competitive advantage. Controlling, like the other managerial tasks, is an ongoing, dynamic, always-changing process that demands constant attention and action. We cover the most important aspects of the control task in Chapters 13 and 14.

The four managerial tasks—planning, organizing, leading, and controlling—are essential parts of a manager's job. At all levels in the managerial hierarchy, and across all jobs and departments in an organization, effective management means performing these four activities successfully—in ways that increase efficiency and effectiveness.

Levels and Skills of Managers

To perform the four managerial tasks efficiently and effectively, organizations group or differentiate their managers in two main ways—by level in hierarchy and by type of skill. First, they differentiate managers according to their level or rank in the organization's hierarchy of authority. The three levels of managers are first-line managers, middle managers, and top managers—arranged in a hierarchy. Typically first-line managers report to middle managers, and middle managers report to top managers.

Second, organizations group managers into different departments (or functions) according to their specific job-related skills, expertise, and experiences, such as a manager's engineering skills, marketing expertise, or sales experience. A department, such as the manufacturing, accounting, engineering, or sales department, is a group of managers and employees who work together because they possess similar skills and experience or use the same kind of knowledge, tools, or techniques to perform their jobs. Within each department are all three levels of management. Next we examine why organizations use a hierarchy of managers and group them, by the jobs they perform, into departments.

department A group of people who work together and possess similar skills or use the same knowledge, tools, or techniques to perform their jobs.

LO 1-3 Differentiate among three levels of management, and understand the tasks and responsibilities of managers at different levels in the organizational hierarchy.

first-line manager A manager who is responsible for the daily supervision of nonmanagerial employees.

Levels of Management

Organizations normally have three levels of management: first-line managers, middle managers, and top managers (see Figure 1.3). Managers at each level have different but related responsibilities for using organizational resources to increase efficiency and effectiveness.

At the base of the managerial hierarchy are first-line managers, often called *supervisors*. They are responsible for daily supervision of the nonmanagerial employees who perform the specific activities necessary to produce goods and services. First-line managers work in all departments or functions of an organization.

Figure 1.3
Levels of Managers

Examples of first-line managers include the supervisor of a work team in the manufacturing department of a car plant, the head nurse in the obstetrics department of a hospital, and the chief mechanic overseeing a crew of mechanics in the service function of a new car dealership. At Dell, first-line managers include the supervisors responsible for controlling the quality of its computers or the level of customer service provided by telephone salespeople. When Michael Dell started his company, he personally controlled the computer assembly process and thus acted as a first-line manager or supervisor.

middle manager
A manager who supervises first-line managers and is responsible for finding the best way to use resources to achieve organizational goals.

Supervising the first-line managers are middle managers, responsible for finding the best way to organize human and other resources to achieve organizational goals. To increase efficiency, middle managers find ways to help first-line managers and nonmanagerial employees better use resources to reduce manufacturing costs or improve customer service. To increase effectiveness, middle managers evaluate whether the organization's goals are appropriate and suggest to top managers how goals should be changed. Often the suggestions that middle managers make to top managers can dramatically increase organizational performance. A major part of the middle manager's job is developing and fine-tuning skills and know-how, such as manufacturing or marketing expertise, that allow the organization to be efficient and effective. Middle managers make thousands of specific decisions about the production of goods and services: Which first-line supervisors should be chosen for this particular project? Where can we find the highest-quality resources? How should employees be organized to allow them to make the best use of resources?

Behind a first-class sales force, look for the middle managers responsible for training, motivating, and rewarding the salespeople. Behind a committed staff of high school teachers, look for the principal who energizes them to find ways to obtain the resources they need to do outstanding and innovative jobs in the classroom.

top manager
A manager who establishes organizational goals, decides how departments should interact, and monitors the performance of middle managers.

In contrast to middle managers, top managers are responsible for the performance of *all* departments.[14] They have *cross-departmental responsibility*. Top managers establish organizational goals, such as which goods and services the company should produce; they decide how the different departments should interact; and they monitor how well middle managers in each department use resources to achieve goals.[15] Top managers are ultimately responsible for the success or failure of an organization, and their performance (like that of Michael Dell or Tim Cook) is continually scrutinized by people inside and outside the organization, such as other employees and investors.[16]

The *chief executive officer (CEO)* is a company's most senior and important manager, the one all other top managers report to. Today the term *chief operating officer (COO)* refers to the company's top manager, such as Tim Cook, who was groomed by Steve Jobs to take over as CEO. Together the CEO and COO are responsible for developing good working relationships among the top managers of various departments (manufacturing and marketing, for example); usually these top managers have the title "vice president." A central concern of the CEO is the creation of a smoothly functioning top management team, a group composed of the CEO, the COO, and the vice presidents most responsible for achieving organizational goals.[17] Tim Cook has worked hard to build such a team at Apple to counter threats from competitors.

top management team A group composed of the CEO, the COO, and the vice presidents of the most important departments of a company.

The relative importance of planning, organizing, leading, and controlling—the four principal managerial tasks—to any particular manager depends on the manager's position in the managerial hierarchy.[18] The amount of time managers

Figure 1.4

Relative Amount of
Time That Managers
Spend on the Four
Managerial Tasks

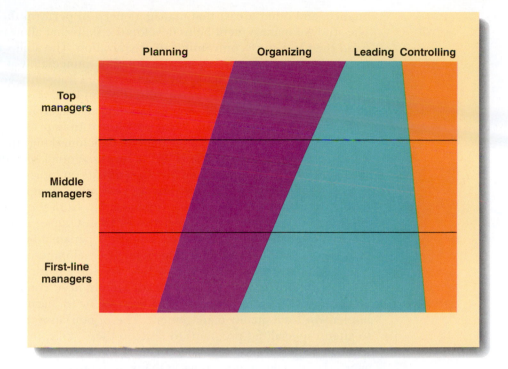

spend planning and organizing resources to maintain and improve organizational performance increases as they ascend the hierarchy (see Figure 1.4).[19] Top managers devote most of their time to planning and organizing, the tasks so crucial to determining an organization's long-term performance. The lower that managers' positions are in the hierarchy, the more time the managers spend leading and controlling first-line managers or nonmanagerial employees.

Managerial Skills

LO 1-4 Distinguish among three kinds of managerial skill, and explain why managers are divided into different departments to perform their tasks more efficiently and effectively.

conceptual skills
The ability to analyze and diagnose a situation and to distinguish between cause and effect.

Both education and experience enable managers to recognize and develop the personal skills they need to put organizational resources to their best use. Michael Dell realized from the start that he lacked sufficient experience and technical expertise in marketing, finance, and planning to guide his company alone. Thus he recruited experienced managers from other IT companies, such as IBM and HP, to help build his company. Research has shown that education and experience help managers acquire and develop three types of skills: *conceptual, human,* and *technical*.[20]

Conceptual skills are demonstrated in the general ability to analyze and diagnose a situation and to distinguish between cause and effect. Top managers require the best conceptual skills because their primary responsibilities are planning and organizing.[21] By all accounts, Steve Jobs was chosen as CEO to transform Apple, and he then picked Tim Cook to succeed him, because of his ability to identify new opportunities and mobilize managers and other resources to take advantage of those opportunities.

Formal education and training are important in helping managers develop conceptual skills. Business training at the undergraduate and graduate (MBA) levels provides many of the conceptual tools (theories and techniques in marketing, finance, and other areas) that managers need to perform their roles effectively. The study of management helps develop the skills that allow managers to understand the big picture confronting an organization. The ability to focus on the big picture lets managers see beyond the situation immediately at hand and consider choices while keeping in mind the organization's long-term goals.

Today continuing management education and training, including training in advanced IT, are an integral step in building managerial skills because theories and techniques are constantly being developed to improve organizational effectiveness, such as total quality management, benchmarking, and web-based organization and business-to-business (B2B) networks. A quick scan through a magazine such as *Forbes* or *Fortune* reveals a host of seminars on topics such as advanced marketing, finance, leadership, and human resource management that are offered to managers at many levels in the organization, from the most senior corporate executives to middle managers. Microsoft, IBM, Oracle, and many other organizations designate a portion of each manager's personal budget to be used at the manager's discretion to attend management development programs.

In addition, organizations may wish to develop a particular manager's abilities in a specific skill area—perhaps to learn an advanced component of departmental skills, such as international bond trading, or to learn the skills necessary to implement total quality management. The organization thus pays for managers to attend specialized programs to develop these skills. Indeed, one signal that a manager is performing well is an organization's willingness to invest in that manager's skill development. Similarly, many nonmanagerial employees who are performing at a high level (because they have studied management) are often sent to intensive management training programs to develop their management skills and to prepare them for promotion to first-level management positions.

human skills The ability to understand, alter, lead, and control the behavior of other individuals and groups.

Human skills include the general ability to understand, alter, lead, and control the behavior of other individuals and groups. The ability to communicate, to coordinate, and to motivate people, and to mold individuals into a cohesive team distinguishes effective from ineffective managers. By all accounts, Tim Cook and Michael Dell possess a high level of these human skills.

Like conceptual skills, human skills can be learned through education and training, as well as be developed through experience.[22] Organizations increasingly utilize advanced programs in leadership skills and team leadership as they seek to capitalize on the advantages of self-managed teams.[23] To manage personal interactions effectively, each person in an organization needs to learn how to empathize with other people—to understand their viewpoints and the problems they face. One way to help managers understand their personal strengths and weaknesses is to have their superiors, peers, and subordinates provide feedback about their job performance. Thorough and direct feedback allows managers to develop their human skills.

technical skills The job-specific knowledge and techniques required to perform an organizational role.

Technical skills are the *job-specific* skills required to perform a particular type of work or occupation at a high level. Examples include a manager's specific manufacturing, accounting, marketing, and increasingly, IT skills. Managers need a range of technical skills to be effective. The array of technical skills managers need depends on their position in their organization. The manager of a restaurant, for example, may need cooking skills to fill in for an absent cook, accounting and bookkeeping skills to keep track of receipts and costs and to administer the payroll, and aesthetic skills to keep the restaurant looking attractive for customers.

As noted earlier, managers and employees who possess the same kinds of technical skills typically become members of a specific department and are known as,

Figure 1.5
Types and Levels of
Managers

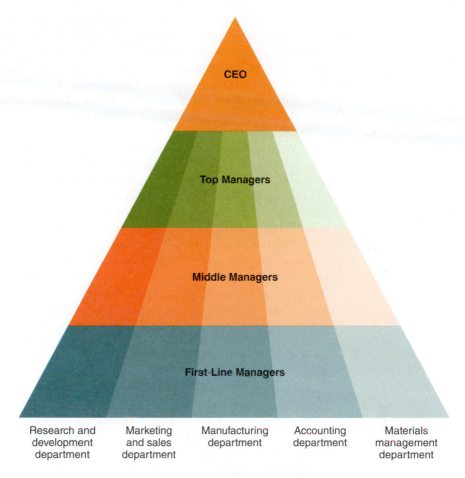

for example, marketing managers or manufacturing managers.[24] Managers are grouped into different departments because a major part of a manager's responsibility is to monitor, train, and supervise employees so their job-specific skills and expertise increase. Obviously this is easier to do when employees with similar skills are grouped into the same department because they can learn from one another and become more skilled and productive at their particular job.

Figure 1.5 shows how an organization groups managers into departments on the basis of their job-specific skills. It also shows that inside each department, a managerial hierarchy of first-line, middle, and top managers emerges. At Dell, for example, Michael Dell hired experienced top managers to take charge of the marketing, sales, and manufacturing departments and to develop work procedures to help middle and first-line managers control the company's explosive sales growth. When the head of manufacturing found he had no time to supervise computer assembly, he recruited experienced manufacturing middle managers from other companies to assume this responsibility.

core competency
The specific set of departmental skills, knowledge, and experience that allows one organization to outperform another.

Today the term core competency is often used to refer to the specific set of departmental skills, knowledge, and experience that allows one organization to outperform its competitors. In other words, departmental skills that create a core competency give an organization a *competitive advantage*. Dell, for example, was the first PC maker to develop a core competency in materials management that allowed it to produce PCs at a much lower cost than its competitors—a major source of competitive advantage. Similarly, 3M is well known for its core competency in research and development (R&D) that allows it to innovate new products at a faster rate than its competitors, and Xerox has been working to strengthen its ability to provide a full-range of imaging services that can be customized to meet the needs of each of the companies it serves.

Effective managers need all three kinds of skills—conceptual, human, and technical—to help their organizations perform more efficiently and effectively. The absence of even one type of managerial skill can lead to failure. One of the biggest problems that people who start small businesses confront, for example, is their lack of appropriate conceptual and human skills. Someone who has the technical skills to start a new business does not necessarily know how to manage the venture successfully. Similarly, one of the biggest problems that scientists or engineers who switch careers from research to management confront is their lack of effective human skills. Ambitious managers or prospective managers are constantly in search of the latest educational contributions to help them develop the conceptual, human, and technical skills they need to perform at a high level in today's changing and increasingly competitive global environment.

Developing new and improved skills through education and training has become a priority for both aspiring managers and the organizations they work for. As we discussed earlier, many people are enrolling in advanced management courses; but many companies, such as Microsoft, GE, and IBM, have established their own colleges to train and develop their employees and managers at all levels. Every year these companies put thousands of their employees through management programs designed to identify the employees who the company believes have the competencies that can be developed to become its future top managers. Most organizations closely link promotion to a manager's ability to acquire the competencies that a particular company believes are important.[25] At Apple and 3M, for example, the ability to successfully lead a new product development team is viewed as a vital requirement for promotion; at Accenture and IBM, the ability to attract and retain clients is viewed as a skill their IT consultants must possess. We discuss the various kinds of skills managers need to develop in most of the chapters of this book.

Recent Changes in Management Practices

The tasks and responsibilities of managers have been changing dramatically in recent years. Two major factors that have led to these changes are global competition and advances in information technology. Stiff competition for resources from organizations both at home and abroad has put increased pressure on all managers to improve efficiency and effectiveness. Increasingly, top managers are encouraging lower-level managers to look beyond the goals of their own departments and take a cross-departmental view to find new opportunities to improve organizational performance. Modern IT gives managers at all levels and in all areas access to more and better information and improves their ability to plan, organize, lead, and control. IT also gives employees more job-related information and allows them to become more skilled, specialized, and productive.[26]

Restructuring and Outsourcing

To utilize IT to increase efficiency and effectiveness, CEOs and top management teams have been restructuring organizations and outsourcing specific organizational activities to reduce the number of employees on the payroll and make more productive use of the remaining workforce.

restructuring

Downsizing an organization by eliminating the jobs of large numbers of top, middle, and first-line managers and nonmanagerial employees.

Restructuring involves simplifying, shrinking, or downsizing an organization's operations to lower operating costs, as both Dell and Xerox have been forced to do. The financial crisis that started in 2009 forced most companies—large and small, and profit and nonprofit—to find ways to reduce costs because their customers are spending less money, so their sales and revenues decrease. Restructuring can be done by eliminating product teams, shrinking departments, and reducing levels in the hierarchy, all of which result in the loss of large numbers of jobs of top, middle, or first-line managers, as well as nonmanagerial employees. Modern IT's ability to improve efficiency has increased the amount of downsizing in recent years because IT makes it possible for fewer employees to perform a particular work task. IT increases each person's ability to process information and make decisions more quickly and accurately, for example. U.S. companies are spending over $100 billion a year to purchase advanced IT that can improve efficiency and effectiveness. We discuss the many dramatic effects of IT on management in Chapter 13 and throughout this book.

Restructuring, however, can produce some powerful negative outcomes. It can reduce the morale of remaining employees, who worry about their own job security. And top managers of many downsized organizations realize that they downsized too far when their employees complain they are overworked and when increasing numbers of customers complain about poor service.[27] Dell faced this charge in the 2010s as it continued to reduce the number of its customer service representatives and outsource their jobs to India to lower costs.

outsourcing

Contracting with another company, usually abroad, to have it perform an activity the organization previously performed itself.

Outsourcing involves contracting with another company, usually in a low-cost country abroad, to have it perform a work activity the organization previously performed itself, such as manufacturing, marketing, or customer service. Outsourcing increases efficiency because it lowers operating costs, freeing up money and resources that can be used in more effective ways—for example, to develop new products.

The need to respond to low-cost global competition has speeded outsourcing dramatically in the 2000s. Over 3 million U.S. jobs in the manufacturing sector have been lost since 2000 as companies have moved their operations to countries such as China, Taiwan, and Malaysia. Tens of thousands of high-paying IT jobs have also moved abroad, to countries like India and Russia, where programmers work for one-third the salary of those in the United States. Dell employs over 12,000 customer service reps in India, for example.[28]

Large for-profit organizations today typically employ 10% to 20% fewer people than they did 10 years ago because of restructuring and outsourcing. Ford, IBM, AT&T, HP, Dell, and DuPont are among the thousands of organizations that have streamlined their operations to increase efficiency and effectiveness. The argument is that the managers and employees who have lost their jobs will find employment in new and growing U.S. companies where their skills and experience will be better utilized. For example, the millions of manufacturing jobs that have been lost overseas will be replaced by higher-paying U.S. jobs in the service sector that are made possible because of the growth in global trade. At the same time, many companies have experienced growing problems with outsourcing in the 2010s, and the move to insource jobs (that is, to bring them back to the United States) has been increasing as discussed in the following "Managing Globally."

MANAGING GLOBALLY

First Outsourcing, Now Insourcing

Outsourcing has become a major global strategic imperative over the last decades; to survive against low-cost competitors U.S. companies have been forced to find ways to reduce costs by moving manufacturing overseas.

First, millions of unskilled manufacturing jobs were outsourced to countries in Asia and Central America; then semiskilled and skilled jobs in engineering and information technology followed. There is a huge talented workforce in countries such as India and China, where millions of workers have the skills to satisfy job requirements and are willing to work for a fraction of what companies must pay workers in the United States.

Boeing embraces insourcing: the first Boeing 787 Dreamliner is being built at Boeing's Paine Field near Everett, Washington.

In some areas, such as the production of clothes and shoes and the assembly of electronic devices such as iPhones and PCs that are labor intensive, countries such as the United States will never be able to regain a competitive advantage because of low labor costs overseas. However, there are other areas in which companies that depend on a reliable supply of high-quality components and finished products have experienced problems with outsourcing production abroad, and many companies have or are in the process of moving back production to the United States—the process of insourcing. There are many reasons for this: Some relate to quality issues and some relate to the enormous problems that most electronics companies experienced after the disastrous flooding in Thailand and the tsunami that struck Japan cut off the supply of vital components. Thousands of U.S. companies were unable to obtain the chips and memory circuits necessary to maintain production, and they became backlogged with orders and lost billions in potential sales.

Boeing experienced firsthand the problems in controlling quality and product development during the building of the Boeing 787 Dreamliner that was finally delivered to its first customer in 2011. Boeing had experienced great success with outsourcing the production of many important components when it developed its previous new airliner, the 777. To tap into the skills of engineers in countries abroad and to reduce costs, Boeing decided early in development of the 787 to work closely with its suppliers who invested in the equipment and facilities necessary to meet Boeing's demands. Its Dreamliner team has about 50 suppliers from the United States and around the world; the partnership features six companies from Japan, six from Britain, five from France, two from Germany, two from Sweden, and one each from South Korea and Italy.[29] They make sections of the fuselage, landing gear, parts of the wing, pumps, valves, engines, brakes, doors, waste systems, escape slides, tires, tubing, cabin lighting, and ducts.

Boeing announced the first of several important delays in delivery dates of key components with overseas suppliers in 2007.[30] A major setback was a problem that arose in 2009 when major structural problems were found in the design of the assembly connecting the wing to the fuselage. Boeing was forced to postpone the date of introduction of the innovative new 787, and when it was finally delivered, it was over two years late to market.

In 2012 it was still having the problem of obtaining components fast enough to ramp up production of the 787 in order to better meet customer demand, and in 2013 the new fleet of Dreamliners was grounded until a major battery problem was solved. It is reevaluating its outsourcing strategy and has already decided to insource production of more components in order to obtain more control over its global supply chain. Like many other companies Boeing has seen the disadvantages of offshore production, including shipping costs, logistical problems, and quality issues. And many U.S. companies are working with their employees and unions to establish pay rates that will make it practical to insource production of many complex or bulky products. For example, GE worked with its unions to establish an agreement that would allow it to bring back to the United States the manufacturing of water heaters and many of the complex components that go into its appliances. Similarly, Caterpillar announced that it would reorganize global production of excavators and triple the volume of excavators made in the United States for export to the Americas. Every manufacturing job brought back to the United States is valuable, especially in a recession.[31] The growing rate of insourcing provides a signal to all U.S. companies that they need to have a second source of supply to ensure they do not suffer when unexpected problems from natural and political factors arise quickly and disrupt their manufacturing activities.

Empowerment and Self-Managed Teams

The second principal way managers have sought to increase efficiency and effectiveness is by empowering lower-level employees and moving to self-managed teams. Empowerment is a management technique that involves giving employees more authority and responsibility over how they perform their work activities. The way in which John Deere, the well-known tractor manufacturer, empowered its employees illustrates how this technique can help raise performance. The employees who assemble Deere's vehicles possess detailed knowledge about how Deere products work. Deere's managers realized these employees could become persuasive salespeople if they were given training. So groups of these employees were given intensive sales training and sent to visit Deere's customers and explain to them how to operate and service the company's new products. While speaking with customers, these newly empowered "salespeople" also collect information that helps Deere develop new products that better meet customers' needs. The new sales jobs are temporary; employees go on assignment but then return to the production line, where they use their new knowledge to find ways to improve efficiency and quality.

empowerment
The expansion of employees' knowledge, tasks, and decision-making responsibilities.

Lonnie Love, an Illinois farmer, checks out the custom wiring job on his John Deere tractor. Technicians, such as the one working on Love's tractor, add irreplaceable know-how to help John Deere's sales force.

LO 1-5 Discuss some major changes in management practices today that have occurred as a result of globalization and the use of advanced information technology (IT).

Often companies find that empowering employees can lead to so many kinds of performance gains that they use their reward systems to promote empowerment. For example, Deere's moves to empower employees were so successful that the company negotiated a new labor agreement with its employees to promote empowerment. The agreement specifies that pay increases will be based on employees' learning new skills and completing college courses in areas such as computer programming that will help the company increase efficiency and quality. Deere has continued to make greater use of teams throughout the 2010s, and its profits have soared because its competitors cannot match its user-friendly machines that are the result of its drive to respond to its customers' needs.

IT is being increasingly used to empower employees because it expands employees' job knowledge and increases the scope of their job responsibilities. Frequently IT allows one employee to perform a task that was previously performed by many employees. As a result, the employee has more autonomy and responsibility. IT also facilitates the use of a self-managed team, a group of employees who assume collective responsibility for organizing, controlling, and supervising their own work activities.[32] Using IT designed to give team members real-time information about each member's performance, a self-managed team can often find ways to accomplish a task more quickly and efficiently. Moreover, self-managed teams assume many tasks and responsibilities previously performed by first-line managers, so a company can better utilize its workforce.[33] First-line managers act as coaches or mentors whose job is not to tell employees what to do but to provide advice and guidance and help teams find new ways to perform their tasks more efficiently.[34] Using the same IT, middle managers can easily monitor what is happening in these teams and make better resource allocation decisions as a result. We discuss self-managed teams in more detail in Chapter 11.

self-managed team A group of employees who assume responsibility for organizing, controlling, and supervising their own activities and monitoring the quality of the goods and services they provide.

Challenges for Management in a Global Environment

Because the world has been changing more rapidly than ever before, managers and other employees throughout an organization must perform at higher and higher levels.[35] In the last 20 years, rivalry between organizations competing domestically (in the same country) and globally (in countries abroad) has increased dramatically. The rise of global organizations, organizations that operate and compete in more than one country, has pressured many organizations to identify better ways to use their resources and improve their performance. The successes of the German chemical companies Schering and Hoechst, Italian furniture manufacturer Natuzzi, Korean electronics companies Samsung and LG, Brazilian plane maker Embraer, and Europe's Airbus Industries are putting pressure on companies in other countries to raise their level of performance to compete successfully against these global organizations.

LO 1-6 Discuss the principal challenges managers face in today's increasingly competitive global environment.

Even in the not-for-profit sector, global competition is spurring change. Schools, universities, police forces, and government agencies are reexamining their operations because looking at how activities are performed in other countries often reveals better ways to do them. For example, many curriculum and teaching changes in the United States have resulted from the study of methods that Japanese and European school systems use. Similarly, European and Asian hospital systems have learned much from the U.S. system—which may be the most effective, though not the most efficient, in the world.

global organizations Organizations that operate and compete in more than one country.

Today managers who make no attempt to learn from and adapt to changes in the global environment find themselves reacting rather than innovating, and their organizations often become uncompetitive and fail. Four major challenges stand out for managers in today's world: building a competitive advantage, maintaining ethical standards, managing a diverse workforce, and utilizing new information systems and technologies.

Building Competitive Advantage

What are the most important lessons for managers and organizations to learn if they are to reach and remain at the top of the competitive environment of business? The answer relates to the use of organizational resources to build a competitive advantage. Competitive advantage is the ability of one organization to outperform other organizations because it produces desired goods or services more efficiently and effectively than its competitors. The four building blocks of competitive advantage are superior *efficiency, quality, innovation,* and *responsiveness to customers* (see Figure 1.6).

Organizations increase their efficiency when they reduce the quantity of resources (such as people and raw materials) they use to produce goods or services. In today's competitive environment, organizations continually search for new ways to use their resources to improve efficiency. Many organizations are training their workforces in the new skills and techniques needed to operate heavily computerized assembly plants. Similarly, cross-training gives employees the range of skills they need to perform many different tasks; and organizing employees in new ways, such as in self-managed teams, lets them make good use of their skills. These are important steps in the effort to improve productivity. Japanese and German companies invest far more in training employees than do American or Italian companies.

Managers must improve efficiency if their organizations are to compete successfully with companies operating in Mexico, China, Malaysia, and other countries where employees are paid comparatively low wages. New methods

competitive advantage The ability of one organization to outperform other organizations because it produces desired goods or services more efficiently and effectively than they do.

Figure 1.6

Building Blocks of Competitive Advantage

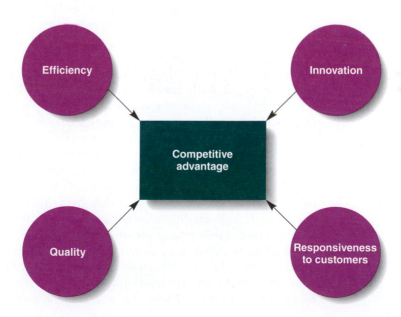

must be devised either to increase efficiency or to gain some other competitive advantage—higher-quality goods, for example—if outsourcing and the loss of jobs to low-cost countries are to be prevented.

The challenge from global organizations such as Korean electronics manufacturers, Mexican agricultural producers, and European design and financial companies also has increased pressure on companies to develop the skills and abilities of their workforces in order to improve the quality of their goods and services. One major thrust to improving quality has been to introduce the quality-enhancing techniques known as *total quality management (TQM)*. Employees involved in TQM are often organized into quality control teams and are responsible for finding new and better ways to perform their jobs; they also must monitor and evaluate the quality of the goods they produce. We discuss ways of managing TQM successfully in Chapter 14.

Today companies can win or lose the competitive race depending on their *speed*—how fast they can bring new products to market—or their *flexibility*—how easily they can change or alter the way they perform their activities to respond to actions of their competitors. Companies that have speed and flexibility are agile competitors: Their managers have superior planning and organizing abilities; they can think ahead, decide what to do, and then speedily mobilize their resources to respond to a changing environment. We examine how managers can build speed and flexibility in their organizations in later chapters. Michael Dell and Tim Cook are working hard to make Dell and Apple agile companies that can react to the technological changes taking place in a digital world—their problem is how to maintain their competitive advantage against HP and Google.

innovation The process of creating new or improved goods and services or developing better ways to produce or provide them.

Innovation, the process of creating new or improved goods and services that customers want or developing better ways to produce or provide goods and services, poses a special challenge. Managers must create an organizational setting in which people are encouraged to be innovative. Typically innovation takes place in small groups or teams; management decentralizes control of work activities to team members and creates an organizational culture that rewards risk taking. For example, a team composed of Apple and Nike employees came up with the idea for a new model of iPod that would be able to record and measure the distance its owner had run, among other things, and the companies formed an alliance to make it.[36] Managing innovation and creating a work setting that encourages risk taking are among the most difficult managerial tasks.

Organizations compete for customers with their products and services, so training employees to be responsive to customers' needs is vital for all organizations, but particularly for service organizations. Retail stores, banks, and hospitals, for example, depend entirely on their employees to perform behaviors that result in high-quality service at a reasonable cost.[37] As many countries (the United States, Canada, and Switzerland are just a few) move toward a more service-based economy (in part because of the loss of manufacturing jobs to China, Malaysia, and other countries with low labor costs), managing behavior in service organizations is becoming increasingly important. Many organizations are empowering their customer service employees and giving them the authority to take the lead in providing high-quality customer service. As noted previously, empowering non-managerial employees and creating self-managed teams change the role of first-line managers and lead to more efficient use of organizational resources.

Sometimes the best efforts of managers to revitalize their organization's fortunes fail; and faced with bankruptcy, the directors of these companies are forced to appoint a new CEO who has a history of success in rebuilding a company.

turnaround management

The creation of a new vision for a struggling company based on a new approach to planning and organizing to make better use of a company's resources and allow it to survive and prosper.

Turnaround management is the creation of a new vision for a struggling company using a new approach to planning and organizing to make better use of a company's resources and allow it to survive and eventually prosper—something Apple's Steve Jobs excelled at. It involves developing radical new strategies such as how to reduce the number of products sold or change how they are made and distributed, or close corporate and manufacturing operations to reduce costs. Organizations that appoint turnaround CEOs are generally experiencing a crisis because they have become inefficient or ineffective; sometimes this is because of poor management over a continuing period, and sometimes it occurs because a competitor introduces a new product or technology that makes their own products unattractive to customers. For example, when Apple introduced the iPhone in 2007, sales of the former best-selling Motorola Razr cell phone plummeted because customers demand state-of-the-art products. Motorola has not recovered although it introduced new phones using Google's Android platform in 2009. Similarly, sales of BlackBerry and Nokia smartphones have plunged while those of Samsung have soared as it has introduced a line of Galaxy smartphones that can compete with the iPhone.

Achieving a competitive advantage requires that managers use all their skills and expertise, as well as their companies' other resources, to find new and improved ways to improve efficiency, quality, innovation, and responsiveness to customers. We revisit this theme often as we examine the ways managers plan strategies, organize resources and activities, and lead and control people and groups to increase efficiency and effectiveness.

Maintaining Ethical and Socially Responsible Standards

Managers at all levels, especially after the recent economic crisis, are under considerable pressure to make the best use of resources to increase the level at which their organizations perform.[38] For example, top managers feel pressure from shareholders to increase the performance of the entire organization to boost its stock price, improve profits, or raise dividends. In turn, top managers may pressure middle managers to find new ways to use organizational resources to increase efficiency or quality and thus attract new customers and earn more revenues—and then middle managers hit on their department's supervisors.

Pressure to increase performance can be healthy for an organization because it leads managers to question how the organization is working, and it encourages them to find new and better ways to plan, organize, lead, and control. However, too much pressure to perform can be harmful.[39] It may induce managers to behave unethically, and even illegally, when dealing with people and groups inside and outside the organization.[40]

A purchasing manager for a nationwide retail chain, for example, might buy inferior clothing as a cost-cutting measure or ignore the working conditions under which products are made to obtain low-priced products. These issues faced the managers of companies that make footwear and clothing in the 1990s, when customers learned about the sweatshop conditions in which garment and shoe workers around the world labored. Today companies such as Nike, Walmart, and Apple are trying to stop sweatshop practices and prevent managers abroad from adopting work practices that harm their workers. They now employ hundreds of inspectors who police the factories overseas that make the products they sell and who can terminate contracts with suppliers when they behave in an unethical or illegal way. Nevertheless, in a 2010 report Apple revealed that its investigations showed that sweatshop conditions still existed in some of the factories it used abroad. Apple said that at least 55 of the 102 factories were ignoring Apple's rule that staff cannot work more than 60 hours a week, for example. Apple is continuing its efforts to reduce these abuses.[41]

Similarly, to secure a large foreign contract, a sales manager in a large company, such as in the defense or electronics industry, might offer bribes to foreign officials to obtain lucrative contracts—even though this is against the law. In 2010, for example, German electronic equipment maker Siemens agreed to pay $1.4 billion in fines to settle claims that it paid bribes and kickbacks to organizations around the world between 2001 and 2007. Securities and Exchange Commission (SEC) Chairman Christopher Cox alleged, "Siemens paid staggering amounts of money to circumvent the rules and gain business. Now, they will pay for it with the largest settlement in the history of the Foreign Corrupt Practices Act since it became law in 1977."[42]

The issue of social responsibility, discussed in Chapter 3, centers on deciding what obligations a company has toward the people and groups affected by its activities—such as employees, customers, or the cities in which it operates. Some companies have strong views about social responsibility; their managers believe they should protect the interests of others. But some managers may decide to act in an unethical way and put their own interests first, hurting others in the process. A recent example showing why managers must always keep the need to act in an ethical and socially responsible way at the forefront of their decision making is profiled in the following "Ethics in Action" box.

ETHICS IN ACTION

"What Goes Around Comes Around": How Dishonest Top Managers Can Corrupt Any Organization—Even a Court

Court judges at the federal, state, or county level are expected to possess the highest ethical standards and abide by the rule of law; they are the top managers who organize and control the legal system and the courts. Why should ordinary citizens believe they are protected by the legal system and their individual rights will be upheld fairly and objectively if they cannot trust their judges? Then imagine the shock citizens of Luzerne County in the heart of Pennsylvania's struggling coal country experienced in 2009 when an FBI investigation revealed that two respected county judges, Mark Ciavarella and Michael Conahan, had conspired to use the managerial power of their office to profit financially by sending thousands of teenagers to jail.

How these managers controlled the county's judicial organization for this unethical and illegal purpose was revealed when investigators found that the number of youths entering detention in Luzerne County was two to three times higher than in similar counties—and these teens were being jailed for trivial violations. A boy who shoplifted a $4 bottle of nutmeg was jailed, for example, and so was the boy with him, who was charged with conspiracy to shoplift because he was physically present. A girl who created a MySpace page that taunted her school administrator was also incarcerated.

Pictured are disgraced former judges Mark Ciavarella and Michael Conahan as they leave the courtroom building during their trial, which accused them of benefiting financially from giving thousands of teenagers illegal jail terms.

Judges Ciavarella and Conahan's plan to subvert the court's organization and control system worked as follows. At that time Conahan controlled the county court and its budget, and Ciavarella controlled sentencing in the juvenile court. As the top managers of the court system, they were largely unsupervised. Over time they worked together to shut down the old county-run juvenile detention center by refusing to send teens there and cutting off its funding. Meanwhile they created their own organization, a privately owned detention center built by the judges' corrupt associates, to replace the facility. Then the judges contracted with the county to pay $58 million to use their detention center for 10 years. The judges admitted they took "at least" $2.6 million in payoffs from their private youth detention center and tried to hide this dishonest income by creating false income tax records.

Most of the teens sentenced were on trial for minor first offenses, and their time in court to defend themselves often lasted for only minutes. Most were unrepresented because their parents were told it was "unnecessary to have a lawyer"; as a consequence one boy remained locked up for over two years. The Pennsylvania Supreme Court has expunged the records of over 2,000 youths who were sent into detention by Ciavarella because of his unethical behavior. "They sold their oath of offices to the highest bidders and engaged in ongoing schemes to defraud the public of honest services that were expected from them," said Deron Roberts, chief of the FBI's Scranton office.[43]

In 2009 these corrupt ex-justices agreed to a plea bargain in which they would spend seven years in jail and pay back millions of dollars. This plea bargain collapsed in 2009 when the presiding judge decided it was too lenient, and in 2010 they faced charges that could lead them to spend decades in jail.[44] In fact, in August 2011, Ciavarella received a 28-year sentence; unethical managers eventually face the consequences of their unsavory actions.

Managing a Diverse Workforce

A major challenge for managers everywhere is to recognize the ethical need and legal requirement to treat human resources fairly and equitably. Today the age, gender, race, ethnicity, religion, sexual preference, and socioeconomic composition of the workforce presents new challenges for managers. To create a highly trained and motivated workforce, as well as to avoid lawsuits, managers must establish human resource management (HRM) procedures and practices that are legal and fair and do not discriminate against any organizational members.[45] Today most organizations understand that to motivate effectively and take advantage of the talents of a diverse workforce, they must make promotion opportunities available to each and every employee.[46] Managers must recognize the performance-enhancing possibilities of a diverse workforce, such as the ability to take advantage of the skills and experiences of different kinds of people.[47] Accenture provides a good example of a company that has utilized the potential of its diverse employees.

Global consulting company Accenture is a first-mover in taking advantage of the diverse skills and knowledge of its consultants to create teams that can provide the customized solutions needed to best satisfy clients such as large overseas companies.

Accenture is a global management consulting company that serves the IT needs of thousands of client companies located in over 120 countries around the world. A major driving force behind Accenture's core organizational vision is to manage and promote diversity in order to improve employee performance and client satisfaction. At Accenture, managers at all levels realize consultants bring distinct experiences, talents, and values to their work, and a major management initiative is to take advantage of that diversity to encourage collaboration between consultants to improve the service Accenture provides to each of its clients. Because Accenture's clients are also diverse by country, religion, ethnicity, and so forth, it tries to match its teams of consultants to the attributes of its diverse clients.

Accenture provides hundreds of diversity management training programs to its consultants each year using its 13 teams of global human capital and diversity experts, who collaborate to create its programs. Accenture also encourages each of its consultants to pursue opportunities to "work across different geographies, workforces, and generations to create agile global leaders."[48] In 2010 one-third of its global workforce was composed of women, who also hold 16% of its management positions at all levels. Accenture chooses to buy from suppliers who can also demonstrate their commitment to diversity, and in 2010 nearly $300 million or 15% of Accenture's purchasing came from small minority- or women-owned suppliers. The firm also provides diversity training programs to its suppliers and prospective suppliers around the world to show them how diversity can increase their efficiency and effectiveness. In all these ways, Accenture uses its expertise in managing diversity to promote individual and organizational performance—one reason it has become the most successful and fast-growing consultancy company in the world.

Managers who value their diverse employees not only invest in developing these employees' skills and capabilities but also succeed best in promoting performance over the long run. Today more organizations are realizing that people are their most important resource and that developing and protecting human resources is the most important challenge for managers in a competitive global environment. Kevin Rollins, a former CEO of Dell, commented, "I've seen firsthand the power of a diverse workforce. Leveraging the similarities and differences of all team members enables Dell to develop the best products, provide a superior customer experience, and contribute in meaningful ways to the communities where we do business."[49] And as Takahiro Moriguchi of Union Bank of California said when accepting a national diversity award for his company when he was its CEO, "By searching for talent from among the disabled, both genders, veterans, gay, all ethnic groups and all nationalities, we gain access to a pool of ideas, energy, and creativity as wide and varied as the human race itself."[50] We discuss the many issues surrounding the management of a diverse workforce in Chapter 3.

Utilizing IT and E-Commerce

As we have discussed, another important challenge for managers is to continually utilize efficient and effective new IT that can link and enable managers and

UPS Dispatch Coordinator Jim McCauley shows driver Muamer Pleh how many stops he will be making in his next delivery run—all made possible by the company's new software that allows each driver to plan the most efficient delivery route each day, which saves the company time and money.

employees to better perform their jobs—whatever their level in the organization. One example of how IT has changed the jobs of people at all organizational levels comes from UPS, where, until 2006, its drivers relied on maps, note cards, and their own experience to plan the fastest way to deliver hundreds of parcels each day. This changed after UPS invested over $600 million to develop a computerized route optimization system that each evening plans each of its 56,000 drivers' routes for the next day in the most efficient way by, for example, minimizing the number of left turns that waste both time and gas. The program has been incredibly successful and has been continuously updated so that by 2010 UPS drivers covered tens of million fewer miles each month while they delivered ever-increasing numbers of packages faster.

Increasingly, new kinds of IT enable not just individual employees but also self-managed teams by giving them important information and allowing virtual interactions around the globe using the Internet. Increased global coordination helps improve quality and increase the pace of innovation. Microsoft, Hitachi, IBM, and most companies now search for new IT that can help them build a competitive advantage. The importance of IT is discussed in detail in Chapters 13 and throughout the text you will find icons that alert you to examples of how IT is changing the way companies operate.

Summary and Review

WHAT IS MANAGEMENT? A manager is a person responsible for supervising the use of an organization's resources to meet its goals. An organization is a collection of people who work together and coordinate their actions to achieve a wide variety of goals. Management is the process of using organizational resources to achieve organizational goals effectively and efficiently through planning, organizing, leading, and controlling. An efficient organization makes the most productive use of its resources. An effective organization pursues appropriate goals and achieves these goals by using its resources to create goods or services that customers want. **[LO 1-1]**

MANAGERIAL TASKS The four principal managerial tasks are planning, organizing, leading, and controlling. Managers at all levels of the organization and in all departments perform these tasks. Effective management means managing these activities successfully. **[LO 1-2]**

LEVELS AND SKILLS OF MANAGERS Organizations typically have three levels of management. First-line managers are responsible for the day-to-day supervision of nonmanagerial employees. Middle managers are responsible for developing and utilizing organizational resources efficiently and effectively. Top managers have cross-departmental responsibility. Three main kinds of managerial skills are conceptual, human, and technical. The need to develop and build technical skills leads organizations to divide managers into departments according to their job-specific responsibilities. Top managers must establish appropriate goals for the entire organization and verify that department managers are using resources to achieve those goals. **[LO 1-3, 1-4]**

RECENT CHANGES IN MANAGEMENT PRACTICES To increase efficiency and effectiveness, many organizations have altered how they operate. Managers have restructured and downsized operations and outsourced activities to reduce costs. Companies are also empowering their workforces and using self-managed teams to increase efficiency and effectiveness. Managers are increasingly using IT to achieve these objectives. **[LO 1-5]**

CHALLENGES FOR MANAGEMENT IN A GLOBAL ENVIRONMENT Today's competitive global environment presents many interesting challenges to managers. One of the main challenges is building a competitive advantage by increasing efficiency; quality; speed, flexibility, and innovation; and customer responsiveness. Other challenges are behaving in an ethical and socially responsible way toward people inside and outside the organization, managing a diverse workforce, and utilizing new IT. **[LO 1-6]**

Management *in Action*

TOPICS FOR DISCUSSION AND ACTION

Discussion

1. Describe the difference between efficiency and effectiveness, and identify real organizations that you think are, or are not, efficient and effective. **[LO 1-1]**

2. In what ways can managers at each of the three levels of management contribute to organizational efficiency and effectiveness? **[LO 1-3]**

3. Identify an organization that you believe is high-performing and one that you believe is low-performing. Give five reasons why you think the performance levels of the two organizations differ so much. **[LO 1-2, 1-4]**

4. What are the building blocks of competitive

advantage? Why is obtaining a competitive advantage important to managers? **[LO 1-5]**

5. In what ways do you think managers' jobs have changed the most over the last 10 years? Why have these changes occurred? **[LO 1-6]**

Action

6. Choose an organization such as a school or a bank; visit it; then list the different organizational resources it uses. How do managers use these resources to maintain and improve its performance? **[LO 1-2, 1-4]**

7. Visit an organization, and talk to first-line, middle, and top managers about their respective management

roles in the organization and what they do to help the organization be efficient and effective. **[LO 1-3, 1-4]**

8. Ask a middle or top manager, perhaps someone you already know, to give examples of how he or she performs the managerial tasks of planning, organizing, leading, and controlling. How much time does he or she spend in performing each task? **[LO 1-3]**

9. Like Mintzberg, try to find a cooperative manager who will allow you to follow him or her around for a day. List the roles the manager plays, and indicate how much time he or she spends performing them. **[LO 1-3, 1-4]**

BUILDING MANAGEMENT SKILLS
Thinking about Managers and Management [LO 1-2, 1-3, 1-4]

Think of an organization that has provided you with work experience and the manager to whom you reported (or talk to someone who has had extensive work experience); then answer these questions:

1. Think about your direct supervisor. Of what department is he or she a member, and at what level of management is this person?

2. How do you characterize your supervisor's approach to management? For example, which particular management tasks and roles does this person perform most often? What kinds of management skills does this manager have?

3. Do you think the tasks, roles, and skills of your supervisor are appropriate for the particular job he or she performs? How could this manager improve his or her task performance? How can IT affect this?

4. How did your supervisor's approach to management affect your attitudes and behavior? For example, how well did you perform as a subordinate, and how motivated were you?

5. Think about the organization and its resources. Do its managers use organizational resources effectively? Which resources contribute most to the organization's performance?

6. Describe how the organization treats its human resources.

How does this treatment affect the attitudes and behaviors of the workforce?

7. If you could give your manager one piece of advice or change one management practice in the organization, what would it be?

8. How attuned are the managers in the organization to the need to increase efficiency, quality, innovation, or responsiveness to customers? How well do you think the organization performs its prime goals of providing the goods or services that customers want or need the most?

MANAGING ETHICALLY [LO 1-1, 1-3]

Think about an example of unethical behavior that you observed in the past. The incident could be something you experienced as an employee or a customer or something you observed informally.

Questions

1. Either by yourself or in a group, give three reasons why you think the behavior was unethical. For example, what rules or norms were broken? Who benefited or was harmed by what took place? What was the outcome for the people involved?

2. What steps might you take to prevent such unethical behavior and encourage people to behave in an ethical way?

SMALL GROUP BREAKOUT EXERCISE [LO 1-2, 1-3, 1-4]
Opening a New Restaurant

Form groups of three or four people, and appoint one group member as the spokesperson who will communicate your findings to the entire class when called on by the instructor. Then discuss the following scenario:

You and your partners have decided to open a large, full-service restaurant in your local community; it will be open from 7 a.m. to 10 p.m. to serve breakfast, lunch, and dinner. Each of you is investing $50,000 in the venture, and together you have secured a bank loan for $300,000 to begin operations. You and your partners have little experience in managing a restaurant beyond serving meals or eating in restaurants, and you now face the task of deciding how you will manage the restaurant and what your respective roles will be.

1. Decide what each partner's managerial role in the restaurant will be. For example, who will be responsible for the necessary departments and specific activities? Describe your managerial hierarchy.

2. Which building blocks of competitive advantage do you need to establish to help your restaurant succeed? What criteria will you use to evaluate how successfully you are managing the restaurant?

3. Discuss the most important decisions that must be made about (a) planning, (b) organizing, (c) leading, and (d) controlling to allow you and your partners to use organizational resources effectively and build a competitive advantage.

4. For each managerial task, list the issues to solve, and decide which roles will contribute the most to your restaurant's success.

BE THE MANAGER [LO 1-2, 1-5]

Problems at Achieva

You have just been called in to help managers at Achieva, a fast-growing Internet software company that specializes in business-to-business (B2B) network software. Your job is to help Achieva solve some management problems that have arisen because of its rapid growth.

Customer demand to license Achieva's software has boomed so much in just two years that more than 50 new software programmers have been added to help develop a new range of software products. Achieva's growth has been so swift that the company still operates informally, its organizational structure is loose and flexible, and programmers are encouraged to find solutions to problems as they go along. Although this structure worked well in the past, you have been told that problems are arising.

There have been increasing complaints from employees that good performance is not being recognized in the organization and that they do not feel equitably treated. Moreover, there have been complaints about getting managers to listen to their new ideas and to act on them. A bad atmosphere is developing in the company, and recently several talented employees left. Your job is to help Achieva's managers solve these problems quickly and keep the company on the fast track.

Questions

1. What kinds of organizing and controlling problems is Achieva suffering from?

2. What kinds of management changes need to be made to solve them?

BLOOMBERG BUSINESSWEEK CASE IN THE NEWS [LO 1-1, 1-2, 1-3, 1-6]

Costco CEO Craig Jelinek Leads the Cheapest, Happiest Company in the World

Joe Carcello has a great job. The 59-year-old has an annual salary of $52,700, gets five weeks of vacation a year, and is looking forward to retiring on the sizable nest egg in his 401(k), which his employer augments with matching funds. After 26 years at his company, he's not worried about layoffs. In 2009, as the recession deepened, his bosses handed out raises. "I'm just grateful to come here to work every day," he says.

This wouldn't be remarkable except that Carcello works in retail, one of the stingiest industries in America, with some of the most dissatisfied workers. On May 29, Wal-Mart Stores (WMT) employees in Miami, Boston, and the San Francisco Bay Area began a week-long strike. (A Walmart spokesman told MSNBC the strike was a "publicity stunt.") Workers at an Amazon.com (AMZN) fulfillment center in Leipzig, Germany, also recently held strikes to demand higher pay and better benefits. (An Amazon spokesman says its employees earn more than the average warehouse worker.) In its 30-year history, Carcello's employer, Costco, has never had significant labor troubles.

Costco Wholesale (COST), the second-largest retailer in the U.S. behind Walmart, is an anomaly in an age marked by turmoil and downsizing. Known for its $55-a-year membership fee and its massive, austere warehouses stocked floor to ceiling with indulgent portions of everything from tilapia to toilet paper, Costco has thrived over the last five years. While competitors lost customers to the Internet and weathered a wave of investor pessimism, Costco's sales have grown 39 percent and its stock price has doubled since 2009. The hot streak continued through last year's retirement of widely admired cofounder and Chief Executive Officer Jim Sinegal. The share price is up 30 percent under the leadership of its new, plain-spoken CEO, Craig Jelinek.

Despite the sagging economy and challenges to the industry, Costco pays its hourly workers an average of $20.89 an hour, not including overtime (vs. the minimum wage of $7.25 an hour). By comparison, Walmart said its average wage for full-time employees in the U.S. is $12.67 an hour. Eighty-eight percent of Costco employees have company-sponsored health insurance; Walmart says that "more than half" of its do. Costco workers with coverage pay premiums that amount to less than 10 percent of the overall cost of their plans. It treats its employees well in the belief that a happier work environment will result in a more profitable company. "I just think people need to make a living wage with health benefits," says Jelinek. "It also puts more money back into the economy and creates a healthier country. It's really that simple."

The Issaquah (Wash.) headquarters of Costco, 20 miles from Seattle, radiate frugality. The floor of the executive wing is covered in faded blue carpet, and in the boardroom, six faux-wood tables—which would look at home in a public school teachers' lounge—are jammed together. On the walls are several Van Gogh and Picasso prints (less than $15 at Art.com), along with two badly staged photographs of the company's board of directors. In one, a picture of Jelinek's head has been awkwardly taped onto the frame, hovering above a Weber grill.

Jelinek earned $650,000 in 2012, plus a $200,000 bonus and stock options worth about $4 million, based on the company's performance. That's more than Sinegal, who made $325,000 a year. By contrast, Walmart CEO Mike Duke's 2012 base salary was $1.3 million; he was also awarded a $4.4 million cash bonus and $13.6 million in stock grants.

No-frills is the defining style of the 627 Costco warehouses around the world. Each stocks around 4,000 different products, and almost everything is marked up 14 percent or less over cost. Items like diapers, suitcases, and wine, which it sells under its in-house Kirkland Signature brand, get a maximum 15 percent bump. All of the stock sits on industrial shelving that the company internally calls "the steel," or in piles that spill from pallets. After accounting for expenses such as real estate costs and wages, Costco barely ekes out a profit on many of its products. Eighty percent of its gross profit comes from membership fees; customers renew their memberships at a rate of close to 90 percent, the company says. It raised its fee by 10 percent in 2011 to few complaints.

"They are buying and selling more olive oil, more cranberry juice, more throw rugs than just about anybody," says David Schick, an analyst at Stifel Nicolaus. And that allows Costco to get bulk discounts from its suppliers, often setting the industry's lowest price. Even Amazon can't beat Costco's prices, which means that "showrooming," or browsing in stores but buying online for the better price, isn't much of a concern for Jelinek.

Costco's constitutional thrift makes its generous pay and health packages all the more remarkable. About 4 percent of its workers, including those who give away samples and sell mobile phones, are part-time and employed by contractors, though Costco says it seeks to ensure they have above-industry-average pay. And while Walmart, Amazon, and others actively avoid unionization, Costco, while not exactly embracing it, is comfortable that the International Brotherhood of Teamsters represents about 15 percent of its U.S. employees. "They are philosophically much better than anyone else I have worked with," says Rome Aloise, a Teamsters vice president.

Costco may be a different species than most big-box chains, but it shares genetic material with Walmart, Kmart, Kohl's (KSS), and Target (TGT), all born in 1962 to cater to the boundless consumer appetites of an expanding middle class. The companies had the same inspiration: FedMart, whose founder, Sol Price, opened some of the first discount department stores in San Diego in the early 1950s, for the first time pairing diverse merchandise and bargain basement prices under a single roof. In the wake of FedMart's collapse after a failed acquisition,

Price and his son Robert created Price Club in 1976. The new store stocked only a few thousand products, all in large quantity, and marked everything up a set amount in the belief that retailers added only limited value; prices should reflect that. Price, who died in 2009, was a demanding boss known for knocking fragile merchandise onto the floor if it blocked customer sightlines. Yet he had a devotion to fair labor practices: He solicited the Teamsters to represent his employees. "Sol's message was always very much the same if you saw through the rough exterior," says Paul Latham, the vice president of marketing and membership services at Costco, who, like many Costco executives, started his career working for Price. "It was about creating value, about treating your employees and customers well, and respecting your vendors—and ultimately rewarding your shareholders in the process."

Sinegal was one of Price's top lieutenants. He brought the Price Club model to Washington in 1983 to start Costco with local attorney Jeff Brotman. Price Club and Costco merged in 1992, and though the combination was troubled and Price left soon after, Sinegal maintained Price's pro-labor principles. Costco went public in 1985, and over the years, Wall Street repeatedly asked it to reduce wages and health benefits. Sinegal instead boosted them every three years.

Jelinek has a strong opinion about one of Costco's best-known products, the $1.50 hot dog the company makes in a facility in California's Central Valley and distributes to all of its North American warehouses. "I'm a purist," he says, noting that he has a hot dog for lunch every day when he's traveling. "No mustard. No ketchup. I savor that hot dog. I eat 'em plain." He says he never touches the pizza. (It's good, he says, he just doesn't care for it.)

Like his predecessor, Jelinek, 59, preaches simplicity, and he has a propensity for aphorisms ending with "good things will happen to you." "This isn't Harvard grad stuff," he says. "We sell quality stuff at the best possible price. If you treat consumers with respect and treat employees with respect, good things are going to happen to you." He vows to continue Sinegal's legacy and doesn't seem to mind a widespread characterization of himself as a "Jim clone." "We don't want to be casualties like some of these other big retailers, like the Sears of the world and Kmart and Circuit City. We are in for the long haul," he says.

As CEO, his biggest move is increasing Costco's international presence. Over the next two years, Costco will open its first locations in France and Spain. Two-thirds of Costco's expansion over the next five years will be international, according to Galanti, with a focus on Japan, Taiwan, and South Korea. Jelinek's strategy is to require Costco's suppliers to give it global deals, even if it upsets their relationships with other retailers in different countries. "If you are going to do business with us, you are not going to say that we can't sell to you in this country," he says. "They are not really respecting our business if they do that." Another challenge for Jelinek is making his voice heard over Sinegal's. Even after his official retirement in early 2012, the co-founder stuck around as an adviser for another year, sitting in on meetings and surreptitiously funneling questions through Joseph Portera, executive vice president of Costco's eastern division. Jelinek concedes he's in a peculiar position, considering Sinegal's presence and the iron-like grip he had over the company, but he says he's happy to have his former boss around. "It's kind of like, your dad is still your dad, no matter how old he is. So it's been great. He lets me run the business, and every once in a while he says, 'Have you rethought this?'"

Another pressing issue is the age of the company's executive team, most of whom are in their late 50s. "We're all old," says Brotman, who is 70. Jelinek says his team talks about succession planning constantly and recently expanded a program to ready the next wave of company leaders. It will have to look inside, since Costco does not hire business school graduates—thanks to another idiosyncrasy meant to preserve its distinct company culture. It cultivates employees who work the floor in its warehouses and sponsors them through graduate school. Seventy percent of its warehouse managers started at the company by pushing carts and ringing cash registers. Employees rarely leave: The company turnover rate is 5 percent among employees who have been there over a year, and less than 1 percent among the executive ranks. That's impressive, but it also suggests the company does not have a regular influx of outside views. Even John Matthews, vice president in charge of human resources, calls the company "awfully inbred."

Sol Price's virtuous cycle continues to work for the company—happy employees are more productive, effective workers. Jelinek is content to focus on the future of Costco, vowing to keep prices low, volumes high, and his employees happy. "As long as you continue to take care of the customer, take care of employees, and keep your expenses in line, good things are going to happen to you," he says. "I don't ever want us to become irrelevant. I hope when I'm 90, and this company is around 30 years from now, I can go eat a hot dog at a Costco food court and hear someone say, 'I remember you.'"

Questions

1. How does CEO Jelinek's management approach resemble that of former CEO Sinegal?

2. How would you describe Costco's approach to planning and strategy?

3. What is Costco's approach to managing its workforce? How has this approach influenced the culture and values of the company?

Source: Brad Stone, "Costco CEO Craig Jelinek Leads the Cheapest, Happiest Company in the World," *Bloomberg Businessweek,* www.businessweek.com, accessed June 6, 2013.

History of Management Thought

The systematic study of management began in the closing decades of the 19th century, after the Industrial Revolution had swept through Europe and America. In the new economic climate, managers of all types of organizations—political, educational, and economic—were increasingly turning their focus toward finding better ways to satisfy customers' needs. Many major economic, technical, and cultural changes were taking place at this time. With the introduction of steam power and the development of sophisticated machinery and equipment, the Industrial Revolution changed the way goods were produced, particularly in the weaving and clothing industries. Small workshops run by skilled workers who produced hand-manufactured products (a system called *crafts production*) were being replaced by large factories in which sophisticated machines controlled by hundreds or even thousands of unskilled or semiskilled workers made products. For example, raw cotton and wool that in the past families or whole villages working together had spun into yarn were now shipped to factories where workers operated machines that spun and wove large quantities of yarn into cloth.

Owners and managers of the new factories found themselves unprepared for the challenges accompanying the change from small-scale crafts production to large-scale mechanized manufacturing. Moreover, many of the managers and supervisors in these workshops and factories were engineers who had only a technical orientation. They were unprepared for the social problems that occur when people work together in large groups (as in a factory or shop system). Managers began to search for new techniques to manage their organizations' resources, and soon they began to focus on ways to increase the efficiency of the worker–task mix. They found help from Frederick W. Taylor.

scientific management
The systematic study of relationships between people and tasks to increase efficiency.

F. W. Taylor and Scientific Management

Frederick W. Taylor (1856–1915) is best known for defining the techniques of scientific management, the systematic study of relationships between people and tasks for the purpose of redesigning the work process to increase efficiency. Taylor was a manufacturing manager who eventually became a consultant and taught other managers how to apply his scientific management techniques. Taylor believed that if the amount of time and effort that each worker expends to produce a unit of output (a finished good or service) can be reduced by increasing specialization and the division of labor, the production process will become more efficient. Taylor believed the way to create the most efficient division of

Frederick W. Taylor, founder of scientific management, and one of the first people to study the behavior and performance of people in the workplace.

labor could best be determined by using scientific management techniques, rather than intuitive or informal rule-of-thumb knowledge. Based on his experiments and observations as a manufacturing manager in a variety of settings, he developed four principles to increase efficiency in the workplace:[1]

- Principle 1: *Study the way workers perform their tasks, gather all the informal job knowledge that workers possess, and experiment with ways of improving the way tasks are performed.*

To discover the most efficient method of performing specific tasks, Taylor studied in great detail and measured the ways different workers went about performing their tasks. One of the main tools he used was a time and motion study, which involves the careful timing and recording of the actions taken to perform a particular task. Once Taylor understood the existing method of performing a task, he then experimented to increase specialization; he tried different methods of dividing up and coordinating the various tasks necessary to produce a finished product. Usually this meant simplifying jobs and having each worker perform fewer, more routine tasks. Taylor also sought to find ways to improve each worker's ability to perform a particular task—for example, by reducing the number of motions workers made to complete the task, by changing the layout of the work area or the type of tool workers used, or by experimenting with tools of different sizes.

- Principle 2: *Codify the new methods of performing tasks into written rules and standard operating procedures.*

Once the best method of performing a particular task was determined, Taylor specified that it should be recorded so that the procedures could be taught to all workers performing the same task. These rules could be used to further standardize and simplify jobs—essentially, to make jobs even more routine. In this way efficiency could be increased throughout an organization.

- Principle 3: *Carefully select workers so that they possess skills and abilities that match the needs of the task, and train them to perform the task according to the established rules and procedures.*

To increase specialization, Taylor believed workers had to understand the tasks that were required and be thoroughly trained in order to perform a task at the required level. Workers who could not be trained to this level were to be transferred to a job where they were able to reach the minimum required level of proficiency.[2]

- Principle 4: *Establish a fair or acceptable level of performance for a task, and then develop a pay system that provides a reward for performance above the acceptable level.*

To encourage workers to perform at a high level of efficiency, and to provide them with an incentive to reveal the most efficient techniques for performing a task, Taylor advocated that workers benefit from any gains in performance. They should be paid a bonus and receive some percentage of the performance gains achieved through the more efficient work process.

By 1910, Taylor's system of scientific management had become nationally known and in many instances faithfully and fully practiced.[3] However, managers in many organizations chose to implement the new principles of scientific management selectively. This decision ultimately resulted in problems. For example, some managers using scientific management obtained increases in performance, but rather than sharing performance gains with workers through bonuses as Taylor had advocated, they simply increased the amount of work that each worker was expected to do. Many workers experiencing the reorganized work system found that as their performance increased, managers required them to do more work for the same pay. Workers also learned that increases in performance often meant fewer jobs and a greater threat of layoffs because fewer workers were needed. In addition, the specialized, simplified jobs were often monotonous and repetitive, and many workers became dissatisfied with their jobs.

From a performance perspective, the combination of the two management practices—(1) achieving the right mix of worker–task specialization and (2) linking people and tasks by the speed of the production line—resulted in huge savings in cost and huge increases in output that occur in large, organized work settings. For example, in 1908, managers at the Franklin Motor Company using scientific management principles redesigned the work process, and the output of cars increased from 100 cars a month to 45 cars a day; workers' wages, however, increased by only 90%.[4]

Taylor's work has had an enduring effect on the management of production systems. Managers in every organization, whether it produces goods or services, now carefully analyze the basic tasks that workers must perform and try to create a work environment that will allow their organizations to operate most efficiently. We discuss this important issue in Chapter 7.

Weber's Bureaucratic Theory

Side by side with scientific managers studying the person–task mix to increase efficiency, other researchers were focusing on how to increase the efficiency with which organizations were managed. Max Weber, a German professor of sociology, outlined his famous principles of bureaucracy—a formal system of organization and administration designed to ensure efficiency and effectiveness—and created bureaucratic theory. A bureaucratic system of administration is based on five principles:

bureaucracy
A formal system of organization and administration designed to ensure efficiency and effectiveness.

authority The power to hold people accountable for their actions and to allocate organizational resources.

- Principle 1: *In a bureaucracy, a manager's formal authority derives from the position he or she holds in the organization.*

  Authority is the power to hold people accountable for their actions and to make decisions concerning the use of organizational resources. Authority gives managers the right to direct and control their subordinates' behavior to achieve organizational goals. In a bureaucratic system of administration, obedience is owed to a manager, not because of any personal qualities—such as personality, wealth, or social status—but because the manager occupies a position that is associated with a certain level of authority and responsibility.[5]

- Principle 2: *In a bureaucracy, people should occupy positions because of their performance, not because of their social standing or personal contacts.*

  This principle was not always followed in Weber's time and is often ignored today. Some organizations and industries are still affected by social networks in which personal contacts and relations, not job-related skills, influence hiring and promotion decisions.

Max Weber developed the principles of bureaucracy during Germany's burgeoning industrial revolution to help organizations increase their efficiency and effectiveness.

- Principle 3: *The extent of each position's formal authority and their responsibilities, and their relationship to other positions in an organization, should be clearly specified.*

When the tasks and authority associated with various positions in the organization are clearly specified, managers and workers know what is expected of them and what to expect from each other. Moreover, an organization can hold all its employees strictly accountable for their actions when they know their exact responsibilities.

- Principle 4: *Authority can be exercised effectively in an organization when positions are arranged hierarchically, so employees know whom to report to and who reports to them.*[6]

Managers must create an organizational hierarchy of authority that makes it clear who reports to whom and to whom managers and workers should go if conflicts or problems arise. This principle is especially important in the armed forces, FBI, CIA, and other organizations that deal with sensitive issues involving possible major repercussions. It is vital that managers at high levels of the hierarchy be able to hold subordinates accountable for their actions.

- Principle 5: *Managers must create a well-defined system of rules, standard operating procedures, and norms so that they can effectively control behavior within an organization.*

rules Formal written instructions specifying to be taken.

standard operating procedures (SOPs) Specific sets of rules about how to perform a particular task.

norms Unwritten informal codes of conduct that prescribe how people should act in particular situations and are considered important by most members of a group or organization.

Rules are formal written instructions that specify actions to be taken under different circumstances to achieve specific goals (for example, if A happens, do B). Standard operating procedures (SOPs) are specific sets of written instructions about how to perform a certain aspect of a task. A rule might state that at the end of the workday employees are to leave their machines in good order, and a set of SOPs specifies exactly how they should do so, itemizing which machine parts must be oiled or replaced. Norms are unwritten, informal codes of conduct that prescribe how people should act in particular situations. For example, an organizational norm in a restaurant might be that waiters should help each other if time permits.

Rules, SOPs, and norms provide behavioral guidelines that increase the performance of a bureaucratic system because they specify the best ways to accomplish organizational tasks. Companies such as McDonald's and Walmart have developed extensive rules and procedures to specify the behaviors required of their employees, such as "Always greet the customer with a smile."

Weber believed that organizations that implement all five principles establish a bureaucratic system that improves organizational performance. The specification of positions and the use of rules and SOPs to regulate how tasks are performed make it easier for managers to organize and control the work of subordinates. Similarly, fair and equitable selection and promotion systems improve managers' feelings of security, reduce stress, and encourage organizational members to act ethically and further promote the interests of the organization.[7]

If bureaucracies are not managed well, many problems can result. Sometimes managers allow rules and SOPs, "bureaucratic red tape," to become so cumbersome that decision making becomes slow and inefficient and organizations are unable to change. When managers rely too much on rules to solve problems and not enough on their own skills and judgment, their behavior becomes inflexible. A key challenge for managers is to use bureaucratic principles to benefit, rather than harm, an organization.

The Work of Mary Parker Follett

If F. W. Taylor is considered the father of management thought, Mary Parker Follett (1868–1933) serves as its mother.[8] Much of her writing about management and the way managers should behave toward workers was a response to her concern that Taylor was ignoring the human side of the organization. She pointed out that management often overlooks the multitude of ways in which employees can contribute to the organization when managers allow them to participate and exercise initiative in their everyday work lives.[9] Taylor, for example, never proposed that managers involve workers in analyzing their jobs to identify better ways to perform tasks, or even ask workers how they felt about their jobs. Instead, he used time and motion experts to analyze workers' jobs for them. Follett, in contrast, argued that because workers know the most about their jobs, they should be involved in job analysis and managers should allow them to participate in the work development process.

Mary Parker Follett, an early management thinker who advocated, "Authority should go with knowledge … whether it is up the line or down."

Follett proposed, "Authority should go with knowledge . . . whether it is up the line or down." In other words, if workers have the relevant knowledge, then workers, rather than managers, should be in control of the work process itself, and managers should behave as coaches and facilitators—not as monitors and supervisors. In making this statement, Follett anticipated the current interest in self-managed teams and empowerment. She also recognized the importance of having managers in different departments communicate directly with each other to speed decision making. She advocated what she called "cross-functioning": members of different departments working together in cross-departmental teams to accomplish projects—an approach that is increasingly utilized today.[10] She proposed that knowledge and expertise, not managers' formal authority deriving from their position in the hierarchy, should decide who would lead at any particular moment. She believed, as do many management theorists today, that power is fluid and should flow to the person who can best help the organization achieve its goals. Follett took a horizontal view of power and authority, rather than viewing the vertical chain of command as being most essential to effective management. Thus, Follett's approach was very radical for its time.

The Hawthorne Studies and Human Relations

Probably because of its radical nature, Follett's work went unappreciated by managers and researchers until quite recently. Most continued to follow in the footsteps of Taylor, and to increase efficiency, they studied ways to improve various characteristics of the work setting, such as job specialization or the kinds of tools workers used.

Workers in a telephone manufacturing plant, in 1931. Around this time, researchers at the Hawthorne Works of the Western Electric Company began to study the effects of work setting characteristics—such as lighting and rest periods—on productivity. To their surprise, they discovered that workers' productivity was affected more by the attention they received from researchers than by the characteristics of the work setting—a phenomenon that became known as the Hawthorne effect.

One series of studies was conducted from 1924 to 1932 at the Hawthorne Works of the Western Electric Company.[11] This research, now known as the Hawthorne studies, was initiated as an attempt to investigate how characteristics of the work setting—specifically the level of lighting or illumination—affect worker fatigue and performance. The researchers conducted an experiment in which they systematically measured worker productivity at various levels of illumination.

The experiment produced some unexpected results. The researchers found that regardless of whether they raised or lowered the level of illumination, productivity increased. In fact, productivity began to fall only when the level of illumination dropped to the level of moonlight, a level at which presumably workers could no longer see well enough to do their work efficiently.

As you can imagine, the researchers found these results very puzzling. They invited a noted Harvard psychologist, Elton Mayo, to help them. Mayo proposed another series of experiments to solve the mystery. These experiments, known as the relay assembly test experiments, were designed to investigate the effects of other aspects of the work context on job performance, such as the effect of the number and length of rest periods and hours of work on fatigue and monotony.[12] The goal was to raise productivity.

During a two-year study of a small group of female workers, the researchers again observed that productivity increased over time, but the increases could not be solely attributed to the effects of changes in the work setting. Gradually, the researchers discovered that, to some degree, the results they were obtaining were influenced by the fact that the researchers themselves had become part of the experiment. In other words, the presence of the researchers was affecting the results because the workers enjoyed receiving attention and being the subject of study and were willing to cooperate with the researchers to produce the results they believed the researchers desired.

Hawthorne effect
Workers' productivity is affected more by observation or attention received than by physical work setting.

human relations movement
Advocates behavior and leadership training of supervisors to elicit worker cooperation and improve productivity.

Subsequently, it was found that many other factors also influence worker behavior, and it was not clear what was actually influencing the Hawthorne workers' behavior. However, this particular effect—which became known as the Hawthorne effect—seemed to suggest that the attitudes of workers toward their managers affect the level of workers' performance. In particular, the significant finding was that a manager's behavior or leadership approach can affect performance. This finding led many researchers to turn their attention to managerial behavior and leadership. If supervisors could be trained to behave in ways that would elicit cooperative behavior from their subordinates, then productivity could be increased. From this view emerged the human relations movement, which advocates that supervisors be behaviorally trained to manage subordinates in ways that elicit their cooperation and increase their productivity.

The importance of behavioral or human relations training became even clearer to its supporters after another series of experiments—the bank wiring room experiments. In a study of workers making telephone-switching equipment, researchers Elton Mayo and F. J. Roethlisberger discovered that the workers, as a group, had deliberately adopted a norm of output restriction to protect their jobs. Other group members subjected workers who violated this informal production norm to sanctions. Those who violated group performance norms and performed above the norm were called "ratebusters"; those who performed below the norm were called "chisellers."

The experimenters concluded that both types of workers threatened the group as a whole. Ratebusters threaten group members because they reveal to managers how fast the work can be done. Chisellers are looked down on because they are not doing their share of the work. Work-group members discipline both ratebusters and chisellers in order to create a pace of work that the workers (not the managers) think is fair. Thus, the work group's influence over output can be as great as the supervisors' influence. Since the work group can influence the behavior of its members, some management theorists argue that supervisors should be trained to behave in ways that gain the goodwill and cooperation of workers so that supervisors, not workers, control the level of work-group performance.

One of the main implications of the Hawthorne studies was that the behavior of managers and workers in the work setting is as important in explaining the level of performance as the technical aspects of the task. Managers must understand the workings of the informal organization, the system of behavioral rules and norms that emerge in a group, when they try to manage or change behavior in organizations. Many studies have found that, as time passes, groups often develop elaborate procedures and norms that bond members together, allowing unified action either to cooperate with management in order to raise performance or to restrict output and thwart the attainment of organizational goals.[13] The Hawthorne studies demonstrated the importance of understanding how the feelings, thoughts, and behavior of work-group members and managers affect performance. It was becoming increasingly clear to researchers that understanding behavior in organizations is a complex process that is critical to increasing performance.[14] Indeed, the increasing interest in the area of management known as organizational behavior, the study of the factors that have an impact on how individuals and groups respond to and act in organizations, dates from these early studies.

informal organization The system of behavioral rules and norms that emerge in work groups.

organizational behavior The study of factors that impact how workers respond to and act in an organization.

Theory X and Theory Y

Several studies after the Second World War revealed how assumptions about workers' attitudes and behavior affect managers' behavior. Douglas McGregor developed the most influential approach. He proposed that two different sets of assumptions about work attitudes and behaviors dominate the way managers think and affect how they behave in organizations. McGregor named these two contrasting sets of assumptions *Theory X* and *Theory Y*.[15]

According to the assumptions of Theory X, the average worker is lazy, dislikes work, and will try to do as little as possible. Moreover, workers have little ambition and wish to avoid responsibility. Thus, the manager's task is to counteract workers' natural tendencies to avoid work. To keep workers' performance at a high level, the manager must supervise them closely and control their behavior by means of "the carrot and stick"—rewards and punishments.

Managers who accept the assumptions of Theory X design and shape the work setting to maximize their control over workers' behaviors and minimize workers'

Theory X The assumption that workers will try to do as little as possible and avoid further responsibility unless rewarded or punished for doing otherwise.

control over the pace of work. These managers believe that workers must be made to do what is necessary for the success of the organization, and they focus on developing rules, SOPs, and a well-defined system of rewards and punishments to control behavior. They see little point in giving workers autonomy to solve their own problems because they think that the workforce neither expects nor desires cooperation. Theory X managers see their role as to closely monitor workers to ensure that they contribute to the production process and do not threaten product quality. Henry Ford, who closely supervised and managed his workforce, fits McGregor's description of a manager who holds Theory X assumptions.

Theory Y The assumption that workers will do what is best for an organization if given the proper work setting, opportunity and encouragement.

In contrast, Theory Y assumes that workers are not inherently lazy, do not naturally dislike work, and, if given the opportunity, will do what is good for the organization. According to Theory Y, the characteristics of the work setting determine whether workers consider work to be a source of satisfaction or punishment; and managers do not need to closely control workers' behavior in order to make them perform at a high level, because workers will exercise self-control when they are committed to organizational goals. The implication of Theory Y, according to McGregor, is that "the limits of collaboration in the organizational setting are not limits of human nature but of management's ingenuity in discovering how to realize the potential represented by its human resources."[16] It is the manager's task to create a work setting that encourages commitment to organizational goals and provides opportunities for workers to be imaginative and to exercise initiative and self-direction.

When managers design the organizational setting to reflect the assumptions about attitudes and behavior suggested by Theory Y, the characteristics of the organization are quite different from those of an organizational setting based on Theory X. Managers who believe that workers are motivated to help the organization reach its goals can decentralize authority and give more control over the job to workers, both as individuals and in groups. In this setting, individuals and groups are still accountable for their activities, but the manager's role is not to control employees but to provide support and advice, to make sure workers have the resources they need to perform their jobs, and to evaluate them on their ability to help the organization meet its goals.

These same kinds of debates are raging today as managers seek to increase both the efficiency and effectiveness of their organizations.

2
Values, Attitudes, Emotions, and Culture: The Manager as a Person

LEARNING OBJECTIVES

After studying this chapter, you should be able to:

1 Describe the various personality traits that affect how managers think, feel, and behave. **[LO 2-1]**

2 Explain what values and attitudes are and describe their impact on managerial action. **[LO 2-2]**

3 Appreciate how moods and emotions influence all members of an organization. **[LO 2-3]**

4 Describe the nature of emotional intelligence and its role in management. **[LO 2-4]**

5 Define organizational culture and explain how managers both create and are influenced by organizational culture. **[LO 2-5]**

No wonder the fabrics perform so well! With an inventor like Kevin Plank, Under Armour's innovative endurance products give larger sporting goods companies a run for their money.

Kevin Plank's Determination at Under Armour

What Does It Take to Succeed Against Tough Odds?

When Kevin Plank was a walk-on fullback football player at the University of Maryland in the 1990s, he often became annoyed that his T-shirt was soaked and weighted down with sweat. Always an original thinker, he wondered why athletic apparel couldn't be made out of some kind of polyester blend that would help athletes' and sports aficionados' muscles stay cool while wicking away, and not holding, moisture from sweat.[1] As he was finishing his undergraduate studies at Maryland, he started experimenting with different fabrics, testing their durability, comfort, and water resistance with the help of a local tailor. A prototype of Under Armour's first product—the 0039 compression shirt—was developed.[2]

Upon graduation from the University of Maryland, Plank was offered a position at Prudential Life Insurance. An entrepreneur at heart willing to risk everything to pursue his bold ideas, Plank realized

that accepting a secure position with an insurance company would have driven him nuts. So, he turned down the Prudential offer and mustered his determination to sell his innovative T-shirt.[3] With little business training or experience, and a lot of perseverance and discipline, Plank pursued the makings of what would become a major competitor of Nike 16 years later with net revenues over $1.8 billion in 2012.[4] Entering and succeeding in the competitive sports apparel industry dominated by huge players like Nike with vast resources and a widely recognized brand would seem like an impossible feat even for a seasoned business person with access to capital. With around $20,000 in the bank and the resolve to turn his idea into a viable venture, Plank succeeded against all odds.[5]

Very outgoing and confident, Plank used his network of athletic contacts from playing on teams in high school, military school, and the University of Maryland to get the word out about the shirt.[6] From the various teams he had played on, he was familiar enough with around 40 NFL players to contact them and tell them about the shirt. Living out of his car with his trunk full of shirts, Plank drove around to

45

training camps and schools to show athletes and managers his new product. Teaming up with two partners, Plank began running his business from the basement of his grandmother's house in Georgetown, Washington DC, with the help of a $250,000 small-business loan. As business and orders picked up, Under Armour outgrew the basement and set up shop on Sharp Street in Baltimore.[7] The rest has literally been history.

Under Armour currently produces and sells apparel, shoes, and accessories for women, men, and youth for athletics, sports, outdoor activities, and fitness.[8] The apparel is focused on regulating body temperature and improving performance under different conditions and is organized into three lines. Each line comes in three styles—tight fit or compression, fitted or athletic fit, and loose fit or relaxed. The HEATGEAR® line is to be worn in hot to warm temperatures singly or under equipment and is made of a microfiber blend that wicks sweat away from the skin, keeping wearers cool and dry. The very first compression T-shirt Plank originally developed and sold was a HEATGEAR® product that remains popular today. COLDGEAR®, which is to be worn in cold temperatures, wicks sweat away from the body and circulates body heat to maintain body temperature so that wearers are both warm and dry in cold weather. ALLSEASONSGEAR®, to be worn in temperatures that change, keeps people warm when it's chilly and cool and dry when it's warm.[9]

As chairman, CEO, and president, Plank has created and maintained a culture at Under Armour that is true to his own personality and values.[10] Just as he and his two partners worked as a team to start Under Armour, a team mentality pervades the culture and the brand. As employee Erin Wendell puts it, "Working here is like being part of a sports team."[11] Accomplishing great feats, taking risks, being active and excited, open minded, ambitious, imaginative, and courageous are important to Plank and part of Under Armour's culture—as is a focus on health. The hard work, determination, and conviction that got Plank through the early days of driving around to schools and training camps with boxes of T-shirts in the trunk of his car are also pervasive.[12]

Today, Under Armour is a global company with over 5,400 employees, operating in North America, Europe, the Middle East, Africa, Asia, and Latin America though most employees work in the United States.[13] Under Armour is currently headquartered in what used to be the 400,000-square-foot Tide Point complex where Procter & Gamble used to manufacture detergent in Baltimore.[14] Some of the original names of the facilities like Joy and Cheer remain and seem apt for a company like Under Armour.[15] Clearly, Plank demonstrates that being original, daring, and taking risks while at the same time being highly determined, disciplined, and persevering can help managers and entrepreneurs succeed against tough odds. As he puts it, "There's an entrepreneur right now, scared to death. . . . Get out of your garage and go take a chance, and start your business."[16]

Overview
Like people everywhere, Kevin Plank has his own distinctive personality, values, ways of viewing things, and personal challenges and disappointments. In this chapter we focus on the manager as a feeling, thinking human being. We start by describing enduring characteristics that influence how managers manage, as well as how they view other people, their organizations, and the world around them. We also discuss how managers' values, attitudes, and moods play out in organizations, shaping organizational culture. By the end of this chapter, you will appreciate how the personal characteristics of managers influence the process of management in general—and organizational culture in particular.

LO 2-1 Describe the various personality traits that affect how managers think, feel, and behave.

Enduring Characteristics: Personality Traits

All people, including managers, have certain enduring characteristics that influence how they think, feel, and behave both on and off the job. These characteristics are personality traits: particular tendencies to feel, think, and act in certain ways that can be used to describe the personality of every individual. It is important to understand the personalities of managers because their personalities influence their behavior and their approach to managing people and resources.

personality traits
Enduring tendencies to feel, think, and act in certain ways.

Some managers are demanding, difficult to get along with, and highly critical of other people. Other managers may be as concerned about effectiveness and efficiency as highly critical managers but are easier to get along with, are likable, and frequently praise the people around them. Both management styles may produce excellent results, but their effects on employees are quite different. Do managers deliberately decide to adopt one or the other of these approaches to management? Although they may do so part of the time, in all likelihood their personalities account for their different approaches. Indeed, research suggests that the way people react to different conditions depends, in part, on their personalities.[17]

The Big Five Personality Traits

We can think of an individual's personality as being composed of five general traits or characteristics: extraversion, negative affectivity, agreeableness, conscientiousness, and openness to experience.[18] Researchers often consider these the Big Five personality traits.[19] Each of them can be viewed as a continuum along which every individual or, more specifically, every manager falls (see Figure 2.1).

Figure 2.1

The Big Five Personality Traits

Managers' personalities can be described by determining where on each of the following continua they fall.

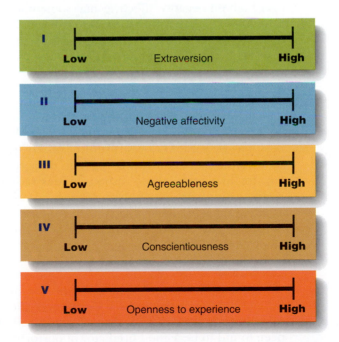

Some managers may be at the high end of one trait continuum, others at the low end, and still others somewhere in between. An easy way to understand how these traits can affect a person's approach to management is to describe what people are like at the high and low ends of each trait continuum. As will become evident as you read about each trait, no single trait is right or wrong for being an effective manager. Rather, effectiveness is determined by a complex interaction between the characteristics of managers (including personality traits) and the nature of the job and organization in which they are working. Moreover, personality traits that enhance managerial effectiveness in one situation may impair it in another.

extraversion

The tendency to experience positive emotions and moods and to feel good about oneself and the rest of the world.

EXTRAVERSION Extraversion is the tendency to experience positive emotions and moods and feel good about oneself and the rest of the world. Managers who are high on extraversion (often called *extraverts*) tend to be sociable, affectionate, outgoing, and friendly. Managers who are low on extraversion (often called *introverts*) tend to be less inclined toward social interactions and to have a less positive outlook. Being high on extraversion may be an asset for managers whose jobs entail especially high levels of social interaction. Managers who are low on extraversion may nevertheless be highly effective and efficient, especially when their jobs do not require much social interaction. Their quieter approach may enable them to accomplish quite a bit of work in limited time. See Figure 2.2 for an example of a scale that can be used to measure a person's level of extraversion.

negative affectivity

The tendency to experience negative emotions and moods, to feel distressed, and to be critical of oneself and others.

NEGATIVE AFFECTIVITY Negative affectivity is the tendency to experience negative emotions and moods, feel distressed, and be critical of oneself and others. Managers high on this trait may often feel angry and dissatisfied and complain about their own and others' lack of progress. Managers who are low on negative affectivity do not tend to experience many negative emotions and moods and are less pessimistic and critical of themselves and others. On the plus side, the critical approach of a manager high on negative affectivity may sometimes spur both the manager and others to improve their performance. Nevertheless, it is probably more pleasant to work with a manager who is low on negative affectivity; the better working relationships that such a manager is likely to cultivate also can be an important asset. Figure 2.3 is an example of a scale developed to measure a person's level of negative affectivity.

agreeableness

The tendency to get along well with other people.

AGREEABLENESS Agreeableness is the tendency to get along well with others. Managers who are high on the agreeableness continuum are likable, tend to be affectionate, and care about other people. Managers who are low on agreeableness may be somewhat distrustful of others, unsympathetic, uncooperative, and even at times antagonistic. Being high on agreeableness may be especially important for managers whose responsibilities require that they develop good, close relationships with others. Nevertheless, a low level of agreeableness may be an asset in managerial jobs that actually require that managers be antagonistic, such as drill sergeants and some other kinds of military managers. See Figure 2.2 for an example of a scale that measures a person's level of agreeableness.

conscientiousness

The tendency to be careful, scrupulous, and persevering.

CONSCIENTIOUSNESS Conscientiousness is the tendency to be careful, scrupulous, and persevering.[20] Managers who are high on the conscientiousness continuum are organized and self-disciplined; those who are low on this trait might sometimes appear to lack direction and self-discipline. Conscientiousness has been found to be a good predictor of performance in many kinds of jobs, including managerial jobs in a variety of organizations.[21] Entrepreneurs who found their own companies, like Kevin Plank profiled in "Management Snapshot," often are

Figure 2.2

Measures of
Extraversion,
Agreeableness,
Conscientiousness, and
Openness to Experience

Listed below are phrases describing people's behaviors. Please use the rating scale below to describe how accurately each statement describes *you*. Describe yourself as you generally are now, not as you wish to be in the future. Describe yourself as you honestly see yourself, in relation to other people you know of the same sex as you are and roughly your same age.

1	2	3	4	5
Very inaccurate	Moderately inaccurate	Neither inaccurate nor accurate	Moderately accurate	Very accurate

_____ 1. Am interested in people.

_____ 2. Have a rich vocabulary.

_____ 3. Am always prepared.

_____ 4. Am not really interested in others.*

_____ 5. Leave my belongings around.*

_____ 6. Am the life of the party.

_____ 7. Have difficulty understanding abstract ideas.*

_____ 8. Sympathize with others' feelings.

_____ 9. Don't talk a lot.*

_____ 10. Pay attention to details.

_____ 11. Have a vivid imagination.

_____ 12. Insult people.*

_____ 13. Make a mess of things.*

_____ 14. Feel comfortable around people.

_____ 15. Am not interested in abstract ideas.*

_____ 16. Have a soft heart.

_____ 17. Get chores done right away.

_____ 18. Keep in the background.*

_____ 19. Have excellent ideas.

_____ 20. Start conversations.

_____ 21. Am not interested in other people's problems.*

_____ 22. Often forget to put things back in their proper place.*

_____ 23. Have little to say.*

_____ 24. Do not have a good imagination.*

_____ 25. Take time out for others.

_____ 26. Like order.

_____ 27. Talk to a lot of different people at parties.

_____ 28. Am quick to understand things.

_____ 29. Feel little concern for others.*

_____ 30. Shirk my duties.*

_____ 31. Don't like to draw attention to myself.*

_____ 32. Use difficult words.

_____ 33. Feel others' emotions.

_____ 34. Follow a schedule.

_____ 35. Spend time reflecting on things.

_____ 36. Don't mind being the center of attention.

_____ 37. Make people feel at ease.

_____ 38. Am exacting in my work.

_____ 39. Am quiet around strangers.*

_____ 40. Am full of ideas.

* Item is reverse-scored: 1 = 5, 2 = 4, 4 = 2, 5 = 1
Scoring: Sum responses to items for an overall scale.
    Extraversion = sum of items 6, 9, 14, 18, 20, 23, 27, 31, 36, 39
    Agreeableness = sum of items 1, 4, 8, 12, 16, 21, 25, 29, 33, 37
    Conscientiousness = sum of items 3, 5, 10, 13, 17, 22, 26, 30, 34, 38
    Openness to experience = sum of items 2, 7, 11, 15, 19, 24, 28, 32, 35, 40

Source: Lewis R. Goldberg, Oregon Research Institute, http://ipip.ori.org/ipip/. Reprinted with permission.

openness to experience

The tendency to be original, have broad interests, be open to a wide range of stimuli, be daring, and take risks.

high on conscientiousness, and their persistence and determination help them to overcome obstacles and turn their ideas into successful new ventures. Figure 2.2 provides an example of a scale that measures conscientiousness.

OPENNESS TO EXPERIENCE Openness to experience is the tendency to be original, have broad interests, be open to a wide range of stimuli, be daring, and take risks.[22] Managers who are high on this trait continuum may be especially likely to take

Figure 2.3

A Measure of Negative Affectivity

Instructions: Listed below are a series of statements a person might use to describe her/his attitudes, opinions, interests, and other characteristics. If a statement is true or largely true, put a "T" in the space next to the item. Or if the statement is false or largely false, mark an "F" in the space.

Please answer every statement, even if you are not completely sure of the answer. Read each statement carefully, but don't spend too much time deciding on the answer.

_____ 1. I worry about things a lot.

_____ 2. My feelings are often hurt.

_____ 3. Small problems often irritate me.

_____ 4. I am often nervous.

_____ 5. My moods often change.

_____ 6. Sometimes I feel bad for no apparent reason.

_____ 7. I often have very strong emotions such as anger or anxiety without really knowing why.

_____ 8. The unexpected can easily startle me.

_____ 9. Sometimes, when I am thinking about the day ahead of me, I feel anxious and tense.

_____ 10. Small setbacks sometimes bother me too much.

_____ 11. My worries often cause me to lose sleep.

_____ 12. Some days I seem to be always "on edge."

_____ 13. I am more sensitive than I should be.

_____ 14. Sometimes I go from feeling happy to sad, and vice versa, for no good reason.

Scoring: Level of negative affectivity is equal to the number of items answered "True."

Source: Auke Tellegen, *Brief Manual for the Differential Personality Questionnaire,* Copyright © 1982. Paraphrased version reproduced by permission of University of Minnesota Press.

risks and be innovative in their planning and decision making. Entrepreneurs who start their own businesses—like Bill Gates of Microsoft, Jeff Bezos of Amazon.com, and Anita Roddick of The Body Shop—are, in all likelihood, high on openness to experience, which has contributed to their success as entrepreneurs and managers. Kevin Plank, discussed in this chapter's "Management Snapshot," founded his own company and continues to explore new ways for it to grow—a testament to his high level of openness to experience. Managers who are low on openness to experience may be less prone to take risks and more conservative in their planning and decision making. In certain organizations and positions, this tendency might be an asset. The manager of the fiscal office in a public university, for example, must ensure that all university departments and units follow the university's rules and regulations pertaining to budgets, spending accounts, and reimbursements of expenses. Figure 2.2 provides an example of a measure of openness to experience.

Successful managers occupy a variety of positions on the Big Five personality trait continua. One highly effective manager may be high on extraversion and negative affectivity; another equally effective manager may be low on both these traits; and still another may be somewhere in between. Members of an organization must understand these differences among managers because they can shed light on how managers behave and on their approach to planning, leading, organizing, or controlling. If subordinates realize, for example, that their manager is low on extraversion, they will not feel slighted when their manager seems to be aloof because they will realize that by nature he or she is simply not outgoing.

Managers themselves also need to be aware of their own personality traits and the traits of others, including their subordinates and fellow managers. A manager who knows that he has a tendency to be highly critical of other people might try to tone down his negative approach. Similarly, a manager who realizes that her chronically complaining subordinate tends to be so negative because of his personality may take all his complaints with a grain of salt and realize that things probably are not as bad as this subordinate says they are.

In order for all members of an organization to work well together and with people outside the organization, such as customers and suppliers, they must understand each other. Such understanding comes, in part, from an appreciation of some fundamental ways in which people differ from one another—that is, an appreciation of personality traits.

Other Personality Traits That Affect Managerial Behavior

Many other specific traits in addition to the Big Five describe people's personalities. Here we look at traits that are particularly important for understanding managerial effectiveness: locus of control; self-esteem; and the needs for achievement, affiliation, and power.

internal locus of control The tendency to locate responsibility for one's fate within oneself.

LOCUS OF CONTROL People differ in their views about how much control they have over what happens to and around them. The locus of control trait captures these beliefs.[23] People with an internal locus of control believe they themselves are responsible for their own fate; they see their own actions and behaviors as being major and decisive determinants of important outcomes such as attaining levels of job performance, being promoted, or being turned down for a choice job assignment. Some managers with an internal locus of control see the success of a whole organization resting on their shoulders. One example is Kevin Plank in the "Management Snapshot." An internal locus of control also helps to ensure ethical behavior and decision making in an organization because people feel accountable and responsible for their own actions.

external locus of control The tendency to locate responsibility for one's fate in outside forces and to believe one's own behavior has little impact on outcomes.

People with an external locus of control believe that outside forces are responsible for what happens to and around them; they do not think their own actions make much of a difference. As such, they tend not to intervene to try to change a situation or solve a problem, leaving it to someone else.

Managers need an internal locus of control because they *are* responsible for what happens in organizations; they need to believe they can and do make a difference, as does Kevin Plank at Under Armour. Moreover, managers are responsible for ensuring that organizations and their members behave in an ethical fashion, and for this as well they need an internal locus of control—they need to know and feel they can make a difference.

self-esteem The degree to which individuals feel good about themselves and their capabilities.

SELF-ESTEEM Self-esteem is the degree to which individuals feel good about themselves and their capabilities. People with high self-esteem believe they are

Confidence matters: A manager who takes difficulties in stride and can effectively lead is able to inspire subordinates while getting the job done.

need for achievement
The extent to which an individual has a strong desire to perform challenging tasks well and to meet personal standards for excellence.

need for affiliation The extent to which an individual is concerned about establishing and maintaining good interpersonal relations, being liked, and having other people get along.

need for power The extent to which an individual desires to control or influence others.

competent, deserving, and capable of handling most situations, as does Kevin Plank. People with low self-esteem have poor opinions of themselves, are unsure about their capabilities, and question their ability to succeed at different endeavors.[24] Research suggests that people tend to choose activities and goals consistent with their levels of self-esteem. High self-esteem is desirable for managers because it facilitates their setting and keeping high standards for themselves, pushes them ahead on difficult projects, and gives them the confidence they need to make and carry out important decisions.

NEEDS FOR ACHIEVEMENT, AFFILIATION, AND POWER Psychologist David McClelland has extensively researched the needs for achievement, affiliation, and power.[25] The need for achievement is the extent to which an individual has a strong desire to perform challenging tasks well and to meet personal standards for excellence. People with a high need for achievement often set clear goals for themselves and like to receive performance feedback. The need for affiliation is the extent to which an individual is concerned about establishing and maintaining good interpersonal relations, being liked, and having the people around him or her get along with one another. The need for power is the extent to which an individual desires to control or influence others.[26]

Research suggests that high needs for achievement and for power are assets for first-line and middle managers and that a high need for power is especially important for upper-level managers.[27] One study found that U.S. presidents with a relatively high need for power tended to be especially effective during their terms of office.[28] A high need for affiliation may not always be desirable in managers because it might lead them to try too hard to be liked by others (including subordinates) rather than doing all they can to ensure that performance is as high as it can and should be. Although most research on these needs has been done in the United States, some studies suggest that these findings may also apply to people in other countries such as India and New Zealand.[29]

Taken together, these desirable personality traits for managers—an internal locus of control, high self-esteem, and high needs for achievement and power—suggest that managers need to be take-charge people who not only believe their own actions are decisive in determining their own and their organizations' fates but also believe in their own capabilities. Such managers have a personal desire for accomplishment and influence over others.

Values, Attitudes, and Moods and Emotions

What are managers striving to achieve? How do they think they should behave? What do they think about their jobs and organizations? And how do they actually feel at work? We can find some answers to these questions by exploring managers' values, attitudes, and moods.

Values, attitudes, and moods and emotions capture how managers experience their jobs as individuals. *Values* describe what managers are trying to achieve through work and how they think they should behave. *Attitudes* capture their thoughts and feelings about their specific jobs and organizations. *Moods and emotions* encompass how managers actually feel when they are managing. Although these three aspects of managers' work experience are highly personal, they also have important implications for understanding how managers behave, how they treat and respond to others, and how, through their efforts, they help contribute to organizational effectiveness through planning, leading, organizing, and controlling.

Values: Terminal and Instrumental

terminal value
A lifelong goal or objective that an individual seeks to achieve.

instrumental value
A mode of conduct that an individual seeks to follow.

norms Unwritten, informal codes of conduct that prescribe how people should act in particular situations and are considered important by most members of a group or organization.

value system
The terminal and instrumental values that are guiding principles in an individual's life.

The two kinds of personal values are *terminal* and *instrumental*. A terminal value is a personal conviction about lifelong goals or objectives; an instrumental value is a personal conviction about desired modes of conduct or ways of behaving.[30] Terminal values often lead to the formation of norms, which are unwritten, informal codes of conduct, such as behaving honestly or courteously, that prescribe how people should act in particular situations and are considered important by most members of a group or organization.

Milton Rokeach, a leading researcher in the area of human values, identified 18 terminal values and 18 instrumental values that describe each person's value system (see Figure 2.4).[31] By rank ordering the terminal values from 1 (most important as a guiding principle in one's life) to 18 (least important as a guiding principle in one's life) and then rank ordering the instrumental values from 1 to 18, people can give good pictures of their value systems—what they are striving to achieve in life and how they want to behave.[32] (You can gain a good understanding of your own values by rank ordering first the terminal values and then the instrumental values listed in Figure 2.4.)

Several of the terminal values listed in Figure 2.4 seem to be especially important for managers—such as *a sense of accomplishment (a lasting contribution), equality (brotherhood, equal opportunity for all),* and *self-respect (self-esteem).* A manager who thinks a sense of accomplishment is of paramount importance might focus on making a lasting contribution to an organization by developing a new product that can save or prolong lives, as is true of managers at Medtronic (a company that makes medical devices such as cardiac pacemakers), or by opening a new foreign subsidiary. A manager who places equality at the top of his or her list of terminal values may be at the forefront of an organization's efforts to support, provide equal opportunities to, and capitalize on the many talents of an increasingly diverse workforce.

Other values are likely to be considered important by many managers, such as *a comfortable life (a prosperous life), an exciting life (a stimulating, active life), freedom (independence, free choice),* and *social recognition (respect, admiration).* The relative importance that managers place on each terminal value helps explain what they are striving to achieve in their organizations and what they will focus their efforts on.

Several of the instrumental values listed in Figure 2.4 seem to be important modes of conduct for managers, such as being *ambitious (hardworking, aspiring), broad-minded (open-minded), capable (competent, effective), responsible (dependable, reliable),* and *self-controlled (restrained, self-disciplined).* Moreover, the relative importance a manager places on these and other instrumental values may be a significant determinant of actual behaviors on the job. A manager who considers being *imaginative (daring, creative)* to be highly important, for example, is more likely to be innovative and take risks than is a manager who considers this to be

Figure 2.4
Terminal and
Instrumental Values

Terminal Values	Instrumental Values
A comfortable life (a prosperous life)	Ambitious (hardworking, aspiring)
An exciting life (a stimulating, active life)	Broad-minded (open-minded)
A sense of accomplishment (lasting contribution)	Capable (competent, effective)
A world at peace (free of war and conflict)	Cheerful (lighthearted, joyful)
A world of beauty (beauty of nature and the arts)	Clean (neat, tidy)
Equality (brotherhood, equal opportunity for all)	Courageous (standing up for your beliefs)
Family security (taking care of loved ones)	Forgiving (willing to pardon others)
Freedom (independence, free choice)	Helpful (working for the welfare of others)
Happiness (contentedness)	Honest (sincere, truthful)
Inner harmony (freedom from inner conflict)	Imaginative (daring, creative)
Mature love (sexual and spiritual intimacy)	Independent (self-reliant, self-sufficient)
National security (protection from attack)	Intellectual (intelligent, reflective)
Pleasure (an enjoyable, leisurely life)	Logical (consistent, rational)
Salvation (saved, eternal life)	Loving (affectionate, tender)
Self-respect (self-esteem)	Obedient (dutiful, respectful)
Social recognition (respect, admiration)	Polite (courteous, well-mannered)
True friendship (close companionship)	Responsible (dependable, reliable)
Wisdom (a mature understanding of life)	Self-controlled (restrained, self-disciplined)

Source: Adapted with the permission of The Free Press, a Division of Simon & Schuster, Inc., from *The Nature of Human Values* by Milton Rokeach. Copyright © 1973 by The Free Press. Copyright renewed © 1991 by Sandra Ball-Rokeach. All rights reserved.

less important (all else being equal). A manager who considers being *honest (sincere, truthful)* to be of paramount importance may be a driving force for taking steps to ensure that all members of a unit or organization behave ethically.

All in all, managers' value systems signify what managers as individuals are trying to accomplish and become in their personal lives and at work. Thus managers' value systems are fundamental guides to their behavior and efforts at planning, leading, organizing, and controlling.

Attitudes

attitude A collection of feelings and beliefs.

An attitude is a collection of feelings and beliefs. Like everyone else, managers have attitudes about their jobs and organizations, and these attitudes affect how they approach their jobs. Two of the most important attitudes in this context are job satisfaction and organizational commitment.

job satisfaction The collection of feelings and beliefs that managers have about their current jobs.

JOB SATISFACTION Job satisfaction is the collection of feelings and beliefs that managers have about their current jobs.[33] Managers who have high levels of job satisfaction generally like their jobs, feel they are fairly treated, and believe their jobs have many desirable features or characteristics (such as interesting work, good pay and job security, autonomy, or nice coworkers). Figure 2.5 shows sample items from two scales that managers can use to measure job satisfaction. Levels of job satisfaction tend to increase as one moves up the hierarchy in an organization. Upper managers, in general, tend to be more satisfied with their jobs than entry-level employees. Managers' levels of job satisfaction can range from very low to very high.

One might think that in tough economic times when unemployment is high and layoffs are prevalent, people who do have jobs might be relatively satisfied with them. However, this is not necessarily the case. For example, in December 2009 the U.S. unemployment rate was 10%, 85,000 jobs were lost from the economy, and the underemployment rate (which includes people who have given up looking for jobs and those who are working part-time because they can't find a full-time position) was 17.3%.[34] During these recessionary conditions, job satisfaction levels in the United States fell to record lows.[35]

Figure 2.5

Sample Items from
Two Measures of Job
Satisfaction

Sample items from the Minnesota Satisfaction Questionnaire:
People respond to each of the items in the scale by checking whether they are:

[ ] Very dissatisfied   [ ] Satisfied
[ ] Dissatisfied   [ ] Very satisfied
[ ] Can't decide whether satisfied or not

On my present job, this is how I feel about . . .

_____ **1.** Being able to do things that don't go against my conscience.

_____ **2.** The way my job provides for steady employment.

_____ **3.** The chance to do things for other people.

_____ **4.** The chance to do something that makes use of my abilities.

_____ **5.** The way company policies are put into practice.

_____ **6.** My pay and the amount of work I do.

_____ **7.** The chances for advancement on this job.

_____ **8.** The freedom to use my own judgment.

_____ **9.** The working conditions.

_____ **10.** The way my coworkers get along with each other.

_____ **11.** The praise I get for doing a good job.

_____ **12.** The feeling of accomplishment I get from the job.

The Faces Scale
Workers select the face which best expresses how they feel about their job in general.

11   10   9   8   7   6   5   4   3   2   1

Source: D. J. Weiss et al., *Manual for the Minnesota Satisfaction Questionnaire.* Copyrighted by the Vocational Psychology Research, University of Minnesota. Copyright © 1975 by the American Psychological Association. Adapted by permission of Randall B. Dunham and J. B. Brett.

The Conference Board has been tracking levels of U.S. job satisfaction since 1987, when 61.1% of workers surveyed indicated that they were satisfied with their jobs.[36] In 2009 only 45% of workers surveyed indicated that they were satisfied with their jobs, an all-time low for the survey.[37] Some sources of job dissatisfaction include uninteresting work, lack of job security, incomes that have not kept pace with inflation, and having to spend more money on health insurance. For example, three times as many workers in 2009 had to contribute to paying for their health insurance and had rising levels of contributions compared to 1980. Only 43% of workers thought their jobs were secure in 2009 compared to 59% in 1987. In the 2000s, average household incomes adjusted for inflation declined.[38]

Of all age groups, workers under 25 were the most dissatisfied with their jobs. More specifically, approximately 64% of workers in this age group were dissatisfied with their jobs, perhaps due to declining opportunities and relatively low earnings. Around 22% of all respondents didn't think they would still have the same job in a year.[39]

Some organizations have combined a concern about protecting the environment with a concern about preserving workers' jobs and avoiding layoffs, as illustrated in the following "Ethics in Action."

ETHICS IN ACTION

Protecting the Environment and Jobs at Subaru of Indiana Automotive

Subaru of Indiana Automotive (SIA) is located in Lafayette, Indiana; produces the Subaru Legacy, Outback, and Tribeca; and has over 3,500 employees.[40] While the U.S. auto industry has had its share of major problems ranging from massive layoffs to huge bankruptcies, SIA has never laid off employees.[41] In fact, SIA employees receive annual raises, premium-free health care, substantial amounts of overtime work, financial counseling, the option of earning a Purdue University degree at the production facility, and pay for volunteer work. While 46,000 auto jobs have been lost in Indiana and several auto manufacturing plants have shut down in the state, SIA appears to be thriving.[42]

At the same time, SIA has been on an uncompromising mission to protect the environment and save money by eliminating waste. Around 98% of the waste at SIA is recycled or composted with considerable efficiencies and cost savings.[43] An on-site broker manages bids for recycled metals, glass, plastic, and paper. Only about 2% of waste is incinerated and this is done locally at an operation that converts waste to fuel. Suppliers are encouraged

More than corn in Indiana? Definitely more benefits for the environment as Subaru of Indiana pioneers efforts to reduce packaging, eliminate waste, and reuse extra materials.

to minimize packaging, which enables SIA to get better deals from them, and boxes and containers shipping parts and materials back and forth from Japan to Indiana are reused, cutting costs. Scrap from welding is sold in copper auctions. Executive Vice President Tom Easterday estimates that SIA saves over $5 million per year from its efforts to eliminate waste, recycle, and compost.[44]

SIA combines its minimal environmental impact philosophy with a commitment to reducing worker injuries and promoting worker health.[45] For example, rather than inspecting the quality of welds by taking cars apart as was customary, SIA now uses ultrasonic technology to check welds. This change reduced worker injuries from jackhammers and metals waste and results in a process that is more effective, quicker, and less expensive. SIA has a free on-site gym with wellness and weight loss programs.[46] Workers receive bonuses for identifying unnecessary packaging and processes, which can cut costs and be a source of rebates from suppliers, the very top bonus being a brand new Subaru Legacy. All these costs savings are used for further plant investments and overtime pay.[47]

SIA's relentless quest for efficiency in terms of reducing waste/protecting the environment and increasing productivity on the assembly line does put a lot of pressure on employees who are expected to work long hours.[48] Nonetheless, they know that their jobs are secure and they receive overtime pay and premium-free health insurance. When the Japanese earthquake in 2011 forced the plant to slow down because of disruptions in the supply of parts from Japan, SIA continued to pay all its employees their full wages to volunteer in the local community. Thus, it is not surprising that there are about 10 applicants for each open position at SIA. Clearly, SIA has demonstrated it is possible to protect the environment and protect jobs to the benefit of all.[49]

In general, it is desirable for managers to be satisfied with their jobs, for at least two reasons. First, satisfied managers may be more likely to go the extra mile for their organization or perform organizational citizenship behaviors (OCBs)— behaviors that are not required of organizational members but that contribute to and are necessary for organizational efficiency, effectiveness, and competitive advantage.[50] Managers who are satisfied with their jobs are more likely to perform these "above and beyond the call of duty" behaviors, which can range from putting in long hours when needed to coming up with truly creative ideas and overcoming obstacles to implement them (even when doing so is not part of the manager's job), or to going out of one's way to help a coworker, subordinate, or superior (even when doing so entails considerable personal sacrifice).[51]

A second reason why it is desirable for managers to be satisfied with their jobs is that satisfied managers may be less likely to quit.[52] A manager who is highly satisfied may never even think about looking for another position; a dissatisfied manager may always be on the lookout for new opportunities. Turnover can hurt an organization because it results in the loss of the experience and knowledge that managers have gained about the company, industry, and business environment.

A growing source of dissatisfaction for many lower- and middle-level managers, as well as for nonmanagerial employees, is the threat of unemployment and increased workloads from organizational downsizings and layoffs. Organizations that try to improve their efficiency through restructuring and layoffs often eliminate a sizable number of first-line and middle management positions. This decision obviously hurts the managers who are laid off, and it also can reduce the job

organizational citizenship behaviors (OCBs)
Behaviors that are not required of organizational members but that contribute to and are necessary for organizational efficiency, effectiveness, and competitive advantage.

Brainstorming for hours and staying late flow naturally when you know your work is appreciated, your job is secure, and you are valued.

satisfaction levels of managers who remain. They might fear being the next to be let go. In addition, the workloads of remaining employees often are dramatically increased as a result of restructuring, and this can contribute to dissatisfaction.

How managers and organizations handle layoffs is of paramount importance, not only for the layoff victims but also for employees who survive the layoff and keep their jobs.[53] Showing compassion and empathy for layoff victims, giving them as much advance notice as possible about the layoff, providing clear information about severance benefits, and helping layoff victims in their job search efforts are a few of the ways in which managers can humanely manage a layoff.[54] For example, when Ron Thomas, vice president of organizational development for Martha Stewart Living Omnimedia, had to lay off employees as a result of closing the organization's catalog business, he personally called all the catalog businesses he knew to find out about potential positions for laid-off employees.[55]

Efforts such as Thomas's to help layoff victims find new jobs can contribute to the job satisfaction of those who survive the layoff. As Thomas puts it, "If you handle a restructuring well, the word gets out that you're a good place to work . . . if we post a job opening today, we'll get 1,500 résumés tomorrow."[56]

Unfortunately, when the unemployment rate is high, laid-off employees sometimes find it difficult to find new jobs and can remain jobless for months.[57] For small businesses, the decision to lay off employees and communicating that decision can be especially painful because managers often have developed close personal relationships with the people they have to let go, know their families, and fear what will happen to them with the loss of a steady income.[58] Shelly Polum, vice president for administration at Ram Tool, a small family-owned manufacturing company in Grafton, Wisconsin, broke down in tears in her office after she had to let employees know they were being laid off.[59] When Charlie Thomas, vice president of Shuqualak Lumber in Shuqualak, Mississippi, had to announce layoffs of close to a quarter of his employees, he wrote a speech that he could not get through without stopping and retreating to his office to pull himself together. As he put it, "I couldn't get it out . . . It just killed my soul."[60] As these managers realize, getting laid off during a recession can be devastating for employees and their families because jobs are few and far between.

organizational commitment

The collection of feelings and beliefs that managers have about their organization as a whole.

ORGANIZATIONAL COMMITMENT Organizational commitment is the collection of feelings and beliefs that managers have about their organization as a whole.[61] Managers who are committed to their organizations believe in what their organizations are doing, are proud of what these organizations stand for, and feel a high degree of loyalty toward their organizations. Committed managers are more likely to go above and beyond the call of duty to help their company and are less likely to quit.[62] Organizational commitment can be especially strong when employees and managers truly believe in organizational values; it also leads to a strong organizational culture, as found in Under Armour.

Organizational commitment is likely to help managers perform some of their figurehead and spokesperson roles (see Chapter 1). It is much easier for a manager to persuade others both inside and outside the organization of the merits of what the organization has done and is seeking to accomplish if the manager truly believes in and is committed to the organization. Figure 2.6 is an example of a scale that can measure a person's level of organizational commitment.

Figure 2.6

A Measure of Organizational Commitment

People respond to each of the items in the scale by checking whether they:
[ ] Strongly disagree   [ ] Slightly agree
[ ] Moderately disagree   [ ] Moderately agree
[ ] Slightly disagree   [ ] Strongly agree
[ ] Neither disagree nor agree

____ 1. I am willing to put in a great deal of effort beyond that normally expected in order to help this organization be successful.

____ 2. I talk up this organization to my friends as a great organization to work for.

____ 3. I feel very little loyalty to this organization.*

____ 4. I would accept almost any type of job assignment in order to keep working for this organization.

____ 5. I find that my values and the organization's values are very similar.

____ 6. I am proud to tell others that I am part of this organization.

____ 7. I could just as well be working for a different organization as long as the type of work was similar.*

____ 8. This organization really inspires the very best in me in the way of job performance.

____ 9. It would take very little change in my present circumstances to cause me to leave this organization.*

____ 10. I am extremely glad that I chose this organization to work for over others I was considering at the time I joined.

____ 11. There's not too much to be gained by sticking with this organization indefinitely.*

____ 12. Often, I find it difficult to agree with this organization's policies on important matters relating to its employees.*

____ 13. I really care about the fate of this organization.

____ 14. For me this is the best of all possible organizations for which to work.

____ 15. Deciding to work for this organization was a definite mistake on my part.*

Scoring: Responses to items 1, 2, 4, 5, 6, 8, 10, 13, and 14 are scored such that 1 = strongly disagree; 2 = moderately disagree; 3 = slightly disagree; 4 = neither disagree nor agree; 5 = slightly agree; 6 = moderately agree; and 7 = strongly agree. Responses to "*" items 3, 7, 9, 11, 12, and 15 are scored 7 = strongly disagree; 6 = moderately disagree; 5 = slightly disagree; 4 = neither disagree nor agree; 3 = slightly agree; 2 = moderately agree; and 1 = strongly agree. Responses to the 15 items are averaged for an overall score from 1 to 7; the higher the score, the higher the level of organizational commitment.

Source: L. W. Porter and F. J. Smith, "Organizational Commitment Questionnaire," in J. D. Cook, S. J. Hepworth, T. D. Wall, and P. B. Warr, eds., *The Experience of Work: A Compendium and Review of 259 Measures and Their Use* (New York: Academic Press, 1961), 85–86.

Do managers in different countries have similar or different attitudes? Differences in the levels of job satisfaction and organizational commitment among managers in different countries are likely because these managers have different kinds of opportunities and rewards and because they face different economic, political, and sociocultural forces in their organizations' general environments. Levels of organizational commitment from one country to another may depend on the extent to which countries have legislation affecting firings and layoffs and the extent to which citizens of a country are geographically mobile.

Moods and Emotions

LO 2-3 Appreciate how moods and emotions influence all members of an organization.

mood A feeling or state of mind.

emotions Intense, relatively short-lived feelings.

Just as you sometimes are in a bad mood and at other times are in a good mood, so too are managers. A *mood* is a feeling or state of mind. When people are in a positive mood, they feel excited, enthusiastic, active, or elated.[63] When people are in a negative mood, they feel distressed, fearful, scornful, hostile, jittery, or nervous.[64] People who are high on extraversion are especially likely to experience positive moods; people who are high on negative affectivity are especially likely to experience negative moods. People's situations or circumstances also determine their moods; however, receiving a raise is likely to put most people in a good mood regardless of their personality traits. People who are high on negative affectivity are not always in a bad mood, and people who are low on extraversion still experience positive moods.[65]

Emotions are more intense feelings than moods, are often directly linked to whatever caused the emotion, and are more short-lived.[66] However, once whatever has triggered the emotion has been dealt with, the feelings may linger in the form of a less intense mood.[67] For example, a manager who gets very angry when a subordinate has engaged in an unethical behavior may find his anger decreasing in intensity once he has decided how to address the problem. Yet he continues to be in a bad mood the rest of the day, even though he is not directly thinking about the unfortunate incident.[68]

Research has found that moods and emotions affect the behavior of managers and all members of an organization. For example, research suggests that the subordinates of managers who experience positive moods at work may perform at somewhat higher levels and be less likely to resign and leave the organization than the subordinates of managers who do not tend to be in a positive mood at work.[69] Other research suggests that under certain conditions creativity might be enhanced by positive moods, whereas under other conditions negative moods might push people to work harder to come up with truly creative ideas.[70] Recognizing that both mood states have the potential to contribute to creativity in different ways, recent research suggests that employees may be especially likely to be creative to the extent that they experience both mood states (at different times) on the job and to the extent that the work environment is supportive of creativity.[71]

Other research suggests that moods and emotions may play an important role in ethical decision making. For example, researchers at Princeton University found that when people are trying to solve difficult personal moral dilemmas, the parts of their brains that are responsible for emotions and moods are especially active.[72]

More generally, emotions and moods give managers and all employees important information and signals about what is going on in the workplace.[73] Positive emotions and moods signal that things are going well and thus can lead to more expansive, and even playful, thinking. Negative emotions and moods signal that there are problems in need of attention and areas for improvement. So when people are in negative moods, they tend to be more detail-oriented and focused on the facts at hand.[74] Some studies suggest that critical thinking and devil's advocacy may be promoted by a negative mood, and sometimes especially accurate judgments may be made by managers in negative moods.[75]

As indicated in the following "Management Insight," emotions can sometimes be the impetus for important changes in an organization.

MANAGEMENT INSIGHT

Emotions as Triggers for Changes in Organizations

In our personal lives, intense emotional experiences can often be triggers for changes for the better. For example, the fear that accompanies a near miss auto accident may prompt a driver to slow down and leave more time to get to destinations. Embarrassment experienced from being underprepared for a major presentation might prompt a student to be more prepared in the future. Anger over being treated poorly can sometimes help people get out of bad personal relationships.

Need to change your culture? Try a tug at the heartstrings—or the gut. A screen saver image of how quickly and how thoroughly medical personnel hands got dirty was the impetus for a turnaround at a hospital with low hand-washing stats.

Interestingly enough, some managers and organizations are using emotions to prompt needed changes. For example, the CEO of North American Tool, Curt Lansbery, was dismayed that employees weren't contributing as much as they could to their 401(k) retirement plans because the company had a matched contribution plan whereby it contributed a percentage of an employee's contribution.[76] North American Tool makes industrial cutting machinery and each year has an annual 401(k) enrollment meeting. Lansbery decided to bring a bag full of money to the next meeting that equaled the amount of money employees did not receive the prior year because they did not contribute the maximum to their 401(k) plans. He dumped the money on a table and told the employees that this really should be their money, not the company's.[77] The negative feelings that this invoked in employees—there's a bunch of money that should be ours and is not—prompted many more to maximize their 401(k) contributions for the coming year and reap the benefits of the matched contribution plan.[78]

Dr. Leon Bender and other colleagues at Cedars-Sinai Medical Center were concerned that doctors and nurses weren't washing their hands as often as they should.[79] Repeated hand-washing by medical staff is a key contributor to keeping patients free of secondary bacterial infections; avoiding these kinds of preventable bacterial infections acquired in hospitals can save patients' lives. Despite their efforts to encourage more hand washing in the Center, their compliance rates with standards was around 80%. The Center was due for an inspection during which a minimum compliance rate of 90% was needed.[80]

After lunch one day, a group of around 20 doctors and staff were requested by the Center's epidemiologist to put their hands on an agar plate.[81] After the agar plates were cultured, they showed that the doctors' and administrators' hands were coated with bacteria. Photos of the cultured plates were circulated and one was made into a screen saver for the computers on the hospital's networks. The disgust experienced by everyone who saw the screen saver and the photos was a powerful impetus for change, and compliance with hand-washing protocols increased to close to 100%. It remained at a high level.[82] Hence, emotions can be useful triggers for needed changes in organizations.[83]

Managers and other members of an organization need to realize that how they feel affects how they treat others and how others respond to them, including their subordinates. For example, a subordinate may be more likely to approach a manager with a somewhat unusual but potentially useful idea if the subordinate thinks the manager is in a good mood. Likewise, when managers are in very bad moods, their subordinates might try to avoid them at all costs. Figure 2.7 is an example of a scale that can measure the extent to which a person experiences positive and negative moods at work.

Figure 2.7

A Measure of Positive and Negative Mood at Work

People respond to each item by indicating the extent to which the item describes how they felt at work during the past week on the following scale:

1 = Very slightly or not at all   4 = Quite a bit
2 = A little   5 = Very much
3 = Moderately

_____ **1.** Active   _____ **7.** Enthusiastic

_____ **2.** Distressed   _____ **8.** Fearful

_____ **3.** Strong   _____ **9.** Peppy

_____ **4.** Excited   _____ **10.** Nervous

_____ **5.** Scornful   _____ **11.** Elated

_____ **6.** Hostile   _____ **12.** Jittery

Scoring: Responses to items 1, 3, 4, 7, 9, and 11 are summed for a positive mood score; the higher the score, the more positive mood is experienced at work. Responses to items 2, 5, 6, 8, 10, and 12 are summed for a negative mood score; the higher the score, the more negative mood is experienced at work.

Source: A. P. Brief, M. J. Burke, J. M. George, B. Robinson, and J. Webster, "Should Negative Affectivity Remain an Unmeasured Variable in the Study of Job Stress?" *Journal of Applied Psychology* 72 (1988), 193–98; M. J. Burke, A. P. Brief, J. M. George, L. Roberson, and J. Webster, "Measuring Affect at Work: Confirmatory Analyses of Competing Mood Structures with Conceptual Linkage in Cortical Regulatory Systems," *Journal of Personality and Social Psychology* 57 (1989), 1091–102.

Emotional Intelligence

LO 2-4 Describe the nature of emotional intelligence and its role in management.

emotional intelligence The ability to understand and manage one's own moods and emotions and the moods and emotions of other people.

In understanding the effects of managers' and all employees' moods and emotions, it is important to take into account their levels of emotional intelligence. Emotional intelligence is the ability to understand and manage one's own moods and emotions and the moods and emotions of other people.[84] Managers with a high level of emotional intelligence are more likely to understand how they are feeling and why, and they are more able to effectively manage their feelings. When managers are experiencing stressful feelings and emotions such as fear or anxiety, emotional intelligence lets them understand why and manage these feelings so they do not get in the way of effective decision making.[85]

Emotional intelligence also can help managers perform their important roles such as their interpersonal roles (figurehead, leader, and liaison).[86] Understanding how your subordinates feel, why they feel that way, and how to manage these feelings is central to developing strong interpersonal bonds with them.[87] More generally, emotional intelligence has the potential to contribute to effective leadership in multiple ways.[88]

For example, emotional intelligence helps managers understand and relate well to other people.[89] It also helps managers maintain their enthusiasm and confidence and energize subordinates to help the organization attain its goals.[90] Recent theorizing and research suggest that emotional intelligence may be especially important in awakening employee creativity.[91] Managers themselves are increasingly recognizing the importance of emotional intelligence. An example of a scale that measures emotional intelligence is provided in Figure 2.8.

Organizational Culture

LO 2-5 Define organizational culture and explain how managers both create and are influenced by organizational culture.

organizational culture The shared set of beliefs, expectations, values, norms, and work routines that influence how individuals, groups, and teams interact with one another and cooperate to achieve organizational goals.

Personality is a way of understanding why all managers and employees, as individuals, characteristically think and behave in different ways. However, when people belong to the same organization, they tend to share certain beliefs and values that lead them to act in similar ways.[92] Organizational culture comprises the shared set of beliefs, expectations, values, norms, and work routines that influence how members of an organization relate to one another and work together to achieve organizational goals. In essence, organizational culture reflects the distinctive ways in which organizational members perform their jobs and relate to others inside and outside the organization. It may, for example, be how customers in a particular hotel chain are treated from the time they are greeted at check-in until they leave; or it may be the shared work routines that research teams use to guide new product development. When organizational members share an intense commitment to cultural values, beliefs, and routines and use them to achieve their goals, a *strong* organizational culture exists.[93] When organizational members are not strongly committed to a shared system of values, beliefs, and routines, organizational culture is weak.

The stronger the culture of an organization, the more one can think about it as being the "personality" of an organization because it influences the way its members behave.[94] Organizations that possess strong cultures may differ on a wide variety of dimensions that determine how their members behave toward one another and perform their jobs. For example, organizations differ in how members relate to each other (formally or informally), how important decisions are made (top-down or bottom-up), willingness to change (flexible or unyielding), innovation (creative or predictable), and playfulness (serious or serendipitous).

Figure 2.8

A Measure of Emotional
Intelligence

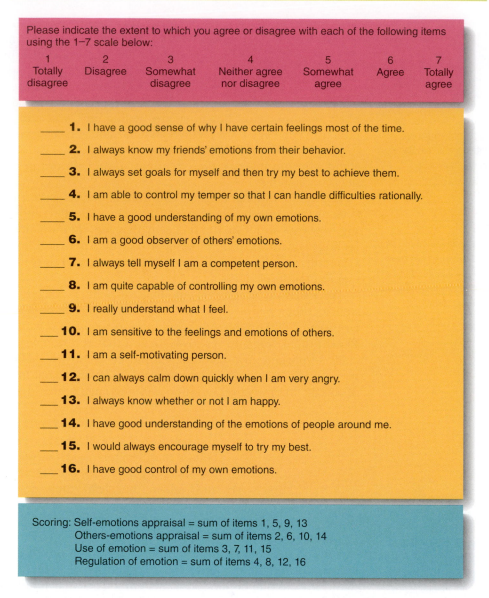

Please indicate the extent to which you agree or disagree with each of the following items using the 1–7 scale below:

1	2	3	4	5	6	7
Totally disagree	Disagree	Somewhat disagree	Neither agree nor disagree	Somewhat agree	Agree	Totally agree

_____ **1.** I have a good sense of why I have certain feelings most of the time.

_____ **2.** I always know my friends' emotions from their behavior.

_____ **3.** I always set goals for myself and then try my best to achieve them.

_____ **4.** I am able to control my temper so that I can handle difficulties rationally.

_____ **5.** I have a good understanding of my own emotions.

_____ **6.** I am a good observer of others' emotions.

_____ **7.** I always tell myself I am a competent person.

_____ **8.** I am quite capable of controlling my own emotions.

_____ **9.** I really understand what I feel.

_____ **10.** I am sensitive to the feelings and emotions of others.

_____ **11.** I am a self-motivating person.

_____ **12.** I can always calm down quickly when I am very angry.

_____ **13.** I always know whether or not I am happy.

_____ **14.** I have good understanding of the emotions of people around me.

_____ **15.** I would always encourage myself to try my best.

_____ **16.** I have good control of my own emotions.

Scoring: Self-emotions appraisal = sum of items 1, 5, 9, 13
        Others-emotions appraisal = sum of items 2, 6, 10, 14
        Use of emotion = sum of items 3, 7, 11, 15
        Regulation of emotion = sum of items 4, 8, 12, 16

Source: K. Law, C. Wong, and L. Song, "The Construct and Criterion Validity of Emotional Intelligence and Its Potential Utility for Management Studies," *Journal of Applied Psychology* 89, no. 3 (June 2004), 496; C. S. Wong and K. S. Law, "The Effects of Leader and Follower Emotional Intelligence on Performance and Attitude: An Exploratory Study," *Leadership Quarterly* 13 (2002), pp. 243–74.

In an innovative design firm like IDEO Product Development in Silicon Valley, employees are encouraged to adopt a playful attitude toward their work, look outside the organization to find inspiration, and adopt a flexible approach toward product design that uses multiple perspectives.[95] IDEO's culture is vastly different from that of companies such as Citibank and ExxonMobil, in which employees treat each other in a more formal or deferential way, employees are expected to adopt a serious approach to their work, and decision making is constrained by the hierarchy of authority.

IDEO employees brainstorming—informal communication, casual attire, and flexibility are all hallmarks of this organization.

Managers and Organizational Culture

While all members of an organization can contribute to developing and maintaining organizational culture, managers play a particularly important part in influencing organizational culture[96] because of their multiple and important roles (see Chapter 1). How managers create culture is most vividly evident in start-ups of new companies. Entrepreneurs who start their own companies are typically also the start-ups' top managers until the companies grow and become profitable. Often referred to as the firms' founders, these managers literally create their organizations' cultures.

The founders' personal characteristics play an important role in the creation of organizational culture. Benjamin Schneider, a well-known management researcher, developed a model that helps to explain the role that founders' personal characteristics play in determining organizational culture.[97] His model, called the attraction–selection–attrition (ASA) framework, posits that when founders hire employees for their new ventures, they tend to be attracted to and choose employees whose personalities are similar to their own.[98] These similar employees are more likely to stay with the organization. Although employees who are dissimilar in personality might be hired, they are more likely to leave the organization over time.[99] As a result of these attraction, selection, and attrition processes, people in the organization tend to have similar personalities, and the typical or dominant personality profile of organizational members determines and shapes organizational culture.[100]

For example, when David Kelley became interested in engineering and product design challenges in the late 1970s, he realized that who he was as a person meant he would not be happy working in a typical corporate environment. Kelley is high on openness to experience, driven to go where his interests take him, and not content to follow others' directives. Kelley recognized that he needed to start

attraction–selection–attrition (ASA) framework
A model that explains how personality may influence organizational culture.

his own business, and with the help of other Stanford-schooled engineers and design experts, IDEO was born.[101]

From the start, IDEO's culture has embodied Kelley's spirited, freewheeling approach to work and design—from colorful and informal workspaces to an emphasis on networking and communicating with as many people as possible to understand a design problem. No project or problem is too big or too small for IDEO; the company designed the Apple Lisa computer and mouse (the precursor of the Mac) and the Palm as well as the Crest Neat Squeeze toothpaste dispenser and the Racer's Edge water bottle.[102] Kelley hates rules, job titles, big corner offices, and all the other trappings of large traditional organizations that stifle creativity. Employees who are attracted to, selected by, and remain with IDEO value creativity and innovation and embrace one of IDEO's mottos: "Fail often to succeed sooner."[103]

Although ASA processes are most evident in small firms such as IDEO, they also can operate in large companies.[104] According to the ASA model, this is a naturally occurring phenomenon to the extent that managers and new hires are free to make the kinds of choices the model specifies. However, while people tend to get along well with others who are similar to themselves, too much similarity in an organization can impair organizational effectiveness. That is, similar people tend to view conditions and events in similar ways and thus can be resistant to change. Moreover, organizations benefit from a diversity of perspectives rather than similarity in perspectives (see Chapter 3). At IDEO Kelley recognized early on how important it is to take advantage of the diverse talents and perspectives that people with different personalities, backgrounds, experiences, and education can bring to a design team. Hence IDEO's design teams include not only engineers but others who might have a unique insight into a problem, such as anthropologists, communications experts, doctors, and users of a product. When new employees are hired at IDEO, they meet many employees who have different backgrounds and characteristics; the focus is not on hiring someone who will fit in but, rather, on hiring someone who has something to offer and can "wow" different kinds of people with his or her insights.[105]

In addition to personality, other personal characteristics of managers shape organizational culture; these include managers' values, attitudes, moods and emotions, and emotional intelligence.[106] For example, both terminal and instrumental values of managers play a role in determining organizational culture. Managers who highly value freedom and equality, for example, might be likely to stress the importance of autonomy and empowerment in their organizations, as well as fair treatment for all. As another example, managers who highly value being helpful and forgiving might not only tolerate mistakes but also emphasize the importance of organizational members' being kind and helpful to one another.

Managers who are satisfied with their jobs, are committed to their organizations, and experience positive moods and emotions might also encourage these attitudes and feelings in others. The result would be an organizational culture emphasizing positive attitudes and feelings. Research suggests that attitudes like job satisfaction and organizational commitment can be affected by the influence of others. Managers are in a particularly strong position to engage in social influence given their multiple roles. Moreover, research suggests that moods and emotions can be contagious and that spending time with people who are excited and enthusiastic can increase one's own levels of excitement and enthusiasm.

The Role of Values and Norms in Organizational Culture

Shared terminal and instrumental values play a particularly important role in organizational culture. *Terminal values* signify what an organization and its employees are trying to accomplish, and *instrumental values* guide how the organization and its members achieve organizational goals. In addition to values, shared norms also are a key aspect of organizational culture. Recall that norms are unwritten, informal rules or guidelines that prescribe appropriate behavior in particular situations. For example, norms at IDEO include not being critical of others' ideas, coming up with multiple ideas before settling on one, and developing prototypes of new products.[107]

Managers determine and shape organizational culture through the kinds of values and norms they promote in an organization. Some managers, like David Kelley of IDEO, cultivate values and norms that encourage risk taking, creative responses to problems and opportunities, experimentation, tolerance of failure in order to succeed, and autonomy.[108] Top managers at organizations such as Microsoft and Google encourage employees to adopt such values to support their commitment to innovation as a source of competitive advantage.

Other managers, however, might cultivate values and norms that tell employees they should be conservative and cautious in their dealings with others and should consult their superiors before making important decisions or any changes to the status quo. Accountability for actions and decisions is stressed, and detailed records are kept to ensure that policies and procedures are followed. In settings where caution is needed—nuclear power stations, oil refineries, chemical plants, financial institutions, insurance companies—a conservative, cautious approach to making decisions might be appropriate.[109] In a nuclear power plant, for example, the catastrophic consequences of a mistake make a high level of supervision vital. Similarly, in a bank or mutual fund company, the risk of losing investors' money makes a cautious approach to investing appropriate.

Managers of different kinds of organizations deliberately cultivate and develop the organizational values and norms that are best suited to their task and general environments, strategy, or technology. Organizational culture is maintained and transmitted to organizational members through the values of the founder, the process of socialization, ceremonies and rites, and stories and language (see Figure 2.9).

VALUES OF THE FOUNDER From the ASA model just discussed, it is clear that founders of an organization can have profound and long-lasting effects on

Figure 2.9

Factors That Maintain
and Transmit
Organizational Culture

organizational culture. Founders' values inspire the founders to start their own companies and, in turn, drive the nature of these new companies and their defining characteristics. Thus an organization's founder and his or her terminal and instrumental values have a substantial influence on the values, norms, and standards of behavior that develop over time within the organization.[110] Founders set the scene for the way cultural values and norms develop because their own values guide the building of the company, and they hire other managers and employees who they believe will share these values and help the organization to attain them. Moreover, new managers quickly learn from the founder what values and norms are appropriate in the organization and thus what is desired of them. Subordinates imitate the style of the founder and, in turn, transmit their values and norms to their subordinates. Gradually, over time, the founder's values and norms permeate the organization.[111]

A founder who requires a great display of respect from subordinates and insists on proprieties such as formal job titles and formal dress encourages subordinates to act in this way toward their subordinates. Often a founder's personal values affect an organization's competitive advantage. For example, McDonald's founder Ray Kroc insisted from the beginning on high standards of customer service and cleanliness at McDonald's restaurants; these became core sources of McDonald's competitive advantage. Similarly, Bill Gates, the founder of Microsoft, pioneered certain cultural values in Microsoft. Employees are expected to be creative and to work hard, but they are encouraged to dress informally and to personalize their offices. Gates also established a host of company events such as cookouts, picnics, and sports events to emphasize to employees the importance of being both an individual and a team player.

SOCIALIZATION Over time, organizational members learn from each other which values are important in an organization and the norms that specify appropriate and inappropriate behaviors. Eventually organizational members behave in accordance with the organization's values and norms—often without realizing they are doing so.

organizational socialization

The process by which newcomers learn an organization's values and norms and acquire the work behaviors necessary to perform jobs effectively.

Organizational socialization is the process by which newcomers learn an organization's values and norms and acquire the work behaviors necessary to perform jobs effectively.[112] As a result of their socialization experiences, organizational members internalize an organization's values and norms and behave in accordance with them not only because they think they have to but because they think these values and norms describe the right and proper way to behave.[113]

At Texas A&M University, for example, all new students are encouraged to go to "Fish Camp" to learn how to be an "Aggie" (the traditional nickname of students at the university). They learn about the ceremonies that have developed over time to commemorate significant events or people in A&M's history. In addition, they learn how to behave at football games and in class and what it means to be an Aggie. As a result of this highly organized socialization program, by the time new students arrive on campus and start their first semester, they have been socialized into what a Texas A&M student is supposed to do, and they have relatively few problems adjusting to the college environment.

Most organizations have some kind of socialization program to help new employees learn the ropes—the values, norms, and culture of the organization. The military, for example, is well known for the rigorous socialization process it uses to turn raw recruits into trained soldiers. Organizations such as the Walt

How does Snow White stay so perfectly in character when meeting her littlest fans? Rigorous training through Disney University, a socialization process Disney requires of all its employees.

Disney Company also put new recruits through a rigorous training program to teach them to perform well in their jobs and play their parts in helping Disneyland visitors have fun in a wholesome theme park. New recruits at Disney are called "cast members" and attend Disney University to learn the Disney culture and their parts in it. Disney's culture emphasizes the values of safety, courtesy, entertainment, and efficiency, and these values are brought to life for newcomers at Disney University. Newcomers also learn about the attraction area they will be joining (such as Adventureland or Fantasyland) at Disney University and then receive on-the-job socialization in the area itself from experienced cast members.[114] Through organizational socialization, founders and managers of an organization transmit to employees the cultural values and norms that shape the behavior of organizational members. Thus the values and norms of founder Walt Disney live on today at Disneyland as newcomers are socialized into the Disney way.

CEREMONIES AND RITES Another way in which managers can create or influence organizational culture is by developing organizational ceremonies and rites—formal events that recognize incidents of importance to the organization as a whole and to specific employees.[115] The most common rites that organizations use to transmit cultural norms and values to their members are rites of passage, of integration, and of enhancement (see Table 2.1).[116]

Rites of passage determine how individuals enter, advance within, and leave the organization. The socialization programs developed by military organizations (such as the U.S. Army) or by large accountancy and law firms are rites of passage. Likewise, the ways in which an organization prepares people for promotion or retirement are rites of passage.

Rites of integration, such as shared announcements of organizational successes, office parties, and company cookouts, build and reinforce common bonds among organizational members. IDEO uses many rites of integration to make its employees feel connected to one another and special. In addition to having wild "end-of-year" celebratory bashes, groups of IDEO employees periodically take time off to go to a sporting event, movie, or meal, or sometimes on a long bike ride or for a sail. These kinds of shared activities not only reinforce IDEO's culture but also can be a source of inspiration on the job (for example, IDEO has been involved in making movies such as *The Abyss* and *Free Willy*). One 35-member design studio

Table 2.1

Organizational Rites

Type of Rite	Example of Rite	Purpose of Rite
Rite of passage	Induction and basic training	Learn and internalize norms and values
Rite of integration	Office holiday party	Build common norms and values
Rite of enhancement	Presentation of annual award	Motivate commitment to norms and values

at IDEO led by Dennis Boyle has bimonthly lunch fests with no set agenda—anything goes. While enjoying great food, jokes, and camaraderie, studio members often end up sharing ideas for their latest great products, and the freely flowing conversation that results often leads to creative insights.[117]

A company's annual meeting also may be used as a ritual of integration, offering an opportunity to communicate organizational values to managers, other employees, and shareholders.[118] Walmart, for example, makes its annual stockholders' meeting an extravagant ceremony that celebrates the company's success. The company often flies thousands of its highest-performing employees to its annual meeting at its Bentonville, Arkansas, headquarters for a huge weekend entertainment festival complete with star musical performances. Walmart believes that rewarding its supporters with entertainment reinforces the company's high-performance values and culture. The proceedings are shown live over closed-circuit television in all Walmart stores so all employees can join in the rites celebrating the company's achievements.[119]

Rites of enhancement, such as awards dinners, newspaper releases, and employee promotions, let organizations publicly recognize and reward employees' contributions and thus strengthen their commitment to organizational values. By bonding members within the organization, rites of enhancement reinforce an organization's values and norms.

Stories and language also communicate organizational culture. Stories (whether fact or fiction) about organizational heroes and villains and their actions provide important clues about values and norms. Such stories can reveal the kinds of behaviors that are valued by the organization and the kinds of practices that are frowned on.[120] At the heart of McDonald's rich culture are hundreds of stories that organizational members tell about founder Ray Kroc. Most of these stories focus on how Kroc established the strict operating values and norms that are at the heart of McDonald's culture. Kroc was dedicated to achieving perfection in McDonald's quality, service, cleanliness, and value for money (QSC&V), and these four central values permeate McDonald's culture. For example, an often retold story describes what happened when Kroc and a group of managers from the Houston region were touring various restaurants. One of the restaurants was having a bad day operationally. Kroc was incensed about the long lines of customers, and he was furious when he realized that the products customers were receiving that day were not up to his high standards. To address the problem, he jumped up and stood on the front counter to get the attention of all customers and operating crew personnel. He introduced himself, apologized for the long wait and cold food, and told the customers they could have freshly cooked food or their money back—whichever they wanted. As a result, the customers left happy; and when Kroc checked on the restaurant later, he found that his message had gotten through to its managers and crew—performance had improved. Other stories describe Kroc scrubbing dirty toilets and picking up litter inside or outside a restaurant. These and similar stories are spread around the organization by McDonald's employees. They are the stories that have helped establish Kroc as McDonald's "hero."

Because spoken language is a principal medium of communication in organizations, the characteristic slang or jargon—that is, organization-specific words or phrases—that people use to frame and describe events provides important clues about norms and values. "McLanguage," for example, is prevalent at all levels of McDonald's. A McDonald's employee described as having "ketchup in his or her blood" is someone who is truly dedicated to the McDonald's way—someone who has been completely socialized to its culture. McDonald's has an extensive training program that teaches new employees "McDonald's speak," and new employees are welcomed into the family with a formal orientation that illustrates Kroc's dedication to QSC&V.

The concept of organizational language encompasses not only spoken language but how people dress, the offices they occupy, the cars they drive, and the degree of formality they use when they address one another. For example, casual dress reflects and reinforces Microsoft's entrepreneurial culture and values. Formal business attire supports the conservative culture found in many banks, which emphasize the importance of conforming to organizational norms such as respect for authority and staying within one's prescribed role. When employees speak and understand the language of their organization's culture, they know how to behave in the organization and what is expected of them.

At IDEO, language, dress, the physical work environment, and extreme informality all underscore a culture that is adventuresome, playful, risk taking, egalitarian, and innovative. For example, at IDEO, employees refer to taking the consumers' perspective when designing products as "being left-handed." Employees dress in T-shirts and jeans, the physical work environment continually evolves and changes depending on how employees wish to personalize their workspace, no one "owns" a fancy office with a window, and rules are nonexistent.[121]

Culture and Managerial Action

While founders and managers play a critical role in developing, maintaining, and communicating organizational culture, this same culture shapes and controls the behavior of all employees, including managers themselves. For example, culture influences how managers perform their four main functions: planning, organizing, leading, and controlling. As we consider these functions, we continue to distinguish between top managers who create organizational values and norms that encourage creative, innovative behavior and top managers who encourage a conservative, cautious approach by their subordinates. We noted earlier that both kinds of values and norms can be appropriate depending on the situation and type of organization.

PLANNING Top managers in an organization with an innovative culture are likely to encourage lower-level managers to participate in the planning process and develop a flexible approach to planning. They are likely to be willing to listen to new ideas and to take risks involving the development of new products. In contrast, top managers in an organization with conservative values are likely to emphasize formal top-down planning. Suggestions from lower-level managers are likely to be subjected to a formal review process, which can significantly slow decision making. Although this deliberate approach may improve the quality of decision making in a nuclear power plant, it can have unintended consequences. In the past, at conservative IBM, the planning process became so formalized that managers spent most of their time assembling complex presentations to defend their current positions rather than thinking about what they should do to keep IBM abreast of the changes taking place in the computer industry. When former CEO Lou Gerstner took over, he used every means at his disposal to abolish this culture, even building a brand-new campus-style headquarters to change managers' mind-sets. IBM's culture underwent further changes initiated by its next CEO, Samuel Palmisano, who is now chairman of the board.[122]

ORGANIZING What kinds of organizing will managers in innovative and in conservative cultures encourage? Valuing creativity, managers in innovative cultures are likely to try to create an organic structure—one that is flat, with few levels in the hierarchy, and one in which authority is decentralized so employees are encouraged to work together to solve ongoing problems. A product team structure may be suitable for an organization with an innovative culture. In contrast, managers in a conservative culture are likely to create a well-defined hierarchy of authority and establish clear reporting relationships so employees know exactly whom to report to and how to react to any problems that arise.

LEADING In an innovative culture, managers are likely to lead by example, encouraging employees to take risks and experiment. They are supportive regardless of whether employees succeed or fail. In contrast, managers in a conservative culture are likely to use management by objectives and to constantly monitor subordinates' progress toward goals, overseeing their every move. We examine leadership in detail in Chapter 10 when we consider the leadership styles that managers can adopt to influence and shape employee behavior.

CONTROLLING The ways in which managers evaluate, and take actions to improve, performance differ depending on whether the organizational culture emphasizes formality and caution or innovation and change. Managers who want to encourage risk taking, creativity, and innovation recognize that there are multiple potential paths to success and that failure must be accepted for creativity to thrive. Thus they are less concerned about employees' performing their jobs in a specific, predetermined manner and in strict adherence to preset goals and more concerned about employees' being flexible and taking the initiative to come up with ideas for improving performance. Managers in innovative cultures are also more concerned about long-term performance than short-term targets because they recognize that real innovation entails much uncertainty that necessitates flexibility. In contrast, managers in cultures that emphasize caution and maintenance of the status quo often set specific, difficult goals for employees, frequently monitor progress toward these goals, and develop a clear set of rules that employees are expected to adhere to.

The values and norms of an organization's culture strongly affect the way managers perform their management functions. The extent to which managers buy into the values and norms of their organization shapes their view of the world and their actions and decisions in particular circumstances. In turn, the actions that managers take can have an impact on the performance of the organization. Thus organizational culture, managerial action, and organizational performance are all linked together.

While our earlier example of IDEO illustrates how organizational culture can give rise to managerial actions that ultimately benefit the organization, this is not always the case. The cultures of some organizations become dysfunctional, encouraging managerial actions that harm the organization and discouraging actions that might improve performance.[123] Corporate scandals at large companies like Enron, Tyco, and WorldCom show how damaging a dysfunctional culture can be to an organization and its members. For example, Enron's arrogant, "success at all costs" culture led to fraudulent behavior on the part of its top managers.[124] Unfortunately hundreds of Enron employees paid a heavy price for the unethical behavior of these top managers and the dysfunctional organizational culture. Not only did these employees lose their jobs, but many also lost their life savings in Enron stock and pension funds, which became worth just a fraction of their former value before the wrongdoing at Enron came to light. We discuss ethics in depth in the next chapter.

Summary and Review

ENDURING CHARACTERISTICS: PERSON-ALITY TRAITS Personality traits are enduring tendencies to feel, think, and act in certain ways. The Big Five general traits are extraversion, negative affectivity, agreeableness, conscientiousness, and openness to experience. Other personality traits that affect managerial behavior are locus of control, self-esteem, and the needs for achievement, affiliation, and power. **[LO 2-1]**

VALUES, ATTITUDES, AND MOODS AND EMOTIONS A terminal value is a personal conviction about lifelong goals or objectives; an instrumental value is a personal conviction about modes of conduct. Terminal and instrumental values have an impact on what managers try to achieve in their organizations and the kinds of behaviors they engage in. An attitude is a collection of feelings and beliefs. Two attitudes important for understanding managerial behaviors include job satisfaction (the collection of feelings and beliefs that managers have about their jobs) and organizational commitment (the collection of feelings and beliefs that managers have about their organizations). A mood is a feeling or state of mind; emotions are intense feelings that are short-lived and directly linked to their causes. Managers' moods and emotions, or how they feel at work on a day-to-day basis, have the potential to impact not only their own behavior and effectiveness but also those of their subordinates. Emotional intelligence is the ability to understand and manage one's own and other people's moods and emotions. **[LO 2-2, 2-3, 2-4]**

ORGANIZATIONAL CULTURE Organizational culture is the shared set of beliefs, expectations, values, norms, and work routines that influence how members of an organization relate to one another and work together to achieve organizational goals. Founders of new organizations and managers play an important role in creating and maintaining organizational culture. Organizational socialization is the process by which newcomers learn an organization's values and norms and acquire the work behaviors necessary to perform jobs effectively. **[LO 2-5]**

Management *in Action*

TOPICS FOR DISCUSSION AND ACTION

Discussion

1. Discuss why managers who have different types of personalities can be equally effective and successful. **[LO 2-1]**

2. Can managers be too satisfied with their jobs? Can they be too committed to their organizations? Why or why not? **[LO 2-2]**

3. Assume that you are a manager of a restaurant. Describe what it is like to work for you when you are in a negative mood. **[LO 2-3]**

4. Why might managers be disadvantaged by low levels of emotional intelligence? **[LO 2-4]**

Action

5. Interview a manager in a local organization. Ask the manager to describe situations in which he or she is especially likely to act in accordance with his or her values. Ask the manager to describe situations in which he or she is less likely to act in accordance with his or her values. **[LO 2-2]**

6. Watch a popular television show, and as you watch it, try to determine the emotional intelligence levels of the characters the actors in the show portray. Rank the characters from highest to lowest in terms of emotional intelligence. As you watched the show, what factors influenced your assessments of emotional intelligence levels? **[LO 2-4]**

7. Go to an upscale clothing store in your neighborhood, and go to a clothing store that is definitely not upscale. Observe the behavior of employees in each store as well as the store's environment. In what ways are the organizational cultures in each store similar? In what ways are they different? **[LO 2-5]**

BUILDING MANAGEMENT SKILLS

Diagnosing Culture [LO 2-5]

Think about the culture of the last organization you worked for, your current university, or another organization or club to which you belong. Then answer the following questions:

1. What values are emphasized in this culture?

2. What norms do members of this organization follow?

3. Who seems to have played an important role in creating the culture?

4. In what ways is the organizational culture communicated to organizational members?

MANAGING ETHICALLY [LO 2-1, 2-2]

Some organizations rely on personality and interest inventories to screen potential employees. Other organizations attempt to screen employees by using paper-and-pencil honesty tests.

Questions

1. Either individually or in a group, think about the ethical implications of using personality and interest inventories to screen potential employees. How might this practice be unfair to potential applicants? How might organizational members who are in charge of hiring misuse it?

2. Because of measurement error and validity problems, some relatively trustworthy people may "fail" an honesty test given by an employer. What are the ethical implications of trustworthy people "failing" honesty tests, and what obligations do you think employers should have when relying on honesty tests for screening?

SMALL GROUP BREAKOUT EXERCISE

Making Difficult Decisions in Hard Times [LO 2-2, 2-3, 2-4, 2-5]

Form groups of three or four people, and appoint one member as the spokesperson who will communicate your findings to the whole class when called on by the instructor. Then discuss the following scenario:

You are on the top management team of a medium-size company that manufactures cardboard boxes, containers, and other cardboard packaging materials. Your company is facing increasing levels of competition for major corporate customer accounts, and profits have declined significantly. You have tried everything you can to cut costs and remain competitive, with the exception of laying off employees. Your company has had a no-layoff policy for the past 20 years, and you believe it is an important part of the organization's culture. However, you are experiencing mounting pressure to increase your firm's performance, and your no-layoff policy has been questioned by shareholders. Even though you haven't decided whether to lay off employees and thus break with a 20-year tradition for your company, rumors are rampant in your organization that something is afoot, and employees are worried. You are meeting today to address this problem.

1. Develop a list of options and potential courses of action to address the heightened competition and decline in profitability that your company has been experiencing.

2. Choose your preferred course of action, and justify why you will take this route.

3. Describe how you will communicate your decision to employees.

4. If your preferred option involves a layoff, justify why. If it doesn't involve a layoff, explain why.

BE THE MANAGER [LO 2-1, 2-2, 2-3, 2-4, 2-5]

You have recently been hired as the vice president for human resources in an advertising agency. One problem that has been brought to your attention is the fact that the creative departments at the agency have dysfunctionally high levels of conflict. You have spoken with members of each of these departments, and in each one it seems that a few members of the department are creating all the problems. All these individuals are valued contributors who have many creative ad campaigns to their credit. The high levels of conflict are creating problems in the departments, and negative moods and emotions are much more prevalent than positive feelings.

Questions

1. What are you going to do to retain valued employees?

2. How will you alleviate the excessive conflict and negative feelings in these departments?

THE WALL STREET JOURNAL CASE IN THE NEWS

[LO 2-1, 2-2, 2-5]

More Action, Less Drama at Disney

Some Hollywood studio chiefs make their mark in a new job by signing deals with big name stars. Others announce their intention to rethink the ways movies are made and released. Alan Horn did it with a talking monkey.

In one of his first moves after being named chairman of Walt Disney Co.'s movie studio last May, Mr. Horn approved reshoots for "Oz: The Great and Powerful," a prequel to the "Wizard of Oz" that comes out Friday. The biggest change was to give star

75

James Franco a wacky sidekick in the form of a chatty flying simian. In the version of the movie shot before Mr. Horn began, the monkey talked only late in the picture.

"Alan took the movie over and really made it his," said producer Joe Roth.

Few in Hollywood would be comfortable during their first weeks in a new job ordering up $15 million of changes to a movie that already cost about $200 million. But insiders say Mr. Horn, a 70-year-old industry veteran, has brought gravitas to the top of a studio embroiled in drama since 2009, when Disney Chief Executive Robert Iger filled the job with Rich Ross, a television executive who had no filmmaking experience. Mr. Ross lasted less than three years.

"There really is a feeling of stability and that is exactly what was needed," said Mr. Roth, who held Mr. Horn's job from 1994 through 2000. "A year or two ago you'd talk to agents and they couldn't figure out what Disney was up to."

Mr. Horn could hardly be more different from Mr. Ross, who came to the movie studio after running Disney Channels Worldwide. Upon taking the top movie job, Mr. Ross ousted most of the studio's senior executives and sought to revamp established marketing and distribution strategies. His brash approach struck filmmakers, agents, and producers as ham-handed, and he won few allies in the creative community.

He was fired last April by Mr. Iger. A spokeswoman for Mr. Iger didn't respond to a request for comment. Messrs. Horn and Ross declined to comment.

By contrast, Mr. Horn has made no changes in Walt Disney Studios' executive ranks, defying typical Hollywood practice. He also is frequently lauded by people who do business with him as courtly and smooth. Mr. Horn was president of Warner Bros. from 1999 until 2011, when he was asked to leave so three younger executives could compete to replace the retiring studio chairman.

Disney's studio—which generated $722 million of operating income on $5.8 billion of revenue in the last fiscal year—is far smaller than the company's television and theme park units, but it creates material that feeds the parks, TV channels, and video games.

That strategy makes it very valuable for Disney to fully own its movies, so the company doesn't use financing partners to temper risk, as most of its competitors do. Last year's flop "John Carter" led to a $200 million write-off.

"Oz" should fare better. While early reviews have been lukewarm, pre-release surveys suggest it will open to about $80 million domestically and that interest is strong in many foreign countries.

Uniquely in Hollywood, many of Disney's movies come not from its namesake studio but corporate siblings including Marvel Studios, Pixar Animation Studios, and, soon, Lucasfilm, the company behind "Star Wars" that Disney acquired last year. Those units all ultimately report to Mr. Horn but have separate management teams. Disney also distributes films from DreamWorks Studios, which it doesn't own.

Mr. Horn has been particularly focused on Disney Studios' own live-action movies—a category that had been languishing. When he took over, the studio had only three such pictures scheduled: "Oz," July's "The Lone Ranger" starring Johnny Depp, and next year's "Maleficent" with Angelina Jolie.

"It had gotten down to where they didn't have many [movies] going on," said John Lasseter, chief creative officer of Pixar and Disney Animation Studios.

Mr. Horn has sped up development and gave the go-ahead to a pair of new big-budget pictures: "Tomorrowland," named after a section of the Disneyland theme park, and a fifth "Pirates of the Caribbean." He has also approved low-budget dramas including December's "Saving Mr. Banks," about the making of Disney's "Mary Poppins."

In addition, Mr. Horn hopes he will have a new "Star Wars" movie every year starting in 2015. Lucasfilm chief Kathy Kennedy is working with a trio of writers on sequels, the first of which will be directed by J.J. Abrams, and spin-offs focused on individual characters.

"I can see how much more active the place has become in the past year," said Mr. Roth.

Mr. Horn's lack of digital-age expertise could be his Achilles' heel. Despite the challenges that new technology and evolving consumer habits pose to the entertainment industry—a topic about which Mr. Iger frequently speaks—Mr. Horn is known as a traditionalist. Unlike his predecessor, he hasn't sought to challenge long-held practices by shortening the "window" between theatrical and DVD release dates or embracing social media in order to spend less on television advertising.

Disney is also the only major studio not to support an initiative to offer movies in the digital cloud in an effort to boost online sales. Its own effort, dubbed Disney Movies

Anywhere, has been in the works for more than three years but has no launch date.

But Mr. Horn has garnered respect as he navigates the potentially treacherous waters of assigning release dates and giving feedback on projects he releases but whose production he doesn't directly supervise.

Marvel President Kevin Feige called his approach "a confidence-booster" and DreamWorks CEO Stacey Snider said a note from Mr. Horn prompted a decision to rework the epilogue of her studio's coming movie "The Fifth Estate," about WikiLeaks founder Julian Assange.

"Alan can check in on anything and anyone at Disney with a great deal of authority," said a producer who works with the studio.

Questions

1. How would you describe Alan Horn's personality in terms of the Big Five personality traits?

2. How would you describe Alan Horn's personality in terms of the other personality traits that affect managerial behavior?

3. Which terminal and instrumental values do you think might be especially important to him?

4. In what ways do you think that Horn might influence the culture of the Walt Disney Co.'s movie studio?

Source: B. Fritz, "More Action, Less Drama at Disney," *The Wall Street Journal,* March 8, 2013, B1–B2.

3 Managing Ethics and Diversity

LEARNING OBJECTIVES

After studying this chapter, you should be able to:

1 Illustrate how ethics help managers determine the right way to behave when dealing with different stakeholder groups. **[LO 3-1]**

2 Explain why managers should behave ethically and strive to create ethical organizational cultures. **[LO 3-2]**

3 Appreciate the increasing diversity of the workforce and of the organizational environment. **[LO 3-3]**

4 Grasp the central role that managers play in the effective management of diversity. **[LO 3-4]**

5 Understand why the effective management of diversity is both an ethical and a business imperative. **[LO 3-5]**

6 Understand the two major forms of sexual harassment and how they can be eliminated. **[LO 3-6]**

Where do your grocery dollars go? Whole Foods Market's goal is to make shopping fun and socially responsible. Customers' money supports an organization that monitors its suppliers, rewards its employees, and seeks to reduce its impact on the environment.

Whole Foods Market Practices What It Preaches

How Do Managers Satisfy the Needs of An Organization's Stakeholders?

The first Whole Foods Market opened in Austin, Texas, in 1980 as a supermarket for natural foods and had 19 employees.[1] Today it is the world's leading retailer of natural and organic foods, with 345 stores in North America and the United Kingdom.[2] Whole Foods specializes in selling chemical- and drug-free meat, poultry, and produce; its products are the "purest" possible, meaning it selects the ones least adulterated by artificial additives, sweeteners, colorings, and preservatives.[3] Despite the high prices it charges for its pure produce, sales per store are growing, and its revenues had grown to over $10 billion by 2012.[4] Sales for the first quaster of 2013 were $3.9 billion.[5] Why has Whole Foods been so successful? Co-founder and CEO John Mackey says it is because of the principles he established to manage his company since its beginning—principles founded on the need to behave in an ethical and socially responsible way toward everybody affected by its business.

Mackey says he started his business for three reasons—to have fun, to make money, and to contribute to the well-being of other people.[6] The company's mission is based on its members' collective responsibility to the well-being of the people and groups it affects, its *stakeholders;* at Whole Foods these are customers, team members, investors, suppliers, the community, and the natural environment. Mackey measures his company's success by how well it satisfies the needs of these stakeholders. His ethical stance toward customers is that they are guaranteed that Whole Foods products are 100% organic, hormone-free, or as represented. To help achieve this promise, Whole Foods insists that its suppliers also behave in an ethical way, so it knows, for example, that the beef it sells comes from cows pastured on grass, not corn-fed in feed lots, and the chicken it sells is from free-range hens and not from hens that have been confined in tiny cages that prevent movement.

Mackey's management approach toward "team members," as Whole Foods employees are called, is also based on a well-defined ethical position. He says, "We put great emphasis at Whole Foods on the 'Whole People' part of the company mission. We believe in helping support our team members to grow as individuals—to become 'Whole People.' We allow tremendous individual initiative at Whole Foods, and that's why our company is so innovative and creative."[7] Mackey claims that each supermarket in the chain is unique because in each one team members are constantly experimenting with new and better ways to serve customers and improve their well-being. As team members learn, they become "self-actualized" or self-fulfilled, and this increase in their well-being translates into a desire to increase the well-being of other stakeholders. Evidence of Whole Foods Market's commitment to team members is the fact that Whole Foods Market has been included in *Fortune* magazine's "100 Best Companies to Work For" for 15 years running. Whole Foods also has been recognized by *Fortune* for being a "Most Diverse" Company.[8]

Mackey's strong views on ethics and social responsibility also serve shareholders. Mackey does not believe the object of being in business is to primarily maximize profits for shareholders; he puts customers first.

He believes, however, that companies that behave ethically and strive to satisfy the needs of customers and employees simultaneously satisfy the needs of investors because high profits are the result of loyal customers and committed employees. Indeed, since Whole Foods issued shares to the public in 1992, the value of those shares has increased substantially. Giving back to local communities and protecting the natural enviroment are also key priorities at Whole Foods.[9] Clearly, taking a strong position on ethics and social responsibility has worked so far at Whole Foods.

Overview

While a strong code of ethics can influence the way employees behave, what causes people to behave unethically in the first place? Moreover, how do managers and employees determine what is ethical or unethical? In this chapter, we examine the nature of the obligations and responsibilities of managers and the companies they work for toward the people and society that are affected by their actions. First, we examine the nature of ethics and the sources of ethical problems. Second, we discuss the major groups of people, called *stakeholders,* who are affected by the way companies operate. Third, we look at four rules or guidelines that managers can use to decide whether a specific business decision is ethical or unethical and why it is important for people and companies to behave in an ethical way.

We then turn to the issue of the effective management of diversity. This first requires that organizations, their managers, and all employees behave ethically and follow legal rules and regulations in the ways diverse employees are hired, promoted, and treated. Second, effectively managing diversity means learning to appreciate and respond appropriately to the needs, attitudes, beliefs, and values that diverse employees bring to an organization and finding ways to use their skills and talents to benefit them and the company they work for. Finally, we discuss steps managers can take to eradicate sexual harassment in organizations. By the end of this chapter you will understand the central role that the effective management of ethics and diversity plays in shaping the practice of business and the life of a people, society, and nation.

 LO 3-1 Illustrate how ethics help managers determine the right way to behave when dealing with different stakeholder groups.

The Nature of Ethics

Suppose you see a person being mugged. Will you act in some way to help, even though you risk being hurt? Will you walk away? Perhaps you might not intervene but will you call the police? Does how you act depend on whether the person being mugged is a fit male, an elderly person, or a street person? Does it depend on whether other people are around so you can tell yourself, Oh well, someone else will help or call the police, I don't need to?

Ethical Dilemmas

ethical dilemma
The quandary people find themselves in when they have to decide if they should act in a way that might help another person or group even though doing so might go against their own self-interest.

The situation just described is an example of an *ethical dilemma*, the quandary people find themselves in when they have to decide if they should act in a way that might help another person or group and is the right thing to do, even though doing so might go against their own self-interest.[10] A dilemma may also arise when a person has to choose between two different courses of action, knowing that whichever course he or she selects will harm one person or group even while it may benefit another. The ethical dilemma here is to decide which course of action is the lesser of two evils.

People often know they are confronting an ethical dilemma when their moral scruples come into play and cause them to hesitate, debate, and reflect upon the rightness or goodness of a course of action. Moral scruples are thoughts and feelings that tell a person what is right or wrong; they are a part of a person's ethics. *Ethics* are the inner guiding moral principles, values, and beliefs that people use to analyze or interpret a situation and then decide what is the right or appropriate way to behave. Ethics also indicate what is inappropriate behavior and how a person should behave to avoid harming another person.

ethics The inner guiding moral principles, values, and beliefs that people use to analyze or interpret a situation and then decide what is the right or appropriate way to behave.

The essential problem in dealing with ethical issues, and thus solving moral dilemmas, is that no absolute or indisputable rules or principles can be developed to decide whether an action is ethical or unethical. Put simply, different people or groups may dispute which actions are ethical or unethical depending on their personal self-interest and specific attitudes, beliefs, and values—concepts we discussed in Chapter 2. How, therefore, are we and companies and their managers and employees to decide what is ethical and so act appropriately toward other people and groups?

Ethics and the Law

The first answer to this question is that society as a whole, using the political and legal process, can lobby for and pass laws that specify what people can and cannot do. Many different kinds of laws govern business—for example, laws against fraud and deception and laws governing how companies can treat their employees and customers. Laws also specify what sanctions or punishments will follow if those laws are broken. Different groups in society lobby for which laws should be passed based on their own personal interests and beliefs about right and wrong. The group that can summon the most support can pass laws that align with its interests and beliefs. Once a law is passed, a decision about what the appropriate behavior is with regard to a person or situation is taken from the personally determined ethical realm to the societally determined legal realm. If you do not conform to the law, you can be prosecuted; and if you are found guilty of breaking the law, you can be punished. You have little say in the matter; your fate is in the hands of the court and its lawyers.

In studying the relationship between ethics and law, it is important to understand that *neither laws nor ethics are fixed principles* that do not change over time. Ethical beliefs change as time passes; and as they do so, laws change to reflect the changing ethical beliefs of a society. It was seen as ethical, and it was legal, for example, to acquire and possess slaves in ancient Rome and Greece and in the United States until the late 19th century. Ethical views regarding whether slavery was morally right or appropriate changed, however. Slavery was made illegal in the United States when those in power decided that slavery degraded the meaning of being human. Slavery makes a statement about the value or worth of human beings and about their right to life, liberty, and the pursuit of happiness. And if we deny these rights to other people, how can we claim to have any natural rights to these things?

Moreover, what is to stop any person or group that becomes powerful enough to take control of the political and legal process from enslaving us and denying us the right to be free and to own property? In denying freedom to others, one risks losing it oneself, just as stealing from others opens the door for them to steal from us in return. "Do unto others as you would have them do unto you" is a common ethical or moral rule that people apply in such situations to decide what is the right thing to do.

Changes in Ethics over Time

There are many types of behavior—such as murder, theft, slavery, rape, and driving while intoxicated—that most people currently believe are unacceptable and unethical and should therefore be illegal. However, the ethics of many other actions and behaviors are open to dispute. Some people might believe a particular behavior—for example, smoking tobacco or possessing guns—is unethical and so should be made illegal. Others might argue that it is up to the individual or group to decide if such behaviors are ethical and thus whether a particular behavior should remain legal.

As ethical beliefs change over time, some people may begin to question whether existing laws that make specific behaviors illegal are still appropriate. They might argue that although a specific behavior is deemed illegal, this does not make it unethical and thus the law should be changed. In the United States, for example, it is illegal to possess or use marijuana (cannabis). To justify this law, it is commonly argued that smoking marijuana leads people to try more dangerous drugs. Once the habit of taking drugs has been acquired, people can get hooked on them. More powerful drugs such as murderous heroin and other narcotics are fearfully addictive, and most people cannot stop using them without help. Thus the use of marijuana, because it might lead to further harm, is an unethical practice.

It has been documented medically, however, that marijuana use can help people with certain illnesses. For example, for cancer sufferers who are undergoing chemotherapy and for those with AIDS who are on potent medications, marijuana offers relief from many treatment side effects, such as nausea and lack of appetite. Yet in the United States it is illegal in many states for doctors to prescribe marijuana for these patients, so their suffering continues. Since 1996, however, 15 states have made it legal to prescribe marijuana for medical purposes; nevertheless, the federal government has sought to stop such state legislation. The U.S. Supreme Court ruled in 2005 that only Congress or the states could decide whether medical marijuana use should be made legal, and people in many states are currently lobbying for a relaxation of state laws against its use for medical purposes.[11] In Canada

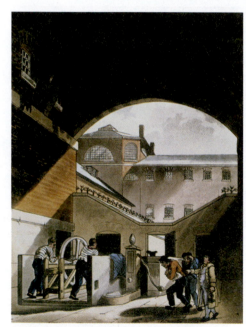

Coldbath Fields Prison, London, circa 1810. The British criminal justice system around this time was severe: There were over 350 different crimes for which a person could be executed, including sheep stealing. As ethical beliefs change over time, so do laws.

there has been a widespread movement to decriminalize marijuana. While not making the drug legal, decriminalization removes the threat of prosecution even for uses that are not medically related and allows the drug to be taxed. In 2012, for example, initiatives were under way in several states to decriminalize the possession of small amounts of marijuana for personal use as well as to make it more widely available to people legally for medical purposes. A major ethical debate is currently raging over this issue in many states and countries.

The important point to note is that while ethical beliefs lead to the development of laws and regulations to prevent certain behaviors or encourage others, laws themselves change or even disappear as ethical beliefs change. In Britain in 1830 a person could be executed for over 350 different crimes, including sheep stealing. Today the death penalty is no longer legal in Britain. Thus both ethical and legal rules are *relative:* No absolute or unvarying standards exist to determine how we should behave, and people are caught up in moral dilemmas all the time. Because of this we have to make ethical choices.

The previous discussion highlights an important issue in understanding the relationship between ethics, law, and business. Throughout the 2010s many scandals plagued major companies such as Guidant, Siemens, Merck, Pfizer, and others. Managers in some of these companies clearly broke the law and used illegal means to defraud investors, market their products to customers, or raise the prices of their products to customers.

In other cases managers took advantage of loopholes in the law to divert hundreds of millions of dollars of company capital into their own personal fortunes. At WorldCom, for example, former CEO Bernie Ebbers used his position to place six personal friends on the 13-member board of directors. Although this is not illegal, obviously these people would vote in his favor at board meetings. As a result of their support, Ebbers received huge stock options and a personal loan of over $150 million from WorldCom. In return, his supporters were well rewarded for being directors; for example, Ebbers allowed them to use WorldCom's corporate jets for a minimal cost, saving them hundreds of thousands of dollars a year.[12] In 2012 a scandal erupted at Chesapeake Energy after it was revealed its CEO Aubrey McClendon had received over $1 billion in loans from the company to fund his personal financial ventures.

In the light of these events some people said, "Well, what these people did was not illegal," implying that because such behavior was not illegal it was also not unethical. However, not being illegal does *not* make behavior ethical; such behavior is clearly unethical.[13] In many cases laws are passed *later* to close loopholes and prevent unethical people, such as Ebbers and McClendon, from taking advantage of them to pursue their own self-interest at the expense of others. Like ordinary people, managers must decide what is appropriate and inappropriate as they use a company's resources to produce goods and services for customers.[14]

Stakeholders and Ethics

Just as people have to work out the right and wrong ways to act, so do companies. When the law does not specify how companies should behave, their managers must decide the right or ethical way to behave toward the people and groups affected by their actions. Who are the people or groups that are affected by a company's business decisions? If a company behaves in an ethical way, how does this benefit people and society? Conversely, how are people harmed by a company's unethical actions?

stakeholders

The people and groups that supply a company with its productive resources and so have a claim on and a stake in the company.

The people and groups affected by how a company and its managers behave are called its stakeholders. Stakeholders supply a company with its productive resources; as a result, they have a claim on and a stake in the company.[15] Because stakeholders can directly benefit or be harmed by its actions, the ethics of a company and its managers are important to them. Who are a company's major stakeholders? What do they contribute to a company, and what do they claim in return? Here we examine the claims of these stakeholders—stockholders; managers; employees; suppliers and distributors; customers; and community, society, and nation-state (Figure 3.1).

Stockholders

Stockholders have a claim on a company because when they buy its stock or shares they become its owners. When the founder of a company decides to publicly incorporate the business to raise capital, shares of the stock of that company are issued. This stock grants its buyers ownership of a certain percentage of the company and the right to receive any future stock dividends. For example, in 2005 Microsoft decided to pay the owners of its 5 billion shares a special dividend payout of $32 billion. Bill Gates received $3.3 billion in dividends based on his stockholding, and he donated this money to the Bill and Melinda Gates Foundation, to which he has reportedly donated over $30 billion to date, with the promise of much more to come; and Warren Buffet committed to donate at least $30 billion to the Gates Foundation over the next decade. The two richest people in the world have decided to give away a large part of their wealth to serve global ethical causes—in particular to address global health concerns such as malnutrition, malaria, tuberculosis, and AIDS.

Stockholders are interested in how a company operates because they want to maximize the return on their investment. Thus they watch the company and its managers closely to ensure that management is working diligently to increase the company's profitability.[16] Stockholders also want to ensure that managers are

Figure 3.1

Types of Company Stakeholders

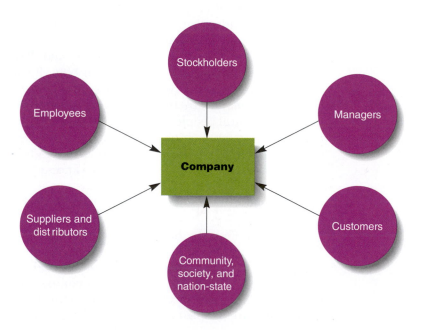

behaving ethically and not risking investors' capital by engaging in actions that could hurt the company's reputation. Managers of companies such as Chesapeake Energy, Goldman Sachs, and WorldCom pursued their own self-interest at the expense of their stakeholders. As a result of these managers' unethical actions, in 2006 WorldCom's ex-CEO Bernie Ebbers was sentenced to a long jail term, in 2012 two Goldman Sachs directors accused of insider trading also received jail sentences, and Aubrey McClendon was forced to resign as CEO and is currently under investigation by the Securities and Exchange Commission.

Managers

Managers are a vital stakeholder group because they are responsible for using a company's financial, capital, and human resources to increase its performance and thus its stock price.[17] Managers have a claim on an organization because they bring to it their skills, expertise, and experience. They have the right to expect a good return or reward by investing their human capital to improve a company's performance. Such rewards include good salaries and benefits, the prospect of promotion and a career, and stock options and bonuses tied to company performance.

Managers are the stakeholder group that bears the responsibility to decide which goals an organization should pursue to most benefit stakeholders and how to make the most efficient use of resources to achieve those goals. In making such decisions, managers are frequently in the position of having to juggle the interests of different stakeholders, including themselves.[18] These sometimes difficult decisions challenge managers to uphold ethical values because some decisions that benefit certain stakeholder groups (managers and stockholders) harm other groups (individual workers and local communities). For example, in economic downturns or when a company experiences performance shortfalls, layoffs may help cut costs (thus benefiting shareholders) at the expense of the employees laid off. Many U.S. managers have recently faced this difficult decision. Until the 2009 financial crisis sent unemployment soaring over 10%, on average about 1.6 million U.S. employees out of a total labor force of 140 million were affected by mass layoffs each year; and over 3 million jobs from the United States, Europe, and Japan have been outsourced to Asia since 2005. Layoff decisions are always difficult: They not only take a heavy toll on workers, their families, and local communities but also mean the loss of the contributions of valued employees to an organization. In 2010, after GM pulled out, Toyota announced it would close down its NUMMI plant in Fremont,

Rajat Kumar Gupta, former Goldman Sachs board member, leaves a Manhattan court after surrendering to federal authorities on October 26, 2011, in New York City. Gupta was charged with conspiracy and securities fraud, stemming from a massive hedge fund insider trading case.

California; the resulting loss of jobs would raise total unemployment to 25% in this community. Whenever decisions such as these are made—benefiting some groups at the expense of others—ethics come into play.

As we discussed in Chapter 1, managers must be motivated and given incentives to work hard in the interests of stockholders. Their behavior must also be scrutinized to ensure they do not behave illegally or unethically, pursuing goals that threaten stockholders and the company's interests.[19] Unfortunately we have seen in the 2010s how easy it is for top managers to find ways to ruthlessly pursue their self-interest at the expense of stockholders and employees because laws and regulations are not strong enough to force them to behave ethically.

In a nutshell, the problem has been that in many companies corrupt managers focus not on building the company's capital and stockholders' wealth but on maximizing their own personal capital and wealth. In an effort to prevent future scandals, the Securities and Exchange Commission (SEC), the government's top business watchdog, has begun to rework the rules governing a company's relationship with its auditor, as well as regulations concerning stock options, and to increase the power of outside directors to scrutinize a CEO. The SEC's goal is to outlaw many actions that were previously classified as merely unethical. For example, companies are now forced to reveal to stockholders the value of the stock options they give their top executives and directors and when they give them these options; this shows how much such payments reduce company profits. Managers and directors can now be prosecuted if they disguise or try to hide these payments. In the 2010s the SEC announced many new rules requiring that companies disclose myriad details of executive compensation packages to investors; already the boards of directors of many companies have stopped giving CEOs perks such as free personal jet travel, membership in exclusive country clubs, and luxury accommodations on "business trips." Also Congress has been considering a major new set of financial regulations that would prevent the many unethical and illegal actions of managers of banks and other financial institutions that led to the 2009 financial crisis; one of these regulations is the "Volcker Rule," which prohibits any "banking entity" from proprietary stock trading and from owning or sponsoring relationships with hedge funds and other private funds.

Indeed, many experts argue that the rewards given to top managers, particularly the CEO and COO, grew out of control in the 2000s. Top managers are today's "aristocrats," and through their ability to influence the board of directors and raise their own pay, they have amassed personal fortunes worth hundreds of millions of dollars. For example, according to a study by the Federal Reserve, U.S. CEOs now get paid about 600 times what the average worker earns, compared to about 40 times in 1980—a staggering increase. In 2011, the average CEO was paid $6.9 million, for example. We noted in Chapter 1 that besides their salaries, top managers often receive tens of millions in stock bonuses and options—even when their companies perform poorly.

Is it ethical for top managers to receive such vast amounts of money from their companies? Do they really earn it? Remember, this money could have gone to shareholders in the form of dividends. It could also have reduced the huge salary gap between those at the top and those at the bottom of the hierarchy. Many people argue that the growing disparity between the rewards given to CEOs and to other employees is unethical and should be regulated. CEO pay has skyrocketed because CEOs are the people who set and control one another's salaries and bonuses; they can do this because they sit on the boards of other companies as outside directors. Others argue that because top managers play an important role in building a company's capital and wealth, they deserve a significant share of its profits. Some recent research has suggested that the companies whose CEO compensation includes a large percentage of stock options tend to experience big share losses more often than big gains, and that on average, company performance improves as stock option use declines.[20] The debate over how much money CEOs and other top managers should be paid is still raging, particularly because the financial crisis beginning in 2009 showed how much money the CEOs of troubled financial companies earned even as their companies' performance and stock prices collapsed. For example, Countrywide Mortgage, which pioneered the subprime business, suffered losses of over $1.7 billion in 2007, and its stock fell 80%; yet its CEO Angelo Mozilo still received $20 million in stock awards and sold stock options worth $121 million before the company's price collapsed.

Employees

A company's employees are the hundreds of thousands of people who work in its various departments and functions, such as research, sales, and manufacturing. Employees expect to receive rewards consistent with their performance. One principal way that a company can act ethically toward employees and meet their expectations is by creating an occupational structure that fairly and equitably rewards employees for their contributions. Companies, for example, need to develop recruitment, training, performance appraisal, and reward systems that do not discriminate against employees and that employees believe are fair.

Suppliers and Distributors

No company operates alone. Every company is in a network of relationships with other companies that supply it with the inputs (such as raw materials, components, contract labor, and clients) that it needs to operate. It also depends on intermediaries such as wholesalers and retailers to distribute its products to the final customers. Suppliers expect to be paid fairly and promptly for their inputs; distributors expect to receive quality products at agreed-upon prices. Once again, many ethical issues arise in how companies contract and interact with their suppliers and distributors. Important issues concerning product quality and safety specifications are governed by the contracts a company signs with its suppliers and distributors.

Many other issues depend on business ethics. For example, numerous products sold in U.S. stores have been outsourced to countries that do not have U.S.-style regulations and laws to protect the workers who make these products. All companies must take an ethical position on the way they obtain and make the products they sell. Commonly this stance is published on a company's website.

Customers

Customers are often regarded as the most critical stakeholder group because if a company cannot attract them to buy its products, it cannot stay in business. Thus managers and employees must work to increase efficiency and effectiveness in order to create loyal customers and attract new ones. They do so by selling customers quality products at a fair price and providing good after-sales service. They can also strive to improve their products over time and provide guarantees to customers about the integrity of their products.

Many laws protect customers from companies that attempt to provide dangerous or shoddy products. Laws allow customers to sue a company whose product causes them injury or harm, such as a defective tire or vehicle. Other laws force companies to clearly disclose the interest rates they charge on purchases—an important hidden cost that customers frequently do not factor into their purchase decisions. Every year thousands of companies are prosecuted for breaking these laws, so "buyer beware" is an important rule customers must follow when buying goods and services.

Community, Society, and Nation

The effects of the decisions made by companies and their managers permeate all aspects of the communities, societies, and nations in which they operate. *Community* refers to physical locations like towns or cities or to social milieus like ethnic neighborhoods in which companies are located. A community provides a company with the physical and social infrastructure that allows it to operate; its utilities and labor force; the homes in which its managers and employees live; the schools, colleges, and hospitals that serve their needs; and so on.

Through the salaries, wages, and taxes it pays, a company contributes to the economy of its town or region and often determines whether the community prospers or declines. Similarly, a company affects the prosperity of a society and a nation and, to the degree that a company is involved in global trade, all the countries it operates in and thus the prosperity of the global economy. We have already discussed the many issues surrounding global outsourcing and the loss of jobs in the United States, for example.

Although the individual effects of the way each McDonald's restaurant operates might be small, for instance, the combined effects of how all McDonald's and other fast-food companies do business are enormous. In the United States alone, over 500,000 people work in the fast-food industry, and many thousands of suppliers like farmers, paper cup manufacturers, builders, and so on depend on it for their livelihood. Small wonder then that the ethics of the fast-food business are scrutinized closely. This industry was the major lobbyer against attempts to raise the national minimum wage (which was last raised to $7.25 an hour in 2009, up from $5.15—a figure that had not changed since 1997), for example, because a higher minimum wage would substantially increase its operating costs. However, responding to protests about chickens raised in cages where they cannot move, McDonald's—the largest egg buyer in the United States—issued new ethical guidelines concerning cage size and related matters that its egg suppliers must abide by if they are to retain its business. What ethical rules does McDonald's use to decide its stance toward minimum pay or minimum cage size?

Business ethics are also important because the failure of a company can have catastrophic effects on a community; a general decline in business activity affects a whole nation. The decision of a large company to pull out of a community, for example, can seriously threaten the community's future. Some companies may attempt to improve their profits by engaging in actions that, although not illegal, can hurt communities and nations. One of these actions is pollution. For example, many U.S. companies reduce costs by trucking their waste to Mexico, where it is legal to dump waste in the Rio Grande. The dumping pollutes the river from the Mexican side, but the U.S. side of the river is increasingly experiencing pollution's negative effects.

Rules for Ethical Decision Making

When a stakeholder perspective is taken, questions on company ethics abound.[21] What is the appropriate way to manage the claims of all stakeholders? Company decisions that favor one group of stakeholders, for example, are likely to harm the interests of others.[22] High prices charged to customers may bring high returns to shareholders and high salaries to managers in the short run. If in the long run customers turn to companies that offer lower-cost products, however, the result may be declining sales, laid-off employees, and the decline of the communities that support the high-priced company's business activity.

When companies act ethically, their stakeholders support them. For example, banks are willing to supply them with new capital, they attract highly qualified job applicants, and new customers are drawn to their products. Thus ethical companies grow and expand over time, and all their stakeholders benefit. The results of unethical behavior are loss of reputation and resources, shareholders selling their shares, skilled managers and employees leaving the company, and customers turning to the products of more reputable companies.

When making business decisions, managers must consider the claims of all stakeholders.[23] To help themselves and employees make ethical decisions and behave in ways that benefit their stakeholders, managers can use four ethical rules or principles to analyze the effects of their business decisions on stakeholders: the *utilitarian, moral rights, justice,* and *practical* rules (Figure 3.2).[24] These rules are useful guidelines that help managers decide on the appropriate way to behave in situations where it is necessary to balance a company's self-interest and the interests of its stakeholders. Remember, the right choices will lead resources

Figure 3.2

Four Ethical Rules

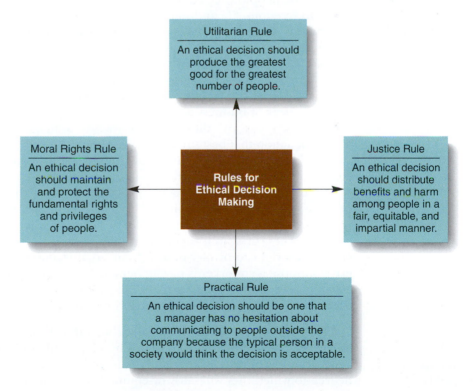

Utilitarian Rule

An ethical decision should produce the greatest good for the greatest number of people.

Moral Rights Rule

An ethical decision should maintain and protect the fundamental rights and privileges of people.

Rules for Ethical Decision Making

Justice Rule

An ethical decision should distribute benefits and harm among people in a fair, equitable, and impartial manner.

Practical Rule

An ethical decision should be one that a manager has no hesitation about communicating to people outside the company because the typical person in a society would think the decision is acceptable.

to be used where they can create the most value. If all companies make the right choices, all stakeholders will benefit in the long run.[25]

utilitarian rule
An ethical decision is a decision that produces the greatest good for the greatest number of people.

UTILITARIAN RULE The utilitarian rule is that an ethical decision is a decision that produces the greatest good for the greatest number of people. To decide which is the most ethical course of business action, managers should first consider how different possible courses of business action would benefit or harm different stakeholders. They should then choose the course of action that provides the most benefits, or, conversely, the one that does the least harm, to stakeholders.[26]

The ethical dilemma for managers is this: How do you measure the benefit and harm that will be done to each stakeholder group? Moreover, how do you evaluate the rights of different stakeholder groups, and the relative importance of each group, in coming to a decision? Because stockholders own the company, shouldn't their claims be held above those of employees? For example, managers might face a choice of using global outsourcing to reduce costs and lower prices or continuing with high-cost production at home. A decision to use global outsourcing benefits shareholders and customers but will result in major layoffs that will harm employees and the communities in which they live. Typically, in a capitalist society such as the United States, the interests of shareholders are put above those of employees, so production will move abroad. This is commonly regarded as being an ethical choice because in the long run the alternative, home production, might cause the business to collapse and go bankrupt, in which case greater harm will be done to all stakeholders.

moral rights rule
An ethical decision is one that best maintains and protects the fundamental or inalienable rights and privileges of the people affected by it.

MORAL RIGHTS RULE Under the moral rights rule, an ethical decision is one that best maintains and protects the fundamental or inalienable rights and privileges of the people affected by it. For example, ethical decisions protect people's rights to freedom, life and safety, property, privacy, free speech, and freedom of conscience. The adage "Do unto others as you would have them do unto you" is a moral rights principle that managers should use to decide which rights to uphold. Customers must also consider the rights of the companies and people who create the products they wish to consume.

From a moral rights perspective, managers should compare and contrast different courses of business action on the basis of how each course will affect the rights of the company's different stakeholders. Managers should then choose the course of action that best protects and upholds the rights of *all* stakeholders. For example, decisions that might significantly harm the safety or health of employees or customers would clearly be unethical choices.

The ethical dilemma for managers is that decisions that will protect the rights of some stakeholders often will hurt the rights of others. How should they choose which group to protect? For example, in deciding whether it is ethical to snoop on employees, or search them when they leave work to prevent theft, does an employee's right to privacy outweigh an organization's right to protect its property? Suppose a coworker is having personal problems and is coming in late and leaving early, forcing you to pick up the person's workload. Do you tell your boss even though you know this will probably get that person fired?

justice rule
An ethical decision distributes benefits and harms among people and groups in a fair, equitable, or impartial way.

JUSTICE RULE The justice rule is that an ethical decision distributes benefits and harms among people and groups in a fair, equitable, or impartial way. Managers should compare and contrast alternative courses of action based on the degree to which they will fairly or equitably distribute outcomes to stakeholders.

For example, employees who are similar in their level of skill, performance, or responsibility should receive similar pay; allocation of outcomes should not be based on differences such as gender, race, or religion.

The ethical dilemma for managers is to determine the fair rules and procedures for distributing outcomes to stakeholders. Managers must not give people they like bigger raises than they give to people they do not like, for example, or bend the rules to help their favorites. On the other hand, if employees want managers to act fairly toward them, then employees need to act fairly toward their companies by working hard and being loyal. Similarly, customers need to act fairly toward a company if they expect it to be fair to them—something people who illegally copy digital media should consider.

PRACTICAL RULE Each of these rules offers a different and complementary way of determining whether a decision or behavior is ethical, and all three rules should be used to sort out the ethics of a particular course of action. Ethical issues, as we just discussed, are seldom clear-cut, however, because the rights, interests, goals, and incentives of different stakeholders often conflict. For this reason many experts on ethics add a fourth rule to determine whether a business decision is ethical: The practical rule is that an ethical decision is one that a manager has no hesitation or reluctance about communicating to people outside the company because the typical person in a society would think it is acceptable. A business decision is probably acceptable on ethical grounds if a manager can answer yes to each of these questions:

1. Does my decision fall within the accepted values or standards that typically apply in business activity today?
2. Am I willing to see the decision communicated to all people and groups affected by it—for example, by having it reported in newspapers or on television?
3. Would the people with whom I have a significant personal relationship, such as family members, friends, or even managers in other organizations, approve of the decision?

Applying the practical rule to analyze a business decision ensures that managers are taking into account the interests of all stakeholders.[27]

Why Should Managers Behave Ethically?

Why is it so important that managers, and people in general, should act ethically and temper their pursuit of self-interest by considering the effects of their actions on others? The answer is that the relentless pursuit of self-interest can lead to a collective disaster when one or more people start to profit from being unethical because this encourages other people to act in the same way.[28] More and more people jump onto the bandwagon, and soon everybody is trying to manipulate the situation to serve their personal ends with no regard for the effects of their action on others. This situation is sometimes called the "tragedy of the commons."

Suppose that in an agricultural community there is common land that everybody has an equal right to use. Pursuing self-interest, each farmer acts to make the maximum use of the free resource by grazing his or her own cattle and sheep. Collectively all the farmers overgraze the land, which quickly becomes worn out. Then a strong wind blows away the exposed topsoil, so the common land is destroyed. The pursuit of individual self-interest with no consideration of societal

practical rule
An ethical decision is one that a manager has no reluctance about communicating to people outside the company because the typical person in a society would think it is acceptable.

LO 3-2 Explain why managers should behave ethically and strive to create ethical organizational cultures.

interests leads to disaster for each individual and for the whole society because scarce resources are destroyed.[29] For example, consider digital piracy; the tragedy that would result if all people were to steal digital media would be the disappearance of music, movie, and book companies as creative people decided there was no point in working hard to produce original songs, stories, and so on.

We can look at the effects of unethical behavior on business activity in another way. Suppose companies and their managers operate in an unethical society, meaning one in which stakeholders routinely try to cheat and defraud one another. If stakeholders expect each other to cheat, how long will it take them to negotiate the purchase and shipment of products? When they do not trust each other, stakeholders will probably spend hours bargaining over fair prices, and this is a largely unproductive activity that reduces efficiency and effectiveness.[30] The time and effort that could be spent improving product quality or customer service are lost to negotiating and bargaining. Thus, unethical behavior ruins business commerce, and society has a lower standard of living because fewer goods and services are produced, as Figure 3.3 illustrates.

On the other hand, suppose companies and their managers operate in an ethical society, meaning stakeholders believe they are dealing with others who are basically moral and honest. In this society stakeholders have a greater reason

Figure 3.3

Some Effects of Ethical and Unethical Behavior

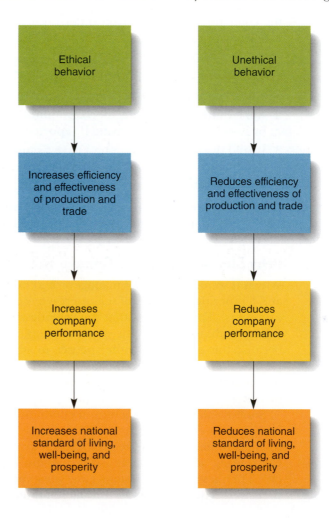

trust The willingness of one person or group to have faith or confidence in the goodwill of another person, even though this puts them at risk.

to trust others. Trust is the willingness of one person or group to have faith or confidence in the goodwill of another person, even though this puts them at risk (because the other might act in a deceitful way). When trust exists, stakeholders are likely to signal their good intentions by cooperating and providing information that makes it easier to exchange and price goods and services. When one person acts in a trustworthy way, this encourages others to act in the same way. Over time, as greater trust between stakeholders develops, they can work together more efficiently and effectively, which raises company performance (see Figure 3.3). As people see the positive results of acting in an honest way, ethical behavior becomes a valued social norm, and society in general becomes increasingly ethical.

As noted in Chapter 1, a major responsibility of managers is to protect and nurture the resources under their control. Any organizational stakeholders—managers, workers, stockholders, suppliers—who advance their own interests by behaving unethically toward other stakeholders, either by taking resources or by denying resources to others, waste collective resources. If other individuals or groups copy the behavior of the unethical stakeholder, the rate at which collective resources are misused increases, and eventually few resources are available to produce goods and services. Unethical behavior that goes unpunished creates incentives for people to put their unbridled self-interests above the rights of others.[31] When this happens, the benefits that people reap from joining together in organizations disappear quickly.

An important safeguard against unethical behavior is the potential for loss of reputation.[32] Reputation, the esteem or high repute that people or organizations gain when they behave ethically, is an important asset. Stakeholders have valuable reputations that they must protect because their ability to earn a living and obtain resources in the long run depends on how they behave.

reputation The esteem or high repute that individuals or organizations gain when they behave ethically.

If a manager misuses resources and other parties regard that behavior as being at odds with acceptable standards, the manager's reputation will suffer. Behaving unethically in the short run can have serious long-term consequences. A manager who has a poor reputation will have difficulty finding employment with other companies. Stockholders who see managers behaving unethically may refuse to invest in their companies, and this will decrease the stock price, undermine the companies' reputations, and ultimately put the managers' jobs at risk.[33]

All stakeholders have reputations to lose. Suppliers who provide shoddy inputs find that organizations learn over time not to deal with them, and eventually they go out of business. Powerful customers who demand ridiculously low prices find that their suppliers become less willing to deal with them, and resources ultimately become harder for them to obtain. Workers who shirk responsibilities on the job find it hard to get new jobs when they are fired. In general, if a manager or company is known for being unethical, other stakeholders are likely to view that individual or organization with suspicion and hostility, creating a poor reputation. But a manager or company known for ethical business practices will develop a good reputation.[34]

In summary, in a complex, diverse society, stakeholders, and people in general, need to recognize they are part of a larger social group. How they make decisions and act not only affects them personally but also affects the lives of many other people. Unfortunately, for some people, the daily struggle to survive and succeed or their total disregard for others' rights can lead them to lose that bigger connection to other people. We can see our relationships to our families and friends, to our school, church, and so on. But we must go further and keep in mind the effects of our actions on other people—people who will be judging our actions and whom we might harm by acting unethically. Our moral scruples are like those "other people" but are inside our heads.

Sources of an Organization's Code of Ethics

Codes of ethics are formal standards and rules, based on beliefs about right or wrong, that managers can use to help themselves make appropriate decisions with regard to the interests of their stakeholders.[35] Ethical standards embody views about abstractions such as justice, freedom, equity, and equality. An organization's code of ethics derives from three principal sources in the organizational environment: *societal* ethics, *professional* ethics, and the *individual* ethics of the organization's managers and employees (see Figure 3.4).

societal ethics
Standards that govern how members of a society are to deal with each other on issues such as fairness, justice, poverty, and the rights of the individual.

SOCIETAL ETHICS Societal ethics are standards that govern how members of a society deal with each other in matters involving issues such as fairness, justice, poverty, and the rights of the individual. Societal ethics emanate from a society's laws, customs, and practices, and from the unwritten attitudes, values, and norms that influence how people interact with each other. People in a particular country may automatically behave ethically because they have internalized values and norms that specify how they should behave in certain situations. Not all values and norms are internalized, however. The typical ways of doing business in a society and laws governing the use of bribery and corruption are the result of decisions made and enforced by people with the power to determine what is appropriate.

Societal ethics vary among societies. For example, ethical standards accepted in the United States are not accepted in all other countries. In many economically poor countries bribery is standard practice to get things done, such as getting a

Figure 3.4

Sources of an Organization's Code of Ethics

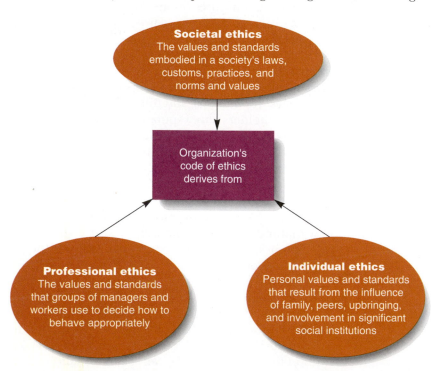

telephone installed or a contract awarded. In the United States and many other Western countries, bribery is considered unethical and often illegal.

Societal ethics control self-interested behavior by individuals and organizations—behavior threatening to society's collective interests. Laws spelling out what is good or appropriate business practice provide benefits to everybody. Free and fair competition among organizations is possible only when laws and rules level the playing field and define what behavior is acceptable or unacceptable in certain situations. For example, it is ethical for a manager to compete with managers in other companies by producing a higher-quality or lower-priced product, but it is not ethical (or legal) to do so by spreading false claims about competitors' products, bribing stores to exclude competitors' products, or blowing up competitors' factories.

professional ethics
Standards that govern how members of a profession are to make decisions when the way they should behave is not clear-cut.

PROFESSIONAL ETHICS Professional ethics are standards that govern how members of a profession, managers or workers, make decisions when the way in which they should behave is not clear-cut.[36] Medical ethics govern the way doctors and nurses are to treat patients. Doctors are expected to perform only necessary medical procedures and to act in the patient's interest and not in their own. The ethics of scientific research require scientists to conduct their experiments and present their findings in ways that ensure the validity of their conclusions. Like society at large, most professional groups can impose punishments for violations of ethical standards. Doctors and lawyers can be prevented from practicing their professions if they disregard professional ethics and put their own interests first.

Within an organization, professional rules and norms often govern how employees such as lawyers, researchers, and accountants make decisions and act in certain situations, and these rules and norms may become part of the organization's code of ethics. When they do, workers internalize the rules and norms of their profession (just as they do those of society) and often follow them automatically when deciding how to behave.[37] Because most people follow established rules of behavior, people often take ethics for granted. However, when professional ethics are violated, such as when scientists fabricate data to disguise the harmful effects of products, ethical issues rise to the forefront of attention.

individual ethics
Personal values and attitudes that govern how individuals interact with other people.

INDIVIDUAL ETHICS Individual ethics are personal values (both terminal and instrumental) and attitudes that govern how individuals interact with other people.[38] Sources of individual ethics include the influence of one's family, peers, and upbringing in general, and an individual's personality and experience. The experiences gained over a lifetime—through membership in significant social institutions such as schools and religions, for example—also contribute to the development of the personal standards and values that a person applies to decide what is right or wrong and whether to perform certain actions or make certain decisions. Many decisions or behaviors that one person finds unethical, such as using animals for cosmetics testing, may be acceptable to another person because of differences in their personalities, values, and attitudes (see Chapter 2).

Ethical Organizational Cultures

Managers can emphasize the importance of ethical behavior and social responsibility by ensuring that ethical values and norms are a central component of organizational culture. An organization's code of ethics guides decision making when ethical questions arise, but managers can go one step farther by ensuring that important ethical values and norms are key features of an organization's culture.

For example, Herb Kelleher and Southwest Airlines' culture value employee well-being; this emphasis translates into norms dictating that layoffs should be avoided.[39] Ethical values and norms such as these that are part of an organization's culture help organizational members resist self-interested action and recognize that they are part of something bigger than themselves.[40]

Managers' role in developing ethical values and standards in other employees is very important. Employees naturally look to those in authority to provide leadership, and managers become ethical role models whose behavior is scrutinized by their subordinates. If top managers are not ethical, their subordinates are not likely to behave in an ethical manner. Employees may think that if it's all right for a top manager to engage in dubious behavior, it's all right for them, too. The actions of top managers such as CEOs and the president of the United States are scrutinized so closely for ethical improprieties because these actions represent the values of their organizations and, in the case of the president, the values of the nation.

Managers can also provide a visible means of support to develop an ethical culture. Increasingly, organizations are creating the role of ethics officer, or ethics ombudsman, to monitor their ethical practices and procedures. The ethics ombudsman is responsible for communicating ethical standards to all employees, for designing systems to monitor employees' conformity to those standards, and for teaching managers and nonmanagerial employees at all levels of the organization how to respond to ethical dilemmas appropriately.[41] Because the ethics ombudsman has organizationwide authority, organizational members in any department can communicate instances of unethical behavior by their managers or coworkers without fear of retribution. This arrangement makes it easier for everyone to behave ethically. In addition, ethics ombudsmen can provide guidance when organizational members are uncertain about whether an action is ethical. Some organizations have an organizationwide ethics committee to provide guidance on ethical issues and help write and update the company code of ethics.

ethics ombudsman An ethics officer who monitors an organization's practices and procedures to be sure they are ethical.

LO 3-3 Appreciate the increasing diversity of the workforce and of the organizational environment.

The Increasing Diversity of the Workforce and the Environment

One of the most important management issues to emerge over the last 40 years has been the increasing diversity of the workforce. Diversity is dissimilarity—differences—among people due to age, gender, race, ethnicity, religion, sexual orientation, socioeconomic background, education, experience, physical appearance, capabilities/disabilities, and any other characteristic that is used to distinguish between people (see Figure 3.5).

Diversity raises important ethical issues and social responsibility issues. It is also a critical issue for organizations, one that if not handled well can bring an organization to its knees, especially in our increasingly global environment. There are several reasons why diversity is such a pressing concern and an issue both in the popular press and for managers and organizations:

- There is a strong ethical imperative in many societies that diverse people must receive equal opportunities and be treated fairly and justly. Unfair treatment is also illegal.

- Effectively managing diversity can improve organizational effectiveness.[42] When managers effectively manage diversity, they not only encourage other managers to treat diverse members of an organization fairly and justly but also

diversity Differences among people due to age, gender, race, ethnicity, religion, sexual orientation, socioeconomic background, education, physical appearance, capabilities, disabilities, and any other characteristic used to distinguish people.

Figure 3.5

Sources of Diversity in the Workplace

realize that diversity is an important organizational resource that can help an organization gain a competitive advantage.

- There is substantial evidence that diverse individuals continue to experience unfair treatment in the workplace as a result of biases, stereotypes, and overt discrimination.[43] In one study, résumés of equally qualified men and women were sent to high-priced Philadelphia restaurants (where potential earnings are high). Though equally qualified, men were more than twice as likely as women to be called for a job interview and more than five times as likely to receive a job offer.[44] Findings from another study suggest that both women and men tend to believe that women will accept lower pay than men; this is a possible explanation for the continuing gap in pay between men and women.[45]

Other kinds of diverse employees may face even greater barriers. For example, the federal Glass Ceiling Commission Report indicated that African Americans have the hardest time being promoted and climbing the corporate ladder, that Asians are often stereotyped into technical jobs, and that Hispanics are assumed to be less well educated than other minority groups.[46] (The term glass ceiling alludes to the invisible barriers that prevent minorities and women from being promoted to top corporate positions.)[47]

Before we can discuss the multitude of issues surrounding the effective management of diversity, we must document just how diverse the U.S. workforce is becoming.

glass ceiling

A metaphor alluding to the invisible barriers that prevent minorities and women from being promoted to top corporate positions.

Age

According to data from the U.S. Census Bureau and the CIA's World Fact Book, the median age of a person in the United States is the highest it has ever been, 36.9 years.[48] Moreover, by 2030 it is projected that close to 20% of the population will be 65 or over.[49] The Age Discrimination in Employment Act of 1967 prohibits

Table 3.1

Major Equal Employment Opportunity Laws Affecting Human Resources Management

Year	Law	Description
1963	Equal Pay Act	Requires that men and women be paid equally if they are performing equal work.
1964	Title VII of the Civil Rights Act	Prohibits discrimination in employment decisions on the basis of race, religion, sex, color, or national origin; covers a wide range of employment decisions, including hiring, firing, pay, promotion, and working conditions.
1967	Age Discrimination in Employment Act	Prohibits discrimination against workers over the age of 40 and restricts mandatory retirement.
1978	Pregnancy Discrimination Act	Prohibits discrimination against women in employment decisions on the basis of pregnancy, childbirth, and related medical decisions.
1990	Americans with Disabilities Act	Prohibits discrimination against disabled individuals in employment decisions and requires that employers make accommodations for disabled workers to enable them to perform their jobs.
1991	Civil Rights Act	Prohibits discrimination (as does Title VII) and allows for the awarding of punitive and compensatory damages, in addition to back pay, in cases of intentional discrimination.
1993	Family and Medical Leave Act	Requires that employers provide 12 weeks of unpaid leave for medical and family reasons, including paternity and illness of a family member.

age discrimination.[50] Major equal employment opportunity legislation that prohibits discrimination among diverse groups is summarized in Table 3.1.

The aging of the population suggests managers need to be vigilant to ensure that employees are not discriminated against because of age. Moreover, managers need to ensure that the policies and procedures they have in place treat all workers fairly, regardless of their ages. Additionally, effectively managing diversity means employees of diverse ages are able to learn from each other, work well together, and take advantage of the different perspectives each has to offer.

At Loft Studio Marcel Weber, a more experienced architect helps guide a new employee—just one example of how respecting and valuing each person's unique contributions actually benefits your bottom line and your long-term success.

Gender

Women and men are almost equally represented in the U.S. workforce (approximately 53.3% of the U.S. workforce is male and 46.7% female),[51] yet women's median weekly earnings are estimated to be $688 compared to $843 for men.[52] Thus the gender pay gap appears to be as alive and well as the glass ceiling. According to the nonprofit organization Catalyst, which studies women in business, while women compose about 51.5% of the employees in managerial and professional positions,[53] only around 14.1% of executive officers in the 500 largest U.S. companies (that is, the *Fortune* 500) are women, and only 7.5% of the top earner executive officers are women.[54] These women, such as Virginia

A female executive enjoying the company plane is not as rare a sight today as it used to be; nevertheless, the glass ceiling remains a very real barrier to women in the business workforce.

Rometty, CEO of IBM, and Indra Nooyi, CEO of PepsiCo, stand out among their male peers and often receive a disparate amount of attention in the media. Women are also very underrepresented on boards of directors—they currently hold 16.1% of the board seats of *Fortune* 500 companies.[55] However, as Sheila Wellington, former president of Catalyst, indicates, "Women either control or influence nearly all consumer purchases, so it's important to have their perspective represented on boards."[56]

Additionally, research conducted by consulting firms suggests that female executives outperform their male colleagues in skills such as motivating others, promoting good communication, turning out high-quality work, and being a good listener.[57] For example, the Hagberg Group performed in-depth evaluations of 425 top executives in a variety of industries, with each executive rated by approximately 25 people. Of the 52 skills assessed, women received higher ratings than men on 42 skills, although at times the differences were small.[58] Results of a study conducted by Catalyst found that organizations with higher proportions of women in top management positions had significantly better financial performance than organizations with lower proportions of female top managers.[59] Another study conducted by Catalyst found that companies with three or more women on their boards of directors performed better in terms of returns on equity, sales, and invested capital than companies with fewer women on their boards or no women.[60] All in all, studies such as these make one wonder why the glass ceiling continues to hamper the progress of women in business.

Race and Ethnicity

The U.S. Census Bureau distinguished among the following races in the 2010 Census: American Indian or Alaska Native; Asian Indian; Black, African American, or Negro; Chinese; Filipino; Japanese; Korean; Vietnamese; Other Asian; Native Hawaiian; Guamanian or Chamorro; Samoan; Other Pacific Islander; White; and other races.[61] Although *ethnicity* refers to a grouping of people based on some shared characteristic such as national origin, language, or culture, the U.S. Census Bureau treats ethnicity in terms of whether a person is Hispanic, Latino, or of Spanish origin or not.[62] Hispanics, also referred to as Latinos, are people whose origins are in Spanish cultures such as those of Cuba, Mexico, Puerto Rico, and South and Central America. Hispanics can be of different races.[63] According to a recent poll, most Hispanics prefer to be identified by their country of origin (such as Mexican, Cuban, or Salvadoran) rather than by the overarching term *Hispanic*.[64]

The racial and ethnic diversity of the U.S. population is increasing at an exponential rate, as is the composition of the workforce.[65] According to the U.S. Census Bureau, approximately one of every three U.S. residents belongs to a minority group (i.e., is not a non-Hispanic White).[66] More specifically, 16.3% of the population is Hispanic or Latino, 83.7% of the population is not Hispanic or Latino, and

63.7% of the population is White alone (i.e., white and not Hispanic or Latino).[67] For those individuals self-identifying one race in the 2010 U.S. Census, approximately 72.4% of the population is White, 12.6% is Black or African American, 0.9% is American Indian or Alaska Native, 4.8% is Asian, 0.2% is Native Hawaiian and Other Pacific Islander, and 6.2% is another race; 2.9% of the population self-identified two or more races.[68] According to projections released by the U.S. Census Bureau, the composition of the U.S. population in 2050 will be quite different from its composition today; in 2050, the U.S. population is projected to be 54% minority.[69]

The increasing racial and ethnic diversity of the workforce and the population as a whole underscores the importance of effectively managing diversity. Statistics compiled by the Bureau of Labor statistics suggest that much needs to be done in terms of ensuring that diverse employees have equal opportunities. For example, median weekly earnings for Black men are approximately 75.8% of median earnings for White men; median weekly earnings for Black women are approximately 84.8% of median earnings for White women.[70] In the remainder of this chapter, we focus on the fair treatment of diverse employees and explore why this is such an important challenge and what managers can do to meet it. We begin by taking a broader perspective and considering how increasing racial and ethnic diversity in an organization's environment (such as customers and suppliers) affects decision making and organizational effectiveness.

At a general level, managers and organizations are increasingly being reminded that stakeholders in the environment are diverse and expect organizational decisions and actions to reflect this diversity. For example, the NAACP (National Association for the Advancement of Colored People) and Children Now (an advocacy group) have lobbied the entertainment industry to increase the diversity in television programming, writing, and producing.[71] The need for such increased diversity is more than apparent. For example, while Hispanics make up 12.5% of the U.S. population (or 35 million potential TV viewers), only about 2% of the characters in prime-time TV shows are Hispanics (of the 2,251 characters in prime-time shows, only 47 are Hispanic), according to a study conducted by Children Now.[72] Moreover, only about 1.3% of the evening network TV news stories are reported by Hispanic correspondents, according to the Center for Media and Public Affairs.[73]

Pressure is mounting on networks to increase diversity for a variety of reasons revolving around the diversity of the population as a whole, TV viewers, and consumers. For example, home and automobile buyers are increasingly diverse, reflecting the increasing diversity of the population as a whole.[74] Moreover, managers have to be especially sensitive to avoid stereotyping different groups when they communicate with potential customers. For example, Toyota Motor Sales USA made a public apology to the Reverend Jesse Jackson and his Rainbow Coalition for using a print advertisement depicting an African American man with a Toyota RAV4 sport utility image embossed on his gold front tooth.[75]

Religion

Title VII of the Civil Rights Act prohibits discrimination based on religion (as well as based on race/ethnicity, country of origin, and sex; see Table 3.1). In addition to enacting Title VII, in 1997 the federal government issued "The White House Guidelines on Religious Exercise and Expression in the Federal Workplace."[76]

These guidelines, while technically applicable only in federal offices, also are frequently relied on by large corporations. The guidelines require that employers make reasonable accommodations for religious practices, such as observances of holidays, as long as doing so does not entail major costs or hardships.[77]

A key issue for managers when it comes to religious diversity is recognizing and being aware of different religions and their beliefs, with particular attention being paid to when religious holidays fall. For example, critical meetings should not be scheduled during a holy day for members of a certain faith, and managers should be flexible in allowing people to have time off for religious observances. According to Lobna Ismail, director of a diversity training company in Silver Spring, Maryland, when managers acknowledge, respect, and make even small accommodations for religious diversity, employee loyalty is often enhanced. For example, allowing employees to leave work early on certain days instead of taking a lunch break or posting holidays for different religions on the company calendar can go a long way toward making individuals of diverse religions feel respected and valued as well as enabling them to practice their faith.[78] According to research conducted by the Tanenbaum Center for Interreligious Understanding in New York, while only about 23% of employees who feel they are victims of religious discrimination actually file complaints, about 45% of these employees start looking for other jobs.[79]

Capabilities/Disabilities

The Americans with Disabilities Act (ADA) of 1990 prohibits discrimination against persons with disabilities and also requires that employers make reasonable accommodations to enable these people to effectively perform their jobs. On the surface, few would argue with the intent of this legislation. However, as managers attempt to implement policies and procedures to comply with the ADA, they face a number of interpretation and fairness challenges.

On one hand, some people with real disabilities warranting workplace accommodations are hesitant to reveal their disabilities to their employers and claim the accommodations they deserve.[80] On the other hand, some employees abuse the ADA by seeking unnecessary accommodations for disabilities that may or may not exist.[81] Thus it is perhaps not surprising that the passage of the ADA does not appear to have increased employment rates significantly for those with disabilities.[82] A key challenge for managers is to promote an environment in which employees needing accommodations feel comfortable disclosing their need and, at the same time, to ensure that the accommodations not only enable those with disabilities to effectively perform their jobs but also are perceived to be fair by those not disabled.[83]

In addressing this challenge, often managers must educate both themselves and their employees about the disabilities, as well as the real capabilities, of those who are disabled. For example, during Disability Awareness Week, administrators at the University of Notre Dame sought to increase the public's knowledge of disabilities while also heightening awareness of the abilities of persons who are disabled.[84] The University of Houston conducted a similar program called "Think Ability."[85] According to Cheryl Amoruso, director of the University of Houston's Center for Students with Disabilities, many people are unaware of the prevalence of disabilities as well as misinformed about their consequences. She suggests, for example, that although students may not be able to see, they can still excel in their coursework and have successful careers.[86] Accommodations enabling such students to perform up to their capabilities are covered under the ADA.

As profiled in the following "Ethics in Action" box, a number of organizations have not only provided employment opportunities for disabled adults but also have benefited from their valuable contributions.[87]

ETHICS IN ACTION

Disabled Employees Make Valuable Contributions

Some large organizations like McDonald's, Walmart, Home Depot, and Walgreens actively recruit disabled employees to work in positions such as cashiers, maintenance workers, greeters, shelf stockers, and floor workers that help customers find items. Home Depot, for example, works with a nonprofit agency called Ken's Krew, Inc., founded by parents of disabled adults, to recruit and place disabled employees in its stores. Thus far, working with Ken's Krew has enabled Home Depot to recruit and place around 100 disabled adults in over 50 of its stores.[88]

Often, when given the opportunity, disabled employees make valuable contributions to their organizations. Walgreens opened an automated distribution center in Anderson, South Carolina, in which more than 40% of its 264 employees are disabled.[89] For disabled employees like 18-year-old Harrison Mullinax, who has autism and checks in merchandise to be distributed to drugstores with a bar code scanner, having a regular job is a godsend. Randy Lewis, senior vice president of distribution and logistics at Walgreens, thought about hiring workers with disabilities when Walgreens was considering using technology to increase automation levels in a distribution center. Lewis, the father of a young adult son who has autism, was aware of how difficult it can be for young adults like his son to find employment. Various accommodations were made, like redesigning workstations and computer displays to suit employees' needs, and employees received appropriate training in how to do their jobs. Some days, disabled employees are actually the most productive in the center. As Lewis puts it, "One thing we found is they can all do the job. . . . What surprised us is the environment that it's created. It's a building where everybody helps each other out."[90]

Walgreens is a large organization, but small organizations also have benefited from the valuable contributions of disabled employees. Habitat International, founded by current CEO David Morris and his father Saul over 30 years ago, is a manufacturer and contractor of indoor–outdoor carpet and artificial grass and a supplier to home improvement

Working through his training as a greeter, Jamie Heal embraces his job at Walmart with gusto. His new-found independence became a catalyst for life changes (going by the name Cameron was one) as well as a deeper sense of self-respect.

companies like Lowe's and Home Depot.[91] Habitat's profits have steadily increased over the years, and the factory's defect rate is less than 0.5%.[92]

Morris attributes Habitat's success to its employees, 75% of whom have either a physical or a mental disability or both.[93] Habitat has consistently provided employment opportunities to people with disabilities such as Down syndrome, schizophrenia, or cerebral palsy.[94] The company has also hired the homeless, recovering alcoholics, and non-English-speaking refugees. And these employees were relied on by plant manager Connie Presnell when she needed to fill a rush order by assigning it to a team of her fastest workers.[95] Habitat pays its employees regionally competitive wages and has low absence and turnover rates. Employees who need accommodations to perform their jobs are provided them, and Habitat has a highly motivated, satisfied, and committed workforce.[96]

While Habitat has actually gained some business from clients who applaud its commitment to diversity, Habitat's ethical values and social responsibility have also led the company to forgo a major account when stereotypes reared their ugly heads. Several years ago CEO Morris dropped the account of a distribution company because its representatives had made derogatory comments about his employees. Although it took Habitat two years to regain the lost revenues from this major account, Morris had no regrets.[97] Habitat's commitment to diversity and fair treatment is a win–win situation; the company is thriving, and so are its employees.[98]

The ADA also protects employees with acquired immune deficiency syndrome (AIDS) from being discriminated against in the workplace. AIDS is caused by the human immunodeficiency virus (HIV) and is transmitted through sexual contact, infected needles, and contaminated blood products. HIV is not spread through casual nonsexual contact. Yet out of ignorance, fear, or prejudice, some people wish to avoid all contact with anyone infected with HIV. Infected individuals may not necessarily develop AIDS, and some individuals with HIV are able to remain effective performers of their jobs while not putting others at risk.[99]

AIDS awareness training can help people overcome their fears and also give managers a tool to prevent illegal discrimination against HIV-infected employees. Such training focuses on educating employees about HIV and AIDS, dispelling myths, communicating relevant organizational policies, and emphasizing the rights of HIV-positive employees to privacy and an environment that allows them to be productive.[100] The need for AIDS awareness training is underscored by some of the problems HIV-positive employees experience once others in their workplace become aware of their condition.[101] Moreover, organizations are required to make reasonable accommodations to enable people with AIDS to effectively perform their jobs.

Thus managers have an obligation to educate employees about HIV and AIDS, dispel myths and the stigma of AIDS, and ensure that HIV-related discrimination is not occurring in the workplace. For example, Home Depot has provided HIV training and education to its store managers; such training was sorely needed given that over half of the managers indicated it was the first time they had the opportunity to talk about AIDS.[102] Moreover, advances in medication and treatment mean that more infected individuals are able to continue working or are able to return to work after their condition improves. Thus managers need to ensure that these employees are fairly treated by all members of their organizations.[103] And managers and organizations that do not treat HIV-positive employees in a fair manner, as well as provide reasonable accommodations (such as allowing time off for doctor visits or to take medicine), risk costly lawsuits.

Socioeconomic Background

The term *socioeconomic background* typically refers to a combination of social class and income-related factors. From a management perspective, socioeconomic diversity (and in particular diversity in income levels) requires that managers be sensitive and responsive to the needs and concerns of individuals who might not be as well off as others. U.S. welfare reform in the middle to late 1990s emphasized the need for single mothers and others receiving public assistance to join or return to the workforce. In conjunction with a strong economy, this led to record declines in the number of families, households, and children living below the poverty level, according to the 2000 U.S. census.[104] However, the economic downturns in the early and late 2000s suggest that some past gains, which lifted families out of poverty, have been reversed. In a strong economy, it is much easier for poor people with few skills to find jobs; in a weak economy, when companies lay off employees in hard times, people who need their incomes the most are unfortunately often the first to lose their jobs.[105] And in recessionary times, it is difficult for laid-off employees to find new positions. For example, in December 2009 there was an average of 6.1 unemployed workers for every open position.[106]

According to statistics released by the US Census Bureau in 2011, the official poverty rate in the United States increased to 15.1% or 46.2 million people in 2010; in 2009, the poverty rate was 14.3% or 43.6 million people.[107] The Census Bureau relies on predetermined threshold income figures, based on family size and composition, adjusted annually for inflation, to determine the poverty level. Families whose income falls below the threshold level are considered poor.[108] For example, in 2010 a family of four was considered poor if their annual income fell below $22,314.[109] When workers earn less than $10 or $15 per hour, it is often difficult, if not impossible, for them to meet their families' needs.[110] Moreover, increasing numbers of families are facing the challenge of finding suitable child care arrangements that enable the adults to work long hours and/or through the night to maintain an adequate income level. New information technology has led to more businesses operating 24 hours a day, creating real challenges for workers on the night shift, especially those with children.[111]

Hundreds of thousands of parents across the country are scrambling to find someone to care for their children while they are working the night shift, commuting several hours a day, working weekends and holidays, or putting in long hours on one or more jobs. This has led to the opening of day care facilities that operate around the clock as well as to managers seeking ways to provide such care for children of their employees. For example, the Children's Choice Learning Center in Las Vegas, Nevada, operates around the clock to accommodate employees working nights in neighboring casinos, hospitals, and call centers. Randy Donahue, a security guard who works until midnight, picks his children up from the center when he gets off work; his wife is a nurse on the night shift.[112]

A father drops off his child at a day care facility before going to work. Managers need to be aware that many employees deal with challenging socioeconomic factors such as long commutes and finding suitable child care arrangements.

Judy Harden, who focuses on families and child care issues for the United Workers Union, indicates that the demands families are facing necessitate around-the-clock and odd-hour child care options. Many parents simply do not have the choice of working at hours that allow them to take care of their children at night and/or on weekends, never mind when the children are sick.[113] Some parents and psychologists feel uneasy having children separated from their families for so much time and particularly at night. Most agree that, unfortunately for many families, this is not a choice but a necessity.[114]

Socioeconomic diversity suggests that managers need to be sensitive and responsive to the needs and concerns of workers who may be less fortunate than themselves in terms of income and financial resources, child care and elder care options, housing opportunities, and existence of sources of social and family support. Moreover—and equally important—managers should try to give such individuals opportunities to learn, advance, and make meaningful contributions to their organizations while improving their economic well-being.

Sexual Orientation

According to research conducted by Gary Gates of the Williams Institute at the UCLA School of Law, approximately 3.5% of adults in the United States or 9 million U.S. residents self-identify as lesbian, gay, bisexual, or transgender (LGBT).[115] Although no federal law prohibits discrimination based on sexual orientation, 20 states have such laws, and a 1998 executive order prohibits sexual orientation discrimination in civilian federal offices.[116] Moreover, an increasing number of organizations recognize the minority status of LGBT employees, affirm their rights to fair and equal treatment, and provide benefits to same-sex partners of gay and lesbian employees.[117] For example, a vast majority of *Fortune* 500 companies prohibit discrimination based on sexual orientation, and a majority of the *Fortune* 500 provide domestic partner benefits.[118] As indicated in the following "Focus on Diversity" box, managers can take many steps to ensure that sexual orientation is not used to unfairly discriminate among employees.

FOCUS ON DIVERSITY

Preventing Discrimination Based on Sexual Orientation

Although gays and lesbians have made great strides in attaining fair treatment in the workplace, much more needs to be done. In a study conducted by Harris Interactive Inc. (a research firm) and Witeck Communications Inc. (a marketing firm), over 40% of gay and lesbian employees indicated that they had been unfairly treated, denied a promotion, or pushed to quit their jobs because of their sexual orientation.[119] Given continued harassment and discrimination despite the progress that has been made,[120] many gay and lesbian employees fear disclosing their sexual orientation in the workplace and thus live a life of secrecy. While there are a few openly gay top managers, such as David Geffen, cofounder of DreamWorks SKG, and Allan Gilmour, former vice chairman

Danish employees of Microsoft raise awareness at Copenhagen's annual Gay Pride Parade. Corporate backing, such as that displayed here, can go a long way toward making sure workplaces are safe and respectful for everyone.

and CFO of Ford and currently a member of the board of directors of DTE Energy Holding Company, many others choose not to disclose or discuss their personal lives, including long-term partners.[121]

Thus it is not surprising that many managers are taking active steps to educate and train their employees about issues of sexual orientation. S. C. Johnson & Sons, Inc., maker of Raid insecticide and Glade air fresheners in Racine, Wisconsin, provides mandatory training to its plant managers to overturn stereotypes; and Eastman Kodak, Merck & Co., Ernst & Young, and Toronto-Dominion Bank all train managers in how to prevent sexual orientation discrimination.[122] Other organizations such as Lucent Technologies, Microsoft, and Southern California Edison send employees to seminars conducted at prominent business schools. And many companies such as Raytheon, IBM, Eastman Kodak, and Lockheed Martin provide assistance to their gay and lesbian employees through gay and lesbian support groups.[123] Recently, JPMorgan Chase, Goldman Sachs Group, and Bank of America were recognized as Best Places to Work 2012 for gay, lesbian, bisexual, and transgender employees by the Human Rights Campaign, a nonprofit organization that advocates for the civil rights of LGBT people.[124]

The Chubb Group of Insurance Companies, a property and casualty insurance company, provides its managers with a two-hour training session to help create work environments that are safe and welcoming for lesbian, gay, bisexual, and transgender (LGBT) people.[125] The sessions are conducted by two Chubb employees; usually one of the trainers is straight and the other is gay. The sessions focus on issues that affect a manager's ability to lead diverse teams, such as assessing how safe and welcoming the workplace is for LGBT people, how to refer to gay employees' significant others, and how to respond if employees or customers use inappropriate language or behavior. The idea for the program originated from one of Chubb's employee resource groups. Managers rate the program highly and say they are better able to respond to the concerns of their LGBT employees while creating a safe and productive work environment for all.[126] In 2012, the Chubb Group was also recognized as one of the Best Places to Work by the Human Right Campaign.[127]

Other Kinds of Diversity

Other kinds of diversity are important in organizations, are critical for managers to deal with effectively, and also are potential sources of unfair treatment. For example, organizations and teams need members with diverse backgrounds and experiences. This is clearly illustrated by the prevalence of cross-functional teams in organizations whose members might come from various departments such as marketing, production, finance, and sales (teams are covered in depth in Chapter 11). A team responsible for developing and introducing a new product, for example, often needs the expertise of employees not only from R&D and engineering but also from marketing, sales, production, and finance.

Other types of diversity can affect how employees are treated in the workplace. For example, employees differ from each other in how attractive they are (based on the standards of the cultures in which an organization operates) and in body weight. Whether individuals are attractive or unattractive, thin or overweight, in most cases has no bearing on their job performance unless they have jobs in which physical appearance plays a role, such as modeling. Yet sometimes these physical sources of diversity end up influencing advancement rates and salaries. A study published in the *American Journal of Public Health* found that highly educated obese women earned approximately 30% less per year than women who were not obese and men (regardless of whether or not the men were obese).[128] Clearly managers need to ensure that all employees are treated fairly, regardless of their physical appearance.

Managers and the Effective Management of Diversity

LO 3-4 Grasp the central role that managers play in the effective management of diversity.

The increasing diversity of the environment—which, in turn, increases the diversity of an organization's workforce—increases the challenges managers face in effectively managing diversity. Each of the kinds of diversity just discussed presents a particular set of issues managers need to appreciate before they can respond to them effectively. Understanding these issues is not always a simple matter, as many informed managers have discovered. Research on how different groups are currently treated and the unconscious biases that might adversely affect them is vital because it helps managers become aware of the many subtle and unobtrusive ways in which diverse employee groups can come to be treated unfairly over time. Managers can take many more steps to become sensitive to the ongoing effects of diversity in their organizations, take advantage of all the contributions diverse employees can make, and prevent diverse employees from being unfairly treated.

Critical Managerial Roles

In each of their managerial roles (see Chapter 1), managers can either promote the effective management of diversity or derail such efforts; thus they are critical to this process. For example, in their interpersonal roles, managers can convey that the effective management of diversity is a valued goal and objective (figurehead role), can serve as a role model and institute policies and procedures to ensure that diverse organizational members are treated fairly (leader role), and can enable diverse individuals and groups to coordinate their efforts and cooperate with each other both inside the organization and at the organization's boundaries (liaison role). In Table 3.2 we summarize some ways managers can ensure that diversity is effectively managed as they perform their different roles.

Given the formal authority that managers have in organizations, they typically have more influence than rank-and-file employees. When managers commit to supporting diversity, their authority and positions of power and status influence other members of an organization to make a similar commitment.[129] Research on social influence supports such a link: People are likely to be influenced and persuaded by others who have high status.[130]

Moreover, when managers commit to diversity, their commitment legitimizes the diversity management efforts of others.[131] In addition, resources are devoted to such efforts, and all members of an organization believe that their diversity-related efforts are supported and valued. Consistent with this reasoning, top management

Table 3.2

Managerial Roles and the Effective Management of Diversity

Type of Role	Specific Role	Example
Interpersonal	Figurehead	Conveys that the effective management of diversity is a valued goal and objective.
	Leader	Serves as a role model and institutes policies and procedures to ensure that diverse members are treated fairly.
	Liaison	Enables diverse individuals to coordinate their efforts and cooperate with one another.
Informational	Monitor	Evaluates the extent to which diverse employees are being treated fairly.
	Disseminator	Informs employees about diversity policies and initiatives and the intolerance of discrimination.
	Spokesperson	Supports diversity initiatives in the wider community and speaks to diverse groups to interest them in career opportunities.
Decisional	Entrepreneur	Commits resources to develop new ways to effectively manage diversity and eliminate biases and discrimination.
	Disturbance handler	Takes quick action to correct inequalities and curtail discriminatory behavior.
	Resource allocator	Allocates resources to support and encourage the effective management of diversity.
	Negotiator	Works with organizations (e.g., suppliers) and groups (e.g., labor unions) to support and encourage the effective management of diversity.

commitment and rewards for the support of diversity are often cited as critical ingredients in the success of diversity management initiatives.[132] Additionally, seeing managers express confidence in the abilities and talents of diverse employees causes other organizational members to be similarly confident and helps reduce any misconceived misgivings they may have as a result of ignorance or stereotypes.[133]

LO 3-5 Understand why the effective management of diversity is both an ethical and a business imperative.

Two other important factors emphasize why managers are so central to the effective management of diversity. The first factor is that women, African Americans, Hispanics, and other minorities often start out at a slight disadvantage due to how they are perceived by others in organizations, particularly in work settings where they are a numerical minority. As Virginia Valian, a psychologist at Hunter College who studies gender, indicates, "In most organizations women begin at a slight disadvantage. A woman does not walk into the room with the same status as an equivalent man, because she is less likely than a man to be viewed as a serious professional."[134]

The second factor is that research suggests that slight differences in treatment can accumulate and result in major disparities over time. Even small differences—such as a very slight favorable bias toward men for promotions—can lead to major differences in the number of male and female managers over time.[135] Thus while women and other minorities are sometimes advised not to make "a mountain out of a molehill" when they perceive they have been unfairly treated, research conducted by Valian and others suggests that molehills (slight differences in treatment based on irrelevant distinctions such as race, gender, or ethnicity) can turn into mountains over time (major disparities in important outcomes such as promotions) if they are ignored.[136] Once again, managers have the obligation, from both an ethical and a business perspective, to prevent any disparities in treatment and outcomes due to irrelevant distinctions such as race or ethnicity.

Effectively Managing Diversity Makes Good Business Sense

Diverse organizational members can be a source of competitive advantage, helping an organization provide customers with better goods and services.[137] The variety of points of view and approaches to problems and opportunities that diverse employees provide can improve managerial decision making. Suppose the Budget Gourmet frozen food company is trying to come up with creative ideas for new frozen meals that will appeal to health-conscious, time-conscious customers tired of the same old frozen fare. Which group do you think is likely to come up with the most creative ideas: a group of white women with marketing degrees from Yale University who grew up in upper-middle-class families in the Northeast or a racially mixed group of men and women who grew up in families with varying income levels in different parts of the country and attended a mix of business schools (New York University, Oklahoma State, University of Michigan, UCLA, Cornell University, Texas A&M University, and Iowa State)? Most people would agree that the diverse group is likely to have a wider range of creative ideas. Although this example is simplistic, it underscores one way in which diversity can lead to a competitive advantage.

Just as the workforce is becoming increasingly diverse, so too are the customers who buy an organization's goods or services. In an attempt to suit local customers' needs and tastes, organizations like Target often vary the selection of products available in stores in different cities and regions.[138]

Diverse members of an organization are likely to be attuned to what goods and services diverse segments of the market want and do not want. Automakers, for example, are increasingly assigning women to their design teams to ensure that the needs and desires of female customers are taken into account in new car design.

For Darden Restaurants, the business case for diversity rests on market share and growth. Darden seeks to satisfy the needs and tastes of diverse customers by providing menus in Spanish in communities with large Hispanic populations.[139] Similarly, market share and growth and the identification of niche markets led Tracey Campbell to cater to travelers with disabilities.[140] She heads InnSeekers, a telephone and online listing resource for bed and breakfasts. Nikki Daruwala works for the Calvert Group in Bethesda, Maryland, a mutual fund that emphasizes social responsibility and diversity. She indicates that profit alone is more than enough of an incentive to effectively manage diversity. As she puts it, "You can look at an automaker. There are more women making decisions about car buying or home buying. . . $3.72 trillion per year are spent by women."[141]

Another way that effective management of diversity can improve profitability is by increasing retention of valued employees, which decreases the costs of hiring replacements for those who quit as well as ensures that all employees are highly motivated. In terms of retention, given the current legal environment, more and more organizations are attuned to the need to emphasize the importance of diversity in hiring. Once hired, if diverse employees think they are being unfairly treated, however, they will be likely to seek opportunities elsewhere. Thus recruiting diverse employees has to be followed up by ongoing effective management of diversity to retain valued organizational members.

If diversity is not effectively managed and turnover rates are higher for members of groups who are not treated fairly, profitability will suffer on several counts. Not only are the future contributions of diverse employees lost when they quit, but the organization also has to bear the costs of hiring replacement workers. According to the Employment Management Association, on average it costs more than $10,000 to hire a new employee; other estimates are significantly higher. For example, Ernst & Young estimates it costs about $1,200,000 to replace 10 professionals, and the diversity consulting firm Hubbard & Hubbard estimates replacement costs average one-and-a-half times an employee's annual salary.[142] Moreover, additional costs from failing to effectively manage diversity stem from time lost due to the barriers diverse members of an organization perceive as thwarting their progress and advancement.[143]

Effectively managing diversity makes good business sense for another reason. More and more, managers and organizations concerned about diversity are insisting that their suppliers also support diversity.[144]

Finally, from both business and ethical perspectives, effective management of diversity is necessary to avoid costly lawsuits such as those settled by Advantica (owner of the Denny's chain) and the Coca-Cola Company. In 2000 Coca-Cola settled a class action suit brought by African American employees, at a cost of $192 million. The damage such lawsuits cause goes beyond the monetary awards to the injured parties; it can tarnish a company's image. One positive outcome of Coca-Cola's 2000 settlement is the company's recognition of the need to commit additional resources to diversity management initiatives. Coca-Cola is increasing its use of minority suppliers, instituting a formal mentoring program, and instituting days to celebrate diversity with its workforce.[145] By now it should be clear that effectively managing diversity is a necessity on both ethical and business grounds.

Sexual Harassment

Sexual harassment seriously damages both the people who are harassed and the reputation of the organization in which it occurs. It also can cost organizations large amounts of money. In 1995, for example, Chevron Corporation agreed to pay $2.2 million to settle a sexual harassment lawsuit filed by four women who worked at the Chevron Information Technology Company in San Ramon, California. One woman involved in the suit said she had received violent pornographic material through the company mail. Another, an electrical engineer, said she had been asked to bring pornographic videos to Chevron workers at an Alaska drill site.[146] More recently, in 2001 TWA settled a lawsuit to the tune of $2.6 million that alleged that female employees were sexually harassed at JFK International Airport in New York. According to the EEOC, not only was sexual harassment tolerated at TWA, but company officials did little to curtail it when it was brought to their attention.[147]

Unfortunately the events at Chevron and TWA are not isolated incidents.[148] In 2011, two lawsuits were filed against American Apparel and its founder and CEO, Dov Charney, alleging sexual harassment.[149] Of the 607 women surveyed by the National Association for Female Executives, 60% indicated that they had experienced some form of sexual harassment.[150] In a survey conducted by the Society for Human Resource Management of 460 companies, 36% of the companies indicated that, within the last 24 months, one or more employees claimed that they had been sexually harassed.[151] Sexual harassment victims can be women or men, and their harassers do not necessarily have to be of the opposite sex.[152] However, women are the most frequent victims of sexual harassment, particularly those in male-dominated occupations or those who occupy positions stereotypically associated with certain gender relationships, such as a female secretary reporting to a male boss. Though it occurs less frequently, men can also be victims of sexual harassment. For instance, several male employees at Jenny Craig filed a lawsuit

LO 3-6 Understand the two major forms of sexual harassment and how they can be eliminated.

claiming they were subject to lewd and inappropriate comments from female coworkers and managers.[153] Sexual harassment is not only unethical; it is also illegal. Managers have an ethical obligation to ensure that they, their coworkers, and their subordinates never engage in sexual harassment, even unintentionally.

Forms of Sexual Harassment

quid pro quo sexual harassment Asking for or forcing an employee to perform sexual favors in exchange for receiving some reward or avoiding negative consequences.

There are two basic forms of sexual harassment: quid pro quo sexual harassment and hostile work environment sexual harassment. Quid pro quo sexual harassment occurs when a harasser asks or forces an employee to perform sexual favors to keep a job, receive a promotion, receive a raise, obtain some other work-related opportunity, or avoid receiving negative consequences such as demotion or dismissal.[154] This "Sleep with me, honey, or you're fired" form of harassment is the more extreme type and leaves no doubt in anyone's mind that sexual harassment has taken place.[155]

hostile work environment sexual harassment Telling lewd jokes, displaying pornography, making sexually oriented remarks about someone's personal appearance, and other sex-related actions that make the work environment unpleasant.

Hostile work environment sexual harassment is more subtle. It occurs when organizational members face an intimidating, hostile, or offensive work environment because of their sex.[156] Lewd jokes, sexually oriented comments or innuendos, vulgar language, displays of pornography, displays or distribution of sexually oriented objects, and sexually oriented remarks about one's physical appearance are examples of hostile work environment sexual harassment.[157] A hostile work environment interferes with organizational members' ability to perform their jobs effectively and has been deemed illegal by the courts. Managers who engage in hostile work environment harassment or allow others to do so risk costly lawsuits for their organizations. For example, in February 2004 a federal jury awarded Marion Schwab $3.24 million after deliberating on her sexual harassment case against FedEx.[158] Schwab was the only female tractor-trailer driver at the FedEx facility serving the Harrisburg International Airport vicinity in Middletown, Pennsylvania, from 1997 to 2000. During that period she was the target of sexual innuendos, was given inferior work assignments, and was the brunt of derogatory comments about her appearance and the role of women in society. On five occasions the brakes on her truck were tampered with. The federal EEOC sued FedEx, and Schwab was part of the suit.[159]

The courts have recently recognized other forms of hostile work environment harassment, in addition to sexual harassment. For example, in June 2006 a California jury awarded $61 million in punitive and compensatory damages to two FedEx Ground drivers. The drivers, who are of Lebanese descent, indicated that they faced a hostile work environment and high levels of stress because a manager harassed them with racial slurs for two years.[160]

Steps Managers Can Take to Eradicate Sexual Harassment

Managers have an ethical obligation to eradicate sexual harassment in their organizations. There are many ways to accomplish this objective. Here are four initial steps managers can take to deal with the problem:[161]

- *Develop and clearly communicate a sexual harassment policy endorsed by top management.* This policy should include prohibitions against both quid pro quo and hostile work environment sexual harassment. It should contain (1) examples of types of behavior that are unacceptable, (2) a procedure for employees to use to report instances of harassment, (3) a discussion of the disciplinary actions that will be taken when harassment has taken place, and (4) a commitment to educate and train organizational members about sexual harassment.

- *Use a fair complaint procedure to investigate charges of sexual harassment.* Such a procedure should (1) be managed by a neutral third party, (2) ensure that complaints are dealt with promptly and thoroughly, (3) protect and fairly treat victims, and (4) ensure that alleged harassers are fairly treated.

- *When it has been determined that sexual harassment has taken place, take corrective actions as soon as possible.* These actions can vary depending on the severity of the harassment. When harassment is extensive, prolonged, of a quid pro quo nature, or severely objectionable in some other manner, corrective action may include firing the harasser.

- *Provide sexual harassment education and training to all organizational members, including managers.* The majority of *Fortune* 500 firms currently provide this education and training for their employees. Managers at DuPont, for example, developed DuPont's "A Matter of Respect" program to help educate employees about sexual harassment and eliminate its occurrence. The program includes a four-hour workshop in which participants are given information that defines sexual harassment, sets forth the company's policy against it, and explains how to report complaints and access a 24-hour hotline. Participants watch video clips showing actual instances of harassment. One clip shows a saleswoman having dinner with a male client who, after much negotiating, seems about to give her company his business when he suddenly suggests that they continue their conversation in his hotel room. The saleswoman is confused about what to do. Will she be reprimanded if she says no and the deal is lost? After watching a video, participants discuss what they have seen, why the behavior is inappropriate, and what organizations can do to alleviate the problem.[162] Throughout the program, managers stress to employees that they do not have to tolerate sexual harassment or get involved in situations in which harassment is likely to occur.

Barry S. Roberts and Richard A. Mann, experts on business law and authors of several books on the topic, suggest a number of additional factors that managers and all members of an organization need to keep in mind about sexual harassment:[163]

- Every sexual harassment charge should be taken seriously.

- Employees who go along with unwanted sexual attention in the workplace can be sexual harassment victims.

- Employees sometimes wait before they file complaints of sexual harassment.

- An organization's sexual harassment policy should be communicated to each new employee and reviewed with current employees periodically.

- Suppliers and customers need to be familiar with an organization's sexual harassment policy.

- Managers should give employees alternative ways to report incidents of sexual harassment.

- Employees who report sexual harassment must have their rights protected; this includes being protected from any potential retaliation.

- Allegations of sexual harassment should be kept confidential; those accused of harassment should have their rights protected.

- Investigations of harassment charges and any resultant disciplinary actions need to proceed in a timely manner.

- Managers must protect employees from sexual harassment from third parties they may interact with while performing their jobs, such as suppliers or customers.[164]

Summary and Review

ETHICS AND STAKEHOLDERS Ethics are moral principles or beliefs about what is right or wrong. These beliefs guide people in their dealings with other individuals and groups (stakeholders) and provide a basis for deciding whether behavior is right and proper. Many organizations have a formal code of ethics derived primarily from societal ethics, professional ethics, and the individual ethics of the organization's top managers. Managers can apply ethical standards to help themselves decide on the proper way to behave toward organizational stakeholders. Ethical organizational cultures are those in which ethical values and norms are emphasized. Ethical organizational cultures can help organizations and their members behave in a socially responsible manner. **[LO 3-1, 3-2]**

INCREASING DIVERSITY OF WORKFORCE AND ENVIRONMENT Diversity is differences among people due to age, gender, race, ethnicity, religion, sexual orientation, socioeconomic background, and capabilities/disabilities. The workforce and the organizational environment have become increasingly diverse. Effectively managing diversity is an ethical imperative and can improve organizational effectiveness. **[LO 3-3, 3-5]**

MANAGING DIVERSITY The effective management of diversity is not only an essential responsibility of managers but an ethical and a business imperative. In each of their managerial roles, managers can encourage organizationwide acceptance and valuing of diversity. **[LO 3-4, 3-5]**

SEXUAL HARASSMENT Two forms of sexual harassment are quid pro quo sexual harassment and hostile work environment sexual harassment. Steps that managers can take to eradicate sexual harassment include development, communication, and enforcement of a sexual harassment policy, use of fair complaint procedures, prompt corrective action when harassment occurs, and sexual harassment training and education. **[LO 3-6]**

Management *in Action*

TOPICS FOR DISCUSSION AND ACTION

Discussion

1. When are ethics and ethical standards especially important in organizations? **[LO 3-1]**

2. Why might managers do things that conflict with their own ethical values? **[LO 3-1]**

3. How can managers ensure that they create ethical organizational cultures? **[LO 3-2]**

4. Why are gay and lesbian workers and workers who test positive for HIV sometimes discriminated against? **[LO 3-3]**

5. Why might some employees resent workplace accommodations that are dictated by the Americans with Disabilities Act? **[LO 3-3]**

Action

6. Choose a *Fortune* 500 company not mentioned in the chapter. Conduct research to determine what steps this organization has taken to effectively manage diversity and eliminate sexual harassment. **[LO 3-4, 3-5, 3-6]**

BUILDING MANAGEMENT SKILLS [LO 3-3, 3-4, 3-5, 3-6]
Solving Diversity-Related Problems

Think about the last time that you (1) were treated unfairly because you differed from a decision maker on a particular dimension of diversity or (2) observed someone else being treated unfairly because that person differed from a decision maker on a particular dimension of diversity. Then answer these questions:

1. Why do you think the decision maker acted unfairly in this situation?

2. In what ways, if any, were biases, stereotypes, or overt discrimination involved in this situation?

3. Was the decision maker aware that he or she was acting unfairly?

4. What could you or the person who was treated unfairly have done to improve matters and rectify the injustice on the spot?

5. Was any sexual harassment involved in this situation? If so, what kind was it?

6. If you had authority over the decision maker (e.g., if you were his or her manager or

supervisor), what steps would you take to ensure that the decision maker no longer treated diverse individuals unfairly?

MANAGING ETHICALLY [LO 3-1]

Some companies require that their employees work very long hours and travel extensively.

Employees with young children, employees taking care of elderly relatives, and employees who have

interests outside the workplace sometimes find that their careers are jeopardized if they try to work more reasonable hours or limit their work-related travel. Some of these employees feel that it is unethical for their manager to expect so much of them in the workplace and not understand their needs as parents and caregivers.

Questions

1. Either individually or in a group, think about the ethical implications of requiring long hours and extensive amounts of travel for some jobs.

2. What obligations do you think managers and companies have to enable employees to have a balanced life and meet nonwork needs and demands?

SMALL GROUP BREAKOUT EXERCISE [LO 3-3, 3-4, 3-5]
Determining If a Problem Exists

Form groups of three or four people, and appoint one member as the spokesperson who will communicate your findings to the whole class when called on by the instructor. Then discuss the following scenario:

You and your partners own and manage a local chain of restaurants, with moderate to expensive prices, that are open for lunch and dinner during the week and for dinner on weekends. Your staff is diverse, and you believe that you are effectively managing diversity. Yet on visits to the different restaurants you have noticed that your African American employees tend to congregate together and communicate mainly with each other. The same is true for your Hispanic employees and your white employees. You are meeting with your partners today to discuss this observation.

1. Discuss why the patterns of communication that you observed might be occurring in your restaurants.

2. Discuss whether your observation reflects an underlying problem. If so, why? If not, why not?

3. Discuss whether you should address this issue with your staff and in your restaurants. If so, how and why? If not, why not?

BE THE MANAGER [LO 3-3, 3-4, 3-5, 3-6]

You are Maria Herrera and have been recently promoted to the position of director of financial analysis for a medium-size consumer goods firm. During your first few weeks on the job, you took the time to have lunch with each of your subordinates to try to get to know them better. You have 12 direct reports who are junior and senior financial analysts who support different product lines. Susan Epstein, one of the female financial analysts you had lunch with, made the following statement: "I'm

so glad we finally have a woman in charge. Now, hopefully things will get better around here." You pressed Epstein to elaborate, but she clammed up. She indicated that she didn't want to unnecessarily bias you and that the problems were pretty self-evident. In fact, Epstein was surprised that you didn't know what she was talking about and jokingly mentioned that perhaps you should spend some time undercover, observing her group and their interactions with others.

You spoke with your supervisor and the former director who had been promoted and had volunteered to be on call if you had any questions. Neither man knew of any diversity-related issues in your group. In fact, your supervisor's response was, "We've got a lot of problems, but fortunately that's not one of them."

Question

1. What are you going to do to address this issue?

Amid the worst flu season in recent years, lawmakers in at least a half-dozen cities and states are intensifying a push for laws requiring paid time off when workers take sick days.

Some 39% of private-sector workers aren't entitled to paid time off when they fall ill, according to the Bureau of Labor Statistics, and 11% of state and local government workers lack the benefit. Low-wage and part-time workers, particularly those at small firms or who work in restaurants, are among the least likely to get paid sick time.

To change that, Democratic lawmakers and their allies in Maryland, Washington, and Massachusetts, and in cities including New York, Philadelphia, and Portland, Ore., are trying to advance measures that would make paid sick time a legal requirement for most firms. In Congress, Sen. Tom Harkin (D., Iowa) plans to reintroduce a federal paid-sick-leave bill this spring.

Such efforts started before this year, but a vicious flu season that sidelined many workers has given them new urgency. Former President Bill Clinton chimed in this month, calling for the first federal paid-sick-leave law. The White House also supports a federal paid-sick-leave law.

Opponents of codifying paid sick leave say such laws weigh on businesses and ultimately hurt workers. In Connecticut, which last year became the first state to mandate paid sick leave, some employers contend the measure has raised costs and harmed workers by prompting cuts in wages or increases. Most firms there with 50 or more workers must provide five paid sick days a year, which employees accrue at a rate of one hour of leave for every 40 worked.

A canvassing of Connecticut businesses from the right-leaning Employment Policies Institute found that, of 156 respondents, more than half had begun complying with the law and most of those said it wasn't good for business. Many said they had offset expected expenses ahead of the law, including by raising prices, cutting workers' hours, and limiting their expansion in the state.

Dan Shackford, owner of Great Beginnings day care in Plainville, Conn., said that before the law, his 50 employees were welcome to call in sick without pay and earn a day off for three months of perfect attendance. Now when someone calls in sick, he has to pay a substitute and the worker. "The law is hurting me," he said.

To cope, he and his wife have lowered the annual raises they selectively give, to 3% from 5%. Mr. Shackford estimates it would cost up to $30,000 annually if his workers used all their sick time. The BLS says that, on average, full-time private-sector workers with a fixed number of days don't use them all.

Proponents contend the benefits outweigh the costs. Connecticut Gov. Dannel Malloy, a Democrat who signed the law, said it has been good for the state as people "aren't going to work and therefore making other people sick." He said he has talked with a variety of employers statewide who "now admit it really wasn't that big of a deal."

Cities with such laws include Seattle, Washington, D.C., and San Francisco, whose policy was enacted in 2007. Research by the left-leaning Institute for Women's Policy Research found that San Francisco's paid-sick ordinance is rarely misused by workers, supported by most employers now, and isn't hurting profits for the vast majority.

The federal Bureau of Labor Statistics also said the benefits of paid sick leave have been shown to help productivity and reduce the spread of workplace disease, but it wasn't specific about the extent.

It is "not only the right thing to do for families, but good for businesses and the economy," said Sen. Harkin, who is chairman of a Senate labor committee. His Healthy Families Act would let workers accrue up to seven paid sick days a year through hours worked to care for themselves or family, including doctor visits.

Tennessee Sen. Lamar Alexander, the top Republican on the labor committee, contends such a requirement "would only make a bad unemployment problem worse" by increasing hiring costs.

The majority of workers who already have paid sick time receive it from employers that provide it voluntarily, usually through a fixed number of days or, less frequently, as needed.

Karen Barnes, a single mother and part-time director of a Philadelphia day care, wants options like that. She is advocating for a paid-sick bill that would broaden the narrow pool of employers in the city that currently must provide the benefit. Ms. Barnes recently missed two weeks of work, unpaid, after being sent to the hospital with a skin infection. Her employer has told her it can't afford the benefit. "They're going to have to re-evaluate their financial situation," she said.

Questions

1. Do you think the provision of paid sick leave is an ethical issue? Why or why not?

2. Do you think managers and organizations should provide workers with paid sick leave on ethical grounds? Why or why not?

3. Which stakeholder groups might be affected by paid sick leave, and how?

4. What might be some implications of the increasing diversity of the workforce for paid sick leave?

Source: M. Trottman, "Legislators Step Up Push for Paid Sick Leave," *The Wall Street Journal,* February 23–24, 2013, A3.

4 Managing in the Global Environment

LEARNING OBJECTIVES

After studying this chapter, you should be able to:

1 Explain why the ability to perceive, interpret, and respond appropriately to the global environment is crucial for managerial success. **[LO 4-1]**

2 Differentiate between the global task and global general environments. **[LO 4-2]**

3 Identify the main forces in both the global task and general environments and describe the challenges that each force presents to managers. **[LO 4-3]**

4 Explain why the global environment is becoming more open and competitive and identify the forces behind the process of globalization that increase the opportunities, complexities, challenges, and threats that managers face. **[LO 4-4]**

5 Discuss why national cultures differ and why it is important that managers be sensitive to the effects of falling trade barriers and regional trade associations on the political and social systems of nations around the world. **[LO 4-5]**

Nokia has closed down its assembly operations around the world, such as this one in Romania, and outsourced all cell phone assembly to companies in China to lower costs.

Nokia Flips Its Approach to Managing the Global Environment

Why is Managing the Global Environment So Complex Today?

Nokia has experienced enormous problems in the 2010s because the popularity of smartphones has soared and companies like Apple, BlackBerry, Samsung, and Motorola (now owned by Google) are competing vigorously to offer customers the smartphone that contains the latest features and technology. In fact, in 2012 Samsung took over from Nokia as the world's largest cell phone maker, and Nokia's stock price has plunged in the 2010s as its attempts to fight back continue to fail and it is losing billions of dollars.

To a large degree the reasons for Nokia's problems center around the way it has traditionally managed the global environment compared to its cell phone competitors. To keep their costs to a minimum, its competitors have outsourced their cell phone production to Asian companies. Nokia did not because historically a major reason for Nokia's dominance in cell phones was its skills in global supply chain management that allowed it to provide low-cost phones that could be customized to the needs of customers in different world regions. Nokia's global strategy was to make its phones in the world region in which they were sold; Nokia built expensive state-of-the-art factories in Germany, Brazil, China, and India. In 2008 it opened a new plant in Romania to make phones for the expanding eastern European and Russian market.

A major reason for beginning operations in Romania was its low labor costs. In fact, once Nokia's Romanian factory was up and running, Nokia closed its factory in Bochum, Germany, in 2008 because it was too expensive to operate. Even so, Nokia was hardheaded about how efficiently it expected its Romanian factory to operate because *all* its global factories were required to operate at the same level of efficiency that its *most* efficient global factory has achieved. Nokia's goal was to continuously improve efficiency over time by encouraging managers to find ways to lower costs and then share this knowledge across the company.

Finally, in 2010, Nokia's CEO Olli-Pekka Kallas-vuo realized that Nokia's strategy had failed and that the company needed to recruit a new CEO who understood how to change the way it managed the environment. Stephen Elop became Nokia's CEO in September 2010, the first non-Finn ever to be named to the top position. Elop left Microsoft, where he had been head of its business division, and announced that Nokia would team up with Microsoft to supply its new smartphone software and dump its own Simian platform. In April 2011 Elop announced it would axe 7,000 jobs and outsource its Symbian software development unit to cut $1.2 billion in costs. The move included laying off 4,000 staff and transferring another 3,000 to services firm Accenture—12% of its phone unit workforce.

Then in September 2011 Elop announced the closure of its assembly plant in Romania and in January 2012 the closure of its operations in Finland, Hungary, and Mexico. In the future all smartphone assembly would be outsourced to Asia with the loss of over 15,000 jobs. In addition, Nokia announced it would cut 17,000 more jobs or almost a quarter of its workforce in its Nokia Siemens Network division, a global telecommunications joint venture with Siemens.

Elop was betting Nokia's future on developing its close ties with Microsoft, and in October 2011 Nokia unveiled two sleek new smartphones based on Microsoft Windows in time for Christmas, a major step in its fight back against Apple and Google.[1] These phones did not sell well despite their reasonable pricing, and Nokia's competitive position continued to deteriorate. In June 2012 Elop announced plans to cut another 10,000 jobs globally and warned its second-quarter loss from its cell phone business would be larger than expected. Its stock price continued to plunge and many analysts wondered if Nokia could survive or whether it would become a takeover target. Despite its new approach to managing the global environment Nokia was still losing the battle against Samsung and Apple and its future looks bleak indeed.

Overview

Top managers of a global company like Nokia operate in an environment where they compete with other companies for scarce and valuable resources. Managers of companies large and small have found that to survive and prosper in the 21st century, most companies must become global organizations, which operate and compete not only domestically, at home, but also globally, in countries around the world. Operating in the global environment is uncertain and unpredictable because it is complex and changes constantly.

If organizations are to adapt successfully to this changing environment, their managers must learn to understand the forces that operate in it and how these forces give rise to opportunities and threats. In this chapter we examine why the environment, both domestically and globally, has become more open, vibrant, and competitive. We examine how forces in the task and general environments affect global organizations and their managers. By the end of this chapter, you will appreciate the changes that are taking place in the environment and understand why it is important for managers to develop a global perspective as they strive to increase organizational efficiency and effectiveness.

global organization
An organization that operates and competes in more than one country.

LO 4-1 Explain why the ability to perceive, interpret, and respond appropriately to the global environment is crucial for managerial success.

What Is the Global Environment?

The global environment is a set of forces and conditions in the world outside an organization's boundary that affect how it operates and shape its behavior.[2] These forces change over time and thus present managers with *opportunities* and *threats*. Some changes in the global environment, such as the development of efficient new production technology, the availability of lower-cost components, or the opening of new global markets, create opportunities for managers to make and sell more products, obtain more resources and capital, and thereby strengthen their organization. In contrast, the rise of new global competitors, a global

global environment
The set of global forces and conditions that operate beyond an organization's boundaries but affect a manager's ability to acquire and utilize resources.

task environment
The set of forces and conditions that originate with suppliers, distributors, customers, and competitors and affect an organization's ability to obtain inputs and dispose of its outputs because they influence managers daily.

economic recession, or an oil shortage poses threats that can devastate an organization if managers are unable to sell its products so that revenues and profits plunge. The quality of managers' understanding of forces in the global environment and their ability to respond appropriately to those forces are critical factors affecting organizational performance.

In this chapter we explore the nature of these forces and consider how managers can respond to them. To identify opportunities and threats caused by forces in the global environment, it is helpful for managers to distinguish between the *task environment* and the more encompassing *general environment* (see Figure 4.1).

The task environment is the set of forces and conditions that originate with global suppliers, distributors, customers, and competitors; these forces and conditions affect an organization's ability to obtain inputs and dispose of its outputs. The task environment contains the forces that have the most *immediate* and *direct* effect on managers because they pressure and influence managers daily. When managers turn on the radio or television, arrive at their offices in the morning, open their mail, or look at their computer screens, they are likely to learn about problems facing them because of changing conditions in their organization's task environment.

Figure 4.1

Forces in the Global Environment

general environment
The wide-ranging global, economic, technological, sociocultural, demographic, political, and legal forces that affect an organization and its task environment.

The general environment includes the wide-ranging global, economic, technological, sociocultural, demographic, political, and legal forces that affect the organization and its task environment. For the individual manager, opportunities and threats resulting from changes in the general environment are often more difficult to identify and respond to than are events in the task environment. However, changes in these forces can have major impacts on managers and their organizations.

The Task Environment

Forces in the task environment result from the actions of suppliers, distributors, customers, and competitors both at home and abroad (see Figure 4.1). These four groups affect a manager's ability to obtain resources and dispose of outputs daily, weekly, and monthly and thus have a significant impact on short-term decision making.

Suppliers

suppliers Individuals and organizations that provide an organization with the input resources it needs to produce goods and services.

Suppliers are the individuals and organizations that provide an organization with the input resources (such as raw materials, component parts, or employees) it needs to produce goods and services. In return, the suppliers receive payment for those goods and services. An important aspect of a manager's job is to ensure a reliable supply of input resources.

Take Dell Computer, for example, the company we focused on in Chapter 1. Dell has many suppliers of component parts such as microprocessors (Intel and AMD) and disk drives (Quantum and Seagate Technologies). It also has suppliers of preinstalled software, including the operating system and specific applications software (Microsoft and Adobe). Dell's providers of capital, such as banks and financial institutions, are also important suppliers. Cisco Systems and Oracle are important providers of Internet hardware and software for dot-coms.

Dell has several suppliers of labor. One source is the educational institutions that train future Dell employees and therefore provide the company with skilled workers. Another is trade unions, organizations that represent employee interests and can control the supply of labor by exercising the right of unionized workers to strike. Unions also can influence the terms and conditions under which labor is employed. Dell's workers are not unionized; when layoffs became necessary after Dell was forced to outsource all its global assembly operations, it had few problems in laying off its global workforce to reduce costs. In organizations and industries where unions are strong, however, such as the transportation industry, an important part of a manager's job is negotiating and administering agreements with unions and their representatives.

Changes in the nature, number, or type of suppliers produce opportunities and threats to which managers must respond if their organizations are to prosper. For example, a major supplier-related threat that confronts managers arises when suppliers' bargaining position is so strong that they can raise the prices of the inputs they supply to the organization. A supplier's bargaining position is especially strong when (1) the supplier is the sole source of an input and (2) the input is vital to the organization.[3] For example, for 17 years G. D. Searle was the sole supplier of Nutra-Sweet, the artificial sweetener used in most diet soft drinks. Not

LO 4-2 Differentiate between the global task and global general environments.

LO 4-3 Identify the main forces in the global task and general environments, and describe the challenges that each force presents to managers.

only was NutraSweet an important ingredient in diet soft drinks, but it also was one for which there was no acceptable substitute (saccharin and other artificial sweeteners raised health concerns). Searle earned its privileged position because it invented and held the patent for NutraSweet, and patents prohibit other organizations from introducing competing products for 17 years. As a result Searle was able to demand a high price for Nutra-Sweet, charging twice the price of an equivalent amount of sugar; and paying that price raised the costs of soft drink manufacturers such as Coca-Cola and PepsiCo. When Searle's patent expired many other companies introduced products similar to NutraSweet, and prices fell.[4] In the 2000s Splenda, which was made by McNeil Nutritionals, owned by Tate & Lyle, a British company, replaced NutraSweet as the artificial sweetener of choice, and NutraSweet's price fell further; Splenda began to command a high price from soft drink companies.[5]

In contrast, when an organization has many suppliers for a particular input, it is in a relatively strong bargaining position with those suppliers and can demand low-cost, high-quality inputs from them. Often an organization can use its power with suppliers to force them to reduce their prices, as Dell frequently does. Dell, for example, is constantly searching for low-cost suppliers abroad to keep its PC prices competitive. At a global level, organizations can buy products from suppliers overseas or become their own suppliers by manufacturing their products abroad.

It is important that managers recognize the opportunities and threats associated with managing the global supply chain. On one hand, gaining access to low-cost products made abroad represents an opportunity for U.S. companies to lower their input costs. On the other hand, managers who fail to use low-cost overseas suppliers create a threat and put their organizations at a competitive disadvantage.[6] Levi Strauss, for example, was slow to realize that it could not compete with the low-priced jeans sold by Walmart and other retailers, but it was eventually forced to close all its U.S. jean factories and outsource manufacturing to low-cost overseas suppliers to cut the price of its jeans to a competitive level. Now it sells its low-priced jeans in Walmart. The downside to global outsourcing is, of course, the loss of millions of U.S. jobs, an issue we have discussed in previous chapters.

A common problem facing managers of large global companies such as Ford, Sony, and Dell is managing the development of a global supplier network that will allow their companies to keep costs down and quality high. For example, Boeing's 777 jet was originally built using 132,500 engineered components made by 545 global suppliers.[7] Although Boeing made the majority of these parts, eight Japanese suppliers made parts for the 777 fuselage, doors, and wings; a Singapore supplier made the doors for the plane's forward landing gear; and three Italian suppliers produced its wing flaps. Boeing decided to buy so many inputs from overseas suppliers because these suppliers were the best in the world at performing their particular activities, and Boeing's goal was to produce a high-quality final product—a vital requirement for aircraft safety and reliability.[8]

The purchasing activities of global companies have become increasingly complicated as a result of the development of a whole range of skills and competencies in different countries around the world. It is clearly in companies' interests to search out the lowest-cost, best-quality suppliers. IT and the Internet are continually making it easier for companies to coordinate complicated, long-distance exchanges involving the purchasing of inputs and the disposal of outputs—something Sony has taken advantage of as it trims the number of its suppliers to reduce costs.

global outsourcing
The purchase or production of inputs or final products from overseas suppliers to lower costs and improve product quality or design.

Global outsourcing occurs when a company contracts with suppliers in other countries to make the various inputs or components that go into its products or to assemble the final products to reduce costs. For example, Apple contracts with companies in Taiwan and China to make inputs such as the chips, batteries, and LCD displays that power its digital devices; then it contracts with outsourcers such as Foxconn to assemble its final products—such as iPods, iPhones, and iPads. Apple also outsources the distribution of its products around the world by contracting with companies such as FedEx or DHL.

The purchasing activities of global companies have become increasingly complicated in recent years. Hundreds of suppliers around the world produce parts for Boeing's new Dreamliner.

Global outsourcing has grown enormously to take advantage of national differences in the cost and quality of resources such as labor or raw materials that can significantly reduce manufacturing costs or increase product quality or reliability. Today such global exchanges are becoming so complex that some companies specialize in managing other companies' global supply chains. Global companies use the services of overseas intermediaries or brokers, which are located close to potential suppliers, to find the suppliers that can best meet the needs of a particular company. They can design the most efficient supply chain for a company to outsource the component and assembly operations required to produce its final products. Because these suppliers are located in thousands of cities in many countries, finding them is difficult. Li & Fung, based in Hong Kong, is one broker that has helped hundreds of major U.S. companies to outsource their component or assembly operations to suitable overseas suppliers, especially suppliers in mainland China.[9]

Although outsourcing to take advantage of low labor costs has helped many companies perform better, in the 2010s its risks have also become apparent, especially when issues such as reliability, quality, and speed are important. For example, as noted in Chapter 1 the introduction of Boeing's 787 Dreamliner plane was delayed for several years because the company increased its reliance on companies abroad to make vital components and many of these had problems in meeting Boeing's delivery requirements. Clearly, outsourcing decisions need to be carefully considered given the nature of a company's products.[10] For example recall from Chapter 1 that Caterpillar decided to "insource" production of excavators back to the United States because lower U.S. labor costs and increasing global shipping costs had made this the most efficient way to do business. On the other hand, some companies do not outsource manufacturing; they prefer to establish their own assembly operations and factories in countries around the world to protect their proprietary technology. For example, most global automakers own their production operations in China to retain control over their global decision making and keep their operations secret. An interesting example of the supply problems that have developed between Nokia and Microsoft is discussed in the following "Managing Globally" box.

MANAGING GLOBALLY

How Microsoft Became a Powerful Nokia Supplier

As discussed at the beginning of this chapter, when Nokia appointed Stephen Elop as CEO, among his first moves was to dump Nokia's free Symbian cell phone software that was powering millions of new phones every year and to introduce new smartphones based on the Windows 7 software phone platform. The Lumina 900 became Nokia's flagship product and was designed to compete with the Apple iPhone and Samsung Galaxy, but sales never took off and only hundreds of thousands were sold compared to millions of its rivals' phones.

In London, Stephen Elop, chief executive officer of Nokia, gestures as Steve Ballmer, chief executive officer of Microsoft, looks on. Nokia, the world's biggest maker of mobile phones, said it's forming a software partnership with Microsoft Corp., a bet that together the two companies can better challenge Google and Apple.

From the start, analysts wondered if Nokia had been smart to put "all its eggs in one basket" by moving to the Windows 7 platform, which, lacking the thousands of developers needed to develop phone applications, was always one step behind Google's Android and Apple's iOS 5 phone software. Poor Lumina smartphone sales and the layoff of over 40,000 employees seemed to suggest Elop's new global initiatives were not working out, and Nokia experienced a major blow in June 2012 when Microsoft made a surprising announcement.

In order to compete effectively against the Android and iOS 5 platforms, it would introduce new advanced phone software—the Windows 8 platform—in late 2012. However, the problem for Nokia was that its flagship Lumina 900 smartphone could not be upgraded to this new software platform. This was because Windows 7 smartphones run on single-core processors but all smartphone makers were moving to use multicore processors and high-definition screens that support more sophisticated video and gaming applications. And these would only run on the Windows 8 phone platform! This was a disaster for Nokia; it made its current Windows smartphones essentially obsolete despite their low pricing.

Essentially, Microsoft had become a powerful supplier (of software) to Nokia and it was riding roughshod over Nokia in order to protect its own global competitive position and was allowing Nokia to "go to the dogs." Windows Phone 8 brings the operating system into parity with Android and iOS smartphones; for Microsoft it was a possible "game-changing" platform that could attract key smartphone makers such as HTC, Samsung, and LG. In fact, Microsoft announced that Samsung, HTC, and Huawei are working on Windows Phone 8 smartphones—so too is Nokia.

However, analysts recognizing the body blow Nokia had experienced drastically cut their estimates of Nokia's 2013 revenues by over 30% and cut estimates of Nokia's Windows Phone unit sales down to 34 million handsets, 41% lower than they had previously predicted! Nokia downplayed the news, arguing its low pricing would help attract customers because they were getting great value. But most analysts felt that Microsoft had used its power to its own advantage and that customers would wait for the Windows 8 platform that would be available from several smartphone makers, so Nokia had lost its competitive advantage, especially because it had not unveiled any new Windows Phone 8 handsets.

Nokia's CEO began to attract a lot of criticism from analysts who argued that Elop had made major mistakes and had no global roadmap for the company to follow; it was losing top talent and replacing it with managers from Microsoft. Moreover, his main focus seems to have been on reducing costs, which is still not working, and he has neglected expensive product development in his drive to keep costs low. In 2013, Nokia was still struggling although sales of its windows-based smartphone were improving and it introduced an inexpensive smartphone to sell in Asia.

Distributors

Distributors are organizations that help other organizations sell their goods or services to customers. The decisions managers make about how to distribute products to customers can have important effects on organizational performance. For example, package delivery companies such as Federal Express, UPS, and the U.S. Postal Service have become vital distributors for the millions of items bought online and shipped to customers by dot-com companies both at home and abroad.

The changing nature of distributors and distribution methods can bring opportunities and threats for managers. If distributors become so large and powerful that they can control customers' access to a particular organization's goods and services, they can threaten the organization by demanding that it reduce the prices of its goods and services.[11] For example, the huge retail distributor Walmart controls its suppliers' access to millions of customers and thus can demand that its suppliers reduce their prices to keep its business. If an organization such as Procter & Gamble refuses to reduce its prices, Walmart might respond by buying products only from Procter & Gamble's competitors—companies such as Unilever and Colgate. To reduce costs, Walmart also has used its power as a distributor to demand that all its suppliers adopt a new wireless radio frequency scanning technology to reduce the cost of shipping and stocking products in its stores; otherwise it would stop doing business with them.[12]

It is illegal for distributors to collaborate or collude to keep prices high and thus maintain their power over buyers; however, this frequently happens. In the early 2000s several European drug companies conspired to keep the price of vitamins artificially high. In 2005 the three largest global makers of flash memory, including Samsung, were found guilty of price fixing (they collaborated to keep prices high); in 2010 the major suppliers of LCD screens were also found guilty of conspiring to keep prices high. All these companies paid hundreds of millions of dollars in fines, and many of their top executives were sentenced to jail terms.

Customers

customers

Individuals and groups that buy the goods and services an organization produces.

Customers are the individuals and groups that buy the goods and services an organization produces. For example, Dell's customers can be segmented into several distinct groups: (1) individuals who purchase PCs for home and mobile use, (2) small companies, (3) large companies, and (4) government agencies and educational institutions. Changes in the number and types of customers or in customers' tastes and needs create opportunities and threats. An organization's success depends on its responsiveness to customers—whether it can satisfy their needs. In the PC industry, customers are demanding thinner computers, better graphics and speed, and increased wireless and Internet connections—and lower prices—and PC makers must respond to the changing types and needs of customers, such as by introducing tablet computers. A school, too, must adapt to the changing needs of its customers. For example, if more Spanish-speaking students enroll, additional classes in English as a second language may need to be scheduled. A manager's ability to identify an organization's main customer groups, and make the products that best satisfy their particular needs, is a crucial factor affecting organizational and managerial success.

The most obvious opportunity associated with expanding into the global environment is the prospect of selling goods and services to millions or billions of new customers, as Amazon.com's CEO Jeff Bezos discovered when he expanded his company's operations in many countries.[13] Similarly, Accenture and Cap Gemini, two large consulting companies, established regional operating centers around the globe, and they recruit and train thousands of overseas consultants to serve the needs of customers in their respective world regions.

Today many products have gained global customer acceptance. This consolidation is occurring both for consumer goods and for business products and has created enormous opportunities for managers. The worldwide acceptance of Coca-Cola, Apple iPods, McDonald's hamburgers, and Samsung smartphones is a sign that the tastes and preferences of customers in different countries may not be so different after all.[14] Likewise, large global markets exist for business products such as telecommunications equipment, electronic components, and computer and financial services. Thus Cisco and Siemens sell their telecommunications equipment; Intel, its microprocessors; and Oracle and SAP, their business systems management software, to customers all over the world.

Competitors

competitors

Organizations that produce goods and services that are similar to a particular organization's goods and services.

One of the most important forces an organization confronts in its task environment is competitors. Competitors are organizations that produce goods and services that are similar and comparable to a particular organization's goods and services. In other words, competitors are organizations trying to attract the same customers. Dell's competitors include other domestic PC makers (such as Apple and HP) as well as overseas competitors (such as Sony and Toshiba in Japan; Lenovo, the Chinese company that bought IBM's PC division; and Acer, the Taiwanese company that bought Gateway). Similarly, dot-com stockbroker E*Trade has other competitors such as Ameritrade, Scottrade, and Charles Schwab.

Rivalry between competitors is potentially the most threatening force managers must deal with. A high level of rivalry typically results in price competition, and falling prices reduce customer revenues and profits. In the early 2000s competition in the PC industry became intense because Dell was aggressively cutting costs and prices to increase its global market share.[15] IBM had to exit the PC business after it lost billions in its battle against low-cost rivals, and Gateway and HP also suffered losses while Dell's profits soared. By 2006, however, HP's fortunes had recovered because it had found ways to lower its costs and offer stylish new PCs, and Apple was growing rapidly, so Dell's profit margins shrunk. In 2009, HP overtook Dell to become the largest global PC maker, and by 2010 Apple's and Acer's sales were also expanding rapidly. Dell's managers had failed to appreciate how fast its global competitors were catching up and had not developed the right strategies to keep the company at the top; in 2013, its future was uncertain.

Although extensive rivalry between existing competitors is a major threat to profitability, so is the potential for new competitors to enter the task environment. Potential competitors are organizations that are not presently in a task environment but have the resources to enter if they so choose. In 2010, Amazon.com, for example, was not in the furniture or large appliance business, but it could enter these businesses if its managers decided it could profitably sell such products online—and in 2013 it does sell furniture and large appliances. When new competitors enter an industry, competition increases and prices and profits decrease—as furniture and electronic stores such as Best Buy have discovered as they battle Amazon.com.

BARRIERS TO ENTRY In general, the potential for new competitors to enter a task environment (and thus increase competition) is a function of barriers to entry.[16] Barriers to entry are factors that make it difficult and costly for a company to enter a particular task environment or industry.[17] In other words, the more difficult and costly it is to enter the task environment, the higher are the barriers to entry. The higher the barriers to entry, the fewer the competitors in an organization's task environment and thus the lower the threat of competition. With fewer competitors, it is easier to obtain customers and keep prices high.

Barriers to entry result from three main sources: economies of scale, brand loyalty, and government regulations that impede entry (see Figure 4.2). Economies of scale are the cost advantages associated with large operations. Economies of

potential competitors
Organizations that presently are not in a task environment but could enter if they so choose.

barriers to entry
Factors that make it difficult and costly for an organization to enter a particular task environment or industry.

economies of scale
Cost advantages associated with large operations.

Figure 4.2

Barriers to Entry and Competition

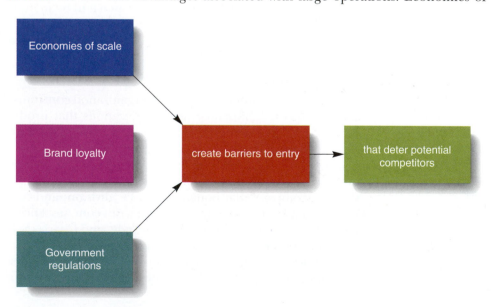

scale result from factors such as manufacturing products in very large quantities, buying inputs in bulk, or making more effective use of organizational resources than do competitors by fully utilizing employees' skills and knowledge. If organizations already in the task environment are large and enjoy significant economies of scale, their costs are lower than the costs that potential entrants will face, and newcomers will find it expensive to enter the industry. Amazon.com, for example, enjoys significant economies of scale relative to most other dot-com companies because of its highly efficient distribution system.[18]

brand loyalty
Customers' preference for the products of organizations currently existing in the task environment.

Brand loyalty is customers' preference for the products of organizations currently in the task environment. If established organizations enjoy significant brand loyalty, a new entrant will find it difficult and costly to obtain a share of the market. Newcomers must bear huge advertising costs to build customer awareness of the goods or services they intend to provide.[19] Today Google, Amazon.com, and eBay enjoy a high level of brand loyalty and have some of the highest website hit rates, which allows them to increase their marketing revenues.

The tyranny of the lower price. A Japanese businessman purchases a frozen U.S.-sourced rice O-bento lunch at a Nippon Tokyo store. Nippon's importing practices have angered Japanese rice farmers.

In some cases, *government regulations* function as a barrier to entry at both the industry and the country levels. Many industries that were deregulated, such as air transport, trucking, utilities, and telecommunications, experienced a high level of new entry after deregulation; this forced existing companies in those industries to operate more efficiently or risk being put out of business. At the national and global levels, administrative barriers are government policies that create barriers to entry and limit imports of goods by overseas companies. Japan is well known for the many ways in which it attempts to restrict the entry of overseas competitors or lessen their impact on Japanese firms. Japan has come under intense pressure to relax and abolish regulations such as those governing the import of rice, for example.

The Japanese rice market, like many other Japanese markets, was closed to overseas competitors until 1993 to protect Japan's thousands of high-cost, low-output rice farmers. Rice cultivation is expensive in Japan because of the country's mountainous terrain, and Japanese consumers have always paid high prices for rice. Under overseas pressure, the Japanese government opened the market; but overseas competitors are allowed to export to Japan only 8% of its annual rice consumption to protect its farmers.

In the 2000s, however, an alliance between organic rice grower Lundberg Family Farms of California and the Nippon Restaurant Enterprise Co. found a new way to break into the Japanese rice market. Because there is no tariff on rice used in processed foods, Nippon converts the U.S. organic rice into "O-bento," an organic hot boxed lunch packed with rice, vegetables, chicken, beef, and salmon, all imported from the United States. The lunches, which cost about $4 compared to a Japanese rice bento that costs about $9, are sold at railway stations and other outlets throughout Japan and have become very popular. A storm of protest from Japanese rice farmers arose because the entry of U.S. rice growers forced them to leave their rice fields idle or grow less profitable crops. Other overseas companies are increasingly forming alliances with Japanese companies to find new ways to break into the high-priced Japanese market, and little by little, Japan's restrictive trade practices are being whittled away.

In summary, intense rivalry among competitors creates a task environment that is highly threatening and makes it increasingly difficult for managers to gain access to the resources an organization needs to make goods and services. Conversely, low rivalry results in a task environment where competitive pressures are more moderate and managers have greater opportunities to acquire the resources they need to make their organizations effective.

The General Environment

Economic, technological, sociocultural, demographic, political, and legal forces in the general environment often have important effects on forces in the task environment that determine an organization's ability to obtain resources—effects that managers may not be aware of. For example, the sudden, dramatic upheavals in the mortgage and banking industry that started in 2007 were brought about by a combination of the development of complex new financial lending instruments called derivatives; a speculative boom in commodities and housing prices; and lax government regulation that allowed unethical bankers and financial managers to exploit the derivatives to make immense short-term profits. These events triggered the economic crisis beginning in 2008 that caused stock markets around the world to plummet, devastating the retirement savings of hundreds of millions of ordinary people, and caused layoffs of millions of employees as companies slashed their workforces because customers reduced their spending. Fortunately, by 2013 sound economic policies resulted in a major recovery.

The implication is clear: Managers must continuously analyze forces in the general environment because these forces affect ongoing decision making and planning. How well managers can perform this task determines how quickly an organization can respond to the changes taking place. Next we discuss the major forces in the general environment and examine their impact on an organization's task environment.

Economic Forces

economic forces
Interest rates, inflation, unemployment, economic growth, and other factors that affect the general health and well-being of a nation or the regional economy of an organization.

Economic forces affect the general health and well-being of a country or world region. They include interest rates, inflation, unemployment, and economic growth. Economic forces produce many opportunities and threats for managers. Low levels of unemployment and falling interest rates give people more money to spend, and as a result organizations can sell more goods and services. Good economic times affect the supply of resources that become easier or more inexpensive to acquire, and organizations have an opportunity to flourish. High-tech companies enjoyed this throughout the 1990s when computer and electronics companies like Sony made record profits as the global economy boomed because of advances in IT and growing global trade.

In contrast, worsening macroeconomic conditions, like those in the 2010s, pose a major threat because they reduce managers' ability to gain access to the resources their organizations need to survive and prosper. Profit-seeking organizations such as hotels and retail stores have fewer customers during economic downturns; hotel rates dropped by 14% in 2009 compared to 2008, for example, just as retail sales plunged. Nonprofits such as charities and colleges also saw donations decline by more than 20% because of the economic downturn.

Poor economic conditions make the environment more complex and managers' jobs more difficult and demanding. Companies often need to reduce the number of their managers and employees, streamline their operations, and identify ways to acquire and use resources more efficiently and effectively. Successful managers realize the important effects that economic forces have on their organizations, and they pay close attention to what is occurring in the economy at the national and regional levels to respond appropriately.

Technological Forces

technology
The combination of skills and equipment that managers use in designing, producing, and distributing goods and services.

Technology is the combination of tools, machines, computers, skills, information, and knowledge that managers use to design, produce, and distribute goods and services; technological forces are outcomes of changes in that technology. The overall pace of technological change has accelerated greatly in the last decades because technological advances in microprocessors and computer hardware and software have spurred technological advances in most businesses and industries. The effects of changing technological forces are still increasing in magnitude.[20]

technological forces Outcomes of changes in the technology managers use to design, produce, or distribute goods and services.

Technological forces can have profound implications for managers and organizations. Technological change can make established products obsolete—for example, cathode-ray tube (CRT) computer monitors and televisions (such as Sony's Trinitron), bound sets of encyclopedias, and newspapers and magazines—forcing managers to find new ways to satisfy customer needs. Although technological change can threaten an organization, it also can create a host of new opportunities for designing, making, or distributing new and better kinds of goods and services. Ever more powerful microprocessors developed by Intel and AMD, which now have 8 or 12 processing cores on each chip, are continuing the IT revolution that has spurred demand for all kinds of new digital computing devices and services and has affected the competitive position of all high-tech companies. Will Google's new suite of software devastate Microsoft, for example, just as Microsoft's devastated IBM in the 1990s? Managers must move quickly to respond to such changes if their organizations are to survive and prosper.

Changes in IT are altering the nature of work itself within organizations, including that of the manager's job. Today telecommuting, videoconferencing, and text messaging are everyday activities that let managers supervise and coordinate geographically dispersed employees. Salespeople in many companies work from home offices and commute electronically to work. They communicate with other employees through companywide electronic communication networks using tablet PCs and smartphones to orchestrate "face-to-face" meetings with coworkers across the country or globe.

Sociocultural Forces

sociocultural forces Pressures emanating from the social structure of a country or society or from the national culture.

social structure
The traditional system of relationships established between people and groups in a society.

Sociocultural forces are pressures emanating from the social structure of a country or society or from the national culture, such as the concern for diversity, discussed in the previous chapter. Pressures from both sources can either constrain or facilitate the way organizations operate and managers behave. Social structure is the traditional system of relationships established between people and groups in a society. Societies differ substantially in social structure. In societies that have a high degree of social stratification, there are many distinctions among individuals and groups. Caste systems in India and Tibet and the recognition of numerous social classes in Great Britain and France produce a multilayered social structure in each of those countries. In contrast, social stratification is lower in relatively egalitarian New Zealand and in the United States, where the social structure reveals few distinctions among people. Most top managers in France come from the upper classes of French society, but top managers in the United States come from all strata of American society.

Societies also differ in the extent to which they emphasize the individual over the group. Such differences may dictate how managers need to motivate and lead employees.

national culture
The set of values that a society considers important and the norms of behavior that are approved or sanctioned in that society.

National culture is the set of values that a society considers important and the norms of behavior that are approved or sanctioned in that society. Societies differ substantially in the values and norms they emphasize. For example, in the United States individualism is highly valued, but in Korea and Japan individuals are expected to conform to group expectations.[21] National culture, discussed at length later in this chapter, also affects how managers motivate and coordinate employees and how organizations do business. Ethics, an important aspect of national culture, were discussed in detail in Chapter 3.

Pick your poison. The American trend toward fitness has prompted traditional soft drink manufacturers to expand their offerings into a staggering array of energy drinks.

Social structure and national culture not only differ across societies but also change within societies over time. In the United States, attitudes toward the roles of women, sex, marriage, and gays and lesbians changed in each past decade. Many people in Asian countries such as Hong Kong, Singapore, Korea, and even China think the younger generation is far more individualistic and "American-like" than previous generations. Currently, throughout much of Eastern Europe, new values that emphasize individualism and entrepreneurship are replacing communist values based on collectivism and obedience to the state. The pace of change is accelerating.

Individual managers and organizations must be responsive to changes in, and differences among, the social structures and national cultures of all the countries in which they operate. In today's increasingly integrated global economy, managers are likely to interact with people from several countries, and many managers live and work abroad. Effective managers are sensitive to differences between societies and adjust their behavior accordingly.

Managers and organizations also must respond to social changes within a society. In the last decades, for example, Americans have become increasingly interested in their personal health and fitness. Managers who recognized this trend early and took advantage of the opportunities that resulted from it were able to reap significant gains for their organizations, such as chains of health clubs. PepsiCo used the opportunity presented by the fitness trend and took market share from archrival Coca-Cola by being the first to introduce diet colas and fruit-based soft drinks. Then Quaker Oats made Gatorade the most popular energy drink, and now others like Red Bull, Monster, and Rockstar are increasing in popularity. The health trend, however, did not offer opportunities to all companies; to some it posed a threat. Tobacco companies came under intense pressure due to consumers' greater awareness of negative health impacts from smoking. The rage for "low-carb" foods in the 2000s increased demand for meat and protein, and bread and doughnut companies such as Kraft and Krispy Kreme suffered—until the ongoing recession boosted the sale of inexpensive products such as macaroni and cheese and hamburger helper.

Demographic Forces

demographic forces Outcomes of changes in, or changing attitudes toward, the characteristics of a population, such as age, gender, ethnic origin, race, sexual orientation, and social class.

Demographic forces are outcomes of changes in, or changing attitudes toward, the characteristics of a population, such as age, gender, ethnic origin, race, sexual orientation, and social class. Like the other forces in the general environment, demographic forces present managers with opportunities and threats and can have major implications for organizations. We examine the nature of these challenges throughout this book.

Today most industrialized nations are experiencing the aging of their populations as a consequence of falling birth and death rates and the aging of the baby boom generation. Consequently, the absolute number of older people has increased substantially, which has generated opportunities for organizations that cater to older people, such as the home health care, recreation, and medical industries, which have seen an upswing in demand for their services. The aging of the population also has several implications for the workplace. Most significant are a relative decline in the number of young people joining the workforce and an increase in the number of active employees who are postponing retirement beyond the traditional age of 65. Indeed, the continuing financial crisis in the 2010s has made it impossible for millions of older people to retire because their savings have been decimated. These changes suggest that organizations need to find ways to motivate older employees and use their skills and knowledge—an issue that many Western societies have yet to tackle.

Political and Legal Forces

political and legal forces Outcomes of changes in laws and regulations, such as deregulation of industries, privatization of organizations, and increased emphasis on environmental protection.

Political and legal forces are outcomes of changes in laws and regulations. They result from political and legal developments that take place within a nation, within a world region, or across the world, and significantly affect managers and organizations everywhere. Political processes shape a nation's laws and the international laws that govern the relationships between nations. Laws constrain the operations of organizations and managers and thus create both opportunities and threats.[22] For example, throughout much of the industrialized world there has been a strong trend toward deregulation of industries previously controlled by the state and privatization of organizations once owned by the state such as airlines, railways, and utility companies.

Another important political and legal force affecting managers and organizations is the political integration of countries that has been taking place during the last decades.[23] Increasingly, nations are forming political unions that allow free exchange of resources and capital. The growth of the European Union (EU) is one example: Common laws govern trade and commerce between EU member countries, and the European Court has the right to examine the business of any global organization and to approve any proposed mergers between overseas companies that operate inside the EU. For example, Microsoft's anticompetitive business practices came under scrutiny, and it was fined hundreds of millions for its uncompetitive practice of bundling its Internet Explorer web browser with its software. As part of its agreement with the European Court, Microsoft agreed that, beginning in 2010, it would ship its Windows 7 software with a choice of 10 web browsers (such as Chrome, Safari, and Mozilla). Also, in 2012, after months of delay, the court allowed the merger between Motorola and Google to proceed although the court was also investigating Google for possible anticompetitive online advertising practices. The North American Free Trade Agreement (NAFTA), discussed later in the chapter, has more modest political goals; but like the EU, it has changed the laws that affect international commerce by lowering barriers to the free flow of goods and services between member nations.[24]

Indeed, international agreements to abolish laws and regulations that restrict and reduce trade between countries have been having profound effects on global organizations. The falling legal trade barriers create enormous opportunities for companies to sell goods and services internationally. But by allowing overseas companies to compete in a nation's domestic market for customers, falling trade barriers also pose a serious threat because they increase competition in the task environment. Between 1980 and 2010, for example, Japanese companies increased their share of the U.S. car market from around 20% to 40%; Taiwanese companies' share grew from 2% to 7%. In essence, removing legal restrictions on global trade has the same effect as deregulating industries and removing restrictions against competition: It increases the intensity of competition in the task environment and forces conservative, slow-moving companies—such as GM and Chrysler—to become more efficient, improve product quality, and learn new values and norms to compete in the global environment. To help turn around their performance, GM was forced to declare bankruptcy in 2009 and Chrysler was bought by Fiat, and the performance of both these companies has improved in the 2010s—indeed they have become profitable.

LO 4-4 Explain why the global environment is becoming more open and competitive, and identify the forces behind the process of globalization that increase the opportunities, complexities, challenges, and threats that managers face.

Deregulation, privatization, and the removal of legal barriers to trade are just a few of the many ways in which changing political and legal forces can challenge organizations and managers. Others include increased emphasis on environmental protection and the preservation of endangered species, increased emphasis on workplace safety, and legal constraints against discrimination on the basis of race, gender, or age. Managers face major challenges when they seek to take advantage of the opportunities created by changing political, legal, and economic forces.

The Changing Global Environment

The 21st century has banished the idea that the world is composed of distinct national countries and markets that are separated physically, economically, and culturally. Managers need to recognize that companies compete in a truly global marketplace, which is the source of the opportunities and threats they must respond to. Managers continually confront the challenges of global competition such as establishing operations in a country abroad, obtaining inputs from suppliers abroad, or managing in a different national culture.[25] (See Figure 4.3.)

In essence, as a result of falling trade barriers, managers view the global environment as open—that is, as an environment in which companies are free to buy goods and services from, and sell goods and services to, whichever companies and countries they choose. They also are free to compete against each other to attract customers around the world. All large companies must establish an international network of operations and subsidiaries to build global competitive advantage. Coca-Cola and PepsiCo, for example, have competed aggressively for decades to

Figure 4.3

The Global Environment

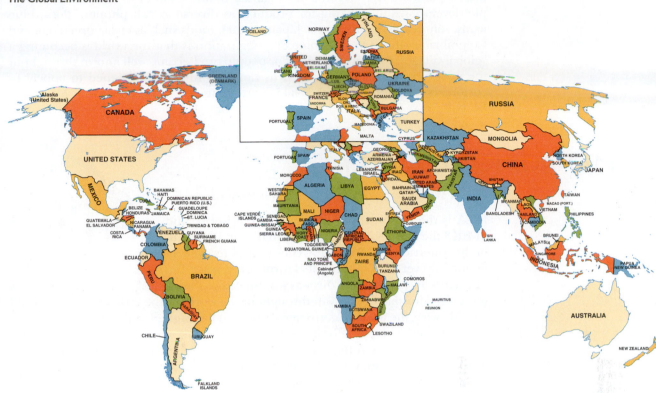

develop the strongest global soft drink empire, just as Toyota and Honda have built hundreds of car plants around the world to provide the vehicles that global customers like.

In this section we first explain how this open global environment is the result of globalization and the flow of capital around the world. Next we examine how specific economic, political, and legal changes, such as the lowering of barriers to trade and investment, have increased globalization and led to greater interaction and exchanges between organizations and countries. Then we discuss how declining barriers of distance and culture have also increased the pace of globalization, and we consider the specific implications of these changes for managers and organizations. Finally we note that nations still differ widely from each other because they have distinct cultural values and norms and that managers must appreciate these differences to compete successfully across countries.

globalization The set of specific and general forces that work together to integrate and connect economic, political, and social systems *across* countries, cultures, or geographical regions so that nations become increasingly interdependent and similar.

The Process of Globalization

Perhaps the most important reason why the global environment has become more open and competitive is the increase in globalization. Globalization is the set of specific and general forces that work together to integrate and connect economic, political, and social systems *across* countries, cultures, or geographic regions. The result of globalization is that nations and peoples become increasingly *interdependent* because the same forces affect them in similar ways. The fates of peoples in different countries become interlinked as the world's markets and businesses become increasingly interconnected. And as nations become more interdependent, they become more similar to one another in the sense that people develop a similar liking for products as diverse as cell phones, iPods, blue jeans, soft drinks, sports teams, Japanese cars, foods such as curry, green tea, and Colombian coffee. One outcome of globalization is that the world is becoming a "global village": Products, services, or people can become well known throughout the world—something IKEA, with its range of furniture designed to appeal to customers around the world, is taking advantage of, as the following "Managing Globally" box describes.

MANAGING GLOBALLY

IKEA Is on Top of the Furniture World

IKEA is the largest furniture chain in the world, and in 2013 the Swedish company operated over 340 stores in 40 countries. In 2012 IKEA sales soared to over $40 billion, or over 23% of the global furniture market; but to its managers and employees this was just the tip of the iceberg. They believed IKEA was poised for massive growth throughout the world in the 2010s because it could provide what the average customer wanted: well-designed and well-made contemporary furniture at an affordable price. IKEA's ability to provide customers with affordable furniture is the result of its approach to globalization, to how it treats its global employees and operates its global store empire. In a nutshell, IKEA's global approach focuses on simplicity, attention to detail, cost-consciousness, and responsiveness in every aspect of its operations and behavior.

IKEA's global approach derives from the personal values and beliefs of its founder, Ingvar Kamprad, about how companies should treat their employees and customers. Kamprad, who is in his 80s (and in 2013 was one of the top 10 richest people in the world), was born in Smaland, a poor Swedish province whose citizens are known for being entrepreneurial, frugal, and hardworking. Kamprad definitely absorbed these values—when he entered the furniture business, he made them the core of his management approach. He teaches store managers and employees his values; his beliefs about the need to operate in a no-frills, cost-conscious way; and his view that they are all in business "together," by which he means that every person who works in his global empire plays an essential role and has an obligation to everyone else.

What does Kamprad's approach mean in practice? All IKEA employees fly coach class on business trips, stay in inexpensive hotels, and keep traveling expenses to a minimum. And IKEA stores operate on the simplest rules and procedures possible, with employees expected to cooperate to solve problems and get the job done. Many famous stories circulate about the frugal Kamprad, such as that he always flies coach class and that when he takes a soda can from the minibar in a hotel room, he replaces it with one bought in a store—despite the fact that he is a multibillionaire.

IKEA's employees see what Kamprad's global approach means as soon as they are recruited to work in a store in one of the many countries in which the company operates. They start learning about IKEA's global corporate culture by performing jobs at the bottom of the ladder, and they are quickly trained to perform

Need a new kitchen table? How about a cute rug to go with it, and while you're at it, a cookie sheet, too? Options await you at any one of the thousands of IKEA stores worldwide.

all the various jobs involved in store operations. During this process they internalize IKEA's global values and norms, which center on the importance the company attaches to their taking the initiative and responsibility for solving problems and for focusing on customers. Employees are rotated between departments and sometimes stores, and rapid promotion is possible for those who demonstrate the enthusiasm and togetherness that show they have bought into IKEA's global culture.

Most of IKEA's top managers rose from its ranks, and the company holds "breaking the bureaucracy weeks," in which managers are required to work in stores and warehouses for a week each year to make sure they and all employees stay committed to IKEA's global values. No matter which country they operate in, all employees wear informal clothes to work at IKEA—Kamprad has always worn an open-neck shirt—and there are no marks of status such as executive dining rooms or private parking places. Employees believe that if they buy into IKEA's work values, behave in ways that keep its growing global operations streamlined and efficient, and focus on being one step ahead of potential problems, they will share in its success. Promotion, training, above-average pay, a generous store bonus system, and the personal well-being that comes from working in a company where people feel valued are some of the rewards that Kamprad pioneered to build and strengthen IKEA's global approach.

Whenever IKEA enters a new country, it sends its most experienced store managers to establish its global approach in its new stores. When IKEA first entered the United States, the attitude of U.S. employees puzzled its managers. Despite their obvious drive to succeed and their good education, employees seemed reluctant to take initiative and assume responsibility. IKEA's managers discovered that their U.S. employees were afraid mistakes would result in the loss of their jobs, so the managers strove to teach employees the "IKEA way." The approach paid off: The United States has become the company's second best country market, and IKEA plans to open many more U.S. stores, as well as stores around the world, over the next decade.[26]

But what drives or spurs globalization? What makes companies like IKEA, Toyota, or Microsoft want to venture into an uncertain global environment? The answer is that the path of globalization is shaped by the ebb and flow of *capital*—valuable wealth-generating assets or resources that people move through companies, countries, and world regions to seek their greatest returns or profits. Managers, employees, and companies like IKEA and Sony are motivated to try to profit or benefit by using their skills to make products customers around the world want to buy. The four principal forms of capital that flow between countries are these:

- *Human capital:* the flow of people around the world through immigration, migration, and emigration.
- *Financial capital:* the flow of money capital across world markets through overseas investment, credit, lending, and aid.

- *Resource capital:* the flow of natural resources, parts, and components between companies and countries, such as metals, minerals, lumber, energy, food products, microprocessors, and auto parts.

- *Political capital:* the flow of power and influence around the world using diplomacy, persuasion, aggression, and force of arms to protect the right or access of a country, world region, or political bloc to the other forms of capital.

Most of the economic advances associated with globalization are the result of these four capital flows and the interactions between them, as nations compete on the world stage to protect and increase their standards of living and to further the political goals and social causes that are espoused by their societies' cultures. The next sections look at the factors that have increased the rate at which capital flows between companies and countries. In a positive sense, the faster the flow, the more capital is being utilized where it can create the most value, such as people moving to where their skills earn them more money, or investors switching to the stocks or bonds that give them higher dividends or interest, or companies finding lower-cost sources of inputs. In a negative sense, however, a fast flow of capital also means that individual countries or world regions can find themselves in trouble when companies and investors move their capital to invest it in more productive ways in other countries or world regions—often those with lower labor costs or rapidly expanding markets. When capital leaves a country, the results are higher unemployment, recession, and a lower standard of living for its people.

Declining Barriers to Trade and Investment

One of the main factors that has speeded globalization by freeing the movement of capital has been the decline in barriers to trade and investment, discussed earlier. During the 1920s and 1930s many countries erected formidable barriers to international trade and investment in the belief that this was the best way to promote their economic well-being. Many of these barriers were high tariffs on imports of manufactured goods. A tariff is a tax that a government imposes on goods imported into one country from another. The aim of import tariffs is to protect domestic industries and jobs, such as those in the auto or steel industry, from overseas competition by raising the price of these products from abroad. In 2009, for example, the U.S. government increased the tariffs on vehicle tires imported from China to protect U.S. tire makers from unfair competition; in 2012 it imposed a 30% tariff on imports of Chinese solar panels after U.S. solar companies complained that the Chinese government was unfairly subsidizing this industry.

The reason for removing tariffs is that, very often, when one country imposes an import tariff, others follow suit and the result is a series of retaliatory moves as countries progressively raise tariff barriers against each other. In the 1920s this behavior depressed world demand and helped usher in the Great Depression of the 1930s and massive unemployment. Beginning with the 2009 economic crisis, the governments of most countries have worked hard in the 2010s not to fall into the trap of raising tariffs to protect jobs and industries in the short run because they know the long-term consequences of this would be the loss of even more jobs. Governments of countries that resort to raising tariff barriers ultimately reduce employment and undermine the economic growth of their countries because capital and resources will always move to their most highly valued use—wherever that is in the world.[27]

tariff A tax that a government imposes on imported or, occasionally, exported goods.

GATT AND THE RISE OF FREE TRADE After World War II, advanced Western industrial countries, having learned from the Great Depression, committed themselves to the goal of removing barriers to the free flow of resources and capital between countries. This commitment was reinforced by acceptance of the principle that free trade, rather than tariff barriers, was the best way to foster a healthy domestic economy and low unemployment.[28]

free-trade doctrine
The idea that if each country specializes in the production of the goods and services that it can produce most efficiently, this will make the best use of global resources.

The free-trade doctrine predicts that if each country agrees to specialize in the production of the goods and services that it can produce most efficiently, this will make the best use of global capital resources and will result in lower prices.[29] For example, if Indian companies are highly efficient in the production of textiles and U.S. companies are highly efficient in the production of computer software, then, under a free-trade agreement, capital would move to India and be invested there to produce textiles, while capital from around the world would flow to the United States and be invested in its innovative computer software companies. Consequently, prices of both textiles and software should fall because each product is being produced where it can be made at the lowest cost, benefiting consumers and making the best use of scarce capital. This doctrine is also responsible for the increase in global outsourcing and the loss of millions of U.S. jobs in textiles and manufacturing as capital has been invested in factories in Asian countries such as China and Malaysia. However, millions of U.S. jobs have also been created because of new capital investments in the high-tech, IT, and service sectors, which in theory should offset manufacturing job losses in the long run.

Historically, countries that accepted this free-trade doctrine set as their goal the removal of barriers to the free flow of goods, services, and capital between countries. They attempted to achieve this through an international treaty known as the General Agreement on Tariffs and Trade (GATT). In the half-century since World War II, there have been eight rounds of GATT negotiations aimed at lowering tariff barriers. The last round, the Uruguay Round, involved 117 countries and succeeded in lowering tariffs by over 30% from the previous level. It also led to the dissolving of GATT and its replacement by the World Trade Organization (WTO), which continues the struggle to reduce tariffs and has more power to sanction countries that break global agreements.[30] On average, the tariff barriers among the governments of developed countries declined from over 40% in 1948 to about 3% today, causing a dramatic increase in world trade.[31]

Declining Barriers of Distance and Culture

Historically, barriers of distance and culture also closed the global environment and kept managers focused on their domestic market. The management problems Unilever, the huge British-based soap and detergent maker, experienced at the turn of the 20th century illustrate the effect of these barriers.

Founded in London during the 1880s by William Lever, a Quaker, Unilever had a worldwide reach by the early 1900s and operated subsidiaries in most major countries of the British Empire, including India, Canada, and Australia. Lever had a very hands-on, autocratic management style and found his far-flung business empire difficult to control. The reason for Lever's control problems was that communication over great distances was difficult. It took six weeks to reach India by ship from England, and international telephone and telegraph services were unreliable.

Another problem Unilever encountered was the difficulty of doing business in societies that were separated from Britain by barriers of language and culture.

Different countries have different sets of national beliefs, values, and norms, and Lever found that a management approach that worked in Britain did not necessarily work in India or Persia (now Iran). As a result, management practices had to be tailored to suit each unique national culture. After Lever's death in 1925, top management at Unilever lowered or *decentralized* (see Chapter 7) decision-making authority to the managers of the various national subsidiaries so they could develop a management approach that suited the country in which they were operating. One result of this strategy was that the subsidiaries grew distant and remote from one another, which reduced Unilever's performance.[32]

Since the end of World War II, a continuing stream of advances in communications and transportation technology has worked to reduce the barriers of distance and culture that affected Unilever and all global organizations. Over the last decades, global communication has been revolutionized by developments in satellites, digital technology, the Internet and global computer networks, and video teleconferencing that allow transmission of vast amounts of information and make reliable, secure, and instantaneous communication possible between people and companies anywhere in the world.[33] This revolution has made it possible for a global organization—a tiny garment factory in Li & Fung's network or a huge company such as IKEA or Unilever—to do business anywhere, anytime, and to search for customers and suppliers around the world.

One of the most important innovations in transportation technology that has opened the global environment has been the growth of commercial jet travel. New York is now closer in travel time to Tokyo than it was to Philadelphia in the days of the 13 colonies—a fact that makes control of far-flung international businesses much easier today than in William Lever's era. In addition to speeding travel, modern communications and transportation technologies have also helped reduce the cultural distance between countries. The Internet and its millions of websites facilitate the development of global communications networks and media that are helping to create a worldwide culture above and beyond unique national cultures. Moreover, television networks such as CNN, MTV, ESPN, BBC, and HBO can now be received in many countries, and Hollywood films are shown throughout the world.

Effects of Free Trade on Managers

The lowering of barriers to trade and investment and the decline of distance and culture barriers has created enormous opportunities for companies to expand the market for their goods and services through exports and investments in overseas countries. The shift toward a more open global economy has created not only more opportunities to sell goods and services in markets abroad but also the opportunity to buy more from other countries. For example, the success of clothing companies such as Lands' End has been based on its managers' willingness to import low-cost clothing and bedding from overseas manufacturers. Lands' End works closely with manufacturers in Hong Kong, Malaysia, Taiwan, and China to make the clothing that its managers decide has the quality and styling its customers want at a price they will pay.[34] A manager's job is more challenging in a dynamic global environment because of the increased intensity of competition that goes hand in hand with the lowering of barriers to trade and investment.

REGIONAL TRADE AGREEMENTS The growth of regional trade agreements such as the North American Free Trade Agreement (NAFTA), and more recently the

Central American Free Trade Agreement (CAFTA), also presents opportunities and threats for managers and their organizations. In North America, NAFTA, which became effective in 1994, aimed to abolish the tariffs on 99% of the goods traded between Mexico, Canada, and the United States by 2004. Although it did not achieve this lofty goal, NAFTA has removed most barriers on the cross-border flow of resources, giving, for example, financial institutions and retail businesses in Canada and the United States unrestricted access to the Mexican marketplace. After NAFTA was signed, there was a flood of investment into Mexico from the United States, as well as many other countries such as Japan. Walmart, Costco, Ford, and many major U.S. retail chains expanded their operations in Mexico; Walmart, for example, is stocking many more products from Mexico in its U.S. stores, and its Mexican store chain is also expanding rapidly.

The establishment of free-trade areas creates an opportunity for manufacturing organizations because it lets them reduce their costs. They can do this either by shifting production to the lowest-cost location within the free-trade area (for example, U.S. auto and textile companies shifting production to Mexico) or by serving the whole region from one location rather than establishing separate operations in each country. Some managers, however, view regional free-trade agreements as a threat because they expose a company based in one member country to increased competition from companies based in the other member countries. NAFTA has had this effect; today Mexican managers in some industries face the threat of head-to-head competition against efficient U.S. and Canadian companies. But the opposite is true as well: U.S. and Canadian managers are experiencing threats in labor-intensive industries, such as the flooring tile, roofing, and textile industries, where Mexican businesses have a cost advantage.

In 2005 the U.S. House of Representatives approved the formation of CAFTA, a regional trade agreement designed to eliminate tariffs on products moving between the United States and all countries in Central America. By 2006 the Dominican Republic, El Salvador, Guatemala, Nicaragua, and Honduras had also approved and implemented the agreement, but Costa Rica still has not. CAFTA is seen as a stepping-stone toward establishing the Free Trade Area of the Americas (FTAA), which is an ambitious attempt to establish a free-trade agreement that would increase economic prosperity throughout the Americas. FTAA would include all South American and Caribbean nations except Cuba, as well as those of North and Central America. However, the economic problems many countries have been experiencing, together with major political and ideological differences—such as the political resistance within the United States because of jobs lost to Mexico and Canada—have slowed the process of integration and globalization. The more competitive environment NAFTA has brought about has increased both the opportunities that managers can take advantage of and the threats they must respond to in performing their jobs effectively.

The Role of National Culture

Despite evidence that countries are becoming more similar because of globalization, and that the world may become "a global village," the cultures of different countries still vary widely because of vital differences in their values, norms, and attitudes. As noted earlier, national culture includes the values, norms, knowledge, beliefs, moral principles, laws, customs, and other practices that unite the citizens of a country.[35] National culture shapes individual behavior by specifying appropriate and inappropriate behavior and interaction with others. People learn national culture in their everyday lives by interacting with those around them. This learning starts at an early age and continues throughout their lives.

Cultural Values and Norms

values Ideas about what a society believes to be good, right, desirable, or beautiful.

The basic building blocks of national culture are values and norms. Values are beliefs about what a society considers to be good, right, desirable, or beautiful—or their opposites. They provide the basic underpinnings for notions of individual freedom, democracy, truth, justice, honesty, loyalty, social obligation, collective responsibility, the appropriate roles for men and women, love, sex, marriage, and so on. Values are more than merely abstract concepts; they are invested with considerable emotional significance. People argue, fight, and even die over values such as freedom or dignity.

Although deeply embedded in society, values are not static; they change over time, but change is often the result of a slow and painful process. For example, the value systems of many formerly communist states such as Georgia, Hungary, and Romania have undergone significant changes as those countries move away from values that emphasize state control toward values that emphasizes individual freedom. Social turmoil often results when countries undergo major changes in their values, as is happening today in Asia, South America, and the Middle East.

norms Unwritten, informal codes of conduct that prescribe how people should act in particular situations and are considered important by most members of a group or organization.

Norms are unwritten, informal codes of conduct that prescribe appropriate behavior in particular situations and are considered important by most members of a group or organization. They shape the behavior of people toward one another. Two types of norms play a major role in national culture: mores and folkways. Mores are norms that are considered to be of central importance to the functioning of society and to social life. Accordingly, the violation of mores brings serious retribution. Mores include proscriptions against murder, theft, adultery, and incest. In many societies mores have been enacted into law. Thus, all advanced societies have laws against murder and theft. However, there are many differences in mores from one society to another.[36] In the United States, for example, drinking alcohol is widely accepted; but in Saudi Arabia consumption of alcohol is viewed as a serious violation of social mores and is punishable by imprisonment.

mores Norms that are considered to be central to the functioning of society and to social life.

folkways The routine social conventions of everyday life.

Folkways are the routine social conventions of everyday life. They concern customs and practices such as dressing appropriately for particular situations, good social manners, eating with the correct utensils, and neighborly behavior. Although folkways define how people are expected to behave, violation of folkways is not a serious or moral matter. People who violate folkways are often thought to be eccentric or ill-mannered, but they are not usually considered immoral or wicked. In many countries, strangers are usually excused for violating folkways because they are unaccustomed to local behavior; but if they repeat the violation, they are censured because they are expected to learn appropriate behavior. Hence the importance for managers working in countries abroad to gain wide experience.

LO 4-5 Discuss why national cultures differ and why it is important that managers be sensitive to the effects of falling trade barriers and regional trade associations on the political and social systems of nations around the world.

Hofstede's Model of National Culture

Researchers have spent considerable time and effort identifying similarities and differences in the values and norms of different countries. One model of national culture was developed by Geert Hofstede.[37] As a psychologist for IBM,

individualism A worldview that values individual freedom and self-expression and adherence to the principle that people should be judged by their individual achievements rather than by their social background.

collectivism A worldview that values subordination of the individual to the goals of the group and adherence to the principle that people should be judged by their contribution to the group.

power distance The degree to which societies accept the idea that inequalities in the power and well-being of their citizens are due to differences in individuals' physical and intellectual capabilities and heritage.

Hofstede collected data on employee values and norms from more than 100,000 IBM employees in 64 countries. Based on his research, Hofstede developed five dimensions along which national cultures can be placed (see Figure 4.4).[38]

INDIVIDUALISM VERSUS COLLECTIVISM The first dimension, which Hofstede labeled "individualism versus collectivism," has a long history in human thought. Individualism is a worldview that values individual freedom and self-expression and adherence to the principle that people should be judged by their individual achievements rather than by their social background. In Western countries, individualism usually includes admiration for personal success, a strong belief in individual rights, and high regard for individual entrepreneurs.[39]

In contrast, collectivism is a worldview that values subordination of the individual to the goals of the group and adherence to the principle that people should be judged by their contribution to the group. Collectivism was widespread in communist countries but has become less prevalent since the collapse of communism in most of those countries. Japan is a noncommunist country where collectivism is highly valued.

Collectivism in Japan traces its roots to the fusion of Confucian, Buddhist, and Shinto thought that occurred during the Tokugawa period in Japanese history (1600–1870s).[40] A central value that emerged during this period was strong attachment to the group—whether a village, a work group, or a company. Strong identification with the group is said to create pressures for collective action in Japan, as well as strong pressure for conformity to group norms and a relative lack of individualism.[41]

Managers must realize that organizations and organizational members reflect their national culture's emphasis on individualism or collectivism. Indeed, one of the major reasons why Japanese and American management practices differ is that Japanese culture values collectivism and U.S. culture values individualism.[42]

POWER DISTANCE By power distance Hofstede meant the degree to which societies accept the idea that inequalities in the power and well-being of their citizens

Figure 4.4

Hofstede's Model of National Culture

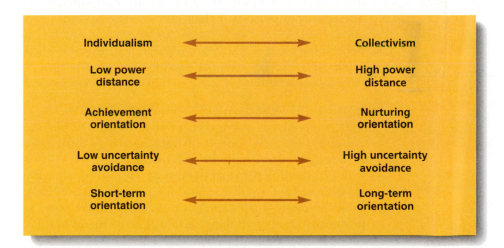

Source: G. Hofstede, B. Nevijen, D. D. Ohayv, and G. Sanders, "Measuring Organizational Cultures: A Qualitative and Quantitative Study across Twenty Cases," *Administrative Science Quarterly* 35, no. 2 (June 1990), 286–316. Copyright © 1990 by Cornell University, Johnson Graduate School of Management. Reproduced with permission of Sage Publications, Inc. via Copyright Clearance Center.

are due to differences in individuals' physical and intellectual capabilities and heritage. This concept also encompasses the degree to which societies accept the economic and social differences in wealth, status, and well-being that result from differences in individual capabilities.

Societies in which inequalities are allowed to persist or grow over time have *high power distance*. In high-power-distance societies, workers who are professionally successful amass wealth and pass it on to their children, and, as a result, inequalities may grow over time. In such societies, the gap between rich and poor, with all the attendant political and social consequences, grows very large. In contrast, in societies with *low power distance*, large inequalities between citizens are not allowed to develop. In low-power-distance countries, the government uses taxation and social welfare programs to reduce inequality and improve the welfare of the least fortunate. These societies are more attuned to preventing a large gap between rich and poor and minimizing discord between different classes of citizens.

Advanced Western countries such as the United States, Germany, the Netherlands, and the United Kingdom have relatively low power distance and high individualism. Economically poor Latin American countries such as Guatemala and Panama, and Asian countries such as Malaysia and the Philippines, have high power distance and low individualism.[43] These findings suggest that the cultural values of richer countries emphasize protecting the rights of individuals and, at the same time, provide a fair chance of success to every member of society.

ACHIEVEMENT VERSUS NURTURING ORIENTATION Societies that have an achievement orientation value assertiveness, performance, success, competition, and results. Societies that have a nurturing orientation value the quality of life, warm personal relationships, and services and care for the weak. Japan and the United States tend to be achievement-oriented; the Netherlands, Sweden, and Denmark are more nurturing-oriented.

UNCERTAINTY AVOIDANCE Societies as well as individuals differ in their tolerance for uncertainty and risk. Societies low on uncertainty avoidance (such as the United States and Hong Kong) are easygoing, value diversity, and tolerate differences in personal beliefs and actions. Societies high on uncertainty avoidance (such as Japan and France) are more rigid and skeptical about people whose behaviors or beliefs differ from the norm. In these societies, conformity to the values of the social and work groups to which a person belongs is the norm, and structured situations are preferred because they provide a sense of security.

LONG-TERM VERSUS SHORT-TERM ORIENTATION The last dimension that Hofstede described is orientation toward life and work.[44] A national culture with a long-term orientation rests on values such as thrift (saving) and persistence in achieving goals. A national culture with a short-term orientation is concerned with maintaining personal stability or happiness and living for the present. Societies with a long-term orientation include Taiwan and Hong Kong, well known for their high rate of per capita savings. The United States and France have a short-term orientation, and their citizens tend to spend more and save less.

National Culture and Global Management

Differences among national cultures have important implications for managers. First, because of cultural differences, management practices that are effective

---

achievement orientation
A worldview that values assertiveness, performance, success, and competition.

nurturing orientation
A worldview that values the quality of life, warm personal friendships, and services and care for the weak.

uncertainty avoidance The degree to which societies are willing to tolerate uncertainty and risk.

long-term orientation A worldview that values thrift and persistence in achieving goals.

short-term orientation
A worldview that values personal stability or happiness and living for the present.

in one country might be troublesome in another. General Electric's managers learned this while trying to manage Tungsram, a Hungarian lighting products company GE acquired for $150 million. GE was attracted to Tungsram, widely regarded as one of Hungary's best companies, because of Hungary's low wage rates and the possibility of using the company as a base from which to export lighting products to western Europe. GE transferred some of its best managers to Tungsram and hoped it would soon become a leader in Europe. Unfortunately many problems arose.

One problem resulted from major misunderstandings between the American managers and the Hungarian workers. The Americans complained that the Hungarians were lazy; the Hungarians thought the Americans were pushy. The Americans wanted strong sales and marketing functions that would pamper customers. In the prior command economy, sales and marketing activities were unnecessary. In addition, Hungarians expected GE to deliver Western-style wages, but GE came to Hungary to take advantage of the country's low-wage structure.[45] As Tungsram's losses mounted, GE managers had to admit that, because of differences in basic attitudes between countries, they had underestimated the difficulties they would face in turning Tungsram around. Nevertheless, by 2001 these problems had been solved, and the increased efficiency of GE's Hungarian operations made General Electric a major player in the European lighting market, causing it to invest another $1 billion.[46]

Often, management practices must be tailored to suit the cultural contexts within which an organization operates. An approach effective in the United States might not work in Japan, Hungary, or Mexico because of differences in national culture. For example, U.S.-style pay-for-performance systems that emphasize the performance of individuals might not work well in Japan, where individual performance in pursuit of group goals is the value that receives emphasis.

Managers doing business with individuals from another country must be sensitive to the value systems and norms of that country and behave accordingly. For example, Friday is the Islamic Sabbath. Thus it would be impolite and inappropriate for a U.S. manager to schedule a busy day of activities for Saudi Arabian managers on a Friday.

A culturally diverse management team can be a source of strength for an organization participating in the global marketplace. Compared to organizations with culturally homogeneous management teams, organizations that employ managers from a variety of cultures have a better appreciation of how national cultures differ, and they tailor their management systems and behaviors to the differences.[47] Indeed, one advantage that many Western companies have over their Japanese competitors is greater willingness to create global teams composed of employees from different countries around the world who can draw on and share their different cultural experiences and knowledge to provide service that is customized to the needs of companies in different countries. For example, because IT services account for more than half of IBM's $90 billion annual revenues, it has been searching for ways to better use its talented workforce to both lower

IT services with an edge: IBM's new competency centers customize teams of workers who can manage their own tasks.

costs and offer customers unique, specialized kinds of services that its competitors cannot. IBM has developed several kinds of techniques to accomplish this.[48]

In the 2000s, IBM created "competency centers" around the world staffed by employees who share the same specific IT skill. In India, for example, today, IBM employs over 20,000 IT personnel who specialize in providing technical customer support for large U.S. companies. These employees work in self-managed teams and are responsible for managing all aspects of a particular client's specific needs. By using teams, IBM can offer high-quality personalized service at a low price and compete effectively in the global marketplace.

Most of IBM's employees are concentrated in competency centers located in the countries in which IBM has the most clients and does the most business. These employees have a wide variety of skills, developed from their previous work experience, and the challenge facing IBM is to use these experts efficiently. To accomplish this, IBM used its own IT expertise to develop sophisticated software that allows it to create self-managed teams composed of IBM experts who have the optimum mix of skills to solve a client's particular problems. First, IBM programmers analyze the skills and experience of its 80,000 global employees and enter the results into the software program. Then they analyze and code the nature of a client's specific problem and input that information. IBM's program matches each specific client problem to the skills of IBM's experts and identifies a list of "best fit" employees. One of IBM's senior managers narrows this list and decides on the actual composition of the self-managed team. Once selected, team members, from wherever they happen to be in the world, assemble as quickly as possible and go to work analyzing the client's problem. Together, team members use their authority. This new IT lets IBM create an ever-changing set of global self-managed teams that form to develop the software and service package necessary to solve the problems of IBM's global clients. At the same time, IBM's IT also optimizes the use of its whole talented workforce because each employee is placed in his or her "most highly valued use"—that is, in the team where the employee's skills can best increase efficiency and effectiveness. In some cases it is not easy for a company to harmonize the skills, attitudes, values, and experience of employees from different countries as the problems Sony has experienced, discussed in the following "Manager as a Person," suggest.

MANAGER AS A PERSON

Kazuo Hirai Replaces Howard Stringer as CEO of Sony

Sony, the Japanese electronics maker, was renowned in the 1990s for using its engineering prowess to develop blockbuster new products such as the Walkman, Trinitron TV, and PlayStation.[49] Sony's engineers were given freedom to pursue their own ideas, and its different product teams pursued their own innovations; but major problems arose with this approach in the 2000s. Companies in Korea and Taiwan (e.g., LG and Samsung) made major innovations in technologies, such as the development of advanced LCD screen displays and flash memory, that made Sony's technologies obsolete. On the product front, companies such as Apple, Samsung, and Nintendo developed new digital devices such as the iPod, smartphones, and the Wii game console that better met customer needs than Sony's old-fashioned and expensive products. Also, all these companies had worked to reduce manufacturing costs and engaged in extensive outsourcing so that Sony lost its competitive advantage in both technology and price and it began to lose billions of dollars.

By 2005 Sony was in serious trouble, and at this crucial point in their company's history, Sony's Japanese top managers turned to a *gaijin*, or non-Japanese, executive to lead their company. Their choice was Sir Howard Stringer, a Welshman, the previous head of Sony's North American operations who had been instrumental in cutting costs and increasing the profits of Sony's U.S. division. Once he became CEO in 2005, Stringer faced the immediate problem of reducing Sony's operating costs that were more than double those of its competitors, even as it was losing its technological leadership. Stringer had to make many radical strategic decisions.

Kazuo Hirai and Sir Howard Stringer are both committed to finding ways to turn around the performance of the flagging multinational.

Japan is a country where large companies traditionally had a policy of lifetime employment, but Stringer made it clear that layoffs were inevitable. Within five years he cut Sony's Japanese workforce by over 25,000 employees and closed 12 factories to reduce costs. Stringer also recognized how widespread power struggles among the top managers of Sony's different product divisions were hurting the company, and he made it clear that these problems had to stop. At Sony, like many other Japanese companies, the top managers of its divisions worked to protect their own divisions' interests—not Sony's. As Sony's performance fell, competition between managers increased, which slowed strategic decision making, made it harder for the company to innovate new products, and increased operating costs as each division fought for the funding necessary to develop new products.

Many top divisional managers, including the manager of Sony's successful PlayStation division, ignored Stringer; he replaced them and worked steadily to downsize Sony's bloated corporate headquarters staff and to change its ineffective culture. In Stringer's own words, the present culture or "business of Sony has been management, not making products." In 2009, to speed change, Stringer announced he would take control of the struggling core electronics division *and* would add the title of president to his existing roles as chairman and CEO to speed the reorganization of Sony's divisions. He also replaced four more top executives with younger managers who had held positions outside Japan and were "familiar with the digital world."

Stringer worked hard to bring the realities of global competition to the forefront and change Sony's managers' values and attitudes; his goal was to cut operating costs by over $10 billion, or 40%. To achieve this, he announced Sony would rapidly expand its use of outsourcing and centralize purchasing. By 2010, financial results suggested that Stringer's initiatives were finally paying off—he had stemmed Sony's huge losses and its products were selling better—and he expected Sony to become profitable by 2011. In 2010, Sony announced a major initiative to push into new digital, but so were its competitors such as Apple and Samsung, which were quickly innovating new kinds of mobile devices such as smartphones and tablet computers; global rivalry was intense and Sony had not regained a competitive advantage.

Stringer, who was now in his late 60s, searched for a successor who would continue to pursue cultural change and change its global strategies; he recommended to the board that Kazuo Hirai replace him as president and CEO while he would become chairman. Hirai, Sony's youngest CEO ever, is fluent in English, has extensive overseas experience, and was not part of Sony's old culture. Hirai has an important advantage over Stringer—a work history that allows him to move effortlessly between Sony's U.S. and Japanese operations. Apparently Stringer, who can't speak Japanese, spent years not realizing many of his directives as CEO were being ignored by the managers of its operating divisions.

Stringer announced that "Kaz is a globally focused executive; I believe his tough-mindedness and leadership skills will be of great benefit to the company and its customers in the months and years ahead."[50] Stringer had appointed Hirai to turn around its struggling gaming division; in 2006, he set about simplifying and outsourcing the manufacture of components, and cut its price by 25%. Hirai pledged to continue to follow Stringer's efforts to streamline costs in all Sony's divisions. Also, he promised to review Sony's businesses to exit those that are uncompetitive, and to focus on producing a narrower range of advanced digital products. In 2013, Sony amanced its first profitable quarter in six years; perhaps it will be able to compete with Apple and Samsung in the future.

Summary and Review

WHAT IS THE GLOBAL ENVIRONMENT? The global environment is the set of forces and conditions that operate beyond an organization's boundaries but affect a manager's ability to acquire and use resources. The global environment has two components: the task environment and the general environment. **[LO 4-1]**

THE TASK ENVIRONMENT The task environment is the set of forces and conditions that originate with global suppliers, distributors, customers, and competitors and influence managers daily. The opportunities and threats associated with forces in the task environment become more complex as a company expands globally. **[LO 4-2, 4-3]**

THE GENERAL ENVIRONMENT The general environment comprises wide-ranging global economic, technological, sociocultural, demographic, political, and legal forces that affect an organization and its task environment. **[LO 4-2, 4-3]**

THE CHANGING GLOBAL ENVIRONMENT In recent years there has been a marked shift toward a more open global environment in which capital flows more freely as people and companies search for new opportunities to create profit and wealth. This has hastened the process of globalization. Globalization is the set of specific and general forces that work together to integrate and connect economic, political, and social systems across countries, cultures, or geographic regions so that nations become increasingly interdependent and similar. The process of globalization has been furthered by declining barriers to international trade and investment and declining barriers of distance and culture. **[LO 4-4, 4-5]**

Management *in Action*

TOPICS FOR DISCUSSION AND ACTION

Discussion

1. Why is it important for managers to understand the forces in the global environment that are acting on them and their organizations? **[LO 4-1]**

2. Which organization is likely to face the most complex task environment—a biotechnology company trying to develop a cure for cancer or a large retailer like The Gap or Macy's? Why? **[LO 4-2, 4-3]**

3. The population is aging because of declining birth rates, declining death rates, and the aging of the baby boom generation. What might some of the implications of

this demographic trend be for (a) a pharmaceutical company and (b) the home construction industry? **[LO 4-1, 4-2, 4-3]**

4. How do political, legal, and economic forces shape national culture? What characteristics of national culture do you think have the most important effect on how successful a country is in doing business abroad? **[LO 4-3, 4-5]**

5. After the passage of NAFTA, many U.S. companies shifted production operations to Mexico to take advantage of lower labor costs and lower standards for environmental and worker protection. As a result, they cut their costs and

were better able to survive in an increasingly competitive global environment. Was their behavior ethical—that is, did the ends justify the means? **[LO 4-4]**

Action

6. Choose an organization, and ask a manager in that organization to list the number and strengths of forces in the organization's task environment. Ask the manager to pay particular attention to identifying opportunities and threats that result from pressures and changes in customers, competitors, and suppliers. **[LO 4-1, 4-2, 4-3]**

BUILDING MANAGEMENT SKILLS **[LO 4-1, 4-2, 4-3]**

Analyzing an Organization's Environment

Pick an organization with which you are familiar. It can be an organization in which you have worked or currently work or one that you interact with regularly as a customer (such as the college you are attending). For this organization do the following:

1. Describe the main forces in the global task environment that are affecting the organization.

2. Describe the main forces in the global general

environment that are affecting the organization.

3. Explain how environmental forces affect the job of an individual manager within this organization. How do they

determine the opportunities and threats that its managers must confront?

MANAGING ETHICALLY [LO 4-4, 4-5]

In recent years the number of U.S. companies that buy their inputs from low-cost overseas suppliers has been growing, and concern about the ethics associated with employing young children in factories has been increasing. In Pakistan and India, children as young as six years old work long hours to make rugs and carpets for export to Western countries or clay bricks for local use. In countries like Malaysia and in Central America, children and teenagers routinely work long hours in factories and sweatshops to produce the clothing that is found in most U.S. discount and department stores.

Questions

1. Either by yourself or in a group, discuss whether it is ethical to employ children in factories and whether U.S. companies should buy and sell products made by these children. What are some arguments for and against child labor?

2. If child labor is an economic necessity, what methods could be employed to make it as ethical a practice as possible? Or is it simply unethical?

SMALL GROUP BREAKOUT EXERCISE [LO 4-1, 4-2]

How to Enter the Copying Business

Form groups of three to five people, and appoint one group member as the spokesperson who will communicate your findings to the whole class when called on by the instructor. Then discuss the following scenario:

You and your partners have decided to open a small printing and copying business in a college town of 100,000 people. Your business will compete with companies like FedEx Kinko's. You know that over 50% of small businesses fail in their first year, so to increase your chances of success, you have decided to perform a detailed analysis of the task environment of the copying business to discover what opportunities and threats you will encounter.

1. Decide what you must know about (a) your future customers, (b) your future competitors, and (c) other critical forces in the task environment if you are to be successful.

2. Evaluate the main barriers to entry into the copying business.

3. Based on this analysis, list some steps you would take to help your new copying business succeed.

BE THE MANAGER [LO 4-1, 4-2]

The Changing Environment of Retailing

You are the new manager of a major clothing store that is facing a crisis. This clothing store has been the leader in its market for the last 15 years. In the last three years, however, two other major clothing store chains have opened, and they have steadily been attracting customers away from your store—your sales are down 30%. To find out why, your store surveyed former customers and learned that they perceive your store as not keeping up with changing fashion trends and new forms of customer service. In examining how the store operates, you found out that the 10 purchasing managers who buy the clothing and accessories for the store have been buying from the same clothing suppliers and have become reluctant to try new ones. Moreover, salespeople rarely, if ever, make suggestions for changing how the store operates, and they don't respond to customer requests; the culture of the store has become conservative and risk-averse.

Questions

1. Analyze the major forces in the task environment of a retail clothing store.

2. Devise a program that will help other managers and employees to better understand and respond to their store's task environment.

BLOOMBERG BUSINESSWEEK CASE IN THE NEWS [LO 4-1, 4-2, 4-3, 4-4]
How Samsung Became the World's No. 1 Smartphone Maker

I'm in a black Mercedes-Benz van with three Samsung Electronics PR people heading toward Yongin, a city about 45 minutes south of Seoul. Yongin is South Korea's Orlando: a nondescript, fast-growing city known for its tourist attractions, especially Everland Resort, the country's largest theme park. But the van isn't going to Everland. We're headed to a far more profitable theme park: the Samsung Human Resources Development Center, where the theme just happens to be Samsung.

The complex's formal name is Changjo Kwan, which translates as Creativity Institute. It's a massive structure with a traditional Korean roof, set in parklike surroundings. In a breezeway, a map carved in stone tiles divides the earth into two categories: countries where Samsung conducts business, indicated by blue lights; and countries where Samsung will conduct business, indicated by red. The map is mostly blue. In the lobby, an engraving in Korean and English proclaims: "We will devote our human resources and technology to create superior products and services, thereby contributing to a better global society." Another sign says in English: "Go! Go! Go!"

More than 50,000 employees pass through Changjo Kwan and its sister facilities in a given year. In sessions that last anywhere from a few days to several months, they are inculcated in all things Samsung: They learn about the three P's (products, process, and people); they learn about "global management" so that Samsung can expand into new markets; some employees go through the exercise of making kimchi together, to learn about teamwork and Korean culture. Samsung's internal practices and external strategies—from how TVs are designed to the company's philosophy of "perpetual crisis"—all spring from the codified teachings of Lee Kun Hee, the 71-year-old chairman of Samsung Electronics. Since Lee took control of Samsung in 1987, sales have surged to over $175 billion, making it the world's largest electronics company. In 1993, Chairman Lee gathered his lieutenants and laid out a plan to transform Samsung, then a second-tier TV manufacturer, into the biggest, most powerful electronics manufacturer on earth. Today, Samsung is dominant in TVs and sells a lot of washing machines, but it's smartphones that made Samsung as recognizable a presence around the world.

Samsung Electronics is the largest part of Samsung, a conglomerate that accounts for 17 percent of South Korea's gross domestic product. It employs 370,000 people in more than 80 countries. Consider the disciplined way Samsung Electronics moves into new product categories, the first step is to start small: make a key component for that industry. Ideally the component will be something that costs a lot of money to manufacture, since costly barriers to entry help limit competition, such as microprocessors and memory chips facilities. Once the facilities are in place Samsung begins selling its components to other companies. This gives the company insight into how the industry works. When Samsung decides to expand operations and start competing with the companies it has been supplying, it makes massive investments in facilities and technologies, leveraging its foothold into a position that other companies have little chance of matching. Last year, Samsung Electronics devoted $21.5 billion to capital expenditures, more than twice what Apple spent in the same period. In 1991, Samsung started making LCD panels it sold to other television brands. In 1994 it started making flash memory for devices such as the iPod and smartphones. Samsung is now the No. 1 maker of LCD televisions and sells more flash memory and RAM chips than any other company in the world. And in 2012 it passed Nokia (NOK) to become the world's largest mobile-phone manufacturer. As Samsung has risen, others have failed, often in spectacular fashion: Motorola was split up and its handset business sold to Google. Nokia watched its long-standing No. 1 position erode when it got blindsided by smartphones. When it comes to mobile hardware, today there's only Apple, Samsung, and a desperate crowd of brands that can't seem to rise above being called "just average."

Such striving for efficiency and excellence wasn't always a priority. In 1995, Chairman Lee was dismayed to learn that cell phones he gave as New Year's gifts were found to be inoperable. He directed underlings to assemble a pile of 150,000 devices in a field outside the Gumi factory. More than 2,000 staff members gathered around the pile. Then it was set on fire. When the flames died down, bulldozers razed whatever was remaining. "If you continue to make poor-quality products like these," Lee Keon Hyok recalls the chairman saying, "I'll come back and do the same thing." The lesson stuck. In May 2012, three weeks before the new Galaxy S III was to be shipped, a Samsung customer told the company that the back covers for the smartphone looked cheaper than the demo models shown to clients earlier. "He was right," says DJ Lee, the marketing chief of Samsung Mobile. "The grain wasn't as fine on the later models." There were 100,000 covers in the warehouse with the inferior design, as well as shipments of the assembled devices waiting at airports. This time, there would be no bonfire—all 100,000 covers, as well as those on the units at the airports, were scrapped and replaced.

In 2010, Samsung introduced the Galaxy S line based on the momentous decision to use bigger screens. The Galaxy S's screen was significantly larger than the original Galaxy and other Android models. "We settled on a 4-inch screen, which people thought was too big," says DJ Lee. "There was a lot of argument about that." But the bigger screens proved to be a major selling point; they grew larger still on the Galaxy S II and S III. Now, Samsung smartphones come in sizes ranging from 2.8 inches to 5 inches (to say nothing of the company's "phablets," which go up to 5.5). "Nobody had any idea what the right screen size was, so Samsung made all of them and saw which one worked," says Benedict Evans, a researcher at Enders Analysis. "When we released the Galaxy S III, our research showed that, for some people in some markets, the handset was too big," says DJ Lee. "So we were able to create the same phone with a 4-inch screen, and we called it the Galaxy S III mini." Getting the smaller device into production took about four to six months, says DJ Lee. "We watch the market, and we immediately respond," he says; the Galaxy S 4 came out only nine months after the GS3.

"Samsung has taken differentiation to a new art," says Michael Gartenberg, an analyst at Gartner (IT). "If I want something in between an iPad and an iPad mini, I can't get that from Apple." Maybe iPhones 6, 7, and 8 will prove so beautiful and compelling, not even Samsung will have an answer. A likelier scenario is that another company, probably from China, will do to Samsung what it has done to its competitors. "The Chinese look like Samsung did five years ago," says Horace Dediu, an independent mobile analyst. He identifies Huawei and ZTE as particular threats (other analysts bring up Lenovo). "Samsung makes less profit per smartphone than Apple," Dediu continues. "The Chinese make even less. If the smartphone is going to become a commodity, how does Samsung play in that game?"

When the mobile business ceases to be profitable, Samsung will have to force its way into some other industry that requires a lot of upfront capital and expertise in mass-manufacturing. The company announced in late 2011 that it would spend $20 billion by 2020 to develop proficiencies in medical devices, solar panels, LED lighting, biotech, and batteries for electric cars. And if Samsung batteries or MRI machines don't take over the market, maybe the chairman will set a huge pile of them on fire. "The chairman is saying all the time, 'This is perpetual crisis,'" says mobile marketing chief DJ Lee. "We are in danger. We are in jeopardy."

Questions

1. What is Samsung's approach toward managing the global environment?

2. What kinds of strategies did Samsung use to become the global leader in the smartphone industry?

3. Search the Internet. Is Samsung still the global leader? Why? How have Apple and other smartphone makers changed their global strategies to better compete with Samsung?

Source: Sam Grobart and Jungah Lee, "How Samsung Became the World's No. 1 Smartphone Maker," *Bloomberg Businessweek,* www.business.com, accessed March 28, 2013.

5 Decision Making, Learning, Creativity, and Entrepreneurship

LEARNING OBJECTIVES

After studying this chapter, you should be able to:

1 Understand the nature of managerial decision making, differentiate between programmed and nonprogrammed decisions, and explain why nonprogrammed decision making is a complex, uncertain process. **[LO 5-1]**

2 Describe the six steps managers should take to make the best decisions, and explain how cognitive biases can lead managers to make poor decisions. **[LO 5-2]**

3 Identify the advantages and disadvantages of group decision making, and describe techniques that can improve it. **[LO 5-3]**

4 Explain the role that organizational learning and creativity play in helping managers to improve their decisions. **[LO 5-4]**

5 Describe how managers can encourage and promote entrepreneurship to create a learning organization, and differentiate between entrepreneurs and intrapreneurs. **[LO 5-5]**

GarageTek franchises design and install custom garage systems like this one.

Decision Making and Learning at GarageTek

Why Is Decision Making and Learning of Utmost Importance for Entrepreneurs and Managers?

All managers must make decisions day in and day out under considerable uncertainty. And sometimes those decisions come back to haunt them if they turn out poorly. Sometimes, even highly effective managers make bad decisions. Other times, factors beyond a manager's control, such as unforeseen changes in the environment, cause a good decision to result in unexpected negative consequences. Effective managers recognize the critical importance of making decisions on an ongoing basis as well as learning from prior decisions.

Decision making has been an ongoing challenge for Marc Shuman, founder and president of GarageTek, headquartered in Melville, New York.[1] Since founding his company less than 15 years ago,[2] he has met this challenge time and time again, recognizing when decisions need to be made and learning from feedback about prior decisions.

Shuman was working with his father in a small business, designing and building interiors of department stores, when he created and installed a series of wall panels with flexible shelving for a store to display its merchandise. When he realized that some of his employees were using the same concept in their own homes to organize the clutter in their basements and garages, he recognized that he had a potential opportunity to start a new business, GarageTek, designing and installing custom garage systems to organize and maximize storage capacities and uses for home garage space.[3] A strong housing market at the time, the popularity of closet organizing systems, and the recognition that many people's lives were getting busier and more complicated led him to believe that homeowners would be glad to pay someone to design and install a system that would help them gain control over some of the clutter in their lives.[4]

Shuman decided to franchise his idea because he feared that other entrepreneurs were probably having similar thoughts and competition could be around the corner.[5] Within three years GarageTek had 57 franchises in 33 states, contributing revenues to the home office of around $12 million. While this would seem to be an enviable track record of success, Shuman recognized that although many of the franchises were succeeding, some were having serious problems. With the help of a consulting company, Shuman and home office managers set about trying to figure out why some franchises were failing. They gathered detailed information about each franchise: the market served, pricing strategies, costs, managerial talent, and franchisee investment. From this information, Shuman learned that the struggling franchises tended either to have lower levels of capital investment behind them or to be managed by nonowners.[6]

Shuman learned from this experience. He now has improved decision criteria for accepting new franchisees to help ensure that their investments of time and money lead to a successful franchise.[7] Shuman also decided to give new franchisees much more training and support than he had in the past. New franchisees now receive two weeks of training at the home office that culminates in their preparing a one-year marketing and business plan;[8] on-site assistance in sales, marketing, and operations; a multivolume training manual; a sales and marketing kit; and access to databases and GarageTek's intranet. Franchisees learn from each other through monthly conference calls and regional and national meetings.[9]

By 2013, GarageTek had franchises covering 60 markets in the United States and also had expanded overseas into the United Kingdom, Australia, New Zealand, South Africa, and Russia.[10] And Shuman continues to make decisions day in and day out; in his words, "We're not, by any stretch, done."[11]

Overview

The "Management Snapshot" illustrates how decision making and learning from prior decisions are an ongoing challenge for managers that can have a profound influence on organizational effectiveness. Shuman's decision to seize an opportunity and start GarageTek and his subsequent decisions along the way have had a profound effect on his business. The decisions managers make at all levels in companies large and small can have a dramatic impact on the growth and prosperity of these companies and the well-being of their employees, customers, and other stakeholders. Yet such decisions can be difficult to make because they are fraught with uncertainty.

In this chapter we examine how managers make decisions, and we explore how individual, group, and organizational factors affect the quality of the decisions they make and ultimately determine organizational performance. We discuss the nature of managerial decision making and examine some models of the decision-making process that help reveal the complexities of successful decision making. Then we outline the main steps of the decision-making process. Next we examine how managers can promote organizational learning and creativity and improve the quality of decision making throughout an organization. Finally we discuss the important role of entrepreneurship in promoting organizational creativity, and we differentiate between entrepreneurs and intrapreneurs. By the end of this chapter you will appreciate the critical role of management decision making in creating a high-performing organization.

LO 5-1 Understand the nature of managerial decision making, differentiate between programmed and nonprogrammed decisions, and explain why nonprogrammed decision making is a complex, uncertain process.

The Nature of Managerial Decision Making

Every time managers act to plan, organize, direct, or control organizational activities, they make a stream of decisions. In opening a new restaurant, for example, managers have to decide where to locate it, what kinds of food to provide, which people to employ, and so on. Decision making is a basic part of every task managers perform.

As we discussed in the previous chapter, one of the main tasks facing a manager is to manage the organizational environment. Forces in the external environment give rise to many opportunities and threats for managers and their organizations. In addition, inside an organization managers must

decision making
The process by which managers respond to opportunities and threats by analyzing options and making determinations about specific organizational goals and courses of action.

address many opportunities and threats that may arise as organizational resources are used. To deal with these opportunities and threats, managers must make decisions—that is, they must select one solution from a set of alternatives. Decision making is the process by which managers respond to opportunities and threats by analyzing the options and making determinations, or *decisions*, about specific organizational goals and courses of action. Good decisions result in the selection of appropriate goals and courses of action that increase organizational performance; bad decisions lower performance.

Decision making in response to opportunities occurs when managers search for ways to improve organizational performance to benefit customers, employees, and other stakeholder groups. In the "Management Snapshot," Marc Shuman seized the opportunities to start his own business and expand internationally. *Decision making in response to threats* occurs when events inside or outside the organization adversely affect organizational performance and managers search for ways to increase performance.[12] When his company was in its early years, Shuman realized that some of his franchisees were having problems and he made a series of decisions to rectify matters.[13] Decision making is central to being a manager, and whenever managers engage in planning, organizing, leading, and controlling—their four principal tasks—they are constantly making decisions.

Managers are always searching for ways to make better decisions to improve organizational performance. At the same time they do their best to avoid costly mistakes that will hurt organizational performance. Examples of spectacularly good decisions include Martin Cooper's decision to develop the first cell phone at Motorola and Apple's decision to develop the iPod.[14] Examples of spectacularly bad decisions include the decision by managers at NASA and Morton Thiokol to launch the *Challenger* space shuttle—a decision that killed six astronauts in 1986—and the decision by NASA to launch the *Columbia* space shuttle in 2003, which killed seven astronauts.

programmed decision making
Routine, virtually automatic decision making that follows established rules or guidelines.

Programmed and Nonprogrammed Decision Making

Regardless of the specific decisions a manager makes, the decision-making process is either programmed or nonprogrammed.[15]

Programmed decisions allow warehouse supervisors such as this one to develop simple rubrics so the job is done consistently and with less error.

PROGRAMMED DECISION MAKING Programmed decision making is a *routine*, virtually automatic process. Programmed decisions are decisions that have been made so many times in the past that managers have developed rules or guidelines to be applied when certain situations inevitably occur. Programmed decision making takes place when a school principal asks the school board to hire a new teacher whenever student enrollment increases by 40 students; when a manufacturing supervisor hires new workers whenever existing workers' overtime increases by more than 10%; and when an office manager orders basic office supplies, such as paper and pens, whenever the inventory of supplies drops below a certain level. Furthermore, in the last example, the office manager probably orders the same amount of supplies each time.

This decision making is called *programmed* because office managers, for example, do not need to repeatedly make new judgments about what should be done. They can rely on long-established decision rules such as these:

- *Rule 1:* When the storage shelves are three-quarters empty, order more copy paper.
- *Rule 2:* When ordering paper, order enough to fill the shelves.

Managers can develop rules and guidelines to regulate all routine organizational activities. For example, rules can specify how a worker should perform a certain task, and rules can specify the quality standards that raw materials must meet to be acceptable. Most decision making that relates to the day-to-day running of an organization is programmed decision making. Examples include deciding how much inventory to hold, when to pay bills, when to bill customers, and when to order materials and supplies. Programmed decision making occurs when managers have the information they need to create rules that will guide decision making. There is little ambiguity involved in assessing when the stockroom is empty or counting the number of new students in class.

NONPROGRAMMED DECISION MAKING Suppose, however, managers are not certain that a course of action will lead to a desired outcome. Or in even more ambiguous terms, suppose managers are not even sure what they are trying to achieve. Obviously rules cannot be developed to predict uncertain events.

Nonprogrammed decision making is required for these *nonroutine* decisions. Nonprogrammed decisions are made in response to unusual or novel opportunities and threats. Nonprogrammed decision making occurs when there are no ready-made decision rules that managers can apply to a situation. Rules do not exist because the situation is unexpected or uncertain and managers lack the information they would need to develop rules to cover it. Examples of nonprogrammed decision making include decisions to invest in a new technology, develop a new kind of product, launch a new promotional campaign, enter a new market, expand internationally, or start a new business as did Marc Shuman in the "Management Snapshot."

nonprogrammed decision making
Nonroutine decision making that occurs in response to unusual, unpredictable opportunities and threats.

intuition Feelings, beliefs, and hunches that come readily to mind, require little effort and information gathering, and result in on-the-spot decisions.

reasoned judgment
A decision that requires time and effort and results from careful information gathering, generation of alternatives, and evaluation of alternatives.

Nonprogrammed decision making covers areas with no previous benchmarks or rubrics, such as seen in this photo.

How do managers make decisions in the absence of decision rules? They may rely on their intuition—feelings, beliefs, and hunches that come readily to mind, require little effort and information gathering, and result in on-the-spot decisions.[16] Or they may make reasoned judgments—decisions that require time and effort and result from careful information gathering, generation of alternatives, and evaluation of alternatives. "Exercising" one's judgment is a more rational process than "going with" one's intuition. For reasons that we examine later in this chapter, both intuition and judgment often are flawed and can result in poor decision making. Thus the likelihood of error is much greater in nonprogrammed decision making than in programmed decision making.[17] In the remainder of this chapter, when we talk about decision making, we are referring to *nonprogrammed* decision making because it causes the most problems for managers and is inherently challenging.

Sometimes managers have to make rapid decisions and don't have time to carefully consider the issues involved. They must rely on their intuition to quickly respond to a pressing concern. For example, when fire chiefs, captains, and lieutenants manage firefighters battling dangerous, out-of-control fires, they often need to rely on their expert intuition to make on-the-spot decisions that will protect the lives of the firefighters and save the lives of others, contain the fires, and preserve property—decisions made in emergency situations entailing high uncertainty, high risk, and rapidly changing conditions.[18] In other cases managers do have time to make reasoned judgments, but there are no established rules to guide their decisions, such as when deciding whether to proceed with a proposed merger.

Regardless of the circumstances, making nonprogrammed decisions can result in effective or ineffective decision making. As indicated in the following "Manager as a Person," managers have to be on their guard to avoid being overconfident in decisions that result from either intuition or reasoned judgment.

MANAGER AS A PERSON

Curbing Overconfidence

Should managers be confident in their intuition and reasoned judgments?[19] Decades of research by Nobel Prize winner Daniel Kahneman, his longtime collaborator the late Amos Tversky, and other researchers suggests that managers (like all people) tend to be overconfident in the decisions they make, whether based on intuition or reasoned judgment.[20] And with overconfidence comes failure to evaluate and rethink the wisdom of the decisions one makes and failure to learn from mistakes.[21]

Kahneman distinguishes between the intuition of managers who are truly expert in the content domain of a decision and the intuition of managers who have some knowledge and experience but are not true experts.[22] Although the intuition of both types can be faulty, that of experts is less likely to be flawed. This is why fire captains can make good decisions and why expert chess players can make good moves, in both cases without spending much time or deliberating carefully on what, for nonexperts, is a complicated set of circumstances. What distinguishes expert managers from those with limited expertise is that the experts have extensive experience under conditions in which they receive quick and clear feedback about the outcomes of their decisions.[23]

Unfortunately managers who have some experience in a content area but are not true experts tend to be overly confident in their intuition and their judgments.[24] As Kahneman puts it, "People jump to statistical conclusions on the basis of very weak evidence. We form powerful intuitions about trends and about the replicability of results on the basis of information that is truly inadequate."[25] Not only do managers, and all people, tend to be overconfident about their intuition and judgments, but they also tend not to learn from mistakes. Compounding this undue optimism is the human tendency to be overconfident in one's own abilities and influence over unpredictable events. Surveys have found that the majority of people think they are above average, make better decisions, and are less prone to making bad decisions than others (of course it is impossible for most people to be above average on any dimension).[26]

Examples of managerial overconfidence abound. Research has consistently found that mergers tend to turn out poorly—postmerger profitability declines, stock prices drop, and so forth. For example, Chrysler had the biggest profits of the three largest automakers in the United States when it merged with Daimler; the merger was a failure and both Chrysler and Daimler would have been better off if it never had happened.[27] One would imagine that top executives and boards of directors would learn from this research and from articles in the business press about the woes of merged companies (such as the AOL–Time Warner merger and the Hewlett-Packard–Compaq merger).[28] Evidently not. Top managers seem to overconfidently believe that they can succeed where others have failed.[29] Similarly, whereas fewer than 35% of new small ventures succeed as viable businesses for more than five years, entrepreneurs, on average, tend to think that they have a 6 out of 10 chance of being successful.[30]

Jeffrey Pfeffer, a professor at Stanford University's Graduate School of Business, suggests that managers can avoid the perils of overconfidence by critically evaluating the decisions they have made and the outcomes of those decisions. They should admit to themselves when they have made a mistake and really learn from their mistakes (rather than dismissing them as flukes or situations out of their control). In addition, managers should be leery of too much agreement at the top. As Pfeffer puts it, "If two people agree all the time, one of them is redundant."[31]

The classical and administrative decision-making models reveal many of the assumptions, complexities, and pitfalls that affect decision making. These models help reveal the factors that managers and other decision makers must be aware of to improve the quality of their decision making. Keep in mind, however, that the classical and administrative models are just guides that can help managers understand the decision-making process. In real life the process is typically not cut-and-dried, but these models can help guide a manager through it.

The Classical Model

One of the earliest models of decision making, the classical model, is *prescriptive,* which means it specifies how decisions *should* be made. Managers using the classical model make a series of simplifying assumptions about the nature of the decision-making process (see Figure 5.1). The premise of the classical model is that once managers recognize the need to make a decision, they should be able to generate a complete list of *all* alternatives and consequences and make the best choice. In other words, the classical model assumes managers have access to *all* the information they need to make the optimum decision, which is the most appropriate decision possible in light of what they believe to be the most desirable consequences for the organization. Furthermore, the classical model assumes managers can easily list their own preferences for each alternative and rank them from least to most preferred to make the optimum decision.

The Administrative Model

James March and Herbert Simon disagreed with the underlying assumptions of the classical model of decision making. In contrast, they proposed that managers in the real world do *not* have access to all the information they need to make a

Figure 5.1

The Classical Model of Decision Making

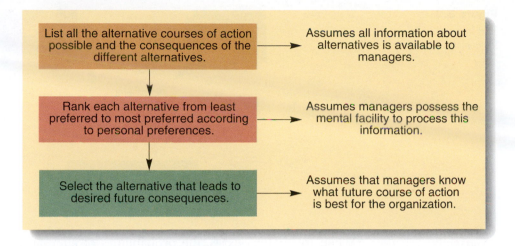

decision. Moreover, they pointed out that even if all information were readily available, many managers would lack the mental or psychological ability to absorb and evaluate it correctly. As a result, March and Simon developed the administrative model of decision making to explain why decision making is always an inherently uncertain and risky process—and why managers can rarely make decisions in the manner prescribed by the classical model. The administrative model is based on three important concepts: *bounded rationality, incomplete information,* and *satisficing.*

BOUNDED RATIONALITY March and Simon pointed out that human decision-making capabilities are bounded by people's cognitive limitations—that is, limitations in their ability to interpret, process, and act on information.[32] They argued that the limitations of human intelligence constrain the ability of decision makers to determine the optimum decision. March and Simon coined the term bounded rationality to describe the situation in which the number of alternatives a manager must identify is so great and the amount of information so vast that it is difficult for the manager to even come close to evaluating it all before making a decision.[33]

INCOMPLETE INFORMATION Even if managers had unlimited ability to evaluate information, they still would not be able to arrive at the optimum decision because they would have incomplete information. Information is incomplete because the full range of decision-making alternatives is unknowable in most situations, and the consequences associated with known alternatives are uncertain.[34] In other words, information is incomplete because of risk and uncertainty, ambiguity, and time constraints (see Figure 5.2).

RISK AND UNCERTAINTY As we saw in Chapter 4, forces in the organizational environment are constantly changing. Risk is present when managers know the possible outcomes of a particular course of action and can assign probabilities to them. For example, managers in the biotechnology industry know that new drugs have a 10% probability of successfully passing advanced clinical trials and a 90% probability of failing. These probabilities reflect the experiences of thousands of drugs that have gone through advanced clinical trials. Thus when managers in the biotechnology industry decide to submit a drug for testing, they know that there is only a 10% chance that the drug will succeed, but at least they have some information on which to base their decision.

---

administrative model An approach to decision making that explains why decision making is inherently uncertain and risky and why managers usually make satisfactory rather than optimum decisions.

bounded rationality Cognitive limitations that constrain one's ability to interpret, process, and act on information.

risk The degree of probability that the possible outcomes of a particular course of action will occur.

Figure 5.2

Why Information Is
Incomplete

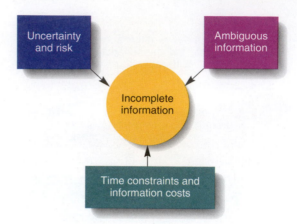

When **uncertainty** Unpredictability.

When **uncertainty** exists, the probabilities of alternative outcomes *cannot* be determined and future outcomes are *unknown*. Managers are working blind. Because the probability of a given outcome occurring is not known, managers have little information to use in making a decision. For example, in 1993, when Apple Computer introduced the Newton, its personal digital assistant (PDA), managers had no idea what the probability of a successful product launch for a PDA might be. Because Apple was the first to market this totally new product, there was no body of well-known data that Apple's managers could draw on to calculate the probability of a successful launch. Uncertainty plagues most managerial decision making.[35] Although Apple's initial launch of its PDA was a disaster due to technical problems, an improved version was more successful.

ambiguous information
Information that can be interpreted in multiple and often conflicting ways.

Ambiguous Information   A second reason why information is incomplete is that much of the information managers have at their disposal is ambiguous information. Its meaning is not clear—it can be interpreted in multiple and often conflicting ways.[36] Take a look at Figure 5.3. Do you see a young woman or an old woman? In a similar fashion, managers often interpret the same piece of information differently and make decisions based on their own interpretations.

Figure 5.3

Ambiguous Information:
Young Woman or Old
Woman?

Time Constraints and Information Costs   The third reason why information is incomplete is that managers have neither the time nor the money to search for all possible alternative solutions and evaluate all the potential consequences of those alternatives. Consider the situation confronting a Ford Motor Company purchasing manager who has one month to choose a supplier for a small engine part. There are 20,000 potential suppliers for this part in the United States alone. Given the time available, the purchasing manager cannot contact all potential suppliers and ask each for its terms (price, delivery schedules, and so on). Moreover, even if the time were available, the costs of obtaining the information, including the manager's own time, would be prohibitive.

SATISFICING   March and Simon argued that managers do not attempt to discover every alternative when faced with bounded rationality, an uncertain future, unquantifiable risks, considerable ambiguity, time constraints, and high information costs. Rather, they use a strategy known as satisficing, which is exploring a limited sample of all potential alternatives.[37] When managers satisfice, they search for and choose acceptable, or satisfactory, ways to respond to problems and opportunities rather than trying to make the optimal decision.[38] In the case of the Ford purchasing manager's search, for example, satisficing may involve asking a limited number of suppliers for their terms, trusting that they are representative of suppliers in general, and making a choice from that set. Although this course of action is reasonable from the perspective of the purchasing manager, it may mean that a potentially superior supplier is overlooked.

March and Simon pointed out that managerial decision making is often more art than science. In the real world, managers must rely on their intuition and judgment to make what seems to them to be the best decision in the face of uncertainty and ambiguity.[39] Moreover, managerial decision making is often fast-paced; managers use their experience and judgment to make crucial decisions under conditions of incomplete information. Although there is nothing wrong with this approach, decision makers should be aware that human judgment is often flawed. As a result, even the best managers sometimes make poor decisions.[40]

> **satisficing** Searching for and choosing an acceptable, or satisfactory, response to problems and opportunities, rather than trying to make the best decision.

Steps in the Decision-Making Process

Using the work of March and Simon as a basis, researchers have developed a step-by-step model of the decision-making process and the issues and problems that managers confront at each step. Perhaps the best way to introduce this model is to examine the real-world nonprogrammed decision making of Scott McNealy at a crucial point in Sun Microsystems' history. McNealy was a founder of Sun Microsystems and was the chairman of the board of directors until Sun was acquired by Oracle in 2010.[41]

In early August 1985, Scott McNealy, then CEO of Sun Microsystems[42] (a hardware and software computer workstation manufacturer focused on network solutions), had to decide whether to go ahead with the launch of the new Carrera workstation computer, scheduled for September 10. Sun's managers had chosen the date nine months earlier when the development plan for the Carrera was first proposed. McNealy knew it would take at least a month to prepare for the September 10 launch, and the decision could not be put off.

Customers were waiting for the new machine, and McNealy wanted to be the first to provide a workstation that took advantage of Motorola's powerful

> **LO 5.2** Describe the six steps managers should take to make the best decisions, and explain how cognitive biases can lead managers to make poor decisions.

16-megahertz 68020 microprocessor. Capitalizing on this opportunity would give Sun a significant edge over Apollo, its main competitor in the workstation market. McNealy knew, however, that committing to the September 10 launch date was risky. Motorola was having production problems with the 16-megahertz 68020 microprocessor and could not guarantee Sun a steady supply of these chips. Moreover, the operating system software was not completely free of bugs.

If Sun launched the Carrera on September 10, the company might have to ship some machines with software that was not fully operational, was likely to crash the system, and utilized Motorola's less powerful 12-megahertz 68020 microprocessor instead of the 16-megahertz version.[43] Of course Sun could later upgrade the microprocessor and operating system software in any machines purchased by early customers, but the company's reputation would suffer. If Sun did not go ahead with the September launch, the company would miss an important opportunity.[44] Rumors were circulating in the industry that Apollo would be launching a new machine of its own in December.

McNealy clearly had a difficult decision to make. He had to decide quickly whether to launch the Carrera, but he did not have all the facts. He did not know, for example, whether the microprocessor or operating system problems could be resolved by September 10; nor did he know whether Apollo was going to launch a competing machine in December. But he could not wait to find these things out—he had to make a decision. We'll see what he decided later in the chapter.

Many managers who must make important decisions with incomplete information face dilemmas similar to McNealy's. Managers should consciously follow six steps to make a good decision (see Figure 5.4).[45] We review these steps in the remainder of this section.

Recognize the Need for a Decision

The first step in the decision-making process is to recognize the need for a decision. Scott McNealy recognized this need, and he realized a decision had to be made quickly.

Figure 5.4

Six Steps in Decision Making

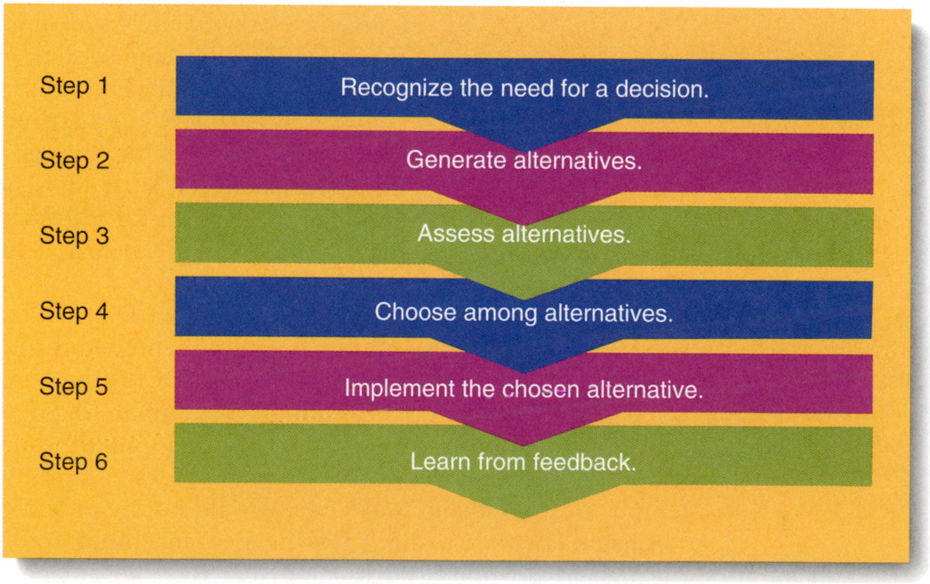

Step 1	Recognize the need for a decision.
Step 2	Generate alternatives.
Step 3	Assess alternatives.
Step 4	Choose among alternatives.
Step 5	Implement the chosen alternative.
Step 6	Learn from feedback.

Some stimuli usually spark the realization that a decision must be made. These stimuli often become apparent because changes in the organizational environment result in new kinds of opportunities and threats. This happened at Sun Microsystems. The September 10 launch date had been set when it seemed that Motorola chips would be readily available. Later, with the supply of chips in doubt and bugs remaining in the system software, Sun was in danger of failing to meet its launch date.

The stimuli that spark decision making are as likely to result from the actions of managers inside an organization as they are from changes in the external environment.[46] An organization possesses a set of skills, competencies, and resources in its employees and in departments such as marketing, manufacturing, and research and development. Managers who actively pursue opportunities to use these competencies create the need to make decisions. Managers thus can be proactive or reactive in recognizing the need to make a decision, but the important issue is that they must recognize this need and respond in a timely and appropriate way.[47]

Generate Alternatives

Having recognized the need to make a decision, a manager must generate a set of feasible alternative courses of action to take in response to the opportunity or threat. Management experts cite failure to properly generate and consider different alternatives as one reason why managers sometimes make bad decisions.[48] In the Sun Microsystems decision, the alternatives seemed clear: to go ahead with the September 10 launch or to delay the launch until the Carrera was 100% ready for market introduction. Often, however, the alternatives are not so obvious or so clearly specified.

One major problem is that managers may find it difficult to come up with creative alternative solutions to specific problems. Perhaps some of them are used to seeing the world from a single perspective—they have a certain "managerial mind-set." Many managers find it difficult to view problems from a fresh perspective. According to best-selling management author Peter Senge, we all are trapped within our personal mental models of the world—our ideas about what is important and how the world works.[49] Generating creative alternatives to solve problems and take advantage of opportunities may require that we abandon our existing mind-sets and develop new ones—something that usually is difficult to do.

The importance of getting managers to set aside their mental models of the world and generate creative alternatives is reflected in the growth of interest in the work of authors such as Peter Senge and Edward de Bono, who have popularized techniques for stimulating problem solving and creative thinking among managers.[50] Later in this chapter, we discuss the important issues of organizational learning and creativity in detail.

Assess Alternatives

Once managers have generated a set of alternatives, they must evaluate the advantages and disadvantages of each one.[51] The key to a good assessment of the alternatives is to define the opportunity or threat exactly and then specify the criteria that *should* influence the selection of alternatives for responding to the problem or opportunity. One reason for bad decisions is that managers often fail to specify the criteria that are important in reaching a decision.[52] In general, successful managers use four criteria to evaluate the pros and cons of alternative courses of action (see Figure 5.5):

1. *Legality:* Managers must ensure that a possible course of action will not violate any domestic or international laws or government regulations.

Figure 5.5

General Criteria for Evaluating Possible Courses of Action

Is the possible course of action . . .

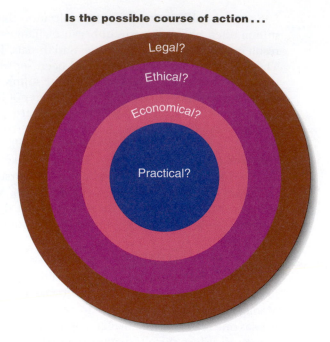

2. *Ethicalness:* Managers must ensure that a possible course of action is ethical and will not unnecessarily harm any stakeholder group. Many decisions managers make may help some organizational stakeholders and harm others (see Chapter 3). When examining alternative courses of action, managers need to be clear about the potential effects of their decisions.

3. *Economic feasibility:* Managers must decide whether the alternatives are economically feasible—that is, whether they can be accomplished given the organization's performance goals. Typically managers perform a cost–benefit analysis of the various alternatives to determine which one will have the best net financial payoff.

4. *Practicality:* Managers must decide whether they have the capabilities and resources required to implement the alternative, and they must be sure the alternative will not threaten the attainment of other organizational goals. At first glance an alternative might seem economically superior to other alternatives; but if managers realize it is likely to threaten other important projects, they might decide it is not practical after all.

Often a manager must consider these four criteria simultaneously. Scott McNealy framed the problem at hand at Sun Microsystems quite well. The key question was whether to go ahead with the September 10 launch date. Two main criteria were influencing McNealy's choice: the need to ship a machine that was as "complete" as possible (the *practicality* criterion) and the need to beat Apollo to market with a new workstation (the *economic feasibility* criterion). These two criteria conflicted. The first suggested that the launch should be delayed; the second, that the launch should go ahead. McNealy's actual choice was based on the relative importance that he assigned to these two criteria. In fact, Sun Microsystems went ahead with the September 10 launch, which suggests that McNealy thought the need to beat Apollo to market was the more important criterion.

Some of the worst managerial decisions can be traced to poor assessment of the alternatives, such as the decision to launch the *Challenger* space shuttle, mentioned earlier. In that case, the desire of NASA and Morton Thiokol managers to demonstrate to the public the success of the U.S. space program in order to ensure future funding (*economic feasibility*) conflicted with the need to ensure the safety of the astronauts (*ethicalness*). Managers deemed the economic criterion more important and decided to launch the space shuttle even though there were unanswered questions about safety. Tragically, some of the same decision-making problems that resulted in the *Challenger* tragedy led to the demise of the *Columbia* space shuttle 17 years later, killing all seven astronauts on board.[53] In both the *Challenger* and the *Columbia* disasters, safety questions were raised before the shuttles were launched; safety concerns took second place to budgets, economic feasibility, and schedules; top decision makers seemed to ignore or downplay the inputs of those with relevant technical expertise; and speaking up was discouraged.[54] Rather than making safety a top priority, decision makers seemed overly concerned with keeping on schedule and within budget.[55]

As indicated in the following "Ethics in Action," in order to help ensure that decisions meet the *ethicalness* criteria, some organizations have created the position of chief sustainability officer.

ETHICS IN ACTION

Helping to Ensure Decisions Contribute to Sustainability

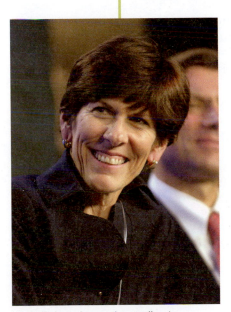

Linda Fisher, shown above, directs DuPont's efforts to ease its impact on the environment, juggling questions of plant waste, carcinogen release, worker safety, and consumer wellness every day.

Some large organizations have added the position of chief sustainability officer to their ranks of top managers reporting to the chief executive officer or chief operating officer. Chief sustainability officers are typically concerned with helping to ensure that decisions that are made in organizations conserve energy and protect the environment.[56] For example, Scott Wicker is the first chief sustainability officer for UPS.[57] Wicker leads a team that presides over a sustainability directors committee and a sustainability working committee focused on developing performance indicators and goals pertaining to sustainability to guide decision making.[58]

Linda Fisher is the vice president of DuPont Safety, Health & Environment and chief sustainability officer at DuPont. Before she joined DuPont, she held a variety of positions related to sustainability, including the position of deputy administrator of the Environmental Protection Agency.[59] Fisher leads efforts at DuPont to make decisions that help to reduce energy consumption, toxins and carcinogens in the air, and greenhouse gas emissions and help DuPont's customers reduce their environmental footprints. Protecting both the environment and human safety is a priority for Fisher and DuPont.[60]

Beatriz Perez is the chief sustainability officer for Coca-Cola, leading a global office of sustainability.[61] While Coca-Cola has 500 different brands yielding 3,500 products, sustainability is a companywide initiative centered around major goals and initiatives.[62] These goals include water conservation and returning to the environment the water that Coca-Cola consumes in making its products, reducing packaging waste and increasing recycling, and protecting the environment from pollution by, for example, using hybrid trucks, having energy efficient manufacturing facilities, and improving the sustainability of refrigeration methods.[63] Clearly, ensuring that decisions contribute to sustainability means much more than simply complying with legal requirements. Having chief sustainability officers with dedicated teams and offices focused on sustainability might be a step in the right direction.

Choose among Alternatives

Once the set of alternative solutions has been carefully evaluated, the next task is to rank the various alternatives (using the criteria discussed in the previous section) and make a decision. When ranking alternatives, managers must be sure *all* the information available is brought to bear on the problem or issue at hand. As the Sun Microsystems case indicates, however, identifying all *relevant* information for a decision does not mean the manager has *complete* information; in most instances, information is incomplete.

Perhaps more serious than the existence of incomplete information is the often-documented tendency of managers to ignore critical information, even when it is available. We discuss this tendency in detail later when we examine the operation of cognitive biases and groupthink.

Implement the Chosen Alternative

Once a decision has been made and an alternative has been selected, it must be implemented, and many subsequent and related decisions must be made. After a course of action has been decided—say, to develop a new line of women's clothing—thousands of subsequent decisions are necessary to implement it. These decisions would involve recruiting dress designers, obtaining fabrics, finding high-quality manufacturers, and signing contracts with clothing stores to sell the new line.

Although the need to make subsequent decisions to implement the chosen course of action may seem obvious, many managers make a decision and then fail to act on it. This is the same as not making a decision at all. To ensure that a decision is implemented, top managers must assign to middle managers the responsibility for making the follow-up decisions necessary to achieve the goal. They must give middle managers sufficient resources to achieve the goal, and they must hold the middle managers accountable for their performance. If the middle managers succeed in implementing the decision, they should be rewarded; if they fail, they should be subject to sanctions.

Learn from Feedback

The final step in the decision-making process is learning from feedback. Effective managers always conduct a retrospective analysis to see what they can learn from past successes or failures. Managers who do not evaluate the results of their decisions do not learn from experience; instead they stagnate and are likely to make the same mistakes again and again.[64] To avoid this problem, managers must establish a formal procedure with which they can learn from the results of past decisions. The procedure should include these steps:

1. Compare what actually happened to what was expected to happen as a result of the decision.
2. Explore why any expectations for the decision were not met.
3. Derive guidelines that will help in future decision making.

Managers who always strive to learn from past mistakes and successes are likely to continuously improve the decisions they make. A significant amount of learning can take place when the outcomes of decisions are evaluated, and this assessment can produce enormous benefits. Learning from feedback is particularly important for entrepreneurs who start their own businesses, as was illustrated in the "Management Snapshot" about GarageTek.

LO 5-3 Identify the advantages and disadvantages of group decision making, and describe techniques that can improve it.

Group Decision Making

When everyone agrees right off the bat, the lack of conflict could be indicative of groupthink.

Many (or perhaps most) important organizational decisions are made by groups or teams of managers rather than by individuals. Group decision making is superior to individual decision making in several respects. When managers work as a team to make decisions and solve problems, their choices of alternatives are less likely to fall victim to the biases and errors discussed previously. They are able to draw on the combined skills, competencies, and accumulated knowledge of group members and thereby improve their ability to generate feasible alternatives and make good decisions. Group decision making also allows managers to process more information and to correct one another's errors. And in the implementation phase, all managers affected by the decisions agree to cooperate. When a group of managers makes a decision (as opposed to one top manager making a decision and imposing it on subordinate managers), the probability that the decision will be implemented successfully increases.

Some potential disadvantages are associated with group decision making. Groups often take much longer than individuals to make decisions. Getting two or more managers to agree to the same solution can be difficult because managers' interests and preferences are often different. In addition, just like decision making by individual managers, group decision making can be undermined by biases. A major source of group bias is *groupthink*.

groupthink

A pattern of faulty and biased decision making that occurs in groups whose members strive for agreement among themselves at the expense of accurately assessing information relevant to a decision.

The Perils of Groupthink

Groupthink is a pattern of faulty and biased decision making that occurs in groups whose members strive for agreement among themselves at the expense of accurately assessing information relevant to a decision.[65] When managers are subject to groupthink, they collectively embark on a course of action without developing appropriate criteria to evaluate alternatives. Typically a group rallies around one central manager, such as the CEO, and the course of action that manager supports. Group members become blindly committed to that course of action without evaluating its merits. Commitment is often based on an emotional, rather than an objective, assessment of the optimal course of action.

The decision President Kennedy and his advisers made to launch the unfortunate Bay of Pigs invasion in Cuba in 1962, the decisions made by President Johnson and his advisers from 1964 to 1967 to escalate the war in Vietnam, the decision made by President Nixon and his advisers in 1972 to cover up the Watergate break-in, and the decision made by NASA and Morton Thiokol in 1986 to launch the ill-fated *Challenger* shuttle—all were likely influenced by groupthink. After the fact, decision makers such as these who may fall victim to groupthink are often surprised that their decision-making process and outcomes were so flawed.

When groupthink occurs, pressures for agreement and harmony within a group have the unintended effect of discouraging individuals from raising issues that run counter to majority opinion. For example, when managers at NASA and Morton Thiokol fell victim to groupthink, they convinced each other that all was well and that there was no need to delay the launch of the *Challenger* space shuttle.

Devil's Advocacy

The existence of groupthink raises the question of how to improve the quality of group and individual decision making so managers make decisions that are realistic and are based on thorough evaluation of alternatives. One technique known to counteract groupthink is devil's advocacy.[66]

devil's advocacy
Critical analysis of a preferred alternative, made in response to challenges raised by a group member who, playing the role of devil's advocate, defends unpopular or opposing alternatives for the sake of argument.

Devil's advocacy is a critical analysis of a preferred alternative to ascertain its strengths and weaknesses before it is implemented.[67] Typically one member of the decision-making group plays the role of devil's advocate. The devil's advocate critiques and challenges the way the group evaluated alternatives and chose one over the others. The purpose of devil's advocacy is to identify all the reasons that might make the preferred alternative unacceptable after all. In this way, decision makers can be made aware of the possible perils of recommended courses of action.

Diversity among Decision Makers

Another way to improve group decision making is to promote diversity in decision-making groups (see Chapter 3).[68] Bringing together managers of both genders from various ethnic, national, and functional backgrounds broadens the range of life experiences and opinions that group members can draw on as they generate, assess, and choose among alternatives. Moreover, diverse groups are sometimes less prone to groupthink because group members already differ from each other and thus are less subject to pressures for uniformity.

LO 5-4 Explain the role that organizational learning and creativity play in helping managers to improve their decisions.

Organizational Learning and Creativity

The quality of managerial decision making ultimately depends on innovative responses to opportunities and threats. How can managers increase their ability to make nonprogrammed decisions that will allow them to adapt to, modify, and even drastically alter their task environments so they can continually increase organizational performance? The answer is by encouraging organizational learning.[69]

organizational learning The process through which managers seek to improve employees' desire and ability to understand and manage the organization and its task environment.

learning organization An organization in which managers try to maximize the ability of individuals and groups to think and behave creatively and thus maximize the potential for organizational learning to take place.

creativity A decision maker's ability to discover original and novel ideas that lead to feasible alternative courses of action.

Organizational learning is the process through which managers seek to improve employees' desire and ability to understand and manage the organization and its task environment so employees can make decisions that continuously raise organizational effectiveness.[70] A learning organization is one in which managers do everything possible to maximize the ability of individuals and groups to think and behave creatively and thus maximize the potential for organizational learning to take place. At the heart of organizational learning is creativity, which is the ability of a decision maker to discover original and novel ideas that lead to feasible alternative courses of action. Encouraging creativity among managers is such a pressing organizational concern that many organizations hire outside experts to help them develop programs to train their managers in the art of creative thinking and problem solving.

Creating a Learning Organization

How do managers go about creating a learning organization? Learning theorist Peter Senge identified five principles for creating a learning organization (see Figure 5.6):[71]

1. For organizational learning to occur, top managers must allow every person in the organization to develop a sense of *personal mastery*. Managers must empower employees and allow them to experiment, create, and explore what they want.

2. As part of attaining personal mastery, organizations need to encourage employees to develop and use *complex mental models*—sophisticated ways of thinking that challenge them to find new or better ways of performing a task—to deepen their understanding of what is involved in a particular activity. Here Senge argued that managers must encourage employees to develop a taste for experimenting and risk taking.[72]

3. Managers must do everything they can to promote group creativity. Senge thought that *team learning* (learning that takes place in a group or team) is more important than individual learning in increasing organizational learning. He pointed out that most important decisions are made in subunits such as groups, functions, and divisions.

4. Managers must emphasize the importance of *building a shared vision*—a common mental model that all organizational members use to frame problems or opportunities.

5. Managers must encourage *systems thinking*. Senge emphasized that to create a learning organization, managers must recognize the effects of one level of

Figure 5.6

Senge's Principles for Creating a Learning Organization

learning on another. Thus, for example, there is little point in creating teams to facilitate team learning if managers do not also take steps to give employees the freedom to develop a sense of personal mastery.

Building a learning organization requires that managers change their management assumptions radically. Developing a learning organization is neither a quick nor an easy process. Senge worked with Ford Motor Company to help managers make Ford a learning organization. Why would Ford want this? Top management believed that to compete successfully Ford must improve its members' ability to be creative and make the right decisions.

Increasingly, managers are being called on to promote global organizational learning. For example, managers at Walmart have used the lessons derived from its failures and successes in one country to promote global organizational learning across the many countries in which it now operates. For instance, when Walmart entered Malaysia, it was convinced customers there would respond to its one-stop shopping format. It found, however, that Malaysians enjoy the social experience of shopping in a lively market or bazaar and thus did not like the impersonal efficiency of the typical Walmart store. As a result, Walmart learned the importance of designing store layouts to appeal specifically to the customers of each country in which it operates.

When purchasing and operating a chain of stores in another country, such as the British ASDA chain, Walmart now strives to retain what customers value in the local market while taking advantage of its own accumulated organizational learning. For example, Walmart improved ASDA's information technology used for inventory and sales tracking in stores and enrolled ASDA in Walmart's global purchasing operations, which has enabled the chain to pay less for certain products, sell them for less, and, overall, significantly increase sales. At the same time Walmart empowered local ASDA managers to run the stores; as the president of ASDA indicates, "This is still essentially a British business in the way it's run day to day."[73] Clearly global organizational learning is essential for companies such as Walmart that have significant operations in multiple countries.

Promoting Individual Creativity

Research suggests that when certain conditions are met, managers are more likely to be creative. People must be given the opportunity and freedom to generate new ideas.[74] Creativity declines when managers look over the shoulders of talented employees and try to "hurry up" a creative solution. How would you feel if your boss said you had one week to come up with a new product idea to beat the competition? Creativity results when employees have an opportunity to experiment, to take risks, and to make mistakes and learn from them. And employees must not fear that they will be looked down on or penalized for ideas that might at first seem outlandish; sometimes those ideas yield truly innovative products and services.[75] Highly innovative companies such as Google, Apple, and Facebook are well known

Get off e-mail and lose the desk! Giving yourself and your employees the time and space to know that contributions off the beaten track are valued increases the ability to think outside the box.

for the wide degree of freedom they give their managers and employees to experiment and develop innovative goods and services.[76]

Once managers have generated alternatives, creativity can be fostered by giving them constructive feedback so they know how well they are doing. Ideas that seem to be going nowhere can be eliminated and creative energies refocused in other directions. Ideas that seem promising can be promoted, and help from other managers can be obtained.[77]

Top managers must stress the importance of looking for alternative solutions and should visibly reward employees who come up with creative ideas. Being creative can be demanding and stressful. Employees who believe they are working on important, vital issues are motivated to put forth the high levels of effort that creativity demands. Creative people like to receive the acclaim of others, and innovative organizations have many kinds of ceremonies and rewards to recognize creative employees.

Employees on the front line are often in a good position to come up with creative ideas for improvements but may be reluctant to speak up or share their ideas. In order to encourage frontline employees to come up with creative ideas and share them, some managers have used contests and rewards.[78] Contests and rewards signal the importance of coming up with creative ideas and encourage employees to share them. Examples of companies that have benefited from contests and rewards for creativity include Hammond's Candies in Denver, Colorado; Borrego Solar Systems in San Diego, California; and Infosurv in Atlanta, Georgia.

Promoting Group Creativity

To encourage creativity at the group level, organizations can use group problem-solving techniques that promote creative ideas and innovative solutions. These techniques can also prevent groupthink and help managers uncover biases. Here we look at three group decision-making techniques: *brainstorming*, the *nominal group technique*, and the *Delphi technique*.

BRAINSTORMING *Brainstorming* is a group problem-solving technique in which managers meet face-to-face to generate and debate a wide variety of alternatives from which to make a decision.[79] Generally from 5 to 15 managers meet in a closed-door session and proceed like this:

- One manager describes in broad outline the problem the group is to address.
- Group members share their ideas and generate alternative courses of action.
- As each alternative is described, group members are not allowed to criticize it; everyone withholds judgment until all alternatives have been heard. One member of the group records the alternatives on a flip chart.
- Group members are encouraged to be as innovative and radical as possible. Anything goes; and the greater the number of ideas put forth, the better. Moreover, group members are encouraged to "piggyback" or build on each other's suggestions.
- When all alternatives have been generated, group members debate the pros and cons of each and develop a short list of the best alternatives.

Brainstorming is very useful in some problem-solving situations—for example, when managers are trying to find a name for a new perfume or car model. But sometimes individuals working alone can generate more alternatives. The main reason for the loss of productivity in brainstorming appears to be

production blocking A loss of productivity in brainstorming sessions due to the unstructured nature of brainstorming.

nominal group technique A decision-making technique in which group members write down ideas and solutions, read their suggestions to the whole group, and discuss and then rank the alternatives.

Delphi technique A decision-making technique in which group members do not meet face-to-face but respond in writing to questions posed by the group leader.

LO 5-5 Describe how managers can encourage and promote entrepreneurship to create a learning organization, and differentiate between entrepreneurs and intrapreneurs.

production blocking, which occurs because group members cannot always simultaneously make sense of all the alternatives being generated, think up additional alternatives, and remember what they were thinking.[80]

NOMINAL GROUP TECHNIQUE To avoid production blocking, the nominal group technique is often used. It provides a more structured way of generating alternatives in writing and gives each manager more time and opportunity to come up with potential solutions. The nominal group technique is especially useful when an issue is controversial and when different managers might be expected to champion different courses of action. Generally a small group of managers meets in a closed-door session and adopts the following procedures:

- One manager outlines the problem to be addressed, and 30 or 40 minutes are allocated for group members, working individually, to write down their ideas and solutions. Group members are encouraged to be innovative.
- Managers take turns reading their suggestions to the group. One manager writes all the alternatives on a flip chart. No criticism or evaluation of alternatives is allowed until all alternatives have been read.
- The alternatives are then discussed, one by one, in the sequence in which they were proposed. Group members can ask for clarifying information and critique each alternative to identify its pros and cons.
- When all alternatives have been discussed, each group member ranks all the alternatives from most preferred to least preferred, and the alternative that receives the highest ranking is chosen.[81]

DELPHI TECHNIQUE Both the nominal group technique and brainstorming require that managers meet to generate creative ideas and engage in joint problem solving. What happens if managers are in different cities or in different parts of the world and cannot meet face-to-face? Videoconferencing is one way to bring distant managers together to brainstorm. Another way is to use the Delphi technique, which is a written approach to creative problem solving.[82] The Delphi technique works like this:

- The group leader writes a statement of the problem and a series of questions to which participating managers are to respond.
- The questionnaire is sent to the managers and departmental experts who are most knowledgeable about the problem. They are asked to generate solutions and mail the questionnaire back to the group leader.
- A team of top managers records and summarizes the responses. The results are then sent back to the participants, with additional questions to be answered before a decision can be made.
- The process is repeated until a consensus is reached and the most suitable course of action is apparent.

Entrepreneurship and Creativity

Entrepreneurs are individuals who notice opportunities and decide how to mobilize the resources necessary to produce new and improved goods and services. Entrepreneurs make all of the planning, organizing, leading, and controlling decisions necessary to start new business ventures. Thus entrepreneurs are an important source of creativity in the organizational

entrepreneur
An individual who notices opportunities and decides how to mobilize the resources necessary to produce new and improved goods and services.

social entrepreneur
An individual who pursues initiatives and opportunities and mobilizes resources to address social problems and needs in order to improve society and well-being through creative solutions.

intrapreneur
A manager, scientist, or researcher who works inside an organization and notices opportunities to develop new or improved products and better ways to make them.

world. These people, such as David Filo and Jerry Yang (founders of Yahoo!), make vast fortunes when their businesses succeed. Or they are among the millions of people who start new business ventures only to lose their money when they fail. Despite the fact that many small businesses fail in the first three to five years, a good portion of men and women in today's workforce want to start their own companies.[83]

Social entrepreneurs are individuals who pursue initiatives and opportunities to address social problems and needs in order to improve society and well-being, such as reducing poverty, increasing literacy, protecting the natural environment, or reducing substance abuse.[84] Social entrepreneurs seek to mobilize resources to solve social problems through creative solutions.[85]

Many managers, scientists, and researchers employed by companies engage in entrepreneurial activity, and they are an important source of organizational creativity. They are involved in innovation, developing new and improved products and ways to make them. Such employees notice opportunities for either quantum or incremental product improvements and are responsible for managing the product development process. These individuals are known as intrapreneurs to distinguish them from entrepreneurs who start their own businesses. But in general, entrepreneurship involves creative decision making that gives customers new or improved goods and services.

There is an interesting relationship between entrepreneurs and intrapreneurs. Many managers with intrapreneurial talents become dissatisfied if their superiors decide neither to support nor to fund new product ideas and development efforts that the managers think will succeed. What do intrapreneurial managers who feel they are getting nowhere do? Often they decide to leave their current organizations and start their own companies to take advantage of their new product ideas! In other words, intrapreneurs become entrepreneurs and found companies that often compete with the companies they left. To avoid losing these individuals, top managers must find ways to facilitate the entrepreneurial spirit of their most creative employees. In the remainder of this section we consider issues involved in promoting successful entrepreneurship in both new and existing organizations.

Entrepreneurship and New Ventures

The fact that a significant number of entrepreneurs were frustrated intrapreneurs provides a clue about the personal characteristics of people who are likely to start a new venture and bear all the uncertainty and risk associated with being an entrepreneur.

CHARACTERISTICS OF ENTREPRENEURS Entrepreneurs are likely to possess a particular set of the personality characteristics we discussed in Chapter 2. First, they are likely to be high on the personality trait of *openness to experience,* meaning they are predisposed to be original, to be open to a wide range of stimuli, to be daring, and to take risks. Entrepreneurs also are likely to have an *internal locus of control,* believing that they are responsible for what happens to them and that their own actions determine important outcomes such as the success or failure of a new business. People with an external locus of control, in contrast, would be unlikely to leave a secure job in an organization and assume the risk associated with a new venture.

Entrepreneurs are likely to have a high level of *self-esteem* and feel competent and capable of handling most situations—including the stress and uncertainty surrounding a plunge into a risky new venture. Entrepreneurs are also likely to have a high *need for achievement* and have a strong desire to perform challenging tasks and meet high personal standards of excellence.

ENTREPRENEURSHIP AND MANAGEMENT Given that entrepreneurs are predisposed to activities that are somewhat adventurous and risky, in what ways can people become involved in entrepreneurial ventures? One way is to start a business from scratch. Taking advantage of modern IT, some people start solo ventures or partnerships.

When people who go it alone succeed, they frequently need to hire other people to help them run the business. Michael Dell, for example, began his computer business as a college student and within weeks had hired several people to help him assemble computers from the components he bought from suppliers. From his solo venture grew Dell Computer.

Some entrepreneurs who start a new business have difficulty deciding how to manage the organization as it grows; entrepreneurship is *not* the same as management. Management encompasses all the decisions involved in planning, organizing, leading, and controlling resources. Entrepreneurship is noticing an opportunity to satisfy a customer need and then deciding how to find and use resources to make a product that satisfies that need. When an entrepreneur has produced something customers want, entrepreneurship gives way to management because the pressing need becomes providing the product both efficiently and effectively. Frequently a founding entrepreneur lacks the skills, patience, and experience to engage in the difficult and challenging work of management. Some entrepreneurs find it hard to delegate authority because they are afraid to risk their company by letting others manage it. As a result they become overloaded and the quality of their decision making declines. Other entrepreneurs lack the detailed knowledge necessary to establish state-of-the-art information systems and technology or to create the operations management procedures that are vital to increase the efficiency of their organizations' production systems. Thus, to succeed, it is necessary to do more than create a new product; an entrepreneur must hire managers who can create an operating system that will let a new venture survive and prosper.

entrepreneurship
The mobilization of resources to take advantage of an opportunity to provide customers with new or improved goods and services.

Intrapreneurs face unique challenges in balancing their championing of new ideas with the company's overall need for stability.

Intrapreneurship and Organizational Learning

The intensity of competition today, particularly from agile small companies, has made it increasingly important for large established organizations to promote and encourage intrapreneurship to raise their level of innovation and organizational learning. As we discussed earlier, a learning organization encourages all employees to identify opportunities and solve problems, thus enabling the organization to continuously experiment, improve, and increase its ability to provide customers with new and improved goods and services. The higher the level of intrapreneurship, the higher will be the level of learning and innovation. How can organizations promote organizational learning and intrapreneurship?

PRODUCT CHAMPIONS One way to promote intrapreneurship is to encourage individuals to assume the role of product champion, a manager who takes "ownership" of a project and provides the leadership and vision that take a product from the idea stage to the final customer. 3M, a company well known for its attempts to promote intrapreneurship, encourages all its managers to become product champions and identify new product ideas. A product champion becomes responsible for developing a business plan for the product. Armed with this business plan, the champion appears before 3M's product development committee, a team of senior 3M managers who probe the strengths and weaknesses of the plan to decide whether it should be funded. If the plan is accepted, the product champion assumes responsibility for product development.

product champion
A manager who takes "ownership" of a project and provides the leadership and vision that take a product from the idea stage to the final customer.

SKUNKWORKS The idea behind the product champion role is that employees who feel ownership for a project are inclined to act like outside entrepreneurs and go to great lengths to make the project succeed. Using skunkworks and new venture divisions can also strengthen this feeling of ownership. A skunkworks is a group of intrapreneurs who are deliberately separated from the normal operation of an organization—for example, from the normal chain of command—to encourage them to devote all their attention to developing new products. The idea is that if these people are isolated, they will become so intensely involved in a project that development time will be relatively brief and the quality of the final product will be enhanced. The term *skunkworks* was coined at the Lockheed Corporation, which formed a team of design engineers to develop special aircraft such as the U2 spy plane. The secrecy with which this unit functioned and speculation about its goals led others to refer to it as "the skunkworks."

skunkworks
A group of intrapreneurs who are deliberately separated from the normal operation of an organization to encourage them to devote all their attention to developing new products.

REWARDS FOR INNOVATION To encourage managers to bear the uncertainty and risk associated with the hard work of entrepreneurship, it is necessary to link performance to rewards. Increasingly companies are rewarding intrapreneurs on the basis of the outcome of the product development process. Intrapreneurs are paid large bonuses if their projects succeed, or they are granted stock options that can make them millionaires if their products sell well. Both Microsoft and Google, for example, have made hundreds of their employees multimillionaires as a result of the stock options they were granted as part of their reward packages. In addition to receiving money, successful intrapreneurs can expect to receive promotion to the ranks of top management. Most of 3M's top managers, for example, reached the executive suite because they had a track record of successful entrepreneurship. Organizations must reward intrapreneurs equitably if they wish to prevent them from leaving and becoming outside entrepreneurs who might form a competitive new venture. Nevertheless, intrapreneurs frequently do so.

Summary and Review

THE NATURE OF MANAGERIAL DECISION MAKING Programmed decisions are routine decisions made so often that managers have developed decision rules to be followed automatically. Nonprogrammed decisions are made in response to situations that are unusual or novel; they are nonroutine decisions. The classical model of decision making assumes that decision makers have complete information; are able to process that information in an objective, rational manner; and make optimum decisions. March and Simon argued that managers exhibit bounded rationality, rarely have access to all the information they need to make optimum decisions, and consequently satisfice and rely on their intuition and judgment when making decisions. **[LO 5-1]**

STEPS IN THE DECISION-MAKING PROCESS When making decisions, managers should take these six steps: recognize the need for a decision, generate alternatives, assess alternatives, choose among alternatives, implement the chosen alternative, and learn from feedback. **[LO 5-2]**

GROUP DECISION MAKING Many advantages are associated with group decision making, but there are also several disadvantages. One major source of poor decision making is groupthink. Afflicted decision makers collectively embark on a dubious course of action without questioning the assumptions that underlie their decision. Managers can improve the quality of group decision making by using techniques such as devil's advocacy and dialectical inquiry and by increasing diversity in the decision-making group. **[LO 5-3]**

ORGANIZATIONAL LEARNING AND CREATIVITY Organizational learning is the process through which managers seek to improve employees' desire and ability to understand and manage the organization and its task environment so employees can make decisions that continuously raise organizational effectiveness. Managers must take steps to promote organizational learning and creativity at the individual and group levels to improve the quality of decision making. **[LO 5-4]**

ENTREPRENEURSHIP Entrepreneurship is the mobilization of resources to take advantage of an opportunity to provide customers with new or improved goods and services. Entrepreneurs find new ventures of their own. Intrapreneurs work inside organizations and manage the product development process. Organizations need to encourage intrapreneurship because it leads to organizational learning and innovation. **[LO 5-5]**

Management *in Action*

TOPICS FOR DISCUSSION AND ACTION

Discussion

1. What are the main differences between programmed decision making and nonprogrammed decision making? **[LO 5-1]**

2. In what ways do the classical and administrative models of decision making help managers appreciate the complexities of real-world decision making? **[LO 5-1]**

3. Why do capable managers sometimes make bad decisions? What can individual managers do to improve their decision-making skills? **[LO 5-1, 5-2]**

4. In what kinds of groups is groupthink most likely to be a problem? When is it least likely to be a problem? What steps can group members take to ward off groupthink? **[LO 5-3]**

5. What is organizational learning, and how can managers promote it? **[LO 5-4]**

6. What is the difference between entrepreneurship and intrapreneurship? **[LO 5-5]**

Action

7. Ask a manager to recall the best and the worst decisions he or she ever made. Try to determine why these decisions were so good or so bad. **[LO 5-1, 5-2, 5-3]**

8. Think about an organization in your local community or your university, or an organization that you are familiar with, that is doing poorly. Now think of questions managers in the organization should ask stakeholders to elicit creative ideas for turning around the organization's fortunes. **[LO 5-4]**

BUILDING MANAGEMENT SKILLS

How Do You Make Decisions? [LO 5-1, 5-2, 5-4]

Pick a decision you made recently that has had important consequences for you. It may be your decision about which college to attend, which major to select, whether to take a part-time job, or which part-time job to take. Using the material in this chapter, analyze how you made the decision.

1. Identify the criteria you used, either consciously or unconsciously, to guide your decision making.

2. List the alternatives you considered. Were they all possible alternatives? Did you unconsciously (or consciously) ignore some important alternatives?

3. How much information did you have about each alternative? Were you making the decision on the basis of complete or incomplete information?

4. Try to remember how you reached the decision. Did you sit down and consciously think through the implications of each alternative, or did you make the decision on the basis of intuition? Did you use any rules of thumb to help you make the decision?

5. Having answered the previous four questions, do you think in retrospect that you made a reasonable decision? What, if anything, might you do to improve your ability to make good decisions in the future?

MANAGING ETHICALLY [LO 5-3]

Sometimes groups make extreme decisions—decisions that are either more risky or more conservative than they would have been if individuals acting alone had made them. One explanation for the tendency of groups to make extreme decisions is diffusion of responsibility. In a group, responsibility for the outcomes of a decision is spread among group members, so each person feels less than fully accountable. The group's decision is extreme because no individual has taken full responsibility for it.

Questions

1. Either alone or in a group, think about the ethical implications of extreme decision making by groups.

2. When group decision making takes place, should members of a group each feel fully accountable for outcomes of the decision? Why or why not?

SMALL GROUP BREAKOUT EXERCISE

Brainstorming [LO 5-3, 5-4]

Form groups of three or four people, and appoint one member as the spokesperson who will communicate your findings to the class when called on by the instructor. Then discuss the following scenario.

You and your partners are trying to decide which kind of restaurant to open in a centrally located shopping center that has just been built in your city. The problem confronting you is that the city already has many restaurants that provide different kinds of food at all price ranges. You have the resources to open any type of restaurant. Your challenge is to decide which type is most likely to succeed.

Use brainstorming to decide which type of restaurant to open. Follow these steps:

1. As a group, spend 5 or 10 minutes generating ideas about the alternative restaurants that the members think will be most likely to succeed. Each group member should be as innovative and creative as possible, and no suggestions should be criticized.

2. Appoint one group member to write down the alternatives as they are identified.

3. Spend the next 10 or 15 minutes debating the pros and cons of the alternatives. As a group, try to reach a consensus on which alternative is most likely to succeed.

After making your decision, discuss the pros and cons of the brainstorming method, and decide whether any production blocking occurred.

When called on by the instructor, the spokesperson should be prepared to share your group's decision with the class, as well as the reasons for the group's decision.

BE THE MANAGER [LO 5-1, 5-2, 5-3, 5-4, 5-5]

You are a top manager who was recently hired by an oil field services company in Oklahoma to help it respond more quickly and proactively to potential opportunities in its market. You report to the chief operating officer (COO), who reports to the CEO, and you have been on the job for eight months. Thus far you have come up with three initiatives you carefully studied, thought were noteworthy, and proposed and justified to the COO. The COO seemed cautiously interested when you presented the proposals, and each time he indicated he would think about them and discuss them with the CEO because considerable resources were involved. Each time you never heard back from the COO, and after a few weeks elapsed, you casually asked the COO if there was any news on the proposal in question. For the first proposal, the COO said, "We think it's a good idea, but the timing is off. Let's shelve it for the time being and reconsider it next year." For the second proposal, the COO said, "Mike [the CEO] reminded me that we tried that two years ago and it wasn't well received in the market. I am surprised I didn't remember it myself when you first described the proposal, but it came right back to me once Mike mentioned it." For the third proposal, the COO simply said, "We're not convinced it will work."

You believe your three proposed initiatives are viable ways to seize opportunities in the marketplace, yet you cannot proceed with any of them. Moreover, for each proposal, you invested considerable time and even worked to bring others on board to support the proposal, only to have it shot down by the CEO.

Question

1. When you interviewed for the position, both the COO and the CEO claimed they wanted "an outsider to help them step out of the box and innovate." Yet your experience to date has been just the opposite. What are you going to do?

In 2011, when the electronics firm Plantronics redesigned its headquarters in Santa Cruz, California, executives decided to remove the desks for a third of the firm's 500 local staff. Employees were given a choice: They could work daily from home; they could commute to headquarters; or they could join one of three Bay Area locations of NextSpace, a four-year-old company that runs a chain of work spaces buzzing with freelancers, salespeople, and entrepreneurs. A dozen or so opted to work regularly at a NextSpace branch tucked inside a former bank building in downtown San Jose, where a sign outside screams *working alone sucks.* Inside were all the comforts of a typical Silicon Valley office, including strong Wi-Fi, stronger coffee, plush couches, individual workstations, communal tables, and the keyboard clatter of 70 people working alone together.

Plantronics is engaged in "coworking"—that is, toiling alongside someone who isn't a colleague. In the past few years, the population of these spaces has moved beyond assorted freelancers and the newly unemployed to something far less marginal. "People are burrowing into their social networks in addition to their organizations," says Chris Mach, a global workplace strategist for AT&T. Mach is placing dozens of his company's best researchers, product developers, and technologists in coworking hubs across the country, and he has invited startups and partners such as Ericsson to work alongside them. The goals: spot talent, inspire creativity, and get products to market faster.

There are now an estimated 90,000 coworkers worldwide, nearly half of whom are in the United States. The number of dedicated spaces for them has doubled every year since 2005, to more than 1,800 locations, reported Deskmag, as of last summer. NextSpace plans to open 25 offices across the United States over the next five years. A startup named Serendipity Labs in Rye, New York, will offer corporate memberships in more than 200 U.S. locations. WeWork, with 3,000 members in nine buildings across three cities, tags itself as "The Physical Social Network."

Plantronics and AT&T are part of a vanguard of corporations placing employees in such spaces. According to the Deskmag survey, nearly one in 10 coworkers are employed by large or medium-size businesses. Accenture, PwC, and Capgemini have all deployed teams to various spaces; so has Twitter in Detroit. In London, Google is backing Campus, a seven-story complex that reserves one floor for Google employees and two for coworking facilities. Google is less interested in saving rent than in meeting smart people. "For companies that seek to acquire a lot of talent, something like this makes a lot of sense," says Elizabeth Varley, CEO of TechHub, an entrepreneurs' collective and another Campus tenant.

Proximity also seems to stimulate innovation. A recent study of some 35,000 academic papers found that the best, most-widely cited research came from coauthors sitting less than 10 meters apart. "How closely they worked mattered as much, if not more, than

their affiliation," says the study's author, Isaac Kohane of Harvard Medical School. Coworking's combination of casual relationships and shared spaces, he suggests, can lead to some of an employee's most fruitful collaborations.

Coworking generally falls into one of three categories. The most typical is the NextSpace model—a big, well-appointed office where the employed and self-employed go to make contacts, stare at a laptop, and sip coffee. A second, newer iteration is sometimes called company-to-company sharing, in which a group of companies pool space, employees, and ideas. The third and arguably most radical type might be described as private-to-public sharing—in effect inviting outsiders to work inside your company building or campus.

At the moment, the world's largest experiment in company-to-company coworking sits at the end of a row of handsome brick warehouses in downtown Grand Rapids, Michigan. The teams stationed in the lofty offices of GRid70, as they're called, have been charged with plotting their employers' futures. The fourth floor houses the growth initiatives team of Steelcase, the world's largest office furniture manufacturer, and Amway, the $10 billion multilevel marketer. The test kitchens of Meijer, the Midwest grocery chain, dominate the ground floor, while the third floor belongs to the footwear designers of Wolverine Worldwide, owner of such brands as Hush Puppies, Keds, and Sperry Top-Sider.

GRid70 is an exercise in engineering serendipity, or "happy accidents," in the words of Wolverine CEO Blake Krueger. The hope is that these disparate residents will use their expertise to help one another in their struggles. To that end, an open-door policy reigns. Amway's Post-it-Note-strewn space has no doors at all. Steelcase eschewed cubicles for a long, double-wide table and a few videoconferencing pods. Downstairs, accessible through an atrium staircase, Wolverine's 50 or so designers wade through shoe samples in their open-plan office, while Meijer's food scientists spend their days sampling vendors' baby-back ribs, candy, and macaroni and cheese in a spotlessly clean kitchen the size of a nightclub (which happens to have been the ground floor's former tenant).

All are encouraged to linger in the office kitchen or in one of the building's many airy conference rooms, including a lounge in which they're invited to crash each other's meetings. Residents have shared trade secrets, trend forecasts, materials science, and even recipes for kielbasa. Steelcase reportedly has given Wolverine tips on controlling odors from cement (a problem plaguing the manufacture of both shoes and furniture) and, in turn, has received Amway's proprietary research on India's emerging middle class. None of the companies are in competition with one another. Thus Steelcase can take Amway's advice without parsing it for office politics.

The setup in Grand Rapids is decidedly different from a coworking experiment now under way in Las Vegas. There, architect Jennifer Magnolfi hit upon the idea of inviting Sin City's 2 million metro area residents to work from Zappos's new headquarters. It is almost certainly the world's largest example of private-to-public sharing. It is also the centerpiece of Zappos CEO Tony Hsieh's

Downtown Project, a $350 million bid to catalyze both the city and the company by deliberately blurring the lines between the two.

Hsieh's thoughts on corporate evolution borrow heavily from the Harvard economist Edward Glaeser, who has described cities as the greatest serendipity machines of all. To Glaeser, as cities grow larger they encourage more chance encounters among citizens, sparking innovation and productivity. With companies, though, the bigger they get, the more sclerotic. For Zappos to avoid a similar fate, Hsieh reasoned, he needed to make the company more like a city, so in August he relocated 200 of his 1,400 employees from a suburban campus to downtown Las Vegas, with the rest to follow this year. As part of Hsieh's plan to make Vegas "the Coworking Capital of the World," Magnolfi proposed creating a coworking space on the building's ground floor, essentially a membrane through which strangers and Zappos employees will pass and hopefully collide. Eventually Hsieh wants to turn the company inside out, transforming every downtown bar and restaurant into an extension of its conference rooms, drawing hundreds of startups, students, and small businesses into the Zappos orbit.

The next step may be learning how to rearrange office space at will. Perhaps the greatest failing of the corporate office has been its inability to change as quickly as the nature of work. Companies often neglect office layouts for years at a time. Compare this with Grind, a year-old coworking space in Manhattan, which constantly monitors the head count and positions of its members, reconfiguring the room when necessary. Cofounder Benjamin Dyett can

tell you Wednesdays are peak and Fridays are dead, and that at more than a hundred occupants, "the room falls apart" as members hunker down under the onslaught of arrivals. Ryan Anderson, director of future technology at Herman Miller, imagines bringing new tech to bear on such spaces, perhaps tracking physical movements of workers with sensors or using social media apps to see which acquaintances are nearby. "A data-driven, highly evolutionary work space is where we're headed," he says.

The challenge will be to accommodate everyone who wants a desk. According to the U.S. Bureau of Labor Statistics, by 2020 about 65 million Americans will be freelancers, temps, and independent contractors—40% of the workforce. That fact inspired the creation of LiquidSpace, which wants to make every coworking space, conference room, and spare cubicle searchable and bookable online. "There is $8 trillion worth of office space worldwide," says CEO Mark Gilbreath, and at any given moment, two-thirds of it is empty because the occupants are elsewhere. Why not fill that space with outsiders? With so many of our coworkers already strangers, it can't hurt to let the right ones in.

Questions

1. What are the potential advantages of coworking?
2. What are the potential disadvantages of coworking?
3. In what ways might coworking affect decision making in organizations?
4. What are the implications of coworking for creativity and entrepreneurship?

Source: G. Lindsay, "Working Beyond the Cube," *Fast Company,* March 2013, 34–38.

6 Planning, Strategy, and Competitive Advantage

LEARNING OBJECTIVES

After studying this chapter, you should be able to:

1 Identify the three main steps of the planning process and explain the relationship between planning and strategy. **[LO 6-1]**

2 Differentiate between the main types of business-level strategies and explain how they give an organization a competitive advantage that may lead to superior performance. **[LO 6-2]**

3 Differentiate between the main types of corporate-level strategies and explain how they are used to strengthen a company's business-level strategy and competitive advantage. **[LO 6-3]**

4 Describe the vital role managers play in implementing strategies to achieve an organization's mission and goals. **[LO 6-4]**

"I'll have a Coke" may not be as easy a decision for much longer, as Cott's and other competitors wedge lower-cost sodas into the big retail chains.

MANAGEMENT SNAPSHOT

Different Ways to Compete in the Soft Drink Business

What Makes It So Hard to Compete in an Industry?

"Coke" and "Pepsi" are household names worldwide. Together Coca-Cola and PepsiCo control over 70% of the global soft drink market and over 75% of the U.S. soft drink market. Their success can be attributed to the differentiation strategies they developed to produce and promote their products—strategies that have made them two of the most profitable global organizations. There are several parts to their differentiation strategies. First, both companies built global brands by manufacturing the soft drink concentrate that gives cola its flavor but then selling the concentrate in a syrup form to bottlers throughout the world. The bottlers are responsible for producing and distributing the actual cola. They add carbonated water to the syrup, package the resulting drinks, and distribute them to vending machines, supermarkets, restaurants, and other retail outlets. The bottlers must also sign an exclusive agreement that prohibits them from bottling or distributing the products of competing soft drink companies. This creates a barrier to entry that helps prevent new companies from entering the industry.

Second, Coca-Cola and PepsiCo charge the bottlers a premium price for the syrup; they then invest a large part of the profits in advertising to build and maintain brand awareness. The hundreds of millions they spend on advertising to develop a global brand name help Coca-Cola and PepsiCo differentiate their products so consumers are more likely to buy a Coke or a Pepsi than a less well-known cola. Moreover, brand loyalty allows both companies to charge a premium or comparatively high price for what is, after all, merely colored water and flavoring.

In the last decade the global soft drink environment has undergone a major change, however, because of Gerald Pencer, a Canadian entrepreneur who came up with a new strategy for competing against these powerful differentiators. Pencer's strategy was to produce a high-quality, low-priced cola, manufactured and bottled by the Cott Corporation, of which he was CEO at the time, but to sell it as the private-label house brand of major retail stores such as Walmart (Sam's Cola brand) and supermarket chains such as Kroger's (Big K brand), thus bypassing the bottlers. Pencer could implement his focused low-cost strategy and charge a low price for his soft drinks because he did not need to spend on advertising (the retail stores did that) and because Cott's soft drinks are distributed by the store chains and retailers using their efficient national distribution systems, such as the nation-wide trucking system developed by giant retailer Walmart. Retailers are willing to do this because Cott's low-cost soft drinks allow them to make much more profit than they receive from selling Coke or Pepsi. At the same time, the products build their store brand image.

Pencer implemented this plan first in Canada and then quickly expanded into the United States as retailers' demand for his products grew. He went on to supply the international market by offering to sell soft drink concentrate to global retailers at prices lower than Coca-Cola and PepsiCo. By 2004 Cott was the world's largest supplier of retailer-branded carbonated soft drinks and it still is in 2012.[1] It has manufacturing facilities in Canada, the United States, and the United Kingdom,

and a syrup concentrate production plant in Columbus, Georgia, that supply most of the private-label grocery store, drugstore, mass merchandising, and convenience store chains in these countries. However, note that while Cott is the leading supplier of retailer-branded sodas, it is still focusing on its low-cost strategy. It makes no attempt to compete with Coke and Pepsi, which pursue differentiation strategies and whose brand-name sodas dominate the global soda market. Indeed, both these companies have acquired their independent bottlers for tens of billions of dollars because this would increase their long-term profits—a strategy known as vertical integration, discussed later in the chapter.[2] But Cott is its own bottler; it knows the value of this strategy and its stock price has soared in the 2010s.

Overview

As the opening case suggests, in a fast-changing competitive environment such as the global soft drink industry in which new flavors and brands emerge rapidly, managers

planning Identifying and selecting appropriate goals and courses of action; one of the four principal tasks of management.

strategy A cluster of decisions about what goals to pursue, what actions to take, and how to use resources to achieve goals.

must continually evaluate how well products are meeting customer needs, and they must engage in thorough, systematic planning to find new strategies to better meet those needs. This chapter explores the manager's role both as planner and as strategist. First, we discuss the nature and importance of planning, the kinds of plans managers develop, and the levels at which planning takes place. Second, we discuss the three major steps in the planning process: (1) determining an organization's mission and major goals, (2) choosing or formulating strategies to realize the mission and goals, and (3) selecting the most effective ways to implement and put these strategies into action. We also examine techniques such as SWOT analysis that can help managers improve the quality of their planning; and we discuss a range of strategies managers can use to give their companies a competitive advantage over their rivals. By the end of this chapter, you will understand the vital role managers carry out when they plan, develop, and implement strategies to create a high-performing organization.

Planning and Strategy

LO 6-1 Identify the three main steps of the planning process and explain the relationship between planning and strategy.

Planning, as we noted in Chapter 1, is a process managers use to identify and select appropriate goals and courses of action for an organization.[3] The organizational plan that results from the planning process details the goals of the organization and the specific strategies managers will implement to attain those goals. Recall from Chapter 1 that a strategy is a cluster of related managerial decisions and actions to help an organization attain one of its goals. Thus planning is both a goal-making and a strategy-making process.

In most organizations, planning is a three-step activity (see Figure 6.1). The first step is determining the organization's mission and goals. A mission statement is a broad declaration of an organization's overriding purpose, what it is seeking to achieve from its activities; this statement also identifies what is *unique or*

Figure 6.1

Three Steps in Planning

DETERMINING THE ORGANIZATION'S MISSION AND GOALS
Define the business
Establish major goals

FORMULATING STRATEGY
Analyze current situation and develop strategies

IMPLEMENTING STRATEGY
Allocate resources and responsibilities to achieve strategies

mission statement
A broad declaration of an organization's purpose that identifies the organization's products and customers and distinguishes the organization from its competitors.

important about its products to its employees and customers; finally it *distinguishes or differentiates* the organization in some ways from its competitors. (Three examples of mission statements, those created by Cisco Systems, Walmart, and AT&T, are illustrated later in Figure 6.4.)

The second step is formulating strategy. Managers analyze the organization's current situation and then conceive and develop the strategies necessary to attain the organization's mission and goals. The third step is implementing strategy. Managers decide how to allocate the resources and responsibilities required to implement the strategies among people and groups within the organization.[4] In subsequent sections of this chapter we look in detail at the specifics of these steps. But first we examine the general nature and purpose of planning.

The Nature of the Planning Process

Essentially, to perform the planning task, managers (1) establish and discover where an organization is at the *present time;* (2) determine where it should be in the future, its *desired future state;* and (3) decide how to *move it forward* to reach that future state. When managers plan, they must forecast what may happen in the future to decide what to do in the present. The better their predictions, the more effective will be the strategies they formulate to take advantage of future opportunities and counter emerging competitive threats in the environment. As previous chapters noted, however, the external environment is uncertain and complex, and managers typically must deal with incomplete information and bounded rationality. This is why planning and strategy making are so difficult and risky; and if managers' predictions are wrong and strategies fail, organizational performance falls.

Why Planning Is Important

Almost all managers participate in some kind of planning because they must try to predict future opportunities and threats and develop a plan and strategies that will result in a high-performing organization. Moreover, the absence of a plan often results in hesitations, false steps, and mistaken changes of direction that can hurt an organization or even lead to disaster. Planning is important for four main reasons:

A group of managers meets to plot their company's strategy. Their ability to assess opportunities and challenges and to forecast the future doesn't just depend on brilliance. Such tools as SWOT analysis can significantly bolster the accuracy of their predictions.

1. *Planning is necessary to give the organization a sense of direction and purpose.*[5] A plan states what goals an organization is trying to achieve and what strategies it intends to use to achieve them. Without the sense of direction and purpose that a formal plan provides, managers may interpret their own specific tasks and jobs in ways that best suit themselves. The result will be an organization that is pursuing multiple and often conflicting goals and a set of managers who do not cooperate and work well together. By stating which organizational goals and strategies are important, a plan keeps managers on track so they use the resources under their control efficiently and effectively.

2. *Planning is a useful way of getting managers to participate in decision making about the appropriate goals and strategies for an organization.* Effective planning gives all managers the opportunity to participate in decision making. At Intel, for example, top managers, as part of their annual planning process, regularly request input from lower-level managers to determine what the organization's goals and strategies should be.

3. *A plan helps coordinate managers of the different functions and divisions of an organization to ensure that they all pull in the same direction and work to achieve its desired future state.* Without a well-thought-out plan, for example, it is possible that the manufacturing function will make more products than the sales function can sell, resulting in a mass of unsold inventory. In fact, this happened to the high-flying Internet equipment supplier Cisco Systems. In the early 2000s, it was able to sell all the routers it produced; but only a few years later Cisco found it had over $2 billion of unwanted inventory that its sales force could not sell. Why? Because customers now wanted new kinds of fast optical routers that Cisco had not planned to develop—even though sales had told manufacturing that customer needs were changing.

4. *A plan can be used as a device for controlling managers within an organization.* A good plan specifies not only which goals and strategies the organization is committed to but also *who* bears the responsibility for putting the strategies into action to attain the goals. When managers know they will be held accountable for attaining a goal, they are motivated to do their best to make sure the goal is achieved.

Henri Fayol, the originator of the model of management we discussed in Chapter 1, said that effective plans should have four qualities: unity, continuity, accuracy, and flexibility.[6] *Unity* means that at any time only one central, guiding plan is put into operation to achieve an organizational goal; more than one plan to achieve a goal would cause confusion and disorder. *Continuity* means that planning is an ongoing process in which managers build and refine previous plans and continually modify plans at all levels—corporate, business, and functional—so they fit together into one broad framework. *Accuracy* means that managers need to make every attempt to collect and use all available information in the planning process.

Of course managers must recognize that uncertainty exists and that information is almost always incomplete (for reasons we discussed in Chapter 5). Despite the need for continuity and accuracy, however, Fayol emphasized that the planning process should be *flexible* enough so plans can be altered and changed if the situation changes; managers must not be bound to a static plan.

Levels of Planning

In large organizations planning usually takes place at three levels of management: corporate, business or division, and department or functional. Consider how General Electric (GE) operates. One of the world's largest global organizations, GE competes in over 150 different businesses or industries.[7] GE has three main levels of management: corporate level, business or divisional level, and functional level (see Figure 6.2). At the corporate level are CEO and Chairman Jeffrey Immelt, his top management team, and their corporate support staff. Together they are responsible for planning and strategy making for the organization as a whole.

Below the corporate level is the business level. At the business level are the different *divisions* or *business units* of the company that compete in distinct industries; GE has over 150 divisions, including GE Aircraft Engines, GE Financial Services, GE Lighting, GE Motors, and GE Plastics. Each division or business unit has its own set of *divisional managers* who control planning and strategy for their particular division or unit. So, for example, GE Lighting's divisional managers plan how to operate globally to reduce costs while meeting the needs of customers in different countries.

Going down one more level, each division has its own set of *functions* or *departments,* such as manufacturing, marketing, human resource management (HRM), and research and development (R&D). For example, GE Aircraft has

Figure 6.2

Levels of Planning at General Electric

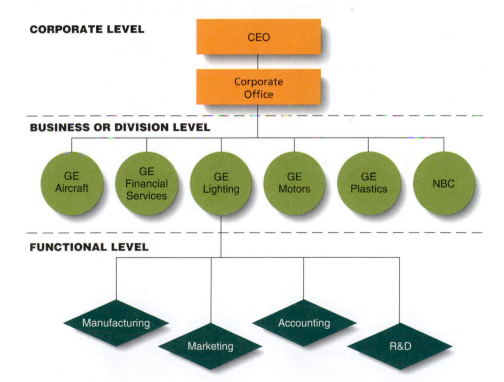

its own marketing function, as do GE Lighting and GE Motors. Each division's *functional managers* are responsible for the planning and strategy making necessary to increase the efficiency and effectiveness of their particular function. So, for example, GE Lighting's marketing managers are responsible for increasing the effectiveness of its advertising and sales campaigns in different countries to improve lightbulb sales.

Levels and Types of Planning

As just discussed, planning at GE, as at all other large organizations, takes place at each level. Figure 6.3 shows the link between these three levels and the three steps in the planning and strategy-making process illustrated in Figure 6.1.

The corporate-level plan contains top management's decisions concerning the organization's mission and goals, overall (corporate-level) strategy, and structure (see Figure 6.3). Corporate-level strategy specifies in which industries and national markets an organization intends to compete and why. One of the goals stated in GE's corporate-level plan is that GE should be first or second in market share in every industry in which it competes. A division that cannot attain this goal may be sold to another company. GE Medical Systems was sold to Thompson of France for this reason. Another GE goal is to acquire other companies that can help a division build its market share to reach its corporate goal of being first or second in an industry. In 2011, GE sold its NBC division to Comcast Cable at an extremely profitable price.

corporate-level plan Top management's decisions pertaining to the organization's mission, overall strategy, and structure.

corporate-level strategy A plan that indicates in which industries and national markets an organization intends to compete.

Figure 6.3

Levels and Types of Planning

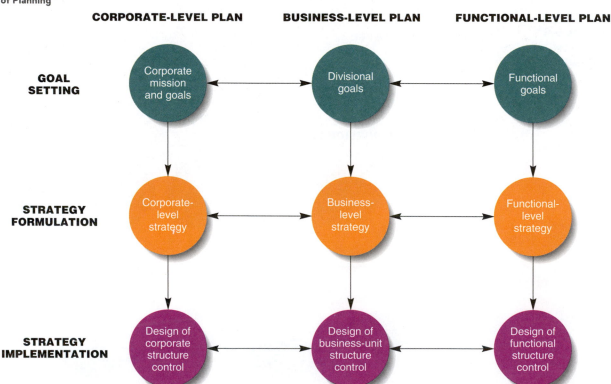

	CORPORATE-LEVEL PLAN	BUSINESS-LEVEL PLAN	FUNCTIONAL-LEVEL PLAN
GOAL SETTING	Corporate mission and goals	Divisional goals	Functional goals
STRATEGY FORMULATION	Corporate-level strategy	Business-level strategy	Functional-level strategy
STRATEGY IMPLEMENTATION	Design of corporate structure control	Design of business-unit structure control	Design of functional structure control

In general, corporate-level planning and strategy are the primary responsibility of top or corporate managers.[8] The corporate-level goal of GE is to be the first or second leading company in every industry in which it competes. Jeffrey Immelt and his top management team decide which industries GE should compete in to achieve this goal. The corporate-level plan provides the framework within which divisional managers create their business-level plans. At the business level, the managers of each division create a business-level plan that details (1) the long-term divisional goals that will allow the division to meet corporate goals and (2) the division's business-level strategy and structure necessary to achieve divisional goals. Business-level strategy outlines the specific methods a division, business unit, or organization will use to compete effectively against its rivals in an industry. Managers at GE's lighting division (currently number two in the global lighting industry, behind the Dutch company Philips NV) develop strategies designed to help their division take over the number one spot and better contribute to GE's corporate goals. The lighting division's specific strategies might focus on ways to reduce costs in all departments to lower prices and so gain market share from Philips. For example, GE has expanded its European lighting operations in Hungary, which is a low-cost location.[9]

business-level plan Divisional managers' decisions pertaining to divisions' long-term goals, overall strategy, and structure.

At the functional level, the business-level plan provides the framework within which functional managers devise their plans. A functional-level plan states the goals that the managers of each function will pursue to help their division attain its business-level goals, which, in turn, will allow the entire company to achieve its corporate goals. Functional-level strategy is a plan of action that managers of individual functions (such as manufacturing or marketing) can follow to improve the ability of each function to perform its task-specific activities in ways that add value to an organization's goods and services and thereby increase the value customers receive. Thus, for example, consistent with the lighting division's strategy of driving down costs, its manufacturing function might adopt the goal "To reduce production costs by 20% over the next three years," and functional strategies to achieve this goal might include (1) investing in state-of-the-art European production facilities and (2) developing an electronic global business-to-business network to reduce the costs of inputs and inventory holding.

functional-level plan Functional managers' decisions pertaining to the goals that they propose to pursue to help the division attain its business-level goals.

functional-level strategy A plan of action to improve the ability of each of an organization's functions to perform its task-specific activities in ways that add value to an organization's goods and services.

In the planning process, it is important to ensure that planning across the three different levels is *consistent*—functional goals and strategies should be consistent with divisional goals and strategies, which, in turn, should be consistent with corporate goals and strategies, and vice versa. When consistency is achieved, the whole company operates in harmony; activities at one level reinforce and strengthen those at the other levels, increasing efficiency and effectiveness. To help accomplish this, each function's plan is linked to its division's business-level plan, which, in turn, is linked to the corporate plan. Although few organizations are as large and complex as GE, most plan in the same way as GE and have written plans, which are frequently updated, to guide managerial decision making.

Time Horizons of Plans

time horizon The intended duration of a plan.

Plans differ in their time horizons, the periods of time over which they are intended to apply or endure. Managers usually distinguish among *long-term plans,* with a time horizon of five years or more; *intermediate-term plans,* with a horizon between one and five years; and *short-term plans,* with a horizon of one year or less.[10] Typically corporate- and business-level goals and strategies require long- and intermediate-term plans, and functional-level goals and strategies require intermediate- and short-term plans.

Although most companies operate with planning horizons of five years or more, this does not mean that managers undertake major planning exercises only once every five years and then "lock in" a specific set of goals and strategies for that period. Most organizations have an annual planning cycle that is usually linked to the annual financial budget (although a major planning effort may be undertaken only every few years). So a corporate- or business-level plan that extends over several years is typically treated as a *rolling plan*—a plan that is updated and amended every year to take account of changing conditions in the external environment. Thus the time horizon for an organization's 2014 corporate-level plan might be 2019; for the 2015 plan it might be 2020, and so on. The use of rolling plans is essential because of the high rate of change in the environment and the difficulty of predicting competitive conditions five years in the future. Rolling plans enable managers to make midcourse corrections if environmental changes warrant or to change the thrust of the plan altogether if it no longer seems appropriate. The use of rolling plans allows managers to plan flexibly without losing sight of the need to plan for the long term.

Standing Plans and Single-Use Plans

Another distinction often made between plans is whether they are standing plans or single-use plans. Managers create standing and single-use plans to help achieve an organization's specific goals. *Standing plans* are used in situations in which programmed decision making is appropriate. When the same situations occur repeatedly, managers develop policies, rules, and standard operating procedures (SOPs) to control the way employees perform their tasks. A policy is a general guide to action; a rule is a formal, written guide to action; and a standing operating procedure is a written instruction describing the exact series of actions that should be followed in a specific situation. For example, an organization may have a standing plan about ethical behavior by employees. This plan includes a policy that all employees are expected to behave ethically in their dealings with suppliers and customers; a rule that requires any employee who receives from a supplier or customer a gift worth more than $50 to report the gift; and an SOP that obliges the recipient of the gift to make the disclosure in writing within 30 days.

In contrast, *single-use plans* are developed to handle nonprogrammed decision making in unusual or one-of-a-kind situations. Examples of single-use plans include *programs,* which are integrated sets of plans for achieving certain goals, and *projects,* which are specific action plans created to complete various aspects of a program. One of NASA's major programs was to reach the moon, and one project in this program was to develop a lunar module capable of landing on the moon and returning to the earth.

Determining the Organization's Mission and Goals

As we discussed earlier, determining the organization's mission and goals is the first step of the planning process. Once the mission and goals are agreed upon and formally stated in the corporate plan, they guide the next steps by defining which strategies are appropriate.[11] Figure 6.4 presents the missions and goals of three companies: Cisco, Walmart, and AT&T.

Figure 6.4
Three Mission
Statements

COMPANY	MISSION STATEMENT
Cisco	Cisco solutions provide competitive advantage to our customers through more efficient and timely exchange of information, which in turn leads to cost savings, process efficiencies, and closer relationships with our customers, prospects, business partners, suppliers, and employees.
Walmart	We work for you. We think of ourselves as buyers for our customers, and we apply our considerable strengths to get the best value for you. We've built Walmart by acting on behalf of our customers, and that concept continues to propel us. We're working hard to make our customers' shopping easy.
AT&T	We are dedicated to being the world's best at bringing people together—giving them easy access to each other and to the information and services they want and need—anytime, anywhere.

Defining the Business

To determine an organization's *mission*—the overriding reason it exists to provide customers with goods or services they value—managers must first *define its business* so they can identify what kind of value customers are receiving. To define the business, managers must ask three related questions about a company's products: (1) *Who* are our customers? (2) *What* customer needs are being satisfied? (3) *How* are we satisfying customer needs?[12] Managers ask these questions to identify the customer needs that the organization satisfies and how the organization satisfies those needs. Answering these questions helps managers identify not only the customer needs they are satisfying now but also the needs they should try to satisfy in the future and who their true competitors are. All this information helps managers plan and establish appropriate goals.

Establishing Major Goals

Once the business is defined, managers must establish a set of primary goals to which the organization is committed. Developing these goals gives the organization a sense of direction or purpose. In most organizations, articulating major goals is the job of the CEO, although other managers have input into the process. For example, at Mattel, CEO Eckert's primary goal is to be the leader in every segment of the toy market in which the company competes, even though this is highly challenging. However, the best statements of organizational goals are ambitious—that is, they *stretch* the organization and require that each of its members work to improve company performance.[13] The role of strategic leadership, the ability of the CEO and top managers to convey a compelling vision of what they want to achieve to their subordinates, is important here. If subordinates buy into the vision and model their behaviors on their leaders, they develop a willingness to undertake the hard, stressful work that is necessary for creative, risk-taking strategy making.[14] Many popular books such as *Built to Last* provide lucid

strategic leadership The ability of the CEO and top managers to convey a compelling vision of what they want the organization to achieve to their subordinates.

accounts of strategic leaders establishing "big, hairy, audacious goals (BHAGs)" that serve as rallying points to unite their subordinates.[15]

Although goals should be challenging, they should also be realistic. Challenging goals give managers at all levels an incentive to look for ways to improve organizational performance, but a goal that is clearly unrealistic and impossible to attain may prompt managers to give up.[16]

Finally, the time period in which a goal is expected to be achieved should be stated. Time constraints are important because they emphasize that a goal must be attained within a reasonable period; they inject a sense of urgency into goal attainment and act as a motivator. For example, Taco Bell's managers committed themselves to reviving the line of its fast-food offerings and to significantly increase sales and by 2013 they had achieved this goal as its tasty treats attracted away customers from McDonald's and KFC.

strategy formulation The development of a set of corporate, business, and functional strategies that allow an organization to accomplish its mission and achieve its goals.

Formulating Strategy

In strategy formulation managers work to develop the set of strategies (corporate, divisional, and functional) that will allow an organization to accomplish its mission and achieve its goals.[17] Strategy formulation begins with managers' systematically analyzing the factors or forces inside an organization and outside in the global environment that affect the organization's ability to meet its goals now and in the future. SWOT analysis and the five forces model are two handy techniques managers can use to analyze these factors.

SWOT Analysis

SWOT analysis A planning exercise in which managers identify organizational strengths (S) and weaknesses (W) and environmental opportunities (O) and threats (T).

SWOT analysis is a planning exercise in which managers identify *internal* organizational strengths (S) and weaknesses (W) and *external* environmental opportunities (O) and threats (T). Based on a SWOT analysis, managers at the different levels of the organization select the corporate, business, and functional strategies to best position the organization to achieve its mission and goals (see Figure 6.5). In Chapter 4 we discussed forces in the task and general environments that have the potential to affect an organization. We noted that changes in these forces can

Figure 6.5

Planning and Strategy Formulation

produce opportunities that an organization might take advantage of and threats that may harm its current situation.

The first step in SWOT analysis is to identify an organization's strengths and weaknesses. Table 6.1 lists many important strengths (such as high-quality skills in marketing and in research and development) and weaknesses (such as rising manufacturing costs and outdated technology). The task facing managers is to identify the strengths and weaknesses that characterize the present state of their organization.

The second step in SWOT analysis begins when managers embark on a full-scale SWOT planning exercise to identify potential opportunities and threats in the environment that affect the organization now or may affect it in the future. Examples of possible opportunities and threats that must be anticipated (many of which were discussed in Chapter 4) are listed in Table 6.1. Scenario planning is often used to strengthen this analysis.

With the SWOT analysis completed, and strengths, weaknesses, opportunities, and threats identified, managers can continue the planning process and determine specific strategies for achieving the organization's mission and goals. The resulting strategies should enable the organization to attain its goals by taking advantage of opportunities, countering threats, building strengths, and

Table 6.1
Questions for SWOT Analysis

Potential Strengths	Potential Opportunities	Potential Weaknesses	Potential Threats
Well-developed strategy?	Expand core business(es)?	Poorly developed strategy?	Attacks on core business(es)?
Strong product lines?	Exploit new market segments?	Obsolete, narrow product lines?	Increase in domestic competition?
Broad market coverage?	Widen product range?	Rising manufacturing costs?	Increase in foreign competition?
Manufacturing competence?	Extend cost or differentiation advantage?	Decline in R&D innovations?	Change in consumer tastes?
Good marketing skills?	Diversify into new growth businesses?	Poor marketing plan?	Fall in barriers to entry?
Good materials management systems?	Expand into foreign markets?	Poor materials management systems?	Rise in new or substitute products?
R&D skills and leadership?	Apply R&D skills in new areas?	Loss of customer goodwill?	Increase in industry rivalry?
Human resource competencies?	Enter new related businesses?	Inadequate human resources?	New forms of industry competition?
Brand-name reputation?	Vertically integrate forward?	Loss of brand name?	Potential for takeover?
Cost of differentiation advantage?	Vertically integrate backward?	Growth without direction?	Changes in demographic factors?
Appropriate management style?	Overcome barriers to entry?	Loss of corporate direction?	Changes in economic factors?
Appropriate organizational structure?	Reduce rivalry among competitors?	Infighting among divisions?	Downturn in economy?
Appropriate control systems?	Apply brand-name capital in new areas?	Loss of corporate control?	Rising labor costs?
Ability to manage strategic change?	Seek fast market growth?	Inappropriate organizational structure and control systems?	Slower market growth?
Others?	Others?	High conflict and politics?	Others?
		Others?	

correcting organizational weaknesses. To appreciate how managers use SWOT analysis to formulate strategy, consider how Douglas Conant, CEO of Campbell Soup since 2001, has used it to find strategies to turn around the performance of the troubled food products maker. In fact, his self-described mission was to take a "bad" company and lift its performance to "extraordinary" by the 2010s— something he has achieved compared to its competitors.[18]

MANAGER AS A PERSON

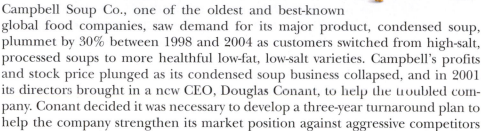

Douglas Conant Keeps Campbell Soup Hot

Campbell Soup Co., one of the oldest and best-known global food companies, saw demand for its major product, condensed soup, plummet by 30% between 1998 and 2004 as customers switched from high-salt, processed soups to more healthful low-fat, low-salt varieties. Campbell's profits and stock price plunged as its condensed soup business collapsed, and in 2001 its directors brought in a new CEO, Douglas Conant, to help the troubled company. Conant decided it was necessary to develop a three-year turnaround plan to help the company strengthen its market position against aggressive competitors such as General Mills, whose Progresso Soup division had attracted away many Campbell customers with its innovative new lines of healthful soup.

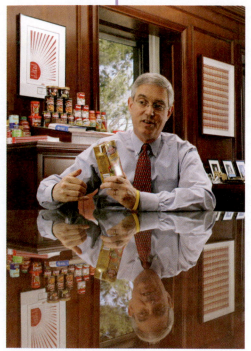

Douglas Conant, CEO of Campbell's, has revitalized the company through SWOT analysis. From SWOT analysis he has learned how to innovate successful new food products, and Campbell's has emerged as a leader in the low-carb, health-conscious, and luxury-food market segments.

One of Conant's first actions was to initiate a thorough SWOT planning exercise. *External analysis* of the environment identified the growth of the organic and health food segment of the food market and the increasing number of other kinds of convenience foods as a threat to Campbell's core soup business. It also revealed three growth opportunities: (1) the growing market for health and sports drinks, in which Campbell already was a competitor with its V8 juice; (2) the growing market for quality bread and cookies, in which Campbell competed with its Pepperidge Farm brand; and (3) chocolate products, where Campbell's Godiva brand had enjoyed increasing sales throughout the 1990s.

With the analysis of the environment complete, Conant turned his attention to his organization's resources and capabilities. His *internal analysis* of Campbell identified a number of major weaknesses. These included staffing levels that were too high relative to its competitors and high costs associated with manufacturing its soups because of the use of outdated machinery.

Also, Conant noted that Campbell had a conservative culture in which people seemed to be afraid to take risks— something that was a real problem in an industry where customer tastes are always changing and new products must be developed constantly. At the same time, the SWOT analysis identified an enormous strength: Campbell enjoyed huge economies of scale because of the enormous quantity of food products that it makes, and it also had a first-rate R&D division capable of developing exciting new food products.

Using the information from this SWOT analysis, Conant and his managers decided that Campbell needed to use its product development skills to revitalize its core products and modify or reinvent them in ways that would appeal to increasingly health-conscious and busy consumers. Conant stressed convenience with microwaveable soups and cans that open with a pull. The recipes became more healthful for its soups, V8 drinks, and Pepperidge Farm snacks because Conant needed to expand Campbell's share of the health, sports, snack, and luxury food market segments. Also, to increase sales, Campbell needed to tap into new food outlets, such as corporate cafeterias, college dining halls, and other mass eateries, to expand consumers' access to its foods. Finally, Conant decided to decentralize authority to managers at lower levels in the organization and make them responsible for developing new soup, bread, and chocolate products that met customers' changing needs. In this way he hoped to revitalize Campbell's slow-moving culture and speed the flow of improved and new products to the market.

Conant put his new plan into action, sales of new soup products increased, and he began to put more emphasis on sales of soup at outlets such as 7-11 and Subway and less on supermarket sales.[19] By 2005 analysts felt that he had made a significant difference in Campbell's performance but that there was still a lot to do—Campbell's operating margins were still shrinking. Carrying on the SWOT analysis, Conant decided Campbell should produce more products to meet the needs of the "low-carb diet," such as new kinds of low-carb bread and cookies. He also decided to shrink the company's operations to lower costs. His goal was to raise profit margins to the level of his major competitors Kraft and General Mills by 2007 using a new three-year plan based on this SWOT analysis.[20]

By 2007 Conant had substantially achieved his goals: Sales of soup had recovered, and the Pepperidge Farm and Godiva divisions were earning record sales and profits.[21] (Sales of Goldfish crackers had increased by 100%!) Campbell's stock price soared, and Conant and employees at all levels received bonuses that rewarded their intense efforts to turn around the company. However, Conant immediately set in motion a new round of SWOT analysis to find fresh opportunities for developing new products.[22]

On the threat side, it was clear that customers wanted more nutritious food and snack products; so Conant set into motion research to make Campbell's food products more appealing to health-conscious customers. One major opportunity was to reformulate a number of its soups to reduce sodium content, and it introduced new kinds of low-salt soup in 2007. Another opportunity was to develop nutritious luxury soups that would command premium prices.[23] Both these initiatives worked well. On the other hand, pursuing his new goal of making Campbell's foods more nutritious led Conant to question if its highly profitable Godiva chocolate brand was still a good fit for the company. He decided it had become a weakness, and in 2008 he sold it for $850 million.[24] He used some of the proceeds of this sale to build new company strengths. For example, he invested in R&D to develop the skills needed to customize Campbell's brands to the needs of customers in countries such as India and China—a move that spearheaded global expansion into major soup-eating nations.

Under Conant, Campbell's profits and stock price increased each year during the 2000s; and with a culture of innovation permeating the organization, in

2013 its future looks even brighter. Thanks to his leadership, employees are more engaged and involved, sales are up, and many new leaders and managers have been promoted to change the company's culture and stretch its employees. How does Conant himself encourage employees to perform at a high level? Obviously he rewards good performance, but he also sends around 20 daily "thank-you" e-mail messages to employees at every level of the organization to show he understands how everyone can contribute to help the company meet its goals and mission over the next three years.

The Five Forces Model

A well-known model that helps managers focus on the five most important competitive forces, or potential threats, in the external environment is Michael Porter's five forces model. We discussed the first four forces in the following list in Chapter 4. Porter identified these five factors as major threats because they affect how much profit organizations competing within the same industry can expect to make:

- *The level of rivalry among organizations in an industry:* The more that companies compete against one another for customers—for example, by lowering the prices of their products or by increasing advertising—the lower is the level of industry profits (low prices mean less profit).

- *The potential for entry into an industry:* The easier it is for companies to enter an industry—because, for example, barriers to entry, such as brand loyalty, are low—the more likely it is for industry prices and therefore industry profits to be low.

- *The power of large suppliers:* If there are only a few large suppliers of an important input, then suppliers can drive up the price of that input, and expensive inputs result in lower profits for companies in an industry.

- *The power of large customers:* If only a few large customers are available to buy an industry's output, they can bargain to drive down the price of that output. As a result, industry producers make lower profits.

- *The threat of substitute products:* Often the output of one industry is a substitute for the output of another industry (plastic may be a substitute for steel in some applications, for example; similarly, bottled water is a substitute for cola). When a substitute for their product exists, companies cannot demand high prices for it or customers will switch to the substitute, and this constraint keeps their profits low.

Porter argued that when managers analyze opportunities and threats, they should pay particular attention to these five forces because they are the major threats an organization will encounter. It is the job of managers at the corporate, business, and functional levels to formulate strategies to counter these threats so an organization can manage its task and general environments, perform at a high level, and generate high profits. At Campbell, Conant performed such analysis to identify the opportunities and threats stemming from the actions of food industry rivals. For example, as noted earlier, General Mills' Progresso Soups division developed more healthful kinds of soups, and this increased rivalry and lowered Campbell's sales and profits until it successfully developed new lines of healthful soups. Both companies have been affected by the threat of rising global food prices as the costs of wheat, corn, rice, and dairy products have increased. Both companies are striving to reduce operating costs to limit food price increases because the company with the lowest prices will attract the most customers and gain a competitive advantage—especially during the recent recession.

Today competition is tough in most industries, whether companies make cars, soup, computers, or dolls. The term hypercompetition applies to industries that are characterized by permanent, ongoing, intense competition brought about by advancing technology or changing customer tastes and fads and fashions.[25] Clearly, planning and strategy formulation are much more difficult and risky when hypercompetition prevails in an industry.

hypercompetition
Permanent, ongoing, intense competition brought about in an industry by advancing technology or changing customer tastes.

Formulating Business-Level Strategies

Michael Porter, the researcher who developed the five forces model, also developed a theory of how managers can select a business-level strategy—a plan to gain a competitive advantage in a particular market or industry.[26] Porter argued that business-level strategy creates a competitive advantage because it allows an organization (or a division of a company) to *counter and reduce* the threat of the five industry forces. That is, successful business-level strategy reduces rivalry, prevents new competitors from entering the industry, reduces the power of suppliers or buyers, and lowers the threat of substitutes—and this raises prices and profits.

LO 6-2 Differentiate between the main types of business-level strategies and explain how they give an organization a competitive advantage that may lead to superior performance.

According to Porter, to obtain these higher profits managers must choose between two basic ways of increasing the value of an organization's products: *differentiating the product* to increase its value to customers or *lowering the costs* of making the product. Porter also argues that managers must choose between serving the whole market or serving just one segment or part of a market. Based on those choices, managers choose to pursue one of four business-level strategies: low cost, differentiation, focused low cost, or focused differentiation (see Table 6.2).

Low-Cost Strategy

low-cost strategy Driving the organization's costs down below the costs of its rivals.

With a low-cost strategy, managers try to gain a competitive advantage by focusing the energy of all the organization's departments or functions on driving the company's costs down below the costs of its industry rivals. This strategy, for example, would require that manufacturing managers search for new ways to reduce production costs, R&D managers focus on developing new products that can be manufactured more cheaply, and marketing managers find ways to lower the costs of

Table 6.2

Porter's Business-Level Strategies

Strategy	Number of Market Segments Served	
	Many	**Few**
Low cost	√	
Focused low cost		√
Differentiation	√	
Focused differentiation		√

attracting customers. According to Porter, companies pursuing a low-cost strategy can sell a product for less than their rivals sell it and yet still make a good profit because of their lower costs. Thus such organizations enjoy a competitive advantage based on their low prices. For example, BIC pursues a low-cost strategy: It offers customers razor blades priced lower than Gillette's and ballpoint pens less expensive than those offered by Cross or Waterman. Also, when existing companies have low costs and can charge low prices, it is difficult for new companies to enter the industry because entering is always an expensive process.

Differentiation Strategy

differentiation strategy
Distinguishing an organization's products from the products of competitors on dimensions such as product design, quality, or after-sales service.

With a differentiation strategy, managers try to gain a competitive advantage by focusing all the energies of the organization's departments or functions on *distinguishing* the organization's products from those of competitors on one or more important dimensions, such as product design, quality, or after-sales service and support. Often the process of making products unique and different is expensive. This strategy, for example, frequently requires that managers increase spending on product design or R&D to differentiate products, and costs rise as a result. Organizations that successfully pursue a differentiation strategy may be able to charge a *premium price* for their products; the premium price lets organizations pursuing a differentiation strategy recoup their higher costs. Coca-Cola, PepsiCo, and Procter & Gamble are some of the many well-known companies that pursue a strategy of differentiation. They spend enormous amounts of money on advertising to differentiate, and create a unique image for, their products. Also, differentiation makes industry entry difficult because new companies have no brand name to help them compete and customers don't perceive other products to be close substitutes, so this also allows premium pricing and results in high profits.

"Stuck in the Middle"

According to Porter's theory, managers cannot simultaneously pursue both a low-cost strategy and a differentiation strategy. Porter identified a simple correlation: Differentiation raises costs and thus necessitates premium pricing to recoup those high costs. For example, if BIC suddenly began to advertise heavily to try to build a strong global brand image for its products, BIC's costs would rise. BIC then could no longer make a profit simply by pricing its blades or pens lower than Gillette or Cross. According to Porter, managers must choose between a low-cost strategy and a differentiation strategy. He refers to managers and organizations that have not made this choice as being "stuck in the middle."

Organizations stuck in the middle tend to have lower levels of performance than do those that pursue a low-cost or a differentiation strategy. To avoid being stuck in the middle, top managers must instruct departmental managers to take actions that will result in either low cost or differentiation.

However, exceptions to this rule can be found. In many organizations managers have been able to drive costs below those of rivals and simultaneously differentiate their products from those offered by rivals.[27] For example, Toyota's production system is the most efficient—and still one of the most reliable—of any global carmaker. This efficiency gives Toyota a low-cost advantage over its rivals in the global car industry. At the same time, Toyota has differentiated its cars from those of rivals on the basis of superior design and quality. This superiority allows the company to charge a premium price for many of its popular models.[28] Thus Toyota seems to be simultaneously pursuing both a low-cost and a differentiated business-level strategy. This example suggests that although Porter's ideas may be valid in most cases, very well managed companies such as Campbell, Toyota, Apple, and McDonald's may have both low costs and differentiated products— and so make the highest profits of any company in an industry.

Focused Low-Cost and Focused Differentiation Strategies

focused low-cost strategy Serving only one segment of the overall market and trying to be the lowest-cost organization serving that segment.

Both the differentiation strategy and the low-cost strategy are aimed at serving many or most segments of a particular market, such as for cars, toys, foods, or computers. Porter identified two other business-level strategies that aim to serve the needs of customers in only one or a few market segments.[29] Managers pursuing a focused low-cost strategy serve one or a few segments of the overall market and aim to make their organization the lowest-cost company serving that segment. By contrast, managers pursuing a focused differentiation strategy serve just one or a few segments of the market and aim to make their organization the most differentiated company serving that segment.

focused differentiation strategy Serving only one segment of the overall market and trying to be the most differentiated organization serving that segment.

Companies pursuing either of these strategies have chosen to *specialize* in some way by directing their efforts at a particular kind of customer (such as serving the needs of babies or affluent customers) or even the needs of customers in a specific geographic region (customers on the East or West Coast). BMW, for example, pursues a focused differentiation strategy, producing cars exclusively for higher-income customers. By contrast, Toyota pursues a differentiation strategy and produces cars that appeal to consumers in almost all segments of the car market, from basic transportation (Toyota Corolla) through the middle of the market (Toyota Camry) to the high-income end of the market (Lexus). An interesting example of how the Cott Corp., pursuing a focused low-cost strategy by specializing in one market segment, can compete with powerful differentiators was discussed in the opening "Management Snapshot."

Increasingly, smaller companies are finding it easier to pursue a focused strategy and compete successfully against large, powerful, low-cost and differentiated companies because of advances in IT that lower costs and enable them to reach and attract customers. By establishing a storefront on the Web, thousands of small, specialized companies have been able to carve out a profitable niche against large bricks-and-mortar competitors. Zara, a Spanish manufacturer of fashionable clothing whose sales have soared in recent years, provides an excellent example of the way even a small bricks-and-mortar company can use IT to pursue a focused strategy and compete globally.[30] Zara has managed to position itself as the low-price, low-cost leader in the fashion segment of the clothing market, against differentiators like Gucci, Dior, and Armani, because it has applied IT to its specific needs. Zara has created IT that allows it to manage its design and manufacturing process in a way that minimizes the inventory it has to carry—the major cost borne by a clothing retailer. However, its IT also gives its designers instantaneous feedback on which clothes are selling well and in which countries, and this gives Zara a competitive advantage from differentiation. Specifically, Zara can manufacture more of a particular kind of dress or suit to meet high customer demand, decide which clothing should be sold in its rapidly expanding network of global stores, and constantly change the mix of clothes it offers customers to keep up with fashion—at low cost.

Zara models an incredibly successful strategy in jumping on trends and turning out new fashion lines in record time, while its smart store layout allows shoppers to quickly find which styles appeal to them.

Zara's IT also lets it efficiently manage the interface between its design and manufacturing operations. Zara takes only five weeks to design a new collection and then a week to make it. Fashion houses like Chanel and Armani, by contrast, can take six or more months to design a collection and then three more months to make it available in stores.[31] This short time to market gives Zara great flexibility and allows the company to respond quickly to the rapidly changing fashion market, in which fashions can change several times a year. Because of the quick manufacturing-to-sales cycle and just-in-time fashion, Zara offers its clothes collections at relatively low prices and still makes profits that are the envy of the fashion clothing industry.[32]

Zara has been able to pursue a focused strategy that is simultaneously low-cost and differentiated because it has developed many strengths in functions such as clothing design, marketing, and IT that have given it a competitive advantage. Developing functional-level strategies that strengthen business-level strategy and increase competitive advantage is a vital managerial task. Discussion of this important issue is left until the next chapter. First, we need to go up one planning level and examine how corporate strategy helps an organization achieve its mission and goals.

Formulating Corporate-Level Strategies

Once managers have formulated the business-level strategies that will best position a company, or a division of a company, to compete in an industry and outperform its rivals, they must look to the future. If their planning has been successful the company will be generating high profits, and their task now is to plan how to invest these profits to increase performance over time.

LO 6-3 Differentiate between the main types of corporate-level strategies and explain how they are used to strengthen a company's business-level strategy and competitive advantage.

Recall that *corporate-level strategy* is a plan of action that involves choosing in which industries and countries a company should invest its resources to achieve its mission and goals. In choosing a corporate-level strategy, managers ask, How should the growth and development of our company be managed to increase its ability to create value for customers (and thus increase its performance) over the long run? Managers of effective organizations actively seek new opportunities to use a company's resources to create new and improved goods and services for customers. Examples of organizations whose product lines are growing rapidly are Google, Intel, Apple, and Toyota, whose managers pursue any feasible opportunity to use their companies' skills to provide customers with new products.

In addition, some managers must help their organizations respond to threats due to changing forces in the task or general environment that have made their business-level strategies less effective and reduced profits. For example, customers may no longer be buying the kinds of goods and services a company is producing (high-salt soup, bulky CRT televisions, or gas-guzzling SUVs), or other organizations may have entered the market and attracted away customers (this happened to Sony in the 2000s after Apple and Samsung began to produce better

MP3 players, laptops, and flat-screen LCD televisions). Top managers aim to find corporate strategies that can help the organization strengthen its business-level strategies and thus respond to these changes and improve performance.

The principal corporate-level strategies that managers use to help a company grow and keep it at the top of its industry, or to help it retrench and reorganize to stop its decline, are (1) concentration on a single industry, (2) vertical integration, (3) diversification, and (4) international expansion. An organization will benefit from pursuing any of these strategies only when the strategy helps further increase the value of the organization's goods and services so more customers buy them. Specifically, to increase the value of goods and services, a corporate-level strategy must help a company, or one of its divisions, either (1) lower the costs of developing and making products or (2) increase product differentiation so more customers want to buy the products even at high or premium prices. Both of these outcomes strengthen a company's competitive advantage and increase its performance.

Concentration on a Single Industry

concentration on a single industry Reinvesting a company's profits to strengthen its competitive position in its current industry.

Most growing companies reinvest their profits to strengthen their competitive position in the industry in which they are currently operating; in doing so, they pursue the corporate-level strategy of concentration on a single industry. Most commonly, an organization uses its functional skills to develop new kinds of products, or it expands the number of locations in which it uses those skills. For example, Apple continuously introduces improved mobile wireless digital devices such as the iPhone and iPad, whereas McDonald's, which began as one restaurant in California, focused all its efforts on using its resources to quickly expand across the globe to become the biggest and most profitable U.S. fast-food company. The way in which Krispy Kreme focuses all its efforts on the doughnut business is discussed in the following "Management Insight" box.

MANAGEMENT INSIGHT

Krispy Kreme Doughnuts Are Hot Again

Founded in 1937 in Newington, Connecticut, Krispy Kreme is a leading specialty retailer of premium-quality yeast-raised doughnuts; it had over 635 stores operating in 2012. Krispy Kreme's doughnuts have a broad customer following and command a premium price because of their unique taste and quality. The way it has developed competences to increase its operating efficiency and responsiveness to customers is instructive. Krispy Kreme calls its store production operations "doughnut theater" because its physical layout is designed so that customers can see and smell the doughnuts being made by its impressive company-built doughnut-making machines.

What are elements of its production competency? The story starts with the 70-year-old company's secret doughnut recipe that it keeps locked up in a vault. None of its franchisees know the recipe for making its dough, and Krispy Kreme sells the ready-made dough and other ingredients to its stores. Even the machines used to make the doughnuts are company designed and produced, so no doughnut maker can imitate its unique cooking methods and thus create a similar competing product. The doughnut-making machines are designed to produce a wide variety of different kinds of doughnuts in small quantities, and each store makes and sells between 4,000 and 10,000 dozen doughnuts per day.

Krispy Kreme constantly refines its production system to improve the efficiency of its small-batch operations. For example, it redesigned its doughnut machine to include a high-tech extruder that uses air pressure to force doughnut dough into row after row of rings or shells. Employees used to have to adjust air pressure manually as the dough load lightened. Now this is all done automatically. A redesigned doughnut icer dips finished pastries into a puddle of chocolate frosting; employees had to dunk the doughnuts two at a time by hand before the machine was invented. Although the effect of these innovations may seem small, its 635 stores worldwide make billions of doughnuts and they add up to significant gains in productivity—and more satisfied customers. Clearly, Krispy Kreme has developed a niche in the fast-food industry where its superior products command a premium price; it is pursuing a focused strategy that in the 2010s resulted in a soaring stock price.

On the other hand, when organizations are performing effectively, they often decide to enter *new industries* in which they can use their growing profits to establish new operating divisions to create and make a wider range of more valuable products. Thus they begin to pursue vertical integration or diversification—such as Coca-Cola, PepsiCo, and Campbell's Soup, discussed earlier.

Vertical Integration

When an organization is performing well in its industry, managers often see new opportunities to create value either by producing the inputs it uses to make its products or by distributing and selling its products to customers. Managers at E. & J. Gallo Winery, for example, realized they could lower Gallo's costs if the company produced its own wine bottles rather than buying bottles from a glass company that was earning good profits from its bottle sales to Gallo. So Gallo established a new division to produce glass bottles more cheaply than buying them; it quickly found it could also produce bottles in new shapes to help differentiate its wines. Vertical integration is a corporate-level strategy in which a company expands its business operations either backward into a new industry that produces inputs for the company's products (*backward vertical integration*) or forward into a new industry that uses, distributes, or sells the company's products (*forward vertical integration*).[33] A steel company that buys iron ore mines and enters the raw materials industry to supply the ore needed to make steel is engaging in backward vertical integration. A PC maker that decides to enter the retail industry and open a chain of company-owned retail outlets to sell its PCs is engaging in forward integration. For example, Apple entered the retail industry when it set up a chain of Apple stores to sell its PCs and other mobile digital devices.

Figure 6.6 illustrates the four main stages in a typical raw material to customer value chain; value is added to the product at each stage by the activities involved in each industry. For a company based in the assembly stage, backward integration would involve establishing a new division in the intermediate manufacturing or raw material production industries; and forward integration would involve establishing a new division to distribute its products to wholesalers or a retail division to sell directly to customers. A division at one stage or one industry receives

vertical integration
Expanding a company's operations either backward into an industry that produces inputs for its products or forward into an industry that uses, distributes, or sells its products.

Figure 6.6

Stages in a Vertical
Value Chain

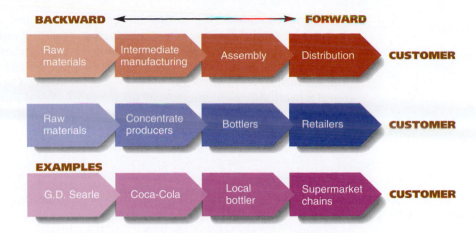

the product produced by the division in the previous stage or industry, transforms it in some way—adding value—and then transfers the output at a higher price to the division at the next stage in the chain.

As an example of how this industry value chain works, consider the cola segment of the soft drink industry. In the raw material industry, suppliers include sugar companies and manufacturers of artificial sweeteners such as NutraSweet and Splenda, which are used in diet colas. These companies sell their products to companies in the soft drink industry that make concentrate—such as Coca-Cola, Cott, and PepsiCo, which mix these inputs with others to produce the cola concentrate. In the process, they add value to these inputs. The concentrate producers then sell the concentrate to companies in the bottling and distribution industry, which add carbonated water to the concentrate and package the resulting drinks—again adding value to the concentrate. Next the bottlers distribute and sell the soft drinks to retailers, including stores such as Costco and Walmart and fast-food chains such as McDonald's. Companies in the retail industry add value by making the product accessible to customers, and they profit from direct sales to customers. Thus value is added by companies at each stage in the raw material to consumer chain.

The reason managers pursue vertical integration is that it allows them either to add value to their products by making them special or unique or to lower the costs of making and selling them. An example of using forward vertical integration to increase differentiation is Apple's decision to open its own stores to make its unique products more accessible to customers who could try them out before they bought them. An example of using forward vertical integration to lower costs is Matsushita's decision to open company-owned stores to sell its Panasonic and JVC products and thus keep the profit that otherwise would be earned by independent retailers.[34] So too is Coca-Cola and PepsiCo's decision to buy their bottlers so they can better differentiate their products and lower costs in the future.

Although vertical integration can strengthen an organization's competitive advantage and increase its performance, it can also reduce an organization's flexibility to respond to changing environmental conditions and create threats that must be countered by changing the organization's strategy. For example, Dell's decision to outsource all its manufacturing and close its U.S. factories to lower costs is an example of how pursuing vertical integration actually lowered the company's performance.[35]

Thus, when considering vertical integration as a strategy to add value, managers must be careful because sometimes it may *reduce* a company's ability to create value when the environment changes. This is why so many companies now outsource the production of component parts to other companies and exit the components industry—by vertically *disintegrating* backward. On the other hand, IBM found a profitable new opportunity for forward vertical integration in the 2000s: It entered the IT consulting services industry to provide advice to global companies about how to install and manage their computer hardware and software, which has become the major source of IBM's profitability in the 2010s.[36]

Diversification

diversification

Expanding a company's business operations into a new industry in order to produce new kinds of valuable goods or services.

Diversification is the corporate-level strategy of expanding a company's business operations into a new industry in order to produce new kinds of valuable goods or services.[37] Examples include PepsiCo's diversification into the snack food business with the purchase of Frito Lay, and Cisco's diversification into consumer electronics when it purchased Linksys. There are two main kinds of diversification: related and unrelated.

related diversification

Entering a new business or industry to create a competitive advantage in one or more of an organization's existing divisions or businesses.

RELATED DIVERSIFICATION Related diversification is the strategy of entering a new business or industry to create a competitive advantage in one or more of an organization's existing divisions or businesses. Related diversification can add value to an organization's products if managers can find ways for its various divisions or business units to share their valuable skills or resources so that synergy is created.[38] Synergy is obtained when the value created by two divisions cooperating is greater than the value that would be created if the two divisions operated separately and independently. For example, suppose two or more divisions of a diversified company can use the same manufacturing facilities, distribution channels, or advertising campaigns—that is, share functional activities. Each division has to invest fewer resources in a shared functional activity than it would have to invest if it performed the functional activity by itself. Related diversification can be a major source of cost savings when divisions share the costs of performing a functional activity.[39] Similarly, if one division's R&D skills can improve another division's products and increase their differentiated appeal, this synergy can give the second division an important competitive advantage over its industry rivals—so the company as a whole benefits from diversification.

synergy Performance gains that result when individuals and departments coordinate their actions.

The way Procter & Gamble's disposable diaper and paper towel divisions cooperate is a good example of the successful production of synergies. These divisions share the costs of procuring inputs such as paper and packaging; a joint sales force sells both products to retail outlets; and both products are shipped using the same distribution system. This resource sharing has enabled both divisions to reduce their costs, and as a result, they can charge lower prices than their competitors and so attract more customers.[40] In addition, the divisions can share the research costs of developing new and improved products, such as finding more absorbent material, that increase both products' differentiated appeal. This is something that is also at the heart of 3M's corporate strategy.[41] From the beginning, 3M has pursued related diversification and created new businesses by leveraging its skills in research and development. Today the company is composed of more than 40 separate divisions positioned in six major business groups: transportation, health care, industrial, consumer and office, electronics and communications, and specialty materials. The company currently operates with the goal

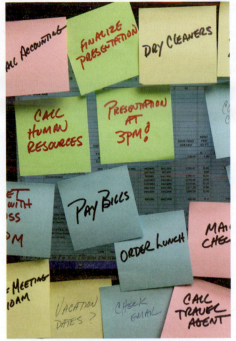

How did we ever survive without Post-it Notes? 3M's intense focus on solving customer problems results in new products that sell well, including countless variations of the original sticky note.

of producing 40% of sales revenues from products introduced within the previous four years.[42]

How does 3M do it? First, the company is a science-based enterprise with a strong tradition of innovation and risk taking. Risk taking is encouraged and failure is not punished but is seen as a natural part of the process of creating new products and business.[43] Second, 3M's management is relentlessly focused on the company's customers and the problems they face. Many of 3M's products have come from helping customers to solve difficult problems. Third, managers set stretch goals that require the company to create new products and businesses at a rapid rate. Fourth, employees are given considerable autonomy to pursue their own ideas; indeed, 15% of employees' time can be spent working on projects of their own choosing without management approval. Many products have resulted from this autonomy, including the ubiquitous Post-it Notes. Fifth, while products belong to business units and business units are responsible for generating profits, the technologies belong to every unit within the company. Anyone at 3M is free to try to develop new applications for a technology developed by its business units. Finally, 3M organizes many companywide meetings where researchers from its different divisions are brought together to share the results of their work. An example of a company that acquired another company to realize the benefits of related diversification is discussed in the following "Management Insight" box.

MANAGEMENT INSIGHT

VF Corp. Acquires Timberland to Realize the Benefits from Related Diversification

In June 2011, U.S.-based VF Corp., the global apparel and clothing maker, announced that it would acquire Timberland, the U.S.-based global footwear maker, for $2 billion.[44] VF is the maker of such established clothing brands as Lee and Wrangler Jeans, Nautica, Kipling, and outdoor apparel makers such as The North Face, JanSport, and Eagle Creek. Timberland is well known for its tough waterproof leather footwear, such as its best-selling hiking boots and its classic boat shoes; it also licenses the right to make clothing and accessories under its brand name. Why would a clothing maker purchase a footwear company that primarily competes in a different industry?

The reason, according to VF's CEO Eric Wiseman, is that the Timberland deal would be a "transformative" acquisition that would add footwear to VF's fastest-growing division, the outdoor and action sports business, which contributed $3.2 billion of VF's total revenues of $7.7 billion.[45] By combining the products of the clothing and footwear division, Wiseman claimed that VF could almost double Timberland's profitability by increasing its global sales by at least 15%. At the same time, the addition of the Timberland brand would increase

Don't forget the shoes: VF's acquistion of Timberland allows them to package their other outdoor clothing goods with the tried-and-true footwear, boosting sales no matter which brand the market knows.

the sales of VF's outdoor brands such as The North Face by 10%. The result would be a major increase in VF's revenues and profitability.

Why would this merger of two very different companies result in so much more value being created? The first reason is that it would allow the company to offer an extended range of outdoor products—clothing, shoes, backpacks, and accessories—that could all be packaged together, distributed to retailers, and marketed and sold to customers. The result would be substantial cost savings because purchasing, distribution, and marketing costs would now be shared between the different brands or product lines in VF's expanded portfolio. In addition, VF would be able to increasingly differentiate its outdoor products by, for example, linking its brand The North Face with the Timberland brand so that customers purchasing outdoor clothing would be more likely to purchase Timberland hiking boots and related accessories such as backpacks offered by VF's other outdoor brands.

In addition, although Timberland is a well-known popular brand in the United States, it generates more than 50% of its revenues from global sales (especially in high-growth markets like China) and it has a niche presence in many countries such as the U.K. and Japan.[46] VF generates only 30% of its revenues from global sales; by taking advantage of the commonalities between its outdoor brands, VF argued that purchasing Timberland would increase its sales in overseas markets, and also increase the brand recognition and sales of its other primary brands such as Wrangler Jeans and Nautica. Thus, the acquisition would allow VF to increase the global differentiated appeal of all its brands, resulting in lower costs. VF would also be able to negotiate better deals with specialist outsourcing companies abroad, and economies of scale would result from reduced global shipping and distribution costs.[47] In a conference call to analysts, Wiseman said, "Timberland has been our Number 1 acquisition priority. It knits together two powerful companies into a new global player in the outdoor and action sports space."

In sum, to pursue related diversification successfully, managers search for new businesses where they can use the existing skills and resources in their departments and divisions to create synergies, add value to new products and businesses, and improve their competitive position and that of the entire company. In addition, managers may try to acquire a company in a new industry because they believe it possesses skills and resources that will improve the performance of one or more of their existing divisions. If successful, such skill transfers can help an organization to lower its costs or better differentiate its products because they create synergies between divisions.

unrelated diversification

Entering a new industry or buying a company in a new industry that is not related in any way to an organization's current businesses or industries.

UNRELATED DIVERSIFICATION Managers pursue unrelated diversification when they establish divisions or buy companies in new industries that are *not* linked in any way to their current businesses or industries. One main reason for pursuing unrelated diversification is that sometimes managers can buy a poorly performing company, transfer their management skills to that company, turn around its business, and increase its performance—all of which create value.

Another reason for pursuing unrelated diversification is that purchasing businesses in different industries lets managers engage in *portfolio strategy,* which is apportioning financial resources among divisions to increase financial returns or spread risks among different businesses, much as individual investors do with their own portfolios. For example, managers may transfer funds from a rich division (a "cash cow") to a new and promising division (a "star") and, by appropriately allocating money between divisions, create value. Though used as a popular explanation in the 1980s for unrelated diversification, portfolio strategy ran into increasing criticism in the 1990s because it simply does not work.[48] Why? As managers expand the scope of their organization's operations and enter more and more industries, it becomes increasingly difficult for top managers to be knowledgeable about all of the organization's diverse businesses. Managers do not have the time to process all of the information required to adequately assess the strategy and performance of each division, and so the performance of the entire company often falls.

This problem has occurred at GE, as its then CEO Reg Jones commented: "I tried to review each business unit plan in great detail. This effort took untold hours and placed a tremendous burden on the corporate executive office. After a while I began to realize that no matter how hard we would work, we could not achieve the necessary in-depth understanding of the 40-odd business unit plans."[49] Unable to handle so much information, top managers are overwhelmed and eventually make important resource allocation decisions on the basis of only a superficial analysis of the competitive position of each division. This usually results in value being lost rather than created.[50]

Thus, although unrelated diversification can potentially create value for a company, research evidence suggests that *too much* diversification can cause managers to lose control of their organization's core business. As a result, diversification can reduce value rather than create it.[51] Because of this, during the last decade there has been an increasing trend for diversified companies to divest many of their unrelated, and sometimes related, divisions. Managers in companies like Tyco, Dial, and Textron have sold off many or most of their divisions and focused on increasing the performance of the core division that remained—in other words, they went back to a strategy of concentrating on a single industry.[52] For example, in 2007 Tyco split into three different companies when it spun off its health care and electronics businesses and focused its activities on engineered and fire and security products, such as its ADT home security business.[53] By 2009 each of the different companies was performing at a higher level under its own team of top managers; by 2012 each division's performance had improved even further.[54]

International Expansion

As if planning whether to vertically integrate, diversify, or concentrate on the core business were not a difficult enough task, corporate-level managers also must decide on the appropriate way to compete internationally. A basic question confronts the managers of any organization that needs to sell its products abroad and compete in more than one national market: To what extent should the organization customize features of its products and marketing campaign to different national conditions?[55]

global strategy
Selling the same standardized product and using the same basic marketing approach in each national market.

multidomestic strategy Customizing products and marketing strategies to specific national conditions.

If managers decide that their organization should sell the same standardized product in each national market in which it competes, and use the same basic marketing approach, they adopt a global strategy.[56] Such companies undertake little, if any, customization to suit the specific needs of customers in different countries. But if managers decide to customize products and marketing strategies to specific national conditions, they adopt a multidomestic strategy. Matsushita, with its Panasonic and JVC brands, has traditionally pursued a global strategy, selling the same basic TVs, camcorders, and DVD and MP3 players in every country in which it does business and often using the same basic marketing approach. Unilever, the European food and household products company, has pursued a multidomestic strategy. Thus, to appeal to German customers, Unilever's German division sells a different range of food products and uses a different marketing approach than its North American division.

Both global and multidomestic strategies have advantages and disadvantages. The major advantage of a global strategy is the significant cost savings associated with not having to customize products and marketing approaches to different national conditions. For example, Rolex watches, Ralph Lauren or Tommy Hilfiger clothing, Chanel or Armani clothing or accessories or perfume, Dell computers, Chinese-made plastic toys and buckets, and U.S.-grown rice and wheat are all products that can be sold using the same marketing across many countries by simply changing the language. Thus, companies can save a significant amount of money. The major disadvantage of pursuing a global strategy is that by ignoring national differences, managers may leave themselves vulnerable to local competitors that differentiate their products to suit local tastes.

Global food makers Kellogg's and Nestlé learned this when they entered the Indian processed food market, which is worth over $100 billion a year. These companies did not understand how to customize their products to the tastes of the Indian market and initially suffered large losses. When Kellogg's launched its breakfast cereals in India, for example, it failed to understand that most Indians eat cooked breakfasts because milk is normally not pasteurized. Today, with the growing availability of pasteurized or canned milk, it offers exotic cereals made from basmati rice and flavored with mango to appeal to customers. Similarly, Nestlé's Maggi noodles failed to please Indian customers until it gave them a "marsala" or mixed curry spice flavor; today its noodles have become a staple in Indian school lunches.

The advantages and disadvantages of a multidomestic strategy are the opposite of those of a global strategy. The major advantage of a multidomestic strategy is that by customizing product offerings and marketing approaches to local conditions, managers may be able to gain market share or charge higher prices for their products. The major disadvantage is that customization raises production costs and puts the multidomestic company at a price disadvantage because it often has to charge prices higher than the prices charged by competitors pursuing a global strategy. Obviously the choice between these two strategies calls for trade-offs.

Managers at Gillette, the well-known razor blade maker that is now part of Procter & Gamble (P&G), created a strategy that combined the best features of both international strategies. Like P&G, Gillette has always been a global organization because its managers quickly saw the advantages of selling its core product, razor blades, in as many countries as possible. Gillette's strategy over the years has been pretty constant: Find a new country with a growing market for razor blades,

A study in contrasts. Matsushita, with its Panasonic brand (shown on the left), has largely pursued a global strategy, selling the same basic TVs and DVD players in every market and using a similar marketing message. Unilever, on the other hand, has pursued a multidomestic strategy, tailoring its product line and marketing approach to specific locations. On the right, the CEO of Hindustan Unilever, Keki Dadiseth, holds a box of Surf detergent designed for local customers.

form a strategic alliance with a local razor blade company and take a majority stake in it, invest in a large marketing campaign, and then build a modern factory to make razor blades and other products for the local market. For example, when Gillette entered Russia after the breakup of the Soviet Union, it saw a huge opportunity to increase sales. It formed a joint venture with a local company called Leninets Concern, which made a razor known as the Sputnik, and then with this base began to import its own brands into Russia. When sales grew sharply, Gillette decided to offer more products in the market and built a new plant in St. Petersburg.[57]

In establishing factories in countries where labor and other costs are low and then distributing and marketing its products to countries in that region of the world, Gillette pursued a global strategy. However, all of Gillette's research and development and design activities are located in the United States. As it develops new kinds of razors, it equips its foreign factories to manufacture them when it decides that local customers are ready to trade up to the new product. So, for example, Gillette's latest razor may be introduced in a country abroad years later than in the United States. Thus Gillette customizes its products to the needs of different countries and so also pursues a multidomestic strategy.

By pursuing this kind of international strategy, Gillette achieves low costs and still differentiates and customizes its product range to suit the needs of each country or world region.[58] P&G pursues a similar international strategy, and the merger between them to create the world's largest consumer products company came about because of the value that could be realized by pursuing related diversification at a global level. For example, P&G's corporate managers realized that substantial global synergies could be obtained by combining their global manufacturing, distribution, and sales operations across countries and world regions. These synergies have saved billions of dollars.[59] At the same time, by pooling their knowledge of the needs of customers in different countries, the combined companies can better differentiate and position products throughout the world. P&G's strategy is working; its principal competitors Colgate and Unilever have not performed well in the 2010s, and P&G has developed a commanding global position.

CHOOSING A WAY TO EXPAND INTERNATIONALLY As we have discussed, a more competitive global environment has proved to be both an opportunity and a threat for organizations and managers. The opportunity is that organizations that expand globally can open new markets, reach more customers, and gain access to new sources of raw materials and to low-cost suppliers of inputs. The threat is that organizations that expand globally are likely to encounter new competitors in the foreign countries they enter and must respond to new political, economic, and cultural conditions.

Before setting up foreign operations, managers of companies such as Amazon.com, Lands' End, GE, P&G, and Boeing needed to analyze the forces in the environment of a particular country (such as Korea or Brazil) to choose the right method to expand and respond to those forces in the most appropriate way. In general, four basic ways to operate in the global environment are importing and exporting, licensing and franchising, strategic alliances, and wholly owned foreign subsidiaries, Gillette's preferred approach. We briefly discuss each one, moving from the lowest level of foreign involvement and investment required of a global organization and its managers, and the least amount of risk, to the high end of the spectrum (see Figure 6.7).[60]

Importing and Exporting   The least complex global operations are exporting and importing. A company engaged in exporting makes products at home and sells them abroad. An organization might sell its own products abroad or allow a local organization in the foreign country to distribute its products. Few risks are associated with exporting because a company does not have to invest in developing manufacturing facilities abroad. It can further reduce its investment abroad if it allows a local company to distribute its products.

A company engaged in importing sells products at home that are made abroad (products it makes itself or buys from other companies). For example, most of the products that Pier 1 Imports and The Limited sell to their customers are made abroad. In many cases the appeal of a product—Irish crystal, French wine, Italian furniture, or Indian silk—is that it is made abroad. The Internet has made it much easier for companies to tell potential foreign buyers about their products; detailed product specifications and features are available online, and informed buyers can communicate easily with prospective sellers.

LICENSING AND FRANCHISING   In licensing, a company (the licenser) allows a foreign organization (the licensee) to take charge of both manufacturing and distributing one or more of its products in the licensee's country or world region in return for a negotiated fee. Chemical maker DuPont might license a local factory in India to produce nylon or Teflon. The advantage of licensing is that the licenser does not have to bear the development costs associated with opening up

exporting Making products at home and selling them abroad.

importing Selling products at home that are made abroad.

licensing Allowing a foreign organization to take charge of manufacturing and distributing a product in its country or world region in return for a negotiated fee.

Figure 6.7

Four Ways to Expand Internationally

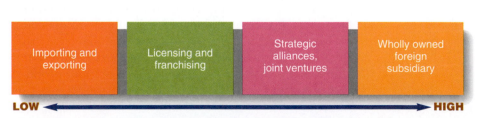

LOW ← Level of foreign involvement and investment and degree of risk → HIGH

Importing and exporting | Licensing and franchising | Strategic alliances, joint ventures | Wholly owned foreign subsidiary

in a foreign country; the licensee bears the costs. The risks associated with this strategy are that the company granting the license has to give its foreign partner access to its technological know-how and so risks losing control of its secrets.

Whereas licensing is pursued primarily by manufacturing companies, franchising is pursued primarily by service organizations. In franchising, a company (the franchiser) sells to a foreign organization (the franchisee) the rights to use its brand name and operating know-how in return for a lump-sum payment and share of the franchiser's profits. Hilton Hotels might sell a franchise to a local company in Chile to operate hotels under the Hilton name in return for a franchise payment. The advantage of franchising is that the franchiser does not have to bear the development costs of overseas expansion and avoids the many problems associated with setting up foreign operations. The downside is that the organization that grants the franchise may lose control over how the franchisee operates, and product quality may fall. In this way franchisers, such as Hilton, Avis, and McDonald's, risk losing their good names. American customers who buy McDonald's hamburgers in Korea may reasonably expect those burgers to be as good as the ones they get at home. If they are not, McDonald's reputation will suffer over time. Once again, the Internet facilitates communication between partners and allows them to better meet each other's expectations.

STRATEGIC ALLIANCES   One way to overcome the loss-of-control problems associated with exporting, licensing, and franchising is to expand globally by means of a strategic alliance. In a strategic alliance, managers pool or share their organization's resources and know-how with those of a foreign company, and the two organizations share the rewards or risks of starting a new venture in a foreign country. Sharing resources allows a U.S. company, for example, to take advantage of the high-quality skills of foreign manufacturers and the specialized knowledge of foreign managers about the needs of local customers and to reduce the risks involved in a venture. At the same time, the terms of the alliance give the U.S. company more control over how the good or service is produced or sold in the foreign country than it would have as a franchiser or licenser.

A strategic alliance can take the form of a written contract between two or more companies to exchange resources, or it can result in the creation of a new organization. A joint venture is a strategic alliance among two or more companies that agree to jointly establish and share the ownership of a new business.[61] An organization's level of involvement abroad increases in a joint venture because the alliance normally involves a capital investment in production facilities abroad in order to produce goods or services outside the home country. Risk, however, is reduced. The Internet and global teleconferencing provide the increased communication and coordination necessary for global partners to work together. For example, Coca-Cola and Nestlé formed a joint venture to market their teas, coffees, and health-oriented beverages in more than 50 countries.[62] Similarly, BP Amoco and Italy's ENI formed a joint venture to build a $2.5 billion gas liquefaction plant in Egypt.[63]

WHOLLY OWNED FOREIGN SUBSIDIARIES   When managers decide to establish a wholly owned foreign subsidiary, they invest in establishing production operations in a foreign country independent of any local direct involvement. Many Japanese car component companies, for example, have established their own operations in the United States to supply U.S.-based Japanese carmakers such as Toyota and Honda with high-quality car components.

---

franchising Selling to a foreign organization the rights to use a brand name and operating know-how in return for a lump-sum payment and a share of the profits.

strategic alliance An agreement in which managers pool or share their organization's resources and know-how with a foreign company, and the two organizations share the rewards and risks of starting a new venture.

joint venture A strategic alliance among two or more companies that agree to jointly establish and share the ownership of a new business.

wholly owned foreign subsidiary Production operations established in a foreign country independent of any local direct involvement.

Operating alone, without any direct involvement from foreign companies, an organization receives all of the rewards and bears all of the risks associated with operating abroad.[64] This method of international expansion is much more expensive than the others because it requires a higher level of foreign investment and presents managers with many more threats. However, investment in a foreign subsidiary or division offers significant advantages: It gives an organization high potential returns because the organization does not have to share its profits with a foreign organization, and it reduces the level of risk because the organization's managers have full control over all aspects of their foreign subsidiary's operations. Moreover, this type of investment allows managers to protect their technology and know-how from foreign organizations. Large well-known companies like DuPont, GM, and P&G, which have plenty of resources, make extensive use of wholly owned subsidiaries.

Obviously, global companies can use many of these different corporate strategies simultaneously to create the most value and strengthen their competitive position. We discussed earlier how P&G pursues related diversification at the global level while it pursues an international strategy that is a mixture of global and multidomestic. P&G also pursues vertical integration: It operates factories that make many of the specialized chemicals used in its products; it operates in the container industry and makes the thousands of different glass and plastic bottles and jars that contain its products; it prints its own product labels; and it distributes its products using its own fleet of trucks. Although P&G is highly diversified, it still puts the focus on its core individual product lines because it is famous for pursuing brand management—it concentrates resources around each brand, which in effect is managed as a "separate company." So P&G is trying to add value in every way it can from its corporate and business strategies.

At the business level P&G aggressively pursues differentiation and charges premium prices for its products. However, it also strives to lower its costs and pursues the corporate-level strategies just discussed to achieve this.

Planning and Implementing Strategy

After identifying appropriate business and corporate strategies to attain an organization's mission and goals, managers confront the challenge of putting those strategies into action. Strategy implementation is a five-step process:

1. Allocating responsibility for implementation to the appropriate individuals or groups.
2. Drafting detailed action plans that specify how a strategy is to be implemented.
3. Establishing a timetable for implementation that includes precise, measurable goals linked to the attainment of the action plan.
4. Allocating appropriate resources to the responsible individuals or groups.
5. Holding specific individuals or groups responsible for the attainment of corporate, divisional, and functional goals.

LO 6-4 Describe the vital role managers play in implementing strategies to achieve an organization's mission and goals.

The planning process goes beyond just identifying effective strategies; it also includes plans to ensure that these strategies are put into action. Normally the plan for implementing a new strategy requires the development of new functional strategies, the redesign of an organization's structure, and the development of new control systems; it might also require a new program to change an organization's culture. These are issues we address in the next three chapters.

Summary and Review

PLANNING Planning is a three-step process: (1) determining an organization's mission and goals; (2) formulating strategy; and (3) implementing strategy. Managers use planning to identify and select appropriate goals and courses of action for an organization and to decide how to allocate the resources they need to attain those goals and carry out those actions. A good plan builds commitment for the organization's goals, gives the organization a sense of direction and purpose, coordinates the different functions and divisions of the organization, and controls managers by making them accountable for specific goals. In large organizations planning takes place at three levels: corporate, business or divisional, and functional or departmental. Long-term plans have a time horizon of five years or more; intermediate-term plans, between one and five years; and short-term plans, one year or less. **[LO 6-1]**

DETERMINING MISSION AND GOALS AND FORMULATING STRATEGY Determining the organization's mission requires that managers define the business of the organization and establish major goals. Strategy formulation requires that managers perform a SWOT analysis and then choose appropriate strategies at the corporate, business, and functional levels. At the business level, managers are responsible for developing a successful low-cost and/or differentiation strategy, either for the whole market or a particular segment of it. At the functional level, departmental managers develop strategies to help the organization either add value to its products by differentiating them or lower the costs of value creation. At the corporate level, organizations use strategies such as concentration on a single industry, vertical integration, related and unrelated diversification, and international expansion to strengthen their competitive advantage by increasing the value of the goods and services provided to customers. **[LO 6-1, 6-2, 6-3]**

IMPLEMENTING STRATEGY Strategy implementation requires that managers allocate responsibilities to appropriate individuals or groups; draft detailed action plans that specify how a strategy is to be implemented; establish a timetable for implementation that includes precise, measurable goals linked to the attainment of the action plan; allocate appropriate resources to the responsible individuals or groups; and hold individuals or groups accountable for the attainment of goals. **[LO 6-4]**

Management *in Action*

TOPICS FOR DISCUSSION AND ACTION

Discussion

1. Describe the three steps of planning. Explain how they are related. **[LO 6-1]**

2. What is the relationship among corporate-, business-, and functional-level strategies, and how do they create value for an organization? **[LO 6-2, 6-3]**

3. Pick an industry and identify four companies in the industry

that pursue one of the four main business-level strategies (low-cost, focused low-cost, etc.). [LO 6-1, 6-2]

4. What is the difference between vertical integration and related diversification? [LO 6-3]

Action

5. Ask a manager about the kinds of planning exercises he or she regularly uses. What are the purposes of these exercises, and what are their advantages or disadvantages? [LO 6-1]

6. Ask a manager to identify the corporate- and business-level strategies used by his or her organization. [LO 6-2, 6-3]

BUILDING MANAGEMENT SKILLS

How to Analyze a Company's Strategy [LO 6-2, 6-3]

Pick a well-known business organization that has received recent press coverage and that provides its annual reports at its website. From the information in the articles and annual reports, answer these questions.

1. What is (are) the main industry(ies) in which the company competes?

2. What business-level strategy does the company seem to be pursuing in this industry? Why?

3. What corporate-level strategies is the company pursuing? Why?

4. Have there been any major changes in its strategy recently? Why?

MANAGING ETHICALLY [LO 6-1, 6-4]

A few years ago, IBM announced that it had fired the three top managers of its Argentine division because of their involvement in a scheme to secure a $250 million contract for IBM to provide and service the computers of one of Argentina's largest state-owned banks. The three executives paid $14 million of the contract money to a third company, CCR, which paid nearly $6 million to phantom companies. This $6 million was then used to bribe the bank executives who agreed to give IBM the contract.

These bribes are not necessarily illegal under Argentine law. Moreover, the three managers argued that all companies have to pay bribes to get new business contracts and they were not doing anything that managers in other companies were not.

Questions

1. Either by yourself or in a group, decide if the business practice of paying bribes is ethical or unethical.

2. Should IBM allow its foreign divisions to pay bribes if all other companies are doing so?

3. If bribery is common in a particular country, what effect would this likely have on the nation's economy and culture?

Form groups of three or four people, and appoint one member as the spokesperson who will communicate your findings to the class when called on by the instructor. Then discuss the following scenario.

You are a team of managers of a major national clothing chain, and you have been charged with finding a way to restore your organization's competitive advantage. Recently, your organization has been experiencing increasing competition from two sources. First, discount stores such as Walmart and Target have been undercutting your prices because they buy their clothes from low-cost foreign manufacturers while you buy most of yours from high-quality domestic suppliers. Discount stores have been attracting your customers who buy at the low end of the price range. Second, small boutiques opening in malls provide high-price designer clothing and are attracting your customers at the high end of the market. Your company has become stuck in the middle, and you have to decide what to do: Should you start to buy abroad so that you can lower your prices and begin to pursue a low-cost strategy? Should you focus on the high end of the market and become more of a differentiator?

Or should you try to pursue both a low-cost strategy and a differentiation strategy?

1. Using SWOT analysis, analyze the pros and cons of each alternative.

2. Think about the various clothing retailers in your local malls and city, and analyze the choices they have made about how to compete with one another along the low-cost and differentiation dimensions.

BE THE MANAGER [LO 6-1, 6-2]

A group of investors in your city is considering opening a new upscale supermarket to compete with the major supermarket chains that are currently dominating the city's marketplace. They have called you in to help them determine what kind of upscale supermarket they should open. In other words, how can they best develop a competitive advantage against existing supermarket chains?

Question

1. List the supermarket chains in your city, and identify their strengths and weaknesses.

2. What business-level strategies are these supermarkets currently pursuing?

3. What kind of supermarket would do best against the competition? What kind of business-level strategy should it pursue?

BLOOMBERG BUSINESSWEEK
CASE IN THE NEWS [LO 6-1, 6-2, 6-3]

GM, Ford, and Chrysler: The Detroit Three Are Back, Right?

Tall and slender, in a minidress that could have been designed by Miuccia Prada for Marvel Comics, "Lady Stingray" towers over her lord, the 2014 Chevrolet Corvette Stingray. Both are being ogled, its the opening day of the New York International Auto Show. Lady Stingray circles the sports car, trailing one hand along it, talking about extruded aluminum and paddle shifters and carbon fiber.

General Motors (GM) is hoping the Corvette's sex appeal draws in a whole new sort of buyer, the kind that currently prowls the roadways in an Audi (NSU) or a BMW (BMW). More important, GM is looking to the car to lend its Chevrolet brand a touch of élan, helping to erase the public's perception of General Motors as a stodgy industrial behemoth that made good trucks but lousy cars. If it succeeds, the Corvette could well become a symbol of a new era, not only at GM, but also for the American auto industry. A better symbol, though, is something less glamorous: a compact like the Chevy Cruze.

Four years ago, GM and Chrysler had to go through bankruptcy, and the federal government was in the process of pouring $80 billion into the industry. Ford Motor, which managed to survive without bailout funds, had asked Congress the year before for an emergency $9 billion credit line. Today, all three boast healthy bottom lines. GM reported record profits of $9.19 billion in 2011, and Ford hit its own third-quarter record last year. In March all three had particularly strong sales—Ford and Chrysler reported their best numbers since before the recession. On one level, the recipe has been simple: They've gotten their labor costs down, and they're building cars people want to buy. After lagging for decades, American cars have closed the gap with their Japanese rivals in quality ratings. And Detroit has become competitive—and profitable—in the small and midsize car market, a segment it used to concede to the competition.

It's been a very good run for three companies that only a few years ago were famed for hubris and mismanagement. As well as they've played their cards, they've been lucky, too, benefiting from government aid, a (slowly) growing economy, and trouble, self-inflicted and otherwise, at Japan's automakers. The durability of the American car resurgence is an open question. And for a variety

of reasons, this year is when it will start to be answered in earnest.

In 1925 a former star executive from GM named Walter Chrysler founded his own car company. Three years later, after he bought Dodge Brothers, the Automotive Daily News coined the term "the Big Three" to describe the dominant troika that Chrysler formed with GM and Ford. In 2006, however, Toyota Motor (TM) displaced Chrysler as third in U.S. auto sales, and two years later Toyota took the title of the world's largest automaker from GM. These days people in the auto industry don't talk about the Big Three; they talk about the Detroit Three. Because the broader economic meltdown of 2008 struck suddenly, it can be easy to forget that American automakers were troubled well before the housing bubble. True, they were the undisputed market leaders in light trucks and SUVs, and the popularity and high margins of Chevy Silverados, Ford Explorers, and Jeep Grand Cherokees helped them regain some of the U.S. market share that the Japanese had taken in the 1980s and early 1990s. The rest of their offerings, however, were another story: Cars like the Chevy Prizm, the Chrysler Sebring, and the briefly revived Ford Thunderbird were uninspired, unreliable, and underperforming on the road and in showrooms.

The mediocrity of those models reflected complacency, as well as the warped economics of Detroit's automakers. GM, Ford, and Chrysler were saddled with union contracts that had been made to preserve labor peace when revenues were far healthier, and were on the hook not only for generous salaries and benefits but retiree health care and pensions. The Center for Automotive Research has calculated that once

all those costs were factored in, GM was spending $78 per hour on each worker. Japanese automakers were spending about $50 per hour at their U.S. factories. When that difference was coming out of the $40,000 price of a Chevy Suburban, there was plenty of profit left. But a $15,000 compact simply couldn't make money with labor that expensive. In other words, the Detroit Three built bad small and midsize cars in part because they didn't see it as worth their while to make them good. "They were basically offending new car buyers in the entry-level and 'move-up' segments," says Kevin Tynan, an auto analyst at Bloomberg Industries. "They didn't care because there was no margin there. They figured it was OK because when you were more affluent and it came time to buy a truck or SUV, they were the only game in town."

Rather than continue to make unloved and low-margin small cars, one sensible option would have been to stop making them, or drastically scale back production and concentrate on higher-margin trucks and SUVs. Two obstacles prevented that. One was the Corporate Average Fuel Economy (CAFE) standard, which requires the average fuel efficiency of a carmaker's fleet, weighted for sales, to be above a certain level; the Obama administration announced that by 2025 the standard will be 54.5 miles per gallon. If the Detroit Three had stopped making compacts and midsize cars, they would have had to pay hefty fines on their profitable pickups and SUVs, so instead the companies opted to keep churning out cars that customers didn't want. To offload the vehicles, dealers had to offer deep discounts and rebates, further cutting into profitability. Or the cars were sold to rental companies, which would use them for a few years then dump them into the used-car market, depressing the cars' resale values and further lessening their appeal. When gas prices shot up in the wake of Hurricane Katrina and buyers fell out of love with gas guzzlers, the Detroit Three's chronic problems grew acute. With the financial crisis, they appeared fatal.

Each of the Detroit Three has followed a different path through the crisis. GM stood on its own, though only after a painful restructuring that forced GM to cut four brands (Pontiac, Hummer, Saturn, and Saab), close or idle 14 plants, and shed more than 1,000 dealers as it went through Chapter 11 bankruptcy. Chrysler also went through Chapter 11 and was sold to Italian carmaker Fiat with similar cuts. The outlier, Ford, didn't require a bailout. In 2006 incoming CEO Alan Mulally had forced the company through a restructuring without bankruptcy, buying out tens of thousands of hourly workers, closing plants, and selling Land Rover and Jaguar to India's Tata Motors. The company went to the capital markets and borrowed $23.4 billion, pledging real estate, factories, even the trademark to its famed blue oval logo as collateral. Although Ford was widely seen as in worse shape than GM at the time—it lost $12.6 billion in 2006—Mulally's actions spared the company from bankruptcy.

One major problem was that GM and Ford had long allowed individual brands and divisions to function as fiefdoms, which created redundancies in everything from research and design to marketing. Now Ford, in particular, has moved toward building more of its cars using the same platforms, taking advantage of its size and globe-spanning reach in ways that

companies such as Toyota and Hyundai Motor do. Such savings have allowed all three American automakers to pay attention to the small cars they'd once disdained. It's an important segment: Entry-level cars are where Japanese models win over customers when they're young and keep them as they trade up. Compacts are even more important now that no one expects dollar-a-gallon gas anymore. "It was unheard of, GM selling a $12,000 Chevy and making money on it," says Adam Jonas, a Morgan Stanley (MS) auto analyst. "Now they can."

Ford enjoyed an advantage in that department, having traditionally been stronger in Europe, where high gas prices made small cars more popular. In 2012 the Ford Focus compact was the best-selling car in the world. In the U.S. in recent months, the midsize Fusion has been selling almost as many units as the longtime segment leaders, the Toyota Camry and Honda Accord. GM has also gotten in the game: The Chevy Cruze has been selling in the 15,000- to 25,000-a-month range and for a couple of stretches in 2011 and 2012 it was the best-selling compact in the country. Chrysler's small cars (think Dodge Neon) have had a reputation as clunkers. Yet under Fiat the company revived the Dodge Dart last summer. The compact impressed the critics and, after a slow start, has caught on with buyers—a little more than 8,000 were sold in March. The desirability of these models has allowed American automakers to address their addiction to discounts and rebates. Holding the line on prices means they make more money from each sale.

Not all the Detroit Three's recent success has been the result of small cars. The two best-selling

vehicles in the country are pickup trucks: the Ford F-Series (67,500 sold in March) and the Chevy Silverado (39,600). But few in the industry expect truck sales to rebound to the numbers of 2004, when Americans bought 940,000 F-Series. Last year's sales were two-thirds that. In addition, many drivers who bought SUVs to ferry the kids to and from school and soccer practice are turning to something called the crossover utility vehicle, part minivan, part SUV on a car chassis. A leader in the U.S. market is the Ford Explorer—once a best-selling SUV, it's now built on the Ford Taurus platform.

To make up for lost revenue on trucks and the still-slim margins on smaller cars, GM and Ford are trying to get consumers to take a second look at the companies' luxury brands. Cadillac has had some success luring drivers from Toyota's Lexus and the German automakers, and its new ATS compact sedan—meant to compete with the BMW 3 series and the Mercedes C-Class—is selling briskly. In March, Cadillac sold 15,800 vehicles, up 50 percent from the previous year. Lincoln, however, is still struggling to generate much excitement despite high-profile redesigns. Sales have been anemic—6,800 last month. At the New York auto show, Lincoln hosted its share of the curious, but nothing like the aspirational throngs at the neighboring BMW and Audi exhibits.

Just as it took time for Americans to give up on American cars, it will take time for them to covet a Lincoln or believe that Chrysler or GM can make a small car as well as Toyota. And the nature of the American car market is changing. Surveys of people in their late teens and early twenties suggest they are less interested in cars than their parents were. The University of Michigan's Transportation Research Institute found that from 1983 to 2008 the percentage of 19-year-olds with a driver's license fell from 87.3 percent to 75.5 percent. Two years later it hit 69.5 percent. Urbanization is partly to blame along with high gas prices and high youth unemployment. In an era of virtual connectivity, being able to drive somewhere doesn't feel as necessary or as liberating as it once did. No one knows exactly what this means for the industry.

While the offerings from GM, Ford, and Chrysler have markedly improved over the past few years, so have everyone else's. "Every year the bar gets set higher on quality metrics," says John Hoffecker, a managing director at the consulting firm AlixPartners. "What you see is that almost everybody is better than the very best were five to 10 years ago." The Detroit Three have caught their competition. Keeping pace will be just as tough.

Questions

1. What kind of planning and strategic errors led to the downfall of the Big Three Detroit carmakers?

2. What new corporate-, business-, and functional-level strategies did the Big Three adopt to help them better compete in the car market? How successful have they been?

3. What kind of new competitive challenges are the Big Three facing today? Search the Internet to see how they are faring against their global competitors.

Source: Drake Bennett, "GM, Ford, and Chrysler: The Detroit Three Are Back, Right?" *Bloomberg BusinessWeek,* April 4, 2013, www.businessweek.com.

7 Designing Organizational Structure

LEARNING OBJECTIVES

After studying this chapter, you should be able to:

1 Identify the factors that influence managers' choice of an organizational structure. **[LO 7-1]**

2 Explain how managers group tasks into jobs that are motivating and satisfying for employees. **[LO 7-2]**

3 Describe the types of organizational structures managers can design, and explain why they choose one structure over another. **[LO 7-3]**

4 Explain why managers must coordinate jobs, functions, and divisions using the hierarchy of authority and integrating mechanisms. **[LO 7-4]**

MANAGEMENT SNAPSHOT

Avon's Global Structure Results in a Disaster

How Should Managers Organize to Improve Performance?

After a decade of profitable growth, Avon suddenly began to experience falling global sales in the mid-2000s both in developing markets in Central Europe, Russia, and China, a major source of its rising sales, and in the United States and Mexico. Avon's stock price plunged in 2007 and its CEO Andrea Jung was shocked by this turn of events.[1] After several months jetting around the globe to visit the managers of its different global divisions, Jung came to a surprising conclusion: Avon's rapid global expansion had given these managers too much autonomy. They had gained so much authority to control operations in their respective geographic regions or countries that they now made decisions to benefit their own divisions—and these decisions had hurt the performance of the whole company.

Avon's country-level managers from Poland to Mexico ran their own factories, made their own product development decisions, and developed their own advertising campaigns. And these decisions were often based on poor marketing knowledge and

with little concern for operating costs; their goal was to increase sales as fast as possible. Also, when too much authority is decentralized to managers lower in an organization's hierarchy, these managers often recruit more managers to help them build their country "empires." The result was that Avon's global organizational hierarchy had exploded—it had risen from 7 levels to 15 levels of managers in a decade as tens of thousands of extra managers were hired around the globe.[2]

Jung realized she had to lay off thousands of Avon's global managers and restructure its organizational hierarchy to reduce costs and increase profitability. She embarked on a program to take away the authority of Avon's country-level managers and transfer authority to managers in charge of global product divisions who were located at corporate headquarters to streamline decision making and reduce costs. She cut out seven levels of management and laid off 25% of Avon's global managers in its 114 worldwide markets. Then, using teams of expert product group managers from corporate headquarters, she examined the way Avon operated to find out how Avon's operating costs could be slashed. In Mexico one team found that country managers' desire to expand their empires led to the development of a staggering 13,000 different products! Not only had this led product development costs to soar but it had also caused major marketing problems: How could Avon's Mexican sales reps learn about the differences between so many products to help customers choose the right ones for them? In Avon's new structure, the goal is to centralize all major new product development.

Jung and all her managers were focused on making operational decisions in the best interests of the whole company, but their continuing efforts to streamline the company's organizational structure failed and losses continued to increase. Continuing efforts to restructure and downsize the company and realign its global value chain operations were not enough to turn the company around. In 2012, after rising shareholder protests, Jung was replaced as CEO by Sherilyn S. McCoy, formerly head of consumer products at Johnson & Johnson.[3] By 2013, after McCoy had instituted another major global reorganization to slash costs, Avon's performance increased sharply and its stock price soared.

Overview

As the "Management Snapshot" suggests, the challenge facing Sherilyn McCoy at Avon was to identify the best way to organize and control managers in the new competitive global environment. In this chapter, we examine how managers can organize and control human and other resources to create high-performing organizations.

By the end of this chapter, you will be familiar not only with the main types of organizational structure but also with the important factors that determine the organizational structure, design choices that managers make. Then, in Chapter 8, we examine issues surrounding the design of an organization's control systems.

Designing Organizational Structure

L07-1 Identify the factors that influence managers' choice of an organizational structure.

organizational structure A formal system of task and reporting relationships that coordinates and motivates organizational members so that they work together to achieve organizational goals.

Organizing is the process by which managers establish the structure of working relationships among employees to allow them to achieve organizational goals efficiently and effectively. Organizational structure is the formal system of task and job reporting relationships that determines how employees use resources to achieve organizational goals.[4] Organizational design is the process by which managers make specific organizing choices about tasks and job relationships that result in the construction of a particular organizational structure.[5]

According to *contingency theory,* managers design organizational structures to fit the factors or circumstances that are affecting the company the most and causing them the most uncertainty.[6] Thus, there is no one best way to design an organization: Design reflects each organization's specific situation, and researchers have argued that in some situations stable, mechanistic structures may be most appropriate while in others flexible, organic structures might be the most effective. Four factors are important determinants of the type of organizational structure or organizing method managers select: the nature of the organizational environment, the type of strategy the organization pursues, the technology (and particularly *information technology*) the organization uses, and the characteristics of the organization's human resources (see Figure 7.1).[7]

The Organizational Environment

In general, the more quickly the external environment is changing and the greater the uncertainty within it, the greater are the problems facing managers in trying

organizational design The process by which managers make specific organizing choices that result in a particular kind of organizational structure.

to gain access to scarce resources. In this situation, to speed decision making and communication and make it easier to obtain resources, managers typically make organizing choices that result in more flexible structures and entrepreneurial cultures.[8] They are likely to decentralize authority, empower lower-level employees to make important operating decisions, and encourage values and norms that emphasize change and innovation—a more organic form of organizing.

In contrast, if the external environment is stable, resources are readily available, and uncertainty is low, then less coordination and communication among people and functions are needed to obtain resources. Managers can make organizing choices that bring more stability or formality to the organizational structure and can establish values and norms that emphasize obedience and being a team player. Managers in this situation prefer to make decisions within a clearly defined hierarchy of authority and to use detailed rules, standard operating procedures (SOPs), and restrictive norms to guide and govern employees' activities— a more mechanistic form of organizing.

As we discussed in Chapter 4, change is rapid in today's global marketplace, and increasing competition both at home and abroad is putting greater pressure on managers to attract customers and increase efficiency and effectiveness. Consequently, interest in finding ways to structure organizations—such as through empowerment and self-managed teams—to allow people and departments to behave flexibly has been increasing.

Strategy

Chapter 6 suggested that once managers decide on a strategy, they must choose the right means to implement it. Different strategies often call for the use of different organizational structures and cultures. For example, a differentiation strategy aimed at increasing the value customers perceive in an organization's goods and services usually succeeds best in a flexible structure with a culture that values innovation; flexibility facilitates a differentiation strategy because managers can develop new or innovative products quickly—an activity that requires extensive cooperation among functions or departments. In contrast, a low-cost strategy that is aimed at driving down costs in all functions usually fares best in a more formal

Figure 7.1

Factors Affecting Organizational Structure

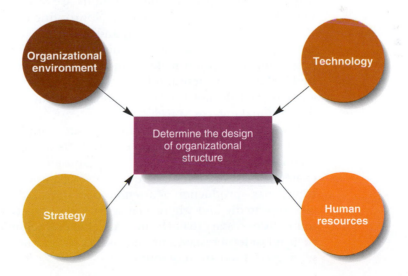

structure with more conservative norms, which gives managers greater control over the activities of an organization's various departments.[9]

In addition, at the corporate level, when managers decide to expand the scope of organizational activities by vertical integration or diversification, for example, they need to design a flexible structure to provide sufficient coordination among the different business divisions.[10] As discussed in Chapter 6, many companies have been divesting businesses because managers have been unable to create a competitive advantage to keep them up to speed in fast-changing industries. By moving to a more flexible structure, managers gain more control over their different businesses. Finally, expanding internationally and operating in many different countries challenges managers to create organizational structures that allow organizations to be flexible on a global level.[11] As we discuss later, managers can group their departments or divisions in several ways to allow them to effectively pursue an international strategy.

Technology

Recall that technology is the combination of skills, knowledge, machines, and computers that are used to design, make, and distribute goods and services. As a rule, the more complicated the technology that an organization uses, the more difficult it is to regulate or control it because more unexpected events can arise. Thus, the more complicated the technology, the greater is the need for a flexible structure and progressive culture to enhance managers' ability to respond to unexpected situations—and give them the freedom and desire to work out new solutions to the problems they encounter. In contrast, the more routine the technology, the more appropriate is a formal structure, because tasks are simple and the steps needed to produce goods and services have been worked out in advance.

What makes a technology routine or complicated? One researcher who investigated this issue, Charles Perrow, argued that two factors determine how complicated or nonroutine technology is: task variety and task analyzability.[12] *Task variety* is the number of new or unexpected problems or situations that a person or function encounters in performing tasks or jobs. *Task analyzability* is the degree to which programmed solutions are available to people or functions to solve the problems they encounter. Nonroutine or complicated technologies are characterized by high task variety and low task analyzability; this means that many varied problems occur and that solving these problems requires significant nonprogrammed decision making. In contrast, routine technologies are characterized by low task variety and high task analyzability; this means that the problems encountered do not vary much and are easily resolved through programmed decision making.

Examples of nonroutine technology are found in the work of scientists in an R&D laboratory who develop new products or discover new drugs, and they are seen in the planning exercises an organization's top-management team uses to chart the organization's future strategy. Examples of routine technology include typical mass–production or assembly operations, where workers perform the same task repeatedly and where managers have already identified the programmed solutions necessary to perform a task efficiently. Similarly, in service organizations such as fast-food restaurants, the tasks that crew members perform in making and serving fast food are very routine.

Human Resources

A final important factor affecting an organization's choice of structure and culture is the characteristics of the human resources it employs. In general, the more highly skilled its workforce, and the greater the number of employees who work together in groups or teams, the more likely an organization is to use a flexible, decentralized structure and a professional culture based on values and norms that foster employee autonomy and self-control. Highly skilled employees, or employees who have internalized strong professional values and norms of behavior as part of their training, usually desire greater freedom and autonomy and dislike close supervision.

Flexible structures, characterized by decentralized authority and empowered employees, are well suited to the needs of highly skilled people. Similarly, when people work in teams, they must be allowed to interact freely and develop norms to guide their own work interactions, which also is possible in a flexible organizational structure. Thus, when designing organizational structure and culture, managers must pay close attention to the needs of the workforce and to the complexity and kind of work employees perform.

In summary, an organization's external environment, strategy, technology, and human resources are the factors to be considered by managers in seeking to design the best structure and culture for an organization. The greater the level of uncertainty in the organization's environment, the more complex its strategy and technologies, and the more highly qualified and skilled its workforce, the more likely managers are to design a structure and a culture that are flexible, can change quickly, and allow employees to be innovative in their responses to problems, customer needs, and so on. The more stable the organization's environment, the less complex and more well understood its strategy or technology, and the less skilled its workforce, the more likely managers are to design an organizational structure that is formal and controlling and a culture whose values and norms prescribe how employees should act in particular situations.

Later in the chapter we discuss how managers can create different kinds of organizational cultures. First, however, we discuss how managers can design flexible or formal organizational structures. The way an organization's structure works depends on the organizing choices managers make about three issues:

job design The process by which managers decide how to divide tasks into specific jobs.

- How to group tasks into individual jobs.
- How to group jobs into functions and divisions.
- How to allocate authority and coordinate or integrate functions and divisions.

Grouping Tasks into Jobs: Job Design

The first step in organizational design is job design, the process by which managers decide how to divide into specific jobs the tasks that have to be performed to provide customers with goods and services. Managers at McDonald's, for example, have decided how best to divide the tasks required to provide customers with fast, cheap food in each McDonald's restaurant. After experimenting with different job arrangements, McDonald's managers decided on a basic division of labor among chefs and food servers. Managers allocated all the tasks involved in actually cooking the food (putting oil in the fat fryers, opening packages of frozen french fries, putting beef patties on the grill, making salads, and so on) to the job of chef. They

LO7-2 Explain how managers group tasks into jobs that are motivating and satisfying for employees.

allocated all the tasks involved in giving the food to customers (such as greeting customers, taking orders, putting fries and burgers into bags, adding salt, pepper, and napkins, and taking money) to food servers. In addition, they created other jobs—the job of dealing with drive-through customers, the job of keeping the restaurant clean, and the job of overseeing employees and responding to unexpected events. The result of the job design process is a *division of labor* among employees, one that McDonald's managers have discovered through experience is most efficient.

At Subway, the roles of chef and server are combined into one, making the job "larger" than the jobs of McDonald's more specialized food servers. The idea behind job enlargement is that increasing the range of tasks performed by employees will reduce boredom.

Establishing an appropriate division of labor among employees is a critical part of the organizing process, one that is vital to increasing efficiency and effectiveness. At McDonald's, the tasks associated with chef and food server were split into different jobs because managers found that, for the kind of food McDonald's serves, this approach was most efficient. It is efficient because when each employee is given fewer tasks to perform (so that each job becomes more specialized), employees become more productive at performing the tasks that constitute each job.

At Subway sandwich shops, however, managers chose a different kind of job design. At Subway, there is no division of labor among the people who make the sandwiches, wrap the sandwiches, give them to customers, and take the money. The roles of chef and food server are combined into one. This different division of tasks and jobs is efficient for Subway and not for McDonald's because Subway serves a limited menu of mostly submarine-style sandwiches that are prepared to order. Subway's production system is far simpler than McDonald's, because McDonald's menu is much more varied and its chefs must cook many different kinds of foods.

Managers of every organization must analyze the range of tasks to be performed and then create jobs that best allow the organization to give customers the goods and services they want. In deciding how to assign tasks to individual jobs, however, managers must be careful not to take job simplification, the process of reducing the number of tasks that each worker performs, too far.[13] Too much job simplification may reduce efficiency rather than increase it if workers find their simplified jobs boring and monotonous, become demotivated and unhappy, and, as a result, perform at a low level.

job simplification
The process of reducing the number of tasks that each worker performs.

Job Enlargement and Job Enrichment

In an attempt to create a division of labor and design individual jobs to encourage workers to perform at a higher level and be more satisfied with their work, several researchers have proposed ways other than job simplification to group tasks into jobs: job enlargement and job enrichment.

job enlargement
Increasing the number of different tasks in a given job by changing the division of labor.

Job enlargement is increasing the number of different tasks in a given job by changing the division of labor.[14] For example, because Subway food servers make the food as well as serve it, their jobs are "larger" than the jobs of McDonald's food servers. The idea behind job enlargement is that increasing the range of tasks performed by a worker will reduce boredom and fatigue and may increase motivation to perform at a high level—increasing both the quantity and the quality of goods and services provided.

job enrichment
Increasing the degree of responsibility a worker has over his or her job.

Job enrichment is increasing the degree of responsibility a worker has over a job by, for example, (1) empowering workers to experiment to find new or better ways of doing the job, (2) encouraging workers to develop new skills, (3) allowing workers to decide how to do the work and giving them the responsibility for deciding how to respond to unexpected situations, and (4) allowing workers to monitor and measure their own performance.[15] The idea behind job enrichment is that increasing workers' responsibility increases their involvement in their jobs and thus increases their interest in the quality of the goods they make or the services they provide, an approach that Dick's Restaurant managers pursue as described in the following "Management Insight."

MANAGEMENT INSIGHT

Dick's Drive-In Restaurants

Dick's Drive-In Restaurants are a five-store family-owned hamburger chain based in Seattle, Washington. Founded in 1954, its owners have pursued an innovative approach to retaining hard-working employees in the fast-food industry—an industry known for its high level of employee turnover rates.[16] From the beginning, Dick's decided to pay its employees well above the industry average and offer them many benefits, too. Dick's pays its 150 part-time employees $11 an hour, covers 100% of the cost of employees' health insurance, and if they work at Dick's for more than six months up to $10,000 toward the cost of their four-year college tuition!

Serving up extraordinary employee benefits along with the burgers, Dick's Drive-In sets the bar high against its larger competitors and proves that looking after one's own pays off!

Dick's competitors, on the other hand—national hamburger chains like Wendy's and McDonald's—pay their part-time employees at the minimum wage of $7.25 an hour and offer them no health insurance or benefits—certainly nothing that can compare to Dick's. When asked why Dick's adopts this approach, Jim Spady, its vice president, answered, "We've been around since 1954 and one thing we've always believed is that there is nothing more important than finding and training and keeping the best people you possibly can."[17] The way to do this is by creating a work structure and culture that motivate and encourage employees to perform at a high level.

Dick's approach to managing its culture begins when it recruits new hires straight from high school. Its managers emphasize that they are looking for hard work and long-term commitment from employees. They stress further that in return Dick's will help and support employees by providing them with above-average pay, health care insurance, and tuition money while they work their way through school. Dick's expects its employees to perform to the best of their abilities to get its burgers, and its customers, out the door as fast as they can. Well-trained employees are expected to perform all of the various tasks involved in the burger restaurant such as taking orders, cooking the food, and cleaning up the premises. When performing their work, Dick's employees don't wait to be asked to do something; they know what to do to provide customers with the freshest burger Seattle has to offer.

Dick's approach to organizing leads to high performance and low turnover that keep operating costs low. Furthermore, Dick's managers have discovered that if employees stay for at least six months, its lower operating costs more than compensate for the extra pay and benefits employees receive. Dick's approach has therefore created a *win-win* situation for the company and its employees. If young people have to work their way through college, then Dick's seems to be a good place to do it.[18]

In general, managers who make design choices that increase job enrichment and job enlargement are likely to increase the degree to which people behave flexibly rather than rigidly or mechanically. Narrow, specialized jobs are likely to lead people to behave in predictable ways; workers who perform a variety of tasks and who are allowed and encouraged to discover new and better ways to perform their jobs are likely to act flexibly and creatively. Thus, managers who enlarge and enrich jobs create a flexible organizational structure, and those who simplify jobs create a more formal structure. If workers are grouped into self-managed work teams, the organization is likely to be flexible because team members provide support for each other and can learn from one another.

The Job Characteristics Model

J. R. Hackman and G. R. Oldham's job characteristics model is an influential model of job design that explains in detail how managers can make jobs more interesting and motivating.[19] Hackman and Oldham's model (see Figure 7.2) also

Figure 7.2

The Job Characteristics Model

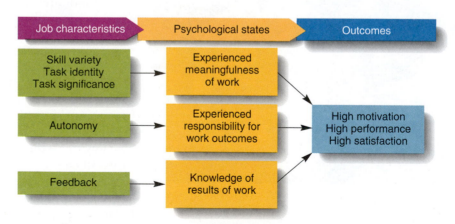

Source: Adapted from J. R. Hackman and G. R. Oldham, *Work Redesign,* Figure 4.2, page 77, © 1980. Reprinted with permission of Pearson Education, Upper Saddle River, NJ.

describes the likely personal and organizational outcomes that will result from enriched and enlarged jobs.

According to Hackman and Oldham, every job has five characteristics that determine how motivating the job is. These characteristics determine how employees react to their work and lead to outcomes such as high performance and satisfaction and low absenteeism and turnover:

- *Skill variety:* The extent to which a job requires that an employee use a wide range of different skills, abilities, or knowledge. Example: The skill variety required by the job of a research scientist is higher than that called for by the job of a McDonald's food server.

- *Task identity:* The extent to which a job requires that a worker perform all the tasks necessary to complete the job, from the beginning to the end of the production process. Example: A craftsworker who takes a piece of wood and transforms it into a custom-made desk has higher task identity than does a worker who performs only one of the numerous operations required to assemble a flat screen TV.

- *Task significance:* The degree to which a worker feels his or her job is meaningful because of its effect on people inside the organization, such as coworkers, or on people outside the organization, such as customers. Example: A teacher who sees the effect of his or her efforts in a well-educated and well-adjusted student enjoys high task significance compared to a dishwasher who monotonously washes dishes as they come to the kitchen.

- *Autonomy:* The degree to which a job gives an employee the freedom and discretion needed to schedule different tasks and decide how to carry them out. Example: Salespeople who have to plan their schedules and decide how to allocate their time among different customers have relatively high autonomy compared to assemblyline workers, whose actions are determined by the speed of the production line.

- *Feedback:* The extent to which actually doing a job provides a worker with clear and direct information about how well he or she has performed the job. Example: An air traffic controller whose mistakes may result in a midair collision receives immediate feedback on job performance; a person who compiles statistics for a business magazine often has little idea of when he or she makes a mistake or does a particularly good job.

Hackman and Oldham argue that these five job characteristics affect an employee's motivation because they affect three critical psychological states (see Figure 7.2). The more employees feel that their work is *meaningful* and that they are *responsible for work outcomes and responsible for knowing how those outcomes affect others,* the more motivating work becomes and the more likely employees are to be satisfied and to perform at a high level. Moreover, employees who have jobs that are highly motivating are called on to use their skills more and to perform more tasks, and they are given more responsibility for doing the job. All of the foregoing are characteristic of jobs and employees in flexible structures where authority is decentralized and where employees commonly work with others and must learn new skills to complete the range of tasks for which their group is responsible.

Grouping Jobs into Functions and Divisions: Designing Organizational Structure

Once managers have decided which tasks to allocate to which jobs, they face the next organizing decision: how to group jobs together to best match the needs of the organization's environment, strategy, technology, and human resources. Typically, managers first decide to group jobs into departments and they design a *functional structure* to use organizational resources effectively. As an organization grows and becomes more difficult to control, managers must choose a more complex organizational design, such as a divisional structure or a matrix or product team structure. The different ways in which managers can design organizational structure are discussed next. Selecting and designing an organizational structure to increase efficiency and effectiveness is a significant challenge. As noted in Chapter 6, managers reap the rewards of a well-thought-out strategy only if they choose the right type of structure to implement the strategy. The ability to make the right kinds of organizing choices is often what differentiates effective from ineffective managers and creates a high-performing organization.

LO7-3 Describe the types of organizational structures managers can design, and explain why they choose one structure over another.

Functional Structure

A *function* is a group of people, working together, who possess similar skills or use the same kind of knowledge, tools, or techniques to perform their jobs. Manufacturing, sales, and research and development are often organized into functional departments. A functional structure is an organizational structure composed of all the departments that an organization requires to produce its goods or services. Figure 7.3 shows the functional structure that Pier 1 Imports, the home furnishings company, uses to supply its customers with a range of goods from around the world to satisfy their desires for new and innovative products.

Pier 1's main functions are finance and administration, merchandising (purchasing the goods), stores (managing the retail outlets), planning and allocations (managing marketing, credit, and product distribution), and human resources. Each job inside a function exists because it helps the function perform the activities necessary for high organizational performance. Thus, within the planning and allocations function are all the jobs necessary to efficiently advertise Pier 1's products to increase their appeal to customers (such as promotion, photography, and visual communication) and then to distribute and transport the products to stores.

There are several advantages to grouping jobs according to function. First, when people who perform similar jobs are grouped together, they can learn from observing one another and thus become more specialized and can perform at a higher level. The tasks associated with one job often are related to the tasks associated with another job, which encourages cooperation within a function. In Pier 1's planning department, for example, the person designing the photography program for an ad campaign works closely with the person responsible for designing store layouts and with visual communication experts. As a result, Pier 1 is able to develop a strong, focused marketing campaign to differentiate its products.

Second, when people who perform similar jobs are grouped together, it is easier for managers to monitor and evaluate their performance.[20] Imagine if marketing experts, purchasing experts, and real-estate experts were grouped together

functional structure An organizational structure composed of all the departments that an organization requires to produce its goods or services.

Figure 7.3   The Functional Structure of Pier 1 Imports

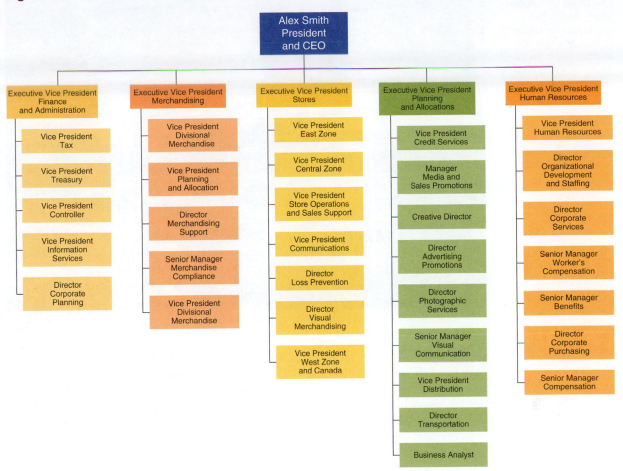

in one function and supervised by a manager from merchandising. Obviously, the merchandising manager would not have the expertise to evaluate all these different people appropriately. However a functional structure allows workers to evaluate how well coworkers are performing their jobs, and if some workers are performing poorly, more experienced workers can help them develop new skills.

Finally, managers appreciate functional structure because it allows them to create the set of functions they need in order to scan and monitor the competitive environment and obtain information about the way it is changing.[21] With the right set of functions in place, managers are then in a good position to develop a strategy that allows the organization to respond to its changing situation. Employees in the marketing group can specialize in monitoring new marketing developments that will allow Pier 1 to better target its customers. Employees in merchandising can monitor all potential suppliers of home furnishings both at home and abroad to find the goods most likely to appeal to Pier 1's customers and manage Pier 1's global outsourcing supply chain.

As an organization grows, and particularly as its task environment and strategy change because it is beginning to produce a wider range of goods and services

Pier 1 organizes its operations by function, which means that employees can more easily learn from one another and improve the service they provide to its customers.

for different kinds of customers, several problems can make a functional structure less efficient and effective.[22] First, managers in different functions may find it more difficult to communicate and coordinate with one another when they are responsible for several different kinds of products, especially as the organization grows both domestically and internationally. Second, functional managers may become so preoccupied with supervising their own specific departments and achieving their departmental goals that they lose sight of organizational goals. If that happens, organizational effectiveness will suffer because managers will be viewing issues and problems facing the organization only from their own, relatively narrow, departmental perspectives.[23] Both of these problems can reduce efficiency and effectiveness.

Divisional Structures: Product, Geographic, and Market

divisional structure
An organizational structure composed of separate business units within which are the functions that work together to produce a specific product for a specific customer.

As the problems associated with growth and diversification increase over time, managers must search for new ways to organize their activities to overcome the problems associated with a functional structure. Most managers of large organizations choose a divisional structure and create a series of business units to produce a specific kind of product for a specific kind of customer. Each *division* is a collection of functions or departments that work together to produce the product. The goal behind the change to a divisional structure is to create smaller, more manageable units within the organization. There are three forms of divisional structure (see Figure 7.4).[24] When managers organize divisions according to the *type of good or service* they provide, they adopt a product structure. When managers organize divisions according to the *area of the country or world* they operate in, they adopt a geographic structure. When managers organize divisions according to *the type of customer* they focus on, they adopt a market structure.

Figure 7.4

Product, Market, and
Geographic Structures

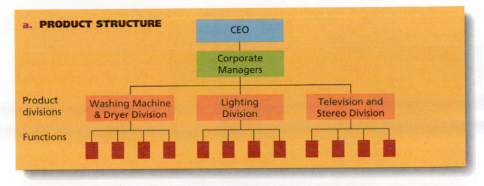

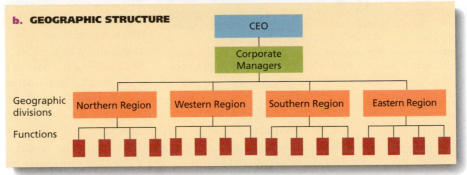

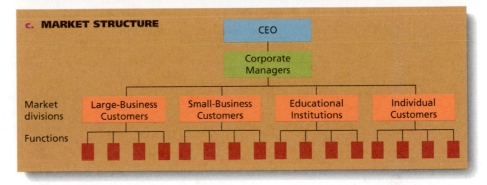

PRODUCT STRUCTURE Imagine the problems that managers at Pier 1 would encounter if they decided to diversify into producing and selling cars, fast food, and health insurance—in addition to home furnishings—and tried to use their existing set of functional managers to oversee the production of all four kinds of products. No manager would have the necessary skills or abilities to oversee those four products. No individual marketing manager, for example, could effectively market cars, fast food, health insurance, and home furnishings at the same time. To perform a functional activity successfully, managers must have experience in specific markets or industries. Consequently, if managers decide to diversify into new industries or to expand their range of products, they commonly design a product structure to organize their operations (see Figure 7.4a).

Using a product structure, managers place each distinct product line or business in its own self-contained division and give divisional managers the responsibility for devising an appropriate business-level strategy to allow the division to

product structure

An organizational structure in which each product line or business is handled by a self-contained division.

When Glaxo Wellcome and SmithKline Beecham merged, managers resolved the problem of how to coordinate the activities of thousands of research scientists by organizing them into product divisions focusing on clusters of diseases.

compete effectively in its industry or market.[25] Each division is self-contained because it has a complete set of all the functions—marketing, R&D, finance, and so on—that it needs to produce or provide goods or services efficiently and effectively. Functional managers report to divisional managers, and divisional managers report to top or corporate managers.

Grouping functions into divisions focused on particular products has several advantages for managers at all levels in the organization. First, a product structure allows functional managers to specialize in only one product area, so they are able to build expertise and fine-tune their skills in this particular area. Second, each division's managers can become experts in their industry; this expertise helps them choose and develop a business-level strategy to differentiate their products or lower their costs while meeting the needs of customers. Third, a product structure frees corporate managers from the need to supervise directly each division's day-to-day operations; this latitude allows corporate managers to create the best corporate-level strategy to maximize the organization's future growth and ability to create value. Corporate managers are likely to make fewer mistakes about which businesses to diversify into or how to best expand internationally, for example, because they are able to take an organizationwide view.[26] Corporate managers also are likely to evaluate better how well divisional managers are doing, and they can intervene and take corrective action as needed.

The extra layer of management, the divisional management layer, can improve the use of organizational resources. Moreover, a product structure puts divisional managers close to their customers and lets them respond quickly and appropriately to the changing task environment. One pharmaceutical company that has recently adopted a new product structure to better organize its activities with great success is GlaxoSmithKline. The need to innovate new kinds of prescription drugs in order to boost performance is a continual battle for pharmaceutical companies. In the 2000s many of these companies have been merging to try to increase their research productivity, and one of them, Glaxo-SmithKline, was created from the merger between Glaxo Wellcome and SmithKline Beecham.[27] Prior to the merger, both companies experienced a steep decline in the number of new prescription drugs their scientists were able to invent. The problem facing the new company's top managers was how to best use and combine the talents of the scientists and researchers from both of the former companies to allow them to quickly innovate promising new drugs.

Top managers realized that after the merger there would be enormous problems associated with coordinating the activities of the thousands of research scientists who were working on hundreds of different kinds of drug research programs. Understanding the problems associated with large size, the top managers decided to group the researchers into eight smaller product divisions to allow them to focus on particular clusters of diseases such as heart disease or viral infections. The members of each product division were told that they would be rewarded based on the number of new prescription drugs they were able to invent and the speed with which they could bring these new drugs to the market. GlaxoSmith-Kline's new product structure has worked well, its research productivity doubled after the reorganization, and a record number of new drugs are moving into clinical trials.[28]

GEOGRAPHIC STRUCTURE When organizations expand rapidly both at home and abroad, functional structures can create special problems because managers in one central location may find it increasingly difficult to deal with the different problems and issues that may arise in each region of a country or area of the world. In these cases, a geographic structure, in which divisions are broken down by geographic location, is often chosen (see Figure 7.4b). To achieve the corporate mission of providing next-day mail service, Fred Smith, CEO of FedEx, chose a geographic structure and divided up operations by creating a division in each region. Large retailers such as Macy's, Neiman Marcus, and Brooks Brothers also use a geographic structure. Since the needs of retail customers differ by region—for example, surfboards in California and down parkas in the Midwest—a geographic structure gives retail regional managers the flexibility they need to choose the range of products that best meets the needs of regional customers.

In adopting a *global geographic structure,* such as shown in Figure 7.5a, managers locate different divisions in each of the world regions where the organization operates. Managers are most likely to do this when they pursue a multidomestic strategy because customer needs vary widely by country or world region. For

geographic structure An organizational structure in which each region of a country or area of the world is served by a self-contained division.

Figure 7.5

Global Geographic and Global Product Structures

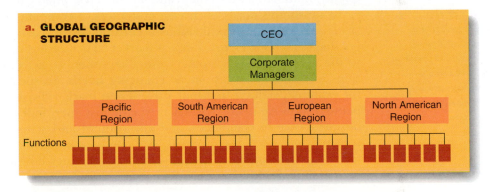

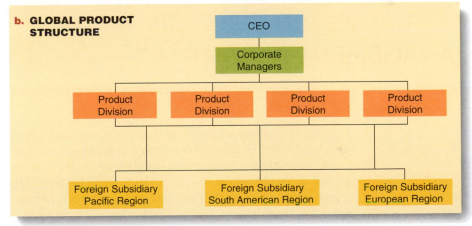

example, if products that appeal to U.S. customers do not sell in Europe, the Pacific Rim, or South America, managers must customize the products to meet the needs of customers in those different world regions; a global geographic structure with global divisions may allow them to do this. Although this approach sometimes works well, it can result in disaster, as the "Management Snapshot" at the beginning of this chapter discusses.

In contrast, to the degree that customers abroad are willing to buy the same kind of product or slight variations thereof, managers are more likely to pursue a global strategy. In this case they are more likely to use a global product structure. In a *global product structure*, each product division, not the country and regional managers, takes responsibility for deciding where to manufacture its products and how to market them in countries worldwide (see Figure 7.5b). Product division managers manage their own global value chains and decide where to establish foreign subsidiaries to distribute and sell their products to customers in foreign countries.

MARKET STRUCTURE Sometimes the pressing issue facing managers is to group functions according to the type of customer buying the product in order to tailor the products the organization offers to each customer's unique demands. A PC maker such as Dell, for example, has several kinds of customers, including large businesses (which might demand networks of computers linked to a mainframe computer), small companies (which may need just a few PCs linked together), educational users in schools and universities (which might want thousands of independent PCs for their students), and individual users (who may want a high-quality multimedia PC so they can play the latest video games).

market structure
An organizational structure in which each kind of customer is served by a self-contained division; also called *customer structure.*

To satisfy the needs of diverse customers, a company might adopt a market structure, which groups divisions according to the particular kinds of customers they serve (see Figure 7.4c). A market structure lets managers be responsive to the needs of their customers and allows them to act flexibly in making decisions in response to customers' changing needs. To spearhead its turnaround, for example, Dell created four streamlined market divisions that each focus on being responsive to one particular type of customer: individual consumers, small businesses, large companies, and government and state agencies. All kinds of organizations need to continually evaluate their structures, as is suggested in the following "Management Insight" box that examines how a major school district increased its performance.

MANAGEMENT INSIGHT

A School District Moves from a Geographic to a Market Structure

Like all organizations, state and city government agencies such as school districts may become too tall and bureaucratic over time and, as they grow, develop ineffective and inefficient organizational structures. This happened to the Houston Independent School District (HISD) when the explosive growth of the city during the last decades added over a million new students to school rolls. As Houston expanded many miles in every direction to become the fourth largest U.S. city, successive HISD superintendents adopted a geographic structure to coordinate and control all the teaching functions involved in creating high-performing elementary, middle, and high schools. The HISD eventually created five different geographic regions or regional school districts. And over time each regional district sought to control more of its own functional activities and became increasingly critical of HISD's central administration. The result was a slowdown in decision making, infighting among districts, an increasingly ineffectual team of district administrators, and falling student academic test scores across the city.

In 2010 a new HISD superintendent was appointed who, working on the suggestions of HISD's top managers, decided to reorganize HISD into a market structure. HISD's new organizational structure is now grouped by the needs of its customers—its students—and three "chief officers" oversee all of Houston's high schools, middle schools, and elementary schools, respectively. The focus is now on the needs of its three types of students, not on the needs of the former five regional managers. Over 270 positions were eliminated in this restructuring, saving over $8 million per year, and many observers hope to see more cost savings ahead.

Many important support functions were recentralized to HISD's headquarters office to eliminate redundancies and reduce costs, including teacher professional development. Also, a new support function called school improvement was formed with managers charged to share ideas and information among schools and oversee their performance on many dimensions to improve service and student performance. HISD administrators also hope that eliminating the regional geographic structure will encourage schools to share best practices and cooperate so that student education and test scores will improve over time.

Matrix and Product Team Designs

Moving to a product, geographic, or market divisional structure allows managers to respond more quickly and flexibly to the particular circumstances they confront. However, when information technology or customer needs are changing rapidly and the environment is uncertain, even a divisional structure may not give managers enough flexibility to respond to the environment quickly. To operate effectively under these conditions, managers must design the most flexible kind of organizational structure available: *a matrix structure* or a *product team structure* (see Figure 7.6).

matrix structure An organizational structure that simultaneously groups people and resources by function and by product.

MATRIX STRUCTURE In a matrix structure, managers group people and resources in two ways simultaneously: by function and by product.[29] Employees are grouped by *functions* to allow them to learn from one another and become more skilled and productive. In addition, employees are grouped into *product teams* in which members of different functions work together to develop a specific product. The result is a complex network of reporting relationships among product teams and functions that makes the matrix structure very flexible (see Figure 7.6a). Each person in a product team reports to two managers: (1) a functional boss, who assigns individuals to a team and evaluates their performance from a functional perspective, and (2) the boss of the product team, who evaluates their performance on the team. Thus team members are known as *two-boss employees*. The functional employees assigned to product teams change over time as the specific

Figure 7.6

Matrix and Product
Team Structures

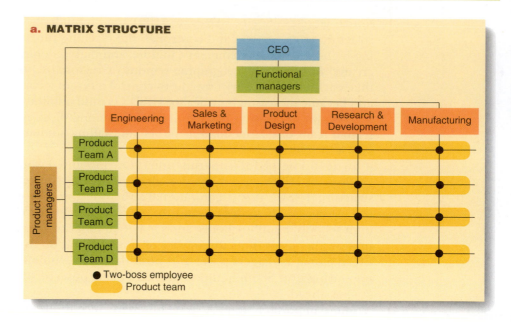

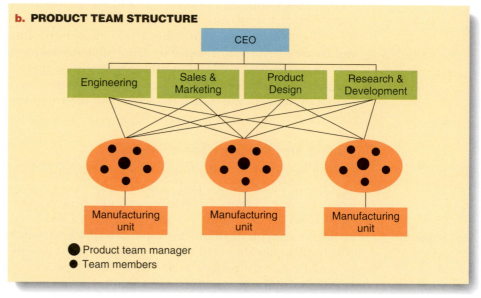

skills that the team needs change. At the beginning of the product development process, for example, engineers and R&D specialists are assigned to a product team because their skills are needed to develop new products. When a provisional design has been established, marketing experts are assigned to the team to gauge how customers will respond to the new product. Manufacturing personnel join when it is time to find the most efficient way to produce the product. As their specific jobs are completed, team members leave and are reassigned to new teams. In this way the matrix structure makes the most use of human resources.

To keep the matrix structure flexible, product teams are empowered and team members are responsible for making most of the important decisions involved in product development.[30] The product team manager acts as a facilitator, controlling the financial resources and trying to keep the project on time and within budget. The functional managers try to ensure that the product is the best it can be to maximize its differentiated appeal.

High-tech companies that operate in environments where new product development takes place monthly or yearly have used matrix structures successfully for many years, and the need to innovate quickly is vital to the organization's survival. The flexibility afforded by a matrix structure lets managers keep pace with a changing and increasingly complex environment.[31]

PRODUCT TEAM STRUCTURE The dual reporting relationships that are at the heart of a matrix structure have always been difficult for managers and employees to deal with. Often the functional boss and the product boss make conflicting demands on team members, who do not know which boss to satisfy first. Also, functional and product team bosses may come into conflict over precisely who is in charge of which team members and for how long. To avoid these problems, managers have devised a way of organizing people and resources that still allows an organization to be flexible but makes its structure easier to operate: a product team structure.

product team structure An organizational structure in which employees are permanently assigned to a cross-functional team and report only to the product team manager or to one of his or her direct subordinates.

The product team structure differs from a matrix structure in two ways: (1) It does away with dual reporting relationships and two-boss employees, and (2) functional employees are permanently assigned to a cross-functional team that is empowered to bring a new or redesigned product to market. A cross-functional team is a group of managers brought together from different departments to perform organizational tasks. When managers are grouped into cross-functional teams, the artificial boundaries between departments disappear, and a narrow focus on departmental goals is replaced with a general interest in working together to achieve organizational goals. The results of such changes have been dramatic: Ford can introduce a new model of car in two years, down from four; Black & Decker can innovate new products in months, not years; and Hallmark Cards can respond to changing customer demands for types of cards in weeks, not months.

cross-functional team A group of managers brought together from different departments to perform organizational tasks.

Members of a cross-functional team report only to the product team manager or to one of his or her direct subordinates. The heads of the functions have only an informal, advisory relationship with members of the product teams—the role of functional managers is only to counsel and help team members, share knowledge among teams, and provide new technological developments that can help improve each team's performance (see Figure 7.6b).[32]

Increasingly, organizations are making empowered cross-functional teams an essential part of their organizational architecture to help them gain a competitive advantage in fast-changing organizational environments. For example, Newell Rubbermaid, the well-known maker of more than 5,000 household products, moved to a product team structure because its managers wanted to speed up the rate of product innovation. Managers created 20 cross-functional teams composed of five to

A committee looks over an artist's work during a meeting at Hallmark in Kansas City. At Hallmark, cross-functional teams like this one can respond quickly to changing customer needs.

seven people from marketing, manufacturing, R&D, and other functions.[33] Each team focuses its energies on a particular product line, such as garden products, bathroom products, or kitchen products. These teams develop more than 365 new products a year.

Coordinating Functions and Divisions

LO7-4 Explain why managers must coordinate jobs, functions, and divisions using the hierarchy of authority and integrating mechanisms.

The more complex the structure a company uses to group its activities, the greater are the problems of *linking and coordinating* its different functions and divisions. Coordination becomes a problem because each function or division develops a different orientation toward the other groups that affects how it interacts with them. Each function or division comes to view the problems facing the company from its own perspective; for example, they may develop different views about the major goals, problems, or issues facing a company.

At the functional level, the manufacturing function typically has a short-term view; its major goal is to keep costs under control and get the product out the factory door on time. By contrast, the product development function has a long-term viewpoint because developing a new product is a relatively slow process and high product quality is seen as more important than low costs. Such differences in viewpoint may make manufacturing and product development managers reluctant to cooperate and coordinate their activities to meet company goals. At the divisional level, in a company with a product structure, employees may become concerned more with making *their* division's products a success than with the profitability of the entire company. They may refuse, or simply not see, the need to cooperate and share information or knowledge with other divisions.

The problem of linking and coordinating the activities of different functions and divisions becomes more acute as the number of functions and divisions increases. We look first at how managers design the hierarchy of authority to coordinate functions and divisions so they work together effectively. Then we focus on integration and examine the different integrating mechanisms managers can use to coordinate functions and divisions.

Allocating Authority

authority The power to hold people accountable for their actions and to make decisions concerning the use of organizational resources.

hierarchy of authority An organization's chain of command, specifying the relative authority of each manager.

span of control The number of subordinates who report directly to a manager.

As organizations grow and produce a wider range of goods and services, the size and number of their functions and divisions increase. To coordinate the activities of people, functions, and divisions and to allow them to work together effectively, managers must develop a clear hierarchy of authority.[34] Authority is the power vested in a manager to make decisions and use resources to achieve organizational goals by virtue of his or her position in an organization. The hierarchy of authority is an organization's *chain of command*—the relative authority that each manager has—extending from the CEO at the top, down through the middle managers and first-line managers, to the nonmanagerial employees who actually make goods or provide services. Every manager, at every level of the hierarchy, supervises one or more subordinates. The term span of control refers to the number of subordinates who report directly to a manager.

Figure 7.7 shows a simplified picture of the hierarchy of authority and the span of control of managers in McDonald's in 2011. At the top of the hierarchy is Jim Skinner, CEO and vice chairman of McDonald's board of directors, who took control in 2004.[35] Skinner is the manager who has ultimate responsibility

Figure 7.7 The Hierarchy of Authority and Span of Control at McDonald's Corporation

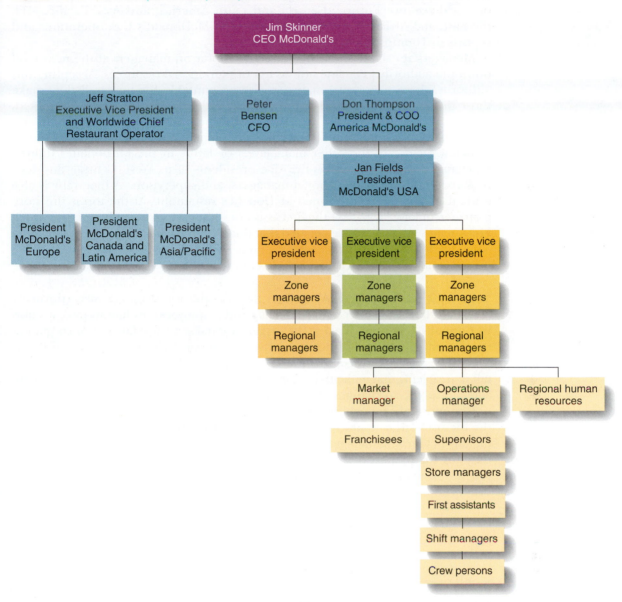

for McDonald's performance, and he has the authority to decide how to use organizational resources to benefit McDonald's stakeholders.[36] Don Thompson, next in line, is president and COO and is responsible for overseeing all of McDonald's global restaurant operations. Thompson reports directly to Skinner, as does chief financial officer Peter Bensen. Unlike the other managers, Bensen is not a line manager, someone in the direct line or chain of command who has formal authority over people and resources. Rather, Bensen is a staff manager, responsible for one of McDonald's specialist functions, finance. Worldwide chief operations officer Jeff Stratton is responsible for overseeing all functional aspects of McDonald's overseas operations, which are headed by the presidents of world regions: Europe; Canada and Latin America; and Asia/Pacific, Middle East, and Africa. Jan Fields is president of McDonald's U.S. operations and reports to Thompson.

Managers at each level of the hierarchy confer on managers at the next level down the authority to decide how to use organizational resources. Accepting this authority, those lower-level managers are accountable for how well they make those decisions. Managers who make the right decisions are typically promoted, and organizations motivate managers with the prospects of promotion and increased responsibility within the chain of command.

Below Fields are the other main levels or layers in the McDonald's domestic chain of command—executive vice presidents of its West, Central, and East regions, zone managers, regional managers, and supervisors. A hierarchy is also evident in each company-owned McDonald's restaurant. At the top is the store manager; at lower levels are the first assistant, shift managers, and crew personnel. McDonald's managers have decided that this hierarchy of authority best allows the company to pursue its business-level strategy of providing fast food at reasonable prices—and its stock price has exploded in the 2000s as its performance increases.

TALL AND FLAT ORGANIZATIONS As an organization grows in size (normally measured by the number of its managers and employees), its hierarchy of authority normally lengthens, making the organizational structure taller. A *tall* organization has many levels of authority relative to company size; a *flat* organization has fewer levels relative to company size (see Figure 7.8).[37] As a hierarchy becomes taller, problems that make the organization's structure less flexible and slow managers' response to changes in the organizational environment may result.

Communication problems may arise when an organization has many levels in the hierarchy. It can take a long time for the decisions and orders of upper-level managers to reach managers further down in the hierarchy, and it can take a long time for top managers to learn how well their decisions worked. Feeling out of touch, top managers may want to verify that lower-level managers are following orders and may require written confirmation from them. Middle managers, who know they will be held strictly accountable for their actions, start devoting too much time to the process of making decisions to improve their chances of being right. They might even try to avoid responsibility by making top managers decide what actions to take.

Another communication problem that can result is the distortion of commands and messages being transmitted up and down the hierarchy, which causes managers at different levels to interpret what is happening differently. Distortion of orders and messages can be accidental, occurring because different managers interpret messages from their own narrow, functional perspectives. Or distortion can be intentional, occurring because managers low in the hierarchy decide to interpret information in a way that increases their own personal advantage.

Another problem with tall hierarchies is that they usually indicate that an organization is employing many managers, and managers are expensive. Managerial salaries, benefits, offices, and secretaries are a huge expense for organizations. Large companies such as IBM and GM pay their managers millions of dollars a year. During the recent recession, hundreds of thousands of managers were laid off as companies restructured and downsized their workforces to reduce costs, and they are still doing this in 2013.

Figure 7.8

Tall and Flat
Organizations

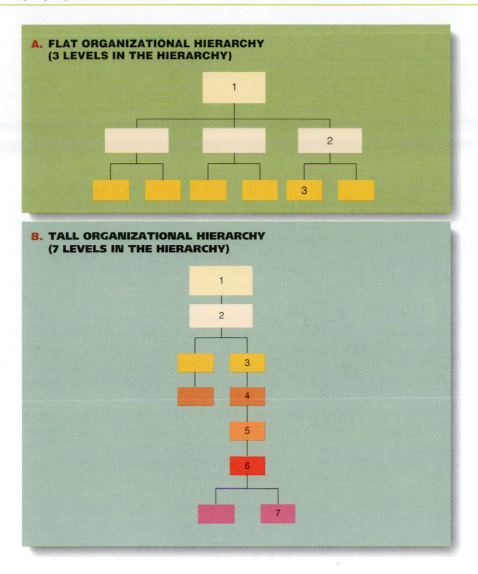

A. FLAT ORGANIZATIONAL HIERARCHY (3 LEVELS IN THE HIERARCHY)

B. TALL ORGANIZATIONAL HIERARCHY (7 LEVELS IN THE HIERARCHY)

THE MINIMUM CHAIN OF COMMAND To ward off the problems that result when an organization becomes too tall and employs too many managers, top managers need to ascertain whether they are employing the right number of middle and first-line managers and whether they can redesign their organizational architecture to reduce the number of managers. Top managers might well follow a basic organizing principle—the principle of the minimum chain of command—which states that top managers should always construct a hierarchy with the fewest levels of authority necessary to efficiently and effectively use organizational resources.

Effective managers constantly scrutinize their hierarchies to see whether the number of levels can be reduced—for example, by eliminating one level and giving the responsibilities of managers at that level to managers above and by empowering employees below. One manager who constantly worked to empower employees and keep the hierarchy flat is Colleen C. Barrett, the highest-ranking woman in the airline industry until she stepped down to become Southwest Airlines's "president emeritus."[38] At Southwest she was well known for continually reaffirming Southwest's message that employees should feel free to go above and beyond their prescribed roles to provide better customer service. Her central message was that Southwest values, trusts, and empowers its employees, who should not look to supervisors for guidance but find their own ways to do the job better. The need to empower workers is increasing as companies work to reduce the number of middle managers to lower costs and to compete with low-cost overseas competitors.

decentralizing authority Giving lower-level managers and nonmanagerial employees the right to make important decisions about how to use organizational resources.

CENTRALIZATION AND DECENTRALIZATION OF AUTHORITY Another way in which managers can keep the organizational hierarchy flat is by decentralizing authority—that is, by giving lower-level managers and nonmanagerial employees the right to make important decisions about how to use organizational resources.[39] If managers at higher levels give lower-level employees the responsibility of making important decisions and only *manage by exception,* then the problems of slow and distorted communication noted previously are kept to a minimum. Moreover, fewer managers are needed because their role is not to make decisions but to act as coach and facilitator and to help other employees make the best decisions. In addition, when decision-making authority is low in the organization and near the customer, employees are better able to recognize and respond to customer needs.

Decentralizing authority allows an organization and its employees to behave in a flexible way even as the organization grows and becomes taller. This is why managers are so interested in empowering employees, creating self-managed work teams, establishing cross-functional teams, and even moving to a product team structure. These design innovations help keep the organizational architecture flexible and responsive to complex task and general environments, complex technologies, and complex strategies.

Although more and more organizations are taking steps to decentralize authority, *too much* decentralization has certain disadvantages. If divisions, functions, or teams are given too much decision-making authority, they may begin to pursue their own goals at the expense of organizational goals. Managers in engineering design or R&D, for example, may become so focused on making the best possible product they fail to realize that the best product may be so expensive few people are willing or able to buy it. Also, too much decentralization can cause lack of communication among functions or divisions; this prevents the synergies of cooperation from ever materializing, and organizational performance suffers.

Top managers must seek the balance between centralization and decentralization of authority that best meets the four major contingencies an organization faces (see Figure 7.1). If managers are in a stable environment, are using well-understood technology, and are producing stable kinds of products (such as cereal, canned soup, or books), there is no pressing need to decentralize authority, and managers at the top can maintain control of much of organizational decision making.[40] However, in uncertain, changing environments where high-tech companies are producing state-of-the-art products, top managers must often empower employees and allow teams to make important strategic decisions so the organization can keep up with the changes taking place. No matter what its environment, a company that fails to control the balance between centralization and decentralization will find its performance suffering.

Integrating and Coordinating Mechanisms

Much coordination takes place through the hierarchy of authority. However, several problems are associated with establishing contact among managers in different functions or divisions. As discussed earlier, managers from different functions and divisions may have different views about what must be done to achieve organizational goals. But if the managers have equal authority (as functional managers typically do), the only manager who can tell them what to do is the CEO, who has the ultimate authority to resolve conflicts. The need to solve everyday conflicts, however, wastes top management time and slows strategic decision making; indeed, one sign of a poorly performing structure is the number of problems sent up the hierarchy for top managers to solve.

To increase communication and coordination among functions or between divisions and to prevent these problems from emerging, top managers incorporate various integrating mechanisms into their organizational architecture. The greater the complexity of an organization's structure, the greater is the need for coordination among people, functions, and divisions to make the organizational structure work efficiently and effectively.[41] Thus when managers adopt a divisional, matrix, or product team structure, they must use complex integrating mechanisms to achieve organizational goals. Several integrating mechanisms are available to managers to increase communication and coordination.[42] Figure 7.9 lists these mechanisms, as well as examples of the individuals or groups who might use them.

LIAISON ROLES Managers can increase coordination among functions and divisions by establishing liaison roles. When the volume of contacts between two functions increases, one way to improve coordination is to give one manager in each function or division the responsibility for coordinating with the other. These

integrating mechanisms

Organizing tools that managers can use to increase communication and coordination among functions and divisions.

Figure 7.9

Types and Examples of
Integrating Mechanisms

SIMPLE

Direct contact

Liaison roles Marketing manager and research and development manager meet to brainstorm new product ideas.

Task forces Representatives from marketing, research and development, and manufacturing meet to discuss launch of new product.

Cross-functional teams A cross-functional team composed of all functions is formed to manage product to its launch in the market.

Integrating roles and departments Senior managers provide members of cross-functional team with relevant information from other teams and from other divisions.

COMPLEX

Liaison role

Task force

Cross-functional team

Integrating role

Washing machine division — Integrating role — Television and stereo division

• Managers responsible for integration

managers may meet daily, weekly, monthly, or as needed. A liaison role is illustrated in Figure 7.9; the small dot represents the person within a function who has responsibility for coordinating with the other function. Coordinating is part of the liaison's full-time job, and usually an informal relationship develops among the people involved, greatly easing strains between functions. Furthermore, liaison roles provide a way of transmitting information across an organization, which is important in large organizations whose employees may know no one outside their immediate function or division.

TASK FORCES When more than two functions or divisions share many common problems, direct contact and liaison roles may not provide sufficient coordination. In these cases, a more complex integrating mechanism, a task force, may be appropriate (see Figure 7.9). One manager from each relevant function or division is assigned to a task force that meets to solve a specific, mutual problem; members are responsible for reporting to their departments on the issues addressed and the solutions recommended. Task forces are often called *ad hoc committees* because they are temporary; they may meet on a regular basis or only a few times. When the problem or issue is solved, the task force is no longer needed; members return to their normal roles in their departments or are assigned to other task forces. Typically task force members also perform many of their normal duties while serving on the task force.

CROSS-FUNCTIONAL TEAMS In many cases the issues addressed by a task force are recurring problems, such as the need to develop new products or find new kinds of customers. To address recurring problems effectively, managers are increasingly using permanent integrating mechanisms such as cross-functional teams. An example of a cross-functional team is a new product development committee that is responsible for the choice, design, manufacturing, and marketing of a new product. Such an activity obviously requires a great deal of integration among functions if new products are to be successfully introduced, and using a complex integrating mechanism such as a cross-functional team accomplishes this. As discussed earlier, in a product team structure people and resources are grouped into permanent cross-functional teams to speed products to market. These teams assume long-term responsibility for all aspects of development and making the product.

INTEGRATING ROLES An integrating role is a role whose only function is to increase coordination and integration among functions or divisions to achieve performance gains from synergies. Usually managers who perform integrating roles are experienced senior managers who can envisage how to use the resources of the functions or divisions to obtain new synergies. One study found that DuPont, the giant chemical company, had created 160 integrating roles to coordinate the different divisions of the company and improve corporate performance.[43] The more complex an organization and the greater the number of its divisions, the more important integrating roles are.

In summary, to keep an organization responsive to changes in its task and general environments as it grows and becomes more complex, managers must increase coordination among functions and divisions by using complex integrating mechanisms. Managers must decide on the best way to organize their structures—that is, choose the structure that allows them to make the best use of organizational resources.

task force A committee of managers from various functions or divisions who meet to solve a specific, mutual problem; also called *ad hoc committee*.

Strategic Alliances, B2B Network Structures, and IT

strategic alliance

An agreement in which managers pool or share their organization's resources and know-how with a foreign company and the two organizations share the rewards and risks of starting a new venture.

network structure

A series of strategic alliances that an organization creates with suppliers, manufacturers, and/or distributors to produce and market a product.

Recently, increasing globalization and the use of new IT have brought about two innovations in organizational architecture that are sweeping through U.S. and European companies: strategic alliances and business-to-business (B2B) network structures. A strategic alliance is a formal agreement that commits two or more companies to exchange or share their resources in order to produce and market a product.[44] Most commonly strategic alliances are formed because the companies share similar interests and believe they can benefit from cooperating. For example, Japanese car companies such as Toyota and Honda have formed many strategic alliances with particular suppliers of inputs such as car axles, gearboxes, and air-conditioning systems. Over time, these car companies work closely with their suppliers to improve the efficiency and effectiveness of the inputs so that the final product—the car produced—is of higher quality and very often can be produced at lower cost. Toyota and Honda have also established alliances with suppliers throughout the United States and Mexico because both companies now build several models of cars in these countries.

The growing sophistication of IT with global intranets and teleconferencing has made it much easier to manage strategic alliances and allow managers to share information and cooperate. One outcome of this has been the growth of strategic alliances into a network structure. A network structure is a series of global strategic alliances that one or several organizations create with suppliers, manufacturers, and/or distributors to produce and market a product. Network structures allow an organization to manage its global value chain in order to find new ways to reduce costs and increase the quality of products—without incurring the high costs of operating a complex organizational structure (such as the costs of employing many managers). More and more U.S. and European companies are relying on global network structures to gain access to low-cost foreign sources of inputs, as discussed in Chapter 6. Shoemakers such as Nike and Adidas are two companies that have used this approach extensively.

Nike is the largest and most profitable sports shoe manufacturer in the world. The key to Nike's success is the network structure that Nike founder and CEO Philip Knight created to allow his company to produce and market shoes. As noted in Chapter 6, the most successful companies today are trying to pursue simultaneously a low-cost and a differentiation strategy. Knight decided early that to do this at Nike he needed organizational architecture that would allow his company to focus on some functions, such as design, and leave others, such as manufacturing, to other organizations.

By far the largest function at Nike's Oregon headquarters is the design function, composed of talented designers who pioneered innovations in sports shoe design such as the air pump and Air Jordans that Nike introduced so successfully. Designers use computer-aided design (CAD) to design Nike shoes, and they electronically store all new product information, including manufacturing instructions. When the designers have finished their work, they electronically transmit all the blueprints for the new products to a network of Southeast Asian suppliers and manufacturers with which Nike has formed strategic alliances.[45] Instructions for the design of a new sole may be sent to a supplier in Taiwan; instructions for the leather uppers, to a supplier in Malaysia. The suppliers produce the shoe parts and send them for final assembly to a manufacturer in China with which

Nike has established another strategic alliance. From China the shoes are shipped to distributors throughout the world. Ninety-nine percent of the 120 million pairs of shoes that Nike makes each year are made in Southeast Asia.

This network structure gives Nike two important advantages. First, Nike is able to respond to changes in sports shoe fashion very quickly. Using its global IT system, Nike literally can change the instructions it gives each of its suppliers overnight, so that within a few weeks its foreign manufacturers are producing new kinds of shoes.[46] Any alliance partners that fail to perform up to Nike's standards are replaced with new partners.

outsource To use outside suppliers and manufacturers to produce goods and services.

Second, Nike's costs are very low because wages in Southeast Asia are a fraction of what they are in the United States, and this difference gives Nike a low-cost advantage. Also, Nike's ability to outsource and use foreign manufacturers to produce all its shoes abroad allows Knight to keep the organization's U.S. structure flat and flexible. Nike is able to use a relatively inexpensive functional structure to organize its activities. However, sports shoe manufacturers' attempts to keep their costs low have led to many charges that Nike and others are supporting sweatshops that harm foreign workers, as the following "Ethics in Action" box suggests.

ETHICS IN ACTION

Of Shoes and Sweatshops

As the production of all kinds of goods and services is being increasingly outsourced to poor regions and countries of the world, the behavior of companies that outsource production to subcontractors in these countries has come under increasing scrutiny. Nike, the giant sports shoe maker with sales of more than $9 billion a year, was one of the first to experience a backlash when critics revealed how workers in these countries were being treated. Indonesian workers were stitching together shoes in hot, noisy factories for only 80 cents a day or about $18 a month.[47] Workers in Vietnam and China fared better; they could earn $1.60 a day. In all cases, however, critics charged that at least $3 a day was needed to maintain an adequate living standard.

Members of United Students against Nike unfurl a banner at the Niketown store in New York accusing Nike of using sweatshop labor to produce its athletic apparel. Nike and other athletic apparel companies have since taken steps to ensure better working conditions for foreign workers.

These facts generated an outcry in the United States, where Nike was roundly attacked for its labor practices; a backlash against sales of Nike products forced Phil Knight, Nike's billionaire owner, to reevaluate Nike's labor practices. Nike announced that henceforth all the factories producing its shoes and clothes would be independently monitored and inspected. After its competitor Reebok, which also had been criticized for similar labor practices, announced that it was raising wages in Indonesia by 20%, Nike raised them by 25%, to $23 a month.[48] Small though this may seem, it was a huge increase to workers in these countries.

In Europe, another sportswear company, Adidas, had largely escaped such criticism. But then newspapers reported that in

El Salvador, a Taiwan-based Adidas subcontractor was employing girls as young as 14 in its factories and making them work for more than 70 hours a week. They were allowed to go to the restroom only twice a day, and if they stayed longer than three minutes, they lost a day's wages.[49] Adidas moved swiftly to avoid the public relations nightmare that Nike had experienced. Adidas announced that henceforth its subcontractors would be required to abide by stricter labor standards.

What happened in the sports shoe industry has happened throughout the clothing industry as well as other industries like electronics and toys in the 2000s. Companies such as Walmart, Target, The Gap, Apple, and Mattel have all been forced to reevaluate the ethics of their labor practices and to promise to keep a constant watch on subcontractors in the future. A statement to this effect can be found on many of these companies' web pages—for example, Nike's (www.nikebiz.com) and The Gap's (www.thegap.com).

The ability of managers to develop a network structure to produce or provide the goods and services customers want, rather than create a complex organizational structure to do so, has led many researchers and consultants to popularize the idea of a boundaryless organization. Such an organization is composed of people linked by IT—computers, faxes, computer-aided design systems, and video teleconferencing—who may rarely, if ever, see one another face-to-face. People are utilized when their services are needed, much as in a matrix structure, but they are not formal members of an organization; they are functional experts who form an alliance with an organization, fulfill their contractual obligations, and then move on to the next project.

Large consulting companies, such as Accenture IBM, SAP, and McKinsey & Co., utilize their global consultants in this way. Consultants are connected by laptops to an organization's knowledge management system, its company-specific information system that systematizes the knowledge of its employees and provides them with access to other employees who have the expertise to solve the problems that they encounter as they perform their jobs.

The use of outsourcing and the development of network structures is increasing rapidly as organizations recognize the many opportunities they offer to reduce costs and increase organizational flexibility. This push to lower costs has led to the development of electronic business-to-business (B2B) networks in which most or all of the companies in an industry (for example, carmakers) use the same software platform to link to each other and establish industry specifications and standards. Then, these companies jointly list the quantity and specifications of the inputs they require and invite bids from the thousands of potential suppliers around the world. Suppliers also use the same software platform, so electronic bidding, auctions, and transactions are possible between buyers and sellers around the world. The idea is that high-volume standardized transactions can help drive down costs at the industry level.

Today, with advances in IT, designing organizational architecture is becoming an increasingly complex management function. To maximize efficiency and effectiveness, managers must assess carefully the relative benefits of having their own organization perform a functional activity versus forming an alliance with

boundaryless organization An organization whose members are linked by computers, faxes, computer-aided design systems, and video teleconferencing and who rarely, if ever, see one another face-to-face.

knowledge management system A company-specific virtual information system that allows workers to share their knowledge and expertise and find others to help solve ongoing problems.

business-to-business (B2B) network A group of organizations that join together and use IT to link themselves to potential global suppliers to increase efficiency and effectiveness.

another organization to perform the activity. It is still not clear how B2B networks and other forms of electronic alliances between companies will develop in the future.

Summary and Review

DESIGNING ORGANIZATIONAL STRUCTURE The four main determinants of organizational structure are the external environment, strategy, technology, and human resources. In general, the higher the level of uncertainty associated with these factors, the more appropriate is a flexible, adaptable structure as opposed to a formal, rigid one. **[LO 7-1]**

GROUPING TASKS INTO JOBS Job design is the process by which managers group tasks into jobs. To create more interesting jobs, and to get workers to act flexibly, managers can enlarge and enrich jobs. The job characteristics model provides a tool managers can use to measure how motivating or satisfying a particular job is. **[LO 7-2]**

GROUPING JOBS INTO FUNCTIONS AND DIVISIONS Managers can choose from many kinds of organizational structures to make the best use of organizational resources. Depending on the specific organizing problems they face, managers can choose from functional, product, geographic, market, matrix, product team, and hybrid structures. **[LO 7-3]**

COORDINATING FUNCTIONS AND DIVISIONS No matter which structure managers choose, they must decide how to distribute authority in the organization, how many levels to have in the hierarchy of authority, and what balance to strike between centralization and decentralization to keep the number of levels in the hierarchy to a minimum. As organizations grow, managers must increase integration and coordination among functions and divisions. Six integrating mechanisms are available to facilitate this: direct contact, liaison roles, task forces, cross-functional teams, integrating roles, and the matrix structure. **[LO 7-3, 7-4]**

STRATEGIC ALLIANCES, B2B NETWORK STRUCTURES, AND IT To avoid many of the communication and coordination problems that emerge as organizations grow, managers are attempting to use IT to develop new ways of organizing. In a strategic alliance, managers enter into an agreement with another organization to provide inputs or to perform a functional activity. If managers enter into a series of these agreements, they create a network structure. A network structure, most commonly based on some shared form of IT, can be formed around one company, or a number of companies can join together to create an industry B2B network. **[LO 7-4]**

Management *in Action*

TOPICS FOR DISCUSSION AND ACTION

Discussion

1. Would a flexible or a more formal structure be appropriate for these organizations: (a) a large department store, (b) a Big Five accountancy firm, (c) a biotechnology company? Explain your reasoning. **[LO 7-1, 7-2]**

2. Using the job characteristics model as a guide, discuss how a manager can enrich or enlarge subordinates' jobs. **[LO 7-2]**

3. How might a salesperson's job or a secretary's job be enlarged or enriched to make it more motivating? **[LO 7-2, 7-3]**

4. When and under what conditions might managers change from a functional to (a) a product, (b) a geographic, or (c) a market structure? **[LO 7-1, 7-3]**

5. How do matrix structures and product team structures differ? Why is the product team structure more widely used? **[LO 7-1, 7-3, 7-4]**

Action

6. Find and interview a manager, and identify the kind of organizational structure that his or her organization uses to coordinate its people and resources. Why is the organization using that structure? Do you think a different structure would be more appropriate? If so which one? **[LO 7-1, 7-3, 7-4]**

7. With the same or another manager, discuss the distribution of authority in the organization. Does the manager think that decentralizing authority and empowering employees are appropriate? **[LO 7-1, 7-3]**

8. Interview some employees of an organization, and ask them about the organization's values and norms, the typical characteristics of employees, and the organization's ethical values and socialization practices. Using this information, try to describe the organization's culture and the way it affects the way people and groups behave. **[LO 7-1, 7-3]**

BUILDING MANAGEMENT SKILLS

Understanding Organizing [LO 7-1, 7-2, 7-3]

Think of an organization with which you are familiar, perhaps one you have worked for—such as a store, restaurant, office, church, or school. Then answer the following questions.

1. Which contingencies are most important in explaining how the organization is organized? Do you think it is organized in the best way?

2. Using the job characteristics model, how motivating do you think the job of a typical employee in this organization is?

3. Can you think of any ways in which a typical job could be enlarged or enriched?

4. What kind of organizational structure does the organization use? If it is part of a chain, what kind of structure does the entire organization use? What other structures discussed in the chapter might allow the organization to operate more effectively? For example, would the move to a product team structure lead to greater efficiency or effectiveness? Why or why not?

5. How many levels are there in the organization's hierarchy? Is authority centralized or decentralized? Describe the

span of control of the top manager and of middle or first-line managers.

6. Is the distribution of authority appropriate for the organization and its activities? Would it be possible to flatten the hierarchy by decentralizing authority and empowering employees?

7. What are the principal integrating mechanisms used in the organization? Do they provide sufficient coordination among individuals and functions? How might they be improved?

8. Now that you have analyzed the way this organization is structured, what advice would you give its managers to help them improve the way it operates?

MANAGING ETHICALLY [LO 7-1, 7-3]

Suppose an organization is downsizing and laying off many of its middle managers. Some top managers charged with deciding whom to terminate might decide to keep the subordinates they like, and who are obedient to them, rather than the ones who are difficult or the best performers. They might also decide to lay off the most highly paid subordinates even if they are high performers. Think of the ethical issues involved in designing a hierarchy, and discuss the following issues.

Questions

1. What ethical rules (see Chapter 3) should managers use to decide which employees to terminate when redesigning their hierarchy?

2. Some people argue that employees who have worked for an organization for many years have a claim on the organization at least as strong as that of its shareholders. What do you think of the ethics of this position—can employees claim to "own" their jobs if they have contributed significantly to the organization's past success? How does a socially responsible organization behave in this situation?

SMALL GROUP BREAKOUT EXERCISE

Bob's Appliances [LO 7-1, 7-3]

Form groups of three or four people, and appoint one member as the spokesperson who will communicate your findings to the class when called on by the instructor. Then discuss the following scenario.

Bob's Appliances sells and services household appliances such as washing machines, dishwashers, ranges, and refrigerators. Over the years, the company has developed a good reputation for the quality of its customer service, and many local builders patronize the store. Recently, some new appliance retailers, including Best Buy, have opened stores that also provide numerous appliances. To attract more customers, however, these stores also carry a complete range of consumer electronics products—televisions, stereos, and computers. Bob Lange, the owner of Bob's Appliances, has decided that if he is to stay in business, he must widen his product range and compete directly with the chains.

In 2007, he decided to build a 20,000-square-foot store and service center, and he is now hiring new employees to sell and service the new line of consumer electronics. Because of his company's increased size, Lange is not sure of the best way to organize the employees. Currently, he uses a functional structure; employees are divided into sales, purchasing and accounting, and repair. Bob is wondering whether selling and servicing consumer electronics is so different from selling and servicing appliances that he should move to a product structure (see the figure) and create separate sets of functions for each of his two lines of business.[50]

Question

1. You are a team of local consultants whom Bob has called in to advise him as he makes this crucial choice. Which structure do you recommend? Why?

FUNCTIONAL STRUCTURE

- Bob Lange
  - Sales
  - Purchasing and Accounting
  - Repair

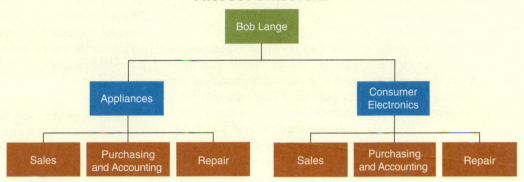

PRODUCT STRUCTURE

- Bob Lange
  - Appliances
    - Sales
    - Purchasing and Accounting
    - Repair
  - Consumer Electronics
    - Sales
    - Purchasing and Accounting
    - Repair

BE THE MANAGER [LO 7-1, 7-3, 7-4]

Speeding Up Website Design

You have been hired by a website design, production, and hosting company whose new animated website designs are attracting a lot of attention and a lot of customers. Currently, employees are organized into different functions such as hardware, software design, graphic art, and website hosting, as well as functions such as marketing and human resources. Each function takes its turn to work on a new project from initial customer request to final online website hosting.

The problem the company is experiencing is that it typically takes one year from the initial idea stage to the time that the website is up and running; the company wants to shorten this time by half to protect and expand its market niche. In talking to other managers, you discover that they believe the company's current functional structure is the source of the problem—it is not allowing employees to develop websites fast enough to satisfy customers' demands. They want you to design a better one.

Questions

1. Discuss ways in which you can improve how the current functional structure operates so that it speeds website development.

2. Discuss the pros and cons of moving to a (a) multidivisional, (b) matrix, or (c) product team structure to reduce website development time.

3. Which of these structures do you think is most appropriate, and why?

BLOOMBERG BUSINESSWEEK CASE IN THE NEWS [LO 7-1, 7-3, 7-4]

Microsoft's Ballmer Said to Plan Broad Restructuring

Microsoft Corp. Chief Executive Officer Steve Ballmer is planning a reorganization aimed at reducing the number of business units and putting more focus on devices and services, according to people familiar with the matter.

The changes would give greater responsibility to executives including Satya Nadella, head of the server business, Don Mattrick, who runs Xbox, Qi Lu, chief of the online group, and Tony Bates, president of Skype, according to two people who asked not to be identified because the discussions are private. Andy Lees, who has overseen corporate development and strategy since November, will probably leave the company in the coming months, the people said.

Ballmer, who is struggling to gain share in mobile-phones and tablets, announced a shift in strategy last year for the world's largest software maker to focus on computing devices and Internet-based services. Any staffing changes will also provide clues as to the executives who may eventually succeed Ballmer.

Plans for the executive shakeup, which Ballmer, 57, has been discussing with the board,

are not final and may still change, the people said. The All Things D blog reported some details of the restructuring yesterday.

The changes are aimed at cutting the number of disparate units and fostering cooperation between products so that Microsoft can better compete against Apple Inc. and Google Inc., said one person.

Peter Wootton, a spokesman for Microsoft, declined to comment on restructuring or staffing changes.

New Structure

One idea under consideration by Ballmer would create four divisions: an enterprise business led by Nadella; a hardware unit overseen by Mattrick; an applications and services division under Lu; and an operating-systems group jointly led by Terry Myerson, Windows phone chief, and Julie Larson-Green, head of Windows engineering, said one person. Bates would also be given a significant role, said the person.

In April, activist investor Value-Act Holdings LP disclosed a stake of about $1.9 billion in Microsoft and said the company should become a leader in Web-based cloud computing, putting more

pressure on Ballmer to focus on that area.

Microsoft, based in Redmond, Washington, currently has eight divisions or units, and six presidents. The Windows business has been run by two vice presidents, Larson-Green and Tami Reller, since Steven Sinofsky was pushed out in November. The Office unit is run by Kurt DelBene.

The reorganization has been under discussion even before Sinofsky's ouster, said the people. Ballmer stressed at the time the need for Microsoft's groups to better cooperate and for executives to make that happen.

Questions

1. Why does Microsoft need to change the way it organizes its functions and divisions?

2. What changes is CEO Ballmer proposing to make? How will they affect the way the company operates?

3. Search the Internet and outline the changes Microsoft has since made to its organizational structure.

Source: Dina Bass, "Microsoft's Ballmer Said to Plan Broad Restructuring," *Bloomberg Businessweek,* www.businessweek.com.

8 Control, Change, and Entrepreneurship

LEARNING OBJECTIVES

After studying this chapter, you should be able to:

1 Define organizational control, and identify the main output and behavior controls managers use to coordinate and motivate employees. **[LO 8-1]**

2 Describe the four steps in the control process and the way it operates over time. **[LO 8-2]**

3 Identify the main output controls, and discuss their advantages and disadvantages as means of coordinating and motivating employees. **[LO 8-3]**

4 Explain how clan control or organizational culture creates an effective organizational architecture. **[LO 8-4]**

5 Discuss the relationship between organizational control and change, and explain why managing change is a vital management task. **[LO 8-5]**

6 Understand the role of entrepreneurship in the control and change process. **[LO 8-6]**

Ford CEO Alan Mulally (left), with former CEO Bill Ford (right), who realized the company needed an outsider at the helm to change Ford's insular, self-protective culture.

How Alan Mulally Transformed Ford

How Can Managers Create a New Culture?

After a loss of more than $13 billion in 2006, William Ford III, who had been Ford Motor's CEO for five years, decided he was not the right person to turn around the company's performance.[1] In fact, it became apparent that he was a part of Ford's problems because he and other Ford top managers tried to build and protect their own corporate empires, and none would ever admit that mistakes had occurred over the years. As a result the whole company's performance had suffered; its future was in doubt. Finally, Ford's board of directors realized they needed an outsider to change Ford's culture and the way it operated, and they recruited Alan Mulally from Boeing to become Ford's new CEO.

After arriving at Ford, Mulally attended hundreds of executive meetings with his new managers; and at one meeting he became confused why one top division manager, who obviously did not know the answer to one of Mulally's questions concerning the performance of his car division, had rambled on for several minutes trying to disguise his ignorance. Mulally turned to his second-in-command, Mark Fields, and asked him why the manager had done that. Fields explained that "at Ford you never admit when you don't know something." He also told Mulally that when he arrived as a middle manager at Ford and wanted to ask his boss to lunch to gain information about divisional operations, he was told, "What rank are you at Ford? Don't you know that a subordinate never asks a superior to lunch?"[2]

It turned out that over the years Ford had developed a tall hierarchy composed of managers whose main goal was to protect their turf and avoid any direct blame for its plunging car sales. When asked why car sales were falling, they did not admit to bad design and poor quality issues in their divisions; instead they hid in the details. They brought thick notebooks and binders to meetings, listing the high prices of components and labor costs to explain why their own particular car models were not selling well—or even why they had to be sold at a loss. Why, Mulally wondered, did Ford's top executives have this inward-looking, destructive mind-set?

Mulally soon realized the problem was the values and norms in Ford's culture that had created a situation in which the managers of its different divisions and functions thought the best way to maintain their jobs, salaries, and status was to hoard, rather than share, information. Thus values and norms of secrecy and ambiguity, and of emphasizing status and rank, to protect their information had developed. The reason only the boss could ask a subordinate to lunch was to allow superiors to protect their information and positions. Ford's culture allowed managers to hide their problems and poor performance. What could Mulally do? He issued a direct order that the managers of every division should share with every other Ford division a detailed statement of the costs they incurred to build each of its vehicles. He insisted that each of Ford's divisional presidents should attend a weekly (rather than a monthly) meeting to share and discuss openly the problems all the company's divisions faced. He also told them they should bring a different subordinate with them to each meeting so every manager in the hierarchy would learn of the problems that had been kept hidden.[3]

Essentially, Mulally's goal was to demolish the dysfunctional values and norms of Ford's culture that focused managers' attention on their own empires at the expense of the whole company. No longer would they be allowed to protect their own careers at the expense of customers. Mulally's goal was to create new values and norms that it was fine to admit mistakes, share information about all aspects of model design and costs, and of course find ways to speed development and reduce costs. He also wanted to emphasize norms of cooperation within and across divisions to improve performance.

How could this situation have gone unchanged in a major car company that has been experiencing increased competition since the mid-1970s? The answer is that the norms and values of an organization's culture are difficult to change; and despite Ford's major problems, no CEO had been able to change the mind-set of the top managers in the company. Ford had become more hierarchical and bureaucratic over time as its problems increased because poor performance led managers to become more defensive and concerned with defending their empires.

By 2010 it was clear that Mulally had changed Ford's values and norms; the company finally reported a profit in the spring of 2010 and has been profitable ever since; in 2013 it was the highest performing U.S. carmaker. The managers who could not or would not conform to Ford's new culture were gone; the others had internalized the need to work toward strengthening Ford's new culture that was now focused on satisfying the needs of customers, not the needs of its top managers.

Overview

As the experience of Ford suggests, the ways in which managers decide to control and regulate the behavior of their employees has important effects on their performance. When managers make choices about how to influence and shape employees' behavior and performance, they are using organizational control. And control is the essential ingredient that is needed to bring about and manage organizational change efficiently and effectively.

As discussed in Chapter 7, the first task facing managers is to establish the structure of task and job reporting relationships that allows organizational members to use resources most efficiently and effectively. Structure alone, however, does not provide the incentive or motivation for people to behave in ways that help achieve organizational goals. The purpose of organizational control is to provide managers with a means of directing and motivating subordinates to work toward achieving organizational goals and to provide managers with specific feedback on how well an organization and its members are performing.

Organizational structure provides an organization with a skeleton, and control and culture give it the muscles, sinews, nerves, and sensations that allow managers to regulate and govern its activities. The managerial functions of organizing and controlling are inseparable, and effective managers must learn to make them work together in a harmonious way.

In this chapter, we look in detail at the nature of organizational control and describe the steps in the control process. We discuss three types of control available to managers to control and influence organizational members—output control, behavior control, and clan control (which operates through the values and norms of an organization's culture).[4] Then we discuss the important issue of organizational change, change that is possible only when managers have put in place a control system that allows them to alter the way people and groups behave. Finally, we look at the role of entrepreneurs and entrepreneurship in changing the way a company operates. By the end of this chapter, you will appreciate the rich variety of control systems available to managers and understand why developing an appropriate control system is vital to increasing the performance of an organization and its members.

What Is Organizational Control?

LO8-1 Define organizational control, and identify the main output and behavior controls managers use to coordinate and motivate employees.

As we noted in Chapter 1, *controlling* is the process whereby managers monitor and regulate how efficiently and effectively an organization and its members are performing the activities necessary to achieve organizational goals. As discussed in previous chapters, when planning and organizing, managers develop the organizational strategy and structure that they hope will allow the organization to use resources most effectively to create value for customers. In controlling, managers monitor and evaluate whether the organization's strategy and structure are working as intended, how they could be improved, and how they might be changed if they are not working.

Control, however, does not mean just reacting to events after they have occurred. It also means keeping an organization on track, anticipating events that might occur, and then changing the organization to respond to whatever opportunities or threats have been identified. Control is concerned with keeping employees motivated, focused on the important problems confronting the organization, and working together to make the changes that will help an organization perform better over time.

The Importance of Organizational Control

To understand the importance of organizational control, consider how it helps managers obtain superior efficiency, quality, responsiveness to customers, and innovation—the four building blocks of competitive advantage.

To determine how efficiently they are using their resources, managers must be able to accurately measure how many units of inputs (raw materials, human resources, and so on) are being used to produce a unit of output, such as a Ford or Toyota vehicle. Managers also must be able to measure how many units of outputs (goods and services) are being produced. A control system contains the measures or yardsticks that let managers assess how efficiently the organization is producing goods and services. Moreover, if managers experiment with changing how the organization produces goods and services to find a more efficient way of producing them, these measures tell managers how successful they have been. Without a control system in place, managers have no idea how well their organization is performing and how its performance can be improved—information that is becoming increasingly important in today's highly competitive environment.

Today much of the competition among organizations centers on increasing the quality of goods and services. In the car industry, for example, cars within each price range compete in features, design, and reliability. Thus whether a customer will buy a Ford Taurus, Toyota Camry, or Honda Accord depends significantly on the quality of each product. Organizational control is important in determining the quality of goods and services because it gives managers feedback on product quality. If the managers of carmakers consistently measure the number of customer complaints and the number of new cars returned for repairs, or if school principals measure how many students drop out of school or how achievement scores on nationally based tests vary over time, they have a good indication of how much quality they have built into their product—be it an educated student or a car that does not break down. Effective managers create a control system that consistently monitors the quality of goods and services so they can continuously improve quality—an approach to change that gives them a competitive advantage.

Managers can help make their organizations more responsive to customers if they develop a control system that allows them to evaluate how well customer-contact employees perform their jobs. Monitoring employee behavior can help managers find ways to increase employees' performance levels, perhaps by revealing areas in which skill training can help employees or in which new procedures can allow employees to perform their jobs better. Also, when employees know their behaviors are being monitored, they have more incentive to be helpful and consistent in how they act toward customers. To improve customer service, for example, Toyota regularly surveys customers about their experiences with particular Toyota dealers. If a dealership receives too many customer complaints, Toyota's managers investigate the dealership to uncover the sources of the problems and suggest solutions; if necessary, they might even threaten to reduce the number of cars a dealership receives to force the dealer to improve the quality of its customer service.

Finally, controlling can raise the level of innovation in an organization. Successful innovation takes place when managers create an organizational setting in which employees feel empowered to be creative and in which authority is decentralized to employees so they feel free to experiment and take control of their work activities. Deciding on the appropriate control systems to encourage risk taking is an important management challenge; organizational culture is vital in this regard. To encourage work teams at Toyota to perform at a high level, for example, top managers monitored the performance of each team, by examining how each team reduced costs or increased quality—and used a bonus system related to performance to reward each team. The team manager then evaluated each team member's individual performance, and the most innovative employees received promotions and rewards based on their superior performance.

Whom would you rather buy a new car from? A company that reinforces and rewards employee responsiveness, consistency, and know-how in customer care, or a company that doesn't? Toyota bets you'll pick the former.

Control Systems and IT

Control systems are formal target-setting, monitoring, evaluation, and feedback systems that provide managers with information about whether the organization's strategy and structure are working efficiently and effectively.[5] Effective control systems alert managers when something is going wrong and give them time to respond to opportunities and threats. An effective control system has three characteristics: It is flexible enough to allow managers to respond as necessary to unexpected events; it provides accurate information about organizational performance; and it gives managers information in a timely manner because making decisions on the basis of outdated information is a recipe for failure.

New forms of IT have revolutionized control systems because they facilitate the flow of accurate and timely information up and down the organizational hierarchy and between functions and divisions. Today employees at all levels of the organization routinely feed information into a company's information system or network and start the chain of events that affect decision making in some other part of the organization. This could be the department store clerk whose scanning of purchased clothing tells merchandise managers what kinds of clothing need to be reordered or the salesperson in the field who feeds into a wireless laptop the information necessary to inform marketing about customers' changing needs.

Control and information systems are developed to measure performance at each stage in the process of transforming inputs into finished goods and services (see Figure 8.1). At the input stage, managers use **feedforward control** to anticipate problems before they arise so problems do not occur later during the conversion process.[6] For example, by giving stringent product specifications to suppliers in advance (a form of performance target), an organization can control the quality of the inputs it receives from its suppliers and thus avoid potential problems during the conversion process. Also, IT can be used to keep in contact with suppliers and to monitor their progress. Similarly, by screening job applicants, often by viewing their résumés electronically and using several interviews to select the most highly skilled people, managers can lessen the chance that they will hire people who lack the necessary skills or experience to perform effectively. In general, the development of management information systems promotes feedforward control that gives managers timely information about changes in the task and general environments that may impact their organization later on. Effective

Figure 8.1
Three Types of Control

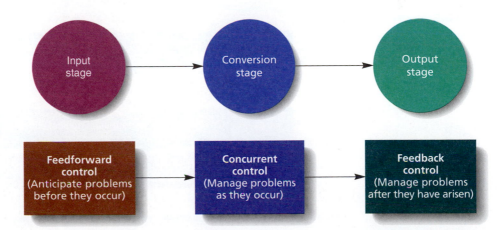

managers always monitor trends and changes in the external environment to try to anticipate problems. (We discuss management information systems in detail in Chapter 13.)

At the conversion stage, concurrent control gives managers immediate feedback on how efficiently inputs are being transformed into outputs so managers can correct problems as they arise. Concurrent control through IT alerts managers to the need to react quickly to whatever is the source of the problem, be it a defective batch of inputs, a machine that is out of alignment, or a worker who lacks the skills necessary to perform a task efficiently. Concurrent control is at the heart of programs to increase quality, in which workers are expected to constantly monitor the quality of the goods or services they provide at every step of the production process and inform managers as soon as they discover problems. One of the strengths of Toyota's production system, for example, is that individual workers have the authority to push a button to stop the assembly line whenever they discover a quality problem. When all problems are corrected, the result is a finished product that is much more reliable.

At the output stage, managers use feedback control to provide information about customers' reactions to goods and services so corrective action can be taken if necessary. For example, a feedback control system that monitors the number of customer returns alerts managers when defective products are being produced, and a management information system (MIS) that measures increases or decreases in relative sales of different products alerts managers to changes in customer tastes so they can increase or reduce the production of specific products.

concurrent control Control that gives managers immediate feedback on how efficiently inputs are being transformed into outputs so managers can correct problems as they arise.

feedback control Control that gives managers information about customers' reactions to goods and services so corrective action can be taken if necessary.

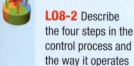

LO8-2 Describe the four steps in the control process and the way it operates over time.

The Control Process

The control process, whether at the input, conversion, or output stage, can be broken down into four steps: establishing standards of performance, and then measuring, comparing, and evaluating actual performance (see Figure 8.2).[7]

- Step 1: *Establish the standards of performance, goals, or targets against which performance is to be evaluated.*

At step 1 in the control process managers decide on the standards of performance, goals, or targets that they will use in the future to evaluate the performance of the entire organization or part of it (such as a division, a function, or an individual). The standards of performance that managers select measure

Figure 8.2

Four Steps in Organizational Control

Step 1	Establish the standards of performance, goals, or targets against which performance is to be evaluated.
Step 2	Measure actual performance.
Step 3	Compare actual performance against chosen standards of performance.
Step 4	Evaluate the result and initiate corrective action if the standard is not being achieved.

efficiency, quality, responsiveness to customers, and innovation.[8] If managers decide to pursue a low-cost strategy, for example, they need to measure efficiency at all levels in the organization.

At the corporate level, a standard of performance that measures efficiency is operating costs, the actual costs associated with producing goods and services, including all employee-related costs. Top managers might set a corporate goal of "reducing operating costs by 10% for the next three years" to increase efficiency. Corporate managers might then evaluate divisional managers for their ability to reduce operating costs within their respective divisions, and divisional managers might set cost-saving targets for functional managers. Thus performance standards selected at one level affect those at the other levels, and ultimately the performance of individual managers is evaluated in terms of their ability to reduce costs.

The number of standards or indicators of performance that an organization's managers use to evaluate efficiency, quality, and so on can run into the thousands or hundreds of thousands. Managers at each level are responsible for selecting standards that will best allow them to evaluate how well the part of the organization they are responsible for is performing.[9] Managers must be careful to choose standards of performance that let them assess how well they are doing with all four building blocks of competitive advantage. If managers focus on just one standard (such as efficiency), and ignore others (such as determining what customers really want and innovating a new line of products to satisfy them), managers may end up hurting their organization's performance.

- Step 2: *Measure actual performance.*

Once managers have decided which standards or targets they will use to evaluate performance, the next step in the control process is to measure actual performance. In practice, managers can measure or evaluate two things: (1) the actual *outputs* that result from the behavior of their members and (2) the *behaviors* themselves (hence the terms *output control* and *behavior control* used in this chapter).[10]

Sometimes both outputs and behaviors can be easily measured. Measuring outputs and evaluating behavior are relatively easy in a fast-food restaurant, for example, because employees are performing routine tasks. Managers at Home Depot are rigorous in using output control to measure how fast inventory flows through stores. Similarly, managers of a fast-food restaurant can easily measure outputs by counting how many customers their employees serve, the time each transaction takes, and how much money each customer spends. Managers can easily observe each employee's behavior and quickly take action to solve any problems that may arise.

When an organization and its members perform complex, nonroutine activities that are intrinsically hard to measure, it is more challenging for managers to measure outputs or behavior.[11] It is difficult, for example, for managers in charge of R&D departments at Intel or AMD, or at Microsoft or Google, to measure performance or to evaluate the performance of individual members because it can take several years to determine whether the new products that engineers and scientists are developing will be profitable. Moreover, it is impossible for a manager to measure how creative an engineer or scientist is by watching his or her actions.

In general, the more nonroutine or complex organizational activities are, the harder it is for managers to measure outputs or behaviors.[12] Outputs, however, are usually easier to measure than behaviors because they are more tangible and objective. Therefore, the first kind of performance measures that managers tend to use are those that measure outputs. Then managers develop performance measures or standards that allow them to evaluate behaviors to determine whether employees at all levels are working toward organizational goals. Some simple behavior measures are (1) whether employees come to work on time and (2) whether employees consistently follow the established rules for greeting and serving customers. The various types of output and behavior control and how they are used at the different organizational levels—corporate, divisional, functional, and individual—are discussed in detail later.

- Step 3: *Compare actual performance against chosen standards of performance.*

During step 3, managers evaluate whether—and to what extent—performance deviates from the standards of performance chosen in step 1. If performance is higher than expected, managers might decide they set performance standards too low and may raise them for the next period to challenge their subordinates.[13] Managers at Japanese companies are well known for the way they try to improve performance in manufacturing settings by constantly raising performance standards to motivate managers and workers to find new ways to reduce costs or increase quality.

However, if performance is too low and standards were not reached, or if standards were set so high that employees could not achieve them, managers must decide whether to take corrective action.[14] It is easy to take corrective action when the reasons for poor performance can be identified—for instance, high labor costs. To reduce costs, managers can search for low-cost overseas suppliers, invest more in technology, or implement cross-functional teams. More often, however, the reasons for poor performance are hard to identify. Changes in the environment, such as the emergence of a new global competitor, a recession, or an increase in interest rates, might be the source of the problem. Within an organization, perhaps the R&D function underestimated the problems it would encounter in developing a new product or the extra costs of doing unforeseen research. If managers are to take any form of corrective action, step 4 is necessary.

- Step 4: *Evaluate the result and initiate corrective action (that is, make changes) if the standard is not being achieved.*

The final step in the control process is to evaluate the results and bring about change as appropriate. Whether or not performance standards have been met, managers can learn a great deal during this step. If managers decide the level of performance is unacceptable, they must try to change how work activities are performed to solve the problem. Sometimes performance problems occur because the work standard was too high—for example, a sales target was too optimistic and impossible to achieve. In this case, adopting more realistic standards can reduce the gap between actual performance and desired performance.

However, if managers determine that something in the situation is causing the problem, then to raise performance they will need to change how resources are utilized.[15] Perhaps the latest technology is not being used; perhaps workers lack the advanced training needed to perform at a higher level; perhaps the organization needs to buy its inputs or assemble its products abroad to compete against low-cost rivals; perhaps it needs to restructure itself or reengineer its work processes to increase efficiency. Or perhaps it needs to change its monitoring and reward systems as suggested by the experience of eBay in the following "Management Insight" box.

MANAGEMENT INSIGHT

Control Problems Arise between eBay and Its Sellers

Since its founding in 1995, eBay has always cultivated good relationships with the millions of sellers that advertise their goods for sale on its website. Over time, however, to increase its revenues and profits, eBay has steadily increased the fees it charges sellers to list their products on its sites, to insert photographs, to use its PayPal online payment service, and so on. Although this caused some grumbling among sellers because it reduced their profit margins, eBay increasingly engaged in extensive advertising that attracted millions more buyers to use its website so that sellers received better prices and their total profits also increased. As a result, they remained largely satisfied with eBay's fee structure.

John Donahoe, new CEO of eBay, learned the hard way that gleaning feedback from a wide range of stakeholders remains absolutely essential when making major changes in organizational control.

This all changed when a new CEO, John Donahoe, took over from eBay's longtime CEO, Meg Whitman, who had built the company into a dot.com giant. By the late 2000s, eBay's revenues and profits had not increased fast enough to keep its investors happy, and its stock price plunged. One of Donahoe's first moves to increase performance was to announce a major overhaul of eBay's fee structure and feedback policy.[16] eBay's new fee structure would reduce upfront listing costs but increase back-end commissions on completed sales and payments. For its small sellers that already had thin profit margins, these fee hikes were painful. In addition, in the future eBay announced it would block sellers from leaving negative feedback about buyers—feedback such as buyers didn't pay for the goods they purchased or took too long to do so. The feedback system that eBay had originally developed has been a major source of its success because it allows buyers to know they are dealing with reputable sellers and vice versa. All sellers and buyers have feedback scores that provide them with a reputation as good—or bad—people to do business with, and these scores reduce the risks involved in online transactions. Donahoe claimed this change was to improve the buyer's experience because many buyers had complained that if they left negative feedback for a seller—the seller would then leave negative feedback for the buyer!

Together, however, these changes resulted in a blaze of conflict between eBay and its millions of sellers who perceived they were being harmed by these changes, that they had lost their prestige and standing at eBay, and their bad feelings resulted in a revolt. Blogs and forums across the Internet were filled with messages claiming that eBay had abandoned its smaller sellers and was pushing them out of business in favor of high-volume "powersellers" who contributed more to eBay's profits. eBay and Donahoe received millions of hostile e-mails, and sellers threatened they would move their business elsewhere, such as onto Amazon.com and Yahoo!, which were both trying to break into eBay's market. Sellers even organized a one-week boycott of eBay during which they would list no items with the company to express their dismay and hostility. Many sellers did shut down their eBay online storefronts and move to Amazon.com, which by 2010 claimed that its network of sites had overtaken eBay in monthly unique viewers or "hits" for the first time.

The bottom line was that the level of conflict between eBay and its buyers had dramatically escalated and eBay's reputation with sellers was suffering; one survey found that while over 50% of buyers thought Amazon.com was an excellent sales channel, only 23% regarded eBay as excellent. In essence, the bitter feelings produced by the changes eBay had made were likely to result in increasing and long-run conflict that would hurt its future performance. Realizing his changes had backfired, Donahoe reversed course in 2009 and eliminated several of eBay's fee increases and revamped its feedback system so that buyers and sellers can now respond to one another's comments in a fairer way.

These moves did improve and smooth over the bad feeling between sellers and eBay, but the old "community relationship" it had enjoyed with buyers in its early years largely disappeared. As this example suggests, finding ways to avoid conflict—such as by testing the waters in advance and asking sellers for their reactions to fee and feedback changes—could have avoided many of the problems that arose. Nevertheless, in the 2010s, eBay's turnaround plan has been successful and its revenues and profits have steadily increased—as has its stock price.

The simplest example of a control system is the thermostat in a home. By setting the thermostat, you establish the standard of performance with which actual temperature is to be compared. The thermostat contains a sensing or monitoring device, which measures the actual temperature against the desired temperature. Whenever there is a difference between them, the furnace or air-conditioning unit is activated to bring the temperature back to the standard. In other words, corrective action is initiated. This is a simple control system: It is entirely self-contained, and the target (temperature) is easy to measure.

Establishing targets and designing measurement systems are much more difficult for managers because the high level of uncertainty in the organizational environment means managers rarely know what might happen in the future. Thus it is vital for managers to design control systems to alert them to problems quickly so they can be dealt with before they become threatening. Another issue is that managers are not just concerned about bringing the organization's performance up to some predetermined standard; they want to push that standard forward to encourage employees at all levels to find new ways to raise performance.

In the following sections, we consider three important types of control systems that managers use to coordinate and motivate employees to ensure that they pursue superior efficiency, quality, innovation, and responsiveness to customers: output control, behavior control, and clan control (see Figure 8.3). Managers use all three to shape, regulate, and govern organizational activities, no matter what specific organizational structure is in place.

Figure 8.3

Three Organizational Control Systems

Type of control	Mechanisms of control
Output control	Financial measures of performance Organizational goals Operating budgets
Behavior control	Direct supervision Management by objectives Rules and standard operating procedures
Organizational culture/clan control	Values Norms Socialization

Output Control

All managers develop a system of output control for their organizations. First they choose the goals or output performance standards or targets that they think will best measure efficiency, quality, innovation, and responsiveness to customers. Then they measure to see whether the performance goals and standards are being achieved at the corporate, divisional, functional, and individual employee levels of the organization. The three main mechanisms that managers use to assess output or performance are financial measures, organizational goals, and operating budgets.

LO8-3 Identify the main output controls, and discuss their advantages and disadvantages as means of coordinating and motivating employees.

Financial Measures of Performance

Top managers are most concerned with overall organizational performance and use various financial measures to evaluate it. The most common are profit ratios, liquidity ratios, leverage ratios, and activity ratios. They are discussed here and summarized in Table 8.1.[17]

- *Profit ratios* measure how efficiently managers are using the organization's resources to generate profits. *Return on investment (ROI)*, an organization's net income before taxes divided by its total assets, is the most commonly used financial performance measure because it allows managers of one organization to compare performance with that of other organizations. ROI lets managers assess an organization's competitive advantage. *Operating margin* is calculated by dividing a company's operating profit (the amount it has left after all the costs of making the product and running the business have been deducted) by sales revenues. This measure tells managers how efficiently an organization is using its resources; every successful attempt to reduce costs will be reflected in increased operating profit, for example. Also, operating margin is a means of comparing one year's performance to another; for example, if managers discover operating margin has improved by 5% from one year to the next, they know their organization is building a competitive advantage.

- *Liquidity ratios* measure how well managers have protected organizational resources to be able to meet short-term obligations. The *current ratio* (current assets divided by current liabilities) tells managers whether they have the resources available to meet the claims of short-term creditors. The *quick ratio* shows whether they can pay these claims without selling inventory.

- *Leverage ratios,* such as the *debt-to-assets ratio* and the *times-covered ratio,* measure the degree to which managers use debt (borrow money) or equity (issue new

Table 8.1

Four Measures of Financial Performance

Profit Ratios

Return on investment $= \dfrac{\text{Net profit before taxes}}{\text{Total assets}}$ — Measures how well managers are using the organization's resources to generate profits.

Operating margin $= \dfrac{\text{Total operating profit}}{\text{Sales revenues}}$ — A measure of how much percentage profit a company is earning on sales; the higher the percentage, the better a company is using its resources to make and sell the product.

Liquidity Ratios

Current ratio $= \dfrac{\text{Current assets}}{\text{Current liabilities}}$ — Do managers have resources available to meet claims of short-term creditors?

Quick ratio $= \dfrac{\text{Current assets} - \text{Inventory}}{\text{Current liabilities}}$ — Can managers pay off claims of short-term creditors without selling inventory?

Leverage Ratios

Debt-to-assets ratio $= \dfrac{\text{Total debt}}{\text{Total assets}}$ — To what extent have managers used borrowed funds to finance investments?

Times-covered ratio $= \dfrac{\text{Profit before interest and taxes}}{\text{Total interest charges}}$ — Measures how far profits can decline before managers cannot meet interest charges. If this ratio declines to less than 1, the organization is technically insolvent.

Activity Ratios

Inventory turnover $= \dfrac{\text{Cost of goods sold}}{\text{Inventory}}$ — Measures how efficiently managers are turning inventory over so that excess inventory is not carried.

Days sales outstanding $= \dfrac{\text{Current accounts receivable}}{\text{Sales for period divided by days in period}}$ — Measures how efficiently managers are collecting revenues from customers to pay expenses.

shares) to finance ongoing operations. An organization is highly leveraged if it uses more debt than equity. Debt can be risky when net income or profit fails to cover the interest on the debt—as some people learn too late when their paychecks do not allow them to pay off their credit cards.

- *Activity ratios* show how well managers are creating value from organizational assets. *Inventory turnover* measures how efficiently managers are turning inventory over so excess inventory is not carried. *Days sales outstanding* reveals how efficiently managers are collecting revenue from customers to pay expenses.

The objectivity of financial measures of performance is the reason why so many managers use them to assess the efficiency and effectiveness of their organizations. When an organization fails to meet performance standards such as ROI, revenue, or stock price targets, managers know they must take corrective action. Thus financial controls tell managers when a corporate reorganization might be necessary, when they should sell off divisions and exit businesses, or when they should rethink their corporate-level strategies.[18] Today financial controls are taught to all organizational employees, as the following "Management Insight" box describes.

MANAGEMENT INSIGHT

Making the Financial Figures Come Alive

You might think financial control is the province of top managers and employees lower in the organization don't need to worry about the numbers or about how their specific activities affect those numbers. However, some top managers make a point of showing employees exactly how their activities affect financial ratios, and they do so because employees' activities directly affect a company's costs and its sales revenues. One of those managers is Michael Dell.

Michael Dell prepares to work the phone lines at Dell's U.S. customer service call center. Dell's emphasis on productivity everywhere means he has no qualms about sitting in an entry-level position for a day both to learn what his employees face and to better teach them.

Dell goes to enormous lengths to convince employees that they need to watch every dime spent in making the PCs that have made his company so prosperous, as well as in saying every word or making every phone call or service call that is needed to sell or repair them. Dell believes all his managers need to have at their fingertips detailed information about Dell's cost structure, including assembly costs, selling costs, and after-sales costs, in order to squeeze out every cent of operating costs. One good reason for this is that Dell puts a heavy emphasis on the operating margin financial ratio in measuring his company's performance. Dell doesn't care about how much profits or sales are growing individually; he cares about how these two figures work together because only if profits are growing faster than sales is the company increasing its long-run profitability by operating more efficiently and effectively.

So he insists that his managers search for every way possible to reduce costs or make customers happier and then help employees learn the new procedures to achieve these goals. At Dell's boot camp for new employees in Austin, Texas, he has been known to bring financial charts that show employees how each minute spent on performing some job activity, or how each mistake made in assembling or packing a PC, affects bottom-line profitability. In the early 2000s Dell's repeated efforts to reduce costs and build customer loyalty boosted its efficiency and operating margins; today, as it battles rivals such as HP and Acer, it is even more important that its employees understand how their specific behaviors affect Dell's bottom-line financial performance. In the 2000s all kinds of companies are training employees at all levels in how their specific job activities, and the way their functions operate, affect the financial ratios used to judge how well an organization is performing.

Although financial information is an important output control, financial information by itself does not tell managers all they need to know about the four building blocks of competitive advantage. Financial results inform managers about the results of decisions they have already made; they do not tell managers how to find new opportunities to build competitive advantage in the future. To encourage a future-oriented approach, top managers must establish organizational goals that encourage middle and first-line managers to achieve superior efficiency, quality, innovation, and responsiveness to customers.

Organizational Goals

Once top managers consult with lower-level managers and set the organization's overall goals, they establish performance standards for the divisions and functions. These standards specify for divisional and functional managers the level at which their units must perform if the organization is to achieve its overall goals.[19] Each division is given a set of specific goals to achieve (see Figure 8.4). We saw in Chapter 6, for example, that Jeffrey Immelt, CEO of GE, has established the goal of having each GE division be first or second in its industry in profit. Divisional managers then develop a business-level strategy (based on achieving superior efficiency or innovation) that they hope will allow them to achieve that goal.[20] In consultation with functional managers, they specify the functional goals that the managers of different functions need to achieve to allow the division to achieve its goals. For example, sales managers might be evaluated for their ability to increase sales; materials management managers, for their ability to increase the quality of inputs or lower their costs; R&D managers, for the number of products they innovate or the number of patents they receive. In turn, functional managers establish goals that first-line managers and nonmanagerial employees need to achieve to allow the function to achieve its goals.

Output control is used at every level of the organization, and it is vital that the goals set at each level harmonize with the goals set at other levels so managers and other employees throughout the organization work together to attain the corporate goals that top managers have set.[21] It is also important that goals be set appropriately so managers are motivated to accomplish them. If goals are set at an impossibly high level, managers might work only half-heartedly to achieve them because they are certain they will fail. In contrast, if goals are set so low that they are too easy to achieve, managers will not be motivated to use all their resources as efficiently and effectively as possible. Research suggests that the best goals are specific, difficult goals—goals that challenge and stretch managers' ability but are not out of reach and do not require an impossibly high expenditure of managerial time and energy. Such goals are often called *stretch goals*.

Figure 8.4

Organizationwide Goal Setting

Corporate-level managers set goals for individual divisions that will allow the organization to achieve corporate goals.

Divisional managers set goals for each function that will allow the division to achieve its goals.

Functional managers set goals for each individual worker that will allow the function to achieve its goals.

Deciding what is a specific, difficult goal and what is a goal that is too difficult or too easy is a skill that managers must develop. Based on their own judgment and work experience, managers at all levels must assess how difficult a certain task is, and they must assess the ability of a particular subordinate manager to achieve the goal. If they do so successfully, challenging, interrelated goals—goals that reinforce one another and focus on achieving overall corporate objectives—will energize the organization.

Operating Budgets

operating budget
A budget that states how managers intend to use organizational resources to achieve organizational goals.

Once managers at each level have been given a goal or target to achieve, the next step in developing an output control system is to establish operating budgets that regulate how managers and workers attain their goals. An operating budget is a blueprint that states how managers intend to use organizational resources to achieve organizational goals efficiently. Typically managers at one level allocate to subordinate managers a specific amount of resources to produce goods and services. Once they have been given a budget, these lower-level managers must decide how to allocate money for different organizational activities. They are then evaluated for their ability to stay within the budget and to make the best use of available resources. For example, managers at GE's washing machine division might have a budget of $50 million to spend on developing and selling a new line of washing machines. They must decide how much money to allocate to the various functions such as R&D, engineering, and sales so the division generates the most customer revenue and makes the biggest profit.

Large organizations often treat each division as a singular or stand-alone responsibility center. Corporate managers then evaluate each division's contribution to corporate performance. Managers of a division may be given a fixed budget for resources and be evaluated on the amount of goods or services they can produce using those resources (this is a cost or expense budget approach). Alternatively, managers may be asked to maximize the revenues from the sales of goods and services produced (a revenue budget approach). Or managers may be evaluated on the difference between the revenues generated by the sales of goods and services and the budgeted cost of making those goods and services (a profit budget approach). Japanese companies' use of operating budgets and challenging goals to increase efficiency is instructive in this context.

In summary, three components—objective financial measures, challenging goals and performance standards, and appropriate operating budgets—are the essence of effective output control. Most organizations develop sophisticated output control systems to allow managers at all levels to keep accurate account of the organization so they can move quickly to take corrective action as needed.[22] Output control is an essential part of management.

Problems with Output Control

When designing an output control system, managers must be careful to avoid some pitfalls. For example, they must be sure the output standards they create motivate managers at all levels and do not cause managers to behave in inappropriate ways to achieve organizational goals.

Suppose top managers give divisional managers the goal of doubling profits over a three-year period. This goal seems challenging and reachable when it is jointly agreed upon, and in the first two years profits go up by 70%. In the third year, however, an economic recession hits and sales plummet. Divisional managers think it is increasingly unlikely that they will meet their profit goal. Failure will mean losing the substantial monetary bonus tied to achieving the goal. How might managers behave to try to preserve their bonuses?

Perhaps they might find ways to reduce costs because profit can be increased either by raising sales revenues or reducing costs. Thus divisional managers might cut back on expensive research activities, delay machinery maintenance, reduce marketing expenditures, and lay off middle managers and workers to reduce costs so that at the end of the year they will make their target of doubling profits and receive their bonuses. This tactic might help them achieve a short-run goal—doubling profits—but such actions could hurt long-term profitability or ROI (because a cutback in R&D can reduce the rate of product innovation, a cutback in marketing will lead to the loss of customers, and so on).

The message is clear: Although output control is a useful tool for keeping managers and employees at all levels motivated and the organization on track, it is only a guide to appropriate action. Managers must be sensitive in how they use output control and must constantly monitor its effects at all levels in the organization—and on customers and other stakeholders.

Behavior Control

Organizational structure by itself does not provide any mechanism that motivates managers and nonmanagerial employees to behave in ways that make the structure work—or even improve how it works: hence the need for control. Put another way, managers can develop an organizational structure that has the right grouping of divisions and functions, and an effective chain of command, but it will work as designed *only* if managers also establish control systems that motivate and shape employee behavior in ways that *match* this structure.[23] Output control is one method of motivating employees; behavior control is another method. This section examines three mechanisms of behavior control that managers can use to keep subordinates on track and make organizational structures work as they are designed to work: direct supervision, management by objectives, and rules and standard operating procedures (see Figure 8.3).

Direct Supervision

The most immediate and potent form of behavior control is direct supervision by managers who actively monitor and observe the behavior of their subordinates, teach subordinates the behaviors that are appropriate and inappropriate, and intervene to take corrective action as needed. Moreover, when managers personally supervise subordinates, they lead by example and in this way can help subordinates develop and increase their own skill levels. (Leadership is the subject of Chapter 10.)

Direct supervision allows managers at all levels to become personally involved with their subordinates and allows them to mentor subordinates and develop their management skills. Thus control through personal supervision can be an effective way of motivating employees and promoting behaviors that increase efficiency and effectiveness.[24]

Nevertheless, certain problems are associated with direct supervision. First, it is expensive because a manager can personally manage only a relatively small number of subordinates effectively. Therefore, if direct supervision is the main kind of control being used in an organization, a lot of managers will be needed and costs will increase. For this reason, output control is usually preferred to behavior control; indeed, output control tends to be the first type of control that managers at all levels use to evaluate performance. Second, direct supervision can *demotivate* subordinates. This occurs if employees feel they are under such close scrutiny that they are not free to make their own decisions or if they feel they are not being evaluated in an accurate and impartial way. Team members and other employees may start to pass the buck, avoid responsibility, and cease to cooperate with other team members if they feel their manager is not accurately evaluating their performance and is favoring some people over others.

Third, as noted previously, for many jobs personal control through direct supervision is simply not feasible. The more complex a job is, the more difficult it is for a manager to evaluate how well a subordinate is performing. The performance of divisional and functional managers, for example, can be evaluated only over relatively long periods (which is why an output control system is developed), so it makes little sense for top managers to continually monitor their performance. However, managers can still communicate the organization's mission and goals to their subordinates and reinforce the values and norms in the organization's culture through their own personal style.

Management by Objectives

management by objectives (MBO)

A goal-setting process in which a manager and each of his or her subordinates negotiate specific goals and objectives for the subordinate to achieve and then periodically evaluate the extent to which the subordinate is achieving those goals.

To provide a framework within which to evaluate subordinates' behavior and, in particular, to allow managers to monitor progress toward achieving goals, many organizations implement some version of management by objectives. Management by objectives (MBO) is a formal system of evaluating subordinates on their ability to achieve specific organizational goals or performance standards and to meet operating budgets.[25] Most organizations use some form of MBO system because it is pointless to establish goals and then fail to evaluate whether they are being achieved. Management by objectives involves three specific steps:

- Step 1: *Specific goals and objectives are established at each level of the organization.*

MBO starts when top managers establish overall organizational objectives, such as specific financial performance goals or targets. Then objective setting cascades down throughout the organization as managers at the divisional and functional levels set their goals to achieve corporate objectives.[26] Finally first-level managers and employees jointly set goals that will contribute to achieving functional objectives.

- Step 2: *Managers and their subordinates together determine the subordinates' goals.*

An important characteristic of management by objectives is its participatory nature. Managers at every level sit down with each of the subordinate managers who report directly to them, and together they determine appropriate and feasible goals for the subordinate and bargain over the budget that the subordinate will need to achieve his or her goals. The participation of subordinates in the objective-setting process is a way of strengthening their commitment to achieving their goals and meeting their budgets.[27] Another reason why it is so important for subordinates (both individuals and teams) to participate in goal setting is that doing so enables them to tell managers what they think they can realistically achieve.[28]

- **Step 3:** *Managers and their subordinates periodically review the subordinates' progress toward meeting goals.*

Once specific objectives have been agreed on for managers at each level, managers are accountable for meeting those objectives. Periodically they sit down with their subordinates to evaluate their progress. Normally salary raises and promotions are linked to the goal-setting process, and managers who achieve their goals receive greater rewards than those who fall short. (The issue of how to design reward systems to motivate managers and other organizational employees is discussed in Chapter 9.)

In the companies that have decentralized responsibility for the production of goods and services to empowered teams and cross-functional teams, management by objectives works somewhat differently. Managers ask each team to develop a set of goals and performance targets that the team hopes to achieve—goals that are consistent with organizational objectives. Managers then negotiate with each team to establish its final goals and the budget the team will need to achieve them. The reward system is linked to team performance, not to the performance of any one team member.

Cypress Semiconductor offers an interesting example of how IT can be used to manage the MBO process quickly and effectively. In the fast-moving semiconductor business, a premium is placed on organizational adaptability. At Cypress, CEO T. J. Rodgers was facing a problem: How could he control his growing 1,500-employee organization without developing a bureaucratic management hierarchy? Rodgers believed that a tall hierarchy hinders the ability of an organization to adapt to changing conditions. He was committed to maintaining a flat and decentralized organizational structure with a minimum of management layers. At the same time he needed to control his employees to ensure that they performed in a manner consistent with the goals of the company.[29] How could he achieve this without resorting to direct supervision and the lengthy management hierarchy that it implies?

To solve this problem, Rodgers implemented an online information system through which he can monitor what every employee and team is doing in his fast-moving and decentralized organization. Each employee maintains a list of 10 to 15 goals, such as "Meet with marketing for new product launch" or "Make sure to check with customer X." Noted next to each goal are when it was agreed upon, when it is due to be finished, and whether it has been finished. All this information is stored on a central computer. Rodgers claims that he can review the goals of all employees in about four hours and that he does so each week.[30] How is this possible? He *manages by exception* and looks only for employees who are falling behind. He then calls them, not to scold but to ask whether there is anything he can do to help them get the job done. It takes only about half an hour each week for employees to review and update their lists. This system allows Rodgers to exercise control over his organization without resorting to the expensive layers of a management hierarchy and direct supervision.

MBO does not always work out as planned, however. Managers and their subordinates at all levels must believe that performance evaluations are accurate and fair. Any suggestion that personal biases and political objectives play a part in the evaluation process can lower or even destroy MBO's effectiveness as a control system. This is why many organizations work so hard to protect the integrity of their systems.

Similarly, when people work in teams, each member's contribution to the team, and each team's contribution to the goals of the organization, must be fairly evaluated. This is no easy thing to do. It depends on managers' ability to create an organizational control system that measures performance accurately and fairly and links performance evaluations to rewards so employees stay motivated and coordinate their activities to achieve the organization's mission and goals.

Bureaucratic Control

bureaucratic control Control of behavior by means of a comprehensive system of rules and standard operating procedures.

When direct supervision is too expensive and management by objectives is inappropriate, managers might turn to another mechanism to shape and motivate employee behavior: bureaucratic control. Bureaucratic control is control by means of a comprehensive system of rules and standard operating procedures (SOPs) that shapes and regulates the behavior of divisions, functions, and individuals. In the appendix to Chapter 1, we discussed Weber's theory of bureaucracy and noted that all organizations use bureaucratic rules and procedures but some use them more than others.[31]

Rules and SOPs guide behavior and specify what employees are to do when they confront a problem that needs a solution. It is the responsibility of a manager to develop rules that allow employees to perform their activities efficiently and effectively. When employees follow the rules that managers have developed, their behavior is standardized—actions are performed the same way time and time again—and the outcomes of their work are predictable. And, to the degree that managers can make employees' behavior predictable, there is no need to monitor the outputs of behavior because standardized behavior leads to standardized outputs.

Suppose a worker at Ford comes up with a way to attach exhaust pipes that reduces the number of steps in the assembly process and increases efficiency. Always on the lookout for ways to standardize procedures, managers make this idea the basis of a new rule that says, "From now on, the procedure for attaching the exhaust pipe to the car is as follows." If all workers followed the rule to the letter, every car would come off the assembly line with its exhaust pipe attached in the new way and there would be no need to check exhaust pipes at the end of the line. In practice, mistakes and lapses of attention do happen, so output control is used at the end of the line, and each car's exhaust system is given a routine inspection. However, the number of quality problems with the exhaust system is minimized because the rule (bureaucratic control) is being followed.

Service organizations such as retail stores, fast-food restaurants, and home-improvement stores attempt to standardize the behavior of employees by instructing them on the correct way to greet customers or the appropriate way to serve and bag food. Employees are trained to follow the rules that have proved to be most effective in a particular situation, and the better trained the employees are, the more standardized is their behavior and the more trust managers can have that outputs (such as food quality) will be consistent.[32]

Problems with Bureaucratic Control

All organizations make extensive use of bureaucratic control because rules and SOPs effectively control routine organizational activities. With a bureaucratic control system in place, managers can manage by exception and intervene and take corrective action only when necessary. However, managers need to be aware of a number of problems associated with bureaucratic control, because such problems can reduce organizational effectiveness.[33]

First, establishing rules is always easier than discarding them. Organizations tend to become overly bureaucratic over time as managers do everything according to the rule book. If the amount of red tape becomes too great, decision making slows and managers react slowly to changing conditions. This sluggishness can imperil an organization's survival if agile new competitors emerge.

Second, because rules constrain and standardize behavior and lead people to behave in predictable ways, there is a danger that people become so used to automatically following rules that they stop thinking for themselves. Thus, too much standardization can actually reduce the level of learning taking place in an organization and get the organization off track if managers and workers focus on the wrong issues. An organization thrives when its members are constantly thinking of new ways to increase efficiency, quality, and customer responsiveness. By definition, new ideas do not come from blindly following standardized procedures. Similarly, the pursuit of innovation implies a commitment by managers to discover new ways of doing things; innovation, however, is incompatible with the use of extensive bureaucratic control.

Managers must therefore be sensitive about the way they use bureaucratic control. It is most useful when organizational activities are routine and well understood and when employees are making programmed decisions—for example, in mass-production settings such as Ford or in routine service settings such as stores like Target or Midas Muffler. Bureaucratic control is much less useful in situations where nonprogrammed decisions have to be made and managers have to react quickly to changes in the organizational environment.

To use output control and behavior control, managers must be able to identify the outcomes they want to achieve and the behaviors they want employees to perform to achieve those outcomes. For many of the most important and significant organizational activities, however, output control and behavior control are inappropriate for several reasons:

- A manager cannot evaluate the performance of workers such as doctors, research scientists, or engineers by observing their behavior on a day-to-day basis.

- Rules and SOPs are of little use in telling a doctor how to respond to an emergency situation or a scientist how to discover something new.

- Output controls such as the amount of time a surgeon takes for each operation or the costs of making a discovery are very crude measures of the quality of performance.

How can managers attempt to control and regulate the behavior of their subordinates when personal supervision is of little use, when rules cannot be developed to tell employees what to do, and when outputs and goals cannot be measured at all or can be measured usefully only over long periods? One source of control increasingly being used by organizations is a strong organizational culture.

Organizational Culture and Clan Control

organizational culture The set of values, norms, and standards of behavior that control the way individuals and groups interact and work together to achieve organizational goals.

clan control The control exerted on individuals and groups by shared organizational values, norms, and standards of behavior.

Organizational culture is another important control system that regulates and governs employee attitudes and behavior. As we discussed in Chapter 2, organizational culture is the shared set of beliefs, expectations, values, norms, and work routines that influences how members of an organization relate to one another and work together to achieve organizational goals. Clan control is the control exerted on individuals and groups in an organization by shared values, norms, standards of behavior, and expectations. Organizational culture is not an externally imposed system of constraints, such as direct supervision or rules and procedures. Rather, employees internalize organizational values and norms and then let these values and norms guide their decisions and actions. Just as people in society at large generally behave in accordance with socially acceptable values and norms—such as the norm that people should line up at the checkout counters in supermarkets—so are individuals in an organizational setting mindful of the force of organizational values and norms.

Organizational culture is an important source of control for two reasons. First, it makes control possible in situations where managers cannot use output or behavior control. Second, and more important, when a strong and cohesive set of organizational values and norms is in place, employees focus on thinking about what is best for the organization in the long run—all their decisions and actions become oriented toward helping the organization perform well. For example, a teacher spends personal time after school coaching and counseling students; an R&D scientist works 80 hours a week, evenings, and weekends to help speed up a late project; a salesclerk at a department store runs after a customer who left a credit card at the cash register. An interesting example of two companies whose CEOs built strong cultures based on close attention to developing the right set of output and behavior controls is profiled in the following "Manager as a Person."

MANAGER AS A PERSON

UPS and Walmart Know How to Build Persuasive Cultures

United Parcel Service (UPS) was founded as a bicycle messenger service in 1907 by James E. Casey. Today it controls more than three-fourths of the U.S. ground and air parcel service, delivering over 10 million packages a day in its fleet of 150,000 trucks. It is also the most profitable company in its industry and employs over 250,000 people globally. Walmart, the largest retailer in the world, was founded by Sam Walton; today it employs over a million people and is the most profitable company in its industry. What do these companies have in common? They were both founded by managers who wanted their employees to take a hands-on approach to their jobs and be completely committed to their mission—total customer satisfaction. And to achieve this both these founders created strong values and norms about how employees should behave and in the process created performance-enhancing organizational cultures.

The 10-foot greeting expectation, the sundown rule, and the Walmart Cheer, shown here, are all parts of Walmart's effective enculturation process. Employees trained into these standards soon learn to pass them along to others, while tales of superior examples work their way into company legends.

At UPS, from the beginning, Casey made efficiency and economy the company's driving values and loyalty, humility, discipline, dependability, and intense effort the key norms its employees should adopt. UPS has always gone to extraordinary lengths to develop and maintain these values and norms in its workforce.[34] First, its control systems from the top of the company down to its trucking operations are the subject of intense scrutiny by the company's 3,000 industrial engineers, who continually search for ways to measure outputs and behaviors to improve efficiency. They time every part of an employee's job. Truck drivers, for example, are told in extraordinary detail how to perform their tasks: They must step from their truck with their right foot first, fold their money face-up, carry packages under their left arm, walk at a pace of 3 feet per second, and slip the key ring holding their truck keys over their third finger. Employees are not allowed to have beards, must be carefully groomed, and are instructed in how to deal with customers. Drivers who perform below average receive visits from training supervisors who accompany them on their delivery routes and teach how to raise their performance level. Not surprisingly, because of this intensive training and close behavior control, UPS employees internalize the company's strong norms about the appropriate ways to behave to help the organization achieve its values of economy and efficiency. In fact, today UPS offers a consulting service to other companies in global supply chain management to teach them how to re-create its values and norms of efficiency and economy that the company has pursued for the last hundred years because these were the values of its founder.

In a similar way, to involve employees (called "associates") at all levels and encourage them to develop work behaviors focused on providing quality customer service, Walton established strong cultural values and norms for Walmart. One of the norms that associates are expected to follow is the "10-foot attitude." This norm encourages associates, in Walton's words, to "promise that whenever you come within 10 feet of a customer, you will look him in the eye, greet him, and ask him if you can help him." The "sundown rule" states that employees should strive to answer customer requests by sundown of the day they are made. The Walmart cheer ("Give me a W; give me an A," and so on) is used in all its stores.[35]

The strong customer-oriented values that Walton created are exemplified in the stories Walmart members tell one another about associates' concern for customers. They include stories like the one about Sheila, who risked her own safety when she jumped in front of a car to prevent a little boy from being struck; about Phyllis, who administered CPR to a customer who had suffered a heart attack in her store; and about Annette, who gave up the Power Ranger she had on lay-away for her own son to fulfill the birthday wish of a customer's son. The strong Walmart culture helps control and motivate employees to achieve the stringent output and financial targets the company has set for itself.

Although both founders are long gone, their companies still seem governed by the values and norms they established. Their new managers take seriously their charge to provide efficient service to customers, and in any delivery by a UPS employee or visit to a Walmart store, it is possible to observe how employees still buy into these values and are rewarded for doing so. Both these companies have taken their values and norms and established them in their overseas divisions around the world so that they have truly global cultures that allow managers and employees to better communicate and work together as they manage their global supply chains to protect their competitive advantage.

Adaptive Cultures versus Inert Cultures

Many researchers and managers believe that employees of some organizations go out of their way to help the organization because it has a strong and cohesive organizational culture—an *adaptive culture* that controls employee attitudes and behaviors. Adaptive cultures, such as those of UPS and Walmart, are cultures whose values and norms help an organization to build momentum and to grow and change as needed to achieve its goals and be effective. By contrast, *inert cultures* are those that lead to values and norms that fail to motivate or inspire employees; they lead to stagnation and often failure over time. What leads to an adaptive or inert culture?

Researchers have found that organizations with strong adaptive cultures, like 3M, UPS, Microsoft, and IBM, invest in their employees. They demonstrate their commitment to their members by, for example, emphasizing the long-term nature of the employment relationship and trying to avoid layoffs. These companies develop long-term career paths for their employees and invest heavily in training and development to increase employees' value to the organization. In these ways, terminal and instrumental values pertaining to the worth of human resources encourage the development of supportive work attitudes and behaviors.

In adaptive cultures employees often receive rewards linked directly to their performance and to the performance of the company as a whole. Sometimes, employee stock ownership plans (ESOPs) are developed in which workers as a group are allowed to buy a significant percentage of their company's stock. Workers who are owners of the company have additional incentive to develop skills that allow them to perform highly and search actively for ways to improve quality, efficiency, and performance.

Some organizations, however, develop cultures with values that do not include protecting and increasing the worth of their human resources as a major goal. Their employment practices are based on short-term employment according to the needs of the organization and on minimal investment in employees who perform simple, routine tasks. Moreover, employees are not often rewarded based on their performance and thus have little incentive to improve their skills or otherwise invest in the organization to help it to achieve goals. If a company has an inert culture, poor working relationships frequently develop between the organization and its employees, and instrumental values of noncooperation, laziness, and loafing and work norms of output restriction are common.

Moreover, an adaptive culture develops an emphasis on entrepreneurship and respect for the employee and allows the use of organizational structures, such as the cross-functional team structure, that empower employees to make decisions and motivate them to succeed. By contrast, in an inert culture, employees are content to be told what to do and have little incentive or motivation to perform beyond minimum work requirements. As you might expect, the emphasis is on close supervision and hierarchical authority, which result in a culture that makes it difficult to adapt to a changing environment.

Organizational Change

LO8-5 Discuss the relationship between organizational control and change, and explain why managing change is a vital management task.

As we have discussed, many problems can arise if an organization's control systems are not designed correctly. One of these problems is that an organization cannot change or adapt in response to a changing environment unless it has effective control over its activities. Companies can lose this control over time, as happened to Ford and Dell, or they can change in ways that make them more effective, as happened to UPS and Walmart.

Interestingly enough, there is a fundamental tension or need to balance two opposing forces in the control process that influences the way organizations change. As just noted, organizations and their managers need to be able to control their activities and make their operations routine and predictable. At the same time, however, organizations have to be responsive to the need to change, and managers and employees have to "think on their feet" and realize when they need to depart from routines to be responsive to unpredictable events. In other words, even though adopting the right set of output and behavior controls is essential for improving efficiency, because the environment is dynamic and uncertain, employees also need to feel that they have the autonomy to depart from routines as necessary to increase effectiveness. (See Figure 8.5.)

For this reason many researchers believe that the highest-performing organizations are those that are constantly changing—and thus become experienced at doing so—in their search to become more efficient and effective. And companies like UPS, and more recently Ford, are constantly changing the mix of their activities to move forward even as they are seeking to make their existing operations more efficient. For example, UPS entered the air express parcel market, bought

Figure 8.5

Organizational Control and Change

Managers must balance the need for an organization to improve the way it currently operates and the need for it to change in response to new, unanticipated events.

a chain of mailbox stores, and began offering a consulting service. At the same time, it has been increasing the efficiency of its ground transport network.

The need to constantly search for ways to improve efficiency and effectiveness makes it vital that managers develop the skills necessary to manage change effectively. Several experts have proposed a model that managers can follow to implement change successfully.[36] **Organization change** is the movement of an organization away from its present state and toward some desired future state to increase its efficiency and effectiveness. Figure 8.6 outlines the steps that managers must take to manage change effectively. In the rest of this section we examine each one.

organization change The movement of an organization away from its present state and toward some desired future state to increase its efficiency and effectiveness.

Assessing the Need for Change

Organizational change can affect practically all aspects of organizational functioning, including organizational structure, culture, strategies, control systems, and groups and teams, as well as the human resource management system and critical organizational processes such as communication, motivation, and leadership. Organizational change can bring alterations in the ways managers carry out the critical tasks of planning, organizing, leading, and controlling and the ways they perform their managerial roles.

Deciding how to change an organization is a complex matter because change disrupts the status quo and poses a threat, prompting employees to resist attempts to alter work relationships and procedures. *Organizational learning,* the process through which managers try to increase organizational members' abilities to understand and appropriately respond to changing conditions, can be an important impetus for change and can help all members of an organization, including managers, effectively make decisions about needed changes.

Assessing the need for change calls for two important activities: recognizing that there is a problem and identifying its source. Sometimes the need for change is obvious, such as when an organization's performance is suffering. Often, however, managers have trouble determining that something is going wrong because problems develop gradually; organizational performance may slip for a number of years before a problem becomes obvious. Thus, during the first step in the change process, managers need to recognize that there is a problem that requires change.

Often the problems that managers detect have produced a gap between desired performance and actual performance. To detect such a gap, managers need to look at performance measures—such as falling market share or profits, rising costs, or employees' failure to meet their established goals or stay within budgets—which indicate whether change is needed. These measures are provided by organizational control systems, discussed earlier in the chapter.

Figure 8.6   Four Steps in the Organizational Change Process

Assess the need for change	Decide on the change to make	Implement the change	Evaluate the change
• Recognize that there is a problem. • Identify the source of the problem.	• Decide what the organization's ideal future state would be. • Identify obstacles to change.	• Decide whether change will occur from the top down or from the bottom up. • Introduce and manage change.	• Compare prechange performance with postchange performance. • Use benchmarking.

To discover the source of the problem, managers need to look both inside and outside the organization. Outside the organization, they must examine how changes in environmental forces may be creating opportunities and threats that are affecting internal work relationships. Perhaps the emergence of low-cost competitors abroad has led to conflict among different departments that are trying to find new ways to gain a competitive advantage. Managers also need to look within the organization to see whether its structure is causing problems between departments. Perhaps a company does not have integrating mechanisms in place to allow different departments to respond to low-cost competition.

Deciding on the Change to Make

Once managers have identified the source of the problem, they must decide what they think the organization's ideal future state would be. In other words, they must decide where they would like their organization to be in the future—what kinds of goods and services it should be making, what its business-level strategy should be, how the organizational structure should be changed, and so on. During this step, managers also must engage in planning how they are going to attain the organization's ideal future state.

This step in the change process also includes identifying obstacles or sources of resistance to change. Managers must analyze the factors that may prevent the company from reaching its ideal future state. Obstacles to change are found at the corporate, divisional, departmental, and individual levels of the organization.

Corporate-level changes in an organization's strategy or structure, even seemingly trivial changes, may significantly affect how divisional and departmental managers behave. Suppose that to compete with low-cost foreign competitors, top managers decide to increase the resources spent on state-of-the-art machinery and reduce the resources spent on marketing or R&D. The power of manufacturing managers would increase, and the power of marketing and R&D managers would fall. This decision would alter the balance of power among departments and might lead to increased conflict as departments start fighting to retain their status in the organization. An organization's present strategy and structure are powerful obstacles to change.

Whether a company's culture is adaptive or inert facilitates or obstructs change. Organizations with entrepreneurial, flexible cultures, such as high-tech companies, are much easier to change than are organizations with more rigid cultures, such as those sometimes found in large, bureaucratic organizations like the military or GM.

The same obstacles to change exist at the divisional and departmental levels as well. Division managers may differ in their attitudes toward the changes that top managers propose and, if their interests and power seem threatened, will resist those changes. Managers at all levels usually fight to protect their power and control over resources. Given that departments have different goals and time horizons, they may also react differently to the changes that other managers propose. When top managers are trying to reduce costs, for example, sales managers may resist attempts to cut back on sales expenditures if they believe that problems stem from manufacturing managers' inefficiencies.

At the individual level, too, people are often resistant to change because change brings uncertainty and uncertainty brings stress. For example, individuals may resist the introduction of a new technology because they are uncertain about their abilities to learn it and effectively use it.

These obstacles make organizational change a slow process. Managers must recognize the potential obstacles to change and take them into consideration. Some obstacles can be overcome by improving communication so that all organizational members are aware of the need for change and of the nature of the changes being made. Empowering employees and inviting them to participate in the planning for change also can help overcome resistance and allay employees' fears. In addition, managers can sometimes overcome resistance by emphasizing group or shared goals such as increased organizational efficiency and effectiveness. The larger and more complex an organization is, the more complex is the change process.

Implementing the Change

top-down change A fast, revolutionary approach to change in which top managers identify what needs to be changed and then move quickly to implement the changes throughout the organization.

Generally, managers implement—that is, introduce and manage—change from the top down or from the bottom up.[37] Top-down change is implemented quickly: Top managers identify the need for change, decide what to do, and then move quickly to implement the changes throughout the organization. For example, top managers may decide to restructure and downsize the organization and then give divisional and departmental managers specific goals to achieve. With top-down change, the emphasis is on making the changes quickly and dealing with problems as they arise; it is revolutionary in nature. Bob Iger, for example, made a major change in Walt Disney's decision making.

In 2006, Iger, who had been COO of Disney under its then-CEO Michael Eisner, took control of the troubled company. For several years Disney had been plagued by slow decision making, and analysts claimed it had made many mistakes in putting its new strategies into action. Its Disney stores were losing money; its Internet properties were not getting many "hits"; and even its theme parks seemed to have lost their luster as few new rides or attractions had been introduced.

Iger believed that one of the main reasons for Disney's declining performance was that it had become too tall and bureaucratic and its top managers were following financial rules that did not lead to innovative strategies. So one of Iger's first moves to turn around the performance of the poorly performing company was to dismantle Disney's central strategic planning office. In this office several levels of managers were responsible for sifting through all the new ideas and innovations sent up by Disney's different business divisions, such as theme parks, movies, and gaming, and then deciding which ones to present to the CEO. Iger saw the strategic planning office as a bureaucratic bottleneck that actually reduced the number of ideas coming from below. So he dissolved the office and reassigned its managers back to the different business units.[38]

The result of cutting out an unnecessary layer in Disney's hierarchy has been that more new ideas are being generated by its different business units. The level of innovation has increased because managers are more willing to speak out and champion their ideas when they know they are dealing directly with the CEO and a top management team searching for innovative new ways to improve

Bob Iger, Disney's CEO, has breathed new life into Disney by removing layers of management and returning creative power to its employees.

performance—rather than a layer of strategic planning "bureaucrats" concerned only with the bottom line.[39] Disney's performance has soared under Iger's control, and its stock price rapidly increased to a new record by 2013.

bottom-up change
A gradual or evolutionary approach to change in which managers at all levels work together to develop a detailed plan for change.

Bottom-up change is typically more gradual or evolutionary. Top managers consult with middle and first-line managers about the need for change. Then, over time, managers at all levels work to develop a detailed plan for change. A major advantage of bottom-up change is that it can co-opt resistance to change from employees. Because the emphasis in bottom-up change is on participation and on keeping people informed about what is going on, uncertainty and resistance are minimized.

Evaluating the Change

The last step in the change process is to evaluate how successful the change effort has been in improving organizational performance.[40] Using measures such as changes in market share, in profits, or in the ability of managers to meet their goals, managers compare how well an organization is performing after the change with how well it was performing before. Managers also can use benchmarking, comparing their performance on specific dimensions with the performance of high-performing organizations, to decide how successful a change effort has been. For example, when Xerox was doing poorly in the 1980s, it benchmarked the efficiency of its distribution operations against that of L. L. Bean, the efficiency of its central computer operations against that of John Deere, and the efficiency of its marketing abilities against that of Procter & Gamble. Those three companies are renowned for their skills in these different areas, and by studying how they performed, Xerox was able to dramatically increase its own performance. Benchmarking is a key tool in total quality management, an important change program discussed in Chapter 14.

benchmarking The process of comparing one company's performance on specific dimensions with the performance of other, high-performing organizations.

In summary, organizational control and change are closely linked because organizations operate in environments that are constantly changing and so managers must be alert to the need to change their strategies and structures. High-performing organizations are those whose managers are attuned to the need to continually modify the way they operate and adopt techniques like empowered work groups and teams, benchmarking, and global outsourcing to remain competitive in a global world.

Entrepreneurship, Control, and Change

As we discussed in Chapter 1, managers are responsible for supervising the use of human and other resources to achieve effective and efficient organizational goals. Entrepreneurs, by contrast, are the people who notice opportunities and take responsibility for mobilizing the resources necessary to produce new and improved goods and services. Essentially, entrepreneurs bring about change to companies and industries because they see new and improved ways to use resources to create products customers will want to buy. At the same time, entrepreneurs who start new business ventures are responsible for all the initial planning, organizing, leading, and controlling necessary to make their idea a reality. If their idea is viable and entrepreneurs do attract customers, then their business grows and then they need to hire managers who will take responsibility for organizing and controlling all the specific functional activities such as marketing, accounting, and manufacturing necessary for a growing organization to be successful.

LO8-6 Understand the role of entrepreneurship in the control and change process.

entrepreneurs

Individuals who notice opportunities and decide how to mobilize the resources necessary to produce new and improved goods and services.

Typically, entrepreneurs assume the substantial risk associated with starting new businesses (many new businesses fail), and they receive all the returns or profits associated with the new business venture. These people are the Bill Gateses, Larry Ellisons, or Liz Claibornes of the world who make vast fortunes when their businesses succeed. Or they are among the millions of people who start new business ventures only to lose their money when their businesses fail. Despite the fact that an estimated 80% of small businesses fail in the first three to five years, by some estimates 38% of men and 50% of women in today's workforce want to start their own companies.

Entrepreneurship does not just end once a new business is founded. Entrepreneurship carries on inside an organization over time, and many people throughout an organization take responsibility for developing innovative goods and services. For example, managers, scientists, or researchers employed by existing companies engage in entrepreneurial activity when they develop new or improved products. To distinguish these individuals from entrepreneurs who found their own businesses, employees of existing organizations who notice opportunities for product or service improvements and are responsible for managing the development process are known as intrapreneurs. In general, then, entrepreneurship is the mobilization of resources to take advantage of an opportunity to provide customers with new or improved goods and services; intrapreneurs engage in entrepreneurship within an existing company.

intrapreneurs

Employees of existing organizations who notice opportunities to develop new or improved products and better ways to make than.

An interesting relationship exists between entrepreneurs and intrapreneurs. Many intrapreneurs become dissatisfied when their superiors decide not to support or to fund new product ideas and development efforts that the intrapreneurs think will succeed. What do intrapreneurs do who feel that they are getting nowhere? Very often intrapreneurs decide to leave their employers and start their own organizations to take advantage of their new product ideas. In other words, intrapreneurs become entrepreneurs and found companies that may compete with the companies they left.

entrepreneurship

The mobilization of resources to take advantage of an opportunity to provide customers with new or improved goods and services.

Many of the world's most successful organizations have been started by frustrated intrapreneurs who became entrepreneurs. William Hewlett and David Packard left Fairchild Semiconductor, an early high-tech industry leader, when managers of that company would not support Hewlett and Packard's ideas; their company now called HP, soon outperformed Fairchild. Compaq Computer was founded by Rod Canion and some of his colleagues, who left Texas Instruments (TI) when managers there would not support Canion's idea that TI should develop its own personal computer, and Compaq was subsequently acquired by HP! To prevent the departure of talented people, organizations need to take steps to promote internal entrepreneurship.

There is also an interesting dynamic between entrepreneurship and management. Very often, it turns out that the entrepreneur who initially founded the business does not have the management skills to successfully control and change the business over time. Entrepreneurs may, for example, lack an understanding of how to create the control structure necessary to manage a successful long-term strategy. Entrepreneurs also may not recognize the need to change their companies because they are so close to them; in other words, they "cannot see the forest for the trees."

Frequently a founding entrepreneur lacks the skills, patience, or experience to engage in the difficult and challenging work of management. Some entrepreneurs find it difficult to delegate authority because they are afraid to risk letting others manage their company. As a result, founding entrepreneurs can become overloaded, and the quality of their decision making declines. Other entrepreneurs lack the detailed knowledge necessary to establish state-of-the-art control systems or to create the organizational culture that is vital to increase organizational effectiveness (discussed in Chapter 14). The following "Management Insight" box describes how Google's founders created a specific kind of company culture that still flourishes today and has made it a global powerhouse.

MANAGEMENT INSIGHT

How Google's Founders Created a Groovy Culture

Google, whose fast-growing product line includes a continuously improving search engine, web-browser, e-mail, and chat has a mission "to organize the world's information and make it universally accessible and useful." The company was started in 1995 when two computer science Stanford graduates, Sergey Brin and Larry Page, collaborated to develop a new kind of search engine technology. They understood the shortcomings of existing search engines and by 1998 they had developed a superior search engine they felt was ready to go online. They raised $1 million from family, friends, and risk-taking "angel" investors to buy the hardware necessary to connect Google's software to the Internet.

At first, Google answered only 10,000 inquiries a day—its plain home page is hardly welcoming—but within a few months it was answering 500,000 inquiries; by the end of 1999, 3 million inquiries, and by the spring of 2001 it reached 100 million inquiries per day! By 2010 Google was the most widely used global search engine, had over a 65% market share and was one of the top five most-used Internet websites. Google's rise has been so rapid that rivals like Yahoo! and Microsoft are struggling to compete and prevent Google from providing all the other services they offer—and doing it better and for free (Google makes billions of dollars of revenues by selling the advertising space used on all kinds of websites).

Google's explosive growth is largely due to the culture or entrepreneurship and innovation its founders cultivated from the start. Although by 2010 Google had grown to over 20,000 employees worldwide, its founders claim that it still maintains a small company feel because its culture empowers employees, whom it calls staffers or "Googlers," to create the best software possible. Brin and Page created Google's entrepreneurial culture in several ways.

From the start, lacking office space and desperate to keep costs low, Google staffers worked in "high-density clusters" that encouraged intensive team interactions. Three or four staffers, each equipped with a powerful server PC, worked at a common desk or on couches or rubber ball chairs to improve its technology. Even when Google moved into more spacious surroundings at its modernistic "Googleplex" headquarters building in Mountain View, California, staffers continued to work in shared spaces.

Google also designed its building so staffers could continually meet each other in places such as Google's funky lobby, the Google Café where everyone eats together, its state-of-the-art recreational facilities, and its "snack rooms" equipped with bins packed with cereals, gummi bears, yogurt, carrots, and of course make-your-own cappuccinos. They also created opportunities for employees to gather together at informal events such as a TGIF open meeting and a twice-weekly outdoor roller-hockey game.

All this attention to creating what just might be the "grooviest" company headquarters in the world did not come about by chance. Brin and Page knew that Google's most important strength would be its ability to attract the best software engineers in the world and motivate them to perform well. Common offices, lobbies, cafes, and so on bring all staffers into close contact with each other, which develops collegiality and encourages them to share their new ideas and to continually work to improve Google's online applications and develop new products (click the Google Labs tab on its website) to grow the company.

The freedom Google gives its staffers to pursue new ideas is a clear signal of its founders' desire to empower them to be innovative and work hard to make Google the software powerhouse of the future. And to motivate staffers to innovate important new software applications, Google's founders reward their achievements by giving them stock in the company, which makes staffers owners as well. Over 10,000 Google staffers have already become millionaires as a result.

In summary, it is necessary to do more than create a new product to succeed; an entrepreneur must hire managers who can create an operating and control system that allows a new venture to survive and prosper. Very often, venture capitalists, the people who provide the capital to fund a new venture, lend entrepreneurs the money only if they agree from the outset to let a professional manager become the CEO of the new company. The entrepreneur then holds a senior planning and advisory role in the company, often chairing its board of directors.

Summary and Review

WHAT IS ORGANIZATIONAL CONTROL? Controlling is the process whereby managers monitor and regulate how efficiently and effectively an organization and its members are performing the activities necessary to achieve organizational goals. Controlling is a four-step process: (1) establishing performance standards, (2) measuring actual performance, (3) comparing actual performance against performance standards, and (4) evaluating the results and initiating corrective action if needed. **[LO 8-1, 8-2]**

OUTPUT CONTROL To monitor output or performance, managers choose goals or performance standards that they think will best measure efficiency, quality, innovation, and responsiveness to customers at the corporate, divisional, departmental or functional, and individual levels. The main mechanisms that managers use to monitor output are financial measures of performance, organizational goals, and operating budgets. **[LO 8-3, 8-4]**

BEHAVIOR CONTROL In an attempt to shape behavior and induce employees to work toward achieving organizational goals, managers utilize direct supervision, management by objectives, and bureaucratic control by means of rules and standard operating procedures. **[LO 8-4]**

ORGANIZATIONAL CULTURE AND CLAN CONTROL Organizational culture is the set of values, norms, standards of behavior, and common expectations that control the ways individuals and groups in an organization interact with one another and work to achieve organizational goals. Clan control is the control exerted on individuals and groups by shared values, norms, standards of behavior, and expectations. Organizational culture is transmitted to employees through the values of the founder, the process of socialization, organizational ceremonies and rites, and stories and language. The way managers perform their management functions influences the kind of culture that develops in an organization. **[LO 8-4]**

ORGANIZATIONAL CONTROL AND CHANGE There is a need to balance two opposing forces in the control process that influences the way organizations change. On the one hand, managers need to be able to control organizational activities and make their operations routine and predictable. On the other hand, organizations have to be responsive to the need to change, and managers must understand when they need to depart from routines to be responsive to unpredictable events. The four steps in managing change are (1) assessing the need for change, (2) deciding on the changes to make, (3) implementing change, and (4) evaluating the results of change. **[LO 8-5]**

ENTREPRENEURSHIP, CONTROL, AND CHANGE Entrepreneurs are people who notice opportunities and decide how to mobilize the resources necessary to produce new and improved goods and services. Intrapreneurs are employees in existing companies who notice opportunities to develop new or improved products and better ways to make them. Both entrepreneurs and intrapreneurs play important roles in the control and change process. **[LO 8-6]**

Management *in Action*

TOPICS FOR DISCUSSION AND ACTION

Discussion

1. What is the relationship between organizing and controlling? **[LO 8-1]**

2. How do output control and behavior control differ? **[LO 8-1, 8-2, 8-3]**

3. Why is it important for managers to involve subordinates in the control process? **[LO 8-3, 8-4, 8-4]**

4. What is organizational culture, and how does it affect the way employees behave? **[LO 8-4]**

5. What kind of controls would you expect to find most used in (a) a hospital, (b) the Navy, (c) a city police force? Why? **[LO 8-1, 8-2, 8-3]**

Action

6. Ask a manager to list the main performance measures that he or she uses to evaluate how well the organization is achieving its goals. **[LO 8-1, 8-3, 8-4]**

7. Interview some employees of an organization, and ask them about the organization's values, norms, socialization practices, ceremonies and rites, and special language and stories. Referring to this information, describe the organization's culture. **[LO 8-3, 8-4, 8-5]**

BUILDING MANAGEMENT SKILLS

Understanding Controlling [LO 8-1, 8-3, 8-4]

For this exercise you will analyze the control systems used by a real organization such as a department store, restaurant, hospital, police department, or small business. Your objective is to uncover all the different ways in which managers monitor and evaluate the performance of the organization and employees.

1. At what levels does control take place in this organization?

2. Which output performance standards (such as financial measures and organizational goals) do managers use most often to evaluate performance at each level?

3. Does the organization have a management-by-objectives system in place? If it does, describe it. If it does not, speculate about why not.

4. How important is behavior control in this organization? For example, how much of managers' time is spent directly supervising employees? How formalized is the organization? Do employees receive a book of rules to instruct them about how to perform their jobs?

5. What kind of culture does the organization have? What are the values and norms? What effect does the organizational culture have on the way employees behave or treat customers?

6. Based on this analysis, do you think there is a fit between the organization's control systems and its culture? What is the nature of this fit? How could it be improved?

MANAGING ETHICALLY [LO 8-4]

Some managers and organizations go to great lengths to monitor their employees' behavior, and they keep extensive records about employees' behavior and performance. Some organizations also seem to possess norms and values that cause their employees to behave in certain ways.

Questions

1. Either by yourself or in a group, think about the ethical implications of organizations' monitoring and collecting information about their employees. What kind of information is it ethical to collect or unethical to collect? Why? Should managers and organizations inform subordinates they are collecting such information?

2. Similarly, some organizations' cultures, like those of Arthur Andersen, the accounting firm, and of Enron, seemed to have developed norms and values that caused their members to behave in unethical ways. When and why does a strong norm that encourages high performance become one that can cause people to act unethically? How can organizations keep their values and norms from becoming "too strong"?

SMALL GROUP BREAKOUT EXERCISE [LO 8-3, 8-4, 8-5]

How Best to Control the Sales Force?

Form groups of three or four people, and appoint one member as the spokesperson who will communicate your findings to the whole class when called on by the instructor. Then discuss the following scenario.

You are the regional sales managers of an organization that supplies high-quality windows and doors to building supply centers nationwide. Over the last three years, the rate of sales growth has slackened. There is increasing evidence that, to make their jobs easier, salespeople are primarily servicing large customer accounts and ignoring small accounts. In addition, the salespeople are not dealing promptly with customer questions and complaints, and this inattention has resulted in a drop in after-sales service. You have talked about these problems, and you are meeting to design a control system to increase both the amount of sales and the quality of customer service.

1. Design a control system that you think will best motivate salespeople to achieve these goals.

2. What relative importance do you put on (a) output control, (b) behavior control, and (c) organizational culture in this design?

BE THE MANAGER [LO 8-1, 8-5]

You have been asked by your company's CEO to find a way to improve the performance of its teams of web-design and web-hosting specialists and programmers. Each team works on a different aspect of website production, and while each is responsible for the quality of its own performance, its performance also depends on how well the other teams perform. Your task is to create a control system that will help to increase the performance of each team separately and facilitate cooperation among the teams. This is necessary because the various projects are interlinked and affect one another just as the different parts of a car must fit together. Since competition in the website production market is intense, it is imperative that each website be up and running as quickly as possible and incorporate all the latest advances in website software technology.

Questions

1. What kind of output controls will best facilitate positive interactions both within the teams and among the teams?

2. What kind of behavior controls will best facilitate positive interactions both within the teams and among the teams?

3. How would you go about helping managers develop a culture to promote high team performance?

BLOOMBERG BUSINESSWEEK
CASE IN THE NEWS [LO 8-1, 8-2, 8-4]
Dish Network, the Meanest Company in America

For 2012, the website 24/7 Wall St. determined that the worst company to work for in America was the Dish Network, the Englewood (Colo.)-based company that provides satellite TV to more than 14 million subscribers. To pick its winner, the site began by sifting entries on glassdoor.com, an online service where people gossip about their jobs. It was hardly the most scientific of methods. Still, the volume of miserable tales about Dish is impressive; 346 former or current employees had taken the time to write not-so-nice things about the company. On a scale of 1 to 5, they ranked their company an average of 2.2, beating Dillard's and RadioShack (RSH) for the spot at the bottom.

The most common complaints were long hours, lack of paid holidays, and way too much mandatory overtime. Some posts suggest that merely setting foot in Dish's headquarters is a danger to the soul. "Quit" was the recommendation to one Dish employee who sought management advice. "You're part of a poisonous environment . . . go find a job where you can use your talents for good rather than evil." The roundup noted one other thing: The share price was up more than 30 percent for most of the year.

Much of the malice, and value generation, can be traced to one man: Charlie Ergen, 59, the founder and chairman of Dish. Although he turned over the role of chief executive officer to former Sirius XM Radio head Joseph Clayton in 2011, Ergen remains the core of Dish—and its largest shareholder, with 53.2 percent of the outstanding shares and 90.4 percent of the voting rights. Ergen founded Dish more than 30 years ago, installing satellite systems with partner Jim

DeFranco. Dish is now the second-largest satellite TV provider in the U.S., with 26,000 employees. Ergen, according to the Bloomberg Billionaires Index, has an estimated net worth of $11 billion.

Michael Neuman knew the risks going in when he accepted Ergen's offer to be Dish's president and chief operating officer in 2005. Before Neuman, no president had lasted more than four years. Still, for Neuman, a man who'd known Ergen for more than a decade and had run a Dish-like satellite service in Canada, the opportunity was too tempting to pass up. Unlike its major competitor, DirecTV (DTV), Dish was fully integrated: It engineered, built, and sold all its own set-top boxes and ran its own installation fleet and customer service. (The company split in 2008, with EchoStar [SATS] building the boxes and Dish doing everything else. Ergen remains chairman of both companies.) "If you're a student of management like I am, it was irresistible," says Neuman. At first, Neuman loved working at Dish but over time he came to realize why former presidents such as John Reardon, who lasted less than a year, described Ergen as "pounding people into submission." The hours were long, yes, but it was Ergen's habit of unilaterally making decisions that most irked Neuman.

Although Dish had more than 100 people employed in its marketing department and reams of customer data to analyze, when it came time to figure out how much it was going to charge for satellite service, Ergen went into his office and came up with the final number alone. "It would be like the CEO of Kraft getting up in the morning and determining how much they were going to charge at retail for 12 slices of American cheese," says

Neuman. "It wasn't that he didn't invite input or share his thought process, because he did both. It's just that he'd had his hands on the wheel for so long that he trusted his own judgment the best." What made it worse, Neuman says, is that Ergen was almost always right. Eight months after accepting the job, Neuman resigned.

Judianne Atencio left Dish not long after. As head of communications for a decade, she had witnessed some of the company's biggest triumphs, including the successful launch of its satellites and the signing of its 10 millionth subscriber. She had also been around for some of its most crushing defeats, such as Murdoch's last-minute cancellation of a planned merger and the federal government's denial of another with competitor DirecTV.

"I didn't have a life for 10 years," she says. "I couldn't even have a dog." There were times when Ergen screamed so loud at Atencio that she packed up her stuff and had to be persuaded in the parking lot to return to work by an apologetic board member. A friend who had worked in the White House even tried to comfort her by saying, "Charlie's like Clinton—he only screams at the ones he cares about."

A self-described "country boy from Tennessee," Ergen is capable of a Warren Buffett–style folksy charm. He often packs his own brown bag lunch and has lived in the same house for 20 years. Ergen and his four siblings grew up in Oak Ridge. His father was an Austrian-born nuclear physicist who worked on the Manhattan Project. Ergen's first real job out of school was as an accountant at Frito-Lay. He quit to work as a professional gambler, with blackjack his preferred game. He was

so good at counting cards that he has told reporters he was once tossed out of a Las Vegas casino. At Dish, he still keeps a counter's eye on the numbers. Up until a few years ago, as he noted at a recent talk at the University of Colorado, Ergen signed every check that left Dish headquarters, a process that took him three to four hours a week and left him with an unparalleled understanding of how money was moving out of the company. He still signs company checks today, though now that Dish has $14.3 billion in annual revenue and $2.4 billion in operating expenses, Ergen reserves his signature for anything over $100,000.

At Dish headquarters in Englewood, a suburb of Denver, the day begins no later than 9 a.m. Badges used to be the preferred method of entry into the building. But a few years ago, after noticing that some employees were taking advantage of the system by having others badge-in for them, Ergen upgraded to fingerprint scanners. If a worker is late, an e-mail is immediately sent to human resources, which then sends another to that person's boss, and sometimes directly to Ergen. Multiple ex-employees say it's not uncommon to see Ergen publicly berate an executive for scanning in a few minutes late, even if that executive had spent the previous 12 hours at home working through the night. Neuman, when he was still president, refused to implement Ergen's proposed strict badge-in policy. He worried it might be "demoralizing."

Employees, both current and former, describe an Ergen-created culture of condescension and distrust. Vikas Arora, a manager on Dish's international content acquisition team, had never worked anywhere else in the U.S. until he left the company last year. That's when he discovered that "outside of Dish, people are actually treated like adults."

Whereas many companies are doing their best to cater to millennials who demand flexibility among other benefits, Dish doesn't allow its employees to work from home. It offers no company credit cards. And according to a former regional manager, for many years, if an employee expensed a meal where they'd tipped more than 15 percent, the extra amount was then subtracted from his paycheck, even if he'd only gone over by a nickel. Turnover is said by many employees to be constant, and while no one knows exactly how many employees are laid off during regular quarterly cullings, all employees are aware of the company's euphemism for the bloodbaths: "talent upgrades." There's a running joke on glassdoor.com that Dish is an acronym for "Did I sleep here?"

"We're a one-trick pony," Ergen has said of Dish, which has a sole product: satellite TV. In a November earnings call, Ergen talked about how his five kids—most of whom don't even have cable subscriptions—think he's "crazy" to be in the pay-TV business. To address that, Ergen has spent nearly $3 billion in the past two years buying wireless spectrum from bankrupt companies and just received word of a favorable Federal Communications Commission decision that may allow him to deliver video to tablets and cell phones. He's also made it clear that he'd like to try again to merge with DirecTV and have his own mobile network to compete with telecom giants such as AT&T and Verizon, though a succession of recent wireless industry consolidations has possibly imperiled those plans.

Since Ergen relinquished the CEO role, Dish employees say the company has relaxed some. It is, according to the former regional manager, now possible to leave a 17 percent tip without incurring a personal charge. But austerity and meanness still have their place. In response to the economic downturn, it takes longer to accrue vacation days, and holiday parties have been scaled back. The company reports earnings on February 22. It's beaten estimates five out of the last eight quarters.

Questions

1. How would you describe CEO Ergen's approach to output control? Give examples to support your view.

2. How would you describe CEO Ergen's approach to behavior control? Give examples to support your view.

3. Given his approach to control, what kind of values, norms, and organizational culture has he created for Dish?

Source: Caleb Hannan, "Dish Network, the Meanest Company in America," *Bloomberg Businessweek,* January 2, 2013 www.businessweek.com.

9 Motivation

LEARNING OBJECTIVES

After studying this chapter, you should be able to:

1 Explain what motivation is and why managers need to be concerned about it. **[LO 9-1]**

2 Describe from the perspectives of expectancy theory and equity theory what managers should do to have a highly motivated workforce. **[LO 9-2]**

3 Explain how goals and needs motivate people and what kinds of goals are especially likely to result in high performance. **[LO 9-3]**

4 Identify the motivation lessons that managers can learn from operant conditioning theory and social learning theory. **[LO 9-4]**

5 Explain why and how managers can use pay as a major motivation tool. **[LO 9-5]**

Customer service with a difference: this employee exhibits the high levels of motivation typical of Enterprise's workers because she knows that everyone in Enterprise cuts their teeth on the same positions, follows the same promotion path, and enjoys the same type of benefits tied to the performance of their specific area.

High Motivation at Enterprise Rent-A-Car

How Can Managers Encourage and Maintain High Levels of Employee Motivation to Provide Excellent Customer Service?

Enterprise Rent-A-Car was founded by Jack Taylor in 1957 in St. Louis, Missouri, as a very small auto leasing business.[1] Today, Enterprise Holdings, which owns and operates Enterprise Rent-A-Car, is the biggest car rental company in the world with over $15 billion in revenues and over 74,000 employees. Enterprise has over 6,000 locations in the United States, Canada, the United Kingdom, France, Spain, Ireland, and Germany.[2] One of the biggest employers of new college graduates in the United States, Enterprise typically hires over 8,000 college graduates each year.[3] While starting salaries tend to be on the low end and the work can be hard (e.g., four assistant managers once sued the company claiming that they should receive overtime pay), Enterprise has been ranked among the top 50 best companies for new college graduates to launch their careers by *Bloomberg Businessweek* magazine.[4]

A privately held company, Enterprise is very much a family business. In its entire history, Enterprise has had only two CEOs, founder Jack Taylor, who is now retired but still involved in the company, and his son Andrew Taylor, who became president in 1980 and CEO in 1991.[5] Nonetheless, Enterprise's policy of promoting from within ensures that all employees who perform well have the opportunity to advance in the company.[6]

One of the keys to Enterprise's success is the way it motivates its employees to provide excellent customer service.[7] Practically all entry-level hires participate in Enterprise's Management Training Program.[8] As part of the program, new hires learn all aspects of the company business, and how to provide excellent customer service. Management trainees first have a four-day training session focused primarily on Enterprise's culture. They are then assigned to a branch office for around 8 to 12 months where they learn all aspects of the business, from negotiating with body shops to helping customers to washing cars. As part of this training, they learn how important high-quality customer service is to Enterprise and how they can personally provide great service, increasing their confidence levels.[9]

All those who do well in the program are promoted after about a year to the position of management assistant. Management assistants who do well are promoted to become assistant branch managers with responsibility for mentoring and supervising employees. Assistant managers who do well can be promoted to become branch managers who are responsible for managing a branch's employees and provision of customer service, rental car fleet, and financial performance. Branch managers with about five years of experience in the position often move on to take up management positions at headquarters or assume the position of area manager overseeing all the branches in a certain geographic region.[10] By training all new hires in all aspects of the business including the provision of excellent customer service, by providing them with valuable experience with increasing levels of responsibility and empowerment, and by providing all new hires who perform well with the opportunity to advance in the company, Enterprise has developed a highly motivated workforce. As Patrick Farrell, vice president of corporate communications indicated, "What's unique about our company is that everyone came up through the same system, from the CEOs on down . . . 100% of our operations personnel started as management trainees."[11]

In addition to motivating high performance and excellent customer service through training and promotional opportunities, Enterprise also uses financial incentives to motivate employees. Essentially, each branch is considered a profit center and the managers overseeing the branch and in charge of all aspects of its functioning have the autonomy and responsibility for the branch's profitability almost as if the branch was their own small business or franchise.[12] All branch employees at the rank of assistant manager and higher earn incentive compensation whereby their monthly pay depends upon the profitability of their branch. Managers at higher levels, such as area managers, have their monthly pay linked to the profitability of the region they oversee. Thus, managers at all levels know that their pay is linked to the profitability of the parts of Enterprise for which they are responsible. And they have the autonomy to make decisions ranging from buying and selling cars to opening new branches.[13]

Another way in which Enterprise motivates its employees is through its philanthropic activities and initiatives to protect the natural environment.[14] For example, the Enterprise Rent-A-Car Foundation has committed $50 million to plant 50 million trees over a 50-year period in public forests.[15] The foundation also focuses on supporting and giving back to the communities in which Enterprise operates.[16] Of all rental car companies, Enterprise has the biggest fleet of fuel-efficient cars.[17] As Andrew Taylor suggests, "We're not going to be able to save the world . . . but we think we can have an effect on the space where we play every day as a business. And we think that's what our customers and especially our employees want us to do."[18] All in all, the multiple ways in which Enterprise motivates its employees and satisfies its customers have contributed to its ongoing success story.[19]

Overview

Even with the best strategy in place and an appropriate organizational architecture, an organization will be effective only if its members are motivated to perform at a high level. Jack and Andrew Taylor in the "Management Snapshot" clearly realize this. One reason why leading is such an important managerial activity is that it entails ensuring that each member of an organization is motivated to perform highly and help the organization achieve its goals. When managers are effective, the outcome of the leading process is a highly motivated workforce. A key challenge for managers of organizations both large and small is to encourage employees to perform at a high level.

In this chapter we describe what motivation is, where it comes from, and why managers need to promote high levels of it for an organization to be effective and achieve its goals. We examine important theories of motivation: expectancy theory, need theories, equity theory, goal-setting theory, and learning theories. Each gives managers important insights about how to motivate organizational members. The theories are complementary in that each focuses on a different aspect of motivation. Considering all the theories together helps managers gain a rich understanding of the many issues and problems involved in encouraging high levels of motivation throughout an organization. Last, we consider the use of pay as a motivation tool. By the end of this chapter you will understand what it takes to have a highly motivated workforce.

The Nature of Motivation

motivation
Psychological forces that determine the direction of a person's behavior in an organization, a person's level of effort, and a person's level of persistence.

intrinsically motivated behavior Behavior that is performed for its own sake.

Motivation may be defined as psychological forces that determine the direction of a person's behavior in an organization, a person's level of effort, and a person's level of persistence in the face of obstacles.[20] The *direction of a person's behavior* refers to the many possible behaviors a person could engage in. For example, employees at Enterprise Rent-A-Car know that they should do whatever is required to provide high-quality customer service such as giving customers rides to pick up and drop off rental cars. *Effort* refers to how hard people work. Employees at Enterprise exert high levels of effort to provide superior customer service. *Persistence* refers to whether, when faced with roadblocks and obstacles, people keep trying or give up. Branch managers at Enterprise Rent-A-Car persistently seek to improve the profitability of their branches while maintaining very high levels of customer service.

Motivation is central to management because it explains *why* people behave the way they do in organizations[21]—why employees at Enterprise Rent-A-Car provide excellent customer service. Motivation also explains why a waiter is polite or rude and why a kindergarten teacher really tries to get children to enjoy learning or just goes through the motions. It explains why some managers truly put their organizations' best interests first, whereas others are more concerned with maximizing their salaries and why—more generally—some workers put forth twice as much effort as others.

Motivation can come from *intrinsic* or *extrinsic* sources. Intrinsically motivated behavior is behavior that is performed for its own sake; the source of motivation is actually performing the behavior, and motivation comes from doing the work itself. Many managers are intrinsically motivated; they derive a sense of accomplishment and achievement from helping the organization achieve its goals and gain competitive advantages. Jobs that are interesting and challenging are more likely to lead to intrinsic motivation than are jobs that are boring or do not use a person's skills and abilities. An elementary school teacher who really enjoys teaching children, a computer programmer who loves solving programming problems, and a commercial photographer who relishes taking creative photographs are all intrinsically motivated. For these individuals, motivation comes from performing their jobs—teaching children, finding bugs in computer programs, and taking pictures.

A lack of intrinsic motivation at work sometimes propels people to make major changes in their lives, as illustrated in the following "Managing Globally" box.

MANAGING GLOBALLY

Seeking Intrinsic Motivation in Far-Flung Places

Dom Jackman and Rob Symington, then in their late 20s, were doing financial consulting work for Ernst & Young in London when they were both struck by how lacking their jobs felt in terms of intrinsic motivation. As Symington put it, "It felt like the work we did, crunching spreadsheets, just didn't matter to anyone, including to our customers or employers."[22] Realizing that they were probably not the only young workers in the finance field who didn't enjoy the work they were doing, Jackman and Symington decided to do something about it. They quit their jobs and created Escape the City, a website devoted to assisting bankers and finance professionals

Escape the City's founders offer a previously untapped motivation to bored young office workers the world over: enjoy meaningful work where they want!

find interesting and exciting work in far-flung places.[23] By the way, "The City" refers to the financial district in London and hence Escape the City is a fitting name for a website oriented toward "escaping unfulfilling corporate jobs."[24]

Employers pay to list positions on the site that entail initiative and adventure while job seekers can sign up for free.[25] Weekly e-mails inform job seekers of interesting opportunities they might want to pursue, ranging from African charity work and employment with venture capital firms in Mongolia to microfinance work in India and surf camps in Morocco. Escape the City earned profits its first year in operation and has expanded to the United States with a New York office led my Mike Howe, who used to work for Merrill Lynch.[26]

Asia Pacific Investment Partners hired an operations manager and a communications manager from listings on the site.[27] Will Tindall landed the latter position and as chief communications officer for Asia Pacific he works out of Hong Kong, Ulan Bator, and London. Harry Minter found a position as the manager of Guludo Beach Lodge in Mozambique—he used to work in the hedge fund field at Headstart Advisers.[28] Of course, not all professionals in finance and the corporate world find their work to be uninteresting and demotivating. Indeed, some are very intrinsically motivated by the work they do. Nonetheless, for those who are not motivated and desire more exciting, interesting, and meaningful work, Escape the City certainly expands the set of options they might want to consider.

extrinsically motivated behavior Behavior that is performed to acquire material or social rewards or to avoid punishment.

Extrinsically motivated behavior is behavior that is performed to acquire material or social rewards or to avoid punishment; the source of motivation is the consequences of the behavior, not the behavior itself. A car salesperson who is motivated by receiving a commission on all cars sold, a lawyer who is motivated by the high salary and status that go along with the job, and a factory worker who is motivated by the opportunity to earn a secure income are all extrinsically motivated. Their motivation comes from the consequences they receive as a result of their work behaviors.

People can be intrinsically motivated, extrinsically motivated, or both intrinsically and extrinsically motivated.[29] A top manager who derives a sense of accomplishment and achievement from managing a large corporation and strives to reach year-end targets to obtain a hefty bonus is both intrinsically and extrinsically motivated. Similarly, a nurse who enjoys helping and taking care of patients and is motivated by having a secure job with good benefits is both intrinsically and extrinsically motivated. At Enterprise Rent-A-Car, employees are both extrinsically motivated, because of opportunities for promotions and having their pay linked to the performance of their branches or units, and intrinsically motivated because they get a sense of satisfaction out of serving customers and learning new things. Whether workers are intrinsically motivated, extrinsically motivated, or both depends on a wide variety of factors: (1) workers' own personal characteristics (such as their personalities, abilities, values, attitudes, and needs), (2) the nature of their jobs (such as whether they have been enriched or where they are on the

Where are you more likely to find prosocial motivation? Here in the classroom as a teacher walks her student through that tricky math problem. Getting companies to foster this type of motivation is a bit trickier!

prosocially motivated behavior Behavior that is performed to benefit or help others.

five core characteristics of the job characteristics model), and (3) the nature of the organization (such as its structure, its culture, its control systems, its human resource management system, and the ways in which rewards such as pay are distributed to employees).

In addition to being intrinsically or extrinsically motivated, some people are prosocially motivated by their work.[30] Prosocially motivated behavior is behavior that is performed to benefit or help others.[31] Behavior can be prosocially motivated in addition to being extrinsically and/or intrinsically motivated. An elementary school teacher who not only enjoys the process of teaching young children (has high intrinsic motivation) but also has a strong desire to give children the best learning experience possible and help those with learning disabilities overcome their challenges, and who keeps up with the latest research on child development and teaching methods in an effort to continually improve the effectiveness of his teaching, has high prosocial motivation in addition to high intrinsic motivation. A surgeon who specializes in organ transplants, enjoys the challenge of performing complex operations, has a strong desire to help her patients regain their health and extend their lives through successful organ transplants, and is also motivated by the relatively high income she earns has high intrinsic, prosocial, and extrinsic motivation. Recent preliminary research suggests that when workers have high prosocial motivation, also having high intrinsic motivation can be especially beneficial for job performance.[32]

outcome Anything a person gets from a job or organization.

Regardless of whether people are intrinsically, extrinsically, or prosocially motivated, they join and are motivated to work in organizations to obtain certain outcomes. An outcome is anything a person gets from a job or organization. Some outcomes, such as autonomy, responsibility, a feeling of accomplishment, and the pleasure of doing interesting or enjoyable work, result in intrinsically motivated behavior. Outcomes, such as improving the lives or well-being of other people and doing good by helping others, result in prosocially motivated behavior. Other outcomes, such as pay, job security, benefits, and vacation time, result in extrinsically motivated behavior.

input Anything a person contributes to his or her job or organization.

Organizations hire people to obtain important inputs. An input is anything a person contributes to the job or organization, such as time, effort, education, experience, skills, knowledge, and actual work behaviors. Inputs such as these are necessary for an organization to achieve its goals. Managers strive to motivate members of an organization to contribute inputs—through their behavior, effort, and persistence—that help the organization achieve its goals. How do managers do this? They ensure that members of an organization obtain the outcomes they desire when they make valuable contributions to the organization. Managers use outcomes to motivate people to contribute their inputs to the organization. Giving people outcomes when they contribute inputs and perform well aligns the interests of employees with the goals of the organization as a whole because when employees do what is good for the organization, they personally benefit.

This alignment between employees and organizational goals as a whole can be described by the motivation equation depicted in Figure 9.1. Managers seek to ensure that people are motivated to contribute important inputs to the

Figure 9.1

The Motivation Equation

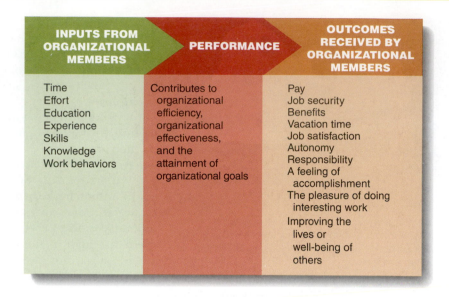

INPUTS FROM ORGANIZATIONAL MEMBERS	PERFORMANCE	OUTCOMES RECEIVED BY ORGANIZATIONAL MEMBERS
Time Effort Education Experience Skills Knowledge Work behaviors	Contributes to organizational efficiency, organizational effectiveness, and the attainment of organizational goals	Pay Job security Benefits Vacation time Job satisfaction Autonomy Responsibility A feeling of accomplishment The pleasure of doing interesting work Improving the lives or well-being of others

organization, that these inputs are put to good use or focused in the direction of high performance, and that high performance results in workers' obtaining the outcomes they desire.

Each of the theories of motivation discussed in this chapter focuses on one or more aspects of this equation. Together, the theories provide a comprehensive set of guidelines for managers to follow to promote high levels of employee motivation. Effective managers, such as Andrew Taylor in the "Management Snapshot," tend to follow many of these guidelines, whereas ineffective managers often fail to follow them and seem to have trouble motivating organizational members.

Expectancy Theory

LO 9-2 Describe from the perspectives of expectancy theory and equity theory what managers should do to have a highly motivated workforce.

expectancy theory The theory that motivation will be high when workers believe that high levels of effort lead to high performance and high performance leads to the attainment of desired outcomes.

Expectancy theory, formulated by Victor H. Vroom in the 1960s, posits that motivation is high when workers believe that high levels of effort lead to high performance and high performance leads to the attainment of desired outcomes. Expectancy theory is one of the most popular theories of work motivation because it focuses on all three parts of the motivation equation: inputs, performance, and outcomes. Expectancy theory identifies three major factors that determine a person's motivation: *expectancy, instrumentality,* and *valence* (see Figure 9.2).[33]

Expectancy

Expectancy is a person's perception about the extent to which effort (an input) results in a certain level of performance. A person's level of expectancy determines whether he or she believes that a high level of effort results in a high level of performance. People are motivated to put forth a lot of effort on their jobs only if they think that their effort will pay off in high performance—that is, if they have high expectancy. Think about how motivated you would be to study for a test if you thought that no matter how hard you tried, you would get a D. Think about how motivated a marketing manager would be who thought that no matter how hard he or she worked, there was no way to increase sales of an unpopular product. In these cases, expectancy is low, so overall motivation is also low.

Figure 9.2

Expectancy, Instrumentality, and Valence

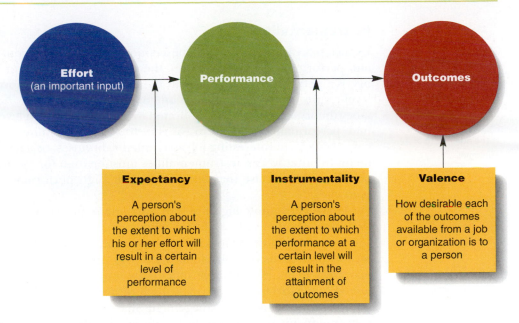

Effort (an important input)

Performance

Outcomes

Expectancy

A person's perception about the extent to which his or her effort will result in a certain level of performance

Instrumentality

A person's perception about the extent to which performance at a certain level will result in the attainment of outcomes

Valence

How desirable each of the outcomes available from a job or organization is to a person

expectancy In expectancy theory, a perception about the extent to which effort results in a certain level of performance.

Members of an organization are motivated to put forth a high level of effort only if they think that doing so leads to high performance.[34] In other words, in order for people's motivation to be high, expectancy must be high. Thus, in attempting to influence motivation, managers need to make sure their subordinates believe that if they do try hard, they can actually succeed. One way managers can boost expectancies is through expressing confidence in their subordinates' capabilities. Managers at The Container Store, for example, express high levels of confidence in their subordinates. As Container Store cofounder Garrett Boone put it, "Everybody we hire, we hire as a leader. Anybody in our store can take an action that you might think of typically being a manager's action."[35]

In addition to expressing confidence in subordinates, other ways for managers to boost subordinates' expectancy levels and motivation are by providing training so people have the expertise needed for high performance and increasing their levels of autonomy and responsibility as they gain experience so they have the freedom to do what it takes to perform at a high level. For example, the Best Buy chain of stores selling electronics, computers, music and movies, and gadgets of all sorts boosts salespeople's expectancies by giving them extensive training in on-site meetings and online. Electronic learning terminals in each department not only help salespeople learn how different systems work and can be sold as an integrated package but also enable them to keep up to date with the latest advances in technology and products. Salespeople also receive extensive training in how to determine customers' needs.[36] At Enterprise Rent-A-Car in the "Management Snapshot" the Management Training Program helps new hires develop high levels of expectancy and these high levels of expectancy are maintained as experienced employees are given more responsibility and autonomy to ensure that their branches are profitable and provide excellent customer service.

Instrumentality

instrumentality
In expectancy theory,
a perception about
the extent to which
performance results
in the attainment of
outcomes.

Expectancy captures a person's perceptions about the relationship between effort and performance. Instrumentality, the second major concept in expectancy theory, is a person's perception about the extent to which performance at a certain level results in the attainment of outcomes (see Figure 9.2). According to expectancy theory, employees are motivated to perform at a high level only if they think high performance will lead to (or is *instrumental* for attaining) outcomes such as pay, job security, interesting job assignments, bonuses, or a feeling of accomplishment. In other words, instrumentalities must be high for motivation to be high—people must perceive that because of their high performance they will receive outcomes.[37]

Managers promote high levels of instrumentality when they link performance to desired outcomes. In addition, managers must clearly communicate this linkage to subordinates. By making sure that outcomes available in an organization are distributed to organizational members on the basis of their performance, managers promote high instrumentality and motivation. When outcomes are linked to performance in this way, high performers receive more outcomes than low performers. In the "Management Snapshot," Andrew Taylor raises levels of instrumentality and motivation for Enterprise Rent-A-Car employees by linking opportunities for promotion and pay to performance.

Valence

Although all members of an organization must have high expectancies and instrumentalities, expectancy theory acknowledges that people differ in their preferences for outcomes. For many people, pay is the most important outcome of working. For others, a feeling of accomplishment or enjoying one's work is more important than pay. The term valence refers to how desirable each of the outcomes available from a job or organization is to a person. To motivate organizational members, managers need to determine which outcomes have high valence for them—are highly desired—and make sure that those outcomes are provided when members perform at a high level.

valence In expectancy
theory, how desirable
each of the outcomes
available from a job
or organization is to a
person.

From the "Management Snapshot," it appears that not only pay but also autonomy, responsibility, and opportunities from promotions are highly valent outcomes for many employees at Enterprise Rent-A-Car.

Bringing It All Together

According to expectancy theory, high motivation results from high levels of expectancy, instrumentality, and valence (see Figure 9.3). If any one of these factors is low, motivation is likely to be low. No matter how tightly desired outcomes are linked to performance, if a person thinks it is practically impossible to perform at a high level, motivation to perform at a high level will be exceedingly low. Similarly, if a person does not think outcomes are linked to high performance, or if a person does not desire the outcomes that are linked to high performance, motivation to perform at a high level will be low. Effective managers realize the importance of high levels of expectancy, instrumentality, and valence and take concrete steps to ensure that their employees are highly motivated.

Figure 9.3

Expectancy Theory

Expectancy is high:

People perceive that if they try hard, they can perform at a high level.

Instrumentality is high:

People perceive that high performance leads to the receipt of certain outcomes.

Valence is high:

People desire the outcomes that result from high performance.

HIGH MOTIVATION

Need Theories

A need is a requirement or necessity for survival and well-being. The basic premise of need theories is that people are motivated to obtain outcomes at work that will satisfy their needs. Need theory complements expectancy theory by exploring in depth which outcomes motivate people to perform at a high level. Need theories suggest that to motivate a person to contribute valuable inputs to a job and perform at a high level, a manager must determine what needs the person is trying to satisfy at work and ensure that the person receives outcomes that help to satisfy those needs when the person performs at a high level and helps the organization achieve its goals.

There are several need theories. Here we discuss Abraham Maslow's hierarchy of needs, Frederick Herzberg's motivator-hygiene theory, and David McClelland's needs for achievement, affiliation, and power. These theories describe needs that people try to satisfy at work. In doing so, they give managers insights about what outcomes motivate members of an organization to perform at a high level and contribute inputs to help the organization achieve its goals.

Maslow's Hierarchy of Needs

Psychologist Abraham Maslow proposed that all people seek to satisfy five basic kinds of needs: physiological needs, safety needs, belongingness needs, esteem needs, and self-actualization needs (see Table 9.1).[38] He suggested that these needs constitute a hierarchy of needs, with the most basic or compelling needs—physiological and safety needs—at the bottom. Maslow argued that these lowest-level needs must be met before a person strives to satisfy needs higher up in the hierarchy, such as self-esteem needs. Once a need is satisfied, Maslow proposed, it ceases to operate as a source of motivation. The lowest level of *unmet* needs in the hierarchy is the prime motivator of behavior; if and when this level is satisfied, needs at the next highest level in the hierarchy motivate behavior.

Although this theory identifies needs that are likely to be important sources of motivation for many people, research does not support Maslow's contention that there is a need hierarchy or his notion that only one level of needs is motivational at a time.[39] Nevertheless, a key conclusion can be drawn from Maslow's theory: People try to satisfy different needs at work. To have a motivated

LO 9-3 Explain how goals and needs motivate people and what kinds of goals are especially likely to result in high performance.

need A requirement or necessity for survival and well-being.

need theories Theories of motivation that focus on what needs people are trying to satisfy at work and what outcomes will satisfy those needs.

Maslow's hierarchy of needs An arrangement of five basic needs that, according to Maslow, motivate behavior. Maslow proposed that the lowest level of unmet needs is the prime motivator and that only one level of needs is motivational at a time.

Table 9.1

Maslow's Hierarchy of Needs

	Needs	Description	Examples of How Managers Can Help People Satisfy These Needs at Work
Highest-level needs ↑	**Self-actualization needs**	The needs to realize one's full potential as a human being.	By giving people the opportunity to use their skills and abilities to the fullest extent possible.
	Esteem needs	The needs to feel good about oneself and one's capabilities, to be respected by others, and to receive recognition and appreciation.	By granting promotions and recognizing accomplishments.
	Belongingness needs	Needs for social interaction, friendship, affection, and love.	By promoting good interpersonal relations and organizing social functions such as company picnics and holiday parties.
	Safety needs	Needs for security, stability, and a safe environment.	By providing job security, adequate medical benefits, and safe working conditions.
Lowest-level needs (most basic or compelling) ↓	**Physiological needs**	Basic needs for things such as food, water, and shelter that must be met in order for a person to survive.	By providing a level of pay that enables a person to buy food and clothing and have adequate housing.

The lowest level of unsatisfied needs motivates behavior; once this level of needs is satisfied, a person tries to satisfy the needs at the next level.

workforce, managers must determine which needs employees are trying to satisfy in organizations and then make sure that individuals receive outcomes that satisfy their needs when they perform at a high level and contribute to organizational effectiveness. By doing this, managers align the interests of individual members with the interests of the organization as a whole. By doing what is good for the organization (that is, performing at a high level), employees receive outcomes that satisfy their needs.

In our increasingly global economy, managers must realize that citizens of different countries might differ in the needs they seek to satisfy through work.[40] Some research suggests, for example, that people in Greece and Japan are especially motivated by safety needs and that people in Sweden, Norway, and Denmark are motivated by belongingness needs.[41] In less developed countries with low standards of living, physiological and safety needs are likely to be the prime motivators of behavior. As countries become wealthier and have higher standards of living, needs related to personal growth and accomplishment (such as esteem and self-actualization) become important motivators of behavior.

No one pumps their fist over their laptop unless it's for a good reason! Clearly, whipping an obnoxious spreadsheet into shape and sending out a calmly worded press release make for satisfied self-actualization needs.

Herzberg's Motivator-Hygiene Theory

Adopting an approach different from Maslow's, Frederick Herzberg focused on two factors: (1) outcomes that can lead to high levels of motivation and job satisfaction and (2) outcomes that can prevent people from being dissatisfied. According to Herzberg's motivator-hygiene theory, people have two sets of needs or requirements: motivator needs and hygiene needs.[42] *Motivator needs* are related to the nature of the work itself and how challenging it is. Outcomes such as interesting work, autonomy, responsibility, being able to grow and develop on the job, and a sense of accomplishment and achievement help to satisfy motivator needs. To have a highly motivated and satisfied workforce, Herzberg suggested, managers should take steps to ensure that employees' motivator needs are being met.

Hygiene needs are related to the physical and psychological context in which the work is performed. Hygiene needs are satisfied by outcomes such as pleasant and comfortable working conditions, pay, job security, good relationships with coworkers, and effective supervision. According to Herzberg, when hygiene needs are not met, workers are dissatisfied, and when hygiene needs are met, workers are not dissatisfied. Satisfying hygiene needs, however, does not result in high levels of motivation or even high levels of job satisfaction. For motivation and job satisfaction to be high, motivator needs must be met.

Many research studies have tested Herzberg's propositions, and, by and large, the theory fails to receive support.[43] Nevertheless, Herzberg's formulations have contributed to our understanding of motivation in at least two ways. First, Herzberg helped to focus researchers' and managers' attention on the important distinction between intrinsic motivation (related to motivator needs) and extrinsic motivation (related to hygiene needs), covered earlier in the chapter. Second, his theory prompted researchers and managers to study how jobs could be designed or redesigned so they are intrinsically motivating.

McClelland's Needs for Achievement, Affiliation, and Power

Psychologist David McClelland extensively researched the needs for achievement, affiliation, and power.[44] The need for achievement is the extent to which an individual has a strong desire to perform challenging tasks well and to meet personal standards for excellence. People with a high need for achievement often set clear goals for themselves and like to receive performance feedback. The need for affiliation is the extent to which an individual is concerned about establishing and maintaining good interpersonal relations, being liked, and having the people around him or her get along with each other. The need for power is the extent to which an individual desires to control or influence others.[45]

Although each of these needs is present in each of us to some degree, their importance in the workplace depends on the position one occupies. For example, research suggests that high needs for achievement and for power are assets for first-line and middle managers and that a high need for power is especially important for upper managers.[46] One study found that U.S. presidents with a relatively high need for power tended to be especially effective during their terms of office.[47] A high need for affiliation may not always be desirable in managers and other leaders because it might lead them to try too hard to be liked by others (including subordinates) rather than doing all they can to ensure that performance is as high as it can and should be. Although most research on

Herzberg's motivator-hygiene theory A need theory that distinguishes between motivator needs (related to the nature of the work itself) and hygiene needs (related to the physical and psychological context in which the work is performed) and proposes that motivator needs must be met for motivation and job satisfaction to be high.

need for achievement The extent to which an individual has a strong desire to perform challenging tasks well and to meet personal standards for excellence.

need for affiliation The extent to which an individual is concerned about establishing and maintaining good interpersonal relations, being liked, and having the people around him or her get along with each other.

need for power The extent to which an individual desires to control or influence others.

these needs has been done in the United States, some studies suggest that the findings may be applicable to people in other countries as well, such as India and New Zealand.[48]

Other Needs

Clearly, more needs motivate workers than the needs described by these three theories. For example, more and more workers are feeling the need for work–life balance and time to take care of their loved ones while simultaneously being highly motivated at work. Thus, for example, not being required to work excessive hours and being able to take time off when needed can help meet needs for work–life balance. Interestingly enough, recent research suggests that being exposed to nature (even just being able to see some trees from an office window) has many salutary effects, and a lack of such exposure can impair well-being and performance.[49] Thus having some time during the day when one can at least see nature may be another important need. Managers of successful companies often strive to ensure that as many of their valued employees' needs as possible are satisfied in the workplace.

Equity Theory

LO 9-2 Describe from the perspectives of expectancy theory and equity theory what managers should do to have a highly motivated workforce.

equity theory A theory of motivation that focuses on people's perceptions of the fairness of their work outcomes relative to their work inputs.

equity The justice, impartiality, and fairness to which all organizational members are entitled.

Equity theory is a theory of motivation that concentrates on people's perceptions of the fairness of their work *outcomes* relative to, or in proportion to, their work *inputs*. Equity theory complements expectancy and need theories by focusing on how people perceive the relationship between the outcomes they receive from their jobs and organizations and the inputs they contribute. Equity theory was formulated in the 1960s by J. Stacy Adams, who stressed that what is important in determining motivation is the *relative* rather than the *absolute* levels of outcomes a person receives and inputs a person contributes. Specifically, motivation is influenced by the comparison of one's own outcome–input ratio with the outcome–input ratio of a referent.[50] The *referent* could be another person or a group of people who are perceived to be similar to oneself; the referent also could be oneself in a previous job or one's expectations about what outcome–input ratios should be. In a comparison of one's own outcome–input ratio to a referent's ratio, one's *perceptions* of outcomes and inputs (not any objective indicator of them) are key.

Equity

Equity exists when a person perceives his or her own outcome–input ratio to be equal to a referent's outcome–input ratio. Under conditions of equity (see Table 9.2), if a referent receives more outcomes than you receive, the referent contributes proportionally more inputs to the organization, so his or her outcome–input ratio still equals your ratio. Maria Sanchez and Claudia King, for example, both work in a shoe store in a large mall. Sanchez is paid more per hour than King but also contributes more inputs, including being responsible for some of the store's bookkeeping, closing the store, and periodically depositing cash in the bank. When King compares her outcome–input ratio to Sanchez's (her referent's), she perceives the ratios to be equitable because Sanchez's higher level of pay (an outcome) is proportional to her higher level of inputs (bookkeeping, closing the store, and going to the bank).

Table 9.2
Equity Theory

Condition	Person		Referent	Example
Equity	$\dfrac{\text{Outcomes}}{\text{Inputs}}$	=	$\dfrac{\text{Outcomes}}{\text{Inputs}}$	An engineer perceives that he contributes more inputs (time and effort) and receives proportionally more outcomes (a higher salary and choice job assignments) than his referent.
Underpayment inequity	$\dfrac{\text{Outcomes}}{\text{Inputs}}$	< (less than)	$\dfrac{\text{Outcomes}}{\text{Inputs}}$	An engineer perceives that he contributes more inputs but receives the same outcomes as his referent.
Overpayment inequity	$\dfrac{\text{Outcomes}}{\text{Inputs}}$	> (greater than)	$\dfrac{\text{Outcomes}}{\text{Inputs}}$	An engineer perceives that he contributes the same inputs but receives more outcomes than his referent.

Similarly, under conditions of equity, if you receive more outcomes than a referent, your inputs are perceived to be proportionally higher. Continuing with our example, when Sanchez compares her outcome–input ratio to King's (her referent's) ratio, she perceives them to be equitable because her higher level of pay is proportional to her higher level of inputs.

When equity exists, people are motivated to continue contributing their current levels of inputs to their organizations to receive their current levels of outcomes. If people wish to increase their outcomes under conditions of equity, they are motivated to increase their inputs.

Inequity

inequity Lack of fairness.

Inequity, or lack of fairness, exists when a person's outcome–input ratio is not perceived to be equal to a referent's. There are two types of inequity: underpayment inequity and overpayment inequity (see Table 9.2). Underpayment inequity exists when a person's own outcome–input ratio is perceived to be *less* than that of a referent. In comparing yourself to a referent, you think you are *not* receiving the outcomes you should be, given your inputs. Overpayment inequity exists when a person perceives that his or her own outcome–input ratio is *greater* than that of a referent. In comparing yourself to a referent, you think you are receiving *more* outcomes than you should be, given your inputs.

underpayment inequity The inequity that exists when a person perceives that his or her own outcome–input ratio is less than the ratio of a referent.

overpayment inequity The inequity that exists when a person perceives that his or her own outcome–input ratio is greater than the ratio of a referent.

Ways to Restore Equity

According to equity theory, both underpayment inequity and overpayment inequity create tension that motivates most people to restore equity by bringing the ratios back into balance.[51] When people experience *underpayment* inequity, they may be motivated to lower their inputs by reducing their working hours, putting forth less effort on the job, or being absent; or they may be motivated to increase their outcomes by asking for a raise or a promotion. Susan Richie, a financial analyst at a large corporation, noticed that she was working longer hours and getting more work accomplished than a coworker who had the same position, yet they both received the exact same pay and other outcomes. To restore equity, Richie decided to stop coming in early and staying late. Alternatively, she could have tried to restore equity by trying to increase her outcomes, perhaps by asking her boss for a raise.

When people experience underpayment inequity and other means of equity restoration fail, they can change their perceptions of their own or the referent's inputs or outcomes. For example, they may realize that their referent is really working on more difficult projects than they are or that they really take more time off from work than their referent does. Alternatively, if people who feel they are underpaid have other employment options, they may leave the organization. As an example, John Steinberg, an assistant principal in a high school, experienced underpayment inequity when he realized all the other assistant principals of high schools in his school district had received promotions to the position of principal even though they had been in their jobs for a shorter time than he had. Steinberg's performance had always been appraised as being high, so after his repeated requests for a promotion went unheeded, he found a job as a principal in a different school district.

When people experience *overpayment* inequity, they may try to restore equity by changing their perceptions of their own or their referent's inputs or outcomes. Equity can be restored when people realize they are contributing more inputs than they originally thought. Equity also can be restored by perceiving the referent's inputs to be lower or the referent's outcomes to be higher than one originally thought. When equity is restored in this way, actual inputs and outcomes are unchanged, and the person being overpaid takes no real action. What is changed is how people think about or view their or the referent's inputs and outcomes. For instance, Mary McMann experienced overpayment inequity when she realized she was being paid $2 an hour more than a coworker who had the same job as she did in a health food store and who contributed the same amount of inputs. McMann restored equity by changing her perceptions of her inputs. She realized she worked harder than her coworker and solved more problems that came up in the store.

Experiencing either overpayment or underpayment inequity, you might decide that your referent is not appropriate because, for example, the referent is too different from yourself. Choosing a more appropriate referent may bring the ratios back into balance. Angela Martinez, a middle manager in the engineering department of a chemical company, experienced overpayment inequity when she realized she was being paid quite a bit more than her friend, who was a middle manager in the marketing department of the same company. After thinking about the discrepancy for a while, Martinez decided that engineering and marketing were so different that she should not be comparing her job to her friend's job even though they were both middle managers. Martinez restored equity by changing her referent; she picked a middle manager in the engineering department as a new referent.

Motivation is highest when as many people as possible in an organization perceive that they are being equitably treated—their outcomes and inputs are in balance. Top contributors and performers are motivated to continue contributing a high level of inputs because they are receiving the outcomes they deserve. Mediocre contributors and performers realize that if they want to increase their outcomes, they have to increase their inputs. Managers of effective organizations, like Andrew Taylor at Enterprise Rent-A-Car, realize the importance of equity for motivation and performance and continually strive to ensure that employees believe they are being equitably treated.

The dot-com boom, its subsequent bust, and two recessions, along with increased global competition, have resulted in some workers putting in longer and longer working hours (increasing their inputs) without any increase in their outcomes. For those whose referents are not experiencing a similar change, perceptions of inequity are likely. According to Jill Andresky Fraser, author of *White Collar Sweatshop,* over 25 million U.S. workers work more than 49 hours per week in the office, almost 11 million work more than 60 hours per week in the office, and many also put in additional work hours at home. Moreover, advances in information technology, such as e-mail and cell phones, have resulted in work intruding on home time, vacation time, and even special occasions.[52]

Goal-Setting Theory

goal-setting theory A theory that focuses on identifying the types of goals that are most effective in producing high levels of motivation and performance and explaining why goals have these effects.

Goal-setting theory focuses on motivating workers to contribute their inputs to their jobs and organizations; in this way it is similar to expectancy theory and equity theory. But goal-setting theory takes this focus a step further by considering as well how managers can ensure that organizational members focus their inputs in the direction of high performance and the achievement of organizational goals.

Ed Locke and Gary Latham, the leading researchers for goal-setting theory, suggested that the goals organizational members strive to attain are prime determinants of their motivation and subsequent performance. A *goal* is what a person is trying to accomplish through his or her efforts and behaviors.[53] Just as you may have a goal to get a good grade in this course, so do members of an organization have goals they strive to meet. For example, salespeople at Neiman Marcus strive to meet sales goals, while top managers pursue market share and profitability goals.

Goal-setting theory suggests that to stimulate high motivation and performance, goals must be *specific* and *difficult*.[54] Specific goals are often quantitative—a salesperson's goal to sell $500 worth of merchandise per day, a scientist's goal to finish a project in one year, a CEO's goal to reduce debt by 40% and increase revenues by 20%, a restaurant manager's goal to serve 150 customers per evening. In contrast to specific goals, vague goals such as "doing your best" or "selling as much as you can" do not have much motivational impact.

Difficult goals are hard but not impossible to attain. In contrast to difficult goals, easy goals are those that practically everyone can attain, and moderate goals are goals that about one-half of the people can attain. Both easy and moderate goals have less motivational power than difficult goals.

Regardless of whether specific, difficult goals are set by managers, workers, or teams of managers and workers, they lead to high levels of motivation and performance. When managers set goals for their subordinates, their subordinates must accept the goals or agree to work toward them; also, they should be committed to them or really want to attain them. Some managers find that having subordinates participate in the actual setting of goals boosts their acceptance of and commitment to the goals. In addition, organizational members need to receive *feedback* about how they are doing; feedback can often be provided by the

Specific, difficult goals can encourage people to exert high levels of effort and to focus efforts in the right direction.

performance appraisal and feedback component of an organization's human resource management system (see Chapter 12).

Specific, difficult goals affect motivation in two ways. First, they motivate people to contribute more inputs to their jobs. Specific, difficult goals cause people to put forth high levels of effort, for example. Just as you would study harder if you were trying to get an A in a course instead of a C, so too will a salesperson work harder to reach a $500 sales goal instead of a $200 sales goal. Specific, difficult goals also cause people to be more persistent than easy, moderate, or vague goals when they run into difficulties. Salespeople who are told to sell as much as possible might stop trying on a slow day, whereas having a specific, difficult goal to reach causes them to keep trying.

A second way in which specific, difficult goals affect motivation is by helping people focus their inputs in the right direction. These goals let people know what they should be focusing their attention on, whether it is increasing the quality of customer service or sales or lowering new product development times. The fact that the goals are specific and difficult also frequently causes people to develop *action plans* for reaching them.[55] Action plans can include the strategies to attain the goals and timetables or schedules for the completion of different activities crucial to goal attainment. Like the goals themselves, action plans also help ensure that efforts are focused in the right direction and that people do not get sidetracked along the way.

Although specific, difficult goals have been found to increase motivation and performance in a wide variety of jobs and organizations both in the United States and abroad, recent research suggests that they may detract from performance under certain conditions. When people are performing complicated and challenging tasks that require them to focus on a considerable amount of learning, specific, difficult goals may actually impair performance.[56] Striving to reach such goals may direct some of a person's attention away from learning about the task and toward trying to figure out how to achieve the goal. Once a person has learned the task and it no longer seems complicated or difficult, then the assignment of specific, difficult goals is likely to have its usual effects. Additionally, for work that is very creative and uncertain, specific, difficult goals may be detrimental.

learning theories Theories that focus on increasing employee motivation and performance by linking the outcomes that employees receive to the performance of desired behaviors and the attainment of goals.

Learning Theories

The basic premise of learning theories as applied to organizations is that managers can increase employee motivation and performance by how they link the outcomes that employees receive to the performance of desired behaviors and the attainment of goals. Thus learning theory focuses on the linkage between performance and outcomes in the motivation equation (see Figure 9.1).

LO 9-4 Identify the motivation lessons that managers can learn from operant conditioning theory and social learning theory.

Learning can be defined as a relatively permanent change in a person's knowledge or behavior that results from practice or experience.[57] Learning takes place in organizations when people learn to perform certain behaviors to receive certain outcomes. For example, a person learns to perform at a higher level than in the past or to come to work earlier because he or she is motivated to obtain the outcomes that result from these behaviors, such as a pay raise or praise from a supervisor. In the "Management Snapshot," Enterprise Rent-A-Car's emphasis on training ensures that new hires learn how to provide excellent customer service and perform all the tasks necessary for successful branch operations.

learning A relatively permanent change in knowledge or behavior that results from practice or experience.

Training can spur learning in all kinds of jobs and organizations, even ones where a good portion of the workforce is working freelance-style, at home, and part-time, as indicated in the following "Management Insight" box.

MANAGEMENT INSIGHT

Training Spurs Learning at Stella & Dot

Stella & Dot, based in San Francisco, is a social selling company that sells jewelry and accessories exclusively through independent stylists who host trunk shows in their homes and online. Founded by Jessica Herrin, who started the firm by designing jewelry, is its current CEO, and was a cofounder of the WeddingChannel.com, Stella & Dot has grown to have over $200 million in sales.[58] Stella & Dot has approximately 10,000 stylists who work out of their homes, many of them part-time. According to Herrin, one of the keys to their success is the training they provide to stylists.[59]

Jessica Herrin knows how important on-the-job training remains for all employees. Her early failure with Stella & Dot taught her that the company could only succeed if it remained nimble, flexible, and was able to foster strong communication among employees to keep the ideas flowing.

The company has its own online learning center, called Stella & Dot University, where stylists have access to interactive videos, guidebooks, tutorials, and audio training. Online quizzes ensure that learning takes place and stylists receive immediate feedback when they master a content area. Weekly phone calls with headquarters also focus on coaching and training stylists to learn how best to market and sell products.[60] Herrin herself makes it a point to send personal e-mails, and she phones a minimum of 10 stylists a day to see how they are doing and to congratulate them when things go well.[61]

There are also many opportunities for stylists to learn from each other. High-performing stylists relate the keys to their own success in webcams in their homes, how they managed the process, and the obstacles they were able to overcome.[62] A national annual conference also enables stylists to learn from each other by providing networking opportunities and training sessions led by high-performing stylists. Training also is provided on a regional basis by local high-performing stylists.[63] In all of its training efforts, Stella & Dot emphasizes treating stylists with respect as the professionals that they are and celebrating successes.[64] All in all, facilitating learning through training has certainly paid off for Stella & Dot.

Of the different learning theories, *operant conditioning theory* and *social learning theory* provide the most guidance to managers in their efforts to have a highly motivated workforce.

Operant Conditioning Theory

operant conditioning theory The theory that people learn to perform behaviors that lead to desired consequences and learn not to perform behaviors that lead to undesired consequences.

According to operant conditioning theory, developed by psychologist B. F. Skinner, people learn to perform behaviors that lead to desired consequences and learn not to perform behaviors that lead to undesired consequences.[65] Translated into motivation terms, Skinner's theory means that people will be motivated to perform at a high level and attain their work goals to the extent that high performance and goal attainment allow them to obtain outcomes they desire. Similarly, people avoid performing behaviors that lead to outcomes they do not desire. By linking the performance of *specific behaviors* to the attainment of *specific outcomes,* managers can motivate organizational members to perform in ways that help an organization achieve its goals.

Operant conditioning theory provides four tools that managers can use to motivate high performance and prevent workers from engaging in absenteeism and other behaviors that detract from organizational effectiveness. These tools are positive reinforcement, negative reinforcement, extinction, and punishment.[66]

positive reinforcement Giving people outcomes they desire when they perform organizationally functional behaviors.

POSITIVE REINFORCEMENT Positive reinforcement gives people outcomes they desire when they perform organizationally functional behaviors. These desired outcomes, called *positive reinforcers,* include any outcomes that a person desires, such as pay, praise, or a promotion. Organizationally functional behaviors are behaviors that contribute to organizational effectiveness; they can include producing high-quality goods and services, providing high-quality customer service, and meeting deadlines. By linking positive reinforcers to the performance of functional behaviors, managers motivate people to perform the desired behaviors.

negative reinforcement Eliminating or removing undesired outcomes when people perform organizationally functional behaviors.

NEGATIVE REINFORCEMENT Negative reinforcement also can encourage members of an organization to perform desired or organizationally functional behaviors. Managers using negative reinforcement actually eliminate or remove undesired outcomes once the functional behavior is performed. These undesired outcomes, called *negative reinforcers,* can range from a manager's constant nagging or criticism to unpleasant assignments or the ever-present threat of losing one's job. When negative reinforcement is used, people are motivated to perform behaviors because they want to stop receiving or avoid undesired outcomes. Managers who try to encourage salespeople to sell more by threatening them with being fired are using negative reinforcement. In this case, the negative reinforcer is the threat of job loss, which is removed once the functional behavior is performed.

Whenever possible, managers should try to use positive reinforcement. Negative reinforcement can create a very unpleasant work environment and even a negative culture in an organization. No one likes to be nagged, threatened, or exposed to other kinds of negative outcomes. The use of negative reinforcement sometimes causes subordinates to resent managers and try to get back at them.

Identifying the Right Behaviors for Reinforcement   Even managers who use positive reinforcement (and refrain from using negative reinforcement) can get into trouble if they are not careful to identify the right behaviors to reinforce—behaviors that are truly functional for the organization. Doing this is not always as straightforward as it might seem. First, it is crucial for managers to choose behaviors over which subordinates have control; in other words, subordinates must have the freedom and opportunity to perform the behaviors that are being reinforced. Second, it is crucial that these behaviors contribute to organizational effectiveness.

EXTINCTION Sometimes members of an organization are motivated to perform behaviors that detract from organizational effectiveness. According to operant conditioning theory, all behavior is controlled or determined by its consequences; one way for managers to curtail the performance of dysfunctional behaviors is to eliminate whatever is reinforcing the behaviors. This process is called extinction.

extinction Curtailing the performance of dysfunctional behaviors by eliminating whatever is reinforcing them.

Suppose a manager has a subordinate who frequently stops by his office to chat—sometimes about work-related matters but at other times about various topics ranging from politics to last night's football game. The manager and the subordinate share certain interests and views, so these conversations can get quite involved, and both seem to enjoy them. The manager, however, realizes that these frequent and sometimes lengthy conversations are causing him to stay at work later in the evenings to make up for the time he loses during the day. The manager also realizes that he is reinforcing his subordinate's behavior by acting interested in the topics the subordinate brings up and responding at length to them. To extinguish this behavior, the manager stops acting interested in these non-work-related conversations and keeps his responses polite and friendly but brief. No longer being reinforced with a pleasurable conversation, the subordinate eventually ceases to be motivated to interrupt the manager during working hours to discuss non-work-related issues.

PUNISHMENT Sometimes managers cannot rely on extinction to eliminate dysfunctional behaviors because they do not have control over whatever is reinforcing the behavior or because they cannot afford the time needed for extinction to work. When employees are performing dangerous behaviors or behaviors that are illegal or unethical, the behavior needs to be eliminated immediately. Sexual harassment, for example, is an organizationally dysfunctional behavior that cannot be tolerated. In such cases managers often rely on punishment, which is administering an undesired or negative consequence to subordinates when they perform the dysfunctional behavior. Punishments used by organizations range from verbal reprimands to pay cuts, temporary suspensions, demotions, and firings. Punishment, however, can have some unintended side effects—resentment, loss of self-respect, a desire for retaliation—and should be used only when necessary.

punishment Administering an undesired or negative consequence when dysfunctional behavior occurs.

To avoid the unintended side effects of punishment, managers should keep in mind these guidelines:

- Downplay the emotional element involved in punishment. Make it clear that you are punishing a person's performance of a dysfunctional behavior, not the person himself or herself.

- Try to punish dysfunctional behaviors as soon as possible after they occur and make sure the negative consequence is a source of punishment for the individuals involved. Be certain that organizational members know exactly why they are being punished.

- Try to avoid punishing someone in front of others because this can hurt a person's self-respect and lower esteem in the eyes of coworkers as well as make coworkers feel uncomfortable.[67] Even so, making organizational members aware that an individual who has committed a serious infraction has been punished can sometimes be effective in preventing future infractions and teaching all members of the organization that certain behaviors are unacceptable. For example, when organizational members are informed that a manager who has sexually harassed subordinates has been punished, they learn or are reminded of the fact that sexual harassment is not tolerated in the organization.

Managers and students alike often confuse negative reinforcement and punishment. To avoid such confusion, keep in mind the two major differences between them. First, negative reinforcement is used to promote the performance of functional behaviors in organizations; punishment is used to stop the performance of dysfunctional behaviors. Second, negative reinforcement entails the *removal* of a negative consequence when functional behaviors are performed; punishment entails the *administration* of negative consequences when dysfunctional behaviors are performed.

Social Learning Theory

social learning theory A theory that takes into account how learning and motivation are influenced by people's thoughts and beliefs and their observations of other people's behavior.

Social learning theory proposes that motivation results not only from direct experience of rewards and punishments but also from a person's thoughts and beliefs. Social learning theory extends operant conditioning's contribution to managers' understanding of motivation by explaining (1) how people can be motivated by observing other people performing a behavior and being reinforced for doing so (*vicarious learning*), (2) how people can be motivated to control their behavior themselves (*self-reinforcement*), and (3) how people's beliefs about their ability to successfully perform a behavior affect motivation (*self-efficacy*).[68] We look briefly at each of these motivators.

vicarious learning Learning that occurs when the learner becomes motivated to perform a behavior by watching another person performing it and being reinforced for doing so; also called *observational learning*.

VICARIOUS LEARNING Vicarious learning, often called *observational learning*, occurs when a person (the learner) becomes motivated to perform a behavior by watching another person (the model) performing the behavior and being positively reinforced for doing so. Vicarious learning is a powerful source of motivation on many jobs in which people learn to perform functional behaviors by watching others. Salespeople learn how to help customers, medical school students learn how to treat patients, law clerks learn how to practice law, and nonmanagers learn how to be managers, in part, by observing experienced members of an organization perform these behaviors properly and be reinforced for them. In general, people are more likely to be motivated to imitate the behavior of models who are highly competent, are (to some extent) experts in the behavior, have high status, receive attractive reinforcers, and are friendly or approachable.[69]

To promote vicarious learning, managers should strive to have the learner meet the following conditions:

- The learner observes the model performing the behavior.
- The learner accurately perceives the model's behavior.
- The learner remembers the behavior.
- The learner has the skills and abilities needed to perform the behavior.
- The learner sees or knows that the model is positively reinforced for the behavior.[70]

SELF-REINFORCEMENT Although managers are often the providers of reinforcement in organizations, sometimes people motivate themselves through self-reinforcement. People can control their own behavior by setting goals for themselves

How do you treat that? When medical students enter residency, they learn vicariously by shadowing a full physician on his or her rounds.

self-reinforcer Any desired or attractive outcome or reward that a person gives to himself or herself for good performance.

and then reinforcing themselves when they achieve the goals.[71] Self-reinforcers are any desired or attractive outcomes or rewards that people can give to themselves for good performance, such as a feeling of accomplishment, going to a movie, having dinner out, buying a new CD, or taking time out for a golf game. When members of an organization control their own behavior through self-reinforcement, managers do not need to spend as much time as they ordinarily would trying to motivate and control behavior through the administration of consequences because subordinates are controlling and motivating themselves. In fact, this self-control is often referred to as the *self-management of behavior.*

When employees are highly skilled and are responsible for creating new goods and services, managers typically rely on self-control and self-management of behavior, as is the case at Google. Employees at Google are given the flexibility and autonomy to experiment, take risks, and sometimes fail as they work on new projects. They are encouraged to learn from their failures and apply what they learn to subsequent projects.[72] Google's engineers are given one day a week to work on their own projects that they are highly involved with, and new products such as Google News often emerge from these projects.[73]

self-efficacy A person's belief about his or her ability to perform a behavior successfully.

SELF-EFFICACY Self-efficacy is a person's belief about his or her ability to perform a behavior successfully.[74] Even with all the most attractive consequences or reinforcers hinging on high performance, people are not going to be motivated if they do not think they can actually perform at a high level. Similarly, when people control their own behavior, they are likely to set for themselves difficult goals that will lead to outstanding accomplishments only if they think they can reach those goals. Thus self-efficacy influences motivation both when managers provide reinforcement and when workers themselves provide it.[75] The greater the self-efficacy, the greater is the motivation and performance. In the "Management Snapshot" managers at Enterprise Rent-A-Car boost self-efficacy by providing employees with training, increasing their levels of autonomy and responsibility as they gain experience with the company, and expressing confidence in their ability to manage their units. Such verbal persuasion, as well as a person's own past performance and accomplishments and the accomplishments of other people, plays a role in determining a person's self-efficacy.

Pay and Motivation

In Chapter 12 we discuss how managers establish a pay level and structure for an organization as a whole. Here we focus on how, once a pay level and structure are in place, managers can use pay to motivate employees to perform at a high level and attain their work goals. Pay is used to motivate entry-level workers, first-line and middle managers, and even top managers such as CEOs. Pay can be used to motivate people to perform behaviors that help an organization achieve its goals, and it can be used to motivate people to join and remain with an organization.

LO 9-5 Explain why and how managers can use pay as a major motivation tool.

Each of the theories described in this chapter alludes to the importance of pay and suggests that pay should be based on performance:

- *Expectancy theory:* Instrumentality, the association between performance and outcomes such as pay, must be high for motivation to be high. In addition, pay is an outcome that has high valence for many people.

- *Need theories:* People should be able to satisfy their needs by performing at a high level; pay can be used to satisfy several different kinds of needs.

- *Equity theory:* Outcomes such as pay should be distributed in proportion to inputs (including performance levels).
- *Goal-setting theory:* Outcomes such as pay should be linked to the attainment of goals.
- *Learning theories:* The distribution of outcomes such as pay should be contingent on the performance of organizationally functional behaviors.

As these theories suggest, to promote high motivation, managers should base the distribution of pay to organizational members on performance levels so that high performers receive more pay than low performers (other things being equal).[76] A compensation plan basing pay on performance is often called a **merit pay plan**.

merit pay plan
A compensation plan that bases pay on performance.

In tough economic times, when organizations lay off employees, and pay levels and benefits of those who are at least able to keep their jobs may be cut while their responsibilities are often increased,[77] managers are often limited in the extent to which they can use merit pay, if at all.[78] Nonetheless, in such times, managers can still try to recognize top performers. Jenny Miller, manager of 170 engineers in the commercial systems engineering department at Rockwell Collins, an aerospace electronics company in Cedar Rapids, Iowa, experienced firsthand the challenge of not being able to recognize top performers with merit pay during tough economic times.[79] Rockwell Collins laid off 8% of its workforce, and the workloads for the engineers Miller managed increased by about 15%. The engineers were working longer hours without receiving any additional pay; there was a salary freeze, so they knew raises were not in store. With a deadline approaching for flight deck software for a customer, she needed some engineers to work over the Thanksgiving holiday and so sent out an e-mail request for volunteers. Approximately 20 employees volunteered. In recognition of their contributions, Miller gave them each a $100 gift card.[80]

A $100 gift card might not seem like much for an employee who is already working long hours to come to work over the Thanksgiving holiday for no additional pay or time off. Yet Steve Nieuwsma, division vice president at Rockwell Collins, indicates that the gift cards at least signaled that managers recognized and appreciated employees' efforts and sought to thank them for it. Not being able to give his employees raises at that time, Nieuwsma also gave gift cards to recognize contributions and top performers in amounts varying between $25 and $500.[81]

Once managers have decided to use a merit pay plan, they face two important choices: whether to base pay on individual, group, or organizational performance and whether to use salary increases or bonuses.

Basing Merit Pay on Individual, Group, or Organizational Performance

Managers can base merit pay on individual, group, or organizational performance. When individual performance (such as the dollar value of merchandise a salesperson sells, the number of loudspeakers a factory worker assembles, and a lawyer's billable hours) can be accurately determined, individual motivation is likely to be highest when pay is based on individual performance.[82] When members of an organization work closely together and individual performance cannot be accurately determined (as in a team of computer programmers developing a single software package), pay cannot be based on individual performance, and a group- or organization-based plan must be used. When the attainment of organizational goals hinges on members' working closely together and cooperating with each other (as in a small construction company that builds custom homes), group- or organization-based plans may be more appropriate than individual-based plans.[83]

It is possible to combine elements of an individual-based plan with a group- or organization-based plan to motivate each individual to perform highly and, at the same time, motivate all individuals to work well together, cooperate with one another, and help one another as needed. Lincoln Electric, a very successful company and a leading manufacturer of welding machines, uses a combination individual- and organization-based plan.[84] Pay is based on individual performance. In addition, each year the size of a bonus fund depends on organizational performance. Money from the bonus fund is distributed to people on the basis of their contributions to the organization, attendance, levels of cooperation, and other indications of performance. Employees of Lincoln Electric are motivated to cooperate and help one another because when the firm as a whole performs well, everybody benefits by having a larger bonus fund. Employees also are motivated to contribute their inputs to the organization because their contributions determine their share of the bonus fund.

Salary Increase or Bonus?

Managers can distribute merit pay to people in the form of a salary increase or a bonus on top of regular salaries. Although the dollar amount of a salary increase or bonus might be identical, bonuses tend to have more motivational impact for at least three reasons. First, salary levels are typically based on performance levels, cost-of-living increases, and so forth, from the day people start working in an organization, which means the absolute level of the salary is based largely on factors unrelated to *current* performance. A 5% merit increase in salary, for example, may seem relatively small in comparison to one's total salary. Second, a current salary increase may be affected by other factors in addition to performance, such as cost-of-living increases or across-the-board market adjustments. Third, because organizations rarely reduce salaries, salary levels tend to vary less than performance levels do. Related to this point is the fact that bonuses give managers more flexibility in distributing outcomes. If an organization is doing well, bonuses can be relatively high to reward employees for their contributions. However, unlike salary increases, bonus levels can be reduced when an organization's performance lags. All in all, bonus plans have more motivational impact than salary increases because the amount of the bonus can be directly and exclusively based on performance.[85]

Consistent with the lessons from motivation theories, bonuses can be linked directly to performance and vary from year to year and employee to employee, as at Gradient Corporation, a Cambridge, Massachusetts, environmental consulting firm.[86] Another organization that successfully uses bonuses is Nucor Corporation. Steelworkers at Nucor tend to be much more productive than steelworkers in other companies—probably because they can receive bonuses tied to performance and quality that can range from 130% to 150% of their regular base pay.[87] During the economic downturn in 2007–2009, Nucor struggled as did many other companies, and bonus pay for steelworkers dropped considerably. However, managers at Nucor avoided having to lay off employees by finding ways to cut costs and having employees work on maintenance activities and safety manuals, along with taking on tasks that used to be performed by independent contractors, such as producing specialty parts and mowing the grass.[88]

employee stock option A financial instrument that entitles the bearer to buy shares of an organization's stock at a certain price during a certain period or under certain conditions.

In addition to receiving pay raises and bonuses, high-level managers and executives are sometimes granted employee stock options. Employee stock options are financial instruments that entitle the bearer to buy shares of an organization's stock at a certain price during a certain period or under certain conditions.[89] For example, in addition to salaries, stock options are sometimes used to attract high-level managers. The exercise price is the stock price at which the bearer can buy the stock, and the vesting conditions specify when the bearer can actually buy the stock at the exercise price. The option's exercise price is generally set equal to the market price of the stock on the date it is granted, and the vesting conditions might specify that the manager has to have worked at the organization for 12 months or perhaps met some performance target (perhaps an increase in profits) before being able to exercise the option. In high-technology firms and start-ups, options are sometimes used in a similar fashion for employees at various levels in the organization.[90]

From a motivation standpoint, stock options are used not so much to reward past individual performance but, rather, to motivate employees to work in the future for the good of the company as a whole. This is true because stock options issued at current stock prices have value in the future only if an organization does well and its stock price appreciates; thus giving employees stock options should encourage them to help the organization improve its performance over time.[91] At high-technology start-ups and dot-coms, stock options have often motivated potential employees to leave promising jobs in larger companies and work for the start-ups. In the late 1990s and early 2000s, many dot-commers were devastated to learn not only that their stock options were worthless, because their companies went out of business or were doing poorly, but also that they were unemployed. Unfortunately stock options have also led to unethical behavior; for example, sometimes individuals seek to artificially inflate the value of a company's stock to increase the value of stock options.

Examples of Merit Pay Plans

Managers can choose among several merit pay plans, depending on the work that employees perform and other considerations. Using *piece-rate pay,* an individual-based merit plan, managers base employees' pay on the number of units each employee produces, whether televisions, computer components, or welded auto parts. Managers at Lincoln Electric use piece-rate pay to determine individual pay levels. Advances in information technology have dramatically simplified the administration of piece-rate pay in a variety of industries.

Using *commission pay,* another individual-based merit pay plan, managers base pay on a percentage of sales. Managers at the successful real estate company Re/Max International Inc. use commission pay for their agents, who are paid a percentage of their sales. Some department stores, such as Neiman Marcus, use commission pay for their salespeople.

Examples of organizational-based merit pay plans include the Scanlon plan and profit sharing. The *Scanlon plan* (developed by Joseph Scanlon, a union leader in a steel and tin plant in the 1920s) focuses on reducing expenses or cutting costs; members of an organization are motivated to propose and implement cost-cutting strategies because a percentage of the cost savings achieved during a specified time is distributed to the employees.[92] Under *profit sharing,* employees receive a share of an organization's profits. Regardless of the specific kind of plan that is used, managers should always strive to link pay to the performance of behaviors that help an organization achieve its goals.

Japanese managers in large corporations have long shunned merit pay plans in favor of plans that reward seniority. However, more and more Japanese companies are adopting merit-based pay due to its motivational benefits; among such companies are SiteDesign,[93] Tokio Marine and Fire Insurance, and Hissho Iwai, a trading organization.[94]

Summary and Review

THE NATURE OF MOTIVATION Motivation encompasses the psychological forces within a person that determine the direction of the person's behavior in an organization, the person's level of effort, and the person's level of persistence in the face of obstacles. Managers strive to motivate people to contribute their inputs to an organization, to focus these inputs in the direction of high performance, and to ensure that people receive the outcomes they desire when they perform at a high level. **[LO 9-1]**

EXPECTANCY THEORY According to expectancy theory, managers can promote high levels of motivation in their organizations by taking steps to ensure that expectancy is high (people think that if they try, they can perform at a high level), instrumentality is high (people think that if they perform at a high level, they will receive certain outcomes), and valence is high (people desire these outcomes). **[LO 9-2]**

NEED THEORIES Need theories suggest that to motivate their workforces, managers should determine what needs people are trying to satisfy in organizations and then ensure that people receive outcomes that satisfy these needs when they perform at a high level and contribute to organizational effectiveness. **[LO 9-3]**

EQUITY THEORY According to equity theory, managers can promote high levels of motivation by ensuring that people perceive that there is equity in the organization or that outcomes are distributed in proportion to inputs. Equity exists when a person perceives that his or her own outcome–input ratio equals the outcome–input ratio of a referent. Inequity motivates people to try to restore equity. **[LO 9-2]**

GOAL-SETTING THEORY Goal-setting theory suggests that managers can promote high motivation and performance by ensuring that people are striving to achieve specific, difficult goals. It is important for people to accept the goals, be committed to them, and receive feedback about how they are doing. **[LO 9-3]**

LEARNING THEORIES Operant conditioning theory suggests that managers can motivate people to perform highly by using positive reinforcement or negative reinforcement (positive reinforcement being the preferred strategy). Managers can motivate people to avoid performing dysfunctional behaviors by using extinction or punishment. Social learning theory suggests that people can also be motivated by observing how others perform behaviors and receive rewards, by engaging in self-reinforcement, and by having high levels of self-efficacy. **[LO 9-4]**

PAY AND MOTIVATION Each of the motivation theories discussed in this chapter alludes to the importance of pay and suggests that pay should be based on performance. Merit pay plans can be individual-, group-, or organization-based and can entail the use of salary increases or bonuses. **[LO 9-5]**

Management *in Action*

TOPICS FOR DISCUSSION AND ACTION

Discussion

1. Discuss why two people with similar abilities may have very different expectancies for performing at a high level. **[LO 9-2]**

2. Describe why some people have low instrumentalities even when their managers distribute outcomes based on performance. **[LO 9-2]**

3. Analyze how professors try to promote equity to motivate students. **[LO 9-2]**

4. Describe three techniques or procedures that managers can use to determine whether a goal is difficult. **[LO 9-3]**

5. Discuss why managers should always try to use positive reinforcement instead of negative reinforcement. **[LO 9-4]**

Action

6. Interview three people who have the same kind of job (such as salesperson, waiter/waitress, or teacher), and determine what kinds of needs each is trying to satisfy at work. **[LO 9-3]**

7. Interview a manager in an organization in your community to determine the extent to which the manager takes advantage of vicarious learning to promote high motivation among subordinates. **[LO 9-3]**

BUILDING MANAGEMENT SKILLS

Diagnosing Motivation [LO 9-1, 9-2, 9-3, 9-4]

Think about the ideal job that you would like to obtain upon graduation. Describe this job, the kind of manager you would like to report to, and the kind of organization you would be working in. Then answer the following questions.

1. What would be your levels of expectancy and instrumentality on this job? Which outcomes would have high valence for you on this job? What steps would your manager take to influence your levels of expectancy, instrumentality, and valence?

2. Whom would you choose as a referent on this job? What steps would your manager take to make you feel that you were being equitably treated? What would you do if, after a year on the job, you experienced underpayment inequity?

3. What goals would you strive to achieve on this job? Why? What role would your manager play in determining your goals?

4. What needs would you strive to satisfy on this job? Why? What role would your manager play in helping you satisfy these needs?

5. What behaviors would your manager positively reinforce on this job? Why? What positive reinforcers would your manager use?

6. Would there be any vicarious learning on this job? Why or why not?

7. To what extent would you be motivated by self-control on this job? Why?

8. What would be your level of self-efficacy on this job? Why would your self-efficacy be at this level? Should your manager take steps to boost your self-efficacy? If not, why not? If so, what would these steps be?

MANAGING ETHICALLY [LO 9-5]

Sometimes pay is so contingent upon performance that it creates stress for employees. Imagine a salesperson who knows that if sales targets are not met, she or he will not be able to make a house mortgage payment or pay the rent.

Questions

1. Either individually or in a group, think about the ethical implications of closely linking pay to performance.

2. Under what conditions might contingent pay be most stressful, and what steps can managers take to try to help their subordinates perform effectively and not experience excessive amounts of stress?

SMALL GROUP BREAKOUT EXERCISE

Increasing Motivation [LO 9-1, 9-2, 9-3, 9-4, 9-5]

Form groups of three or four people, and appoint one member as the spokesperson who will communicate your findings to the class when called on by the instructor. Then discuss the following scenario.

You and your partners own a chain of 15 dry-cleaning stores in a medium-size town. All of you are concerned about a problem in customer service that has surfaced recently. When any one of you spends the day, or even part of the day, in a particular store, clerks seem to provide excellent customer service, spotters make sure all stains are removed from garments, and pressers do a good job of pressing difficult items such as silk blouses. Yet during those same visits customers complain to you about such things as stains not being removed and items being poorly pressed in some of their previous orders; indeed, several customers have brought garments in to be redone. Customers also sometimes comment on having waited too long for service on previous visits. You and your partners are meeting today to address this problem.

1. Discuss the extent to which you believe that you have a motivation problem in your stores.

2. Given what you have learned in this chapter, design a plan to increase the motivation of clerks to provide prompt service to customers even when they are not being watched by a partner.

3. Design a plan to increase the motivation of spotters to remove as many stains as possible even when they are not being watched by a partner.

4. Design a plan to increase the motivation of pressers to do a top-notch job on all clothes they press, no matter how difficult.

BE THE MANAGER [LO 9-1, 9-2, 9-3, 9-4, 9-5]

You supervise a team of marketing analysts who work on different snack products in a large food products company. The marketing analysts have recently received undergraduate degrees in business or liberal arts and have been on the job between one and three years. Their responsibilities include analyzing the market for their respective products, including competitors; tracking current marketing initiatives; and planning future marketing campaigns. They also need to prepare quarterly sales and expense reports for their products and estimated budgets for the next three quarters; to prepare these reports, they need to obtain data from financial and accounting analysts assigned to their products.

When they first started on the job, you took each marketing

323

analyst through the reporting cycle, explaining what needs to be done and how to accomplish it and emphasizing the need for timely reports. Although preparing the reports can be tedious, you think the task is pretty straightforward and easily accomplished if the analysts plan ahead and allocate sufficient time for it. When reporting time approaches, you remind the analysts through e-mail messages and emphasize the need for accurate and timely reports in team meetings.

You believe this element of the analysts' jobs couldn't be more straightforward. However, at the end of each quarter, the majority of the analysts submit their reports a day or two late, and, worse yet, your own supervisor (to whom the reports are eventually given) has indicated that information is often missing and sometimes the reports contain errors. Once you started getting flak from your supervisor about this problem, you decided you had better fix things quickly. You met with the marketing analysts,

explained the problem, told them to submit the reports to you a day or two early so you could look them over, and more generally emphasized that they really needed to get their act together. Unfortunately, things have not improved much and you are spending more and more of your own time doing the reports.

Question

1. How can you motivate the analysts to ensure accurate and timely reporting?

THE NEW YORK TIMES
CASE IN THE NEWS [LO 9-1, LO 9-2, LO 9-3]
Yahoo's In-Office Policy Aims to Bolster Morale

When Marissa Mayer took over as chief executive at Yahoo last summer, she confronted a Silicon Valley campus that was very different from the one she had left at Google.

Parking lots and entire floors of cubicles were nearly empty because some employees were working as little as possible and leaving early.

Then there were the 200 or so people who had work-at-home arrangements. Although they collected Yahoo paychecks, some did little work for the company and a few had even begun their own start-ups on the side.

These were among the factors that led Ms. Mayer to announce last week that she was abolishing Yahoo's work-from-home policy, saying that to create a new culture of innovation and collaboration at the company, employees had to report to work.

The announcement ignited a national debate over workplace flexibility—and within Yahoo has inspired much water cooler conversation and some concern.

But former and current Yahoo employees said that Ms. Mayer made the decision not as a referendum on working remotely, but to address problems particular to Yahoo. They painted a picture of a company where employees were aimless and morale was low, and a bloated bureaucracy had taken Yahoo out of competition with its more nimble rivals.

"In the tech world it was such a bummer to say you worked for Yahoo," said a former senior employee who, like many Yahoo insiders, would speak only anonymously to preserve professional relationships. The employee added, "I've heard she wants to make Yahoo young and cool."

Restoring Yahoo's cool—from revitalizing behind-the-times products to reversing deteriorating morale and culture—is hard to do if people are not there, Ms. Mayer concluded. That view was reflected in Yahoo's only statement on the work-at-home policy change: "This isn't a broad industry view on working from home. This is about what is right for Yahoo, right now."

Yahoo declined to comment further.

On Monday, another ailing company, Best Buy, announced that it, too, would no longer permit employees to work remotely, reversing one of the most permissive flexible workplace policies in the business world.

Inside Yahoo, there has been mixed reaction to the policy change. Some employees said that they were able to be highly productive by working remotely, and that it helped them concentrate on work instead of the chaos inside Yahoo.

Brandon Holley, former editor of Shine, Yahoo's women's site, said she built the site and signed on big-name advertisers while she and most of her team worked from homes across the country.

"It grew very rapidly," said Ms. Holley, who is now editor of Lucky, Condé Nast's shopping magazine. "A lot of that had to do with the lack of distraction in a very distracted company."

The change to the work-at-home policy initially angered some employees who had such arrangements, and worried others who occasionally stayed home to care for a sick child or receive a delivery. Reports that Ms. Mayer built a nursery for her young son next to her office made parents working at Yahoo even angrier.

This week, the policy continued to be the topic of much discussion at the company, as people wondered aloud whether they would lose that flexibility, said employees who spoke anonymously because they were not authorized to speak to the media.

But for the most part, those employees said, those concerns have been eased by managers who assured them that the real targets of Yahoo's memo were the approximately 200 employees who work from home full time.

One manager said he told his employees, "Be here when you can. Use your best judgment. But if you have to stay home for the cable guy or because your kid is sick, do it."

Many of Yahoo's problems are visible to people outside the company. It missed the two biggest trends on the Internet—social networking and mobile. Its home page and e-mail services had become relics used by people who had never bothered to change their habits. It ceded its crown as the biggest seller of display ads to Facebook and Google. Its stock price was plummeting.

Inside the company, though, there were deeper cultural issues invisible from the outside. For Ms. Mayer's ambitious plans to turn around the company to work, employees briefed on her strategy said, she believed Yahoo needed "all hands on deck."

Jackie Reses, Yahoo's director of human resources and the author of the new policy, is an extreme example of this philosophy. She commutes to Yahoo's campus in Sunnyvale, Calif., from her home in New York, where she lives with her children.

"Morale was terrible because the company was thought to be dying," said a former manager at Yahoo, who would speak only anonymously to preserve business relationships. "When you have those root issues, an employee workforce that is not terribly motivated, it built bad habits over years."

Yahoo has withstood many changes over the years, starting with a turnover of six chief executives in five years, each with his or her own deputies and missions for the company. This led to confusion among the workforce about the company's goals and frustration that projects would be pulled midstream by a new chief executive.

The company had hired many managers to oversee new tech products, but the extra levels of management slowed product development, former employees said.

"Where Yahoo competes, with companies like Facebook churning out a new release every single day, there was a lot of bloat slowing down product decisions," the former manager said.

The new policy is the first unpopular big move Ms. Mayer has made. Yahoo insiders said they did not expect the employee and media outcry that followed.

Employees said that unlike previous chief executives, who focused outside Yahoo, she has prioritized fixing the company internally and motivating employees.

She introduced free food in the cafeterias, swapped employees' BlackBerrys for iPhones and Android phones, and started a Friday all-employee meeting where executives take questions and speak candidly.

A recent internal employee survey found that 95 percent of employees were optimistic about the company's future, a 32 percent bump from the previous survey, Ms. Mayer said in a call with analysts in January.

Résumés have begun arriving from employees at competitors like Facebook and Google, which rarely happened in the past, according to one person briefed on Yahoo hiring.

Since Ms. Mayer made food free, there are now crowds in the cafeterias, lingering to talk about new ideas, employees say— exactly what she wants to encourage by requiring people to work in the office.

"I understand why Marissa Mayer would want to call everybody back into work," Ms. Holley said. "It's kind of a necessary step."

Questions

1. How might the abolishment of Yahoo's work-from-home policy influence employee motivation?

2. Why did employee motivation appear to be low at Yahoo when Marissa Mayer took over as CEO?

3. What steps has Mayer taken to improve employee motivation at Yahoo?

4. What are the potential motivational advantages and disadvantages of work-from-home policies from expectancy, equity, and need theory perspectives?

Source: C. Cain Miller and N. Perlroth, "Yahoo's In-Office Policy Aims to Bolster Morale," *The New York Times,* March 6, 2013, B1–B2.

10

Leaders and Leadership

LEARNING OBJECTIVES

After studying this chapter, you should be able to:

1 Explain what leadership is, when leaders are effective and ineffective, and the sources of power that enable managers to be effective leaders. **[LO 10-1]**

2 Identify the traits that show the strongest relationship to leadership, the behaviors leaders engage in, and the limitations of the trait and behavior models of leadership. **[LO 10-2]**

3 Explain how contingency models of leadership enhance our understanding of

effective leadership and management in organizations. **[LO 10-3]**

4 Describe what transformational leadership is, and explain how managers can engage in it. **[LO 10-4]**

5 Characterize the relationship between gender and leadership and explain how emotional intelligence may contribute to leadership effectiveness. **[LO 10-5]**

Leapfrogs: Doreen Lorenzo knows how to empower her highly skilled employees to continually achieve more. With respect, listening, and the willingness to make changes based on feedback, Lorenzo enables Frog Design to keep its innovations one jump ahead of everyone else.

MANAGEMENT SNAPSHOT

Lorenzo Effectively Leads Frog Design

How Can a Leader Continuously Transform an Innovative Company in a Rapidly Changing Environment?

As president of Frog Design, Doreen Lorenzo is very accustomed to change.[1] In fact, the mission of Frog Design is "to change the world"; this is also part of Lorenzo's vision for the company as is doing all that can be done to keep employees passionate about this vision and mission.[2] Frog Design assists organizations with the design, engineering, and marketing of innovative services and products in a wide variety of industries ranging from personal electronics, entertainment, and media to energy, telecommunications, and health care. When Lorenzo first joined Frog, the company had around 50 employees.[3] Today, Frog Design employs over 1,000 designers, software engineers, and strategists.[4] Headquartered in San Francisco, California, Frog has offices around the world. Disney, MTV, Intel, and Microsoft, are just a few of Frog's many clients. Frog has innovated throughout its history from designing the e-commerce site that generated the most revenues in 2000 (Dell.com) to developing the

Roku digital video player.[5] And new clients continue to partner with Frog for help in creating innovative products and services.[6]

One key aspect of Lorenzo's personal leadership style is the ways she empowers employees at Frog. Frog strives to hire very creative and passionate designers, engineers, and strategists and Lorenzo recognizes the importance of giving them the autonomy to pursue big ideas. Employees often work in teams and these teams enjoy the challenge of working on difficult and interesting projects that end up going to market; they appreciate having their ideas listened to and heard.[7]

In addition to being empowered to work on projects for clients, employees at Frog are also empowered to make changes internally. For example, a few years back Frog relied on a software package for its own performance appraisal reviews. Employees griped about the package, complaining that the software was cumbersome and it took too much time to enter information into the system.[8] When employees complain about something like this at Frog, managers really listen. In the case of the performance appraisal software, Lorenzo let employees know that if they thought the program that was being used was problematic, perhaps someone could develop a better one. A Frog designer took to the task and designed new performance appraisal software. As Lorenzo puts it, "Organizations of all sizes can encourage everyone, from C-level leaders to junior hires, to pursue their convictions."[9]

Lorenzo also emphasizes the importance of communicating with and listening to employees and being genuinely concerned about their well-being. Through company-wide phone chats, town hall meetings, and visits to the studios, Lorenzo lets employees know how the company is doing and finds out what is on employees' minds. She strives to meet with employees individually so they will feel free to speak their minds and not defer to someone who might be more outgoing in a group setting. She seeks to really learn about her employees, including changes they might like to see in the workplace and about their personal lives. For example, after chatting individually with employees, she realized that many of them were having children and/or had young families. Thus, Frog has incorporated more family-oriented activities into studio life such as some studios having "kid days" when employees can bring their children to the studio for arts and crafts.[10]

While Lorenzo empowers employees, she also recognizes that she needs to provide them with the tools they need to best serve their clients. A firm believer in being honest (to both employees and clients), Lorenzo emphasizes that you cannot communicate too much information to a client.[11] Clients should know everything there is to know about their projects and should never be surprised; each client has a dedicated project website that they can access anytime and anywhere. Employees receive training in the best ways to present to clients and pitch their ideas. Lorenzo also encourages designers to have a curious mind, be willing to take risks, and have opinions that they are able to communicate and justify.[12]

A very outgoing person by nature, Lorenzo realizes how building in opportunities for people to get together during the workday in a relaxed fashion is important. Each day each Frog studio has coffee time at 4 p.m. when everyone stops working for a while and socializes.[13] In some studios they play games like ping pong, foosball, or pool. Other studios use the time differently. As Lorenzo indicates, "These are intense people. This is a time for them to take a break, talk to people they might not work with, and to listen to things."[14] At 10 a.m. meetings on Mondays at each studio, employees get together to celebrate birthdays and anniversaries as well as talk about projects and what's going on at other studios. Studios are also encouraged to develop their own rituals to enhance well-being, foster good communication, and keep passion and creativity alive. For example, employees at some studios take regular field trips.[15]

All in all, Doreen Lorenzo's approach to leadership has helped Frog Design grow and continue to change and innovate while providing a stimulating and supportive environment for creative types to flourish.[16]

Overview

Doreen Lorenzo exemplifies the many facets of effective leadership. In Chapter 1 we explained that one of the four primary tasks of managers is leading. Thus it should come as no surprise that leadership is a key ingredient in effective management. When leaders are effective, their subordinates or followers are highly motivated, committed, and high-performing. When leaders are ineffective, chances are good that their subordinates do not perform up to their capabilities, are demotivated, and may be dissatisfied as well. Doreen Lorenzo is a leader at the very top of an organization, but leadership is an important ingredient for managerial success at all levels of organizations: top management, middle management, and first-line management. Moreover, leadership is a key ingredient of managerial success for organizations large and small.

In this chapter we describe what leadership is and examine the major leadership models that shed light on the factors that contribute to a manager's being an effective leader. We look at trait and behavior models, which focus on what leaders are like and what they do, and contingency models—Fiedler's contingency model, path–goal theory, and the leader substitutes model—each of which takes into account the complexity surrounding leadership and the role of the situation in leader effectiveness. We also describe how managers can use transformational leadership to dramatically affect their organizations. By the end of this chapter, you will appreciate the many factors and issues that managers face in their quest to be effective leaders.

The Nature of Leadership

LO 10-1 Explain what leadership is, when leaders are effective and ineffective, and the sources of power that enable managers to be effective leaders.

leadership The process by which an individual exerts influence over other people and inspires, motivates, and directs their activities to help achieve group or organizational goals.

leader An individual who is able to exert influence over other people to help achieve group or organizational goals.

Leadership is the process by which a person exerts influence over other people and inspires, motivates, and directs their activities to help achieve group or organizational goals.[17] The person who exerts such influence is a **leader**. When leaders are effective, the influence they exert over others helps a group or organization achieve its performance goals. When leaders are ineffective, their influence does not contribute to, and often detracts from, goal attainment. As the "Management Snapshot" makes clear, Doreen Lorenzo is taking multiple steps to inspire and motivate Frog's employees so they help Frog Design achieve its goals.

Beyond facilitating the attainment of performance goals, effective leadership increases an organization's ability to meet all the contemporary challenges discussed throughout this book, including the need to obtain a competitive advantage, the need to foster ethical behavior, and the need to manage a diverse workforce fairly and equitably. Leaders who exert influence over organizational members to help meet these goals increase their organizations' chances of success.

In considering the nature of leadership, we first look at leadership styles and how they affect managerial tasks and at the influence of culture on leadership styles. We then focus on the key to leadership, *power*, which can come from a variety of sources. Finally we consider the contemporary dynamic of empowerment and how it relates to effective leadership.

Personal Leadership Style and Managerial Tasks

A manager's *personal leadership style*—that is, the specific ways in which a manager chooses to influence other people—shapes how that manager approaches planning, organizing, and controlling (the other principal tasks of managing). Consider Doreen Lorenzo's personal leadership style in the "Management Snapshot": She empowers employees, emphasizes being open and honest with employees and clients alike, fosters open two-way communication, and really cares about the well-being of employees and fostering their creativity and passion.

Managers at all levels and in all kinds of organizations have their own personal leadership styles that determine not only how they lead their subordinates but also how they perform the other management tasks. Michael Kraus, owner and manager of a dry cleaning store in the northeastern United States, for example, takes a hands-on approach to leadership. He has the sole authority for determining work schedules and job assignments for the 15 employees in his store (an organizing task), makes all important decisions by himself (a planning task), and closely monitors his employees' performance and rewards top performers with pay increases (a control task). Kraus's personal leadership style is effective in his organization. His employees generally are motivated, perform highly, and are satisfied; and his store is highly profitable.

Developing an effective personal leadership style often is a challenge for managers at all levels in an organization. This challenge is often exacerbated when times are tough, due, for example, to an economic downturn or a decline in customer demand. The recession in the late 2000s provided many managers with just such a challenge.

Although leading is one of the four principal tasks of managing, a distinction is often made between managers and leaders. When this distinction is made, managers are thought of as those organizational members who establish and implement procedures and processes to ensure smooth functioning and are accountable for goal accomplishment.[18] Leaders look to the future, chart the course for the organization, and attract, retain, motivate, inspire, and develop relationships with employees based on trust and mutual respect.[19] Leaders provide meaning and purpose, seek innovation rather than stability, and impassion employees to work together to achieve the leaders' vision.[20]

As part of their personal leadership style, some leaders strive to truly serve others. Robert Greenleaf, who was director of management research at AT&T and upon his retirement in 1964 embarked on a second career focused on writing, speaking, and consulting, came up with the term *servant leadership* to describe these leaders.[21] Servant leaders, above all else, have a strong desire to serve and work for the benefit of others.[22] Servant leaders share power with followers and strive to ensure that followers' most important needs are met, they are able to develop as individuals, and their well-being is enhanced, and that attention is paid to those who are least well-off in a society.[23] Greenleaf founded a nonprofit organization called the Greenleaf Center for Servant Leadership (formerly called the Center for Applied Ethics) to foster leadership focused on service to others, power sharing, and a sense of community between organizations and their multiple stakeholders.[24] Some entrepreneurs strive to incorporate servant leadership into their personal leadership styles, as profiled in the following "Ethics in Action" box.

servant leader

A leader who has a strong desire to serve and work for the benefit of others.

ETHICS IN ACTION

Servant Leadership at Zingerman's

Ari Weinzweig and Paul Saginaw founded Zingerman's Delicatessen in Ann Arbor, Michigan, in 1982.[25] Food lovers at heart, Weinzweig and Saginaw delighted in finding both traditional and exotic foods from around the world, making delicious sandwiches to order, and having extensive selections of food items ranging from olives, oils, and vinegars to cheeses, smoked fish, and salami. As their business grew, and to maintain an intimate atmosphere with excellent customer service, Weinzweig and Saginaw expanded from their original deli into a community of related businesses called Zingerman's Community of Businesses. In addition to the original deli, Zingerman's Community of Businesses now includes a mail-order business, a bakery, a catering business, a creamery, a restaurant, a wholesale coffee business, and a training business and has combined annual sales of around $36 million.[26] From the start, Weinzweig and Saginaw have been devoted to excellent customer service, great food, and a commitment to people and community.[27]

Paul Saginaw (left) and Ari Weinzweig have incorporated servant leadership into their personal leadership styles at Zingerman's.

As part of their commitment to people and community, Weinzweig and Saginaw have incorporated servant leadership into their personal leadership styles. As their business has grown and prospered, they have realized that increasing success means greater responsibility to serve others. They strive to treat their employees as well as they treat their customers and give their employees opportunities for growth and development on the job. They have also realized that when their own needs or desires differ from what is best for their company, they should do what is best for the company.[28]

To this day, the cofounders encourage their employees to let them know how they can help them and what they can do for them. And given Zingerman's culture of mutual respect and trust, employees do not hesitate to communicate how their leaders can serve them in many and varied ways. For example, when Weinzweig visited the Zingerman's Roadhouse restaurant and the staff was very busy, they asked him to help out by serving customers or cleaning off tables. As he indicated, "People give me assignments all the time. Sometimes I'm the note-taker. Sometimes I'm the cleaner-upper. . . . Sometimes I'm on my hands and knees wiping up what people spilled."[29]

Weinzweig and Saginaw also have a strong sense of commitment to serving the local community; Zingerman's founded the nonprofit organization Food Gatherers to eliminate hunger and distribute food to the needy, and Food Gatherers is now an independent nonprofit responsible for the Washtenaw County Food Bank with over 5,000 volunteers and a 22-member staff.[30] On Zingerman's 20th anniversary, 13 nonprofit community organizations in Ann Arbor erected a plaque next to Zingerman's Delicatessen with a dedication that read, "Thank you for feeding, sheltering, educating, uplifting, and inspiring an entire community."[31] Clearly, for Weinzweig and Saginaw, leadership entails being of service to others.[32]

Leadership Styles across Cultures

Some evidence suggests that leadership styles vary not only among individuals but also among countries or cultures. Some research indicates that European managers tend to be more humanistic or people-oriented than both Japanese and American managers. The collectivistic culture in Japan places prime emphasis on the group rather than the individual, so the importance of individuals' own personalities, needs, and desires is minimized. Organizations in the United States tend to be very profit-oriented and thus tend to downplay the importance of individual employees' needs and desires. The cultures of many countries in Europe have a more individualistic perspective than Japan and a more humanistic perspective than the United States, and it is this that may result in European managers' being more people-oriented than their Japanese or American counterparts. European managers, for example, tend to be reluctant to lay off employees, and when a layoff is absolutely necessary, they take careful steps to make it as painless as possible.[33]

Another cross-cultural difference occurs in time horizons. While managers in any one country often differ in their time horizons, there are also national differences. For example, U.S. organizations tend to have a short-term profit orientation, and thus U.S. managers' personal leadership styles emphasize short-term performance. Japanese organizations tend to have a long-term growth orientation, so Japanese managers' personal leadership styles emphasize long-term performance. Justus Mische, a personnel manager at the European organization Hoechst, suggests that "Europe, at least the big international firms in Europe, have a philosophy between the Japanese, long term, and the United States, short term."[34] Research on these and other global aspects of leadership is in its infancy; as it continues, more cultural differences in managers' personal leadership styles may be discovered.

Power: The Key to Leadership

No matter what one's leadership style, a key component of effective leadership is found in the *power* the leader has to affect other people's behavior and get them to act in certain ways.[35] There are several types of power: legitimate, reward, coercive, expert, and referent power (see Figure 10.1).[36] Effective leaders take steps to ensure that they have sufficient levels of each type and that they use the power they have in beneficial ways.

legitimate power The authority that a manager has by virtue of his or her position in an organization's hierarchy.

LEGITIMATE POWER Legitimate power is the authority a manager has by virtue of his or her position in organization's hierarchy. Personal leadership style often influences how a manager exercises legitimate power. Take the case of Carol Loray, who is a first-line manager in a greeting card company and leads a group of 15 artists and designers. Loray has the legitimate power to hire new employees, assign projects to the artists and designers, monitor their work, and appraise their performance. She uses this power effectively. She always makes sure her project assignments match the interests of her subordinates as much as possible so they will enjoy their work. She monitors their work to make sure they are on track but does not engage in close supervision, which can hamper creativity. She makes sure her performance appraisals are developmental, providing concrete advice for areas where improvements could be made. Recently Loray negotiated with

Figure 10.1
Sources of Managerial
Power

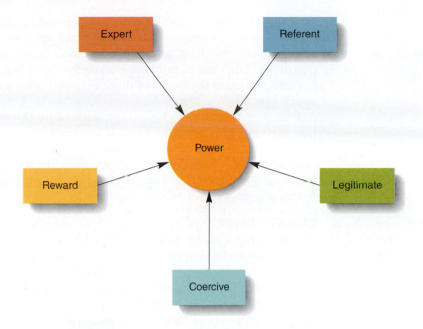

her manager to increase her legitimate power so she can now initiate and develop proposals for new card lines.

reward power The ability of a manager to give or withhold tangible and intangible rewards.

REWARD POWER Reward power is the ability of a manager to give or withhold tangible rewards (pay raises, bonuses, choice job assignments) and intangible rewards (verbal praise, a pat on the back, respect). As you learned in Chapter 9, members of an organization are motivated to perform at a high level by a variety of rewards. Being able to give or withhold rewards based on performance is a major source of power that allows managers to have a highly motivated workforce. Managers of salespeople in retail organizations like Neiman Marcus, Nordstrom, and Macy's[37] and in car dealerships such as Mazda, Ford, and Volvo often use their reward power to motivate their subordinates. Subordinates in organizations such as these often receive commissions on whatever they sell and rewards for the quality of their customer service, which motivate them to do the best they can.

Effective managers use their reward power to show appreciation for subordinates' good work and efforts. Ineffective managers use rewards in a more controlling manner (wielding the "stick" instead of offering the "carrot") that signals to subordinates that the manager has the upper hand. Managers also can take steps to increase their reward power.

coercive power The ability of a manager to punish others.

COERCIVE POWER Coercive power is the ability of a manager to punish others. Punishment can range from verbal reprimands to reductions in pay or working hours to actual dismissal. In the previous chapter we discussed how punishment can have negative side effects, such as resentment and retaliation, and should be used only when necessary (for example, to curtail a dangerous behavior). Managers who rely heavily on coercive power tend to be ineffective as leaders and sometimes even get fired themselves. William J. Fife is one example; he was fired from his position as CEO of Giddings and Lewis Inc., a manufacturer of factory equipment, because of his overreliance on coercive power. In meetings Fife often verbally criticized, attacked, and embarrassed top managers. Realizing how destructive Fife's use of punishment was for them and the company, these managers complained to the board of directors, who, after a careful consideration of the issues, asked Fife to resign.[38]

Excessive use of coercive power seldom produces high performance and is questionable ethically. Sometimes it amounts to a form of mental abuse, robbing workers of their dignity and causing excessive levels of stress. Overuse of coercive power can even result in dangerous working conditions. Better results and, importantly, an ethical workplace that respects employee dignity can be obtained by using reward power.

expert power Power that is based on the special knowledge, skills, and expertise that a leader possesses.

EXPERT POWER Expert power is based on the special knowledge, skills, and expertise that a leader possesses. The nature of expert power varies, depending on the leader's level in the hierarchy. First-level and middle managers often have technical expertise relevant to the tasks their subordinates perform. Their expert power gives them considerable influence over subordinates. Doreen Lorenzo in the "Management Snapshot" has expert power from being an effective leader at Frog Design for over 14 years. As indicated in the following "Manager as a Person" box, managers with expert power nonetheless need to recognize that they are not always right and seek and encourage input from others.

MANAGER AS A PERSON

Gregory Maffei and Expert Power

Gregory Maffei is the president and chief executive officer of Liberty Media Corporation, which has operations in the communications, e-commerce, media, technology, and entertainment industries.[39] Liberty owns or has interests in a variety of companies in these industries, such as SiriusXM, Live Nation, True Position, Inc., Expedia, QVC, HSN, Starz, Red Envelope, Evite, ProFlowers, backcountry.com, Barnes & Noble, bodybuilding.com, and the Atlanta National League Baseball Club, Inc.[40]

Judging from his background and experience, Maffei would certainly appear to possess considerable amounts of expert power. With a bachelor's degree from Dartmouth College and an MBA from the Harvard Business School, Maffei held a number of important leadership positions before joining Liberty.[41] For example, he worked with Bill Gates as the chief financial officer of Microsoft and

Polling the experts gives Gregory Maffei the extra information and know-how to succeed. Rather than assuming his experience and knowledge guarantee being right, Maffei asks for help to make sure no stone is left unturned.

was the chairman of Expedia, the chairman and CEO of 360networks, and the president and chief financial officer for Oracle.[42] He is active in terms of serving on boards of directors and also in the community. For example, he was the president of the Seattle Public Library and currently heads up the budget task force for the governor of Colorado.[43]

Interestingly enough, Maffei is the first to admit that he often doesn't have all the answers.[44] In fact, when he worked with Bill Gates, he realized that Gates often sought input from others and never thought that his ideas were necessarily the right ideas just because he had them.[45] Rather, Gates would ask other managers what they thought about his ideas. Maffei realizes the value of getting multiple inputs on ideas and having two-way conversations in which everyone feels free to speak their minds and ask probing questions, even if it is of the CEO. The first manager Maffei promoted at Liberty was a colleague who would consistently question and sometimes critique his ideas; having valuable insights, Maffei recognized how constructive the exchanges of ideas were with this manager. And he strives to have all employees feel comfortable asking him questions and having a two-way conversation with him.[46] While expert power has certainly helped Maffei as CEO of Liberty, so too has his recognition that he is not always right just because he is CEO.[47]

Some top managers derive expert power from their technical expertise. Craig Barrett, chairman of the board of directors of Intel from 2005 to 2009, has a PhD in materials science from Stanford University and is very knowledgeable about the ins and outs of Intel's business—producing semiconductors and microprocessors.[48] Similarly, Bill Gates, chairman of Microsoft, and CEO Steve Ballmer have expertise in software design; and Tachi Yamada, former president of the Bill and Melinda Gates Foundation's Global Health Program and former chairman of research and development at GlaxoSmithKline, has an MD.[49] Many top-level managers, however, lack technical expertise and derive their expert power from their abilities as decision makers, planners, and strategists. Jack Welch, the former well-known leader and CEO of General Electric, summed it up this way: "The basic thing that we at the top of the company know is that we don't know the business. What we have, I hope, is the ability to allocate resources, people, and dollars."[50]

Effective leaders take steps to ensure that they have an adequate amount of expert power to perform their leadership roles. They may obtain additional training or education in their fields, make sure they keep up with the latest developments and changes in technology, stay abreast of changes in their fields through involvement in professional associations, and read widely to be aware of momentous changes in the organization's task and general environments. Expert power tends to be best used in a guiding or coaching manner rather than in an arrogant, high-handed manner.

referent power
Power that comes from subordinates' and coworkers' respect, admiration, and loyalty.

REFERENT POWER Referent power is more informal than the other kinds of power. Referent power is a function of the personal characteristics of a leader; it is the power that comes from subordinates' and coworkers' respect, admiration, and loyalty. Leaders who are likable and whom subordinates wish to use as a role model are especially likely to possess referent power, as is true of Doreen Lorenzo in the "Management Snapshot."

In addition to being a valuable asset for top managers like Lorenzo, referent power can help first-line and middle managers be effective leaders as well. Sally Carruthers, for example, is the first-level manager of a group of secretaries in the finance department of a large state university. Carruthers's secretaries are known to be among the best in the university. Much of their willingness to go above and beyond the call of duty has been attributed to Carruthers's warm and caring nature, which makes each of them feel important and valued. Managers can take steps to increase their referent power, such as taking time to get to know their subordinates and showing interest in and concern for them.

Empowerment: An Ingredient in Modern Management

empowerment The expansion of employees' knowledge, tasks, and decision-making responsibilities.

More and more managers today are incorporating into their personal leadership styles an aspect that at first glance seems to be the opposite of being a leader. In Chapter 1 we described how empowerment—the process of giving employees at all levels the authority to make decisions, be responsible for their outcomes, improve quality, and cut costs—is becoming increasingly popular in organizations. When leaders empower their subordinates, the subordinates typically take over some responsibilities and authority that used to reside with the leader or manager, such as the right to reject parts that do not meet quality standards, the right to check one's own work, and the right to schedule work activities. Empowered subordinates are given the power to make some decisions that their leaders or supervisors used to make.

Empowerment might seem to be the opposite of effective leadership because managers are allowing subordinates to take a more active role in leading themselves. In actuality, however, empowerment can contribute to effective leadership for several reasons:

- Empowerment increases a manager's ability to get things done because the manager has the support and help of subordinates who may have special knowledge of work tasks.

- Empowerment often increases workers' involvement, motivation, and commitment; and this helps ensure that they are working toward organizational goals.

- Empowerment gives managers more time to concentrate on their pressing concerns because they spend less time on day-to-day supervision.

Effective managers like Doreen Lorenzo realize the benefits of empowerment. The personal leadership style of managers who empower subordinates often entails developing subordinates' ability to make good decisions as well as being their guide, coach, and source of inspiration. Empowerment is a popular trend in the United States and is a part of servant leadership. Empowerment is also taking off around the world.[51] For instance, companies in South Korea (such as Samsung, Hyundai, and Daewoo), in which decision making typically was centralized with the founding families, are now empowering managers at lower levels to make decisions.[52]

An empowered employee, like this auto assembly line worker, can halt the production process to correct an error rather than wasting time and money by waiting for a supervisor.

Trait and Behavior Models of Leadership

Leading is such an important process in all organizations—nonprofit organizations, government agencies, and schools, as well as for-profit corporations—that it has been researched for decades. Early approaches to leadership, called the *trait model* and the *behavior model*, sought to determine what effective leaders are like as people and what they do that makes them so effective.

The Trait Model

The trait model of leadership focused on identifying the personal characteristics that cause effective leadership. Researchers thought effective leaders must have certain personal qualities that set them apart from ineffective leaders and from people who never become leaders. Decades of research (beginning in the 1930s) and hundreds of studies indicate that certain personal characteristics do appear to be associated with effective leadership. (See Table 10.1 for a list of these.)[53] Notice that although this model is called the "trait" model, some of the personal characteristics that it identifies are not personality traits per se but, rather, are concerned with a leader's skills, abilities, knowledge, and expertise. As the "Management Snapshot" shows, Doreen Lorenzo certainly appears to possess many of these characteristics (such as intelligence, knowledge and expertise, self-confidence, high energy, and integrity and honesty). Leaders who do not possess these traits may be ineffective.

Traits alone are not the key to understanding leader effectiveness, however. Some effective leaders do not possess all these traits, and some leaders who possess them are not effective in their leadership roles. This lack of a consistent relationship between leader traits and leader effectiveness led researchers to shift their attention away from traits and to search for new explanations for effective

Table 10.1

Traits and Personal Characteristics Related to Effective Leadership

Trait	Description
Intelligence	Helps managers understand complex issues and solve problems.
Knowledge and expertise	Help managers make good decisions and discover ways to increase efficiency and effectiveness.
Dominance	Helps managers influence their subordinates to achieve organizational goals.
Self-confidence	Contributes to managers' effectively influencing subordinates and persisting when faced with obstacles or difficulties.
High energy	Helps managers deal with the many demands they face.
Tolerance for stress	Helps managers deal with uncertainty and make difficult decisions.
Integrity and honesty	Help managers behave ethically and earn their subordinates' trust and confidence.
Maturity	Helps managers avoid acting selfishly, control their feelings, and admit when they have made a mistake.

leadership. Rather than focusing on what leaders are like (the traits they possess), researchers began looking at what effective leaders actually do—in other words, at the behaviors that allow effective leaders to influence their subordinates to achieve group and organizational goals.

The Behavior Model

After extensive study in the 1940s and 1950s, researchers at The Ohio State University identified two basic kinds of leader behaviors that many leaders in the United States, Germany, and other countries engaged in to influence their subordinates: *consideration* and *initiating structure*.[54]

consideration
Behavior indicating that a manager trusts, respects, and cares about subordinates.

CONSIDERATION Leaders engage in consideration when they show their subordinates that they trust, respect, and care about them. Managers who truly look out for the well-being of their subordinates, and do what they can to help subordinates feel good and enjoy their work, perform consideration behaviors. In the "Management Snapshot," Doreen Lorenzo engages in consideration when she communicates with and listens to employees and ensures that their concerns are being addressed and that they have opportunities to socialize and relax.

initiating structure
Behavior that managers engage in to ensure that work gets done, subordinates perform their jobs acceptably, and the organization is efficient and effective.

INITIATING STRUCTURE Leaders engage in initiating structure when they take steps to make sure that work gets done, subordinates perform their jobs acceptably, and the organization is efficient and effective. Assigning tasks to individuals or work groups, letting subordinates know what is expected of them, deciding how work should be done, making schedules, encouraging adherence to rules and regulations, and motivating subordinates to do a good job are all examples of initiating structure.[55]

Michael Teckel, the manager of an upscale store selling imported men's and women's shoes in a midwestern city, engages in initiating structure when he establishes weekly work, lunch, and break schedules to ensure that the store has enough salespeople on the floor. Teckel also initiates structure when he discusses the latest shoe designs with his subordinates so they are knowledgeable with customers, when he encourages adherence to the store's refund and exchange policies, and when he encourages his staff to provide high-quality customer service and to avoid a hard-sell approach.

Initiating structure and consideration are independent leader behaviors. Leaders can be high on both, low on both, or high on one and low on the other. Many effective leaders, like Doreen Lorenzo of Frog Design, engage in both of these behaviors.

You might expect that effective leaders and managers would perform both kinds of behaviors, but research has found that this is not necessarily the case. The relationship between performance of consideration and initiating-structure behaviors and leader effectiveness is not clear-cut. Some leaders are effective even when they do not perform consideration or initiating-structure behaviors, and some leaders are ineffective even when they perform both kinds of behaviors. Like the trait model of leadership, the behavior model alone cannot explain leader effectiveness. Realizing this, researchers began building more complicated models of leadership, focused not only on the leader and what he or she does but also on the situation or context in which leadership occurs.

Contingency Models of Leadership

LO 10-3 Explain how contingency models of leadership enhance our understanding of effective leadership and management in organizations.

Simply possessing certain traits or performing certain behaviors does not ensure that a manager will be an effective leader in all situations calling for leadership. Some managers who seem to possess the right traits and perform the right behaviors turn out to be ineffective leaders. Managers lead in a wide variety of situations and organizations and have various kinds of subordinates performing diverse tasks in a multiplicity of environmental contexts. Given the wide variety of situations in which leadership occurs, what makes a manager an effective leader in one situation (such as certain traits or behaviors) is not necessarily what that manager needs to be equally effective in a different situation. An effective army general might not be an effective university president; an effective restaurant manager might not be an effective clothing store manager; an effective football team coach might not be an effective fitness center manager; and an effective first-line manager in a manufacturing company might not be an effective middle manager. The traits or behaviors that may contribute to a manager's being an effective leader in one situation might actually result in the same manager being an ineffective leader in another situation.

Contingency models of leadership take into account the situation or context within which leadership occurs. According to contingency models, whether a manager is an effective leader is the result of the interplay between what the manager is like, what he or she does, and the situation in which leadership takes place. Contingency models propose that whether a leader who possesses certain traits or performs certain behaviors is effective depends on, or is contingent on, the situation or context. In this section we discuss three prominent contingency models developed to shed light on what makes managers effective leaders: Fred Fiedler's contingency model, Robert House's path–goal theory, and the leader substitutes model. As you will see, these leadership models are complementary; each focuses on a somewhat different aspect of effective leadership in organizations.

Fiedler's Contingency Model

Fred E. Fiedler was among the first leadership researchers to acknowledge that effective leadership is contingent on, or depends on, the characteristics of the leader *and* of the situation. Fiedler's contingency model helps explain why a manager may be an effective leader in one situation and ineffective in another; it also suggests which kinds of managers are likely to be most effective in which situations.[56]

LEADER STYLE As with the trait approach, Fiedler hypothesized that personal characteristics can influence leader effectiveness. He used the term *leader style* to refer to a manager's characteristic approach to leadership and identified two basic leader styles: *relationship-oriented* and *task-oriented*. All managers can be described as having one style or the other.

relationship-oriented leaders Leaders whose primary concern is to develop good relationships with their subordinates and to be liked by them.

Relationship-oriented leaders are primarily concerned with developing good relationships with their subordinates and being liked by them. Relationship-oriented managers focus on having high-quality interpersonal relationships with subordinates. This does not mean, however, that the job does not get done when such leaders are at the helm. But it does mean that the quality of interpersonal relationships with subordinates is a prime concern for relationship-oriented leaders.

task-oriented leaders Leaders whose primary concern is to ensure that subordinates perform at a high level.

Task-oriented leaders are primarily concerned with ensuring that subordinates perform at a high level and focus on task accomplishment. While task-oriented leaders also may be concerned about having good interpersonal relationships with their subordinates, task accomplishment is their prime concern.

SITUATIONAL CHARACTERISTICS According to Fiedler, leadership style is an enduring characteristic; managers cannot change their style, nor can they adopt different styles in different kinds of situations. With this in mind, Fiedler identified three situational characteristics that are important determinants of how favorable a situation is for leading: leader–member relations, task structure, and position power. When a situation is favorable for leading, it is relatively easy for a manager to influence subordinates so they perform at a high level and contribute to organizational efficiency and effectiveness. In a situation unfavorable for leading, it is much more difficult for a manager to exert influence.

Leader–Member Relations   The first situational characteristic Fiedler described, leader–member relations, is the extent to which followers like, trust, and are loyal to their leader. Situations are more favorable for leading when leader–member relations are good.

leader-member relations The extent to which followers like, trust, and are loyal to their leader; a determinant of how favorable a situation is for leading.

Task Structure   The second situational characteristic Fiedler described, task structure, is the extent to which the work to be performed is clear-cut so that a leader's subordinates know what needs to be accomplished and how to go about doing it. When task structure is high, the situation is favorable for leading. When task structure is low, goals may be vague, subordinates may be unsure of what they should be doing or how they should do it, and the situation is unfavorable for leading.

Task structure was low for Geraldine Laybourne when she was a top manager at Nickelodeon, the children's television network. It was never precisely clear what would appeal to her young viewers, whose tastes can change dramatically, or how to motivate her subordinates to come up with creative and novel ideas.[57] In contrast, Herman Mashaba, founder of Black Like Me, a hair care products company based in South Africa, seemed to have relatively high task structure when he started his company. His company's goals were to produce and sell inexpensive hair care products to native Africans, and managers accomplished these goals by using simple yet appealing packaging and distributing the products through neighborhood beauty salons.[58]

task structure The extent to which the work to be performed is clear-cut so that a leader's subordinates know what needs to be accomplished and how to go about doing it; a determinant of how favorable a situation is for leading.

position power The amount of legitimate, reward, and coercive power that a leader has by virtue of his or her position in an organization; a determinant of how favorable a situation is for leading.

Position Power   The third situational characteristic Fiedler described, position power, is the amount of legitimate, reward, and coercive power a leader has by virtue of his or her position in an organization. Leadership situations are more favorable for leading when position power is strong.

COMBINING LEADER STYLE AND THE SITUATION By considering all possible combinations of good and poor leader–member relations, high and low task structure, and strong and weak position power, Fiedler identified eight leadership situations, which vary in their favorability for leading (see Figure 10.2). After extensive research, he determined that relationship-oriented leaders are most effective in moderately favorable situations (IV, V, VI, and VII in Figure 10.2) and task-oriented leaders are most effective in situations that are either very favorable (I, II, and III) or very unfavorable (VIII).

Figure 10.2

Fiedler's Contingency Theory of Leadership

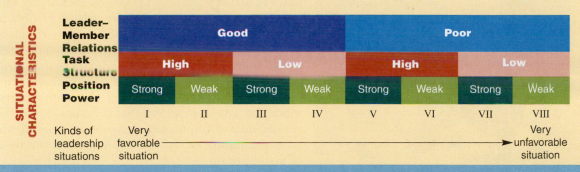

Leader–Member Relations	**Good**				**Poor**			
Task Structure	**High**		**Low**		**High**		**Low**	
Position Power	Strong	Weak	Strong	Weak	Strong	Weak	Strong	Weak
	I	II	III	IV	V	VI	VII	VIII

SITUATIONAL CHARACTERISTICS

Kinds of leadership situations

Very favorable situation ⟶ Very unfavorable situation

Relationship-oriented leaders are most effective in moderately favorable situations for leading (IV, V, VI, VII).
Task-oriented leaders are most effective in very favorable situations (I, II, III) or very unfavorable situations (VIII) for leading.

PUTTING THE CONTINGENCY MODEL INTO PRACTICE Recall that, according to Fiedler, leader style is an enduring characteristic that managers cannot change. This suggests that for managers to be effective, either managers need to be placed in leadership situations that fit their style or situations need to be changed to suit the managers. Situations can be changed, for example, by giving a manager more position power or taking steps to increase task structure, such as by clarifying goals.

Take the case of Mark Compton, a relationship-oriented leader employed by a small construction company, who was in a very unfavorable situation and was having a rough time leading his construction crew. His subordinates did not trust him to look out for their well-being (poor leader–member relations); the construction jobs he supervised tended to be novel and complex (low task structure); and he had no control over the rewards and disciplinary actions his subordinates received (weak position power). Recognizing the need to improve matters, Compton's supervisor gave him the power to reward crew members with bonuses and overtime work as he saw fit and to discipline crew members for poor-quality work and unsafe on-the-job behavior. As his leadership situation improved to moderately favorable, so too did Compton's effectiveness as a leader and the performance of his crew.

Research studies tend to support some aspects of Fiedler's model but also suggest that, like most theories, it needs some modifications.[59] Some researchers have questioned what the LPC scale really measures. Others find fault with the model's premise that leaders cannot alter their styles. That is, it is likely that at least some leaders can diagnose the situation they are in and, when their style is inappropriate for the situation, modify their style so that it is more in line with what the leadership situation calls for.

House's Path–Goal Theory

In what he called path–goal theory, leadership researcher Robert House focused on what leaders can do to motivate their subordinates to achieve group and

path-goal theory A contingency model of leadership proposing that leaders can motivate subordinates by identifying their desired outcomes, rewarding them for high performance and the attainment of work goals with these desired outcomes, and clarifying for them the paths leading to the attainment of work goals.

You could stand over your subordinate and berate him or you could empower him to find the solution by working to see where the issue developed. Supportive managers make a world of difference in retaining and motivating employees.

organizational goals.[60] The premise of path–goal theory is that effective leaders motivate subordinates to achieve goals by (1) clearly identifying the outcomes that subordinates are trying to obtain from the workplace, (2) rewarding subordinates with these outcomes for high performance and the attainment of work goals, and (3) clarifying for subordinates the *paths* leading to the attainment of work *goals*. Path–goal theory is a contingency model because it proposes that the steps managers should take to motivate subordinates depend on both the nature of the subordinates and the type of work they do.

Path–goal theory identifies four kinds of leadership behaviors that motivate subordinates:

- *Directive behaviors* are similar to initiating structure and include setting goals, assigning tasks, showing subordinates how to complete tasks, and taking concrete steps to improve performance.

- *Supportive behaviors* are similar to consideration and include expressing concern for subordinates and looking out for their best interests.

- *Participative behaviors* give subordinates a say in matters and decisions that affect them.

- *Achievement-oriented behaviors* motivate subordinates to perform at the highest level possible by, for example, setting challenging goals, expecting that they be met, and believing in subordinates' capabilities.

Which of these behaviors should managers use to lead effectively? The answer to this question depends, or is contingent on, the nature of the subordinates and the kind of work they do.

Directive behaviors may be beneficial when subordinates are having difficulty completing assigned tasks, but they might be detrimental when subordinates are independent thinkers who work best when left alone. *Supportive* behaviors are often advisable when subordinates are experiencing high levels of stress. *Participative* behaviors can be particularly effective when subordinates' support of a decision is required. *Achievement-oriented* behaviors may increase motivation levels of highly capable subordinates who are bored from having too few challenges, but they might backfire if used with subordinates who are already pushed to their limit.

The Leader Substitutes Model

leadership substitute

A characteristic of a subordinate or of a situation or context that acts in place of the influence of a leader and makes leadership unnecessary.

The leader substitutes model suggests that leadership is sometimes unnecessary because substitutes for leadership are present. A leadership substitute is something that acts in place of the influence of a leader and makes leadership unnecessary. This model suggests that under certain conditions managers do not have to play a leadership role—members of an organization sometimes can perform at a high level without a manager exerting influence over them.[61] The leader substitutes model is a contingency model because it suggests that in some situations leadership is unnecessary.

Take the case of David Cotsonas, who teaches English at a foreign language school in Cyprus, an island in the Mediterranean Sea. Cotsonas is fluent in Greek, English, and French; is an excellent teacher; and is highly motivated. Many of his students are businesspeople who have some rudimentary English skills and wish to increase their fluency to be able to conduct more of their business in English. He enjoys not only teaching them English but also learning about the work they do, and he often keeps in touch with his students after they finish his classes. Cotsonas meets with the director of the school twice a year to discuss semiannual class schedules and enrollments.

With practically no influence from a leader, Cotsonas is a highly motivated top performer at the school. In his situation, leadership is unnecessary because substitutes for leadership are present. Cotsonas's teaching expertise, his motivation, and his enjoyment of his work are substitutes for the influence of a leader—in this case the school's director. If the school's director were to try to influence how Cotsonas performs his job, Cotsonas would probably resent this infringement on his autonomy, and it is unlikely that his performance would improve because he is already one of the school's best teachers.

As in Cotsonas's case, *characteristics of subordinates*—such as their skills, abilities, experience, knowledge, and motivation—can be substitutes for leadership.[62] *Characteristics of the situation or context*—such as the extent to which the work is interesting and enjoyable—also can be substitutes. When work is interesting and enjoyable, as it is for Cotsonas, jobholders do not need to be coaxed into performing because performing is rewarding in its own right. Similarly, when managers *empower* their subordinates or use *self-managed work teams* (discussed in detail in Chapter 11), the need for leadership influence from a manager is decreased because team members manage themselves.

Substitutes for leadership can increase organizational efficiency and effectiveness because they free up some of managers' valuable time and allow managers to focus their efforts on discovering new ways to improve organizational effectiveness. The director of the language school, for example, was able to spend much of his time making arrangements to open a second school in Rhodes, an island in the Aegean Sea, because of the presence of leadership substitutes, not only for Cotsonas but for most other teachers at the school as well.

Bringing It All Together

Effective leadership in organizations occurs when managers take steps to lead in a way that is appropriate for the situation or context in which leadership occurs and for the subordinates who are being led. The three contingency models of leadership just discussed help managers focus on the necessary ingredients for effective leadership. They are complementary in that each one looks at the leadership question from a different angle. Fiedler's contingency model explores how a manager's leadership style needs to be matched to that person's leadership situation for maximum effectiveness. House's path–goal theory focuses on how managers should motivate subordinates and describes the specific kinds of behaviors managers can engage in to have a highly motivated workforce. The leadership substitutes model alerts managers to the fact that sometimes they do not need to exert influence over subordinates and thus can free up their time for other important activities. Table 10.2 recaps these three contingency models of leadership.

Table 10.2

Contingency Models of Leadership

Model	Focus	Key Contingencies
Fiedler's contingency model	Describes two leader styles, relationship-oriented and task-oriented, and the kinds of situations in which each kind of leader will be most effective.	Whether a relationship-oriented or a task-oriented leader is effective is contingent on the situation.
House's path–goal theory	Describes how effective leaders motivate their followers.	The behaviors that managers should engage in to be effective leaders are contingent on the nature of the subordinates and the work they do.
Leader substitutes model	Describes when leadership is unnecessary.	Whether leadership is necessary for subordinates to perform highly is contingent on characteristics of the subordinates and the situation.

Transformational Leadership

LO 10-4 Describe what transformational leadership is, and explain how managers can engage in it.

Time and time again, throughout business history, certain leaders seem to literally transform their organizations, making sweeping changes to revitalize and renew operations. For example, when Sue Nokes became senior vice president of sales and customer service at T-Mobile USA in 2002, the quality of T-Mobile's customer service was lower than that of its major competitors; on average, 12% of employees were absent on any day; and annual employee turnover was over 100%.[63] T-Mobile USA is a subsidiary of Deutsche Telekom; has 36,000 employees; and provides wireless voice, messaging, and data services.[64] When Nokes arrived at T-Mobile, valuable employees were quitting their jobs and customers weren't receiving high-quality service; neither employees nor customers were satisfied with their experience with the company.[65] However, by the late 2000s T-Mobile was regularly receiving highest rankings for customer care and satisfaction in the wireless category by J. D. Power and Associates, absence and turnover rates substantially declined, and around 80% of employees indicated that they were satisfied with their jobs.[66] In fact, when Nokes visited call centers, it was not uncommon for employees to greet her with cheers and accolades.[67]

transformational leadership

Leadership that makes subordinates aware of the importance of their jobs and performance to the organization and aware of their own needs for personal growth and that motivates subordinates to work for the good of the organization.

Nokes transformed T-Mobile into a company in which satisfied employees provide excellent service to customers.[68] When managers have such dramatic effects on their subordinates and on an organization as a whole, they are engaging in transformational leadership. Transformational leadership occurs when managers change (or transform) their subordinates in three important ways:[69]

1. *Transformational managers make subordinates aware of how important their jobs are for the organization and how necessary it is for them to perform those jobs as best they can so the organization can attain its goals.* At T-Mobile, Nokes visited call centers, conducted focus groups, and had town hall meetings to find out what employees and customers were unhappy with and what steps she could take to improve matters.[70] Her philosophy was that when employees are satisfied with their jobs and view their work as important, they are much more likely to

Sue Nokes exhibited transformational leadership at T-Mobile.

provide high-quality customer service. She made employees aware of how important their jobs were by the many steps she took to improve their working conditions, ranging from providing them with their own workspaces to substantially raising their salaries.[71] She emphasized the importance of providing excellent customer service by periodically asking employees what was working well and what was not working well, asking them what steps could be taken to improve problem areas, and taking actions to ensure that employees were able to provide excellent customer service. Nokes also instituted a performance measurement system to track performance in key areas such as quality of service and speed of problem resolution.[72] She sincerely told employees, "You are No. 1, and the customer is why."[73]

2. *Transformational managers make their subordinates aware of the subordinates' own needs for personal growth, development, and accomplishment.* Nokes made T-Mobile's employees aware of their own needs in this regard by transforming training and development at T-Mobile and increasing opportunities for promotions to more responsible positions. Employees now spend over 130 hours per year in training and development programs and team meetings. Nokes also instituted a promote-from-within policy, and around 80% of promotions are given to current employees.[74]

3. *Transformational managers motivate their subordinates to work for the good of the organization as a whole, not just for their own personal gain or benefit.* Nokes emphasized that employees should focus on what matters to customers, coworkers, and T-Mobile as a whole. She let employees know that when they were unnecessarily absent from their jobs, they were not doing right by their coworkers. And she emphasized the need to try to resolve customer problems in a single phone call so customers can get on with their busy lives.[75]

When managers transform their subordinates in these three ways, subordinates trust the managers, are highly motivated, and help the organization achieve its goals. How do managers such as Nokes transform subordinates and produce dramatic effects in their organizations? There are at least three ways in which transformational leaders can influence their followers: by being a charismatic leader, by intellectually stimulating subordinates, and by engaging in developmental consideration (see Table 10.3).

Being a Charismatic Leader

charismatic leader An enthusiastic, self-confident leader who is able to clearly communicate his or her vision of how good things could be.

Transformational managers such as Nokes are charismatic leaders. They have a vision of how good things could be in their work groups and organizations that is in contrast with the status quo. Their vision usually entails dramatic improvements in group and organizational performance as a result of changes in the organization's structure, culture, strategy, decision making, and other critical processes and factors. This vision paves the way for gaining a competitive advantage. From the "Management Snapshot," it is clear that part of Doreen Lorenzo's vision for Frog Design is to help Frog change the world.

Table 10.3

Transformational Leadership

Transformational managers
- Are charismatic.
- Intellectually stimulate subordinates.
- Engage in developmental consideration.

Subordinates of transformational managers
- Have increased awareness of the importance of their jobs and high performance.
- Are aware of their own needs for growth, development, and accomplishment.
- Work for the good of the organization and not just their own personal benefit.

Charismatic leaders are excited and enthusiastic about their vision and clearly communicate it to their subordinates, as does Doreen Lorenzo. The excitement, enthusiasm, and self-confidence of a charismatic leader contribute to the leader's being able to inspire followers to enthusiastically support his or her vision.[76] People often think of charismatic leaders or managers as being "larger than life." The essence of charisma, however, is having a vision and enthusiastically communicating it to others. Thus managers who appear to be quiet and earnest can also be charismatic.

Stimulating Subordinates Intellectually

Transformational managers openly share information with their subordinates so they are aware of problems and the need for change. The manager causes subordinates to view problems in their groups and throughout the organization from a different perspective, consistent with the manager's vision. Whereas in the past subordinates might not have been aware of some problems, may have viewed problems as a "management issue" beyond their concern, or may have viewed problems as insurmountable, the transformational manager's intellectual stimulation leads subordinates to view problems as challenges that they can and will meet and conquer. The manager engages and empowers subordinates to take personal responsibility for helping to solve problems, as did Nokes at T-Mobile.[77]

intellectual stimulation Behavior a leader engages in to make followers aware of problems and view these problems in new ways, consistent with the leader's vision.

Engaging in Developmental Consideration

When managers engage in developmental consideration, they not only perform the consideration behaviors described earlier, such as demonstrating true concern for the well-being of subordinates, but go one step further. The manager goes out of his or her way to support and encourage subordinates, giving them opportunities to enhance their skills and capabilities and to grow and excel on the job.[78] As mentioned earlier, Nokes did this in numerous ways. In fact, after she first met with employees in a call center in Albuquerque, New Mexico, Karen Viola, the manager of the call center, said, "Everyone came out crying. The people said that they had never felt so inspired in their lives, and that they had never met with any leader at that level who [they felt] cared."[79]

developmental consideration Behavior a leader engages in to support and encourage followers and help them develop and grow on the job.

All organizations, no matter how large or small, successful or unsuccessful, can benefit when their managers engage in transformational leadership. Moreover, while the benefits of transformational leadership are often most apparent when an organization is in trouble, transformational leadership can be an enduring approach to leadership, leading to long-term organizational effectiveness.

The Distinction between Transformational and Transactional Leadership

transactional leadership
Leadership that motivates subordinates by rewarding them for high performance and reprimanding them for low performance.

Transformational leadership is often contrasted with transactional leadership. In transactional leadership, managers use their reward and coercive powers to encourage high performance. When managers reward high performers, reprimand or otherwise punish low performers, and motivate subordinates by reinforcing desired behaviors and extinguishing or punishing undesired ones, they are engaging in transactional leadership.[80] Managers who effectively influence their subordinates to achieve goals, yet do not seem to be making the kind of dramatic changes that are part of transformational leadership, are engaging in transactional leadership.

Many transformational leaders engage in transactional leadership. They reward subordinates for a job well done and notice and respond to substandard performance. But they also have their eyes on the bigger picture of how much better things could be in their organizations, how much more their subordinates are capable of achieving, and how important it is to treat their subordinates with respect and help them reach their full potential.

Research has found that when leaders engage in transformational leadership, their subordinates tend to have higher levels of job satisfaction and performance.[81] Additionally, subordinates of transformational leaders may be more likely to trust their leaders and their organizations and feel that they are being fairly treated, and this, in turn, may positively influence their work motivation (see Chapter 9).[82]

Gender and Leadership

The increasing number of women entering the ranks of management, as well as the problems some women face in their efforts to be hired as managers or promoted into management positions, has prompted researchers to explore the relationship between gender and leadership. Although there are relatively more women in management positions today than there were 10 years ago, there are still relatively few women in top management and, in some organizations, even in middle management. As indicated in Chapter 3, while around 51.5% of the employees in managerial and professional jobs in the United States are women, only about 14.1% of corporate officers in the *Fortune* 500 are women, and only 7.5% of the top earners are women.[83]

LO 10-5 Characterize the relationship between gender and leadership and explain how emotional intelligence may contribute to leadership effectiveness.

When women do advance to top management positions, special attention often is focused on them and the fact that they are women. Those who make it to the top post, such as Indra Nooyi of PepsiCo[84] and Meg Whitman of Hewlett-Packard, are salient. As business writer Linda Tischler puts it, "In a workplace where women CEOs of major companies are so scarce . . . they can be identified, like rock stars, by first name only."[85]

A widespread stereotype of women is that they are nurturing, supportive, and concerned with interpersonal relations. Men are stereotypically viewed as being directive and focused on task accomplishment. Such stereotypes suggest that women tend to be more relationship-oriented as managers and engage in more consideration behaviors, whereas men are more task-oriented and engage in more initiating-structure behaviors. Does the behavior of actual male and female managers bear out these stereotypes? Do women managers lead in different ways than men do? Are male or female managers more effective as leaders?

Research suggests that male and female managers who have leadership positions in organizations behave in similar ways.[86] Women do not engage in more consideration than men, and men do not engage in more initiating structure than women. Research does suggest, however, that leadership style may vary between women and men. Women tend to be somewhat more participative as leaders than are men, involving subordinates in decision making and seeking their input.[87] Male managers tend to be less participative than are female managers, making more decisions on their own and wanting to do things their own way. Moreover, research suggests that men tend to be harsher when they punish their subordinates than do women.[88]

There are at least two reasons why female managers may be more participative as leaders than are male managers.[89] First, subordinates may try to resist the influence of female managers more than they do the influence of male managers. Some subordinates may never have reported to a woman before; some may incorrectly see a management role as being more appropriate for a man than for a woman; and some may just resist being led by a woman. To overcome this resistance and encourage subordinates' trust and respect, women managers may adopt a participative approach.

A second reason why female managers may be more participative is that they sometimes have better interpersonal skills than male managers.[90] A participative approach to leadership requires high levels of interaction and involvement between a manager and his or her subordinates, sensitivity to subordinates' feelings, and the ability to make decisions that may be unpopular with subordinates but necessary for goal attainment. Good interpersonal skills may help female managers have the effective interactions with their subordinates that are crucial to a participative approach.[91] To the extent that male managers have more difficulty managing interpersonal relationships, they may shy away from the high levels of interaction with subordinates necessary for true participation.

The key finding from research on leader behaviors, however, is that male and female managers do *not* differ significantly in their propensities to perform different leader behaviors. Even though they may be more participative, female managers do not engage in more consideration or less initiating structure than male managers.

Perhaps a question even more important than whether male and female managers differ in the leadership behaviors they perform is whether they differ in effectiveness. Consistent with the findings for leader behaviors, research suggests that across different kinds of organizational settings, male and female managers tend to be *equally effective* as leaders.[92] Thus there is no logical basis for stereotypes favoring male managers and leaders or for the existence of the "glass ceiling" (an invisible barrier that seems to prevent women from advancing as far as they should in some organizations). Because women and men are equally effective as leaders, the increasing number of women in the workforce should result in a larger pool of highly qualified candidates for management positions in organizations, ultimately enhancing organizational effectiveness.[93]

Emotional Intelligence and Leadership

Do the moods and emotions leaders experience on the job influence their behavior and effectiveness as leaders? Research suggests this is likely to be the case. For example, one study found that when store managers experienced positive moods at work, salespeople in their stores provided high-quality customer service and were less likely to quit.[94] Another study found that groups whose leaders experienced positive moods had better coordination, whereas groups whose leaders experienced negative moods exerted more effort; members of groups with leaders in positive moods also tended to experience more positive moods themselves; and members of groups with leaders in negative moods tended to experience more negative moods.[95]

A leader's level of emotional intelligence (see Chapter 2) may play a particularly important role in leadership effectiveness.[96] For example, emotional intelligence may help leaders develop a vision for their organizations, motivate their subordinates to commit to this vision, and energize them to enthusiastically work to achieve this vision. Moreover, emotional intelligence may enable leaders to develop a significant identity for their organization and instill high levels of trust and cooperation throughout the organization while maintaining the flexibility needed to respond to changing conditions.[97]

Emotional intelligence also plays a crucial role in how leaders relate to and deal with their followers, particularly when it comes to encouraging followers to be creative.[98] Creativity in organizations is an emotion-laden process; it often entails challenging the status quo, being willing to take risks and accept and learn from failures, and doing much hard work to bring creative ideas to fruition in terms of new products, services, or procedures and processes when uncertainty is bound to be high.[99] Leaders who are high on emotional intelligence are more likely to understand all the emotions surrounding creative endeavors, to be able to awaken and support the creative pursuits of their followers, and to provide the kind of support that enables creativity to flourish in organizations.[100]

Summary and Review

THE NATURE OF LEADERSHIP Leadership is the process by which a person exerts influence over other people and inspires, motivates, and directs their activities to help achieve group or organizational goals. Leaders can influence others because they possess power. The five types of power available to managers are legitimate power, reward power, coercive power, expert power, and referent power. Many managers are using empowerment as a tool to increase their effectiveness as leaders. **[LO 10-1]**

TRAIT AND BEHAVIOR MODELS OF LEADERSHIP The trait model of leadership describes personal characteristics or traits that contribute to effective leadership. However, some managers who possess these traits are not effective leaders, and some managers who do not possess all the traits are nevertheless effective leaders. The behavior model of leadership describes two kinds of behavior that most leaders engage in: consideration and initiating structure. **[LO 10-2]**

CONTINGENCY MODELS OF LEADERSHIP Contingency models take into account the complexity surrounding leadership and the role of the situation in determining whether a manager is an effective leader. Fiedler's contingency model explains why managers may be effective leaders in one situation and ineffective in another. According to Fiedler's model, relationship-oriented leaders are most effective in situations that are moderately favorable for leading, and task-oriented leaders are most effective in situations that are very favorable or very unfavorable for leading. House's path–goal theory describes how effective managers motivate their subordinates by determining what outcomes their subordinates want, rewarding subordinates with these outcomes when they achieve their goals and perform at a high level, and clarifying the paths to goal attainment. Managers can engage in four kinds of behaviors to motivate subordinates: directive, supportive, participative, and achievement-oriented behaviors. The leader substitutes model suggests that sometimes managers do not have to play a leadership role because their subordinates perform at a high level without the manager having to exert influence over them. **[LO 10-3]**

TRANSFORMATIONAL LEADERSHIP Transformational leadership occurs when managers have dramatic effects on their subordinates and on the organization as a whole, and inspire and energize subordinates to solve problems and improve performance. These effects include making subordinates aware of the importance of their own jobs and high performance; making subordinates aware of their own needs for personal growth, development, and accomplishment; and motivating subordinates to work for the good of the organization and not just their own personal gain. Managers can engage in transformational leadership by being charismatic leaders, by intellectually stimulating subordinates, and by engaging in developmental consideration. Transformational managers also often engage in transactional leadership by using their reward and coercive powers to encourage high performance. **[LO 10-4]**

GENDER AND LEADERSHIP Female and male managers do not differ in the leadership behaviors they perform, contrary to stereotypes suggesting that women are more relationship-oriented and men more task-oriented. Female managers sometimes are more participative than male managers, however. Research has found that women and men are equally effective as managers and leaders. **[LO 10-5]**

EMOTIONAL INTELLIGENCE AND LEADERSHIP The moods and emotions leaders experience on the job, and their ability to effectively manage these feelings, can influence their effectiveness as leaders. Moreover, emotional intelligence can contribute to leadership effectiveness in multiple ways, including encouraging and supporting creativity among followers. **[LO 10-5]**

Management *in Action*

TOPICS FOR DISCUSSION AND ACTION

Discussion

1. Describe the steps managers can take to increase their power and ability to be effective leaders. **[LO 10-1]**

2. Think of specific situations in which it might be especially important for a manager to engage in consideration and in initiating structure. **[LO 10-2]**

3. Discuss why managers might want to change the behaviors they engage in, given their situation, their subordinates, and the nature of the work being done. Do you think managers can readily change their leadership behaviors? Why or why not? **[LO 10-3]**

4. Discuss why substitutes for leadership can contribute to organizational effectiveness. **[LO 10-3]**

5. Describe what transformational leadership is, and explain how managers can engage in it. **[LO 10-4]**

6. Imagine that you are working in an organization in an

entry-level position after graduation and have come up with what you think is a great idea for improving a critical process in the organization that relates to your job. In what ways might your supervisor encourage you to implement your idea? How might your supervisor discourage you from even sharing your idea with others? **[LO 10-4, 10-5]**

Action

7. Interview a manager to find out how the three situational characteristics that Fiedler identified affect his or her ability to provide leadership. **[LO 10-3]**

8. Find a company that has dramatically turned around its fortunes and improved its performance. Determine whether a transformational manager was behind the turnaround and, if one was, what this manager did. **[LO 10-4]**

BUILDING MANAGEMENT SKILLS

Analyzing Failures of Leadership [LO 10-1, 10-2, 10-3, 10-4]

Think about a situation you are familiar with in which a leader was very ineffective. Then answer the following questions.

1. What sources of power did this leader have? Did the leader have enough power to influence his or her followers?

2. What kinds of behaviors did this leader engage in? Were they appropriate for the situation? Why or why not?

3. From what you know, do you think this leader was a task-oriented leader or a relationship-oriented leader? How favorable was this leader's situation for leading?

4. What steps did this leader take to motivate his or her followers? Were these steps appropriate or inappropriate? Why?

5. What signs, if any, did this leader show of being a transformational leader?

MANAGING ETHICALLY [LO 10-1]

Managers who verbally criticize their subordinates, put them down in front of their coworkers, or use the threat of job loss to influence behavior are exercising coercive power. Some employees subject to coercive power believe that using it is unethical.

Questions

1. Either alone or in a group, think about the ethical implications of the use of coercive power.

2. To what extent do managers and organizations have an ethical obligation to put limits on the amount of coercive power that is exercised?

SMALL GROUP BREAKOUT EXERCISE

Improving Leadership Effectiveness [LO 10-1, 10-2, 10-3, 10-4]

Form groups of three to five people, and appoint one member as the spokesperson who will communicate your findings and conclusions to the class when called on by the instructor. Then discuss the following scenario.

You are a team of human resource consultants who have been hired by Carla Caruso, an entrepreneur who has started her own interior decorating business. A highly competent and creative interior decorator, Caruso has established a working relationship with most of the major home builders in her community. At first she worked on her own as an independent contractor. Then because of a dramatic increase in the number of new homes being built, she became swamped with requests for her services and decided to start her own company.

She hired a secretary–bookkeeper and four interior decorators, all of whom are highly competent. Caruso still does decorating jobs herself and has adopted a hands-off approach to leading the four decorators who report to her because she feels that interior design is a very personal, creative endeavor. Rather than pay the decorators on some kind of commission basis (such as a percentage of their customers' total billings), she pays them a premium salary, higher than average, so they are motivated to do what's best for a customer's needs and not what will result in higher billings and commissions.

Caruso thought everything was going smoothly until customer complaints started coming in. The complaints ranged from the decorators' being hard to reach, promising unrealistic delivery times, and being late for or failing to keep appointments to their being impatient and rude when customers had trouble making up their minds. Caruso knows her decorators are competent and is concerned that she is not effectively leading and managing them. She wonders, in particular, if her hands-off approach is to blame and if she should change the manner in which she rewards or pays her decorators. She has asked for your advice.

1. Analyze the sources of power that Caruso has available to her to influence the decorators. What advice can you give her to either increase her power base or use her existing power more effectively?

2. Given what you have learned in this chapter (for example, from the behavior model and path–goal theory), does Caruso seem to be performing appropriate leader behaviors in this situation? What advice can you give her about the kinds of behaviors she should perform?

3. What steps would you advise Caruso to take to increase the decorators' motivation to deliver high-quality customer service?

4. Would you advise Caruso to try to engage in transformational leadership in this situation? If not, why not? If so, what steps would you advise her to take?

BE THE MANAGER [LO 10-1, 10-2, 10-3, 10-4, 10-5]

You are the CEO of a medium-size company that makes window coverings similar to Hunter Douglas blinds and Duettes. Your company has a real cost advantage in terms of being able to make custom window coverings at costs that are relatively low in the industry. However, the performance of your company has been lackluster. To make needed changes and improve performance, you met with the eight other top managers in your company and charged them with identifying problems and missed opportunities in each of their areas and coming up with an action plan to address the problems and take advantage of opportunities.

Once you gave the managers the ok, they were charged with implementing their action plans in a timely fashion and monitoring the effects of their initiatives monthly for the next 8 to 12 months.

You approved each of the managers' action plans, and a year later most of the managers were reporting that their initiatives had been successful in addressing the problems and opportunities they had identified a year ago. However, overall company performance continues to be lackluster and shows no signs of improvement. You are confused and starting to question your leadership capabilities and approach to change.

Question

1. What are you going to do to improve the performance and effectiveness of your company?

THE WALL STREET JOURNAL
CASE IN THE NEWS [LO 10-1, LO 10-2, LO 10-4]
This CEO Used to Have an Office

Bob Flexon, chief executive of Dynegy Inc., occupies a 64-square-foot cubicle, identical to the ones used by the 235 colleagues who surround him at its Houston headquarters. Hourly employees sometimes stop by his desk to chat.

It's a long way from the expansive office suite, $15,000 marble desk and Oriental rugs that Mr. Flexon inherited when he arrived at Dynegy in July 2011, four months before the power producer filed for bankruptcy.

Under his command, Dynegy shifted its headquarters last May to a single, open floor in a different building.

The move, which saved $5 million a year, is the most visible symbol of Mr. Flexon's attempts to overhaul the company's culture. He aims to transform a business previously focused on day-to-day survival into an agile operator poised for growth.

Among other changes, he made frequent visits to the company's power plants, banned employees from checking email and phones during meetings and restored annual performance reviews. "The idea was to instill a winning spirit," Mr. Flexon says. Though Dynegy emerged from bankruptcy last October, its cultural restructuring remains a work in progress.

Increasingly, leaders of troubled businesses try to fix the company's culture along with its bottom line. Since the financial crisis struck in 2008, CEOs have sought to improve collaboration and decision making, recognizing that a strong culture is "a critical component of their long-term success," says Nick Neuhausel, a partner at consulting firm Senn Delaney, which advised Dynegy.

"The right culture change can—without question—improve results," says John Kotter, co-author of the book "Corporate Culture and Performance" and head of research at consulting firm Kotter International. But putting a sick business on a healthier strategic path while changing its culture "is much more difficult than most executives realize," he cautions.

At British bank Barclays PLC, whose misconduct has cost it billions of pounds, CEO Antony Jenkins recently said he was "shredding" a self-serving and aggressive culture—by abolishing commissions on financial-product sales, among other things. He said, however, that results would take time. The bank's top management team disintegrated last summer after it admitted trying to rig interest rates.

One of the highest-profile attempts at cultural renewal is under way at Internet company Yahoo Inc., where new CEO Marissa Mayer has upgraded workers' mobile devices, introduced free food at company cafeterias and abolished work-from-home arrangements.

Chief executives don't always succeed in reshaping corporate culture. Randy Michaels ran Tribune Co. for less than a year during the media company's bankruptcy. Under his leadership, executives shook up Tribune in ways that often clashed with its traditionally staid management. Mr. Michaels quit in October 2010.

A spokeswoman for Mr. Michaels said Tuesday that he was unavailable for comment.

Mr. Flexon joined the debt-burdened Dynegy after investors rejected two buyout offers, prompting senior officers and the board to jump ship. Demoralized employees wondered "what will go wrong next," says Julius Cox, vice president of human resources. "It was hard for staffers to focus and be engaged."

Many bosses were equally downbeat. In a May survey by Senn Delaney, Dynegy executives and middle managers scored low on questions such as whether they felt valued, proud to work there or committed to the company's future.

In June, the company's 37 highest-ranking executives participated in a two-day offsite meeting led by Senn Delaney, which included trust-building exercises. In one drill, a pair of managers spent one minute expressing appreciation for each other's work, then spent the next giving constructive criticism.

More than a few executives rolled their eyes. Some appeared "skeptical about this cultural change 'mumbo jumbo,'" says Kevin Howell, then chief operating officer, who remains a Dynegy adviser.

Others initially resisted swapping their private offices for cubicles.

Management soon drafted a new purpose statement ("Energizing You, Powering our Communities") and put more emphasis on certain core values, such as safety, accountability and agility. Dynegy estimates it will have spent $425,000 by year-end to train 300 managers in culture change.

Mr. Flexon unveiled the cultural overhaul two days after the company emerged from bankruptcy court. The CEO and management-team members visited the company's 11 plants to discuss the changes with rank-and-file workers.

Then, executives tried to carry out their pledges. Employees got performance reviews for the first time in two years, with bosses judging their subordinates in part on whether they embraced the core values.

Jesse Strausser, an operations technician at a power plant near Reading, Pa., says the company now evaluates him partly on his involvement in devising company-wide cost-saving measures.

Meanwhile, 15 specially trained "culture champions" are attempting to reinforce the message. At meetings, one such champion, Chief Administrative Officer Carolyn J. Burke, says she sometimes chastens a colleague for tapping on his BlackBerry by declaring, "Hey Joe, be here now."

Mr. Flexon has mounted a "Be Here Now" plaque underneath his monitor as a reminder to avoid checking email during calls.

Several hourly workers say the top brass heeds their suggestions faster than previous management did. "What I have to say counts," says Mike Kelley, a site safety coordinator for a Dynegy power plant in Minooka, Ill.

During a plant-safety conference last year, Mr. Kelley persuaded Mr. Flexon that the facility badly needed an intercom. The intercom is being installed.

Morale is up, Mr. Kelley says, adding that plant workers "know that safety is taken seriously."

Employee turnover also has dropped—to 5.8% last year from nearly 8% in 2011, according to Mr. Cox, the human-resources executive. "People are cautiously starting to believe that we can win again," Mr. Flexon says.

Culture changes aside, Dynegy isn't out of danger. It is scheduled to report year-end earnings Thursday after racking up losses of $1.19 billion for the first nine months of 2012, compared with a year-earlier loss of $324 million. Dynegy investors count on senior management to deliver results, Mr. Flexon says. But "our ongoing focus on culture is what will make the difference," he adds.

Questions

1. How would you describe Bob Flexon's personal leadership style?

2. What sources of power does Flexon possess?

3. What leader behaviors does he appear to engage in?

4. In what ways is Flexon engaging in transformational leadership at Dynegy? Be specific.

Source: J. S. Lublin, "This CEO Used to Have an Office," *The Wall Street Journal*, March 13, 2013, B1, B8.

11

Effective Team Management

LEARNING OBJECTIVES

After studying this chapter, you should be able to:

1 Explain why groups and teams are key contributors to organizational effectiveness. **[LO 11-1]**

2 Identify the different types of groups and teams that help managers and organizations achieve their goals. **[LO 11-2]**

3 Explain how different elements of group dynamics influence the functioning and effectiveness of groups and teams. **[LO 11-3]**

4 Explain why it is important for groups and teams to have a balance of conformity and deviance and a moderate level of cohesiveness. **[LO 11-4]**

5 Describe how managers can motivate group members to achieve organizational goals and reduce social loafing in groups and teams. **[LO 11-5]**

Talk about hands-on inspiration! Here, Boeing's team system seats the group responsible for the plane nose right under a "work in progress" in order to better make decisions.

Using Teams to Innovate at Boeing

How Can Managers Cut Costs, Increase Efficiency, and Promote Innovation?

Managers at Boeing have increased their reliance on using teams of employees to promote innovation while cutting costs and improving efficiency.[1] Boeing's 737 is a top-selling jetliner and, faced with high demand, managers at Boeing charged teams with innovating to cut costs, increase efficiency, and increase the number of 737s that could be produced each month in Boeing's Renton, Washington, manufacturing facility. As Eric Lindblad, vice president in charge of manufacturing 737s, put it, "How do you produce more aircraft without expanding the building? . . . Space is the forcing function that means you've got to be creative."[2]

Self-managing, cross-functional teams of around 7 to 10 members typically concentrate on a particular segment of the plane such as the galley, where food and drinks are prepared and stored. Team members have diverse backgrounds and experiences, and thus it is not uncommon for mechanics to be working alongside engineers on the same team. Teams meet as often as their members think it

is called for with some teams meeting as frequently as once per week. Some team projects are completed in a relatively short time period, whereas others can take years with missteps along the way. For example, it took a team about five years to develop and design a new, more efficient way to install the hydraulic tubes in the 737 landing gear wheel well area. In the past, four mechanics were crowded into the wheel well, assembling over 600 tubes for a one-day shift and also a segment of the night shift for a single jet. Boeing employees working on other assembly tasks had to navigate around the mechanics installing the tubes. The team trying to improve this process figured out that around 25 clusters of tubes could be put together at another Boeing plant so that mechanics would be installing 25 larger assemblies and less than 100 individual tubes. The new process resulted in around 30 hours less mechanics' time being taken up by tube installation per plane and fewer leaks in the hydraulic system when planes were operational.[3]

Engineer Jay Dorhrmann worked on a team trying to solve a persistent problem—when planes moved along the assembly line, metal parts and fasteners scattered about the plant's floor would occasionally puncture a tire on a plane.[4] The team's first solution to the problem was to install sweepers on the planes' landing gear so that as the plane was moved along the line, the metal parts would be swept out of the way of the tires. Unfortunately, the sweepers didn't work very well and bolts and other metal parts were still puncturing tires. When Dorhrmann was watching a motorcycle race on his day off, he noticed that race crews put covers on tires before races so that they would warm up and have better traction during the race. This gave him an idea for the problem his team had been struggling with—canvas wheel covers that would encircle the four major landing gear tires on the planes as they were moved along the line. This innovation resulted in cost savings of around $10,000 per punctured tire, resulting in about $250,000 per year cost savings as well as savings resulting from mechanics not having to stop their work and take the time to change out a punctured tire. Team members like Dorhrmann get a real sense of accomplishment when their teams succeed. As Dorhrmann indicates, "It's a good feeling. . . . You hated to see these airplanes jacked at the end of the line and people pulling off tires."[5]

Across all commercial jet programs, Boeing has approximately 1,300 teams focused on innovation, cutting costs, and improving efficiency.[6] Mechanics, engineers, and other Boeing employees who work on the jets on a day-to-day basis, or work on designing new models, are often in a good position to figure out ways to improve the design and assembly process. A big drive behind these efforts is to decrease the amount of time it takes to build a jet and increase the number of jets Boeing can build each month.[7]

With a backlog of orders for around 3,700 jetliners, of which about 2,300 are 737s, it is understandable why managers at Boeing are using teams to spur innovation and increase efficiency while cutting costs.[8] And teams certainly seem to be helping Boeing do just that. At the Renton plant, Boeing used to make 31.5 737 jetliners per month; now the plant is making 38 737s per month. The goal is to increase this number to 42 by 2014. Thus, it is not surprising that Boeing has been hiring additional workers to help fuel the increase in production of jetliners.[9] All in all, teams certainly seem to be contributing to innovation and efficiency at Boeing.[10]

Overview

Boeing is not alone in using groups and teams to improve organizational effectiveness. Managers in companies large and small are using groups and teams to enhance performance, increase responsiveness to customers, spur innovation, and motivate employees. In this chapter we look in detail at how groups and teams can contribute to organizational effectiveness and the types of groups and teams used in organizations. We discuss how different elements of group dynamics influence the functioning and effectiveness of groups, and we describe how managers can motivate group members to achieve organizational goals and reduce social loafing in groups and teams. By the end of this chapter you will appreciate why the effective management of groups and teams is a key ingredient for organizational performance and effectiveness.

 LO 11-1 Explain why groups and teams are key contributors to organizational effectiveness.

Groups, Teams, and Organizational Effectiveness

A group may be defined as two or more people who interact with each other to accomplish certain goals or meet certain needs.[11] A team is a group whose members work *intensely* with one another to achieve a specific common goal or objective. As these definitions imply, all teams are groups, but not all groups are teams. The two characteristics that distinguish teams from groups are the *intensity* with which team members work together and the presence of a *specific, overriding team goal or objective.*

group Two or more people who interact with each other to accomplish certain goals or meet certain needs.

team A group whose members work intensely with one another to achieve a specific common goal or objective.

Recall from the "Management Snapshot" how the teams at Boeing had the goal of improving the manufacturing process for a particular part of the 737 jetliner. In contrast, the accountants who work in a small CPA firm are a group: They may interact with one another to achieve goals such as keeping up-to-date on the latest changes in accounting rules and regulations, maintaining a smoothly functioning office, satisfying clients, and attracting new clients. But they are not a team because they do not work intensely with one another. Each accountant concentrates on serving the needs of his or her own clients.

Because all teams are also groups, whenever we use the term *group* in this chapter, we are referring to both groups *and* teams. As you might imagine, because members of teams work intensely together, teams can sometimes be difficult to form, and it may take time for members to learn how to effectively work together. Groups and teams can help an organization gain a competitive advantage because they can (1) enhance its performance, (2) increase its responsiveness to customers, (3) increase innovation, and (4) increase employees' motivation and satisfaction (see Figure 11.1). In this section we look at each of these contributions in turn.

Groups and Teams as Performance Enhancers

synergy Performance gains that result when individuals and departments coordinate their actions.

One of the main advantages of using groups is the opportunity to obtain a type of synergy: People working in a group can produce more or higher-quality outputs than would have been produced if each person had worked separately and all their individual efforts were later combined. The essence of synergy is captured in the saying "The whole is more than the sum of its parts." Factors that can contribute to synergy in groups include the ability of group members to bounce ideas off one another, to correct one another's mistakes, to solve problems immediately as they arise, to bring a diverse knowledge base to bear on a problem or goal, and to accomplish work that is too vast or all-encompassing for any individual to achieve on his or her own.

To take advantage of the potential for synergy in groups, managers need to make sure that groups are composed of members who have complementary skills and knowledge relevant to the group's work. For example, at Hallmark Cards, synergies are created by bringing together all the different functions needed to create and produce a greeting card in a cross-functional team (a team composed of members from different departments or functions). For instance, artists,

Figure 11.1

Groups' and Teams' Contributions to Organizational Effectiveness

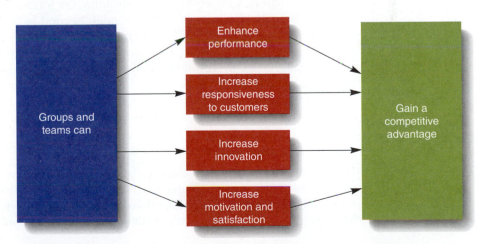

Getting multiple perspectives and departmental inputs on a project can enhance performance.

writers, designers, and marketing experts work together as team members to develop new cards.[12]

At Hallmark the skills and expertise of the artists complement the contributions of the writers and vice versa. Managers also need to give groups enough autonomy so that the groups, rather than the manager, are solving problems and determining how to achieve goals and objectives, as is true in the cross-functional teams at Hallmark and the teams at Boeing in the "Management Snapshot." To promote synergy, managers need to empower their subordinates and to be coaches, guides, and resources for groups while refraining from playing a more directive or supervisory role. The potential for synergy in groups may be why more and more managers are incorporating empowerment into their personal leadership styles (see Chapter 10).

Groups, Teams, and Responsiveness to Customers

Being responsive to customers is not always easy. In manufacturing organizations, for example, customers' needs and desires for new and improved products have to be balanced against engineering constraints, production costs and feasibilities, government safety regulations, and marketing challenges. In service organizations such as health maintenance organizations (HMOs), being responsive to patients' needs and desires for prompt, high-quality medical care and treatment has to be balanced against meeting physicians' needs and desires and keeping health care costs under control. Being responsive to customers often requires the wide variety of skills and expertise found in different departments and at different levels in an organization's hierarchy. Sometimes, for example, employees at lower levels in an organization's hierarchy, such as sales representatives for a computer company, are closest to its customers and the most attuned to their needs. However, lower-level employees like salespeople often lack the technical expertise needed for new product ideas; such expertise is found in the research and development department. Bringing salespeople, research and development experts, and members of other departments together in a group or cross-functional team can enhance responsiveness to customers. Consequently, when managers form a team, they must make sure the diversity of expertise and knowledge needed to be responsive to customers exists within the team; this is why cross-functional teams are so popular.

In a cross-functional team, the expertise and knowledge in different organizational departments are brought together in the skills and knowledge of the team members. Managers of high-performing organizations are careful to determine which types of expertise and knowledge are required for teams to be responsive to customers, and they use this information in forming teams.

Teams and Innovation

Innovation—the creative development of new products, new technologies, new services, or even new organizational structures—is a topic we introduced in Chapter 1. Often an individual working alone does not possess the extensive and diverse skills, knowledge, and expertise required for successful innovation. Managers can better encourage innovation by creating teams of diverse individuals who together have the knowledge relevant to a particular type of innovation, as has been the case at Boeing, rather than by relying on individuals working alone.

Using teams to innovate has other advantages. First, team members can often uncover one another's errors or false assumptions; an individual acting alone would not be able to do this. Second, team members can critique one another's approaches and build off one another's strengths while compensating for weaknesses—an advantage of devil's advocacy discussed in Chapter 5.

To further promote innovation, managers can empower teams and make their members fully responsible and accountable for the innovation process. The manager's role is to provide guidance, assistance, coaching, and the resources that team members need and *not* to closely direct or supervise their activities. To speed innovation, managers also need to form teams in which each member brings some unique resource to the team, such as engineering prowess, knowledge of production, marketing expertise, or financial savvy. Successful innovation sometimes requires that managers form teams with members from different countries and cultures.

Amazon uses teams to spur innovation, and many of the unique features on its website that enable it to be responsive to customers and meet their needs have been developed by teams, as indicated in the following "Information Technology Byte" box.

INFORMATION TECHNOLOGY BYTE

Pizza Teams Innovate at Amazon

Jeff Bezos, founder, CEO, and chairman of the board of Amazon, is a firm believer in the power of teams to spur innovation.[13] At Amazon, teams have considerable autonomy to develop their ideas and experiment without interference from managers or other groups. And teams are kept deliberately small. According to Bezos, no team should need more than two pizzas to feed its members.[14] If more than two pizzas are needed to nourish a team, the team is too large. Thus teams at Amazon typically have no more than about five to seven members.[15]

"Pizza teams" have come up with unique and popular innovations that individuals working alone might never have thought of. A team developed the "Gold Box" icon that customers can click on to receive special offers that expire within a certain time period. Another team developed "Search Inside This Book," which allows customers to search and read content from over 100,000 books.[16] And a team developed the Amazon Kindle, a wireless reader that weighs less than 10 ounces, can hold thousands of titles, can receive automatic delivery of major newspapers and blogs, and has a high-resolution screen that looks like and can be read like paper.[17]

While Bezos gives teams autonomy to develop and run with their ideas, he also believes in careful analysis and testing of ideas. A great advocate of the power of facts, data, and analysis, Bezos feels that whenever an idea can be tested through

Pepperoni or plain cheese? At Amazon, pizza teams are small enough to need just one of each.

analysis, analysis should rule the day. When an undertaking is just too large or too uncertain or when data are lacking, Bezos and other experienced top managers make the final call.[18] But to make such judgment calls about implementing new ideas (either by data analysis or expert judgment), truly creative ideas are needed. To date, teams have played a very important role in generating ideas that have helped Amazon to be responsive to its customers, to have a widely known Internet brand name, and to be the highly successful and innovative company it is today.[19]

Groups and Teams as Motivators

Managers often form groups and teams to accomplish organizational goals and then find that using groups and teams brings additional benefits. Members of groups, and especially members of teams (because of the higher intensity of interaction in teams), are likely to be more satisfied than they would have been if they were working on their own. The experience of working alongside other highly charged and motivated people can be stimulating and motivating: Team members can see how their efforts and expertise directly contribute to the achievement of team and organizational goals, and they feel personally responsible for the outcomes or results of their work. This has been the case at Hallmark Cards.

The increased motivation and satisfaction that can accompany the use of teams can also lead to other outcomes, such as lower turnover. This has been Frank B. Day's experience as founder and chairman of the board of Rock Bottom Restaurants Inc.[20] To provide high-quality customer service, Day has organized the restaurants' employees into waitstaff teams, whose members work together to refill beers, take orders, bring hot chicken enchiladas to the tables, or clear off the tables. Team members share the burden of undesirable activities and unpopular shift times, and customers no longer have to wait until a particular waitress or waiter is available. Motivation and satisfaction levels in Rock Bottom restaurants seem to be higher than in other restaurants, and turnover is about half that experienced in other U.S. restaurant chains.[21]

Working in a group or team can also satisfy organizational members' needs for engaging in social interaction and feeling connected to other people. For workers who perform highly stressful jobs, such as hospital emergency and operating room staff, group membership can be an important source of social support and motivation. Family members or friends may not be able to fully understand or appreciate some sources of work stress that these group members experience firsthand. Moreover, group members may cope better with work stressors when they can share them with other members of their group. In addition, groups often devise techniques to relieve stress, such as the telling of jokes among hospital operating room staff.

Why do managers in all kinds of organizations rely so heavily on groups and teams? Effectively managed groups and teams can help managers in their quest for high performance, responsiveness to customers, and employee motivation. Before explaining how managers can effectively manage groups, however, we will describe the types of groups that are formed in organizations.

Types of Groups and Teams

formal group
A group that managers establish to achieve organizational goals.

informal group
A group that managers or nonmanagerial employees form to help achieve their own goals or meet their own needs.

top management team A group composed of the CEO, the president, and the heads of the most important departments.

To achieve their goals of high performance, responsiveness to customers, innovation, and employee motivation, managers can form various types of groups and teams (see Figure 11.2). Formal groups are those that managers establish to achieve organizational goals. The formal work groups are *cross-functional* teams composed of members from different departments, such as those at Hallmark Cards, and *cross-cultural* teams composed of members from different cultures or countries, such as the teams at global carmakers. As you will see, some of the groups discussed in this section also can be considered to be cross-functional (if they are composed of members from different departments) or cross-cultural (if they are composed of members from different countries or cultures).

Sometimes organizational members, managers or nonmanagers, form groups because they feel that groups will help them achieve their own goals or meet their own needs (for example, the need for social interaction). Groups formed in this way are informal groups. Four nurses who work in a hospital and have lunch together twice a week constitute an informal group.

The Top Management Team

A central concern of the CEO and president of a company is to form a top management team to help the organization achieve its mission and goals. Top management teams are responsible for developing the strategies that result in an organization's competitive advantage; most have between five and seven members. In forming their top management teams, CEOs are well advised to stress diversity in expertise, skills, knowledge, and experience. Thus many top management teams are also cross-functional teams: They are composed of members from different departments, such as finance, marketing, production, and engineering. Diversity helps ensure that the top management team will have all the background and resources it needs to make good decisions. Diversity also helps guard against *groupthink*—faulty group decision making that results when group members strive for agreement at the expense of an accurate assessment of the situation (see Chapter 5).

Figure 11.2

Types of Groups and Teams in Organizations

Research and Development Teams

research and development team
A team whose members have the expertise and experience needed to develop new products.

Managers in pharmaceuticals, computers, electronics, electronic imaging, and other high-tech industries often create research and development teams to develop new products. Managers select R&D team members on the basis of their expertise and experience in a certain area. Sometimes R&D teams are cross-functional teams with members from departments such as engineering, marketing, and production in addition to members from the research and development department.

Command Groups

command group
A group composed of subordinates who report to the same supervisor; also called *department* or *unit*.

Subordinates who report to the same supervisor compose a command group. When top managers design an organization's structure and establish reporting relationships and a chain of command, they are essentially creating command groups. Command groups, often called *departments* or *units*, perform a significant amount of the work in many organizations. In order to have command groups that help an organization gain a competitive advantage, managers not only need to motivate group members to perform at a high level but also need to be effective leaders.

task force A committee of managers or nonmanagerial employees from various departments or divisions who meet to solve a specific, mutual problem; also called *ad hoc committee*.

Task Forces

Managers form task forces to accomplish specific goals or solve problems in a certain time period; task forces are sometimes called *ad hoc committees*. For example, Michael Rider, owner and top manager of a chain of six gyms and fitness centers in the Midwest, created a task force composed of the general managers of the six gyms to determine whether the fitness centers should institute a separate fee schedule for customers who wanted to use the centers only for aerobics classes (and not use other facilities such as weights, steps, tracks, and swimming pools). The task force was given three months to prepare a report summarizing the pros and cons of the proposed change in fee schedules. After the task force completed its report and reached the conclusion that the change in fee structure probably would reduce revenues rather than increase them and thus should not be implemented, it was disbanded. As in Rider's case, task forces can be a valuable tool for busy managers who do not have the time to personally explore an important issue in depth.

Figuring out if the new pharmaceutical drug is a go takes a strong R&D team made up of medical experts who know the science as well as the market needs.

Self-Managed Work Teams

Self-managed work teams are teams in which members are empowered and have the responsibility and autonomy to complete identifiable pieces of work. On a day-to-day basis, team members decide what the team will do, how it will do it, and which members will perform which specific tasks.[22] Managers assign self-managed work teams' overall goals (such as assembling defect-free computer keyboards) but let team members decide how to meet those goals. Managers usually form self-managed work teams to improve quality, increase motivation and satisfaction, and lower costs. Often, by creating self-managed work

self-managed work team A group of employees who supervise their own activities and monitor the quality of the goods and services they provide.

teams, they combine tasks that individuals working separately used to perform, so the team is responsible for the whole set of tasks that yields an identifiable output or end product.

Managers can take a number of steps to ensure that self-managed work teams are effective and help an organization achieve its goals:[23]

- Give teams enough responsibility and autonomy to be truly self-managing. Refrain from telling team members what to do or solving problems for them even if you (as a manager) know what should be done.

- Make sure a team's work is sufficiently complex so that it entails a number of different steps or procedures that must be performed and results in some kind of finished end product.

- Carefully select members of self-managed work teams. Team members should have the diversity of skills needed to complete the team's work, have the ability to work with others, and want to be part of a team.

- As a manager, realize that your role vis-à-vis self-managed work teams calls for guidance, coaching, and supporting, not supervising. You are a resource for teams to turn to when needed.

- Analyze what type of training team members need and provide it. Working in a self-managed work team often requires that employees have more extensive technical and interpersonal skills.

Managers in a wide variety of organizations have found that self-managed work teams help the organization achieve its goals,[24] as profiled in the following "Management Insight" box.

MANAGEMENT INSIGHT

Self-Managed Teams at Louis Vuitton and Nucor Corporation

Managers at Louis Vuitton, the most valuable luxury brand in the world, and managers at Nucor Corporation, the largest producer of steel and biggest recycler in the United States, have succeeded in effectively using self-managed teams to produce luxury accessories and steel, respectively. Self-managed teams at both companies not only are effective but truly excel and have helped make the companies leaders in their respective industries.[25]

Teams with between 20 and 30 members make Vuitton handbags and accessories. The teams work on only one product at a time; a team with 24 members might produce about 120 handbags per day. Team members are empowered to take ownership of the goods they produce, are encouraged to suggest improvements, and are kept up-to-date on key facts such as products' selling prices and popularity. As Thierry Nogues, a team leader at a Vuitton factory in Ducey, France, put it, "Our goal is to make everyone as multiskilled and autonomous as possible."[26]

Production workers at Nucor are organized into teams ranging in size from 8 to 40 members based on the kind of work the team is responsible for, such as rolling steel or operating a furnace. Team members have considerable autonomy to make decisions and creatively respond to problems and opportunities, and there are

A team member assembles classic Louis Vuitton bags at the company's fine leather goods factory in the Normandy town of Ducey in France.

relatively few layers in the corporate hierarchy, supporting the empowerment of teams.[27] Teams develop their own informal rules for behavior and make their own decisions. As long as team members follow organizational rules and policies (such as those for safety) and meet quality standards, they are free to govern themselves. Managers act as coaches or advisers rather than supervisors, helping teams when needed.[28]

To ensure that production teams are motivated to help Nucor achieve its goals, team members are eligible for weekly bonuses based on the team's performance. Essentially, these production workers receive base pay that does not vary and are eligible to receive weekly bonus pay that can average from 80% to 150% of their regular pay.[29] The bonus rate is predetermined by the work a team performs and the capabilities of the machinery they use. Given the immediacy of the bonus and its potential magnitude, team members are motivated to perform at a high level, develop informal rules that support high performance, and strive to help Nucor reach its goals. Moreover, because all members of a team receive the same amount of weekly bonus money, they are motivated to do their best for the team, cooperate, and help one another out.[30] Of course, in tough economic times such as the recession in the late 2000s, Nucor's production workers' bonuses fall as demand for Nucor's products drops. Nonetheless, Nucor has been able to avoid laying off employees (unlike a lot of other large corporations).[31]

Crafting a luxury handbag and making steel joists couldn't be more different from each other in certain ways. Yet the highly effective self-managed teams at Louis Vuitton and Nucor share some fundamental qualities. These teams really do take ownership of their work and are highly motivated to perform effectively. Team members have the skills and knowledge they need to be effective, they are empowered to make decisions about their work, and they know their teams are making vital contributions to their organizations.[32]

Sometimes employees have individual jobs but also are part of a self-managed team that is formed to accomplish a specific goal or work on an important project. Employees need to perform their own individual job tasks and also actively contribute to the self-managed team so that the team achieves its goal.

Like all groups self-managed work teams sometimes run into trouble. Members may be reluctant to discipline one another by withholding bonuses from members who are not performing up to par or by firing members.[33] Buster Jarrell, a manager who oversaw self-managed work teams in AES Corporation's Houston plant, found that although the self-managed work teams were highly effective, they had a difficult time firing team members who were performing poorly.[34]

Virtual Teams

virtual team A team whose members rarely or never meet face-to-face but, rather, interact by using various forms of information technology such as e-mail, computer networks, telephone, fax, and videoconferences.

Virtual teams are teams whose members rarely or never meet face-to-face but, rather, interact by using various forms of information technology such as e-mail, text messaging, computer networks, telephone, fax, and videoconferences. As organizations become increasingly global, and as the need for specialized knowledge increases due to advances in technology, managers can create virtual teams to solve problems or explore opportunities without being limited by team members needing to work in the same geographic location.[35]

Take the case of an organization that has manufacturing facilities in Australia, Canada, the United States, and Mexico and is encountering a quality problem in a complex manufacturing process. Each of its facilities has a quality control team headed by a quality control manager. The vice president for production does not try to solve the problem by forming and leading a team at one of the four manufacturing facilities; instead she forms and leads a virtual team composed of the quality control managers of the four plants and the plants' general managers. When these team members communicate via e-mail, the company's networking site, and videoconferencing, a wide array of knowledge and experience is brought to solve the problem.

The principal advantage of virtual teams is that they enable managers to disregard geographic distances and form teams whose members have the knowledge, expertise, and experience to tackle a particular problem or take advantage of a specific opportunity.[36] Virtual teams also can include members who are not actually employees of the organization itself; a virtual team might include members of a company that is used for outsourcing. More and more companies, including BP PLC, Nokia Corporation, and Ogilvy & Mather, are using virtual teams.[37]

Members of virtual teams rely on two forms of information technology: synchronous technologies and asynchronous technologies.[38] *Synchronous technologies* let virtual team members communicate and interact with one another in real time simultaneously and include videoconferencing, teleconferencing, and electronic meetings. *Asynchronous technologies* delay communication and include e-mail, electronic bulletin boards, and Internet websites. Many virtual teams use both kinds of technology depending on what projects they are working on.

Increasing globalization is likely to result in more organizations relying on virtual teams to a greater extent.[39] One challenge members of virtual teams face is building a sense of camaraderie and trust among team members who rarely, if ever, meet face-to-face. To address this challenge, some organizations schedule recreational activities, such as ski trips, so virtual team members can get together. Other organizations make sure virtual team members have a chance to meet in person soon after the team is formed and then schedule periodic face-to-face meetings to promote trust, understanding, and cooperation in the teams.[40] The need for such meetings is underscored by research suggesting that while some virtual teams can be as effective as teams that meet face-to-face, virtual team members might be less satisfied with teamwork efforts and have fewer feelings of camaraderie or cohesion. (Group cohesiveness is discussed in more detail later in the chapter.)[41]

Research also suggests that it is important for managers to keep track of virtual teams and intervene when necessary by, for example, encouraging members of teams who do not communicate often enough to monitor their team's progress and making sure team members actually have the time, and are recognized for, their virtual teamwork.[42] Additionally, when virtual teams are experiencing downtime or rough spots, managers might try to schedule face-to-face team time to bring team members together and help them focus on their goals.[43]

Researchers at the London Business School, including Professor Lynda Gratton, recently studied global virtual teams to try to identify factors that might help such teams be effective.[44] Based on their research, Gratton suggests that when forming virtual teams, it is helpful to include a few members who already know each other, other members who are well connected to people outside the team, and when possible, members who have volunteered to be a part of the team.[45] It is also advantageous for companies to have some kind of online site where team members can learn more about each other and the kinds of work they are engaged in, and in particular, a shared online workspace that team members can access around the clock.[46] Frequent communication is beneficial. Additionally, virtual team projects should be perceived as meaningful, interesting, and important by their members to promote and sustain their motivation.[47]

friendship group
An informal group composed of employees who enjoy one another's company and socialize with one another.

A recycling interest group organizes like-minded colleagues to help pick up the slack where the formal organization may be lacking.

Friendship Groups

The groups described so far are formal groups created by managers. Friendship groups are informal groups composed of employees who enjoy one another's company and socialize with one another. Members of friendship groups may have lunch together, take breaks together, or meet after work for meals, sports, or other activities. Friendship groups help satisfy employees' needs for interpersonal interaction, can provide needed social support in times of stress, and can contribute to people's feeling good at work and being satisfied with their jobs. Managers themselves often form friendship groups. The informal relationships that managers build in friendship groups can often help them solve work-related problems because members of these groups typically discuss work-related matters and offer advice.

Interest Groups

interest group An informal group composed of employees seeking to achieve a common goal related to their membership in an organization.

Employees form informal interest groups when they seek to achieve a common goal related to their membership in an organization. Employees may form interest groups, for example, to encourage managers to consider instituting flexible working hours, providing on-site child care, improving working conditions, or more proactively supporting environmental protection. Interest groups can give managers valuable insights into the issues and concerns that are foremost in employees' minds. They also can signal the need for change.

Group Dynamics

How groups function and, ultimately, their effectiveness hinge on group characteristics and processes known collectively as *group dynamics*. In this section we discuss five key elements of group dynamics: group size and roles, group leadership, group development, group norms, and group cohesiveness.

LO 11-3 Explain how different elements of group dynamics influence the functioning and effectiveness of groups and teams.

Group Size and Roles

Managers need to take group size and group roles into account as they create and maintain high-performing groups and teams.

GROUP SIZE The number of members in a group can be an important determinant of members' motivation and commitment and group performance. There are several advantages to keeping a group relatively small—between two and nine members. Compared with members of large groups, members of small groups tend to (1) interact more with each other and find it easier to coordinate their efforts, (2) be more motivated, satisfied, and committed, (3) find it easier to share information, and (4) be better able to see the importance of their personal contributions for group success. A disadvantage of small rather than large groups is that members of small groups have fewer resources available to accomplish their goals.

Large groups—with 10 or more members—also offer some advantages. They have more resources at their disposal to achieve group goals than small groups do. These resources include the knowledge, experience, skills, and abilities of group members as well as their actual time and effort. Large groups also let managers obtain the advantages stemming from the division of labor—splitting the work to be performed into particular tasks and assigning tasks to individual workers. Workers who specialize in particular tasks are likely to become skilled at performing those tasks and contribute significantly to high group performance.

The disadvantages of large groups include the problems of communication and coordination and the lower levels of motivation, satisfaction, and commitment that members of large groups sometimes experience. It is clearly more difficult to share information with, and coordinate the activities of, 16 people rather than 8 people. Moreover, members of large groups might not think their efforts are really needed and sometimes might not even feel a part of the group.

In deciding on the appropriate size for any group, managers attempt to gain the advantages of small group size and, at the same time, form groups with sufficient resources to accomplish their goals and have a well-developed division of labor. As a general rule of thumb, groups should have no more members than necessary to achieve a division of labor and provide the resources needed to achieve group goals. In R&D teams, for example, group size is too large when (1) members spend more time communicating what they know to others than applying what they know to solve problems and create new products, (2) individual productivity decreases, and (3) group performance suffers.[48]

division of labor Splitting the work to be performed into particular tasks and assigning tasks to individual workers.

GROUP ROLES A group role is a set of behaviors and tasks that a member of a group is expected to perform because of his or her position in the group. Members of cross-functional teams, for example, are expected to perform roles relevant to their special areas of expertise. In our earlier example of cross-functional teams at Hallmark Cards, it is the role of writers on the teams to create verses for new cards, the role of artists to draw illustrations, and the role of designers to put verse and artwork together in an attractive and appealing card design. The roles of members of top management teams are shaped primarily by their areas of expertise—production, marketing, finance, research and development—but members of top management teams also typically draw on their broad expertise as planners and strategists.

In forming groups and teams, managers need to clearly communicate to group members the expectations for their roles in the group, what is required of them, and how the different roles in the group fit together to accomplish group goals. Managers also need to realize that group roles often change and evolve as a group's tasks and goals change and as group members gain experience and knowledge. Thus, to get the performance gains that come from experience or "learning by doing," managers should encourage group members

group role A set of behaviors and tasks that a member of a group is expected to perform because of his or her position in the group.

role making Taking the initiative to modify an assigned role by assuming additional responsibilities.

to take the initiative to assume additional responsibilities as they see fit and modify their assigned roles. This process, called role making, can enhance individual and group performance.

In self-managed work teams and some other groups, group members themselves are responsible for creating and assigning roles. Many self-managed work teams also pick their own team leaders. When group members create their own roles, managers should be available to group members in an advisory capacity, helping them effectively settle conflicts and disagreements. At Johnsonville Foods, for example, the position titles of first-line managers were changed to "advisory coach" to reflect the managers' role vis-à-vis the self-managed work teams they oversaw.[49]

Group Leadership

All groups and teams need leadership. Indeed, as we discussed in detail in Chapter 10, effective leadership is a key ingredient for high-performing groups, teams, and organizations. Sometimes managers assume the leadership role in groups and teams, as is the case in many command groups and top management teams. Or a manager may appoint a member of a group who is not a manager to be group leader or chairperson, as is the case in a task force or standing committee. In other cases, group or team members may choose their own leaders, or a leader may emerge naturally as group members work together to achieve group goals. When managers empower members of self-managed work teams, they often let group members choose their own leaders. Some self-managed work teams find it effective to rotate the leadership role among their members. Whether or not leaders of groups and teams are managers, and whether they are appointed by managers (often referred to as *formal leaders*) or emerge naturally in a group (often referred to as *informal leaders*), they play an important role in ensuring that groups and teams perform up to their potential.

Group Development over Time

As many managers overseeing self-managed teams have learned, it sometimes takes a self-managed work team two or three years to perform up to its true capabilities.[50] As their experience suggests, what a group is capable of achieving depends in part on its stage of development. Knowing that it takes considerable time for self-managed work teams to get up and running has helped managers have realistic expectations for new teams and know that they need to give new team members considerable training and guidance.

Although every group's development over time is unique, researchers have identified five stages of group development that many groups seem to pass through (see Figure 11.3).[51] In the first stage, *forming*, members try to get to know one another and reach a common understanding of what the group is trying to accomplish and how group members should behave. During this stage, managers should strive to make each member feel that he or she is a valued part of the group.

In the second stage, *storming*, group members experience conflict and disagreements because some members do not wish to submit to the demands of other group members. Disputes may arise over who should lead the group. Self-managed work teams can be particularly vulnerable during the storming stage. Managers need to keep an eye on groups at this stage to make sure conflict does not get out of hand.

Figure 11.3

Five Stages of Group
Development

Forming → Storming → Norming → Performing → Adjourning

During the third stage, *norming*, close ties between group members develop, and feelings of friendship and camaraderie emerge. Group members arrive at a consensus about what goals they should seek to achieve and how group members should behave toward one another. In the fourth stage, *performing*, the real work of the group gets accomplished. Depending on the type of group in question, managers need to take different steps at this stage to help ensure that groups are effective. Managers of command groups need to make sure that group members are motivated and effectively led. Managers overseeing self-managed work teams have to empower team members and make sure teams are given enough responsibility and autonomy at the performing stage.

The last stage, *adjourning*, applies only to groups that eventually are disbanded, such as task forces. During adjourning a group is dispersed. Sometimes adjourning takes place when a group completes a finished product, such as when a task force evaluating the pros and cons of providing on-site child care produces a report supporting its recommendation.

Managers should have a flexible approach to group development and should keep attuned to the different needs and requirements of groups at the various stages.[52] Above all else, and regardless of the stage of development, managers need to think of themselves as *resources* for groups. Thus managers always should strive to find ways to help groups and teams function more effectively.

Group Norms

LO 11-4 Explain why it is important for groups and teams to have a balance of conformity and deviance and a moderate level of cohesiveness.

group norms Shared guidelines or rules for behavior that most group members follow.

All groups, whether top management teams, self-managed work teams, or command groups, need to control their members' behaviors to ensure that the group performs at a high level and meets its goals. Assigning roles to each group member is one way to control behavior in groups. Another important way in which groups influence members' behavior is through the development and enforcement of group norms.[53] Group norms are shared guidelines or rules for behavior that most group members follow. Groups develop norms concerning a wide variety of behaviors, including working hours, the sharing of information among group members, how certain group tasks should be performed, and even how members of a group should dress.

Managers should encourage members of a group to develop norms that contribute to group performance and the attainment of group goals. For example, group norms dictating that each member of a cross-functional team should always be available for the rest of the team when his or her input is needed, return phone calls as soon as possible, inform other team members of travel plans, and give team members a phone number at which he or she can be reached when traveling on business help to ensure that the team is efficient, performs at a high level, and achieves its goals. A norm in a command group of secretaries that dictates that secretaries who happen to have a light workload in any given week should help out secretaries with heavier workloads helps to ensure that the group completes all assignments in a timely and efficient manner. And a norm in a top management team that dictates that team members should always consult with one another before making major decisions helps to ensure that good decisions are made with a minimum of errors.

CONFORMITY AND DEVIANCE Group members conform to norms for three reasons: (1) They want to obtain rewards and avoid punishments; (2) they want to imitate group members whom they like and admire; (3) they have internalized the norm and believe it is the right and proper way to behave.[54] Consider the case of Robert King, who conformed to his department's norm of attending a fund-raiser for a community food bank. King's conformity could be due to (1) his desire to be a member of the group in good standing and to have friendly relationships with other group members (rewards), (2) his copying the behavior of other members of the department whom he respects and who always attend the fund-raiser (imitating other group members), or (3) his belief in the merits of supporting the activities of the food bank (believing that is the right and proper way to behave).

Failure to conform, or deviance, occurs when a member of a group violates a group norm. Deviance signals that a group is not controlling one of its members' behaviors. Groups generally respond to members who behave deviantly in one of three ways:[55]

1. The group might try to get the member to change his or her deviant ways. Group members might try to convince the member of the need to conform, or they might ignore or even punish the deviant. For example, in a Jacksonville Foods plant, Liz Senkbiel, a member of a self-managed work team responsible for weighing sausages, failed to conform to a group norm dictating that group members should periodically clean up an untidy interview room. Because Senkbiel refused to take part in the team's cleanup efforts, team members reduced her monthly bonus by about $225 for a two-month period. Senkbiel clearly learned the costs of deviant behavior in her team.

2. The group might expel the member.

3. The group might change the norm to be consistent with the member's behavior.

This last alternative suggests that some deviant behavior can be functional for groups. Deviance is functional for a group when it causes group members to evaluate norms that may be dysfunctional but are taken for granted by the group. Often group members do not think about why they behave in a certain way or why they follow certain norms. Deviance can cause group members to reflect on their norms and change them when appropriate.

Consider a group of receptionists in a beauty salon who followed the norm that all appointments would be handwritten in an appointment book and, at the end of each day, the receptionist on duty would enter the appointments into the salon's computer system, which printed out the hairdressers' daily schedules. One day a receptionist decided to enter appointments directly into the computer system when they were being made, bypassing the appointment book. This deviant behavior caused the other receptionists to think about why they were using the appointment book at all. After consulting with the owner of the salon, the group changed its norm. Now appointments are entered directly into the computer, which saves time and reduces scheduling errors.

ENCOURAGING A BALANCE OF CONFORMITY AND DEVIANCE To effectively help an organization gain a competitive advantage, groups and teams need the right balance of conformity and deviance (see Figure 11.4). A group needs a certain level of conformity to ensure that it can control members' behavior and channel it in the direction of high performance and group goal accomplishment.

Figure 11.4

Balancing Conformity
and Deviance in Groups

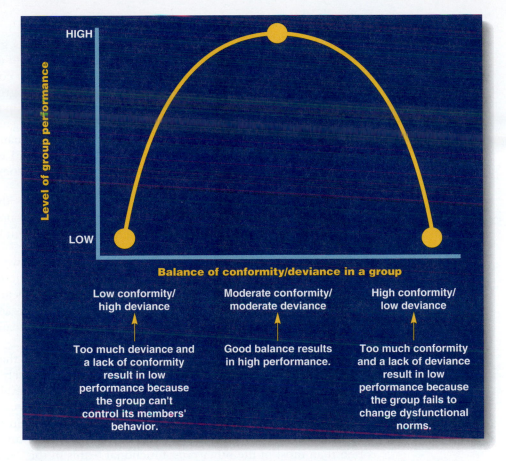

Balance of conformity/deviance in a group

Low conformity/ high deviance	Moderate conformity/ moderate deviance	High conformity/ low deviance
Too much deviance and a lack of conformity result in low performance because the group can't control its members' behavior.	Good balance results in high performance.	Too much conformity and a lack of deviance result in low performance because the group fails to change dysfunctional norms.

A group also needs a certain level of deviance to ensure that dysfunctional norms are discarded and replaced with functional ones. Balancing conformity and deviance is a pressing concern for all groups, whether they are top management teams, R&D teams, command groups, or self-managed work teams.

The extent of conformity and reactions to deviance within groups are determined by group members themselves. The three bases for conformity just described are powerful forces that more often than not result in group members' conforming to norms. Sometimes these forces are so strong that deviance rarely occurs in groups, and when it does, it is stamped out.

Managers can take several steps to ensure adequate tolerance of deviance in groups so that group members are willing to deviate from dysfunctional norms and, when deviance occurs in their group, reflect on the appropriateness of the violated norm and change the norm if necessary. First, managers can be role models for the groups and teams they oversee. When managers encourage and accept employees' suggestions for changes in procedures, do not rigidly insist that tasks be accomplished in a certain way, and admit when a norm they once supported is no longer functional, they signal to group members that conformity should not come at the expense of needed changes and improvements. Second, managers should let employees know that there are always ways to improve group processes and performance levels and thus opportunities to replace existing norms with norms that will better enable a group to achieve its goals and perform at a high level. Third, managers should encourage members of groups and teams to periodically assess the appropriateness of their norms.

Group Cohesiveness

Another important element of group dynamics that affects group performance and effectiveness is group cohesiveness, which is the degree to which members are attracted to or loyal to their group or team.[56] When group cohesiveness is high, individuals strongly value their group membership, find the group appealing, and have strong desires to remain a part of the group. When group cohesiveness is low, group members do not find their group particularly appealing and have little desire to retain their group membership. Research suggests that managers should strive to have a moderate level of cohesiveness in the groups and teams they manage because that is most likely to contribute to an organization's competitive advantage.

CONSEQUENCES OF GROUP COHESIVENESS There are three major consequences of group cohesiveness: level of participation within a group, level of conformity to group norms, and emphasis on group goal accomplishment (see Figure 11.5).[57]

Level of Participation Within a Group   As group cohesiveness increases, the extent of group members' participation within the group increases. Participation contributes to group effectiveness because group members are actively involved in the group, ensure that group tasks get accomplished, readily share information with each other, and have frequent and open communication (the important topic of communication is covered in depth in Chapter 13).

A moderate level of group cohesiveness helps ensure that group members actively participate in the group and communicate effectively with one another. The reason why managers may not want to encourage high levels of cohesiveness is illustrated by the example of two cross-functional teams responsible for developing new toys. Members of the highly cohesive Team Alpha often have lengthy meetings that usually start with non-work-related conversations and jokes, meet more often than most of the other cross-functional teams in the company, and spend a good portion of their time communicating the ins and outs of their department's contribution to toy development to other team members. Members of the moderately cohesive Team Beta generally have efficient meetings in which ideas are communicated and discussed as needed, do not meet more often than necessary, and share the ins and outs of their expertise with one another to the extent needed

Figure 11.5

Sources and Consequences of Group Cohesiveness

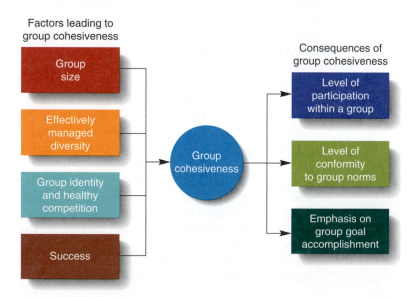

for the development process. Teams Alpha and Beta have both developed some top-selling toys. However, it generally takes Team Alpha 30% longer to do so than Team Beta. This is why too much cohesiveness can be too much of a good thing.

Level of Conformity to Group Norms   Increasing levels of group cohesiveness result in increasing levels of conformity to group norms, and when cohesiveness becomes high, there may be so little deviance in groups that group members conform to norms even when they are dysfunctional. In contrast, low cohesiveness can result in too much deviance and undermine the ability of a group to control its members' behaviors to get things done.

Teams Alpha and Beta in the toy company both had the same norm for toy development. It dictated that members of each team would discuss potential ideas for new toys, decide on a line of toys to pursue, and then have the team member from R&D design a prototype. Recently a new animated movie featuring a family of rabbits produced by a small film company was an unexpected hit, and major toy companies were scrambling to reach licensing agreements to produce toy lines featuring the rabbits. The top management team in the toy company assigned Teams Alpha and Beta to develop the new toy lines quickly to beat the competition.

Members of Team Alpha followed their usual toy development norm even though the marketing expert on the team believed the process could have been streamlined to save time. The marketing expert on Team Beta urged the team to deviate from its toy development norm. She suggested that the team not have R&D develop prototypes but, instead, modify top-selling toys the company already made to feature rabbits and then reach a licensing agreement with the film company based on the high sales potential (given the company's prior success). Once the licensing agreement was signed, the company could take the time needed to develop innovative and unique rabbit toys with more input from R&D.

As a result of the willingness of the marketing expert on Team Beta to deviate from the norm for toy development, the toy company obtained an exclusive licensing agreement with the film company and had its first rabbit toys on the shelves of stores in a record three months. Groups need a balance of conformity and deviance, so a moderate level of cohesiveness often yields the best outcome, as it did in the case of Team Beta.

Emphasis on Group Goal Accomplishment   As group cohesiveness increases, the emphasis placed on group goal accomplishment also increases within a group. A strong emphasis on group goal accomplishment, however, does not always lead to organizational effectiveness. For an organization to be effective and gain a competitive advantage, the different groups and teams in the organization must cooperate with one another and be motivated to achieve *organizational goals,* even if doing so sometimes comes at the expense of the achievement of group goals. A moderate level of cohesiveness motivates group members to accomplish both group and organizational goals. High levels of cohesiveness can cause group members to be so focused on group goal accomplishment that they may strive to achieve group goals no matter what—even when doing so jeopardizes organizational performance.

At the toy company, the major goal of the cross-functional teams was to develop new toy lines that were truly innovative, utilized the latest in technology, and were in some way fundamentally distinct from other toys on the market. When it came to the rabbit project, Team Alpha's high level of cohesiveness contributed to its continued emphasis on its group goal of developing an innovative line of toys; thus the team stuck with its usual design process. Team Beta, in contrast, realized that developing the new line of toys quickly was an important organizational goal

How much cohesiveness is too much? You can answer that question when you evaluate whether a group actually gets something done in its meetings or whether most of the conversation drifting out of the room consists of jokes, life experiences, or comparisons of the last company dinner's entrees.

that should take precedence over the group's goal of developing groundbreaking new toys, at least in the short term. Team Beta's moderate level of cohesiveness contributed to team members' doing what was best for the toy company in this case.

FACTORS LEADING TO GROUP COHESIVENESS

Four factors contribute to the level of group cohesiveness (see Figure 11.5).[58] By influencing these *determinants of group cohesiveness,* managers can raise or lower the level of cohesiveness to promote moderate levels of cohesiveness in groups and teams.

Group Size   As we mentioned earlier, members of small groups tend to be more motivated and committed than members of large groups. Thus to promote cohesiveness in groups, when feasible, managers should form groups that are small to medium in size (about 2 to 15 members). If a group is low in cohesiveness and large in size, managers might want to consider dividing the group in half and assigning different tasks and goals to the two newly formed groups.

Effectively Managed Diversity   In general, people tend to like and get along with others who are similar to themselves. It is easier to communicate with someone, for example, who shares your values, has a similar background, and has had similar experiences. However, as discussed in Chapter 3, diversity in groups, teams, and organizations can help an organization gain a competitive advantage. Diverse groups often come up with more innovative and creative ideas. One reason why cross-functional teams are so popular in organizations like Hallmark Cards is that the diverse expertise represented in the teams results in higher levels of team performance.

In forming groups and teams, managers need to make sure the diversity in knowledge, experience, expertise, and other characteristics necessary for group goal accomplishment is represented in the new groups. Managers then have to make sure this diversity in group membership is effectively managed so groups will be cohesive (see Chapter 3).

Group Identity and Healthy Competition   When group cohesiveness is low, managers can often increase it by encouraging groups to develop their own identities or personalities and engage in healthy competition. This is precisely what managers at Eaton Corporation's manufacturing facility in Lincoln, Illinois, did. Eaton's employees manufacture products such as engine valves, gears, truck axles, and circuit breakers. Managers at Eaton created self-managed work teams to cut costs and improve performance. They realized, however, that the teams would have to be cohesive to ensure that they would strive to achieve their goals. Managers promoted group identity by having the teams give themselves names such as "The Hoods," "The Worms," and "Scrap Attack" (a team striving to reduce costly scrap metal waste by 50%). Healthy competition among groups was promoted by displaying measures of each team's performance and the extent to which teams met their goals on a large TV screen in the cafeteria and by rewarding team members for team performance.[59]

If groups are too cohesive, managers can try to decrease cohesiveness by promoting organizational (rather than group) identity and making the organization as a whole the focus of the group's efforts. Organizational identity can be promoted by making group members feel that they are valued members of the organization and by stressing cooperation across groups to promote the achievement of organizational goals. Excessive levels of cohesiveness also can be reduced by reducing or eliminating competition among groups and rewarding cooperation.

Success   When it comes to promoting group cohesiveness, there is more than a grain of truth to the saying "Nothing succeeds like success." As groups become more successful, they become increasingly attractive to their members, and their cohesiveness tends to increase. When cohesiveness is low, managers can increase cohesiveness by making sure a group can achieve some noticeable and visible successes.

Consider a group of salespeople in the housewares department of a medium-size department store. The housewares department was recently moved to a corner of the store's basement. Its remote location resulted in low sales because of infrequent customer traffic in that part of the store. The salespeople, who were generally evaluated favorably by their supervisors and were valued members of the store, tried various initiatives to boost sales, but to no avail. As a result of this lack of success and the poor performance of their department, their cohesiveness started to plummet. To increase and preserve the cohesiveness of the group, the store manager implemented a group-based incentive across the store. In any month, members of the group with the best attendance and punctuality records would have their names and pictures posted on a bulletin board in the cafeteria and would each receive a $50 gift certificate. The housewares group frequently had the best records, and their success on this dimension helped to build and maintain their cohesiveness. Moreover, this initiative boosted attendance and discouraged lateness throughout the store.

Managing Groups and Teams for High Performance

Now that you understand why groups and teams are so important for organizations, the types of groups managers create, and group dynamics, we consider some additional steps managers can take to make sure groups and teams perform at a high level and contribute to organizational effectiveness. Managers striving to have top-performing groups and teams need to motivate group members to work toward the achievement of organizational goals and reduce social loafing.

LO 11-5 Describe how managers can motivate group members to achieve organizational goals and reduce social loafing in groups and teams.

Motivating Group Members to Achieve Organizational Goals

When work is difficult, tedious, or requires a high level of commitment and energy, managers cannot assume group members will always be motivated to work toward the achievement of organizational goals. Consider a group of house painters who paint the interiors and exteriors of new homes for a construction company and are paid on an hourly basis. Why should they strive to complete painting jobs quickly and efficiently if doing so will just make them feel more tired at the end of the day and they will not receive any tangible benefits? It makes more sense for the painters to adopt a relaxed approach, to take frequent breaks, and to work at a leisurely pace. This relaxed approach, however, impairs the construction company's ability to gain a competitive advantage because it raises costs and increases the time needed to complete a new home.

Managers can motivate members of groups and teams to achieve organizational goals by making sure the members themselves benefit when the group or team performs highly. For example, if members of a self-managed work team know they will receive a weekly bonus based on team performance, they will be motivated to perform at a high level.

Managers often rely on some combination of individual and group-based incentives to motivate members of groups and teams to work toward the achievement of organizational goals. When individual performance within a group can be assessed, pay is often determined by individual performance or by both individual and group performance. When individual performance within a group cannot be accurately assessed, group performance should be the key determinant of pay levels. Many companies that use self-managed work teams base team members' pay in part on team performance.[60] A major challenge for managers is to develop a fair pay system that will lead to both high individual motivation and high group or team performance.

Other benefits managers can make available to high-performance group members—in addition to monetary rewards—include extra resources such as equipment and computer software, awards and other forms of recognition, and choice of future work assignments. For example, members of self-managed work teams that develop new software at companies such as Microsoft often value working on interesting and important projects; members of teams that have performed at a high level are rewarded by being assigned to interesting and important new projects.

At IDEO, an innovative design firm, managers motivate team members by making them feel important. As Tom Kelley, IDEO's general manager, put it, "When people feel special, they'll perform beyond your wildest dreams."[61] To make IDEO team members feel special, IDEO managers plan unique and fun year-end parties, give teams the opportunity to take time off if they feel they need or want to, encourage teams to take field trips, and see pranks as a way to incorporate fun into the workplace.[62]

Valero Energy motivates groups and teams to achieve organizational goals by valuing its employees, looking out for their well-being, and standing by them in crisis situations.[63] For example, employees with medical emergencies can use Valero's corporate jet if they need to, and Valero covers the complete cost of employee's health insurance premiums.[64] In turn, group members put forth high levels of effort to help Valero achieve its goals. As former Valero CEO and chairman Bill Greehey put it, "The more you do for your employees, the more they do for shareholders and the more they do for the community."[65]

When Hurricane Katrina hit the Louisiana coastline in 2005, the way Valero stood by employees in its St. Charles oil refinery near New Orleans, and the way employees stood by each other and the company, brought plant manager Jonathan Stuart to tears as he was briefing Greehey and other top managers a few days after the hurricane hit.[66] Stuart led a 50- person crew that rode out the hurricane in the shut-down refinery. The day before the storm hit, a supervisor used his personal credit card to buy supplies and stayed up all night preparing meals for the crew. Crew members worked round the clock, putting up new power poles, repairing power lines, and replacing motors. The refinery was up and running within eight days (while a Shell refinery close by was still shut down), and the crew had located all of the plant's 570 employees.[67]

Valero's headquarters had supplies delivered to employees whose homes were damaged; trucks brought in food, water, generators, chain saws, refrigerators, shovels, and Nextel phones (the only cell phone system that was still working). Sixty mobile homes were brought in for employees whose houses were unlivable. Employees and law enforcement personnel were given free fuel, and employees were given up to $10,000 in aide from Valero's SAFE fund. Valero continued issuing paychecks to its employees while other affected refineries did not.[68]

Reducing Social Loafing in Groups

We have been focusing on the steps managers can take to encourage high levels of performance in groups. Managers, however, need to be aware of an important downside to group and team work: the potential for social loafing, which reduces group performance. Social loafing is the tendency of individuals to put forth less effort when they work in groups than when they work alone.[69] Have you ever worked on a group project in which one or two group members never seemed to be pulling their weight? Have you ever worked in a student club or committee in which some members always seemed to be missing meetings and never volunteered for activities? Have you ever had a job in which one or two of your coworkers seemed to be slacking off because they knew you or other members of your work group would make up for their low levels of effort? If so, you have witnessed social loafing in action.

Social loafing can occur in all kinds of groups and teams and in all kinds of organizations. It can result in lower group performance and may even prevent a group from attaining its goals. Fortunately managers can take steps to reduce social loafing and sometimes completely eliminate it; we will look at three (see Figure 11.6):

1. *Make individual contributions to a group identifiable.* Some people may engage in social loafing when they work in groups because they think they can hide in the crowd—no one will notice if they put forth less effort than they should. Other people may think if they put forth high levels of effort and make substantial

social loafing The tendency of individuals to put forth less effort when they work in groups than when they work alone.

Figure 11.6

Three Ways to Reduce Social Loafing

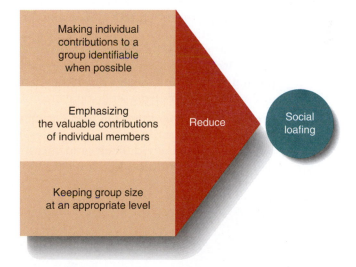

contributions to the group, their contributions will not be noticed and they will receive no rewards for their work—so why bother.[70]

One way that managers can effectively eliminate social loafing is by making individual contributions to a group identifiable so that group members perceive that low and high levels of effort will be noticed and individual contributions evaluated.[71] Managers can accomplish this by assigning specific tasks to group members and holding them accountable for their completion. Take the case of a group of eight employees responsible for reshelving returned books in a large public library in New York. The head librarian was concerned that there was always a backlog of seven or eight carts of books to be reshelved, even though the employees never seemed to be particularly busy and some even found time to sit down and read newspapers and magazines. The librarian decided to try to eliminate the apparent social loafing by assigning each employee sole responsibility for reshelving a particular section of the library. Because the library's front desk employees sorted the books by section on the carts as they were returned, holding the shelvers responsible for particular sections was easily accomplished. Once the shelvers knew the librarian could identify their effort or lack thereof, there were rarely any backlogs of books to be reshelved.

Sometimes the members of a group can cooperate to eliminate social loafing by making individual contributions identifiable. For example, in a small security company, members of a self-managed work team who assemble control boxes for home alarm systems start each day by deciding who will perform which tasks that day and how much work each member and the group as a whole should strive to accomplish. Each team member knows that, at the end of the day, the other team members will know exactly how much he or she has accomplished. With this system in place, social loafing never occurs in the team. Remember, however, that in some teams, individual contributions cannot be made identifiable.

2. *Emphasize the valuable contributions of individual members.* Another reason why social loafing may occur is that people sometimes think their efforts are unnecessary or unimportant when they work in a group. They feel the group will accomplish its goals and perform at an acceptable level whether or not they personally perform at a high level. To counteract this belief, when managers form groups, they should assign individuals to a group on the basis of the valuable contributions that *each* person can make to the group as a whole. Clearly communicating to group members why each person's contributions are valuable to the group is an effective means by which managers and group members themselves can reduce or eliminate social loafing.[72] This is most easily accomplished in cross-functional teams, where each member's valuable contribution to the team derives from a personal area of expertise.

3. *Keep group size at an appropriate level.* Group size is related to the causes of social loafing we just described. As size increases, identifying individual contributions becomes increasingly difficult, and members are increasingly likely to think their individual contributions are not important. To overcome this, managers

should form groups with no more members than are needed to accomplish group goals and perform at a high level.[73]

Summary and Review

GROUPS, TEAMS, AND ORGANIZATIONAL EFFECTIVENESS A group is two or more people who interact with each other to accomplish certain goals or meet certain needs. A team is a group whose members work intensely with one another to achieve a specific common goal or objective. Groups and teams can contribute to organizational effectiveness by enhancing performance, increasing responsiveness to customers, increasing innovation, and being a source of motivation for their members. **[LO 11-1]**

TYPES OF GROUPS AND TEAMS Formal groups are groups that managers establish to achieve organizational goals; they include cross-functional teams, cross-cultural teams, top management teams, research and development teams, command groups, task forces, self-managed work teams, and virtual teams. Informal groups are groups that employees form because they believe the groups will help them achieve their own goals or meet their needs; they include friendship groups and interest groups. **[LO 11-2]**

GROUP DYNAMICS Key elements of group dynamics are group size and roles, group leadership, group development, group norms, and group cohesiveness. The advantages and disadvantages of large and small groups suggest that managers should form groups with no more members than are needed to provide the group with the human resources it needs to achieve its goals and use a division of labor. A group role is a set of behaviors and tasks that a member of a group is expected to perform because of his or her position in the group. All groups and teams need leadership. **[LO 11-3]**

Five stages of development that many groups pass through are forming, storming, norming, performing, and adjourning. Group norms are shared rules for behavior that most group members follow. To be effective, groups need a balance of conformity and deviance. Conformity allows a group to control its members' behavior to achieve group goals; deviance provides the impetus for needed change. **[LO 11-3, 11-4]**

Group cohesiveness is the attractiveness of a group or team to its members. As group cohesiveness increases, so do the level of participation and communication within a group, the level of conformity to group norms, and the emphasis on group goal accomplishment. Managers should strive to achieve a moderate level of group cohesiveness in the groups and teams they manage. **[LO 11-4]**

MANAGING GROUPS AND TEAMS FOR HIGH PERFORMANCE

To make sure groups and teams perform at a high level, managers need to motivate group members to work toward the achievement of organizational goals and reduce social loafing. Managers can motivate members of groups and teams to work toward the achievement of organizational goals by making sure members personally benefit when the group or team performs at a high level. **[LO 11-5]**

Management *in Action*

TOPICS FOR DISCUSSION AND ACTION

Discussion

1. Why do all organizations need to rely on groups and teams to achieve their goals and gain a competitive advantage? [LO 11-1]

2. What kinds of employees would prefer to work in a virtual team? What kinds of employees would prefer to work in a team that meets face-to-face? [LO 11-2]

3. Think about a group that you are a member of, and describe that group's current stage of development.

Does the development of this group seem to be following the forming, storming, norming, performing, and adjourning stages described in the chapter? [LO 11-3]

4. Discuss the reasons why too much conformity can hurt groups and their organizations. [LO 11-4]

5. Why do some groups have very low levels of cohesiveness? [LO 11-4]

6. Imagine that you are the manager of a hotel. What

steps will you take to reduce social loafing by members of the cleaning staff who are responsible for keeping all common areas and guest rooms spotless? [LO 11-5]

Action

7. Interview one or more managers in an organization in your local community to identify the types of groups and teams that the organization uses to achieve its goals. What challenges do these groups and teams face? [LO 11-2]

BUILDING MANAGEMENT SKILLS

Diagnosing Group Failures [LO 11-1, 11-2, 11-3, 11-4, 11-5]

Think about the last dissatisfying or discouraging experience you had as a member of a group or team. Perhaps the group did not accomplish its goals, perhaps group members could agree about nothing, or perhaps there was too much social loafing. Now answer the following questions.

1. What type of group was this?
2. Were group members motivated to achieve group goals? Why or why not?
3. How large was the group and what group roles did members play?
4. What were the group's norms? How much conformity

and deviance existed in the group?

5. How cohesive was the group? Why do you think the group's cohesiveness was at this level? What consequences did this level of group cohesiveness have for the group and its members?

6. Was social loafing a problem in this group? Why or why not?

7. What could the group's leader or manager have done differently to increase group effectiveness?

8. What could group members have done differently to increase group effectiveness?

MANAGING ETHICALLY [LO 11-1, 11-2, 11-3, 11-4, 11-5]

Some self-managed teams encounter a vexing problem: One or more members engage in

social loafing, and other members are reluctant to try to rectify the situation. Social loafing can

be especially troubling if team members' pay is based on team performance and social loafing reduces the team's performance and thus the pay of all members (even the highest performers). Even if managers are aware of the problem, they may be reluctant to take action because the team is supposedly self-managing.

Questions

1. Either individually or in a group, think about the ethical implications of social loafing in a self-managed team.

2. Do managers have an ethical obligation to step in when they are aware of social loafing in a self-managed team? Why or why not? Do other team members have an obligation to try to curtail the social loafing? Why or why not?

SMALL GROUP BREAKOUT EXERCISE

Creating a Cross-Functional Team [LO 11-1, 11-2, 11-3, 11-4, 11-5]

Form groups of three or four people, and appoint one member as the spokesperson who will communicate your findings to the class when called on by the instructor. Then discuss the following scenario.

You are a group of managers in charge of food services for a large state university in the Midwest. Recently a survey of students, faculty, and staff was conducted to evaluate customer satisfaction with the food services provided by the university's eight cafeterias. The results were disappointing, to put it mildly. Complaints ranged from dissatisfaction with the type and range of meals and snacks provided, operating hours, and food temperature to frustration about unresponsiveness to current concerns about healthful diets and the needs of vegetarians. You have decided to form a cross-functional team that will further evaluate reactions to the food services and will develop a proposal for changes to be made to increase customer satisfaction.

1. Indicate who should be on this important cross-functional team, and explain why.

2. Describe the goals the team should strive to achieve.

3. Describe the different roles that will need to be performed on this team.

4. Describe the steps you will take to help ensure that the team has a good balance between conformity and deviance and has a moderate level of cohesiveness.

BE THE MANAGER [LO 11-1, 11-2, 11-3, 11-4, 11-5]

You were recently hired in a boundary-spanning role for the global unit of an educational and professional publishing company. The company is headquartered in New York (where you work) and has divisions in multiple countries. Each division is responsible for translating, manufacturing, marketing, and selling a set of books in its country. Your responsibilities include interfacing with managers in each of the divisions in your region (Central and South America), overseeing their budgeting and financial reporting to headquarters, and leading a virtual team consisting of the top managers in charge of each of the divisions in your region. The virtual team's mission is to promote global learning, explore new potential opportunities and markets, and address ongoing problems. You communicate directly with division managers via telephone and e-mail, as well as written reports, memos, and faxes. When virtual team meetings are convened, videoconferencing is often used.

After your first few virtual team meetings, you noticed that the managers seemed to be reticent about speaking up. Interestingly enough, when each manager communicates with you individually, primarily in telephone conversations and e-mails, she or he tends to be forthcoming and frank, and you feel you have a good rapport with each of them. However, getting the managers to communicate with one another as a virtual team has been a real challenge. At the last meeting you tried to prompt some of the managers to raise issues relevant to the agenda that you knew were on their minds from your individual conversations with them. Surprisingly, the managers skillfully avoided informing their teammates about the heart of the issues in question. You are confused and troubled. Although you feel your other responsibilities are going well, you know your virtual team is not operating like a team at all; and no matter what you try, discussions in virtual team meetings are forced and generally unproductive.

Question

1. What are you going to do to address this problem?

THE WALL STREET JOURNAL
CASE IN THE NEWS [LO 11-1, LO 11-2, LO 11-3]

Tracking Sensors Invade the Workplace

A few years ago when Bank of America Corp. wanted to study whether face time mattered among its call-center teams, the big bank asked about 90 workers to wear badges for a few weeks with tiny sensors to record their movements and the tone of their conversations.

The data showed that the most productive workers belonged to close-knit teams and spoke frequently with their colleagues. So, to get more employees mingling, the bank scheduled workers for group breaks, rather than solo ones.

Productivity rose by at least 10%, says former Bank of America human-resources executive Michael Arena, who helped conduct its study.

As Big Data becomes a fixture of office life, companies are turning to tracking devices to gather real-time information on how teams of employees work and interact. Sensors, worn on lanyards or placed on office furniture, record how often staffers get up from their desks, consult other teams and hold meetings.

Businesses say the data offer otherwise hard-to-glean insights about how workers do their jobs, and are using the information to make changes large and small, ranging from the timing of coffee breaks to how work groups are composed, to spur collaboration and productivity.

"Surveys measure a point in time—what's happening right now with my emotions. [Sensors] measure actual behavior in an objective way," says Mr. Arena.

But there's a fine line between Big Data and Big Brother, at least in the eyes of some employees, who might shudder at the idea of the boss tracking their every move. Sensor proponents, however, argue that smartphones and corporate ID badges already can transmit their owner's location. In many cases, workers can opt out of participating in the sensor studies.

"Gathering big data about human behaviors can be a sensitive topic," says Dave Lathrop, director of workspace futures and strategy at Steelcase Inc., which has used sensor data with its own employees and is developing sensor products for businesses.

Along with addressing privacy concerns, companies must also be ready to make sense of the data, managers say.

Last year, Cubist Pharmaceuticals Inc. did a sensor study of 30 sales and marketing employees at its Lexington, Mass., offices to learn about interactions between team members and various departments, says Eric Kimble, a Cubist executive.

For four weeks, company employees wore iPhone-size badges, supplied by Boston startup Sociometric Solutions Inc., that collected data on their motions, whereabouts, voice levels and conversational patterns.

The information was merged with email-traffic data, along with the results of weekly surveys in which employees rated how energetic and productive they felt.

Like Bank of America, Cubist discovered a correlation between higher productivity and face-to-face interactions. It found that social activity dropped off significantly during lunch time, as many employees retreated to their desks to check emails, rather than chatting with one another.

In response, the company decided to make its once-dingy cafeteria more inviting, improving the lighting and offering better food, to encourage workers to lunch together, instead of at their desks.

Cubist also scaled back to a lone coffee station and water cooler for the sales and marketing group, forcing employees to huddle and mix. It set a 3 p.m. daily coffee break, both to prop up sagging energy levels and to boost social interactions.

In such studies, Sociometric Solutions and its clients say, workers typically get a report on their group's overall interactions, with no names attached, though individuals get to see their own data.

Ben Waber, chief executive of Sociometric Solutions, which he based on his doctoral research at Massachusetts Institute of Technology, says a handful of managers have wanted to see the data on an individual employee, but that his clients must sign contracts and consent forms prohibiting them from doing so.

Individual data can be revealing, however: Dr. Waber says he can divine from a worker's patterns of movement whether that employee is likely to leave the company, or score a promotion.

Ben Lin, an analyst at Cubist, says he didn't find the badges creepy once his bosses explained how the data would be used. His own report showed he changed his tone and gestures based on his conversation partner. "Subconsciously, you mirror who you are talking to," he says.

Rather than radical changes, sensor studies often show that simple tweaks can improve operations. Dr. Waber says his work with one client, a tech company, revealed that the size of a lunch table matters. Workers who ate at 12-person tables were more productive and collaborative than those who dined at tables with four seats. Data collected from sensors showed the larger lunch groups had more social interactions with teams across the company.

About 90% of workers at the 50 large and medium-size organizations that have done sensor studies with Dr. Waber's firm agree to don the badges, which are intended to be worn the entire workday. (Bathroom breaks are optional.) Those who opt out can wear a dummy badge, which appears identical but doesn't record or transmit data, he says.

Lewis Maltby, president of the National Workrights Institute, an employee advocacy group, says current sensing technologies don't seem to violate employment laws. "It's not illegal to track your own employees inside your own building," he says, adding that the data could be helpful in improving firm and worker performance.

But he cautions that employers are likely to want data on individual workers. "Not many service providers are going to refuse to give information to an employer that's paying the bill," says Mr. Maltby. "It would be very surprising if some provider doesn't start giving employers data about individual employees when they ask for it. That's not illegal. But do you really want your employers following around what you are doing? It's a creepy way to work."

Sensors also can reveal how workers use office space. Kimberly-Clark Corp. employees frequently griped that the consumer-product company's Neenah, Wis., offices were short on meeting space. Kimberly-Clark placed space-usage sensors offered by furniture maker Herman Miller Inc. beneath chairs and in conference rooms. It found that groups of three to four employees were gathering in meeting rooms designed for much larger numbers, says Mike Dietzen, a facilities planner.

As a result, the company carved out more and smaller conference spaces designed for small groups. Space-availability complaints have gone down significantly since, Mr. Dietzen says.

Putting badges on workers is just the beginning of a broader trend, researchers say. As companies rethink their offices, many are looking into "smart buildings," wired with technologies that show workers' location in real time and suggest meetings with colleagues nearby.

Philip Ross, CEO of workplace consulting firm UnWork.com, says these features will encourage "engineered serendipity."

To be sure, companies lured by the promise of fine-grained data on their workforces must figure out what to do with it.

Chuck Kelly, a senior vice president at Jones Lang LaSalle, relied on space-use sensors this past fall to see how workers used the property-management firm's downtown Chicago workspace.

"We wanted to see if the perception of how they were using their space matched up to the reality of how they are using their space," he says.

The project generated a slew of graphs and spreadsheets, but about three months later, Mr. Kelly is still trying to extract relevant insights from the noise. It's been a challenge, he says, "getting your head around all that data and what it means."

Questions

1. What ethical issues are involved in the use of tracking sensors?
2. How might the use of tracking sensors help organizations to use groups and teams to enhance motivation and performance?
3. How might the use of tracking sensors help organizations to use groups to increase innovation?
4. How might members of different types of groups and teams react to the use of tracking sensors in organizations?

Source: R. E. Silverman, "Tracking Sensors Invade the Workplace," *The Wall Street Journal,* March 7, 2013, B1–B2.

12

Building and Managing Human Resources

LEARNING OBJECTIVES

After studying this chapter, you should be able to:

1 Explain why strategic human resource management can help an organization gain a competitive advantage. **[LO 12-1]**

2 Describe the steps managers take to recruit and select organizational members. **[LO 12-2]**

3 Discuss the training and development options that ensure organizational members can effectively perform their jobs. **[LO 12-3]**

4 Explain why performance appraisal and feedback are such crucial activities, and list the choices managers must make in designing effective performance appraisal and feedback procedures. **[LO 12-4]**

5 Explain the issues managers face in determining levels of pay and benefits. **[LO 12-5]**

6 Understand the role that labor relations play in the effective management of human resources. **[LO 12-6]**

Mission: Create fun and a little weirdness—accomplished! If you'd like to work in a T-shirt surrounded by your favorite plants, a plastic skull, and personalized balloons while getting the chance to develop your business savvy, check out Zappos's job openings.

Effectively Managing Human Resources at Zappos

How Can Managers Ensure that Employees Will Provide Exceptional Service and Be Happy Doing So?

Nothing is conventional about the online retailer Zappos, headquartered in Henderson, Nevada.[1] Think accountants running Pinewood Derby car races during the workday, employees ringing cowbells and blowing horns during visitor tours, costume parades, and managers spending time socializing with their subordinates.[2] And the list could go on. Yet Zappos, founded in 1999 as a struggling online shoe shop, rode out the dot-com bust to earn over $1.6 billion in annual revenues in 2010 and be ranked 31st on *Fortune* magazine's list of the "One Hundred Best Companies to Work For" in 2013.[3] In 2009 Amazon.com purchased Zappos for shares worth $1.2 billion.[4] As a wholly owned subsidiary of Amazon, Zappos continues to be led by its long-standing CEO Tony Hsieh.[5]

Key to Zappos's success is a focus on people—having happy employees provide exceptional service to customers.[6] In fact, Hsieh's own experiences helped him realize the importance of employees being happy and having fun at work. Hsieh started his first company, LinkExchange, when he was in his early 20s. When he was 24, Hsieh sold LinkExchange to Microsoft for $265 million. Despite this phenomenal early success, Hsieh felt uneasy because he no longer enjoyed going to work, and the people around him seemed more interested in cashing out than building something long-term.[7]

Hsieh decided to build something long-lasting and a workplace to which happy employees wanted to come each day. Zappos was one of 27 start-ups that Hsieh invested in along with his partner and former classmate, Alfred Lin. When Zappos was struggling, Hsieh stepped in with more funds and became involved in running the company.[8]

Zappos has expanded from selling shoes to selling a wide range of products.[9] What is distinctive about Zappos is not so much the products it sells but rather the exceptional service it provides customers.[10] Customers receive free shipping on products both ways and Zappos has a 365-day return policy. Its website displays a toll-free telephone number that customers can call to speak to a member of the Customer Loyalty Team (CLT) 24 hours a day.[11] CLT members have autonomy to keep customers happy the way they think is best. Their call times are not monitored, and they do not read from scripts. They make decisions on their own, such as providing refunds for defective goods, without having to consult a manager. And they strive to make personal connections with their customers. Some calls last for hours, and team members regularly send personal notes to customers.[12] Providing exceptional service that leads to repeat business from happy customers and good word-of-mouth advertising is central to Zappos's approach to business.[13]

Unfortunately, Zappos had to temporarily shut down its phones in January of 2012 when hackers accessed data pertaining to customers from one of Zappos's servers in Kentucky. As a security precaution, Zappos expired customers' passwords and instructed them on how to create new passwords via an e-mail message from Hsieh, who also encouraged them to change passwords for other sites that might have been the same as their Zappos's passwords.[14] Hsieh explained the need to temporarily respond to customers' inquiries via e-mail given the high volume of calls expected from Zappos's more than 24 million customers.[15]

Central to the guiding philosophy at Zappos is having a happy workforce of satisfied employees who have fun on and off the job.[16] Because of the importance of having happy employees, Zappos goes to great lengths to effectively manage human resources. Potential new hires are interviewed by human resources, to make sure they will work well in Zappos's culture and support its values, as well as by the department doing the hiring, to determine their suitability for the position they are interviewing for.[17]

Newly hired employees receive extensive training. For example, the CLT new hires who answer calls have two weeks of classroom training followed by two weeks of training in answering calls. Once the training is completed, they are given the opportunity to receive $2,000 and pay for the time they spent in training if they want to quit.[18] This way only new hires who want to stay with the company remain.

Experienced employees are encouraged to continue to grow and develop on the job. For example, employees who have worked at Zappos for two or fewer years have over 200 hours of classroom training and development during their work hours and are required to read nine books about business. Zappos has a company library with business books and books about personal growth for employees to borrow and read. As Hsieh indicated, "The vision is that three years from now, almost all our hires will be entry-level people. . . . We'll provide them with training and mentorship, so that within five to seven years, they can become senior leaders within the company."[19]

Although pay for entry-level employees is not high, Zappos pays for all their health care.[20] All in all, Zappos's growth in revenues and being ranked among the "100 Best Companies to Work For" in 2013 suggest that human resources are being effectively managed to promote happiness among customers and employees alike.[21]

Overview

Managers are responsible for acquiring, developing, protecting, and utilizing the resources an organization needs to be efficient and effective. One of the most important resources in all organizations is human resources—the people involved in producing and distributing goods and services. Human resources include all members of an organization, ranging from top managers to entry-level employees. Effective managers like Tony Hsieh in the "Management Snapshot" realize how valuable human resources are and take active steps to make sure their organizations build and fully utilize their human resources to gain a competitive advantage.

This chapter examines how managers can tailor their human resource management system to their organization's strategy and structure. We discuss in particular the major components of human resource management: recruitment and selection, training and development, performance appraisal, pay and benefits, and labor relations. By the end of this chapter you will understand the central role human resource management plays in creating a high-performing organization.

Strategic Human Resource Management

human resource management (HRM) Activities that managers engage in to attract and retain employees and to ensure that they perform at a high level and contribute to the accomplishment of organizational goals.

strategic human resource management The process by which managers design the components of an HRM system to be consistent with each other, with other elements of organizational architecture, and with the organization's strategy and goals.

Human resource management (HRM) includes all the activities managers engage in to attract and retain employees and to ensure that they perform at a high level and contribute to the accomplishment of organizational goals. These activities make up an organization's human resource management system, which has five major components: recruitment and selection, training and development, performance appraisal and feedback, pay and benefits, and labor relations (see Figure 12.1).

Strategic human resource management is the process by which managers design the components of an HRM system to be consistent with each other, with other elements of organizational architecture, and with the organization's strategy and goals.[22] The objective of strategic HRM is the development of an HRM system that enhances an organization's efficiency, quality, innovation, and responsiveness to customers—the four building blocks of competitive advantage. At Zappos in the "Management Snapshot," HRM practices ensure that all employees provide excellent customer service.

As part of strategic human resource management, some managers have adopted "Six Sigma" quality improvement plans. These plans ensure that an organization's products and services are as free of errors or defects as possible through a variety of human resource–related initiatives. Jack Welch, former CEO of General Electric Company, has indicated that these initiatives saved his company millions of dollars; and other companies, such as Whirlpool and Motorola, also have implemented Six Sigma initiatives. For such initiatives to be effective, however, top managers have to be committed to Six Sigma, employees must be motivated, and there must be demand for the products or services of the organization in the

Figure 12.1   Components of a Human Resource Management System

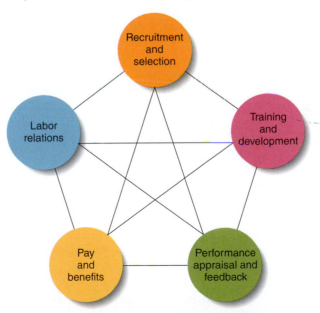

Each component of an HRM system influences the others, and all five must fit together.

first place. David Fitzpatrick, head of Deloitte Consulting's Lean Enterprise Practice, estimates that most Six Sigma plans are not effective because the conditions for effective Six Sigma are not in place. For example, if top managers are not committed to the quality initiative, they may not devote the necessary time and resources to make it work and may lose interest in it prematurely.[23]

Overview of the Components of HRM

Managers use *recruitment and selection,* the first component of an HRM system, to attract and hire new employees who have the abilities, skills, and experiences that will help an organization achieve its goals. Microsoft Corporation, for example, has the goal of remaining the premier computer software company in the world. To achieve this goal, managers at Microsoft realize the importance of hiring only the best software designers: Hundreds of highly qualified candidates are interviewed and rigorously tested. This careful attention to selection has contributed to Microsoft's competitive advantage. Microsoft has little trouble recruiting top programmers because candidates know they will be at the forefront of the industry if they work for Microsoft.[24]

After recruiting and selecting employees, managers use the second component, *training and development,* to ensure that organizational members develop the skills and abilities that will enable them to perform their jobs effectively in the present and the future. Training and development compose an ongoing process; changes in technology and the environment, as well as in an organization's goals and strategies, often require that organizational members learn new techniques and ways of working. At Microsoft, newly hired program designers receive on-the-job training by joining small teams that include experienced employees who serve as mentors or advisers. New recruits learn firsthand from team members how to go about developing computer systems that are responsive to customers' programming needs.[25]

The third component, *performance appraisal and feedback,* serves two different purposes in HRM. First, performance appraisal can give managers the information they need to make good human resources decisions—decisions about how to train, motivate, and reward organizational members.[26] Second, feedback from performance appraisal serves a developmental purpose for members of an organization. When managers regularly evaluate their subordinates' performance, they can provide employees with valuable information about their strengths and weaknesses and the areas in which they need to concentrate.

On the basis of performance appraisals, managers distribute *pay* to employees, which is part of the fourth component of an HRM system. By rewarding high-performing organizational members with pay raises, bonuses, and the like, managers increase the likelihood that an organization's most valued human resources will be motivated to continue their high levels of contribution to the organization. Moreover, if pay is linked to performance, high-performing employees are more likely to stay with the organization, and managers are more likely to fill positions that become open with highly talented individuals. *Benefits* such as health insurance are important outcomes that employees receive by virtue of their membership in an organization.

Last, but not least, *labor relations* encompass the steps that managers take to develop and maintain good working relationships with the labor unions that may represent their employees' interests. For example, an organization's labor relations component can help managers establish safe working conditions and fair labor practices in their offices and plants.

Managers must ensure that all five of these components fit together and complement their company's structure and control systems.[27] For example, if managers decide to decentralize authority and empower employees, they need to invest in training and development to ensure that lower-level employees have the knowledge and expertise they need to make the decisions that top managers would make in a more centralized structure.

Each of the five components of HRM influences the others (see Figure 12.1).[28] The kinds of people that the organization attracts and hires through recruitment and selection, for example, determine (1) the kinds of training and development that are necessary, (2) the way performance is appraised, and (3) the appropriate levels of pay and benefits. Managers at Microsoft ensure that their organization has highly qualified program designers by (1) recruiting and selecting the best candidates, (2) guiding new hires with experienced team members, (3) appraising program designers' performance in terms of their individual contributions and their teams' performance, and (4) basing programmers' pay on individual and team performance.

The Legal Environment of HRM

In the rest of this chapter we focus in detail on the choices managers must make in strategically managing human resources to attain organizational goals and gain a competitive advantage. Effectively managing human resources is a complex undertaking for managers, and we provide an overview of some major issues they face. First, however, we need to look at how the legal environment affects human resource management.

The local, state, and national laws and regulations that managers and organizations must abide by add to the complexity of HRM. For example, the U.S. government's commitment to equal employment opportunity (EEO) has resulted in the creation and enforcement of a number of laws that managers must abide by. The goal of EEO is to ensure that all citizens have an equal opportunity to obtain employment regardless of their gender, race, country of origin, religion, age, or disabilities. Table 12.1 summarizes some of the major EEO laws affecting HRM. Other laws, such as the Occupational Safety and Health Act of 1970, require that managers ensure that employees are protected from workplace hazards and safety standards are met.

equal employment opportunity (EEO) The equal right of all citizens to the opportunity to obtain employment regardless of their gender, age, race, country of origin, religion, or disabilities.

In Chapter 3 we explained how effectively managing diversity is an ethical and business imperative, and we discussed the many issues surrounding diversity. EEO laws and their enforcement make the effective management of diversity a legal imperative as well. The Equal Employment Opportunity Commission (EEOC) is the division of the Department of Justice that enforces most EEO laws and handles discrimination complaints. In addition, the EEOC issues guidelines for managers to follow to ensure that they are abiding by EEO laws. For example, the Uniform Guidelines on Employee Selection Procedures issued by the EEOC (in conjunction with the Departments of Labor and Justice and the Civil Service Commission) guide managers on how to ensure that the recruitment and selection component of human resource management complies with Title VII of the Civil Rights Act (which prohibits discrimination based on gender, race, color, religion, and national origin).[29]

Table 12.1

Major Equal Employment Opportunity Laws Affecting HRM

Year	Law	Description
1963	Equal Pay Act	Requires that men and women be paid equally if they are performing equal work.
1964	Title VII of the Civil Rights Act	Prohibits employment discrimination on the basis of race, religion, sex, color, or national origin; covers a wide range of employment decisions, including hiring, firing, pay, promotion, and working conditions.
1967	Age Discrimination in Employment Act	Prohibits discrimination against workers over the age of 40 and restricts mandatory retirement.
1978	Pregnancy Discrimination Act	Prohibits employment discrimination against women on the basis of pregnancy, childbirth, and related medical decisions.
1990	Americans with Disabilities Act	Prohibits employment discrimination against individuals with disabilities and requires that employers make accommodations for such workers to enable them to perform their jobs.
1991	Civil Rights Act	Prohibits discrimination (as does Title VII) and allows the awarding of punitive and compensatory damages, in addition to back pay, in cases of intentional discrimination.
1993	Family and Medical Leave Act	Requires that employers provide 12 weeks of unpaid leave for medical and family reasons, including paternity and illness of a family member.

Contemporary challenges that managers face related to the legal environment include how to eliminate sexual harassment (see Chapter 3 for an in-depth discussion of sexual harassment), how to accommodate employees with disabilities, how to deal with employees who have substance abuse problems, and how to manage HIV-positive employees and employees with AIDS.[30] HIV-positive employees are infected with the virus that causes AIDS but may show no AIDS symptoms and may not develop AIDS in the near future. Often such employees are able to perform their jobs effectively, and managers must take steps to ensure that they are allowed to do so and are not discriminated against in the workplace.[31] Employees with AIDS may or may not be able to perform their jobs effectively, and, once again, managers need to ensure that they are not unfairly discriminated against.[32] Many organizations have instituted AIDS awareness training programs to educate organizational members about HIV and AIDS, dispel myths about how HIV is spread, and ensure that individuals infected with the HIV virus are treated fairly and are able to be productive as long as they can be while not putting others at risk.[33]

LO 12-2 Describe the steps managers take to recruit and select organizational members.

Recruitment and Selection

Recruitment includes all the activities managers engage in to develop a pool of qualified candidates for open positions.[34] Selection is the process by which managers determine the relative qualifications of job applicants and their

recruitment Activities that managers engage in to develop a pool of qualified candidates for open positions.

selection The process that managers use to determine the relative qualifications of job applicants and their potential for performing well in a particular job.

human resource planning Activities that managers engage in to forecast their current and future needs for human resources.

outsource To use outside suppliers and manufacturers to produce goods and services.

potential for performing well in a particular job. Before actually recruiting and selecting employees, managers need to engage in two important activities: human resource planning and job analysis (Figure 12.2).

Human Resource Planning

Human resource planning includes all the activities managers engage in to forecast their current and future human resource needs. Current human resources are the employees an organization needs today to provide high-quality goods and services to customers. Future human resource needs are the employees the organization will need at some later date to achieve its longer-term goals.

As part of human resource planning, managers must make both demand forecasts and supply forecasts. *Demand forecasts* estimate the qualifications and numbers of employees an organization will need given its goals and strategies. *Supply forecasts* estimate the availability and qualifications of current employees now and in the future, as well as the supply of qualified workers in the external labor market.

As a result of their human resource planning, managers sometimes decide to outsource to fill some of their human resource needs. Instead of recruiting and selecting employees to produce goods and services, managers contract with people who are not members of their organization to produce goods and services. Managers in publishing companies, for example, frequently contract with freelance editors to copyedit books that they intend to publish. Kelly Services is an organization that provides the services of technical and professional employees to managers who want to use outsourcing to fill some of their human resource requirements in these areas.[35]

Two reasons why human resource planning sometimes leads managers to outsource are flexibility and cost. First, outsourcing can give managers increased flexibility, especially when accurately forecasting human resource needs is difficult, human resource needs fluctuate over time, or finding skilled workers in a particular area is difficult. Second, outsourcing can sometimes allow managers to use human resources at a lower cost. When work is outsourced, costs can be lower for a number of reasons: The organization does not have to provide benefits to workers; managers can contract for work only when the work is needed; and managers do not have to invest in training. Outsourcing can be used for functional activities such as after-sales service on appliances and equipment, legal work, and the management of information systems.[36]

Outsourcing has disadvantages, however.[37] When work is outsourced, managers may lose some control over the quality of goods and services. Also, individuals performing outsourced work may have less knowledge of organizational practices, procedures, and goals and less commitment to an organization than regular employees. In addition, unions resist outsourcing because it has the potential to eliminate some of their members. To gain some of the flexibility and cost savings of outsourcing and avoid some of its disadvantages, a number of organizations,

Figure 12.2
The Recruitment and Selection System

such as Microsoft and IBM, rely on a pool of temporary employees to, for example, debug programs.

A major trend reflecting the increasing globalization of business is the outsourcing of office work, computer programming, and technical jobs from the United States and countries in western Europe, with high labor costs, to countries like India and China, with low labor costs.[38] For example, computer programmers in India and China earn a fraction of what their U.S. counterparts earn. Outsourcing (or *offshoring,* as it is also called when work is outsourced to other countries) has also expanded into knowledge-intensive work such as engineering, research and development, and the development of computer software. According to a study conducted by The Conference Board and Duke University's Offshoring Research Network, more than half of U.S. companies surveyed have some kind of offshoring strategy related to knowledge-intensive work and innovation.[39] Why are so many companies engaged in offshoring, and why are companies that already offshore work planning to increase the extent of offshoring? While cost savings continue to be a major motivation for offshoring, managers also want to take advantage of an increasingly talented global workforce and be closer to the growing global marketplace for goods and services.[40]

Major U.S. companies often earn a substantial portion of their revenues overseas. For example, Hewlett-Packard, Caterpillar, and IBM earn over 60% of their revenues from overseas markets. And many large companies employ thousands of workers overseas. For example, IBM employs close to 100,000 workers in India and Hewlett-Packard, over 25,000.[41] Managers at some smaller companies have offshored work to Sri Lanka, Russia, and Egypt.[42] Key challenges for managers who offshore are retaining sufficient managerial control over activities and employee turnover.[43] In recent times, there have been some interesting developments in outsourcing to other countries as profiled in the following "Managing Globally."

MANAGING GLOBALLY

Recent Trends in Outsourcing

Countries in Latin America and Eastern Europe are becoming increasingly popular outsourcing destinations for skilled professional workers in the areas of finance, accounting, research, and procurement. For example, São Paulo, Brazil, has a sizable population of engineering and business school graduates who speak English and can perform a diverse set of tasks ranging from financial analysis to video game development.[44] A Brazilian trade group for technology, Brasscom, indicates that there are more Java programmers in Brazil than in any other country and Brazil has the second highest number of COBOL programmers. Thus, perhaps it is not surprising that IBM's ninth research center is located in São Paulo.[45]

It typically costs more to outsource work to Latin American countries than to India. For example, outsourcing an entry-level accounting job to India costs around 51% less than hiring a worker in the United States; outsourcing the same job to Argentina costs about 13% less than hiring a U.S. worker.[46] However, if the Argentinian has a better understanding of business and is more skilled at interacting with clients, bearing the added costs might make sense. Additionally, if client

Indian office workers face a downswing in the amount of outsourced jobs from the United States in certain fields. Argentina offers stiff competition with skilled workers whose hours are more closely aligned to the U.S. time zones but who can still be paid less than their U.S. counterparts.

interaction levels are high, it is advantageous for outsourcing countries and home countries to be in similar time zones. The time difference between New York and Argentina, for example, is much smaller than the time difference between New York and India.[47]

Copal Partners, an outsourcing company in Gurgaon, India, that provides research services on investments, recently opened an office in Buenos Aires, in part because of the benefits of being in a closer time zone with clients. As Rishi Khosla, the CEO of Copal puts it, "If you're working with a hedge fund manager where you have to interact 10 to 15 times a day, having someone in about the same time zone is important."[48] Tata Consultancy Services, the Indian outsourcing giant, has over 8,000 employees in South American countries, including Peru and Paraguay.[49]

Countries in Eastern Europe are also seeing surges in outsourcing. For example, Microsoft, Ernst & Young, and IBM have all opened outsourcing facilities in Wroclaw, Poland. Ernst & Young actually has six outsourcing centers in cities in Poland that together have around 1,300 employees.[50] Young people in Poland are more likely to be college educated than in India and they tend to be very multilingual. Jacek Levernes, who manages outsourcing to Europe, Africa, and the Middle East for Hewlett-Packard's Wroclaw, Poland, facility indicates that having 26 different languages spoken in the center is very advantageous for interacting with clients in different countries in these regions. Guatemala is also an outsourcing destination for companies like Capgemini Consulting and Coca-Cola enterprises. Evidently the trend toward "nearshoring" to countries closer to home certainly has its advantages.[51]

Job Analysis

job analysis

Identifying the tasks, duties, and responsibilities that make up a job and the knowledge, skills, and abilities needed to perform the job.

Job analysis is a second important activity that managers need to undertake prior to recruitment and selection.[52] Job analysis is the process of identifying (1) the tasks, duties, and responsibilities that make up a job (the *job description*) and (2) the knowledge, skills, and abilities needed to perform the job (the *job specifications*).[53] For each job in an organization, a job analysis needs to be done.

Job analysis can be done in a number of ways, including observing current employees as they perform the job or interviewing them. Often managers rely on questionnaires compiled by jobholders and their managers. The questionnaires ask about the skills and abilities needed to perform the job, job tasks and the amount of time spent on them, responsibilities, supervisory activities, equipment used, reports prepared, and decisions made.[54] A trend, in some organizations, is toward more flexible jobs in which tasks and responsibilities change and cannot be clearly specified in advance. For these kinds of jobs, job analysis focuses more on determining the skills and knowledge workers need to be effective and less on specific duties.

After managers have completed human resource planning and job analyses for all jobs in an organization, they will know their human resource needs and

Many colleges and universities hold job fairs to connect employers with students looking for jobs.

the jobs they need to fill. They will also know what knowledge, skills, and abilities potential employees need to perform those jobs. At this point, recruitment and selection can begin.

External and Internal Recruitment

As noted earlier, recruitment is what managers do to develop a pool of qualified candidates for open positions.[55] They traditionally have used two main types of recruiting, external and internal, which are now supplemented by recruiting over the Internet.

EXTERNAL RECRUITING When managers recruit externally to fill open positions, they look outside the organization for people who have not worked for the organization previously. There are multiple means through which managers can recruit externally: advertisements in newspapers and magazines, open houses for students and career counselors at high schools and colleges or on-site at the organization, career fairs at colleges, and recruitment meetings with groups in the local community.

Many large organizations send teams of interviewers to college campuses to recruit new employees. External recruitment can also take place through informal networks, as occurs when current employees inform friends about open positions in their companies or recommend people they know to fill vacant spots. Some organizations use employment agencies for external recruitment, and some external recruitment takes place simply through walk-ins—job hunters coming to an organization and inquiring about employment possibilities.

With all the downsizing and corporate layoffs that have taken place in recent years, you might think external recruiting would be a relatively easy task for managers. However, it often is not, because even though many people may be looking for jobs, many jobs that are open require skills and abilities that these job hunters do not have. Managers needing to fill vacant positions and job hunters seeking employment opportunities are increasingly relying on the Internet to connect with each other through employment websites such as Monster.com[56] and JobLine International.[57] Major corporations such as Coca-Cola, Cisco, Ernst & Young, Canon, and Telia have relied on JobLine to fill global positions.[58]

External recruiting has both advantages and disadvantages for managers. Advantages include having access to a potentially large applicant pool, being able to attract people who have the skills, knowledge, and abilities that an organization needs to achieve its goals, and being able to bring in newcomers who may have a fresh approach to problems and be up to date on the latest technology. These advantages have to be weighed against the disadvantages, including the relatively high costs of external recruitment. Employees recruited externally also lack knowledge about the inner workings of the organization and may need to receive more training than those recruited internally. Finally, when employees are recruited externally, there is always uncertainty concerning whether they will actually be good performers. Nonetheless, there are steps managers can take to reduce some of the uncertainty surrounding external recruitment, as profiled in the following "Information Technology Byte" box.

INFORMATION TECHNOLOGY BYTE

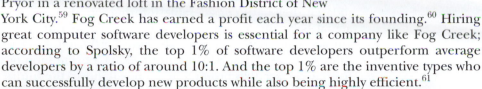

Fog Creek Software's Approach to Recruiting

Fog Creek Software is a small, privately owned software company founded in 2000 by Joel Spolsky and Michael Pryor in a renovated loft in the Fashion District of New York City.[59] Fog Creek has earned a profit each year since its founding.[60] Hiring great computer software developers is essential for a company like Fog Creek; according to Spolsky, the top 1% of software developers outperform average developers by a ratio of around 10:1. And the top 1% are the inventive types who can successfully develop new products while also being highly efficient.[61]

Fog Creek Software uses paid summer internships to help identify and attract promising software developers.

Finding, never mind recruiting, the top 1% is a real challenge for a small company like Fog Creek because many of these people already have great jobs and are not looking to switch employers. Realizing that the top 1% of developers might rarely apply for positions with Fog Creek (or any other company), Fog Creek uses paid summer internships to recruit over 50% of its developers while they are still in college; they are hired full-time after graduation.[62]

In the fall of every year, Fog Creek sends personalized letters to computer science majors across the country who have the potential to be top developers in the future, contacts professors at leading computer science programs for recommendations, and also seeks applications through their website.[63] This process yields hundreds of applicants for internships, the best of whom are then given a phone interview. During the interview, the candidates describe themselves and their classes, are asked how they would go about solving a software development problem or challenge, and then can ask anything they want about the company or living in New York City.[64]

Those who do well in the phone interview are flown to New York for an all-expense paid visit to Fog Creek—they are met at the airport in a limousine, stay in a hip hotel, receive welcoming gifts in their rooms, have a full day of interviews at Fog Creek, and then are given the option of staying two extra nights (at no cost to themselves) to get a feel for New York City. Typically only one out of every three recruits who has an on-site visit receives an internship offer.[65]

Interns perform real software development work—several summers ago, a team of four interns developed a new successful technology support product called Fog Creek Copilot.[66] This both motivates the interns and helps managers decide which interns they would like to hire. The interns are treated well—in addition to being paid, they receive free housing and are invited to outings, parties, and cultural events in New York City. At the conclusion of the internships, managers have a good sense of which interns are great programmers. These top programmers are offered jobs upon graduation with generous salaries, excellent working conditions, and great benefits. Although Fog Creek's approach to external recruitment is lengthy and expensive, it more than pays for itself by identifying and attracting top programmers. As Spolsky indicates, "An internship program creates a pipeline for great employees. It's a pretty long pipeline, so you need to have a long-term perspective, but it pays off in spades."[67]

INTERNAL RECRUITING When recruiting is internal, managers turn to existing employees to fill open positions. Employees recruited internally are either seeking lateral moves (job changes that entail no major changes in responsibility or authority levels) or promotions. Internal recruiting has several advantages. First, internal applicants are already familiar with the organization (including its goals, structure, culture, rules, and norms). Second, managers already know the candidates; they have considerable information about their skills and abilities and actual behavior on the job. Third, internal recruiting can help boost levels of employee motivation and morale, both for the employee who gets the job and for other workers. Those who are not seeking a promotion or who may not be ready for one can see that promotion is a possibility in the future; or a lateral move can alleviate boredom once a job has been fully mastered and can also be a useful way to learn new skills. Finally, internal recruiting is normally less time-consuming and expensive than external recruiting.

Given the advantages of internal recruiting, why do managers rely on external recruiting as much as they do? The answer lies in the disadvantages of internal recruiting—among them, a limited pool of candidates and a tendency among those candidates to be set in the organization's ways. Often the organization simply does not have suitable internal candidates. Sometimes, even when suitable internal applicants are available, managers may rely on external recruiting to find the very best candidate or to help bring new ideas and approaches into their organization. When organizations are in trouble and performing poorly, external recruiting is often relied on to bring in managerial talent with a fresh approach.

> **lateral move**
>
> A job change that entails no major changes in responsibility or authority levels.

The Selection Process

Once managers develop a pool of applicants for open positions through the recruitment process, they need to find out whether each applicant is qualified for the position and likely to be a good performer. If more than one applicant meets these two conditions, managers must further determine which applicants are likely to be better performers than others. They have several selection tools to help them sort out the relative qualifications of job applicants and appraise their potential for being good performers in a particular job. These tools include background information, interviews, paper-and-pencil tests, physical ability tests, performance tests, and references (see Figure 12.3).[68]

BACKGROUND INFORMATION To aid in the selection process, managers obtain background information from job applications and from résumés. Such information might include the highest levels of education obtained, college majors and minors, type of college or university attended, years and type of work experience, and mastery of foreign languages. Background information can be helpful both to screen out applicants who are lacking key qualifications (such as a college degree) and to determine which qualified applicants are more promising than others. For example, applicants with a BS may be acceptable, but those who also have an MBA may be preferable.

Increasing numbers of organizations are performing background checks to verify the background information prospective employees provide (and also to uncover any negative information such as crime convictions).[69] According to Automatic Data Processing, Inc. (ADP), an outsourcing company that

Figure 12.3
Selection Tools

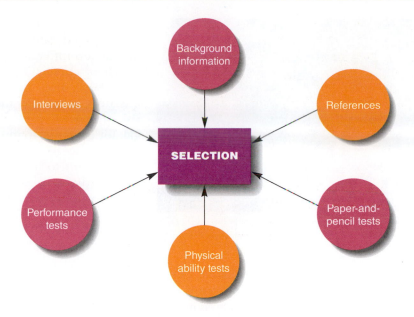

INTERVIEWS

Background information

References

SELECTION

Performance tests

Paper-and-pencil tests

Physical ability tests

performs payroll and human resource functions for organizations, more and more companies are performing background checks on prospective employees and are uncovering inaccuracies, inconsistencies, and negative information not reported on applications.[70] According to ADP, about 30% of applicants provide some form of false information with regards to their employment history.[71] And in some cases, background checks reveal prior convictions.[72]

INTERVIEWS Virtually all organizations use interviews during the selection process, as is true at Zappos in the "Management Snapshot." Interviews may be structured or unstructured. In a *structured interview,* managers ask each applicant the same standard questions (such as "What are your unique qualifications for this position?" and "What characteristics of a job are most important to you?"). Particularly informative questions may be those that prompt an interviewee to demonstrate skills and abilities needed for the job by answering the question. Sometimes called *situational interview questions,* these often present interviewees with a scenario they would likely encounter on the job and ask them to indicate how they would handle it.[73] For example, applicants for a sales job may be asked to indicate how they would respond to a customer who complains about waiting too long for service, a customer who is indecisive, and a customer whose order is lost.

An *unstructured interview* proceeds more like an ordinary conversation. The interviewer feels free to ask probing questions to discover what the applicant is like and does not ask a fixed set of questions determined in advance. In general, structured interviews are superior to unstructured interviews because they are

Practically all organizations use some kind of interview during the selection process.

Yes, it still exists! Employees struggle to get in the doors by completing, on paper, an ability and personality exam.

more likely to yield information that will help identify qualified candidates, are less subjective, and may be less influenced by the interviewer's biases.

When conducting interviews, managers cannot ask questions that are irrelevant to the job in question; otherwise their organizations run the risk of costly lawsuits. It is inappropriate and illegal, for example, to inquire about an interviewee's spouse or to ask questions about whether an interviewee plans to have children. Because questions such as these are irrelevant to job performance, they are discriminatory and violate EEO laws (see Table 12.1). Thus interviewers need to be instructed in EEO laws and informed about questions that may violate those laws.

PAPER-AND-PENCIL TESTS The two main kinds of paper-and-pencil tests used for selection purposes are ability tests and personality tests; both kinds of tests can be administered in hard copy or electronic form. *Ability tests* assess the extent to which applicants possess the skills necessary for job performance, such as verbal comprehension or numerical skills. Autoworkers hired by General Motors, Chrysler, and Ford, for example, are typically tested for their ability to read and to do mathematics.[74]

Personality tests measure personality traits and characteristics relevant to job performance. Some retail organizations, for example, give job applicants honesty tests to determine how trustworthy they are. The use of personality tests (including honesty tests) for hiring purposes is controversial. Some critics maintain that honesty tests do not really measure honesty (that is, they are not valid) and can be faked by job applicants. Before using any paper-and-pencil tests for selection purposes, managers must have sound evidence that the tests are actually good predictors of performance on the job in question. Managers who use tests without such evidence may be subject to costly discrimination lawsuits.

PHYSICAL ABILITY TESTS For jobs requiring physical abilities, such as firefighting, garbage collecting, and package delivery, managers use physical ability tests that measure physical strength and stamina as selection tools. Autoworkers are typically tested for mechanical dexterity because this physical ability is an important skill for high job performance in many auto plants.[75]

PERFORMANCE TESTS *Performance tests* measure job applicants' performance on actual job tasks. Applicants for secretarial positions, for example, typically are required to complete a keyboarding test that measures how quickly and accurately they type. Applicants for middle and top management positions are sometimes given short-term projects to complete—projects that mirror the kinds of situations that arise in the job being filled—to assess their knowledge and problem-solving capabilities.[76]

Assessment centers, first used by AT&T, take performance tests one step further. In a typical assessment center, about 10 to 15 candidates for managerial positions participate in a variety of activities over a few days. During this time they are assessed for the skills an effective manager needs—problem-solving, organizational, communication, and conflict resolution skills. Some of the activities are performed individually; others are performed in groups. Throughout the process, current managers observe the candidates' behavior and measure performance. Summary evaluations are then used as a selection tool.

REFERENCES Applicants for many jobs are required to provide references from former employers or other knowledgeable sources (such as a college instructor or adviser) who know the applicants' skills, abilities, and other personal characteristics. These individuals are asked to provide candid information about the applicant. References are often used at the end of the selection process to confirm a decision to hire. Yet the fact that many former employers are reluctant to provide negative information in references sometimes makes it difficult to interpret what a reference is really saying about an applicant.

In fact, several recent lawsuits filed by applicants who felt that they were unfairly denigrated or had their privacy invaded by unfavorable references from former employers have caused managers to be increasingly wary of providing any negative information in a reference, even if it is accurate. For jobs in which the jobholder is responsible for the safety and lives of other people, however, failing to provide accurate negative information in a reference does not just mean that the wrong person might get hired; it may also mean that other people's lives will be at stake.

THE IMPORTANCE OF RELIABILITY AND VALIDITY Whatever selection tools a manager uses need to be both reliable and valid. Reliability is the degree to which a tool or test measures the same thing each time it is administered. Scores on a selection test should be similar if the same person is assessed with the same tool on two different days; if there is quite a bit of variability, the tool is unreliable. For interviews, determining reliability is more complex because the dynamic is personal interpretation. That is why the reliability of interviews can be increased if two or more different qualified interviewers interview the same candidate. If the interviews are reliable, the interviewers should come to similar conclusions about the interviewee's qualifications.

reliability The degree to which a tool or test measures the same thing each time it is used.

Validity is the degree to which a tool measures what it purports to measure—for selection tools, it is the degree to which the test predicts performance on the tasks or job in question. Does a physical ability test used to select firefighters, for example, actually predict on-the-job performance? Do assessment center ratings actually predict managerial performance? Do keyboarding tests predict secretarial performance? These are all questions of validity. Honesty tests, for example, are controversial because it is not clear that they validly predict honesty in such jobs as retailing and banking.

validity The degree to which a tool or test measures what it purports to measure.

Managers have an ethical and legal obligation to use reliable and valid selection tools. Yet reliability and validity are matters of degree rather than all-or-nothing characteristics. Thus managers should strive to use selection tools in such a way that they can achieve the greatest degree of reliability and validity. For ability tests of a particular skill, managers should keep up to date on the latest advances in the development of valid paper-and-pencil tests and use the test with the highest reliability and validity ratings for their purposes. Regarding interviews, managers can improve reliability by having more than one person interview job candidates.

Training and Development

Training and development help to ensure that organizational members have the knowledge and skills needed to perform jobs effectively, take on new responsibilities, and adapt to changing conditions. Training focuses primarily on teaching organizational members how to perform their current jobs and helping them acquire the knowledge and skills they need to be effective performers. Development focuses on building the knowledge and skills of organizational members so they are prepared to take on new responsibilities and challenges. Training tends to be used more frequently at lower levels of an organization; development tends to be used more frequently with professionals and managers.

LO 12-3 Discuss the training and development options that ensure organizational members can effectively perform their jobs.

Before creating training and development programs, managers should perform a needs assessment to determine which employees need training or development and what type of skills or knowledge they need to acquire (see Figure 12.4).[77]

Types of Training

There are two types of training: classroom instruction and on-the-job training.

All in this together! New employees gathered in a small room listen to their instructor going over the basics before they complete an on-screen assessment of what they have learned.

CLASSROOM INSTRUCTION Through classroom instruction, employees acquire knowledge and skills in a classroom setting. This instruction may take place within the organization or outside it, such as through courses at local colleges and universities. Many organizations establish their own formal instructional divisions—some are even called "colleges"—to provide needed classroom instruction. For example, at Disney, classroom instruction and other forms of training and developing are provided to employees at Disney University.[78]

training Teaching organizational members how to perform their current jobs and helping them acquire the knowledge and skills they need to be effective performers.

Classroom instruction frequently uses videos and role playing in addition to traditional written materials, lectures, and group discussions. *Videos* can demonstrate appropriate and inappropriate job behaviors. For example, by watching an experienced salesperson effectively deal with a loud and angry customer, inexperienced salespeople can develop skills in handling similar situations. During *role playing*, trainees either directly participate in or watch others perform actual job activities in a simulated setting. At McDonald's Hamburger University, for example, role playing helps franchisees acquire the knowledge and skills they need to manage their restaurants.

development Building the knowledge and skills of organizational members so they are prepared to take on new responsibilities and challenges.

Simulations also can be part of classroom instruction, particularly for complicated jobs that require an extensive amount of learning and in which errors carry a high cost. In a simulation, key aspects of the work situation and job tasks are duplicated as closely as possible in an artificial setting. For example, air traffic controllers are trained by simulations because of the complicated nature of the work, the extensive amount of learning involved, and the very high costs of air traffic control errors.

needs assessment An assessment of which employees need training or development and what type of skills or knowledge they need to acquire.

ON-THE-JOB TRAINING In on-the-job training, learning occurs in the work setting as employees perform their job tasks. On-the-job training can be provided by coworkers or supervisors or can occur simply as jobholders gain experience and

Figure 12.4   **Training and Development**

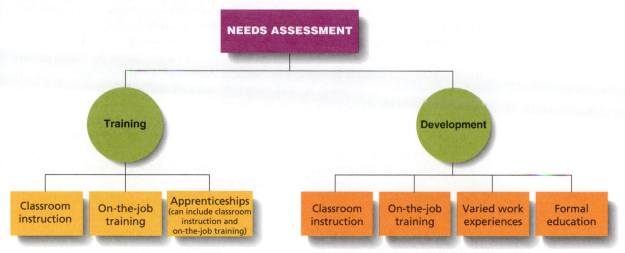

on-the-job training
Training that takes place in the work setting as employees perform their job tasks.

knowledge from doing the work. Newly hired waiters and waitresses in chains such as Red Lobster or the Olive Garden often receive on-the-job training from experienced employees. The supervisor of a new bus driver for a campus bus system may ride the bus for a week to ensure that the driver has learned the routes and follows safety procedures. For all on-the-job training, employees learn by doing.

Managers often use on-the-job training on a continuing basis to ensure that their subordinates keep up to date with changes in goals, technology, products, or customer needs and desires. For example, sales representatives at Mary Kay Cosmetics Inc. receive ongoing training so they not only know about new cosmetic products and currently popular colors but also are reminded of Mary Kay's guiding principles. Mary Kay's expansion into Russia has succeeded in part because of the ongoing training that Mary Kay's Russian salespeople receive.[79]

At many restaurants, new employees receive on-the-job training by shadowing more experienced waiters and waitresses as they go about their work.

Types of Development

Although both classroom instruction and on-the-job training can be used for development as well as training, development often includes additional activities such as varied work experiences and formal education.

VARIED WORK EXPERIENCES Top managers need to develop an understanding of, and expertise in, a variety of functions, products and services, and markets. To develop executives who will have this expertise, managers frequently make sure that employees with high potential have a wide variety of different job experiences, some in line positions and some in staff positions. Varied work experiences broaden employees' horizons and help them think about the big picture. For example, one- to three-year stints overseas are being used increasingly to provide managers with international work experiences. With organizations becoming more global, managers need to understand the different values, beliefs, cultures, regions, and ways of doing business in different countries.

Another development approach is mentoring. (A *mentor* is an experienced member of an organization who provides advice and guidance to a less experienced member, called a *protégé*.) Having a mentor can help managers seek out work experiences and assignments that will contribute to their development and can enable them to gain the most possible from varied work experiences.[80] Although some mentors and protégés hook up informally, organizations have found that formal mentoring programs can be valuable ways to contribute to the development of managers and all employees.

Formal mentoring programs ensure that mentoring takes place in an organization, structure the process, and make sure diverse organizational members have equal access to mentors. Participants receive training, efforts are focused on matching mentors and protégés so meaningful developmental relationships ensue, and organizations can track reactions and assess the potential benefits of mentoring. Formal mentoring programs can also ensure that diverse members of an organization receive the benefits of mentoring. A study conducted by David A. Thomas, a professor at the Harvard Business School, found that members of racial minority groups at three large corporations who were very successful in their careers had the benefit of mentors. Formal mentoring programs help organizations make this valuable development tool available to all employees.[81]

When diverse members of an organization lack mentors, their progress in the organization and advancement to high-level positions can be hampered. Ida Abott, a lawyer and consultant on work-related issues, presented a paper to the Minority Corporate Counsel Association in which she concluded, "The lack of adequate mentoring has held women and minority lawyers back from achieving professional success and has led to high rates of career dissatisfaction and attrition."[82]

Mentoring can benefit all kinds of employees in all kinds of work.[83] John Washko, a manager at the Four Seasons hotel chain, benefited from the mentoring he received from Stan Bromley on interpersonal relations and how to deal with employees; mentor Bromley, in turn, found that participating in the Four Seasons' mentoring program helped him develop his own management style.[84] More generally, development is an ongoing process for all managers, and mentors often find that mentoring contributes to their own personal development.

FORMAL EDUCATION Many large corporations reimburse employees for tuition expenses they incur while taking college courses and obtaining advanced degrees. This is not just benevolence on the part of the employer or even a simple reward given to the employee; it is an effective way to develop employees who can take on new responsibilities and more challenging positions. For similar reasons, corporations spend thousands of dollars sending managers to executive development programs such as executive MBA programs. In these programs, experts teach managers the latest in business and management techniques and practices.

To save time and travel costs, some managers rely on *long-distance learning* to formally educate and develop employees. Using videoconferencing technologies, business schools such as the Harvard Business School, the University of Michigan, and Babson College teach courses on video screens in corporate conference rooms. Business schools also customize courses and degrees to fit the development needs of employees in a particular company and/or a particular geographic region.[85]

Transfer of Training and Development

Whenever training and development take place off the job or in a classroom setting, it is vital for managers to promote the transfer of the knowledge and skills acquired *to the actual work situation*. Trainees should be encouraged and expected to use their newfound expertise on the job.

Performance Appraisal and Feedback

The recruitment/selection and training/development components of a human resource management system ensure that employees have the knowledge and skills needed to be effective now and in the future. Performance appraisal and feedback complement recruitment, selection, training, and development. Performance appraisal is the evaluation of employees' job performance and contributions to the organization. Performance feedback is the process through which managers share performance appraisal information with their subordinates, give subordinates an opportunity to reflect on their own performance, and develop, with subordinates, plans for the future. Before performance feedback, performance appraisal must take place. Performance appraisal could take place without providing performance feedback, but wise managers are careful to provide feedback because it can contribute to employee motivation and performance.

Performance appraisal and feedback contribute to the effective management of human resources in several ways. Performance appraisal gives managers important information on which to base human resource decisions.[86] Decisions about pay raises, bonuses, promotions, and job moves all hinge on the accurate appraisal of performance. Performance appraisal can also help managers determine which workers are candidates for training and development and in what areas. Performance feedback encourages high levels of employee motivation and performance. It lets good performers know that their efforts are valued and appreciated. It also lets poor performers know that their lackluster performance needs improvement. Performance feedback can give both good and poor performers insight on their strengths and weaknesses and ways in which they can improve their performance in the future.

performance appraisal
The evaluation of employees' job performance and contributions to their organization.

performance feedback The process through which managers share performance appraisal information with subordinates, give subordinates an opportunity to reflect on their own performance, and develop, with subordinates, plans for the future.

Types of Performance Appraisal

Performance appraisal focuses on the evaluation of traits, behaviors, and results.[87]

TRAIT APPRAISALS When trait appraisals are used, managers assess subordinates on personal characteristics that are relevant to job performance, such as skills, abilities, or personality. A factory worker, for example, may be evaluated based on her ability to use computerized equipment and perform numerical calculations. A social worker may be appraised based on his empathy and communication skills.

Three disadvantages of trait appraisals often lead managers to rely on other appraisal methods. First, possessing a certain personal characteristic does not ensure that the personal characteristic will actually be used on the job and result in high performance. For example, a factory worker may possess superior computer and numerical skills but be a poor performer due to low motivation. The second disadvantage of trait appraisals is linked to the first. Because traits do not always show a direct association with performance, workers and courts of law may view them as unfair and potentially discriminatory. The third disadvantage of trait appraisals is that they often do not enable managers to give employees feedback they can use to improve performance. Because trait appraisals focus on relatively enduring human characteristics that change only over the long term, employees can do little to change their behavior in response to performance feedback from a trait appraisal. Telling a social worker that he lacks empathy says little about how he can improve his interactions with clients, for example. These disadvantages suggest that managers should use trait appraisals only when they can demonstrate that the assessed traits are accurate and important indicators of job performance.

BEHAVIOR APPRAISALS Through behavior appraisals, managers assess how workers perform their jobs—the actual actions and behaviors that workers exhibit on the job. Whereas trait appraisals assess what workers *are like,* behavior appraisals assess what workers *do.* For example, with a behavior appraisal, a manager might evaluate a social worker on the extent to which he looks clients in the eye when talking with them, expresses sympathy when they are upset, and refers them to community counseling and support groups geared toward the specific problems they are encountering. Behavior appraisals are especially useful when *how* workers perform their jobs is important. In educational organizations such as high schools, for example, the numbers of classes and students taught are important, but also important is how they are taught or the methods teachers use to ensure that learning takes place.

Behavior appraisals have the advantage of giving employees clear information about what they are doing right and wrong and how they can improve their performance. And because behaviors are much easier for employees to change than traits, performance feedback from behavior appraisals is more likely to lead to improved performance.

RESULTS APPRAISALS For some jobs, *how* people perform the job is not as important as *what* they accomplish or the results they obtain. With results appraisals, managers appraise performance by the results or the actual outcomes of work behaviors. Take the case of two new car salespeople. One salesperson strives to develop personal relationships with her customers. She spends hours talking to them and frequently calls them to see how their decision-making process is going. The other salesperson has a much more hands-off approach. He is very knowledgeable, answers customers' questions, and then waits for them to come to him. Both salespersons sell, on average, the same number of cars, and the customers of both are satisfied with the service they receive, according to postcards the dealership mails to customers asking for an assessment of their satisfaction. The manager of the dealership appropriately uses results appraisals (sales and customer satisfaction) to evaluate the salespeople's performance because it does not matter which behavior salespeople use to sell cars as long as they sell the desired number and satisfy customers. If one salesperson sells too few cars, however, the manager can give that person performance feedback about his or her low sales.

OBJECTIVE AND SUBJECTIVE APPRAISALS Whether managers appraise performance in terms of traits, behaviors, or results, the information they assess is either *objective* or *subjective.* Objective appraisals are based on facts and are likely to be numerical—the number of cars sold, the number of meals prepared, the number of times late, the number of audits completed. Managers often use objective appraisals when results are being appraised because results tend to be easier to quantify than traits or behaviors. When *how* workers perform their jobs is important, however, subjective behavior appraisals are more appropriate than results appraisals.

objective appraisal
An appraisal that is based on facts and is likely to be numerical.

subjective appraisal
An appraisal that is based on perceptions of traits, behaviors, or results.

Subjective appraisals are based on managers' perceptions of traits, behaviors, or results. Because subjective appraisals rest on managers' perceptions, there is always the chance that they are inaccurate. This is why both researchers and managers have spent considerable time and effort on determining the best way to develop reliable and valid subjective measures of performance.

Who Appraises Performance?

We have been assuming that managers or the supervisors of employees evaluate performance. This is a reasonable assumption: Supervisors are the most common appraisers of performance.[88] Performance appraisal is an important part of most managers' job duties. Managers are responsible for not only motivating their subordinates to perform at a high level but also making many decisions hinging on performance appraisals, such as pay raises or promotions. Appraisals by managers can be usefully augmented by appraisals from other sources (see Figure 12.5).

SELF, PEERS, SUBORDINATES, AND CLIENTS When self-appraisals are used, managers supplement their evaluations with an employee's assessment of his or her own performance. Peer appraisals are provided by an employee's coworkers. Especially when subordinates work in groups or teams, feedback from peer appraisals can motivate team members while giving managers important information for decision making. A growing number of companies are having subordinates appraise their managers' performance and leadership as well. And sometimes customers or clients assess employee performance in terms of responsiveness to customers and quality of service. Although appraisals from these sources can be useful, managers need to be aware of potential issues that may arise when they are used. Subordinates sometimes may be inclined to inflate self-appraisals, especially if organizations are downsizing and they are worried about job security. Managers who are appraised by their subordinates may fail to take needed but unpopular actions out of fear that their subordinates will appraise them negatively. Some of these potential issues can be mitigated to the extent that there are high levels of trust in an organization.

Figure 12.5
Who Appraises Performance?

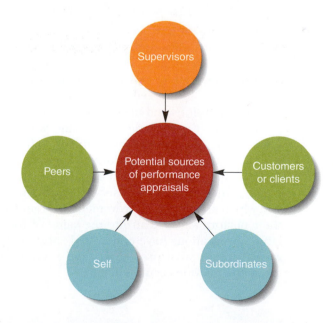

How am I doing? Sitting down for an honest and open performance appraisal with your immediate supervisor can help keep you on track.

360-degree appraisal

A performance appraisal by peers, subordinates, superiors, and sometimes clients who are in a position to evaluate a manager's performance.

360-DEGREE PERFORMANCE APPRAISALS To improve motivation and performance, some organizations include 360-degree appraisals and feedback in their performance appraisal systems, especially for managers. In a 360-degree appraisal a variety of people, beginning with the manager and including peers or coworkers, subordinates, superiors, and sometimes even customers or clients, appraise a manager's performance. The manager receives feedback based on evaluations from these multiple sources.

Companies in a variety of industries rely on 360-degree appraisals and feedback.[89] For 360-degree appraisals and feedback to be effective, there has to be trust throughout an organization. More generally, trust is a critical ingredient in any performance appraisal and feedback procedure. In addition, research suggests that 360-degree appraisals should focus on behaviors rather than traits or results and that managers need to carefully select appropriate raters. Moreover, appraisals tend to be more honest when made anonymously and when raters have been trained in how to use 360-degree appraisal forms.[90] Additionally, managers need to think carefully about the extent to which 360-degree appraisals are appropriate for certain jobs and be willing to modify any appraisal system they implement if they become aware of unintended problems it creates.[91]

Even when 360-degree appraisals are used, it is sometimes difficult to design an effective process by which subordinates' feedback can be communicated to their managers; but advances in information technology can solve this problem. For example, ImproveNow.com has online questionnaires that subordinates fill out to evaluate the performance of their managers and give the managers feedback. Each subordinate of a particular manager completes the questionnaire independently, all responses are tabulated, and the manager is given specific feedback on behaviors in a variety of areas, such as rewarding good performance, looking out for subordinates' best interests and being supportive, and having a vision for the future.[92]

Effective Performance Feedback

formal appraisal

An appraisal conducted at a set time during the year and based on performance dimensions and measures that were specified in advance.

For the appraisal and feedback component of a human resource management system to encourage and motivate high performance, managers must give their subordinates feedback. To generate useful information to feed back to their subordinates, managers can use both formal and informal appraisals. Formal appraisals are conducted at set times during the year and are based on performance dimensions and measures that have been specified in advance.

Managers in most large organizations use formal performance appraisals on a fixed schedule dictated by company policy, such as every six months or every year. An integral part of a formal appraisal is a meeting between the manager and the subordinate in which the subordinate is given feedback on performance. Performance feedback lets subordinates know which areas they are excelling in and which areas need improvement; it should also tell them *how* they can improve their performance. Realizing the value of formal appraisals, managers in many large corporations have committed substantial resources to updating their performance appraisal procedures and training low-level managers in how to use them and provide accurate feedback to employees.[93]

Formal performance appraisals supply both managers and subordinates with valuable information; but subordinates often want more frequent feedback, and managers often want to motivate subordinates as the need arises. For these reasons many companies supplement formal performance appraisal with frequent informal appraisals, for which managers and their subordinates meet as the need arises to discuss ongoing progress and areas for improvement. Moreover, when job duties, assignments, or goals change, informal appraisals can give workers timely feedback concerning how they are handling their new responsibilities.

informal appraisal
An unscheduled appraisal of ongoing progress and areas for improvement.

Managers often dislike providing performance feedback, especially when the feedback is negative, but doing so is an important managerial activity.[94] Here are some guidelines for giving effective performance feedback that contributes to employee motivation and performance:

- *Be specific and focus on behaviors or outcomes that are correctable and within a worker's ability to improve.* Example: Telling a salesperson that he is too shy when interacting with customers is likely to lower his self-confidence and prompt him to become defensive. A more effective approach would be to give the salesperson feedback about specific behaviors to engage in—greeting customers as soon as they enter the department, asking customers whether they need help, and volunteering to help customers find items.

- *Approach performance appraisal as an exercise in problem solving and solution finding, not criticizing.* Example: Rather than criticizing a financial analyst for turning in reports late, the manager helps the analyst determine why the reports are late and identify ways to better manage her time.

- *Express confidence in a subordinate's ability to improve.* Example: Instead of being skeptical, a first-level manager tells a subordinate that he is confident that the subordinate can increase quality levels.

- *Provide performance feedback both formally and informally.* Example: The staff of a preschool receives feedback from formal performance appraisals twice a year. The school director also provides frequent informal feedback such as complimenting staff members on creative ideas for special projects, noticing when they do a particularly good job handling a difficult child, and pointing out when they provide inadequate supervision.

- *Praise instances of high performance and areas of a job in which a worker excels.* Example: Rather than focusing on just the negative, a manager discusses the areas her subordinate excels in as well as the areas in need of improvement.

- *Avoid personal criticisms and treat subordinates with respect.* Example: An engineering manager acknowledges her subordinates' expertise and treats them as professionals. Even when the manager points out performance problems to subordinates, she refrains from criticizing them personally.

- *Agree to a timetable for performance improvements.* Example: A first-level manager and his subordinate decide to meet again in one month to determine whether quality levels have improved.

In following these guidelines, managers need to remember *why* they are giving performance feedback: to encourage high levels of motivation and performance. Moreover, the information that managers gather through performance appraisal and feedback helps them determine how to distribute pay raises and bonuses.

Pay and Benefits

Pay includes employees' base salaries, pay raises, and bonuses and is determined by a number of factors such as characteristics of the organization and the job and levels of performance. Employee *benefits* are based on membership in an organization (and not necessarily on the particular job held) and include sick days, vacation days, and medical and life insurance. In Chapter 9 we discussed how pay can motivate organizational members to perform at a high level, as well as the different kinds of pay plans managers can use to help an organization achieve its goals and gain a competitive advantage. As you will learn, it is important to link pay to behaviors or results that contribute to organizational effectiveness. Next we focus on establishing an organization's pay level and pay structure.

LO 12-5 Explain the issues managers face in determining levels of pay and benefits.

Pay Level

pay level The relative position of an organization's pay incentives in comparison with those of other organizations in the same industry employing similar kinds of workers.

Pay level is a broad comparative concept that refers to how an organization's pay incentives compare, in general, to those of other organizations in the same industry employing similar kinds of workers. Managers must decide if they want to offer relatively high wages, average wages, or relatively low wages. High wages help ensure that an organization is going to be able to recruit, select, and retain high performers, but high wages also raise costs. Low wages give an organization a cost advantage but may undermine the organization's ability to select and recruit high performers and to motivate current employees to perform at a high level. Either of these situations may lead to inferior quality or inadequate customer service.

In determining pay levels, managers should take into account their organization's strategy. A high pay level may prohibit managers from effectively pursuing a low-cost strategy. But a high pay level may be worth the added costs in an organization whose competitive advantage lies in superior quality and excellent customer service. As one might expect, hotel and motel chains with a low-cost strategy, such as Days Inn and Hampton Inns, have lower pay levels than chains striving to provide high-quality rooms and services, such as the Four Seasons.

Pay Structure

pay structure The arrangement of jobs into categories reflecting their relative importance to the organization and its goals, levels of skill required, and other characteristics.

After deciding on a pay level, managers have to establish a pay structure for the different jobs in the organization. A pay structure clusters jobs into categories reflecting their relative importance to the organization and its goals, levels of skill required, and other characteristics managers consider important. Pay ranges are established for each job category. Individual jobholders' pay within job categories is then determined by factors such as performance, seniority, and skill levels.

There are some interesting global differences in pay structures. Large corporations based in the United States tend to pay their CEOs and top managers higher salaries than do their European or Japanese counterparts. Also, the pay differential between employees at the bottom of the corporate hierarchy and those higher up is much greater in U.S. companies than in European or Japanese companies.[95]

Concerns have been raised over whether it is equitable or fair for CEOs of large companies in the United States to be making millions of dollars in years when their companies are restructuring and laying off a large portion of their workforces.[96] Additionally, the average CEO in the United States typically earns over 360 times what the average hourly worker earns.[97] Is a pay structure with such a huge pay differential ethical? Shareholders and the public are increasingly asking this very question and asking large corporations to rethink their pay structures.[98] Also troubling are the millions of dollars in severance packages that some CEOs receive when they leave their organizations. When many workers are struggling to find and keep jobs and make ends meet, more and more people are questioning whether it is ethical for some top managers to be making so much money.[99]

Benefits

Organizations are legally required to provide certain benefits to their employees, including workers' compensation, Social Security, and unemployment insurance. Workers' compensation helps employees financially if they become unable to work due to a work-related injury or illness. Social Security provides financial assistance to retirees and disabled former employees. Unemployment insurance provides financial assistance to workers who lose their jobs due to no fault of their own. The legal system in the United States views these three benefits as ethical requirements for organizations and thus mandates that they be provided.

Other benefits such as health insurance, dental insurance, vacation time, pension plans, life insurance, flexible working hours, company-provided day care, and employee assistance and wellness programs have traditionally been provided at the option of employers. The Health Care Reform Bill signed by President Barack Obama in March 2010 contains provisions whereby, starting in 2014, employers with 50 or more employees may face fines if they don't provide their employees with health insurance coverage.[100] Recall that an attractive benefit at Zappos in the "Management Snapshot" is that Zappos pays for all health care costs. Benefits enabling workers to balance the demands of their jobs and of their lives away from the office or factory are of growing importance for many workers who have competing demands on their scarce time and energy.

cafeteria-style benefit plan
A plan from which employees can choose the benefits they want.

In some organizations, top managers determine which benefits might best suit the employees and organization and offer the same benefit package to all employees. Other organizations, realizing that employees' needs and desires might differ, offer cafeteria-style benefit plans that let employees themselves choose the benefits they want. Cafeteria-style benefit plans sometimes help managers deal with employees who feel unfairly treated because they are unable to take advantage of certain benefits available to other employees who, for example, have children. Some organizations have success with cafeteria-style benefit plans; others find them difficult to manage.

As health care costs escalate and overstretched employees find it hard to take time to exercise and take care of their health, more companies are providing benefits and incentives to promote employee wellness. AstraZeneca International offers its employees on-site counseling with a nutritionist and pays employees $125 for voluntarily taking a health risk assessment that covers wellness-related factors such as weight and nutrition.[101] Dole Food Company rewards employees with points toward gift certificates for participating in wellness activities provided on-site, such as yoga classes.[102] For working parents, family-friendly benefits are often attractive.

Same-sex domestic partner benefits are also being used to attract and retain valued employees. Gay and lesbian workers are reluctant to work for companies that do not provide the same kinds of benefits for their partners as those provided for partners of the opposite sex.[103]

Labor Relations

Labor relations are the activities managers engage in to ensure that they have effective working relationships with the labor unions that represent their employees' interests. Although the U.S. government has responded to the potential for unethical and unfair treatment of workers by creating and enforcing laws regulating employment (including the EEO laws listed in Table 12.1), some workers believe a union will ensure that their interests are fairly represented in their organizations.

Before we describe unions in more detail, let's take a look at some examples of important employment legislation. In 1938 the government passed the Fair Labor Standards Act, which prohibited child labor and provided for minimum wages, overtime pay, and maximum working hours to protect workers' rights. In 1963 the Equal Pay Act mandated that men and women performing equal work (work requiring the same levels of skill, responsibility, and effort performed in the same kind of working conditions) receive equal pay (see Table 12.1). In 1970 the Occupational Safety and Health Act mandated procedures for managers to follow to ensure workplace safety. These are just a few of the U.S. government's efforts to protect workers' rights. State legislatures also have been active in promoting safe, ethical, and fair workplaces.

LO 12-6 Understand the role that labor relations play in the effective management of human resources.

labor relations
The activities managers engage in to ensure that they have effective working relationships with the labor unions that represent their employees' interests.

Unions

Unions exist to represent workers' interests in organizations. Given that managers have more power than rank-and-file workers and that organizations have multiple stakeholders, there is always the potential that managers might take steps that benefit one set of stakeholders such as shareholders while hurting another such as employees. For example, managers may decide to speed up a production line to lower costs and increase production in the hopes of increasing returns to shareholders. Speeding up the line, however, could hurt employees forced to work at a rapid pace and may increase the risk of injuries. Also, employees receive no additional pay for the extra work they are performing. Unions would represent workers' interests in a scenario such as this one.

Congress acknowledged the role that unions could play in ensuring safe and fair workplaces when it passed the National Labor Relations Act of 1935. This act made it legal for workers to organize into unions to protect their rights and interests and declared certain unfair or unethical organizational practices to be illegal. The act also established the National Labor Relations Board (NLRB) to oversee union activity. Currently the NLRB conducts certification elections, which are held among the employees of an organization to determine whether they want a union to represent their interests. The NLRB also makes judgments concerning unfair labor practices and specifies practices that managers must refrain from.

Employees might vote to have a union represent them for any number of reasons.[104] They may think their wages and working conditions need improvement. They may believe managers are not treating them with respect. They may think their working hours are unfair or they need more job security or a safer work environment. Or they may be dissatisfied with management and find it difficult to communicate their concerns to their bosses. Regardless of the specific reason, one overriding reason is power: A united group inevitably wields more power than an individual, and this type of power may be especially helpful to employees in some organizations.

Although these would seem to be potent forces for unionization, some workers are reluctant to join unions. Sometimes this reluctance is due to the perception that union leaders are corrupt. Some workers may simply believe that belonging to a union might not do them much good or may actually cause more harm than good while costing them money in membership dues. Employees also might not want to be forced into doing something they do not want to, such as striking because the union thinks it is in their best interest. Moreover, although unions can be a positive force in organizations, sometimes they also can be a negative force, impairing organizational effectiveness. For example, when union leaders resist needed changes in an organization or are corrupt, organizational performance can suffer.

The percentage of U.S. workers represented by unions today is smaller than it was in the 1950s, an era when unions were especially strong.[105] In the 1950s, around 35% of U.S. workers were union members; in 2012, 11.3% of workers were members of unions.[106] The American Federation of Labor–Congress of Industrial Organizations (AFL-CIO) includes 57 voluntary member unions representing over 12 million workers.[107] Overall, approximately 14.4 million workers in the United States belong to unions.[108] Union influence in manufacturing and heavy industries has been on the decline; more generally, approximately 6.6% of private sectors workers are union members.[109] However, around 35.9% of government workers belong to unions.[110] Unions have made inroads in other segments of the workforce, particularly the low-wage end. Garbage collectors in New Jersey, poultry plant workers in North Carolina, and janitors in Baltimore are among the growing numbers of low-paid workers who are currently finding union membership attractive. North Carolina poultry workers voted in a union partly because they thought it was unfair that they had to buy their own gloves and hairnets used on the job and had to ask their supervisors' permission to go to the restroom.[111]

Collective Bargaining

collective bargaining
Negotiations between labor unions and managers to resolve conflicts and disputes about issues such as working hours, wages, benefits, working conditions, and job security.

Collective bargaining is negotiation between labor unions and managers to resolve conflicts and disputes about important issues such as working hours, wages, working conditions, and job security. Before sitting down with management to negotiate, union members sometimes go on strike to drive home their concerns to managers. Once an agreement that union members support has been reached (sometimes with the help of a neutral third party called a *mediator*), union leaders and managers sign a contract spelling out the terms of the collective bargaining agreement.

Summary and Review

STRATEGIC HUMAN RESOURCE MANAGEMENT Human resource management (HRM) includes all the activities managers engage in to ensure that their organizations can attract, retain, and effectively use human resources. Strategic HRM is the process by which managers design the components of a human resource management system to be consistent with each other, with other elements of organizational architecture, and with the organization's strategies and goals. **[LO 12-1]**

RECRUITMENT AND SELECTION Before recruiting and selecting employees, managers must engage in human resource planning and job analysis. Human resource planning includes all the activities managers engage in to forecast their current and future needs for human resources. Job analysis is the process of identifying (1) the tasks, duties, and responsibilities that make up a job and (2) the knowledge, skills, and abilities needed to perform the job. Recruitment includes all the activities managers engage in to develop a pool of qualified applicants for open positions. Selection is the process by which managers determine the relative qualifications of job applicants and their potential for performing well in a particular job. **[LO 12-2]**

TRAINING AND DEVELOPMENT Training focuses on teaching organizational members how to perform effectively in their current jobs. Development focuses on broadening organizational members' knowledge and skills so they are prepared to take on new responsibilities and challenges. **[LO 12-3]**

PERFORMANCE APPRAISAL AND FEEDBACK Performance appraisal is the evaluation of employees' job performance and contributions to the organization. Performance feedback is the process through which managers share performance appraisal information with their subordinates, give them an opportunity to reflect on their own performance, and develop with them plans for the future. Performance appraisal gives managers useful information for decision making. Performance feedback can encourage high levels of motivation and performance. **[LO 12-4]**

PAY AND BENEFITS Pay level is the relative position of an organization's pay incentives in comparison with those of other organizations in the same industry employing similar workers. A pay structure clusters jobs into categories according to their relative importance to the organization and its goals, the levels of skill required, and other characteristics. Pay ranges are then established for each job category. Organizations are legally required to provide certain benefits to their employees; other benefits are provided at the discretion of employers. **[LO 12-5]**

LABOR RELATIONS Labor relations include all the activities managers engage in to ensure that they have effective working relationships with the labor unions that represent their employees' interests. The National Labor Relations Board oversees union activity. Collective bargaining is the process through which labor unions and managers resolve conflicts and disputes and negotiate agreements. **[LO 12-6]**

Management *in Action*

TOPICS FOR DISCUSSION AND ACTION

Discussion

1. Discuss why it is important for human resource management systems to be in sync with an organization's strategy and goals and with each other. **[LO 12-1]**

2. Discuss why training and development are ongoing activities for all organizations. **[LO 12-3]**

3. Describe the type of development activities you think middle managers are most in need of. **[LO 12-3]**

4. Evaluate the pros and cons of 360-degree performance appraisals and feedback.

Would you like your performance to be appraised in this manner? Why or why not? **[LO 12-4]**

5. Discuss why two restaurants in the same community might have different pay levels. **[LO12-5]**

Action

6. Interview a manager in a local organization to determine how that organization recruits and selects employees. **[LO12-2]**

BUILDING MANAGEMENT SKILLS

Analyzing Human Resource Management Systems [LO 12-1, 12-2, 12-3, 12-4, 12-5]

Think about your current job or a job you have had in the past. If you have never had a job, interview a friend or family member who is currently working. Answer the following questions about the job you have chosen.

1. How are people recruited and selected for this job? Are the recruitment and selection procedures the organization uses effective or ineffective? Why?

2. What training and development do people who hold this job receive? Are the training and development appropriate? Why or why not?

3. How is performance of this job appraised? Does

performance feedback contribute to motivation and high performance on this job?

4. What levels of pay and benefits are provided on this job? Are these levels appropriate? Why or why not?

MANAGING ETHICALLY [LO 12-4, 12-5]

Some managers do not want to become overly friendly with their subordinates because they are afraid that if they do so their objectivity when conducting performance appraisals and making decisions about pay raises and promotions will be impaired. Some subordinates resent it when they see one or more of their coworkers being very friendly with the boss; they are concerned about the potential for favoritism. Their reasoning runs something like this: If two subordinates are equally qualified for a promotion and one is a good friend of the boss's and the other is a mere acquaintance, who is more likely to receive the promotion?

Questions

1. Either individually or in a group, think about the ethical

implications of managers' becoming friendly with their subordinates.

2. Do you think managers should feel free to socialize and become good friends with their subordinates outside the workplace if they so desire? Why or why not?

SMALL GROUP BREAKOUT EXERCISE

Building a Human Resource Management System [LO 12-1, 12-2, 12-3, 12-4, 12-5]

Form groups of three or four people, and appoint one group member as the spokesperson who will communicate your findings to the class when called on by the instructor. Then discuss the following scenario.

You and your three partners are engineers who minored in business at college and have decided to start a consulting business. Your goal is to provide manufacturing process engineering and other engineering services to large and small organizations. You forecast that there will be an increased use of outsourcing for these activities. You discussed with managers in several large organizations the services you plan to offer, and they expressed considerable interest. You have secured funding to start your business and now are building the HRM system. Your human resource planning suggests that you need to hire between five and eight experienced engineers with good communication skills, two clerical/secretarial workers, and two MBAs who between them have financial, accounting, and human resource skills. You are striving to develop your human resources in a way that will enable your new business to prosper.

1. Describe the steps you will take to recruit and select (a) the engineers, (b) the clerical/secretarial workers, and (c) the MBAs.

2. Describe the training and development the engineers, the clerical/secretarial workers, and the MBAs will receive.

3. Describe how you will appraise the performance of each group of employees and how you will provide feedback.

4. Describe the pay level and pay structure of your consulting firm.

BE THE MANAGER [LO 12-4]

You are Walter Michaels and have just received some disturbing feedback. You are the director of human resources for Maxi Vision Inc., a medium-size window and glass door manufacturer. You recently initiated a 360-degree performance appraisal system for all middle and upper managers at Maxi Vision, including yourself, but excluding the most senior executives and the top management team.

You were eagerly awaiting the feedback you would receive from the managers who report to you; you had recently implemented several important initiatives that affected them and their subordinates, including a complete overhaul of the organization's performance appraisal system. While the managers who report to you were evaluated based on 360-degree appraisals, their subordinates were evaluated using a 20-question behavior appraisal scale you recently created that focuses on behaviors. Conducted annually, appraisals are an important input into pay raise and bonus decisions.

You were so convinced that the new performance appraisal procedures were highly effective that you hoped your own subordinates would mention them in their feedback to you. And boy did they! You were amazed to learn that the managers *and* their subordinates thought the new scale was unfair, inappropriate, and a waste of time. In fact, the managers' feedback to you was that their own performance was suffering, based on the 360-degree appraisals they received, because their subordinates hated the new appraisal system and partially blamed their bosses, who were part of management. Some managers even admitted giving all their subordinates approximately the same scores on the scales so their pay raises and bonuses would not be affected by their performance appraisals.

You couldn't believe your eyes when you read these comments. You spent so much time developing what you thought was the ideal rating scale for this group of employees. Evidently, for some unknown reason, they wouldn't give it a chance.

Question

1. Your supervisor is aware of the complaints and told you to make "fixing your mess" your top priority. What are you going to do?

THE WALL STREET JOURNAL
CASE IN THE NEWS [LO 12-4, 12-5]

Psst . . . This Is What Your Co-Worker Is Paid

Office workers have grown accustomed to knowing the intimate details of each other's lives—from a colleague's favorite cat video to a boss's vacation fiasco.

Now a small but growing number of private-sector firms are letting employees in on closely held company secrets: revealing details of company financials, staff performance reviews, even individual pay—and in doing so, walking a tightrope between information and TMI, or too much information.

The warts-and-all approach, most often found in startups, builds trust among workers and makes employees more aware of how their particular contribution affects the company as a whole, advocates say.

Employees at SumAll, a Manhattan data-analytics company, can click on a shared drive to peruse investor agreements, company financials, performance appraisals, hiring decisions and employee pay, along with each worker's equity and bonuses.

SumAll Chief Executive Dane Atkinson says the company was launched as an open enterprise. He and his co-founders reasoned that people work more efficiently when freed of doubts about salary, and better understand their individual contribution to the whole group.

Anyone hired into the company must be comfortable with the system, he says.

The company's 30 or so employees are each assigned to one of nine fixed salaries, which range from about $35,000 for the lowest paid to $120,000 for the highest. Raises occur company-wide, determined by performance and market conditions.

"It's not like you come in and [pay] is posted on your forehead," but having the figures in the open alleviates co-workers' curiosity and anxiety, says Kimi Mongello, SumAll's office manager. "When it's a secret you want to know it more," she says, noting that she and her colleagues rarely look at the data.

Ms. Mongello is in a low salary band, and is fine with it. "I shouldn't be paid as much as an engineer," she says. SumAll workers who feel they're unfairly paid can easily bring it up, she adds.

Little privacy remains in most offices, and as work becomes more collaborative, a move toward greater openness may be inevitable, even for larger firms. Companies "don't really have a choice," says Ed Lawler, director of the Center for Effective Organizations at the University of Southern California. (Public companies and government agencies, meanwhile, generally have disclosure requirements about firm performance or pay.)

But open management can be expensive and time consuming: If any worker's pay is out of line with his or her peers, the firm should be ready to even things up or explain why it's so, says Dr. Lawler. Management should also show employees how to read the company's financial and performance data, he adds.

And because workers can see information normally kept under wraps, they may weigh in on decisions, which can slow things down, company executives say.

Once employees have access to more information, however, they can feel more motivated.

At Tenmast Software, a Lexington, Ky., database software maker, the company's 70 employees have access to company financials and participate in monthly strategic-planning sessions, though individual salaries are kept private. Every new employee must attend a financial literacy course to understand how to interpret accounting statements and business decisions.

That literacy paid off last year when the staff acquired the business through an employee stock ownership plan, giving workers an even greater stake in their decisions.

Angela Lee, a Tenmast support team coordinator, says understanding her impact on the bottom line is empowering. She contrasts that to her previous job, where her

project was shuttered, but employees weren't aware anything was amiss until the last minute.

"I know where we are. I know the bottom line and how it's going to affect the bonus I get at the end of the year," she says.

Giving negative feedback—already challenging for many—can be even harder out in the open.

Tim Ogilvie, co-founder and CEO of Peer Insight, a Washington, D.C., innovation-consulting company, says the firm's dozen employees know one another's salaries, bonuses and performance appraisals, along with detailed company financials, down to how much money the company has in the bank. Employees have a say on whether to take on any one client or project and can weigh in on new hires, he says.

Jessica Dugan, a senior design consultant at Peer Insight, says it can be "totally awkward" conducting project evaluations with the entire office listening in. "You want to be a good colleague and give feedback that will help people improve, but that's hard to do in a public forum," says Ms. Dugan.

While sensitive discussions about performance concerns are held privately, she says that open reviews "ensure everyone on a project is on the same page."

But such openness isn't for everyone.

In 2010, Slava Akhmechet, the CEO and co-founder of RethinkDB, a Mountain View, Calif., database firm, experimented with open pay, sharing salary ranges internally and posting them (without names) on the company's website. He had hoped the transparency would give employees a fuller picture of the company and engender a sense of fair play.

But potential recruits saw the salary figures as a starting point, and bargained for pay beyond the fixed limits. Mr. Akhmechet also found he couldn't hire prized applicants without raising everyone else's salaries or getting them to agree to exceptions, he says.

Mr. Akhmechet eventually took salary data offline; now, only he and two other employees know everyone's pay. "I still think an open salary model might work in a larger company with significant resources," he says, but "it is not an effective use of time in early-stage companies."

Questions

1. What are the potential advantages of open management?

2. What are the potential disadvantages of open management?

3. Are there any kinds of information that you think should never be openly available in organizations? If so, why not? If not, why?

4. Why might some managers or employees be resistant to open management?

Source: R. E. Silverman, "Psst . . . This Is What Your Co-Worker Is Paid," *The Wall Street Journal,* January 30, 2013, B6.

Communication and Information Technology Management

LEARNING OBJECTIVES

After studying this chapter, you should be able to:

1 Differentiate between data and information, list the attributes of useful information, and describe three reasons why managers must have access to information to perform their tasks and roles effectively. **[LO 13-1]**

2 Explain why effective communication—the sharing of information—helps an organization gain a competitive advantage, and describe the communication process. **[LO 13-2]**

3 Define information richness, and describe the information richness of communication media available to managers. **[LO 13-3]**

4 Differentiate among four kinds of management information systems. **[LO 13-4]**

Takes one to know one! Marc Benioff's dedication to effective communication within Salesforce.com equips the company's products and processes, enabling Salesforce.com to grow leaps and bounds beyond competitors simply by being the best in their arena.

How IT Facilitates Communication at Salesforce.com

How Can Managers Use IT to Foster Effective Communication?

Marc Benioff, cofounder, chairman of the board of directors, and chief executive officer of Salesforce.com, not only fosters effective communication and collaboration in his company, but his company provides its customers with the tools to promote effective communication in their own organizations and with their own customers. An effective communicator himself, Benioff well knows the importance of building a common understanding, trust, and a collaborative atmosphere for effective communication.[1]

Salesforce.com was founded in 1999 and provides its subscribing companies with customer relationship management software and applications via cloud computing. Cloud computing entails the delivery of software, services, data management, and storage over the Internet.[2] Thus, Salesforce.com subscribers need not purchase, install, upgrade, or maintain software to manage communications and business activities.

Salesforce.com has over 100,000 subscribers ranging from Dell, Cisco, and Google to NBCUniversal.[3] Its growth trajectory has been remarkable.[4] As Benioff was quoted in a recent press release, "Last year we became the first enterprise cloud computing company to achieve $2 billion in revenue, and we're now poised to deliver the first ever $3 billion year in fiscal 2013."[5]

With over 7,000 employees and more than 100,000 customers, Salesforce.com is a leader in the move toward social enterprises that use mobile, social, and cloud technology to better serve customers.[6] Salesforce.com offers its subscribers (or customers) access to different kinds of social networks to facilitate the sharing of information, communication, and coordination both internally among employees and externally with customers. For example, Salesforce.com's Chatter is a social networking application (or "app")[7] similar to Facebook for internal use by a company's employees. On computers and mobile devices like smartphones and tablets, and in news feeds and groups open to all employees, employees can communicate with each other, work on drafts, collaborate, get feedback on new ideas, and perform data analyses in real time. Inside Salesforce.com, some groups bring together employees from different functions and hierarchical ranks to share thoughts and ideas about their own work experiences such as the groups named Airing of Grievances and Tribal Knowledge.[8]

Each day, employees at Salesforce.com post approximately 3,000 entries on Chatter, with their identities known to all.[9] Thus, while posts cannot get out of hand, this open forum for real-time communication certainly seems to facilitate collaboration and shared understandings. After Salesforce.com developed and adopted Chatter, managers found that around 30% fewer internal e-mails were being sent among employees. Chatter seems to keep both employees and managers more informed about what is going on in the company. Benioff himself indicated that "I learned more about my company in a few months through using Chatter than I had in the last three years."[10] Chatter is used by the vast majority of Salesforce.com customers without any extra charge.[11]

While Salesforce.com excels in the arena of electronic communication and social networking, Benioff, a consummate salesman, nonetheless recognizes the importance of face-to-face communication as well. As a case in point, consider how he managed the acquisition of Rypple, a Canadian start-up that develops human resources applications.[12] Rypple was founded by Daniel Debow and David Stein, who were speaking at the same conference as Benioff in New York City. Even though Benioff already had had several discussions with the pair about Salesforce.com's potentially acquiring Rypple, the night before the meeting, Benioff took Debow and Stein to one of his favorite Italian restaurants in midtown Manhattan. The next day after the conference events were finished, Benioff took Debow (Stein had a flight back home to catch) to the 2nd Avenue Deli for a tasty deli spread at the counter. Rather than talk business, the two just had a casual conversation. Building a good sense of rapport and a common understanding with the CEO of the company that was going to acquire their company evidently meant a lot to Debow and Stein. Even though they had a better offer to acquire their company from one of Salesforce.com's competitors, they decided to accept Salesforce.com's $60 million bid for Rypple. As Debow puts it, "It wasn't only about deal terms, but corporate culture. . . . We barely met the other CEO . . . we entrepreneurs could be part of their family. Nobody can keep up the artifice over a couple of hours of sharing pickles."[13] All in all, Salesforce.com appears to be helping many people and organizations be better communicators.[14]

Overview

Even with all the advances in information technology provided by companies like Salesforce.com that are available to managers, ineffective communication continues to take place in organizations. Ineffective communication is detrimental for managers, employees, and organizations; it can lead to poor performance, strained interpersonal relations, poor service, and dissatisfied customers. For an organization to be effective and gain a competitive advantage, managers at all levels need to be good communicators—and the use of new IT is vital.

In this chapter we survey information systems and information technology in general, looking at the relationship between information and the manager's job. Then we describe the nature of communication and explain why it is so important for all managers and their subordinates to be effective communicators. We describe the communication media available to managers and the factors they need to consider when selecting a communication medium for each message they send. We consider the communication networks that organizational members rely on, and we explore how advances in information technology have expanded managers' communication options.

Finally, we discuss several types of information systems that managers can use to help themselves perform their jobs, and we examine the impact that rapidly evolving information systems and technologies may have on managers' jobs and on an organization's competitive advantage. By the end of this chapter, you will understand the profound ways in which new developments in information systems and technology are shaping the way managers communicate and their functions and roles.

Information and the Manager's Job

LO 13-1 Differentiate between data and information, list the attributes of useful information, and describe three reasons why managers must have access to information to perform their tasks and roles effectively.

data Raw, unsummarized, and unanalyzed facts.

information Data that are organized in a meaningful fashion.

Managers cannot plan, organize, lead, and control effectively unless they have access to information. Information is the source of the knowledge and intelligence that they need to make the right decisions. Information, however, is not the same as data.[15] Data are raw, unsummarized, and unanalyzed facts such as volume of sales, level of costs, or number of customers. Information is data that are organized in a meaningful fashion, such as in a graph showing changes in sales volume or costs over time. Alone, data do not tell managers anything; information, in contrast, can communicate a great deal of useful knowledge to the person who receives it—such as a manager who sees sales falling or costs rising. The distinction between data and information is important because one of the uses of information technology is to help managers transform data into information in order to make better managerial decisions.

Consider the case of a manager in a supermarket who must decide how much shelf space to allocate to two breakfast cereal brands for children: Dentist's Delight and Sugar Supreme. Most supermarkets use checkout scanners to record individual sales and store the data on a computer. Accessing this computer, the manager might find that Dentist's Delight sells 50 boxes per day and Sugar Supreme sells 25 boxes per day. These raw data, however, are of little help in assisting the manager to decide how to allocate shelf space. The manager also needs to know how much shelf space each cereal currently occupies and how much profit each cereal generates for the supermarket.

Suppose the manager discovers that Dentist's Delight occupies 10 feet of shelf space and Sugar Supreme occupies 4 feet and that Dentist's Delight generates 20 cents of profit a box while Sugar Supreme generates 40 cents of profit a box. By putting these three bits of data together (number of boxes sold, amount of shelf space, and profit per box), the manager gets some useful information on which to base a decision: Dentist's Delight generates $1 of profit per foot of shelf space per day ([50 boxes @ $.20]/10 feet), and Sugar Supreme generates $2.50 of profit per foot of shelf space per day ([25 boxes @ $.40]/4 feet). Armed with this information, the manager might decide to allocate less shelf space to Dentist's Delight and more to Sugar Supreme.

Attributes of Useful Information

Four factors determine the usefulness of information to a manager: quality, timeliness, completeness, and relevance (see Figure 13.1).

QUALITY Accuracy and reliability determine the quality of information.[16] The greater its accuracy and reliability, the higher is the quality of information. Modern IT gives managers access to high-quality real-time information that they can use to improve long-term decision making and alter short-term operating decisions, such as how much of a particular product to make daily or monthly. Supermarket managers, for example, use handheld bar code readers linked to a

Figure 13.1

Factors Affecting
the Usefulness of
Information

server to monitor and record how demand for particular products such as milk, chicken, or bread changes daily so they know how to restock their shelves to ensure the products are always available.

TIMELINESS Information that is timely is available when it is required to allow managers to make the optimal decision—not after the decision has been made. In today's rapidly changing world, the need for timely information often means information must be available on a real-time basis—hence the enormous growth in the demand for mobile computing devices such as smartphones.[17] Real-time information is information that reflects current changes in business conditions. In an industry that experiences rapid changes, real-time information may need to be updated frequently.

Airlines use real-time information about the number of flight bookings and competitors' prices to adjust their prices hourly to maximize their revenues. Thus, for example, the fare for flights from New York to Seattle might change from one hour to the next as fares are reduced to fill empty seats and raised when most seats have been sold. U.S. airlines make more than 100,000 fare changes each day. Obviously the managers who make such pricing decisions need real-time information about current market demand.

COMPLETENESS Information that is complete gives managers all the information they need to exercise control, achieve coordination, or make an effective decision. Recall from Chapter 5, however, that managers rarely have access to complete information. Instead, because of uncertainty, ambiguity, and bounded rationality, they have to make do with incomplete information.[18] One function of IT is to increase the completeness of managers' information.

RELEVANCE Information that is relevant is useful and suits a manager's particular needs and circumstances. Irrelevant information is useless and may actually hurt the performance of a busy manager who has to spend valuable time determining whether information is relevant. Given the massive amounts of information that managers are now exposed to and their limited information-processing capabilities, a company's information systems designers need to ensure that managers receive only relevant information.

real-time information

Frequently updated information that reflects current conditions.

What Is Information Technology?

Information technology (IT) is the set of methods or techniques for acquiring, organizing, storing, manipulating, and transmitting information.[19] A management information system (MIS) is a specific form of IT that managers select and use to generate the specific, detailed information they need to perform their roles effectively. Management information systems have existed for as long as there have been organizations, which is a long time indeed: Merchants in ancient Egypt used clay tablets to record their transactions. Before the computing age, most systems were paper-based: Clerks recorded important information on paper documents (often in duplicate or triplicate) in words and numbers; sent copies of the documents to superiors, customers, or suppliers; and stored other copies in filing cabinets for future reference.

Rapid advances in the power of IT—specifically the development of ever more powerful and sophisticated computer hardware and software—have had a fundamental impact on organizations and managers. Some recent IT developments, such as inventory management and customer relationship management (CRM) systems, contribute so much to performance that organizations that do *not* adopt them, or that implement them ineffectively, become uncompetitive compared with organizations that do adopt them.[20] In the 2010s much of the increasing productivity and efficiency of business in general has been attributed to the way organizations and their employees use advancing IT to improve their performance.

Managers need information for three reasons: to make effective decisions, to control the activities of the organization, and to coordinate the activities of the organization. Next we examine these uses of information in detail.

Information and Decisions

Much of management (planning, organizing, leading, and controlling) is about making decisions. For example, the marketing manager must decide what price to charge for a product, what distribution channels to use, and what promotional messages to emphasize to maximize sales. The manufacturing manager must decide how much of a product to make and how to make it. The purchasing manager must decide from whom to purchase inputs and what inventory of inputs to hold. The human relations manager must decide how much employees should be paid, how they should be trained, and what benefits they should be given. The engineering manager must make decisions about new product design. Top managers must decide how to allocate scarce financial resources among competing projects, how best to structure and control the organization, and what business-level strategy the organization should be pursuing. And regardless of their functional orientation, all managers have to make decisions about matters such as what performance evaluation to give to a subordinate.

Charts and graphs may be the clichéd centerpieces of managerial meetings, but the data they represent are key for making informed decisions.

To make effective decisions, managers need information both from inside the organization and from external stakeholders. When deciding how to price a product, for example, marketing managers need information about how consumers will react to different prices. They need information about unit costs because they do not want to set the price below the cost of production. And they need information about competitive strategy because pricing strategy should be consistent with an organization's competitive strategy. Some of this information will come from outside the organization (for example, from consumer surveys) and some from inside the organization (information about production costs comes from manufacturing). As this example suggests, managers' ability to make effective decisions rests on their ability to acquire and process information.

Information and Control

As discussed in Chapter 8, controlling is the process through which managers regulate how efficiently and effectively an organization and its members perform the activities necessary to achieve its stated goals.[21] Managers achieve control over organizational activities by taking four steps (see Figure 8.2): (1) They establish measurable standards of performance or goals; (2) they measure actual performance; (3) they compare actual performance against established goals; and (4) they evaluate the results and take corrective action if necessary.[22] The package delivery company UPS, for example, has a delivery goal: to deliver 95% of the overnight packages it picks up by noon the next day.[23] UPS has thousands of U.S. ground stations (branch offices that coordinate the pickup and delivery of packages in a particular area) that are responsible for the physical pickup and delivery of packages. UPS managers monitor the delivery performance of these stations regularly; if they find that the 95% goal is not being attained, they determine why and take corrective action if necessary.

To achieve control over any organizational activity, managers must have information. To control ground station activities, a UPS manager might need to know what percentage of packages each station delivers by noon. To obtain this information the manager uses UPS's own IT; UPS is also a leader in developing proprietary in-house IT. All packages to be shipped to the stations have been scanned with handheld scanners by the UPS drivers who pick them up; then all this information is sent wirelessly through UPS servers to its headquarters' mainframe computer. When the packages are scanned again at delivery, this information is also transmitted through its computer network. Managers can access this information to quickly discover what percentage of packages were delivered by noon of the day after they were picked up, and also how this information breaks down station by station so they can take corrective action if necessary.

Management information systems are used to control all divisional and functional operations. In accounting, for example, information systems are used to monitor expenditures and compare them against budgets.[24] To track expenditures against budgets, managers need information about current expenditures, broken down by relevant organizational units; accounting IT is designed to give managers this information. An example of IT used to monitor and control the daily activities of employees is the online MBO information system used by T. J. Rodgers at Cypress Semiconductor, discussed in Chapter 8. Rodgers implemented IT that allows him to review the goals of all his employees in about four hours.[25] At first glance it might seem that advances in IT would have a limited impact on the business of an office furniture maker; however, this assumption would be incorrect, as the following "Management Insight" box suggests.

MANAGEMENT INSIGHT

Herman Miller's Office of the Future

Managers at Herman Miller have been finding countless ways to use IT and the Internet to give their company a competitive advantage over rival office furniture makers such as Steelcase and Hon.[26] Early on, Miller's managers saw the potential of the Internet for selling its furniture to business customers. Other furniture companies' websites were simply online advertisements for their products, services, and other marketing information. But Miller's managers quickly realized the true potential of using both the company's intranet and the Internet to reach customers to gain competitive advantage.

First Miller's managers developed IT that linked all the company's dealers and salespeople to its manufacturing hub so sales orders could be coordinated with the custom design department and with manufacturing, enabling customers to receive pricing and scheduling information promptly. Then, with this customer delivery system in place, Miller developed IT to link its manufacturing operations with its network of suppliers so its input supply chain would be coordinated with its customer needs.

When Miller's managers noticed that competitors were imitating its IT, they searched for new ways to maintain their competitive advantage. Soon they realized IT could transform the office furniture business itself. When they began to define Herman Miller as a digital enterprise infused with e-business, they realized IT could not only improve efficiency but also change how the customer experienced Herman Miller and increase value for the customer. A major web initiative was the establishment of an e-learning tool, Uknowit.com, which became Herman Miller's online university. Via the web thousands of Miller's employees and dealers are currently enrolled in Uknowit.com, where they choose from 85 courses covering technology, products and services, product applications, selling skills, and industry competitive knowledge. The benefits to Miller and its dealers and customers from this IT initiative are improved speed to market and ability to respond to competitors' tactics. Salespeople and dealers now have the information and tools they need to better compete for and keep customers.

Moreover, the office furniture business offers highly customized solutions to its customers. A main source of competitive advantage is the ability to give customers exactly what they want at the right price. Using its new IT, Miller's salespeople give design and manufacturing more accurate and timely information, which has reduced specification errors during the selling process. Also, with the new systems time to market has been reduced, and Miller is committed to being able to offer customers highly customized furniture in 10 or fewer business days.

Of course all these IT initiatives have been costly to Herman Miller. Thousands of hours of management time have been spent

Herman Miller's custom-made ergonomic office furniture arrives on time due to the company's use of IT that links its dealers with its manufacturing hub.

developing the IT and providing content, such as information about competitors, for the company's online classes. Herman Miller's managers are looking at the long term; they believe they have created a real source of competitive advantage for their company that will sustain it in the years ahead. And the company was voted as one of the most admired companies by *Fortune* because its managers try to keep their IT one step ahead of its competitors.[27]

Information and Coordination

Coordinating department and divisional activities to achieve organizational goals is another basic task of management. As an example of the size of the coordination task that managers face, consider the coordination effort necessary to build Boeing's 787 Dreamliner jet aircraft, which is assembled from over 3 million individual parts.[28] Managers at Boeing have to coordinate the production and delivery of all these parts so every part arrives at Boeing's Everett, Washington, facility exactly when it is needed (for example, the wings should arrive before the engines). To achieve this high level of coordination, managers need information about which global supplier is producing what part, and when it will be produced. To meet this need, managers at Boeing created global IT that links Boeing to all its suppliers and can track the flow of the 3 million components through the production process around the world in real time—an immense task. Indeed, as we noted in earlier chapters, Boeing's IT system could not match the enormous complexity of the task, and the launch of its new airliner was delayed because of IT glitches that affected communication with suppliers.

To deal with such global coordination problems, managers have been adopting ever more sophisticated computer-based information systems that help them coordinate the flow of materials, semifinished goods, and finished products around the world.

LO 13-2 Explain why effective communication—the sharing of information—helps an organization gain a competitive advantage, and describe the communication process.

Communication, Information, and Management

communication
The sharing of information between two or more individuals or groups to reach a common understanding.

Communication is the sharing of information between two or more people or groups to reach a common understanding.[29] First and foremost, communication, no matter how electronically based, is a human endeavor and involves individuals and groups sharing information and coordinating their actions. Second, communication does not take place unless a common understanding is reached. Thus, if you try to call a business to speak to a person in customer service or billing and you are bounced back and forth between endless automated messages and menu options and eventually hang up in frustration, communication has not taken place.

The Importance of Good Communication

In Chapter 1, we described how in order for an organization to gain a competitive advantage, managers must strive to increase efficiency, quality, responsiveness to customers, and innovation. Good communication is essential for attaining each of these four goals and thus is a necessity for gaining a competitive advantage.

Managers can *increase efficiency* by updating the production process to take advantage of new and more efficient technologies and by training workers to operate the new technologies and expand their skills. Good communication is necessary for managers to learn about new technologies, implement them in their organizations, and train workers in how to use them. Similarly, *improving quality* hinges on effective communication. Managers need to communicate to all members of an organization the meaning and importance of high quality and the routes to attaining it. Subordinates need to communicate quality problems and suggestions for increasing quality to their superiors, and members of self-managed work teams need to share their ideas for improving quality with each other.

Good communication can also help to increase *responsiveness to customers.* When the organizational members who are closest to customers, such as salespeople in department stores and tellers in banks, are empowered to communicate customers' needs and desires to managers, managers are better able to respond to these needs. Managers, in turn, must communicate with other organizational members to determine how best to respond to changing customer preferences.

Innovation, which often takes place in cross-functional teams, also requires effective communication. Members of a cross-functional team developing a new kind of video game console, for example, must communicate effectively with each other to develop a console that customers will want, that will be of high quality, and that can be produced efficiently. Members of the team also must communicate with managers to secure the resources they need to develop the console and keep the managers informed of progress on the project.

Effective communication is necessary for managers and all members of an organization to increase efficiency, quality, responsiveness to customers, and innovation and thus gain a competitive advantage for their organization. Managers therefore must have a good understanding of the communication process if they are to perform effectively. Collaboration software is IT that aims to promote highly interdependent interactions among members of a team and provide the team with an electronic meeting site for communication.[30] Work that is truly team-based involves team members with distinct areas of expertise who need to closely coordinate their efforts, and collaboration software can be a powerful communication tool.

Collaboration software provides members of a team with an online work site where they can post, share, and save data, reports, sketches, and other documents; keep calendars; have team-based online conferences; and send and receive messages. The software can also keep and update progress reports, survey team members about different issues, forward documents to managers, and let users know which of their team members are also online and at the site.[31] Having an integrated online work area can help to organize and centralize the work of a team, help to ensure that information is readily available as needed, and also help team members to make sure that important information is not overlooked. Collaboration software can be much more efficient than e-mail or instant messaging for managing ongoing team collaboration and interaction that is not face-to-face. Moreover, when a team does meet face-to-face, all documents the team might need in the course of the meeting are just a click away.[32]

The New York–based public relations company Ketchum Inc. uses collaboration software for some of its projects. For example, Ketchum is managing public relations, marketing, and advertising for a new charitable program that Fireman's Fund Insurance Co. has undertaken. By using the eRoom software provided by Documentum (a part of EMC Corporation), Ketchum employees working on the project at six different locations, employee representatives from

Fireman's, and a graphics company that is designing a website for the program can share plans, documents, graphic designs, and calendars at an online work site.[33] Members of the Ketchum–Fireman team get e-mail alerts when something has been modified or added to the site. As Ketchum's chief information officer Andy Roach puts it, "The fact that everyone has access to the same document means Ketchum isn't going to waste time on the logistics and can focus on the creative side."[34]

Another company taking advantage of collaboration software is Honeywell International Inc. Managers at Honeywell decided to use the SharePoint collaboration software provided by Microsoft, in part because it can be integrated with other Microsoft software such as Outlook. So, for example, if a team using SharePoint makes a change to the team's calendar, that change will be automatically made in team members' Outlook calendars.[35] Clearly, collaboration software has the potential to enhance communication efficiency and effectiveness in teams.

The Communication Process

The communication process consists of two phases. In the *transmission phase,* information is shared between two or more individuals or groups. In the *feedback phase,* a common understanding is assured. In both phases, a number of distinct stages must occur for communication to take place (see Figure 13.2).[36]

Starting the transmission phase, the sender, the person or group wishing to share information with some other person or group, decides on the message, what information to communicate. Then the sender translates the message into symbols or language, a process called encoding; often messages are encoded into words. Noise is a general term that refers to anything that hampers any stage of the communication process.

Once encoded, a message is transmitted through a medium to the receiver, the person or group for which the message is intended. A medium is simply the pathway, such as a phone call, a letter, a memo, or face-to-face communication in a meeting, through which an encoded message is transmitted to a receiver. At the next stage, the receiver interprets and tries to make sense of the message, a process called decoding. This is a critical point in communication.

sender The person or group wishing to share information.

message The information that a sender wants to share.

encoding Translating a message into understandable symbols or language.

noise Anything that hampers any stage of the communication process.

receiver The person or group for which a message is intended.

medium The pathway through which an encoded message is transmitted to a receiver.

decoding Interpreting and trying to make sense of a message.

Figure 13.2

The Communication Process

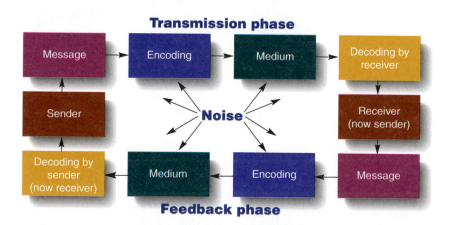

The feedback phase is initiated by the receiver (who becomes a sender). The receiver decides what message to send to the original sender (who becomes a receiver), encodes it, and transmits it through a chosen medium (see Figure 13.2). The message might contain a confirmation that the original message was received and understood or a restatement of the original message to make sure that it has been correctly interpreted; or it might include a request for more information. The original sender decodes the message and makes sure that a common understanding has been reached. If the original sender determines that a common understanding has not been reached, sender and receiver cycle through the whole process as many times as are needed to reach a common understanding.

verbal communication

The encoding of messages into words, either written or spoken.

nonverbal communication

The encoding of messages by means of facial expressions, body language, and styles of dress.

The encoding of messages into words, written or spoken, is verbal communication. We also encode messages without using written or spoken language. Nonverbal communication shares information by means of facial expressions (smiling, raising an eyebrow, frowning, dropping one's jaw), body language (posture, gestures, nods, shrugs), and even style of dress (casual, formal, conservative, trendy). For example, to communicate or signal that General Motors' old bureaucracy has been dismantled and the company is decentralized and more informal than it used to be, top managers at GM wear slacks and sport jackets rather than business suits when they walk around GM plants.[37] The trend toward increasing empowerment of the workforce has led GM and other managers to dress informally to communicate that all employees of an organization are team members, working together to create value for customers.

Nonverbal communication can be used to back up or reinforce verbal communication. Just as a warm and genuine smile can back up words of appreciation for a job well done, a concerned facial expression can back up words of sympathy for a personal problem. In such cases, the congruence between verbal and nonverbal communication helps to ensure that a common understanding is reached.

Sometimes when members of an organization decide not to express a message verbally, they inadvertently do so nonverbally. People tend to have less control over nonverbal communication, and often a verbal message that is withheld gets expressed through body language or facial expressions. A manager who agrees to a proposal that she or he actually is not in favor of may unintentionally communicate disfavor by grimacing.

Sometimes nonverbal communication is used to send messages that cannot be sent through verbal channels. Many lawyers are well aware of this communication tactic. Lawyers are often schooled in techniques of nonverbal communication such as choosing where to stand in the courtroom for maximum effect and using eye contact during different stages of a trial. Lawyers sometimes get into trouble for using inappropriate nonverbal

Nonverbal cues, such as the intense look being exchanged by these people, can provide managers and employees with vital information that helps them make better decisions.

communication in an attempt to influence juries. In a Louisiana court, prosecuting attorney Thomas Pirtle was admonished and fined $2,500 by Judge Yada Magee for shaking his head in an expression of doubt, waving his arms indicating disfavor, and chuckling when attorneys for the defense were stating their case.[38]

The Dangers of Ineffective Communication

Because managers must communicate with others to perform their various roles and tasks, managers spend most of their time communicating, whether in meetings, in telephone conversations, through e-mail, or in face-to-face interactions. Indeed, some experts estimate that managers spend approximately 85% of their time engaged in some form of communication.[39] Effective communication is so important that managers cannot just be concerned that they themselves are effective communicators; they also have to help their subordinates be effective communicators. When all members of an organization are able to communicate effectively with each other and with people outside the organization, the organization is much more likely to perform highly and gain a competitive advantage.

When managers and other members of an organization are ineffective communicators, organizational performance suffers, and any competitive advantage the organization might have is likely to be lost. Moreover, poor communication sometimes can be downright dangerous and even lead to tragic and unnecessary loss of human life. For example, researchers from Harvard University studied the causes of mistakes, such as a patient receiving the wrong medication, in two large hospitals in the Boston area. They discovered that some mistakes in hospitals occur because of communication problems—physicians not having the information they need to correctly order medications for their patients or nurses not having the information they need to correctly administer medications. The researchers concluded that some of the responsibility for these mistakes lies with hospital management, which has not taken active steps to improve communication.[40] Indeed, in 2008 over 400,000 recorded events of mistakes were documented. The following "Management Insight" shows how some managers are trying to promote effective communication.

MANAGEMENT INSIGHT

Why Managers Need Feedback from Employees

As managers advance in the corporate hierarchy and assume positions with increased responsibility, they often become removed from the day-to-day operations of their organizations. Thus, they are less likely to notice or become aware of problems with existing processes and procedures and sources of inefficiencies as well as how customers and clients are reacting to the goods and services the organization provides. Moreover, ideas for ways to improve goods and services sometimes occur to those who are most closely and immediately linked to producing and delivering products and services. Some of these ideas may rarely occur to upper-level managers who are not engaged in these activities on a day-to-day basis.[41]

Thus, it is crucial that managers receive and listen to feedback from employees. While this might seem pretty straightforward and easily accomplished, managers are sometimes the last ones to know about problems for a number of reasons. Employees sometimes fear that they will be blamed for problems that they make their bosses aware of, that they will be seen as "troublemakers," or that managers will perceive their well-intentioned feedback as a personal criticism or attack.[42] Moreover, if employees feel that their feedback, even suggestions for improvements or ways to seize new opportunities, will fall on deaf ears and be ignored, they will be reluctant to speak up.

Effective managers recognize the importance of receiving feedback from employees and take active steps to ensure that this happens. When Yogesh Gupta accepted the position of president and CEO of FatWire Software, one of his priorities was to ensure that his employees provided him with feedback on an ongoing basis.[43] FatWire Software, headquartered in Mineola, New York, has 200 employees, offices in over 10 countries, and over 450 customers such as 3M, *The New York Times*, and Best Buy. In his career, Gupta has often witnessed managers inadvertently discouraging employees from providing feedback, even when the managers desired it.[44] As he indicates, "I've heard so many executives tell employees to be candid and then jump down their throats if they bring up a problem or ask a critical question."[45]

Gupta spends a lot of time talking with FatWire employees and managers to get their perspectives and feedback. He holds individual meetings with managers so they feel more comfortable providing him with frank and honest feedback. And he explicitly asks them if he is doing anything wrong, if there is a better way for him to do things. As a result of listening to the feedback he has received, Gupta realized that FatWire might benefit from having more employees focused on product development and marketing and that customer support services and processes could be enhanced.[46]

When Gupta receives valuable feedback, he makes it a point to positively reinforce the manager or employee who provided it in a public fashion, so other employees realize he really wants their feedback. As he indicates, "I know I have to say, 'You did the right thing to speak up' again and again, because employees fear they'll get blamed if they say anything negative."[47]

At Intuit Inc., a major provider of accounting and financial software, managers receive valuable feedback from employees in a number of ways. An annual employee survey is used to find out what employees think about Intuit's practices and procedures.[48] Managers are advised to have what are called "skip level" meetings throughout the year whereby they meet with the subordinates of the managers who report to them to get their feedback on how things are going.[49] Jim Grenier, vice president for human resources at Intuit, suggests that obtaining employee feedback through this process leads to improved decision making.[50] As he puts it, "You're looking for more input so you can make a better decision. Employees know that we are serious about asking for their feedback, and we listen and we do something about it."[51]

Information Richness and Communication Media

LO 13-3 Define information richness, and describe the information richness of communication media available to managers.

information richness The amount of information that a communication medium can carry and the extent to which the medium enables the sender and receiver to reach a common understanding.

To be effective communicators, managers (and other members of an organization) need to select an appropriate communication medium for *each* message they send. Should a change in procedures be communicated to subordinates in a memo sent through e-mail? Should a congratulatory message about a major accomplishment be communicated in a letter, in a phone call, or over lunch? Should a layoff announcement be made in a memo or at a plant meeting? Should the members of a purchasing team travel to Europe to cement a major agreement with a new supplier, or should they do so through faxes? Managers deal with these questions day in and day out.

There is no one best communication medium for managers to rely on. In choosing a communication medium for any message, managers need to consider three factors. The first and most important is the level of information richness that is needed. Information richness is the amount of information a communication medium can carry and the extent to which the medium enables the sender and receiver to reach a common understanding.[52] The communication media that managers use vary in their information richness (see Figure 13.3).[53] Media high in information richness are able to carry an extensive amount of information and generally enable receivers and senders to come to a common understanding.

The second factor that managers need to take into account in selecting a communication medium is the *time* needed for communication, because managers' and other organizational members' time is valuable. Managers at UPS, for example, dramatically reduced the amount of time they spent by using videoconferences instead of face-to-face communication, which required managers to travel overseas.[54]

The third factor that affects the choice of a communication medium is the *need for a paper or electronic trail* or some kind of written documentation that a message was sent and received. A manager may wish to document in writing, for example, that a subordinate was given a formal warning about excessive lateness.

Figure 13.3

The Information Richness of Communication Media

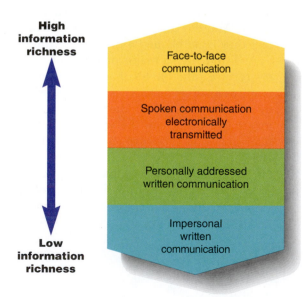

In the remainder of this section we examine four types of communication media that vary along the three dimensions of information richness, time, and the availability of a paper or electronic trail.[55]

Face-to-Face Communication

Face-to-face communication is the medium that is highest in information richness. When managers communicate face-to-face, they not only can take advantage of verbal communication but they also can interpret each other's nonverbal signals such as facial expressions and body language. A look of concern or puzzlement can sometimes tell more than a thousand words, and managers can respond to these nonverbal signals on the spot. Face-to-face communication also enables managers to receive instant feedback. Points of confusion, ambiguity, or misunderstanding can be resolved, and managers can cycle through the communication process as many times as they need to, to reach a common understanding.

management by wandering around

A face-to-face communication technique in which a manager walks around a work area and talks informally with employees about issues and concerns.

Management by wandering around is a face-to-face communication technique that is effective for many managers at all levels in an organization.[56] Rather than scheduling formal meetings with subordinates, managers walk around work areas and talk informally with employees about issues and concerns that both employees and managers may have. These informal conversations provide managers and subordinates with important information and at the same time foster the development of positive relationships. William Hewlett and David Packard, founders and former top managers of Hewlett-Packard, found management by wandering around a highly effective way to communicate with their employees.

Because face-to-face communication is highest in information richness, you might think that it should always be the medium of choice for managers. This is not the case, however, because of the amount of time it takes and the lack of a paper or electronic trail resulting from it. For messages that are important, personal, or likely to be misunderstood, it is often well worth managers' time to use face-to-face communication and, if need be, supplement it with some form of written communication documenting the message.

Advances in information technology are providing managers with new and close alternative communication media for face-to-face communication. Like UPS, other organizations such as American Greetings Corp. and Hewlett-Packard are using *videoconferences* to capture some of the advantages of face-to-face communication (such as access to facial expressions) while saving time and money because managers in different locations do not have to travel to meet with one another. During a videoconference, managers in two or more locations communicate with each other over large TV or video screens; they not only hear each other but also see each other throughout the meeting.

In addition to saving travel costs, videoconferences sometimes have other advantages. Managers at American Greetings have found that decisions get made more quickly when videoconferences are used, because more managers can be involved in the decision-making process and therefore fewer managers

In spite of the popularity of electronic communication, face-to-face communication is still the medium that is highest in information richness.

have to be consulted outside the meeting itself. Managers at HP have found that videoconferences have shortened new product development time by 30% for similar reasons. Videoconferences also seem to lead to more efficient meetings. Some managers have found that their meetings are 20% to 30% shorter when videoconferences are used instead of face-to-face meetings.[57]

Taking videoconferencing a leap forward, Cisco Systems has developed its TelePresence line of products, which enables individuals and teams in different locations to communicate live and in real time over the Internet with high-definition and life-size video and excellent-quality audio that makes it feel like all the people taking part, no matter where they are, are in the same room.[58] One morning, Cisco CEO John Chambers was able to participate in meetings with employees and teams in India, Japan, Cleveland, and London in less than four hours by using TelePresence.[59] Other companies, such as HP, have developed similar products. What distinguishes these products from older videoconferencing systems is the fact that there are no delays in transmission and the video quality is sharp, clear, lifelike, and life-size.[60]

Spoken Communication Electronically Transmitted

After face-to-face communication, spoken communication electronically transmitted over phone lines is second highest in information richness (see Figure 13.3). Although managers communicating over the telephone do not have access to body language and facial expressions, they do have access to the tone of voice in which a message is delivered, the parts of the message the sender emphasizes, and the general manner in which the message is spoken, in addition to the actual words themselves. Thus, telephone conversations have the capacity to convey extensive amounts of information. Managers also can ensure that mutual understanding is reached because they can get quick feedback over the phone and answer questions.

Voice mail systems and answering machines also allow managers to send and receive verbal electronic messages over telephone lines. Voice mail systems are companywide systems that enable senders to record messages for members of an organization who are away from their desks and allow receivers to access their messages when away from the office. Such systems are obviously a necessity when managers are frequently out of the office, and managers on the road are well advised to periodically check their voice mail.

Personally Addressed Written Communication

Lower than electronically transmitted verbal communication in information richness is personally addressed written communication (see Figure 13.3). One of the advantages of face-to-face communication and verbal communication electronically transmitted is that they both tend to demand attention, which helps ensure that receivers pay attention. Personally addressed written communications such as memos and letters also have this advantage. Because they are addressed to a particular person, the chances are good that the person will actually pay attention to (and read) them. Moreover, the sender can write the message in a way that the receiver is most likely to understand. Like voice mail, written communication does not enable a receiver to have his or her questions answered immediately, but when messages are clearly written and feedback is provided, common understandings can still be reached.

Cisco Systems conducts a press conference with Yao Ming using TelePresence's videoconferencing system with life-size imaging.

Even if managers use face-to-face communication, a follow-up in writing is often needed for messages that are important or complicated and need to be referred to later. This is precisely what Karen Stracker, a hospital administrator, did when she needed to tell one of her subordinates about an important change in the way the hospital would be handling denials of insurance benefits. Stracker met with the subordinate and described the changes face-to-face. Once she was sure that the subordinate understood them, she handed her a sheet of instructions to follow, which essentially summarized the information they had discussed.

E-mail also fits into this category of communication media because senders and receivers are communicating through personally addressed written words. The words, however, are appearing on their personal computer screens rather than on pieces of paper. E-mail is becoming so widespread in the business world that managers are even developing their own e-mail etiquette. To save time, Andrew Giangola, a manager at Simon & Schuster, a book publisher, used to type all his e-mail messages in capital letters. He was surprised when a receiver of one of his messages responded, "Why are you screaming at me?" Messages in capital letters are often perceived as being shouted or screamed, and thus Giangola's routine use of capital letters was bad e-mail etiquette. Here are some other guidelines from polite e-mailers: Always punctuate messages; do not ramble on or say more than you need to; do not act as though you do not understand something when in fact you do understand it; and pay attention to spelling and format (put a memo in memo form). To avoid embarrassments like Giangola's, managers at Simon & Schuster created a task force to develop guidelines for e-mail etiquette.[61]

The growing popularity of e-mail has also enabled many workers and managers to become telecommuters, people who are employed by organizations and work out of offices in their own homes. There are approximately 8.4 million telecommuters in the United States. Many telecommuters indicate that the flexibility of working at home enables them to be more productive while giving them a chance to be closer to their families and not waste time traveling to and from the office.[62] A study conducted by Georgetown University found that 75% of the telecommuters surveyed said their productivity increased and 83% said their home life improved once they started telecommuting.[63]

Unfortunately, the growing use of e-mail has been accompanied by growing abuse of e-mail. Some employees sexually harass coworkers through e-mail, and divorcing spouses who work together sometimes sign their spouse's name to e-mail and send insulting or derogatory messages to the spouse's boss. Robert Mirguet, information systems manager at Eastman Kodak, has indicated that some Kodak employees have used Kodak's e-mail system to try to start their own businesses during working hours. Kodak managers monitor employees' e-mail messages when they suspect some form of abuse. Top managers also complain that sometimes their e-mail is clogged with junk mail. In a recent survey over half of the organizations contacted acknowledged some problems with their e-mail systems.[64]

To avoid these and other costly forms of e-mail abuse, managers need to develop a clear policy specifying what company e-mail can and should be used for and what is out of bounds. Managers also should clearly communicate this policy to all members of an organization, as well as the procedures that will be used when e-mail abuse is suspected and the consequences that will result when e-mail abuse is confirmed.

Impersonal Written Communication

Impersonal written communication is lowest in information richness and is well suited for messages that need to reach a large number of receivers. Because such messages are not addressed to particular receivers, feedback is unlikely, so managers must make sure that messages sent by this medium are written clearly in language that all receivers will understand.

Managers often find company newsletters useful vehicles for reaching large numbers of employees. Many managers give their newsletters catchy names to spark employee interest and also to inject a bit of humor into the workplace. Managers at the pork-sausage maker Bob Evans Farms Inc. called their newsletter "The Squealer" for many years but recently changed the title to "The Homesteader" to reflect the company's broadened line of products. Managers at American Greetings Corp., at Yokohama Tire Corp., and at Eastman Kodak call their newsletters "Expressions," "TreadLines," and "Kodakery," respectively. Managers at Quaker State Corp. held a contest to rename their newsletter. Among the 1,000 submitted names were "The Big Q Review," "The Pipeline," and "Q. S. Oil Press"; the winner was "On Q."[65]

Managers can use impersonal written communication for various types of messages, including rules, regulations, policies, newsworthy information, and announcements of changes in procedures or the arrival of new organizational members. Impersonal written communication also can be used to communicate instructions about how to use machinery or how to process work orders or customer requests. For these kinds of messages, the paper or electronic trail left by this communication medium can be invaluable for employees.

Like personal written communication, impersonal written communication can be delivered and retrieved electronically, and this is increasingly being done in companies large and small. Unfortunately, the ease with which electronic messages can be spread has led to their proliferation. The electronic inboxes of many managers and workers are backlogged, and they rarely have time to read all the electronic work-related information available to them. The problem with such information overload—a superabundance of information—is the potential for important information to be ignored or overlooked while tangential information receives attention. Moreover, information overload can result in thousands of hours and millions of dollars in lost productivity.

information overload

A superabundance of information that increases the likelihood that important information is ignored or overlooked and tangential information receives attention.

Realizing the hazards of overload, Nathan Zeldes, computing productivity manager for Intel's division in Israel, decided to tackle this problem head on.[66] In Zeldes's division, some 3 million e-mails are sent or received each day, and some employees receive more than 300 messages a day. On average, employees spend around two and a half hours a day dealing with this barrage of information. To combat this problem, Zeldes developed a training program to educate employees about how e-mail can improve productivity and how it can be used in ways that limit overload.[67] Reactions to the training program have been positive, and it is now used in Intel divisions around the globe.[68]

Advances in Information Technology

Computer-based IT can greatly facilitate and improve the communication process. It has allowed managers to develop computer-based management information systems that provide timely, complete, relevant, and high-quality information. As we have discussed, IT allows companies to improve their responsiveness to customers, minimize costs, and thus improve their competitive position. The link between information systems, communication, and competitive position is an important one that may determine the success or failure of organizations in an increasingly competitive global environment. To better explain the current revolution in information technology, in this section we examine several key aspects of computer-based information technology.

The Effects of Advancing IT

The IT revolution began with the development of the first computers—the hardware of IT—in the 1950s. The language of computers is a digital language of zeros and ones. Words, numbers, images, and sound can all be expressed in zeros and ones. Each letter in the alphabet has its own unique code of zeros and ones, as does each number, each color, and each sound. For example, the digital code for the number 20 is 10100. In the language of computers it takes a lot of zeros and ones to express even a simple sentence, to say nothing of complex color graphics or moving video images. Nevertheless, modern computers can read, process, and store trillions of instructions per second (an *instruction* is a line of software code) and thus vast amounts of zeros and ones. This awesome number-crunching power forms the foundation of the ongoing IT revolution.

The products and services that result from advancing IT are all around us—ever more powerful microprocessors and PCs, high-bandwidth smartphones, sophisticated word-processing software, ever-expanding computer networks, inexpensive digital cameras and game consoles, and more and more useful online information and retailing services that did not exist a generation ago. These products are commonplace and are being continuously improved. Many managers and companies that helped develop the new IT have reaped enormous gains.

However, while many companies have benefited from advancing IT, others have been threatened. Traditional landline telephone companies such as AT&T, Verizon, and other long-distance companies the world over have seen their market dominance threatened by companies offering Internet, broadband, and wireless telephone technology. They responded by buying wireless cellphone companies, building their own high-powered broadband networks, and forming alliances with companies such as Apple and Samsung. So advancing IT is both an opportunity and a threat, and managers have to move quickly to protect their companies and maintain their competitive advantage.[69] Clearly, developing the right strategies to provide advanced IT solutions is a complicated, never-ending process.

On one hand, IT helps create new product opportunities that managers and their organizations can take advantage of—such as online travel and vacation booking. On the other hand, IT creates new and improved products that reduce or destroy demand for older, established products—such as the services provided by bricks-and-mortar travel agents. Walmart, by developing its own sophisticated proprietary IT, has been able to reduce retailing costs so much that it has put hundreds of thousands of small and medium-size stores out of business. Similarly, thousands of small, specialized U.S. bookstores have closed in the last decade as a result of advances in IT that made online bookselling possible.

IT and the Product Life Cycle

product life cycle
The way demand for a product changes in a predictable pattern over time.

When IT is advancing, organizational survival requires that managers quickly adopt and apply it. One reason for this is how IT affects the length of the product life cycle, which is the way demand for a product changes in a predictable pattern over time.[70] In general, the product life cycle consists of four stages: the embryonic, growth, maturity, and decline stages (see Figure 13.4).

Figure 13.4

A Product Life Cycle

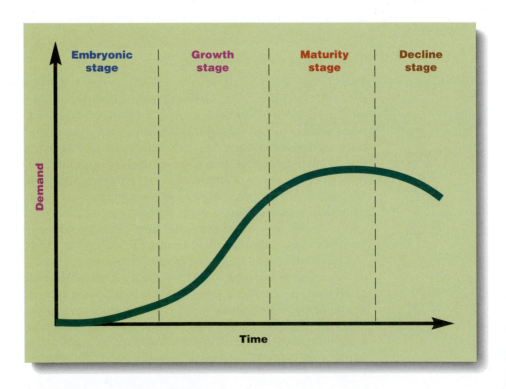

In the *embryonic stage* a product has yet to gain widespread acceptance; customers are unsure what a product, such as a new smartphone, has to offer, and demand for it is minimal. As a product, like Apple's iPod, becomes accepted by customers (although many products are *not,* like Dell's defunct MP3 player), demand takes off and the product enters its growth stage. In the *growth stage* many consumers are entering the market and buying the product for the first time, and demand increases rapidly. This is the stage iPhones and iPads passed through with great success. Of course these products' future success will depend on the value customers see in the collection of IT applications they offer—and how fast competitors such as Samsung and Google move to offer similar and less expensive tablet computers and smartphones.

The growth stage ends and the *maturity stage* begins when market demand peaks because most customers have already bought the product (there are relatively few first-time buyers left). At this stage, demand is typically replacement demand. In the PC market, for example, people who already have a PC trade up to a more powerful model. The iPod is currently in this stage; its users decide whether to trade up to a more powerful version that offers greater capabilities. Products such as laptops and smartphones and services such as Internet broadband and digital TV services are currently in this stage; for example, AT&T, Comcast, and Direct TV are battling to increase their market share.

Once demand for a product starts to fall, the *decline stage* begins; this typically occurs when advancing IT leads to the development of a more advanced product, making the old one obsolete, such as when the iPod destroyed Sony's Walkman franchise. In general, demand for every generation of a digital device such as a PC, cell phone, or MP3 music player falls off when the current leaders' technology is superseded by new products that incorporate the most recent IT advances. For example, 3G or 4G smartphones and tablet computers with broadband capability permit superfast web browsing and downloading of videos, books, and all kinds of digital media. Thus one reason the IT revolution has been so important for managers is that advances in IT are one of the most significant determinants of the length of a product's life cycle, and therefore of competition in an industry.[71] In more and more industries advances in IT are shortening product life cycles as customers jump on the latest fad or fashion—such as smaller tablet computers.

Apple's iPhone 4S claims that it changes everything, again. Boasting the revolutionary Siri app and HD video, Steve Jobs may not have exaggerated. The new iPhone 4S sold 4 million units in its first weekend of sale in October 2011.

The message for managers is clear: The shorter a product's life cycle because of advancing IT, the more important it is to innovate products quickly and continuously. A PC company that cannot develop a new and improved product line every three to six months will soon find itself in trouble. Increasingly managers are trying to outdo their rivals by being the first to market with a product that incorporates some advance in IT, such as cars with advanced stability or steering control that prevents vehicle wrecks.[72] In sum, the tumbling price of information brought about by advances in IT is at the heart of the IT revolution. So how can managers use all this computing power to their advantage?

The Network of Computing Power

The tumbling price of computing power and applications (brought about by ever more powerful microprocessors or "chips" from Intel and AMD) has allowed all kinds of organizations, large and small, to develop more powerful networks of computer servers or to follow the route of cloud computing described in the following "Management Insight."

MANAGEMENT INSIGHT

Cloud Computing, Bricks-and-Mortar, and Mobile Container Data Center Storage Solutions

Server computers (servers) are designed to provide powerful information-intensive computing solutions that in the past could have been executed only on huge, expensive mainframe computers. Servers also link networks of desktop and laptop PCs, and they link to wireless personal digital assistants (PDAs) such as netbooks, tablet computers, and smartphones. Using this array of computing devices, a company's employees can access its installed software applications and databases to obtain the real-time information they need to manage ongoing activities. Today servers can process staggering amounts of data to execute highly complex software applications, and they can access and store amazing amounts of information. Server sales have increased greatly over time (the server market was $30 billion in 2011) because of their ever-increasing computing power and low cost

Blackbox server racks, such as this one created by Sun Microsystems, now part of Oracle, offer a significant safeguard to companies looking for cost- and space-conscious ways to back up their information.

compared to mainframes—although most large companies still use a single mainframe as the "brain" that stores the most essential, secret, and important operating routines and to coordinate the companywide computing network.

As large companies began to buy hundreds and then thousands of servers to meet their increasing need to process and store information, server makers such as HP, Dell, and IBM designed *rack servers* that link individual servers together to increase their joint power. For example, a rack server links an individual server into a rack of 10 connected servers; then 10 racks create a network of 100 servers; 100 racks create a network of a thousand servers, and so on. Using software from specialized companies such as IBM and Oracle to link the operations of these server racks, large companies developed "server farms," which are bricks-and-mortar (B&M) operating facilities that are remote and physically separate from company headquarters. Server farms are database centers composed of thousands of networked server racks that are constantly monitored, maintained, and upgraded by a company's IT engineers (or specialized outsourcers such as IBM) to protect a company's information and databases. Should a company lose such information, it would be helpless; it would have no record of its transactions with its employees, customers, suppliers, and so on. IT storage and database storage are the lifeblood of a global company, which cannot function without them. But a growing concern of managers today is how to reduce the costs of database storage, which are hundreds of millions of dollars for large companies.

As of the late 2000s a new way to offer companies a quick, efficient way to enlarge and upgrade their database center capabilities to respond to the vast increase in Internet use is to house these server racks in standard-size storage containers—the same kind of containers hauled on trucks or stacked on cargo ships. The first U.S. server maker to offer such a mobile database solution was Sun (now part of Oracle), which launched its "Blackbox" data center containing its proprietary Solaris rack servers in a 20-foot shipping container. Each Blackbox contains a mobile data center that can deliver the computing capability of a 9,000-square-foot physical data center but costs only about one-fifth as much. Another company called SGI quickly announced its own new "Concentro" mobile server container—the first self-contained data center based on custom-designed, high-density server racks and data storage housed in a larger 40×20-foot shipping container.[73] Because SGI's space-saving rack servers are half as deep as standard servers, it can cram in twice as many individual servers into a 40-foot container as can its competitors. The immense processing power of SGI's Concentro containers, equivalent to a 30,000-square-foot B&M data center, allows companies to rethink their need for high-cost bricks-and-mortar data centers, especially given the relatively low operating costs of SGI containers compared to physical data centers. Mobile data centers offer companies a low-cost solution and have been snapped up by companies such as Google, Yahoo!, and Amazon.

Also in the late 2000s the term *cloud computing* was popularized by companies like IBM, Microsoft, and Google to refer to a new way to offer companies computing and data storage service similar to how they used and paid for utilities like water or electricity. The strategy behind cloud computing was to create (1) a cost-effective Internet-based global platform of hardware and software provided by (2) a network of thousands of interlinked IT companies that had (3) the capability to provide a full range of on-demand software applications, computing services, and database storage to millions of companies and individuals around the world. The advantage of cloud-based web services is that the cost of running applications or storing data through the Internet is much less than the cost of purchasing hardware and installing software on in-house servers. Cloud computing is like an alliance in which IT companies pool their resources to share processing power and applications that let them offer better prices to customers. For example, installing and managing the software and hardware to operate a specialized software application might cost $50,000 a year; in cloud computing the same service can be rented for $500 a month—this is why Amazon, Google, and Microsoft push cloud computing so vigorously.

Cloud computing essentially offers outsourced, pay-as-you-go, on-demand Internet software capabilities to companies for a fee. Of course a major concern of users is information reliability and security. If cloud computing expands, even the largest companies may cease to operate their own database centers and outsource all their information and computing operations to web-based IT providers because they can perform these IT activities at a significantly lower cost than any particular company. The problem facing managers is to choose the most efficient and effective method to manage their companywide computing networks and database storage operations to reduce operating costs by millions or billions of dollars a year.

Companies can buy networks of server racks that are customized with the mix of hardware and software applications that best meet the needs of their current value chain management activities. The typical organizationwide computing network that has emerged over time is a four-tier network solution that consists of "external" mobile computing devices such as netbooks, smartphones, and tablet computers, connected to desktops and laptops, and then through "internal" rack servers to a company's mainframe (see Figure 13.5). Through wireless and wired communication an employee with the necessary permissions can hook into a company's IT system from any location—in the office, at home, on a boat, on the beach, in the air—anywhere a wireless or wired link can be established.

The internal network is composed of "client" desktop and laptop PCs connected by Ethernet to the company's system of rack servers. The client computers

Figure 13.5

A Four-Tier Information System with Cloud Computing

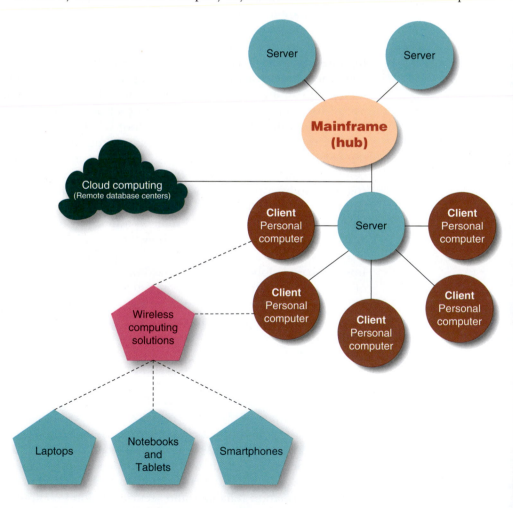

that are linked directly to a server constitute a *local area network* (LAN), and most companies have many LANs—for example, one in every division and function. Large companies that need immense processing power have a mainframe computer at the center or hub of the network that can quickly process vast amounts of information, issue commands, and coordinate computing devices at the other levels. The mainframe can also handle electronic communications between servers and PCs situated in different LANs, and the mainframe can connect to the mainframes of other companies. The mainframe is the master computer that controls the operations of all the other types of computers and digital devices as needed and can link them into one integrated system. It also provides the connection to the *external* IT networks outside the organization; for example, it gives a user access to an organization's cloud computing services—but with high security and reliability and only from recognized and protected computing devices. For instance, a manager with a mobile devices or PC hooked into a four-tier system can access data and software stored in the local server, in the mainframe, or through the Internet to a cloud-based computing solution hosted by an outsourcer whose B&M database might be located anywhere in the world.

Just as computer hardware has been advancing rapidly, so has computer software. *Operating system software* tells the computer hardware how to run. *Applications software,* such as programs for word processing, spreadsheets, graphics, and database management, is developed for a specific task or use. The increase in the power of computer hardware has allowed software developers to write increasingly powerful programs that are also increasingly user-friendly. By harnessing the rapidly growing power of microprocessors, applications software has vastly increased the ability of managers to acquire, organize, and communicate information. In doing so, it also has improved the ability of managers to coordinate and control the activities of their organization and to make better decisions, as discussed earlier.

Types of Management Information Systems

Four types of computer-based management information systems can be particularly helpful in providing managers with the information they need to make decisions and to coordinate and control organizational resources: transaction-processing systems, operations information systems, decision support systems, and expert systems. In Figure 13.6 on the next page, these systems are arranged along a continuum according to their increasing usefulness in providing managers with the information they need to make nonprogrammed decisions. (Recall from Chapter 5 that nonprogrammed decision making occurs in response to unusual, unpredictable opportunities and threats.) We examine each of these systems after focusing on the management information system that preceded them all: the organizational hierarchy.

LO 13-4 Differentiate among four kinds of management information systems.

The Organizational Hierarchy: The Traditional Information System

Traditionally, managers have used the organizational hierarchy as a system for gathering the information they need to achieve coordination and control and make decisions (see Chapter 7 for a discussion of organizational structure and hierarchy). According to business historian Alfred Chandler, the use of the hierarchy as an information network was perfected by railroad companies in the

Figure 13.6

Four Computer-
Based Management
Information Systems

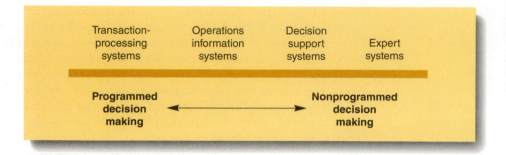

United States during the 1850s.[74] At that time, the railroads were the largest industrial organizations in the United States. By virtue of their size and geographical spread, they faced unique problems of coordination and control. In the 1850s, they started to solve these problems by designing hierarchical management structures that provided senior managers with the information they needed to achieve coordination and control and to make decisions about running the railroads.

Daniel McCallum, superintendent of the Erie Railroad in the 1850s, realized that the lines of authority and responsibility defining the Erie's management hierarchy also represented channels of communication along which information traveled. McCallum established what was perhaps the first modern management information system. Regular daily and monthly reports were fed up the management chain so that top managers could make decisions about, for example, controlling costs and setting freight rates. Decisions were then relayed back down the hierarchy so they could be carried out. Imitating the railroads, most other organizations used their hierarchies as systems for collecting and channeling information. This practice began to change only when electronic information technologies became more reasonably priced in the 1960s.

Although the organizational hierarchy is a useful information system, several drawbacks are associated with it. First, in organizations with many layers of managers, it can take a long time for information to travel up the hierarchy and for decisions to travel back down. This slow pace can reduce the timeliness and usefulness of information and prevent an organization from responding quickly to changing market conditions.[75] Second, information can be distorted as it moves from one layer of management to another. Information distortion, changes in meaning that occur as information passes through a series of senders and receivers, reduces the quality of information.[76] Third, because managers have only a limited span of control, as an organization grows larger, its hierarchy lengthens and this tall structure can make the hierarchy a very expensive information system. The popular idea that companies with tall management hierarchies are bureaucratic and unresponsive to the needs of their customers arises from the inability of tall hierarchies to effectively process data and provide managers with timely, complete, relevant, and high-quality information. Until modern computer-based information systems came along, however, the management hierarchy was the best information system available.

information distortion Changes in meaning that occur as information passes through a series of senders and receivers.

transaction-processing system A management information system designed to handle large volumes of routine, recurring transactions.

Transaction-Processing Systems

A transaction-processing system is a system designed to handle large volumes of routine, recurring transactions. Transaction-processing systems began to appear in the early 1960s with the advent of commercially available mainframe computers. They were the first type of computer-based management information system adopted by many organizations, and today they are commonplace. Bank managers use a transaction-processing system to record deposits into, and payments out of, bank accounts. Supermarket managers use a transaction-processing system to record the sale of items and to track inventory levels. More generally, most managers in large organizations use a transaction-processing system to handle tasks such as payroll preparation and payment, customer billing, and payment of suppliers.

Operations Information Systems

operations information system A management information system that gathers, organizes, and summarizes comprehensive data in a form that managers can use in their nonroutine coordinating, controlling, and decision-making tasks.

Many types of management information systems followed hard on the heels of transaction-processing systems in the 1960s. An operations information system is a system that gathers comprehensive data, organizes it, and summarizes it in a form that is of value to managers. Whereas a transaction-processing system processes routine transactions, an operations information system provides managers with information that they can use in their nonroutine coordinating, controlling, and decision-making tasks. Most operations information systems are coupled with a transaction-processing system. An operations information system typically accesses data gathered by a transaction-processing system, processes those data into useful information, and organizes that information into a form accessible to managers. Managers often use an operations information system to obtain sales, inventory, accounting, and other performance-related information. For example, the information that T. J. Rodgers at Cypress Semiconductor gets on individual employee goals and performance is provided by an operations information system.

FedEx uses an operations information system to track the performance of its 1,500 or so ground stations. Each ground station is evaluated according to four criteria: delivery (the goal is to deliver 100% of all packages by noon the day after they were picked up), productivity (measured by the number of packages shipped per employee-hour), controllable cost, and station profitability. Each ground station also has specific delivery, efficiency, cost, and profitability targets that it must attain. Every month FedEx's operations information system is used to gather information on these four criteria and summarize it for top managers, who are then able to compare the performance of each station against its previously established targets. The system quickly alerts senior managers to underperforming ground stations, so they can intervene selectively to help solve any problems that may have given rise to the poor performance.[77]

Decision Support Systems

decision support system An interactive computer-based management information system with model-building capability that managers can use when they must make nonroutine decisions.

A decision support system is an interactive computer-based system that provides models that help managers make better nonprogrammed decisions.[78] Recall from Chapter 5 that nonprogrammed decisions are decisions that are relatively unusual or novel, such as decisions to invest in new productive capacity, develop a new product, launch a new promotional campaign, enter a new market, or expand internationally. Although an operations information system organizes important information for managers, a decision support system gives managers a model-building capability and so provides them with the ability to manipulate information in a variety of ways. Managers might use a decision support system to help them decide whether to cut prices for a product. The decision support system might contain models of how customers and competitors would respond to a price cut. Managers could run these models and use the results as an *aid* to decision making.

The stress on the word *aid* is important, for in the final analysis a decision support system is not meant to make decisions for managers. Rather, its function is to provide valuable information that managers can use to improve the quality of their decision making.

Expert Systems and Artificial Intelligence

Expert systems are the most advanced management information systems available. An expert system is a system that employs human knowledge captured in a computer to solve problems that ordinarily require human expertise.[79] Expert systems are a variant of artificial intelligence.[80] Mimicking human expertise (and intelligence) requires a computer that can at a minimum (1) recognize, formulate, and solve a problem; (2) explain the solution; and (3) learn from experience.

Recent developments in artificial intelligence that go by names such as "fuzzy logic" and "neural networks" have resulted in computer programs that, in a primitive way, try to mimic human thought processes. Although artificial intelligence is still at a fairly early stage of development, an increasing number of business applications are beginning to emerge in the form of expert systems. General Electric, for example, has developed an expert system to help trouble-shoot problems in the diesel locomotive engines it manufactures. The expert system was originally based on knowledge collected from David Smith, GE's top locomotive troubleshooter, who retired in the 1980s after 40 years of service at GE. A novice engineer or technician can use the system to uncover a fault by spending only a few minutes at a computer terminal. The system can explain to the user the logic of its advice, thereby serving as a teacher as well as a problem solver. The system is based on a flexible, humanlike thought process, and it can be updated to incorporate new knowledge as it becomes available. GE has installed the system in every railroad repair shop that it serves, thus eliminating delays and boosting maintenance productivity.[81] Today, companies like IBM, Accenture and SAP provide expert systems for most industries, for example, the retail, pharmaceutical, and manufacturing industries. These systems are continually improved and have resulted in major increases in efficiency and effectiveness.

expert system

A management information system that employs human knowledge captured in a computer to solve problems that ordinarily require human expertise.

Limitations of Information Systems

Despite their usefulness, information systems have some limitations. A serious potential problem is the one noted at the beginning of this chapter. In all of the enthusiasm for management information systems, electronic communication by means of a computer network, and the like, a vital human element of communication may be lost. Some kinds of information cannot be aggregated and summarized on an MIS report because of issues surrounding information richness. Very rich information is often required to coordinate and control an enterprise and to make informed decisions, far beyond that which can be quantified and aggregated.

The importance of information richness is a strong argument in favor of using electronic communication to *support* face-to-face communication, not to replace it. For example, it would be wrong to make a judgment about an individual's performance merely by "reading the numbers" provided by a management information system. Instead, the numbers should be used to alert managers to individuals who may have a performance problem. The nature of this performance problem should then be explored in a face-to-face meeting, during which rich information can be gathered. As a top Boeing manager noted, "In our company, the use of e-mail and videoconferencing has not reduced the need to visit people at other sites; it has increased it. E-mail has facilitated the establishment of communications channels between people who previously would not communicate, which is good, but direct visits are still required to cement any working relationships that evolve out of these electronic meetings."

Summary and Review

INFORMATION AND THE MANAGER'S JOB Computer-based information systems are central to the operation of most organizations. By providing managers with high-quality, timely, relevant, and relatively complete information, properly implemented information systems can improve managers' ability to coordinate and control the operations of an organization and to make effective decisions. Moreover, information systems can help the organization to attain a competitive advantage through their beneficial impact on productivity, quality, innovation, and responsiveness to customers. **[LO 13-1]**

COMMUNICATION AND MANAGEMENT Communication is the sharing of information between two or more individuals or groups to reach a common understanding. Good communication is necessary for an organization to gain a competitive advantage. Communication occurs in a cyclical process that entails two phases, transmission and feedback. **[LO 13-2]**

INFORMATION RICHNESS AND COMMUNICATION MEDIA Information richness is the amount of information a communication medium can carry and the extent to which the medium enables the sender and receiver to reach a common understanding. Four categories of communication media in descending order of information richness are face-to-face communication (includes videoconferences), spoken communication electronically transmitted (includes voice mail), personally addressed written communication (includes e-mail), and impersonal written communication (includes newsletters). **[LO 13-3]**

THE INFORMATION TECHNOLOGY REVOLUTION Over the last 30 years there have been rapid advances in the power, and rapid declines in the cost, of information technology. Falling prices, wireless communication, computer networks, and software developments have all radically improved the power and efficacy of computer-based information systems. **[LO 13-4]**

TYPES OF MANAGEMENT INFORMATION SYSTEMS Traditionally managers used the organizational hierarchy as the main system for gathering the information they needed to coordinate and control the organization and to make effective decisions. Today, managers use four types of computer-based information systems. Listed in ascending order of sophistication, they are transaction-processing systems, operations information systems, decision support systems, and expert systems. **[LO 13-4]**

Management *in Action*

TOPICS FOR DISCUSSION AND ACTION

Discussion

1. What is the relationship between information systems and competitive advantage? **[LO 13-2]**

2. Which medium (or media) do you think would be appropriate for each of the following kinds of messages that a subordinate could receive from a boss: (a) a raise, (b) not receiving a promotion, (c) an error in a report prepared by the subordinate, (d) additional job responsibilities, and (e) the schedule for company holidays for the upcoming year? Explain your choices. **[LO 13-3]**

3. Because of the growth of high-powered low-cost computing, wireless communications, and technologies such as videoconferencing, many managers soon may not need to come into the office; they will be able to work at home. What are the pros and cons of such an arrangement? **[LO 13-3]**

4. Many companies have reported that it is difficult to implement advanced management information and decision support systems. Why do you think this is so? How might the roadblocks to implementation be removed? **[LO 13-4]**

5. Why is face-to-face communication between managers still important in an organization? **[LO 13-2, 13-3]**

Action

6. Ask a manager to describe the main kinds of information systems that he or she uses on a routine basis at work. **[LO 13-1, 13-2]**

BUILDING MANAGEMENT SKILLS **[LO 13-2, 13-3]**
Diagnosing Ineffective Communication

Think about the last time you experienced very ineffective communication with another person—someone you work with, a classmate, a friend, a member of your family. Describe the incident. Then answer these questions.

1. Why was your communication ineffective in this incident?

2. What stages of the communication process were particularly problematic and why?

3. Describe any filtering or information distortion that occurred.

4. How could you have handled this situation differently so that communication would have been effective?

MANAGING ETHICALLY **[LO 13-2, 13-3]**

In organizations today, employees often take advantage of their company's information systems. E-mail abuse is increasing, and so is the amount of time employees spend surfing the Internet on company time. Indeed, statistics suggest that approximately 70% of the total amount of time spent surfing the Internet is company time.

Questions

1. Either by yourself or in a group, explore the ethics of using IT for personal uses

at work. Should employees have some rights to use these resources? When does their behavior become unethical?

2. Some companies keep track of the way their employees use IT and the Internet. Is it ethical for managers to read employees' private e-mail or to record the sites that employees visit on the World Wide Web?

SMALL GROUP BREAKOUT EXERCISE [LO 13-2, 13-4]
Using New Information Systems

Form groups of three or four people, and appoint one member as the spokesperson who will communicate your findings to the whole class when called upon by the instructor. Then discuss the following scenario.

You are a team of managing partners of a large firm of accountants. You are responsible for auditing your firm's information systems to determine whether they are appropriate and up-to-date. To your surprise, you find that although your organization does have an e-mail system in place and accountants are connected into a powerful local area network (LAN), most of the accountants (including partners) are not using this technology. You also find that the organizational hierarchy is still the preferred information system of the managing partners.

Given this situation, you are concerned that your organization is not exploiting the opportunities offered by new information systems to obtain a competitive advantage. You have discussed this issue and are meeting to develop an action plan to get accountants to appreciate the need to learn, and to take advantage of, the potential of the new information technology.

1. What advantages can you tell accountants they will obtain when they use the new information technology?

2. What problems do you think you may encounter in convincing accountants to use the new information technology?

3. Discuss how you might make it easy for accountants to learn to use the new technology.

BE THE MANAGER [LO 13-2, 13-3]

A Problem in Communication

Mark Chen supervises support staff for an Internet merchandising organization that sells furniture over the Internet. Chen has always thought that he should expand his staff. When he was about to approach his boss with such a request, the economy slowed, and other areas of the company experienced layoffs. Thus, Chen's plans for trying to add to his staff are on indefinite hold.

Chen has noticed a troubling pattern of communication with his staff. Ordinarily, when he wants one of his staff members to work on a task, he e-mails the pertinent information to that person. For the last few months, his e-mail requests have gone unheeded, and his subordinates comply with his requests only after he visits with them in person and gives them a specific deadline. Each time, they apologize for the delay but say that they are so overloaded with requests that they sometimes stop answering their phones. Unless someone asks for something more than once, they feel a request is not particularly urgent and can be put on hold.

Chen thinks this state of affairs is deplorable. He realizes, however, that his subordinates have no way of prioritizing tasks and that is why some very important projects were put on hold until he inquired about them. Knowing that he cannot add to his staff in the short term, Chen has come to you for advice. He wants to develop a system whereby his staff will provide some kind of response to requests within 24 hours, will be able to prioritize tasks, identifying their relative importance, and will not feel so overloaded that they ignore their boss's requests and don't answer their phones.

Question

1. As an expert in communication, how would you advise Chen?

Netflix, Reed Hastings Survive Missteps to Join Silicon Valley's Elite

On a normal weeknight, Netflix accounts for almost a third of all Internet traffic entering North American homes. That's more than YouTube, Hulu, Amazon.com, HBO Go, iTunes, and BitTorrent combined. Traffic to Netflix usually peaks at around 10 p.m. in each time zone, at which point a chart of Internet consumption looks like a python that swallowed a cow. By midnight Pacific time, streaming volume falls off dramatically.

As prime time wound down on Jan. 31, though, there was an unusual amount of tension at Netflix. That was the night the company premièred House of Cards, its political thriller set in Washington. Before midnight about 40 engineers gathered in a conference room at Netflix's headquarters. They sat before a collection of wall-mounted monitors that displayed the status of Netflix's computing systems. On the conference table, a few dozen laptops, tablets, smartphones, and other devices had the Netflix app loaded and ready to stream.

When the clocks hit 12 a.m., the entire season of House of Cards started appearing on the devices, as well as in the recommendation lists of millions of customers chosen by an algorithm. The opening scene, a dog getting run over by an SUV, came and went. At 12:15 a.m., around the time Kevin Spacey's character says, "I'm livid," everything was working fine. "That's when the champagne comes," says Yury Izrailevsky, the vice president in charge of cloud computing at Netflix, which has a history of self-inflicted catastrophes. Izrailevsky stayed until the wee hours of the morning—just in case—as thousands of customers binge-watched the show. The midnight ritual repeated itself on April 19, when Netflix premièred its werewolf horror series Hemlock Grove.

Netflix has more than 36 million subscribers. They watch about 4 billion hours of programs every quarter on more than 1,000 different devices. To meet this demand, the company uses specialized video servers scattered around the world. When a subscriber clicks on a movie to stream, Netflix determines within a split second which server containing that movie is closest to the user, then picks from dozens of versions of the video file, depending on the device the viewer is using. At company headquarters in Los Gatos, Calif., teams of mathematicians and designers study what people watch and build algorithms and interfaces to present them with the collection of videos that will keep them watching.

Netflix is one of the world's biggest users of cloud computing, which means running a data center on someone else's equipment. The company rents server and storage systems by the hour, and it rents all this computing power from Amazon Web Services, the cloud division of Amazon.com, which runs its own video-streaming service that competes with Netflix. It's a mutually beneficial frenemy relationship. Over the years, Netflix has built an array of sophisticated tools to make its software perform well on Amazon's cloud. Amazon has mimicked the advances and offered them to other business customers.

At any moment, Netflix draws upon 10,000 to 20,000 servers running in Amazon data centers somewhere. The computers handle customer information, video recommendations, digital rights management, encoding of video files into different formats, and monitoring the performance of the systems. When a new device like an upgraded Xbox or a Samsung (005930) smartphone comes along, Netflix uses thousands of extra servers to reformat movie files and deal with the new users. By day, some servers handle the grunt work tied to streaming video; by night, they're repurposed to analyze data. The company has been pushing Amazon Web Services to its limits. "We're using Amazon more efficiently than the retail arm of Amazon is," says Adrian Cockcroft, Netflix's cloud architect. "We're pretty sure about that."

Few relationships in the technology industry are as complex as Netflix and Amazon's. Netflix's status as Amazon's biggest customer has earned it favorable pricing and direct lines of communication to Amazon's top engineers. When Netflix wants a new software feature, Amazon is quick to deliver it, and other customers eventually benefit from that work. "There's no question in my mind that our platform is stronger from a performance and functional standpoint because of the collaboration we have with Netflix," says Andy Jassy, who heads Amazon's cloud business.

Netflix has been forced to build from scratch much of the software it needs to survive. Since it relies on Amazon for data centers, its 700 engineers focus on coming up with tools for, say, automating the ways in which thousands of cloud servers get started and configured. In Silicon Valley, Netflix has become best known for its so-called Simian Army, a facetiously named set of applications that test the resilience of its systems. Chaos Monkey, for instance, simulates small outages by randomly turning services off, while Chaos Kong takes down an entire data center.

Netflix can now hire just about any engineer it wants. That's a function of the computer science the company does and its reputation as the highest payer in Silicon Valley. Managers routinely survey salary trends in Silicon Valley and pay their employees 10 percent to 20 percent more than the going rate for a given skill.

Each night, Netflix performs an analysis to see which shows were the most popular where. From 2 a.m. to 5 a.m. local time, it fills its servers with the appropriate programs. If Battlestar Galactica is popular in Houston on Tuesday, then servers in Texas will be loaded up with more episodes in time for Wednesday night. The most popular videos go on high-speed flash storage drives; everything else gets stored on cheaper, slower hard disks. "We use this predictive model to make sure the content is there before the user asks for it," says Ken Florance, vice president for content delivery at Netflix.

The biggest bets Netflix is making now are on its original shows. The company won't disclose how much it paid for two seasons of House of Cards, though the Hollywood blog Deadline.com says it was about $100 million. Rather than make it a weekly show, Netflix released all 13 episodes at once. That meant viewers could watch the whole season in one marathon sitting. It also meant the producers didn't have to alter the plot to give every episode a cliffhanger ending. "If you give people a more creative format, then they can tell their stories better," says Ted Sarandos, the company's Beverly Hills–based content chief. He adds that Netflix's goal is, in part, to become HBO before HBO can become Netflix. "They do great content that people love. What are the things we do well? It's the delivery technology, the user interface stuff, the integration into computing devices, and the seamless streaming." Amazon is introducing its own series, too, and Hollywood is abuzz with hope that Netflix and Amazon will spend wild sums of money on even more shows.

Netflix's critics argue that the company has sacrificed too much control over its technology in its effort to get ahead of rivals. "The problem with Netflix is that they are inextricably bound into Amazon for all eternity," says Paul Maritz, a computing infrastructure veteran and CEO of the cloud computing startup Pivotal. "If they want to go somewhere else, it will be hard." Hastings and his staff characterize such criticism as sour grapes. Another concern is that the studios will stop licensing content now that Netflix is in the originals business. Hollywood is right to remain wary of letting any single entity get too powerful. As Netflix expands overseas, it intends to strike worldwide licensing deals instead of hammering them out country-by-country. From a studio perspective, that could give Netflix the ability to come up with lucrative terms that no regional competitor could match.

Over the past five years a chart of Netflix's share price has shifted from a smooth, upward curve to more of a scribble. Hastings seems unperturbed. The experimentation is a goal in itself, whether it's big things like corporate missions or little things like the personal technology he uses. For one month, he'll only use products made by Apple and the next he's on to phones, tablets, and laptops running Windows. May is Google month, and Hastings has one of the company's touchscreen Chromebook Pixel laptops. "I just keep it rotating," he says.

Questions

1. What different kinds of IT software and hardware is Netflix using to promote its competitive advantage?

2. What are the advantages and disadvantages of its heavy use of Amazon.com's IT skills to help it manage its own IT?

3. Search the Internet to see how Netflix has been performing against Amazon and RedBox.

Source: Ashlee Vance, "Netflix, Reed Hastings Survive Missteps to Join Silicon Valley's Elite," *Bloomberg Businessweek,* May 9, 2013.

14

Operations Management: Managing Vital Operations and Processes

LEARNING OBJECTIVES

After studying this chapter, you should be able to:

1 Explain the role of operations management in achieving superior quality, efficiency, and responsiveness to customers. **[LO 14-1]**

2 Describe what customers want, and explain why it is so important for managers to be responsive to their needs. **[LO 14-2]**

3 Explain why achieving superior quality is so important. **[LO 14-3]**

4 Explain why achieving superior efficiency is so important. **[LO 14-4]**

Moving fast—some might say, too fast to gain lasting traction—and staying light on personnel has pushed Zynga into the arena of online gaming competition. But can they successfully transition to other platforms than Facebook? Your clicks will determine their future.

Zynga Develops New Operational Strategies in Online Social Gaming

How Can Managers Increase Operating Performance?

Zynga Inc., based near Marina del Rey, California, is the most popular maker of online social games—a rapidly growing and highly competitive segment of the game software and content industry. Every month, 1 out of 10 users of the WWW play one or more of Zynga's 55 games, which include Farmville, Cityville, Zynga Poker, and Mafia Wars. About four-fifths of the U.S. population, around 250 million people, play its games each month.

In 2011, Zynga rolled out a new online game, Empires & Allies, which took the company into the "action and strategy" gaming arena, one that has been dominated by leading game developer Electronic Arts (EA), some of whose blockbuster games include Crysis 2, Star Wars, The Sims, and Portal 2. Also, Microsoft, Nintendo, and Sony are major developers of action games that can be played on their proprietary gaming consoles—the Xbox, Wii, and PlayStation, respectively.

The strategy of leading game developers like EA and Sony is to innovate blockbuster games that may each sell millions of copies at a price of $50 to $75 each, so they generate billions of dollars in revenues and profits. Each of these games is the result of the creativity and skills of hundreds of developers who work together for two or more years to create a new game before it is released for sale. The popularity of the games they innovate determines their companies' success; customers are responding to their strategy of innovating a unique game that can be sold at a premium price.

How did Zynga manage to enter and compete successfully in the highly competitive social gaming industry against giants such as EA and Nintendo? Because its principal founder, Mark Pincus, armed with only $29 million in venture capital raised from investors, decided to pursue a strategy to develop its games using an approach that was unique in the software gaming industry. Pincus's approach was to start small, and a score or more of game developers worked interactively in small teams to continuously innovate, develop, and then perfect a new game such as Farmville that better met customer needs. As each new game was launched and revenue from online users started to come in, Pincus could recruit new game developers, who worked to

455

innovate a variety of games in a relaxed, campus-like environment.

Mark Skaggs, Zynga's senior vice president of product design, describes the company's strategy toward game making as "fast, light, and right."[1] Zynga's games take only a few weeks or months to design because its teams of developers work in self-managed groups that have around 30 members. All the ongoing work of each team member, and the way they continuously make changes to a game, is immediately obvious to other team members because they are connected through interactive real-time software that allows them to evaluate how the changes being made will affect the overall nature of the game. Team members can continuously approve, disapprove, or find ways to improve the way a game works, modify its objectives, and add new features over time to help increase the appeal of the game to Zynga's hundreds of millions of online users when it is released.

However, the other aspect of its strategy that works so well for Zynga lies in its competency to continue to customize and change every game it develops to better appeal to the likes and dislikes of its users—even *after* the game has been released online. Unlike the leading game makers who cannot change their games after they have been released, much of the game development at Zynga takes place *after* a Zynga game is released. Its designers work round the clock to add content, correct errors, test new features, and constantly adjust a new game based upon real-time feedback about how game players are "interacting" with it; and this feedback allows developers to discover what users enjoy the most.

This amazing interactive approach to online game development is quite different from the approach of the industry leaders and so is the way it monetizes or obtains revenues from its games. All Zynga's online games are provided free of charge to hundreds of millions of online users—but to be able to use each game's advanced features, users have to pay for them or agree to participate in some form of online marketing exercise. The popularity of online social games is based on the number of daily active users, which in Zynga's case is 50 to 60 million a day (it has an audience of 240 million players on Facebook alone). So if only 2% to 5% of its players spend money on the extra game features (that can be bought cheaply) with 50 million users a day, Zynga can obtain revenues of over $300 million a year. And the more games that Zynga can encourage users to play, the more money it earns! When Zynga announced a public offering of its shares in December 2011 at $10 a share, all the shares were sold valuing the company at $10 billion and the stock rose to $14 by March 2012.

However, investors' enthusiasm quickly soured in April 2012 when it became clear how dependent Zynga was on obtaining revenues from Facebook users, and they also began to worry about the lasting appeal of Zynga's games when the company announced a decline in its user base by 8%. Does Zynga have the competencies to allow it to continue to create value for its customers in the future? Zynga's stock price has plunged since 2012—only time will tell.

Overview

As the "Management Snapshot" suggests, the companies that dominate an industry can never take their leading position for granted. A new competitor can emerge with novel or superior operational strategies that can change the nature of industry competition. In the 2010s gaming industry leaders like EA, Sony, and Nintendo have experienced major problems because of the increasing use of mobile computing devices such as smartphones and laptops in the social gaming market.

In this chapter we focus on operations management techniques that managers can use to increase the quality of an organization's products, the efficiency of production, and the organization's responsiveness to customers. By the end of this chapter, you will understand the vital role operations management plays in building competitive advantage and creating a high-performing organization.

Operations Management and Competitive Advantage

Operations management is the management of any aspect of the production system that transforms inputs into finished goods and services. A **production system** is the system that an organization uses to acquire inputs, convert inputs into outputs, and dispose of the outputs (goods or services). **Operations managers** are managers who are responsible for managing an organization's production system. They do whatever it takes to transform inputs into outputs. Their job is to manage the three stages of production—acquisition of inputs, control of conversion processes, and disposal of goods and services—and to determine where operating improvements might be made in order to increase quality, efficiency, and responsiveness to customers and so give an organization a competitive advantage (see Figure 14.1).

Quality refers to goods and services that are reliable, dependable, or psychologically satisfying: They do the job they were designed for and do it well, or they possess some attribute that gives their users something they value.[2] *Efficiency* refers to the amount of inputs required to produce a given output. *Responsiveness to customers* refers to actions taken to meet the demands and needs of customers. Operations managers are responsible for ensuring that an organization has sufficient supplies of high-quality, low-cost inputs, and they are responsible for designing a production system that creates high-quality, low-cost products that customers are willing to buy.

Notice that achieving superior efficiency and quality is part of attaining superior responsiveness to customers. Customers want value for their money, and an organization whose efficient production system creates high-quality, low-cost products is best able to deliver this value. For this reason, we begin by discussing how operations managers can design the production system to increase responsiveness to customers.

operations management

The management of any aspect of the production system that transforms inputs into finished goods and services.

production system

The system that an organization uses to acquire inputs, convert the inputs into outputs, and dispose of the outputs.

operations manager

A manager who is responsible for managing an organization's production system and for determining where operating improvements might be made.

Figure 14.1

The Purpose of Operations Management

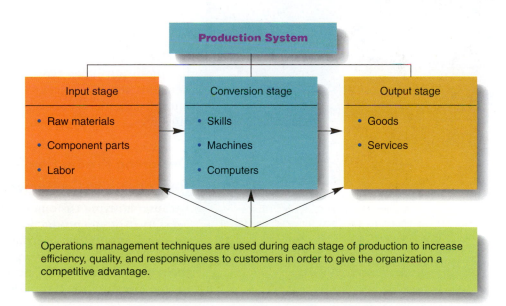

Operations management techniques are used during each stage of production to increase efficiency, quality, and responsiveness to customers in order to give the organization a competitive advantage.

Improving Responsiveness to Customers

Organizations produce outputs—goods or services—that are consumed by customers. All organizations, profit seeking or not-for-profit, have customers. Without customers, most organizations would cease to exist. Because customers are vital to the survival of most organizations, managers must correctly identify customers and promote organizational strategies that respond to their needs. This is why management writers recommend that organizations define their business in terms of which customer *wants* or *needs* they are satisfying, not the type of products they are producing.[3]

LO 14-1 Explain the role of operations management in achieving superior quality, efficiency, and responsiveness to customers.

LO 14-2 Describe what customers want, and explain why it is so important for managers to be responsive to their needs.

What Do Customers Want?

Given that satisfying customer demands is central to the survival of an organization, an important question is, What do customers want? To specify exactly what they want is not possible because their wants vary from industry to industry. However, it is possible to identify some universal product attributes that most customers in most industries want. Generally, other things being equal, most customers prefer

1. A lower price to a higher price.
2. High-quality products to low-quality products.
3. Quick service to slow service. (They will always prefer good after-sales service and support to poor after-sales support.)
4. Products with many features to products with few features. (They will prefer a laptop with a built-in webcam, lots of memory, and a powerful micro-processor to one without these features.)
5. Products that are, as far as possible, customized or tailored to their unique needs.

A Southwest ticket agent assists a customer. Southwest's operating system is geared toward satisfying customer demands for low-priced, reliable, and convenient air travel, making it one of the most consistently successful airlines in recent years. To help keep flights on schedule, Southwest's workforce has been cross-trained to perform multiple tasks. For example, the person who checks tickets might also help with baggage loading.

Of course, the problem is that other things are not equal. For example, providing high quality, quick service, after-sales service and support, products with many features, and products that are customized raises costs and thus the price that must be charged to cover costs. So customers' demands for these attributes typically conflict with their demands for low prices. Accordingly, customers must make a trade-off between price and preferred attributes, and so must managers.

Designing Production Systems to Be Responsive to Customers

Because satisfying customers is so important, managers try to design production systems that can produce the outputs that have the attributes customers desire. The attributes of an organization's outputs—their quality, cost, and features—are determined by the organization's production system.[4] Since the ability of an organization to satisfy the demands of its customers derives from its production system, managers need to devote considerable attention to constantly improving production systems. Managers' desire to attract customers with improved products explains their adoption of many new operations management techniques in recent years. These include flexible manufacturing systems, just-in-time inventory, and, of course, the new information systems and technologies discussed in Chapter 13.

As an example of the link between responsiveness to customers and an organization's production system, consider the success of Southwest Airlines. One of the most consistently successful airlines in the United States, Southwest Airlines has been expanding rapidly. One reason for Southwest's success is that its managers created a production system uniquely tailored to satisfy the demands of its customers for low-priced, reliable (on-time), and convenient air travel. Southwest commands high customer loyalty precisely because its production system delivers products, such as flights from Houston to Dallas, that have all the desired attributes: reliability, convenience, and low price.

Southwest's low-cost production system focuses not only on improving the maintenance of aircraft but also on the company's ticket reservation system, route structure, flight frequency, baggage-handling system, and in-flight services. For example, Southwest offers a no-frills approach to in-flight customer service. No meals are served on board, and there are no first-class seats. Southwest does not subscribe to the big reservation computers used by travel agents because the booking fees are too costly. Also, the airline flies only one aircraft, the fuel-efficient Boeing 737, which keeps training and maintenance costs down. All this translates into low prices for customers.

Southwest's reliability derives from the fact that it has the quickest aircraft turnaround time in the industry. A Southwest ground crew needs only 15 minutes to turn around an incoming aircraft and prepare it for departure. This speedy operation helps to keep flights on time. Southwest has such quick turnaround because it has a flexible workforce that has been cross-trained to perform multiple tasks. Thus, the person who checks tickets might also help with baggage loading if time is short.

Southwest's convenience comes from its scheduling multiple flights every day between its popular locations, such as Dallas and Houston, and its use of airports that are close to downtown (Hobby at Houston and Love Field at Dallas) instead of more distant major airports.[6] Southwest's excellent value chain management has given it a competitive advantage in the airline industry. Another company that has found a way to be responsive to customers by offering them faster service is First Global Xpress, profiled in the following "Management Insight" box.

MANAGEMENT INSIGHT

First Global Xpress Delivers Packages Faster, Cheaper, and Greener

First Global Xpress (FGX) is a small, $10 million global package shipping company that claims it can ship packages from the 12 largest U.S. cities on the East Coast anywhere around the globe 24 hours faster and more reliably

Can upstart company FGX successfully compete with FedEx and UPS? Direct shipping routes and alliances with major airlines are two of the ways FGX believes it can become a major player in the package delivery industry.

(its package loss rate is 1% compared to the industry average of over 8%) than large competitors such as FedEx and UPS. Also, FGX claims it can ship its over 400 customers' packages at a 20% lower cost than its large rivals and in a "greener way" because it uses less fuel oil with a 30% savings in CO_2 emissions.[7] How has it created the value chain strategies to achieve this?

Large shipping companies like FedEx and DHL rely on a "hub-and-spoke" package distribution system so that no matter where a package is collected or its destination it has to go through a central hub first, where packages from all over the United States are sorted for shipment to their final destination. This means that a customer's shipment, say from New York to London, has to take two different flights—one to get to a hub, such as FedEx's hub in Memphis, Tennessee, and then another to get to England. FGX does not own aircraft; it has been rapidly forming alliances with over 100 different global airlines that can ship its customers' packages directly from city to city—from New York to London, for example, which saves time and money.

Customer Relationship Management

customer relationship management (CRM) A technique that uses IT to develop an ongoing relationship with customers to maximize the value an organization can deliver to them over time.

One operations strategy managers can use to get close to customers and understand their needs is customer relationship management (CRM). CRM is a technique that uses IT to develop an ongoing relationship with customers to maximize the value an organization can deliver to them over time. By the 2000s most large companies had installed sophisticated CRM IT to track customers' changing demands for a company's products; this became a vital tool to maximize responsiveness to customers. CRM IT monitors, controls, and links each of the functional activities involved in marketing, selling, and delivering products to customers, such as monitoring the delivery of products through the distribution channel, monitoring salespeople's selling activities, setting product pricing, and coordinating after-sales service. CRM systems have three interconnected components: sales and selling, after-sales service and support, and marketing.

Suppose a sales manager has access only to sales data that show the total sales revenue each salesperson generated in the last 30 days. This information does not break down how much revenue came from sales to existing customers versus sales to new customers. What important knowledge is being lost? First, if most revenues are earned from sales to existing customers, this suggests that the money being spent by a company to advertise and promote its products is not attracting new customers and so is being wasted. Second, important dimensions involved in sales are pricing, financing, and order processing. In many companies, to close a deal, a salesperson has to send the paperwork to a central sales office that handles matters such as approving the customer for special financing and determining specific shipping and delivery dates. In some companies, different departments handle these activities, and it can take a long time to get a response from them; this keeps customers waiting—something that often leads to lost sales. Until CRM systems were introduced, these kinds of problems were widespread and resulted in missed sales and higher operating costs. Today the sales and selling CRM software contains *best sales practices* that analyze this information and then recommend ways to improve how the sales process operates.

One company that has improved its sales and after-sales practices by implementing CRM is Empire HealthChoice Inc., the largest health insurance provider in New York, which sells its policies through 1,800 sales agents. For years these agents were responsible for collecting all the customer-specific information needed to determine the price of each policy. Once they had collected the necessary information, the agents called Empire to get price quotes. After waiting days for these quotes, the agents relayed them back to customers, who often then modified their requests to reduce the cost of their policies. When this occurred, the agents had to telephone Empire again to get revised price quotes. Because this frequently happened several times with each transaction, it often took more than 20 days to close a sale and another 10 days for customers to get their insurance cards.[8]

Recognizing that these delays were causing lost sales, Empire decided to examine how a CRM system could improve the sales process. Its managers chose a web-based system so agents themselves could calculate the insurance quotes online. Once an agent enters a customer's data, a quote is generated in just a few seconds. The agent can continually modify a policy while sitting face-to-face with the customer until the policy and price are agreed upon. As a result, the sales process can now be completed in a few hours, and customers receive their insurance cards in 2 to 3 days rather than 10.[9]

When a company implements after-sales service and support CRM software, salespeople are required to input detailed information about their follow-up visits to customers. Because the system tracks and documents every customer's case history, salespeople have instant access to a record of everything that occurred during previous phone calls or visits. They are in a much better position to respond to customers' needs and build customer loyalty, so a company's after-sales service improves. Cell phone companies like T-Mobile and Sprint, for example, require that telephone sales reps collect information about all customers' inquiries, complaints, and requests, and this is recorded electronically in customer logs. The CRM module can analyze the information in these logs to evaluate whether the customer service reps are meeting or exceeding the company's required service standards.

A CRM system can also identify the top 10 reasons for customer complaints. Sales managers can then work to eliminate the sources of these problems and improve after-sales support procedures. The CRM system also identifies the top 10 best service and support practices, which can then be taught to all sales reps.

Finally, as a CRM system processes information about changing customer needs, this improves marketing in many ways. Marketing managers, for example, have access to detailed customer profiles, including data about purchases and the reasons why individuals were or were not attracted to a company's products. Armed with this knowledge, marketing can better identify customers and the specific product attributes they desire. It may become clear, for example, that a targeted customer group has a specific need that is not satisfied by a product—such as a need for a cell phone containing a 20-megapixel video camera and a GPS system. With real-time information, marketing can work with product development to redesign the product to better meet customer needs. In sum, a CRM system is a comprehensive method of gathering crucial information about how customers respond to a company's products. It is a powerful functional strategy used to align a company's products with customer needs.

Improving Quality

LO 14-3 Explain why achieving superior quality is so important.

As noted earlier, high-quality products possess attributes such as superior design, features, reliability, and after-sales support; these products are designed to better meet customer requirements.[10] Quality is a concept that can be applied to the products of both manufacturing and service organizations—goods such as a Toyota car or services such as Southwest Airlines flight service or customer service in a Citibank branch. Why do managers seek to control and improve the quality of their organizations' products?[11] There are two reasons (see Figure 14.2).

First, customers usually prefer a higher-quality product to a lower-quality product. So an organization able to provide, *for the same price,* a product of higher quality than a competitor's product is serving its customers better—it is being more responsive to its customers. Often, providing high-quality products creates a brand-name reputation for an organization's products. In turn, this enhanced reputation may allow the organization to charge more for its products than its competitors are able to charge, and thus it makes even greater profits. In 2013 Lexus was ranked number one, as it has been for over a decade, on the J. D. Power list of the 10 most reliable carmakers, and Toyota was close behind.[12] The high quality of Toyota/Lexus vehicles enables the company to charge higher prices for its cars than the prices charged by rival carmakers.

The second reason for trying to boost product quality is that higher product quality can increase efficiency and thereby lower operating costs and boost profits. Achieving high product quality lowers operating costs because of the effect of quality on employee productivity: Higher product quality means less employee time is wasted in making defective products that must be discarded or in providing substandard services, and thus less time has to be spent fixing mistakes. This translates into higher employee productivity, which means lower costs.

To increase quality, managers need to develop strategic plans that state goals exactly and spell out how they will be achieved. Managers should embrace the philosophy that mistakes, defects, and poor-quality materials are not acceptable and should be eliminated. First-line managers should spend more time working with nonmanagerial employees and providing them with the tools they need to do the job. Managers should create an environment in which subordinates will not be afraid to report problems or recommend improvements. Output goals

Figure 14.2

The Impact of Increased Quality on Organizational Performance

and targets need to include not only numbers or quotas but also some notion of quality to promote the production of defect-free output. Managers also need to train employees in new skills to keep pace with changes in the workplace. Finally, achieving better quality requires managers to develop organizational values and norms centered on improving quality. The Six Sigma approach discussed in the following "Management Insight" is one technique that is being used increasingly by managers to improve quality.

MANAGEMENT INSIGHT

How Starwood Uses Six Sigma to Improve Hotel Performance

Starwood Hotels & Resorts, based in White Plains, New York, is one of the largest global hotel chains and one of the most profitable—its profit margins are nearly 15% higher than rivals such as Hilton and Marriott. Why? Starwood attributes a significant part of its high performance to its use of Six Sigma, which it began to use in 2001 to improve the quality of service it provides its guests.[13]

The company's Six Sigma group is led by Brian Mayer, the vice president of "Six Sigma Operations Management & Room Support," whose father and grandfather both worked in the hospitality industry. Mayer, a Six Sigma expert, helped by a small group of other experts he recruited, implemented the program in 2001. Since then they have trained 150 Starwood employees as "black belts" and another 2,700 as "green belts" in the practices of Six Sigma. Black belts are the

Guests and a bellhop share a laugh at a Starwood resort. The Starwood company remains one of the most highly profitable in the entire industry based on its rigorous Six Sigma program, listening ear toward customers, and attention to employee needs.

lead change agents in Starwood hotels who take responsibility for managing the change process to meet its main objectives—increasing quality customer service and responsiveness.[14] Green belts are the employees trained by Mayer's experts and each hotel's black belt to become the Six Sigma team in each hotel who work together to develop new ideas or programs that will improve customer responsiveness, and to find the work procedures and processes that will implement the new programs most effectively to improve customer service quality.

Almost all the new initiatives that have permeated the thousands of individual hotels in the Starwood chain come from these Six Sigma teams—whose work has improved the company's performance by hundreds of millions of dollars. For example, the "Unwind Program" was an initiative developed to cater to the interests of the 34% of hotel guests that a study found felt lonely and isolated in overnight hotel stays. Its purpose was to make guests feel at home so they would become return customers. The chain's Six Sigma teams began brainstorming ideas for new kinds of activities and services that would encourage nightly guests to leave their rooms and gather in the lobby, where they could meet and mingle with other guests and so feel more at home. They came up with hundreds of potential new programs. An initial concept was to offer guests short complimentary massages in the lobby, hoping to encourage them to book massage sessions that would boost hotel revenues. Teams at each hotel then dreamed up other programs that they felt would best meet guest needs. These ranged from fire dancing in hotels in Fiji to Chinese watercolor painting in hotels in Beijing.[15] These ideas are shared across all the hotels in the chain using Starwood's proprietary "E-Tool," which contains thousands of successful projects that have worked—and the specific work procedures needed to perform them successfully.

In another major project, Starwood's managers were concerned about the number of injuries hotel employees sustained during their work, such as back strain injuries common among the housekeepers who cleaned rooms. The black and green belt teams studied how housekeepers worked in the various hotels and, pooling their knowledge, realized several changes could reduce injuries. For example, they found that a large number of back strains occurred early in housekeepers' shifts because they were not "warmed up," so one central coordinating team developed a series of job-related stretching exercises. This team also looked at the cleaning tools used, and after experimenting with different sizes and types found that curved, longer-handled tools, which required less bending and stretching, could significantly reduce injuries. The program has reduced the accident rate from 12 to 2 for every 200,000 work hours—a major achievement.

As Starwood has found, having teams of Six Sigma specialists trained to always be alert for opportunities to improve the tens of thousands of different work procedures that help create high-quality customer service pays off. For guests and employees, the result is greater satisfaction and loyalty to the hotel chain in the form of both repeat guest visits and reduced employee turnover.

Improving Efficiency

The third goal of operations management is to increase the efficiency of an organization's production system. The fewer the inputs required to produce a given output, the higher will be the efficiency of the production system. Managers can measure efficiency at the organization level

LO 14-4 Explain why achieving superior efficiency is so important.

in two ways. The measure, known as *total factor productivity*, looks at how well an organization utilizes all of its resources—such as labor, capital, materials, or energy—to produce its outputs. It is expressed in the following equation:

$$\text{Total factor productivity} = \frac{\text{Outputs}}{\text{All inputs}}$$

The problem with total factor productivity is that each input is typically measured in different units: Labor's contribution to producing an output is measured by hours worked; the contribution of materials is measured by the amount consumed (for example, tons of iron ore required to make a ton of steel); the contribution of energy is measured by the units of energy consumed (for example, kilowatt-hours); and so on. To compute total factor productivity, managers must convert all the inputs to a common unit, such as dollars, before they can work the equation.

Though sometimes a useful measure of efficiency overall, total factor productivity obscures the exact contribution of an individual input—such as labor—to the production of a given output. Consequently, most organizations focus on specific measures of efficiency, known as *partial productivity*, that measure the efficiency of an individual unit. For example, the efficiency of labor inputs is expressed as

$$\text{Labor productivity} = \frac{\text{Outputs}}{\text{Direct labor}}$$

Labor productivity is most commonly used to draw efficiency comparisons between different organizations. For example, one study found that in 1994 it took the average Japanese automobile components supplier half as many labor-hours to produce a part, such as a car seat or exhaust system, as the average British company.[16] Thus, the study concluded, Japanese companies use labor more efficiently than British companies.

The management of efficiency is an extremely important issue in most organizations, because increased efficiency lowers production costs, thereby allowing the organization to make a greater profit or to attract more customers by lowering its price. For example, in 1990 the price of the average personal computer sold in the United States was $3,000, by 1995 the price was around $1,800, and in 2005 it was $550. This decrease occurred despite the fact that the power and capabilities of the average personal computer increased dramatically during this time period (microprocessors became more powerful, memory increased, modems were built in, and multimedia capability was added).

Why was the decrease in price possible? Manufacturers of personal computers such as Compaq and Dell focused on quality and boosted their efficiency by improving the quality of their components and making PCs easier to assemble. This allowed them to lower their costs and prices yet still make a profit.[17]

Facilities Layout, Flexible Manufacturing, and Efficiency

Another factor that influences efficiency is the way managers decide to lay out or design an organization's physical work facilities. This is important for two reasons. First, the way in which machines and workers are organized or grouped together into workstations affects the efficiency of the production system. Second, a major determinant of efficiency is the cost associated with setting up the equipment

facilities layout

The operations management technique whose goal is to design the machine–worker interface to increase production system efficiency.

flexible manufacturing

Operations management techniques that attempt to reduce the setup costs associated with a production system.

needed to make a particular product. Facilities layout is the operations management technique whose goal is to design the machine–worker interface to increase production system efficiency. Flexible manufacturing is the set of operations management techniques that attempt to reduce the setup costs associated with a production system.

FACILITIES LAYOUT The way in which machines, robots, and people are grouped together affects how productive they can be. Figure 14.3 shows three basic ways of arranging workstations: product layout, process layout, and fixed-position layout.

In a *product layout,* machines are organized so that each operation needed to manufacture a product is performed at workstations arranged in a fixed sequence. Typically, workers are stationary in this arrangement, and a moving conveyor belt takes the product being worked on to the next workstation so that it is progressively assembled. Mass production is the familiar name for this layout; car assembly lines are probably the best-known example. Formerly product layout was efficient only when products were created in large quantities; however, the introduction of modular assembly lines controlled by computers makes it efficient to make products in small batches.

In a *process layout,* workstations are not organized in a fixed sequence. Rather, each workstation is relatively self-contained, and a product goes to whichever workstation is needed to perform the next operation to complete the product. Process layout is often suited to manufacturing settings that produce a variety of custom-made products, each tailored to the needs of a different kind of customer. For example, a custom furniture manufacturer might use a process layout so that different teams of workers can produce different styles of chairs or tables made from different kinds of woods and finishes. A process layout provides the flexibility needed to change the product. Such flexibility, however, often reduces efficiency because it is expensive.

Figure 14.3 **Three Facilities Layouts**

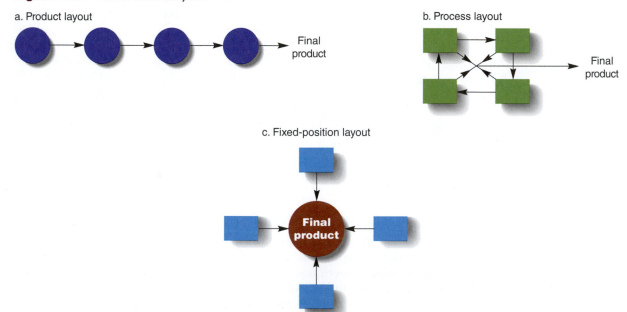

a. Product layout

Final product

b. Process layout

Final product

c. Fixed-position layout

Final product

In a *fixed-position layout*, the product stays in a fixed position. Its component parts are produced in remote workstations and brought to the production area for final assembly. Increasingly, self-managed teams are using fixed-position layouts. Different teams assemble each component part and then send these parts to the final assembly team, which makes the final product. A fixed-position layout is commonly used for products such as jet airlines, mainframe computers, and gas turbines—products that are complex and difficult to assemble or so large that moving them from one workstation to another would be difficult. The effects of moving from one facilities layout to another can be dramatic, as the following "Manager as a Person" suggests.

MANAGER AS A PERSON

How to Improve Facilities Layout

Paddy Hopkirk established his car accessories business in Bedfordshire, England, shortly after he had shot to motor car racing fame by winning the Monte Carlo Rally. Sales of Hopkirk's accessories, such as bicycle racks and axle stands, were always brisk, but Hopkirk was the first to admit that his production system left a lot to be desired, so he invited consultants to help reorganize his production system.

After analyzing his factory's production system, the consultants realized that the source of the problem was the facilities layout Hopkirk had established. Over time, as sales grew, Hopkirk simply added new workstations to the production system as they were needed. The result was a process layout in which the product being assembled moved in the irregular sequences shown in the "Before Change" half of Figure 14.4 (see next page). The consultants suggested that to save time and effort, the workstations should be reorganized into the sequential product layout shown in the "After Change" illustration of Figure 14.4.

Once this change was made, the results were dramatic. One morning the factory was an untidy sprawl of workstations surrounded by piles of crates holding semifinished components. Two days later, when the 170-person workforce came back to work, the machines had been brought together into tightly grouped workstations arranged in the fixed sequence shown in the illustration. The piles of components had disappeared, and the newly cleared floor space was neatly marked with color-coded lines mapping out the new flow of materials between workstations.

In the first full day of production, efficiency increased by as much as 30%. The space needed for some operations had been cut in half, and work-in-progress had been cut considerably. Moreover, the improved layout allowed for some jobs to be combined, freeing operators for deployment elsewhere in the factory. An amazed Hopkirk exclaimed, "I was expecting a change but nothing as dramatic as this . . . it is fantastic."[18]

FLEXIBLE MANUFACTURING In a manufacturing company, a major source of costs is the costs associated with setting up the equipment needed to make a particular product. One of these costs is the cost of production that is forgone because nothing is produced while the equipment is being set up. For example, components manufacturers often need as much as half a day to set up automated

Figure 14.4   **Changing a Facilities Layout**

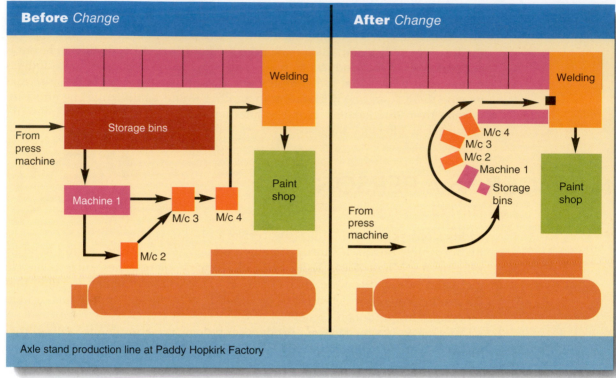

Axle stand production line at Paddy Hopkirk Factory

Source: Reprinted from *Financial Times* of January 4, 1994, by permission of Financial Times Syndication, London.

production equipment when switching from production of one component part (such as a washer ring for the steering column of a car) to another (such as a washer ring for the steering column of a truck). During this half-day, a manufacturing plant is not producing anything, but employees are paid for this "nonproductive" time.

It follows that if setup times for complex production equipment can be reduced, so can setup costs, and efficiency will rise. In other words, if setup times can be reduced, the time that plant and employees spend actually producing something will increase. This simple insight has been the driving force behind the development of flexible manufacturing techniques.

Flexible manufacturing aims to reduce the time required to set up production equipment.[19] Redesigning the manufacturing process so that production equipment geared for manufacturing one product can be quickly replaced with equipment geared to make another product can dramatically reduce setup times and costs. Another favorable outcome from flexible manufacturing is that a company is able to produce many more varieties of a product than before in the same amount of time. Thus, flexible manufacturing increases a company's ability to be responsive to its customers.

Increasingly, organizations are experimenting with new designs for production systems that not only allow workers to be more productive but also make the work process more flexible, thus reducing setup costs. Some Japanese companies are experimenting with facilities layouts arranged as a spiral, as the letter Y, and as the number 6, to see how these various configurations affect setup costs and worker

Assisted by web-based online work instructions, an operator at Dell Computer determines the sequence in which Dell's custom-built computers are to be assembled by its computer-controlled flexible manufacturing system. This flexible system makes possible Dell's low-cost strategy.

productivity. At a camcorder plant in Kohda, Japan, for example, Sony changed from a fixed-position layout in which 50 workers sequentially built a camcorder to a flexible spiral process design in which four workers perform all the operations necessary to produce the camcorder. This new layout allows the most efficient workers to work at the highest pace, and it reduces setup costs because workers can easily switch from one model to another, increasing efficiency by 10%.[20]

MANAGING GLOBALLY

Igus's Factory of the Future

Igus Inc., headquartered in Cologne, Germany, makes over 28,000 polymer bearings and energy supply cable products used in applications the world over. In the 1990s, the company's managers realized they needed to build a new factory that could handle the company's rapidly growing product line.[21]

Igus's product line changes constantly as new products are developed and old ones become obsolete. At Igus new products are often introduced on a daily basis, so the need for flexibility is great. Moreover, because many of its products are highly customized, the specific and changing needs of customers drive new product development.

Igus's new factory—as big as three football fields—was designed with the need for flexibility in mind. Nothing in the factory is tied down or bolted to the floor. All the machines, computers, and equipment can be moved and repositioned to suit changing product requirements. Moreover, all Igus employees are trained to be flexible and can perform many different production tasks. For example, when one new product line proved popular with customers, employees and production operations were relocated four times into increasingly larger spaces. Igus can change its production system at a moment's notice and with minimal disruption, and because the company operates seven days a week, 24 hours a day, these changes are occurring constantly.

To facilitate these changes, workers are equipped with power scooters so they can move around the plant quickly to reconfigure operations. The scooters also allow them to move quickly to wherever in the factory their skills are most needed. Employees also carry mobile phones so they are always on call.

Igus's decision to create a flexible factory has paid off. In the last five years its sales have increased from $10 million to $100 million, and its global staff has tripled.

Just-in-Time Inventory and Efficiency

Inventory is the stock of raw materials, inputs, and component parts that an organization has on hand at a particular time. Just-in-time (JIT) inventory systems play a major role in the process of identifying and finding the source of defects in inputs. When an organization has a just-in-time inventory system, parts or supplies arrive at the organization when they are needed, not before. Under a JIT inventory system, defective parts enter an organization's production system immediately; they are not warehoused for months before use. This means that defective inputs can be quickly spotted. Managers can then trace a problem to the supply source and fix it before more defective parts are produced.

JIT systems, such as Toyota's *kanban* system, were originally developed as part of the effort to improve product quality; they have major implications for efficiency. Toyota's system is based on the delivery of components to the production line just as they are needed. This leads to major cost savings from increasing inventory turnover and reducing inventory holding costs, such as warehousing and storage costs and the cost of capital tied up in inventory. Although companies that manufacture and assemble products can obviously use JIT to great advantage, so can service organizations. Walmart, the biggest retailer in the United States, uses JIT systems to replenish the stock in its stores at least twice a week. Many Walmart stores receive daily deliveries. Walmart's main competitors, Kroger and Target, typically replenish their stock every two weeks. Walmart can maintain the same service levels as these competitors but at one-fourth the inventory-holding cost, a major source of cost savings. Faster inventory turnover has helped Walmart achieve an efficiency-based competitive advantage in the retailing industry.[22]

One drawback of JIT systems is that they leave an organization without a buffer stock of inventory.[23] Although buffer stocks of inventory can be expensive to store, they can help an organization when it is affected by shortages of inputs brought about by a disruption among suppliers (such as a labor dispute in a key supplier). Moreover, buffer stocks can help an organization respond quickly to increases in customer demand—that is, they can increase an organization's responsiveness to customers.

Even a small company can benefit from a kanban, as the experience of United Electric suggests. United Electric Controls, headquartered in Watertown, Massachusetts, is the market leader in the application of threshold detection and switching technology. Once the company simply warehoused its inputs and dispensed them as needed. Then it decided to reduce costs by storing these inputs at their point of use in the production system. However, this practice caused problems because inventories of some inputs actually started to increase while other inputs were used up without anyone knowing which input caused a stoppage in production. Thus, managers decided to experiment with a supplier kanban system even though United Electric had fewer than 40 suppliers who were totally up-to-date with the company's input requirements.

Managers decided to store a three-week supply of parts in a central storeroom, a supply large enough to avoid unexpected shortages.[24] They began by asking their casting supplier to deliver inputs in kanbans and bins. Once a week, this supplier checks up on the bins to determine how much stock needs to be delivered the following week. Other suppliers were then asked to participate in this system, and now more than 35 of United Electric's major suppliers operate some form of the kanban system. By all measures of performance, the results have been successful. Inventory-holding costs have fallen sharply. Products are delivered to all customers on time. And even new products' design-to-production cycles have dropped by 50% because suppliers are now involved much earlier in the design process, so they can supply new inputs as needed.

Self-Managed Work Teams and Efficiency

Another efficiency-boosting technique is the use of self-managed work teams (see Chapter 11).[25] The typical team consists of from 5 to 15 employees who produce an entire product instead of only parts of it.[26] Team members learn all team tasks and move from job to job. The result is a flexible workforce because team members can fill in for absent coworkers. The members of each team also assume responsibility for work and vacation scheduling, ordering materials, and hiring new members—previously all responsibilities of first-line managers. Because people often respond well to being given greater autonomy and responsibility, the use of empowered self-managed teams can increase productivity and efficiency. Moreover, cost savings arise from eliminating supervisors and creating a flatter organizational hierarchy, which further increases efficiency.

The effect of introducing self-managed teams is often an increase in efficiency of 30% or more, sometimes much more. After the introduction of flexible manufacturing technology and self-managed teams, a GE plant in Salisbury, North Carolina, increased efficiency by 250% compared with other GE plants producing the same products.[27]

Process Reengineering and Efficiency

process reengineering
The fundamental rethinking and radical redesign of business processes to achieve dramatic improvements in critical measures of performance such as cost, quality, service, and speed.

Think of the major activities of businesses as processes that take one or more kinds of inputs and create an output that is of value to the customer.[28] Process reengineering is the fundamental rethinking and radical redesign of business processes to achieve dramatic improvements in critical measures of performance such as cost, quality, service, and speed.[29] Customer relationship management can be thought of as a business process: Once a customer's order is received (the input), all the activities necessary to process the order are performed, and the ordered goods are delivered to the customer (the output). Process reengineering can boost efficiency because it eliminates the time devoted to activities that do not add value.

As an example of process reengineering in practice, consider how Ford Motor Company used it. One day a manager from Ford was working at its Japanese partner Mazda and discovered quite by accident that Mazda had only five people in its accounts payable department. The Ford manager was shocked, for Ford's U.S. operation had 500 employees in accounts payable. He reported his discovery to Ford's U.S. managers, who decided to form a task force to figure out why the difference existed.

Ford managers discovered that procurement began when the purchasing department sent a purchase order to a supplier and sent a copy of the purchase order to Ford's accounts payable department. When the supplier shipped the goods and they arrived at Ford, a clerk at the receiving dock completed a form describing the goods and sent the form to accounts payable. The supplier, meanwhile, sent accounts payable an invoice. Thus, accounts payable received three documents relating to these goods: a copy of the original purchase order, the receiving document, and the invoice. If the information in all three was in agreement (most of the time it was), a clerk in accounts payable issued payment. Occasionally, however, all three documents did not agree. Ford discovered that accounts payable clerks spent most of their time straightening out the 1% of instances in which the purchase order, receiving document, and invoice contained conflicting information.[30]

Ford managers decided to reengineer the procurement process to simplify it. Now when a buyer in the purchasing department issues a purchase order to

Managers at Ford Motor Company used process reengineering to improve the efficiency of their procurement process by simplifying it. Now, when one of Ford's dealers issues a purchase order to buy a collection of Ford vehicles for delivery to its lot, the dealer also enters the order into an online database. When the vehicles ordered arrive at the receiving dock for shipment by train, a clerk checks on a computer terminal to ensure that the specific shipment matches the purchase order and checks online with the dealer that the order is still correct. If it is, the vehicles are shipped. The use of process engineering has significantly cut down on the time accounts payable clerks spend to rectify complex vehicle orders that contain conflicting information.

a supplier, that buyer also enters the order into an online database. As before, suppliers send goods to the receiving dock. When the goods arrive, the clerk at the receiving dock checks a computer terminal to see whether the received shipment matches the description on the purchase order. If it does, the clerk accepts the goods and pushes a button on the terminal keyboard that tells the database the goods have arrived. Receipt of the goods is recorded in the database, and a computer automatically issues and sends a check to the supplier. If the goods do not correspond to the description on the purchase order in the database, the clerk at the dock refuses the shipment and sends it back to the supplier.

Payment authorization, which used to be performed by accounts payable, is now accomplished at the receiving dock. The new process has come close to eliminating the need for an accounts payable department. In some parts of Ford, the size of the accounts payable department has been cut by 95%. By reducing the head count in accounts payable, the reengineering effort reduced the amount of time wasted on unproductive activities, thereby increasing the efficiency of the total organization.

In sum, managers at all levels have important roles to play in a company's effort to boost efficiency. Top management's role is to encourage efficiency improvements by, for example, emphasizing the need for continuous improvement or reengineering. Top management also must ensure that managers from different functional departments work together to find ways to increase efficiency. However, while top managers might recognize the need for such actions, functional-level managers are in the best position to identify opportunities for making efficiency-enhancing improvements to an organization's production systems. They are the managers who are involved in an organization's production system on a day-to-day basis. Improving efficiency, like quality, is an ongoing, never-ending process.

Operations Management: Some Remaining Issues

Achieving superior responsiveness to customers through quality and efficiency often requires a profound shift in management operations and in the culture of an organization. Many reports have appeared in the popular press about widespread disillusionment with JIT, flexible manufacturing, and reengineering. It is possible that many of the disillusioned organizations are those that failed to understand that implementing these systems requires a marked shift in organizational culture.[31] None of these systems is a panacea that can be taken once, like a pill, to cure industrial ills. Making these techniques work within an organization can pose a significant challenge that calls for hard work and years of persistence by the sponsoring managers.

Managers also need to understand the ethical implications of the adoption of many of the production techniques discussed here. JIT, flexible manufacturing, and reengineering can all increase quality, efficiency, and responsiveness to customers, but they may do so at great cost to employees. Employees may see the demands of their job increase, or, worse, they may see themselves reengineered out of a job. For example, Toyota is the most efficient car manufacturer in the world, but some of its gains have been achieved at a significant cost to its employees, as discussed in the following "Ethics in Action."

ETHICS IN ACTION

The Human Cost of Improving Productivity

Hisashi Tomiki is the leader of a four-man self-managed team in a Toyota production plant, 200 miles south of Tokyo, Japan. Tomiki and his team work at a grueling pace to build cowls (steel chambers onto which windshields and steering columns are attached). Consider this description of Tomiki at work:

> In two minutes Tomiki fits 24 metal pieces into designated slots on three welding machines; runs two large metal sheets through each of the machines, which weld on the parts; and fuses the two sheets together with two spot welds. There is little room for error. Once or twice an hour a mistake is made or a machine sticks, causing the next machine in line to stop. A yellow light flashes. Tomiki runs over. The squad must fix the part and work faster to catch up. A red button halts the production line if the problems are severe, but there is an unspoken rule against pushing it. Only once this day does Tomiki call in a special maintenance worker.[32]

The experience of workers like Tomiki has become increasingly common. Workers are heard to complain that constant attempts to increase quality and reduce costs really mean continuous speedup and added job stress from the increased pressure on employees to perform. Although some pressure is good, past a certain point it can seriously harm employees. Moreover, consider the following comment by Jerry Miller, a former employee of US West, whose team of billing clerks reengineered themselves out of a job: "When we first formed our teams, the company came in talking teams and empowerment and promised that we wouldn't lose any jobs. It turns out all this was a big cover. The company had us all set up for reengineering. We showed them how to streamline the work, and now 9,000 people are gone. It was cut-your-own-throat. It makes you feel used."[33]

Is it ethical to continually increase the demands placed on employees, regardless of the human cost in terms of job stress? Obviously, the answer is no. Employee support is vital if an organization is to function effectively. What kinds of work pressures are legitimate, and what pressures are excessive? There is no clear answer to this question. Ultimately the issue comes down to the judgment of responsible managers seeking to act ethically.

Summary and Review

OPERATIONS MANAGEMENT AND COMPETITIVE ADVANTAGE To achieve high performance, managers try to improve their responsiveness to customers, the quality of their products, and the efficiency of their organization. To achieve these goals, managers can use a number of operations management techniques to improve the way an organization's production system operates. **[LO 14-1]**

IMPROVING RESPONSIVENESS TO CUSTOMERS To achieve high performance in a competitive environment, it is imperative that the production system of an organization responds to customer demands. Managers try to design production systems that produce outputs that have the attributes customers desire. One of the central tasks of operations management is to develop new and improved production systems that enhance the ability of the organization to deliver economically more of the product attributes that customers desire for the same price. Techniques such as JIT, flexible manufacturing, and process reengineering are popular because they promise to do this. Managers should analyze carefully the links between responsiveness to customers and the production system of an organization. The ability of an organization to satisfy the demands of its customers for lower prices, acceptable quality, better features, and so on depends critically on the nature of the organization's production system. As important as responsiveness to customers is, however, managers need to recognize that there are limits to how responsive an organization can be and still cover its costs. **[LO 14-2]**

IMPROVING QUALITY Managers seek to improve the quality of their organization's output because it enables them to better serve customers, to raise prices, and to lower production costs. The attempt to improve quality requires an organizationwide commitment; managers emphasize a strong customer focus, find ways to measure quality, set quality improvement goals, solicit input from employees about how to improve product quality, and design products for ease of manufacture. **[LO 14-3]**

IMPROVING EFFICIENCY Improving efficiency requires one or more of the following: improve quality, adopt flexible manufacturing technologies, introduce just-in-time inventory systems, establish self-managed work teams, and use process reengineering. Top management is responsible for setting the context within which efficiency improvements can take place by, for example, emphasizing the need for continuous improvement. Functional-level managers bear prime responsibility for identifying and implementing efficiency-enhancing improvements in production systems. **[LO 14-4]**

Management *in Action*

TOPICS FOR DISCUSSION AND ACTION

Discussion

1. What is efficiency, and what are some of the techniques that managers can use to increase it? **[LO 14-4]**

2. Why is it important for managers to pay close attention to their organization's production system if they wish to be responsive to their customers? **[LO 14-1]**

3. "Total customer service is the goal toward which most organizations should strive." To what degree is this statement correct? **[LO 14-2]**

Action

4. Ask a manager how quality, efficiency, and responsiveness to customers are defined and measured in his or her organization. **[LO 14-2, 14-3, 14-4]**

5. Go into a local store, restaurant, or supermarket, and list the ways in which you think the organization is being responsive or unresponsive to the needs of its customers. How could this business's responsiveness to customers be improved? **[LO 14-2]**

BUILDING MANAGEMENT SKILLS [LO 14-1]

Managing a Production System

Choose an organization with which you are familiar—one that you have worked in or patronized or one that has received extensive coverage in the popular press. The organization should be involved in only one industry or business. Answer these questions about the organization.

1. What is the output of the organization?

2. Describe the production system that the organization uses to produce this output.

3. What product attributes do customers of the organization desire?

4. Does its production system allow the organization to deliver the desired product attributes?

5. Try to identify improvements that might be made to the organization's production system to boost the organization's responsiveness to customers, quality, and efficiency.

MANAGING ETHICALLY [LO 14-1]

Review "Ethics in Action: The Human Cost of Improving Productivity." After the implementing of many operations management techniques, layoffs occur in many companies, and, frequently, employees must perform more tasks more quickly, which can generate employee stress and other work-related problems.

Questions

1. Either by yourself or in a group, discuss how to think through the ethical implications of using a new operations management technique to improve organizational performance.

2. What criteria would you use to decide what kind of technique is ethical to adopt and how far to push employees to raise the level of their performance?

3. How big a layoff, if any, would be acceptable? If layoffs are acceptable, what could be done to reduce their harm to employees?

SMALL GROUP BREAKOUT EXERCISE [LO 14-1, 14-2, 14-3, 14-4]

How to Compete in the Sandwich Business

Form groups of three or four people, and appoint one member as the spokesperson who will communicate your findings to the whole class when called on by the instructor. Then discuss the following scenario.

You and your partners are thinking about opening a new kind of sandwich shop that will compete head-to-head with Subway and Thundercloud Subs. Because these chains have good brand-name recognition, it is vital that you find some source of competitive advantage for your new sandwich shop, and you are meeting to brainstorm ways of obtaining one.

1. Identify the product attributes that a typical sandwich shop customer most wants.

2. In what ways do you think you will be able to improve on the operations and processes of existing sandwich shops and achieve a competitive advantage through better (a) product quality, (b) efficiency, or (c) responsiveness to customers?

BE THE MANAGER [LO 14-1, 14-3]

How to Build Flat-Panel Displays

You are an operations management consultant who has been called in by the management team of a start-up company that will produce flat-screen displays for personal computer manufacturers like Dell and Compaq. The flat-screen display market is highly competitive; there is considerable pressure to reduce costs because prices fall rapidly due to competition. Also, personal computer makers are demanding ever higher quality and better features to please customers, and they demand delivery of your product to meet their production schedules. Managers want your advice on how to best meet these requirements. They are in the process of recruiting new workers and building a production facility.

Questions

1. What kinds of techniques discussed in the chapter can help these managers to increase efficiency?

2. In what ways can these managers go about developing a program to increase quality?

3. What critical lessons can these managers learn from operations management?

BLOOMBERG BUSINESSWEEK
CASE IN THE NEWS [LO 14-1, 14-2, 14-3, 14-4]

Inside Google's Secret Lab

Last February, Teller, the director of Google's secretive research lab, Google X, went to seek approval from Chief Executive Officer Larry Page for an unlikely acquisition. Teller was proposing that Google buy Makani Power, a startup that develops wind turbines mounted on unmanned, fixed-wing aircraft tethered to the ground like a kite. The startup, Teller told Page, was seeing promising results, and, he added proudly, its prototypes had survived all recent tests intact.

Page approved Google X's acquisition of Makani, which was being completed for an undisclosed amount at press time. He also had a demand. "He said we could have the budget and the people to go do this," Teller says, "but that we had to make sure to crash at least five of the devices in the near future."

As the polymath engineers and scientists who work there are fond of saying, Google X is the search giant's factory for moonshots, those million-to-one scientific bets that require generous amounts of capital, massive leaps of faith, and a willingness to break things. Google X (the official spelling is Google [x]) is home to the self-driving car initiative and the Internet-connected eyeglasses, Google Glass, among other improbable projects.

The biggest moonshot of all may be the skunkworks itself: With X, Google has created a laboratory whose mandate is to come up with technologies that sound more like plot contrivances from *Star Trek* than products that might satisfy the short-term demands of Google's shareholders. "Google X is very consciously looking at things that Google in its right mind wouldn't do," says Richard DeVaul, a "rapid evaluator" at the lab. "They built the rocket pad far away from the widget factory, so if the rocket blows up, it's hopefully not disrupting the core business."

Since its creation in 2010, Google has kept X largely hidden from view. Over the past month, *Bloomberg Businessweek* spoke to many of X's managers and project leaders, who work with abundant resources and few of the constraints that smothered similar corporate research efforts in the past. "Anything which is a huge problem for humanity we'll sign up for, if we can find a way to fix it," Teller says.

Google X seeks to be an heir to the classic research labs, such as the Manhattan Project, which created the first atomic bomb, and Bletchley Park, where code breakers cracked German ciphers and gave birth to modern cryptography. After the war, the spirit of these efforts was captured in pastoral corporate settings: AT&T's Bell Labs and Xerox PARC, for example, became synonymous with breakthroughs (the transistor and the personal computer among them) and the inability of each company to capitalize on them.

Google X occupies a pair of otherwise ordinary two-story red-brick buildings about a half-mile from Google's main campus. There's a burbling fountain out front and rows of company-issued bikes, which employees use to shuttle to the main campus. Inside one of the buildings, frosted glass covers the conference room windows. A race car tricked out with self-driving technology is parked in the lobby. The car doesn't actually work; it was put there as an April Fools' joke. Some of the hallway whiteboards are filled with diagrams of that multigenerational nerd fantasy: space elevators. Media outlets have speculated that Google X is working on such contraptions, which would involve giant cables that connect the earth to orbiting space platforms. Google X is working on no such project, but employees have embraced the concept. It keeps everyone guessing.

Sitting in the passenger seat of a Google driverless car is a test of faith. The car, a white Lexus RX450h with a $65,000 laser range finder on the roof, is cruising at 55 miles per hour on Silicon Valley's crowded 101 freeway when a giant bus passes—as it happens, a double-decker Google bus, ferrying employees home. As the car weaves to get out of the way, Chris Urmson, the head of the autonomous cars project, is unperturbed. "Google believes in and enables us to do things that wouldn't be possible in academia," says Urmson, a former assistant research professor at Carnegie Mellon, his hands resting comfortably in his lap. Google co-founders Page and Sergey Brin "have this idea that incremental improvements are not good enough. The standard for success is whether we can get these into the world and do audacious things."

If it weren't for the robo-cars, there might be no such thing as Google X. The lab's origins reach back to 2005, when Page first met the Stanford computer scientist Sebastian Thrun at the Darpa Grand Challenge, where Thrun's team of graduate students was competing to send an autonomous vehicle through a 7-mile obstacle course in the Mojave Desert. The two men shared a belief in the promise of artificial intelligence and robotics and became friends. Two years later, Page convinced Thrun and several of his students to help with its Street View mapping project. Thrun had grown disenchanted with the pace of academia, where professors are motivated to publish papers rather than build products. He started the self-driving car project at Google in early 2009. Page and Brin gave him a target: Build one that could flawlessly drive 1,000 miles of open California highways and serpentine city streets. Thrun and his team of a dozen engineers met that goal in 15 months. Their car successfully navigated the jammed streets of Los Angeles and Silicon Valley, and the lower span of the San Francisco–Oakland Bay Bridge, where the car had no GPS reception.

As progress exceeded their expectations, Thrun, Brin, and Page began to talk about expanding the project into a full-fledged research lab. For Page and Brin, it was a way to indulge their longtime interest in technologies beyond search—which generated $44 billion in revenue last year—while keeping the perennially restless Thrun in the fold.

Thrun always thought of corporate labs as playgrounds for lifetime employees who were overly absorbed by the abstractions of pure research. He wanted to focus on research that was at least commercially plausible and let talent come and go as projects evolved. Thrun says he seriously considered calling the new group the Google Research Institute, but that carried exactly the kind of sleepy connotations he was trying to avoid. Google X, he says, was a placeholder, a variable to be filled in later.

Brin decreed early on that the new lab would focus most of its energies on creating hardware. The company's board of directors funded Google X in January 2010. (Google does not disclose the lab's budget, but its R&D budget was $6.8 billion in 2012, up 79 percent since 2010.) Google Glass was X's second project. Babak Parviz, an electrical engineering professor at the University of Washington, who was working on wearable computers, caught the attention of Brin and Page with a paper about the possibility of contact lenses with built-in electronics that could project images onto the wearer's eye. Combining cars and wearable computing in Thrun's budding laboratory somehow seemed appropriate. The first Google Glass prototype was a 10-pound head-mounted display with multiple cables snaking down to a box attached to the wearer's belt. The latest incarnation of Glass weighs about the same as a normal pair of glasses and is considerably more discreet. The device, which is currently available only to developers, costs $1,500, hangs the equivalent of an HD display over the right eye, and is capable of taking photos and video, displaying e-mail, and subjecting its owner to ridicule. Critics have piled on about Google Glass's dorkiness and, more seriously, its potential for surreptitious surveillance.

Some of the real projects in Google X sound almost as outlandish. Makani Power's newest airborne turbine prototype, called Wing 7, is a 26-foot-long carbon-fiber contraption with four electricity-generating propellers that flies in circles at altitudes of 800 to 2,000 feet, sending power down a lightweight tether to a base station. "If we're successful, we can get rid of a huge part of the fossil fuels we use," says Damon Vander Lind, the startup's chief engineer. Vander Lind acknowledges it might not work, but: "If you don't take that chance, and put a decade of your life trying to do it, no progress will get made." Then there's X's still-secret project to bring Internet access to undeveloped parts of the world. A decade ago, David Grace, a senior research fellow at the University of York, spearheaded a project to mount broadband transmitters on high-altitude balloons, as part of a multicountry initiative backed by the European Commission, called the Capanina Consortium. The initiative never progressed beyond the experimental stage. Google announced it was working on such balloon-based broadband technology in June 2013.

The expansion of Google X is enough to give some Google investors a touch of heartburn. Brian Wieser, an analyst at the Pivotal Research Group, calls Google X a "benign to positive" factor for shareholders but wonders why the company doesn't license technology such as Google Glass. "When it comes to creating businesses that are arguably a strategic overreach and likely margin-eroding, that is when you get concerned," he says. Other investors remember that the founders' ranging curiosity is what led to winning bets on businesses that seemed irrelevant at the time—Android, for example, which runs on 75 percent of all smartphones shipped around the world in the first quarter, according to the research firm IDC. "It's a culture that has enabled them to not get caught flat-footed by transitions," says Nabil Elsheshai, an analyst at Thrivent Financial for Lutherans, which holds Google stock.

Teller says he wants Google X to be judged not only on its financial return but on the progress it makes toward clean energy or wiring the world, or on its other projects. "We are still in our adolescence," he says. "We are still figuring out how to do things, like how to kill projects or amplify them when we decide they need to go into the next stage." For now, X will take on two or three new moonshots a year. "If there's an enormous problem with the world, and we can convince ourselves that over some long but not unreasonable period of time we can make that problem go away, then we don't need a business plan," Teller says. "We should be focused on making the world a better place, and once we do that, the money will come back and find us."

Questions

1. Google's operations management system is based on its ability to create innovative new products. In what ways does Google X help it to (a) improve responsiveness to customers; (b) improve the quality of its products; (c) improve efficiency?

2. Operations management is also about improving existing products. In what ways does Google X help the company to achieve these objectives, for example, improving quality or customer responsiveness?

3. In what ways might Google's huge investment in its research center hurt the company if the operations management process is not managed effectively?

Source: Brad Stone, "Inside Google's Secret Lab," *Bloomberg Businessweek*, May 22, 2013.

B Career Development

career The sum total of work-related experiences throughout a person's life.

Managers face several challenges both in the course of their own careers and in facilitating effective career management for their subordinates. A career is the sum total of work-related experiences throughout a person's life.[1] Careers encompass all of the different jobs people hold and the different organizations they work for. Careers are important to most people for at least two reasons. First, a career is a means to support oneself and one's loved ones, providing basic necessities and opportunities to pursue outside interests. Second, a career can be a source of personal fulfillment and meaning. Many managers find that making a difference in an organization and helping improve organizational efficiency and effectiveness are personally as well as financially rewarding.

Career development is a concern for managers both in terms of how their own careers unfold over time and how careers are managed in their organizations. In the development of their own careers, managers seek out challenging and interesting jobs that will develop their skills, lead to future opportunities, and allow them the opportunity to do the kind of work that will be personally meaningful. Similarly, in motivating and leading subordinates, managers need to be attuned to subordinates' career development. When careers (of both managers and rank-and-file employees) are effectively managed in an organization, the organization makes the best use of its human resources and employees tend to be motivated by, and satisfied with, their jobs.

Both employees and managers play an important role in effectively managing careers. For example, employees need to understand themselves, the kind of work they find motivating and fulfilling, and their own future aspirations for their careers. Employees then need to proactively seek the education, training, and kinds of work experiences that will help them to have the careers they want. Managers can motivate employees to make meaningful contributions to organizations by providing them with work assignments, experiences, training, and opportunities that contribute to employees' career development.[2]

Hewlett-Packard CEO (Meg) Whitman served in different posts for an array of companies, such as Stride Rite, FTD, Procter & Gamble, Disney, Hasbro, and eBay, before leading HP.

Types of Careers

While every person's career is unique, the different types of careers that people have fall into four general categories: steady-state careers, linear careers, spiral careers, and transitory careers.[3]

steady-state career
A career consisting of the same kind of job during a large part of an individual's work life.

STEADY-STATE CAREERS   A person with a steady-state career makes a one-time commitment to a certain kind of job that he or she maintains throughout his or her working life.[4] People with steady-state careers can become very skilled and expert at their work. A playwright who starts writing plays upon graduation from college and continues to write plays until retiring at age 70 has a steady-state career. So too does a dentist who maintains a steady dental practice upon graduation from dental school until retirement.

Some managers choose to have a steady-state career, holding the same kind of job during a large part of their work life, often becoming highly skilled and expert in what they do. A talented and creative graphic artist at a magazine publishing company, for example, may turn down promotions and other "opportunities" so that he can continue to work on designing attractive magazine spreads and covers, what he really likes to do. Similarly, some managers at Dillard's have steady-state careers as area sales managers because they enjoy the direct supervision of salespeople and the opportunity to "stay close to" customers.

linear career   A career consisting of a sequence of jobs in which each new job entails additional responsibility, a greater impact on an organization, new skills, and upward movement in an organization's hierarchy.

LINEAR CAREERS   A person who has a linear career moves through a sequence of jobs in which each new job entails additional responsibility, a greater impact on an organization, new skills, and upward movement in an organization's hierarchy.[5] The careers of many managers are linear, whether they stay with the same company or frequently switch organizations. A linear career traces a line of upward progress in the positions held.

Top managers in large corporations have moved through a series of lower-level positions in a variety of organizations before they became CEOs. Similarly, the assistant manager at the Red Lobster in College Station, Texas, started out in an entry-level position as a cashier. A linear career at Dillard's department stores may include the following sequencing of positions: executive trainee, area sales manager, assistant buyer, buyer, assistant store manager of merchandising, store manager, and divisional merchandise manager.[6] Managers' subordinates also may have linear careers, although some subordinates may have other types of careers.

spiral career   A career consisting of a series of jobs that build on each other but tend to be fundamentally different.

SPIRAL CAREERS   A person who has a spiral career tends to hold jobs that, while building off of each other, tend to be fundamentally different.[7] An associate professor of chemical engineering who leaves university teaching and research to head up the R&D department of a chemical company for 10 years and then leaves that position to found her own consulting firm has a spiral career. Similarly, a marketing manager in a large corporation who transfers to a job in public relations and then, after several years in that position, takes a job in an advertising firm has a spiral career. Those three jobs tend to be quite different from each other and do not necessarily entail increases in levels of responsibility.

transitory career
A career in which a person changes jobs frequently and in which each job is different from the one that precedes it.

TRANSITORY CAREERS   Some people change jobs frequently and each job is different from the one that precedes it; this kind of career is a transitory career.[8] A middle school teacher who leaves teaching after two years to work as an administrative assistant in a consumer products company for a year and then moves on to do carpentry work has a transitory career.

Career Stages

Every person's career is unique, but there are certain career stages that people generally appear to progress through. Even if a person does not progress through all the stages, typically some of the stages are experienced. Each stage is associated with certain kinds of activities, hurdles, and potential opportunities. Regardless of the extent to which a person experiences each stage, and regardless of the exact number of the stages, about which there is some disagreement among researchers, here we discuss five stages (see Exhibit A) that are useful to understand and manage careers.[9]

These career stages apply to managers and nonmanagers alike. Thus, understanding the stages is important for managers both in terms of their own career development and in terms of the career development of their subordinates. Importantly, and increasingly, these career stages are experienced by most people in a variety of organizations. That is, while in the past, at least some people might have spent most of their careers in a single organization (or in just a few organizations), this is becoming increasingly rare. Rapid changes in technology, increased global competition, environmental uncertainty, outsourcing, and the layoffs many organizations resort to at one point or another to reduce costs are just some of the factors responsible for people's careers unfolding in a series of positions in a number of different organizations. Thus, a boundaryless career, or a career that is not attached or bound to a single organization, is becoming increasingly common, and most people have a variety of work experiences in multiple organizations throughout their careers.[10]

boundaryless career A career that is not attached to or bound to a single organization and consists of a variety of work experiences in multiple organizations.

PREPARATION FOR WORK

During this stage, people decide what kind of career they desire and learn what qualifications and experiences they will need in order to pursue their chosen career.[11] Deciding on a career is no easy task and requires a certain degree of self-awareness and reflection. Sometimes people turn to professional career counselors to help them discover the kinds of careers in which they are most likely to be happy. A person's personality, values, attitudes, and moods impact the initial choice of a career.[12]

After choosing a career area, a person must gain the knowledge, skills, and education necessary to get a good starting position. A person may need an undergraduate or graduate degree or may be able to acquire on-the-job training through an apprenticeship program (common in Germany and some other countries).

ORGANIZATIONAL ENTRY

At this stage, people are trying to find a good first job. The search entails identifying potential opportunities in a variety of ways (such as reading advertisements, attending career/job fairs, and mining personal contacts), finding out as much as possible about alternative positions, and making oneself an attractive candidate for prospective employers. Organizational entry is a more challenging stage for some kinds of careers than for others. An accounting major who knows she wants to work for an accounting firm already has a good idea of her opportunities and of how to make herself attractive to such firms. An English major who wants a career as an editor for a book publisher may find entry-level positions that seem a "good" start to such a career few and far

Exhibit A Career Stages

between and may decide her best bet is to take a position as a sales representative for a well-respected publisher. More often than not, managers do not start out in management positions but rather begin their careers in an entry-level position in a department such as finance, marketing, or engineering.

EARLY CAREER   The early-career stage begins after a person obtains a first job in his or her chosen career. At this stage there are two important steps: establishment and achievement. *Establishment* means learning the ropes of one's new job and organization—learning, for example, specific job responsibilities and duties, expected and desired behaviors, and important values of other organizational members such as the boss.[13] A person who has acquired the basic know-how to perform a job and function in the wider organization is ready to take the second step. *Achievement* means making one's mark, accomplishing something noteworthy, or making an important contribution to the job or organization.[14]

The achievement step can be crucial for future career progression. It is a means of demonstrating one's potential and standing out from others who are aspiring to become managers and are competing for desired positions. Downsizing and restructuring have reduced the number of management positions at many large companies, making it very important for individuals to manage the early-career stage effectively and thus increase their chances of advancement. By identifying where and how you can make a truly significant contribution to an organization, you can enhance your career prospects both inside and outside the organization.

Some people find that seeking out and gaining the assistance of a mentor can be a valuable asset for the early-career and subsequent stages. A mentor is an experienced member of an organization who provides advice and guidance to a less experienced worker (the protégé, or mentee). The help that a mentor provides can range from advice about handling a tricky job assignment, dealing with a disagreement with a supervisor, and what kind of subsequent positions to strive for, to information about appropriate behavior and what to wear in various situations. Mentors often seek out protégés, but individuals also can be proactive and try to enlist the help of a potential mentor. Generally, especially good potential mentors are successful managers who have had a variety of experiences, genuinely desire to help junior colleagues, and are interpersonally compatible with the would-be protégé. Research has found that receiving help from a mentor is associated with an increase in pay, pay satisfaction, promotion, and feeling good about one's accomplishments.[15]

mentor An experienced member of an organization who provides advice and guidance to a less experienced worker.

MIDCAREER   The midcareer stage generally occurs when people have been in the workforce between 20 and 35 years. Different managers experience this stage in quite different ways. For some managers, the midcareer stage is a high point—a time of major accomplishment and success. For other managers, the midcareer stage is a letdown because their careers plateau.

Managers reach a career plateau when their chances of being promoted into a higher position in their current organizations or of obtaining a more responsible position in another organization dwindle.[16] Some managers inevitably will experience a career plateau because fewer and fewer managerial positions are available as one moves up an organization's hierarchy. In some organizations upper-level positions are especially scarce because of downsizing and restructuring.

Plateaued managers who are able to come to terms with their situation can continue to enjoy their work and make important contributions to their organization. Some plateaued managers, for example, welcome lateral moves, which give

career plateau A position from which the chances of being promoted or obtaining a more responsible job are slight.

them the chance to learn new things and contribute in different ways to the organization. Some find being a mentor especially appealing and a chance to share their wisdom and make a difference for someone starting out in their field.

LATE CAREER   This stage lasts as long as a person continues to work and has an active career. Many managers remain productive at this stage and show no signs of slowing down.

Effective Career Management

effective career management
Ensuring that at all levels in the organization there are well-qualified workers who can assume more responsible positions as needed.

Managers face the challenge of ensuring not only that they have the kind of career they personally desire but also that effective career management exists for all employees in their organization. Effective career management means that at all levels in the organization there are well-qualified workers who can assume more responsible positions as needed and that as many members of the organization as possible are highly motivated and satisfied with their jobs and careers. As you might imagine, effectively managing careers in a whole organization is no easy task. At this point, however, it is useful to discuss two important foundations of effective career management in any organization: a commitment to ethical career practices and accommodations for workers' multidimensional lives.

COMMITMENT TO ETHICAL CAREER PRACTICES   Ethical career practices are among the most important ingredients in effective career management and, at a basic level, rest on honesty, trust, and open communication among organizational members. Ethical career practices include basing promotions on performance, not on irrelevant considerations such as personal friendships and ties, and ensuring that diverse members of an organization receive the career opportunities they deserve. Supervisors must never abuse their power to make career decisions affecting others and must never behave unethically to advance their own careers. Managers at all levels must abide by and be committed to ethical career practices and actively demonstrate this commitment; they must communicate that violation of these practices will not be tolerated; and they must make sure that organizational members who feel that they were not ethically treated can communicate their concerns without fear of retaliation.

ACCOMMODATIONS FOR WORKERS' MULTIDIMENSIONAL LIVES
Effectively managing careers also means being sensitive to and providing accommodations for the multiple demands that many organizational members face in their lives. The dual-career couple is now the norm rather than the exception, the number of single parents is at an all-time high, and more and more midcareer workers need to care for their elderly and infirm parents. By limiting unnecessary moves and travel, adopting flexible work arrangements and schedules, providing on-site day care, and allowing workers to take time off to care for children or elderly parents, managers make it possible for workers to have satisfying and productive careers while fulfilling their other commitments.

Careers are as important for managers' subordinates as they are for managers themselves. Understanding the many issues involved in effectively managing careers helps ensure that both managers and their subordinates will have the kinds of careers they want while helping an organization achieve its goals.

Glossary

A

ACHIEVEMENT ORIENTATION   A worldview that values assertiveness, performance, success, and competition.

ADMINISTRATIVE MANAGEMENT   The study of how to create an organizational structure and control system that leads to high efficiency and effectiveness.

ADMINISTRATIVE MODEL   An approach to decision making that explains why decision making is inherently uncertain and risky and why managers usually make satisfactory rather than optimum decisions.

AGREEABLENESS   The tendency to get along well with other people.

AMBIGUOUS INFORMATION   Information that can be interpreted in multiple and often conflicting ways.

APPLICATIONS SOFTWARE   Software designed for a specific task or use.

ARBITRATOR   A third-party negotiator who can impose what he or she thinks is a fair solution to a conflict that both parties are obligated to abide by.

ARTIFICIAL INTELLIGENCE   Behavior performed by a machine that, if performed by a human being, would be called "intelligent."

ATTITUDE   A collection of feelings and beliefs.

ATTRACTION-SELECTION-ATTRITION (ASA) FRAMEWORK   A model that explains how personality may influence organizational culture.

AUTHORITY   The power to hold people accountable for their actions and to make decisions concerning the use of organizational resources.

B

B2B MARKETPLACE   An Internet-based trading platform set up to connect buyers and sellers in an industry.

B2B NETWORK STRUCTURE   A series of global strategic alliances that an organization creates with suppliers, manufacturers, and/or distributors to produce and market a product.

BARRIERS TO ENTRY   Factors that make it difficult and costly for an organization to enter a particular task environment or industry.

BEHAVIORAL MANAGEMENT   The study of how managers should behave to motivate employees and encourage them to perform at high levels and be committed to the achievement of organizational goals.

BENCHMARKING   The process of comparing one company's performance on specific dimensions with the performance of other high-performing organizations.

BOTTOM-UP CHANGE   A gradual or evolutionary approach to change in which managers at all levels work together to develop a detailed plan for change.

BOUNDARY SPANNING   Interacting with individuals and groups outside the organization to obtain valuable information from the environment.

BOUNDARYLESS CAREER   A career that is not attached to or bound to a single organization and consists of a variety of work experiences in multiple organizations.

BOUNDARYLESS ORGANIZATION   An organization whose members are linked by computers, faxes, computer-aided design systems, and video teleconferencing and who rarely, if ever, see one another face-to-face.

BOUNDED RATIONALITY   Cognitive limitations that constrain one's ability to interpret, process, and act on information.

BRAND LOYALTY   Customers' preference for the products of organizations currently existing in the task environment.

BUREAUCRACY   A formal system of organization and administration designed to ensure efficiency and effectiveness.

BUREAUCRATIC CONTROL   Control of behavior by means of a comprehensive system of rules and standard operating procedures.

BUSINESS-LEVEL PLAN   Divisional managers' decisions pertaining to divisions' long-term goals, overall strategy, and structure.

BUSINESS-LEVEL STRATEGY   A plan that indicates how a division intends to compete against its rivals in an industry.

BUSINESS-TO-BUSINESS (B2B) COMMERCE   Trade that takes place between companies using IT and the Internet to link and coordinate the value chains of different companies.

BUSINESS-TO-CUSTOMER (B2C) COMMERCE   Trade that takes place between a company and individual customers using IT and the Internet.

C

CAFETERIA-STYLE BENEFIT PLAN   A plan from which employees can choose the benefits that they want.

CAREER   The sum total of work-related experiences throughout a person's life.

CAREER PLATEAU   A position from which the chances of being promoted or obtaining a more responsible job are slight.

CENTRALIZATION   The concentration of authority at the top of the managerial hierarchy.

CHARISMATIC LEADER   An enthusiastic, self-confident leader who is able to clearly communicate his or her vision of how good things could be.

CLAN CONTROL   The control exerted on individuals and groups in an organization by shared values, norms, standards of behavior, and expectations.

CLASSICAL DECISION-MAKING MODEL   A prescriptive approach to decision making based on the assumption that the decision maker can identify and evaluate all possible alternatives and their consequences and rationally choose the most appropriate course of action.

COERCIVE POWER   The ability of a manager to punish others.

COLLECTIVE BARGAINING   Negotiations between labor unions and managers to resolve conflicts and disputes about issues such as working hours, wages, benefits, working conditions, and job security.

COLLECTIVISM   A worldview that values subordination of the individual to the goals of the group and adherence to the principle that people should be judged by their contribution to the group.

COMMAND GROUP   A group composed of subordinates who report to the same supervisor; also called department or unit.

COMMUNICATION   The sharing of information between two or more individuals or groups to reach a common understanding.

COMMUNICATION NETWORKS   The pathways along which information flows in groups and teams and throughout the organization.

COMPETITIVE ADVANTAGE   The ability of one organization to outperform other organizations because it produces desired goods or services more efficiently and effectively than they do.

COMPETITORS   Organizations that produce goods and services that are similar to a particular organization's goods and services.

CONCENTRATION ON A SINGLE INDUSTRY   Reinvesting a company's profits to strengthen its competitive position in its current industry.

CONCEPTUAL SKILLS   The ability to analyze and diagnose a situation and to distinguish between cause and effect.

CONCURRENT CONTROL   Control that gives managers immediate feedback on how efficiently inputs are being transformed into outputs so that managers can correct problems as they arise.

CONSCIENTIOUSNESS   The tendency to be careful, scrupulous, and persevering.

CONSIDERATION   Behavior indicating that a manager trusts, respects, and cares about subordinates.

CONTINGENCY THEORY   The idea that the organizational structures and control systems managers choose depend on—are contingent on—characteristics of the external environment in which the organization operates.

CONTROL SYSTEMS   Formal target-setting, monitoring, evaluation, and feedback systems that provide managers with information about how well the organization's strategy and structure are working.

CONTROLLING   Evaluating how well an organization is achieving its goals and taking action to maintain or improve performance; one of the four principal tasks of management.

CORE COMPETENCY   The specific set of departmental skills, knowledge, and experience that allows one organization to outperform another.

CORE MEMBERS   The members of a team who bear primary responsibility for the success of a project and who stay with a project from inception to completion.

CORPORATE-LEVEL PLAN   Top management's decisions pertaining to the organization's mission, overall strategy, and structure.

CORPORATE-LEVEL STRATEGY   A plan that indicates in which industries and national markets an organization intends to compete.

CREATIVITY   A decision maker's ability to discover original and novel ideas that lead to feasible alternative courses of action.

CROSS-FUNCTIONAL TEAM   A group of managers brought together from different departments to perform organizational tasks.

CUSTOMER RELATIONSHIP MANAGEMENT (CRM)   A technique that uses IT to develop an ongoing relationship with customers to maximize the value an organization can deliver to them over time.

CUSTOMERS   Individuals and groups that buy the goods and services that an organization produces.

D

DATA   Raw, unsummarized, and unanalyzed facts.

DECENTRALIZING AUTHORITY   Giving lower-level managers and nonmanagerial employees the right to make important decisions about how to use organizational resources.

DECISION MAKING   The process by which managers respond to opportunities and threats by analyzing options and making determinations about specific organizational goals and courses of action.

DECISION SUPPORT SYSTEM   An interactive computer-based management information system that managers can use to make nonroutine decisions.

DECODING   Interpreting and trying to make sense of a message.

DEFENSIVE APPROACH   Companies and their managers behave ethically to the degree that they stay within the law and abide strictly with legal requirements.

DELPHI TECHNIQUE   A decision-making technique in which group members do not meet face-to-face but respond in writing to questions posed by the group leader.

DEMOGRAPHIC FORCES   Outcomes of changes in, or changing attitudes toward, the characteristics of a population, such as age, gender, ethnic origin, race, sexual orientation, and social class.

DEPARTMENT   A group of people who work together and possess similar skills or use the same knowledge, tools, or techniques to perform their jobs.

DEVELOPMENT   Building the knowledge and skills of organizational members so that they are prepared to take on new responsibilities and challenges.

DEVELOPMENTAL CONSIDERATION   Behavior a leader engages in to support and encourage followers and help them develop and grow on the job.

DEVIL'S ADVOCACY   Critical analysis of a preferred alternative, made in response to challenges raised by a group member who, playing the role of devil's advocate, defends unpopular or opposing alternatives for the sake of argument.

DIFFERENTIATION STRATEGY   Distinguishing an organization's products from the products of competitors on dimensions such as product design, quality, or after-sales service.

DISTRIBUTIVE JUSTICE   A moral principle calling for the distribution of pay raises, promotions, and other organizational resources to be based on meaningful contributions that individuals have made and not on personal characteristics over which they have no control.

DISTRIBUTORS   Organizations that help other organizations sell their goods or services to customers.

DIVERSIFICATION   Expanding a company's business operations into a new industry in order to produce new kinds of valuable goods or services.

DIVERSITY   Differences among people in age, gender, race, ethnicity, religion, sexual orientation, socioeconomic background, and capabilities/disabilities.

DIVISIONAL STRUCTURE   An organizational structure composed of separate business units within which are the functions that work together to produce a specific product for a specific customer.

DIVISION OF LABOR   Splitting the work to be performed into particular tasks and assigning tasks to individual workers.

E

E-COMMERCE   Trade that takes place between companies, and between companies and individual customers, using IT and the Internet.

ECONOMIC FORCES   Interest rates, inflation, unemployment, economic growth, and other factors that affect the general health and well-being of a nation or the regional economy of an organization.

ECONOMIES OF SCALE   Cost advantages associated with large operations.

EFFECTIVE CAREER MANAGEMENT   Ensuring that at all levels in the organization there are well-qualified workers who can assume more responsible positions as needed.

EFFECTIVENESS   A measure of the appropriateness of the goals an organization is pursuing and of the degree to which the organization achieves those goals.

EFFICIENCY   A measure of how well or how productively resources are used to achieve a goal.

EMOTIONAL INTELLIGENCE The ability to understand and manage one's own moods and emotions and the moods and emotions of other people.

EMOTIONS Intense, relatively short-lived feelings.

EMPLOYEE STOCK OPTION A financial instrument that entitles the bearer to buy shares of an organization's stock at a certain price during a certain period of time or under certain conditions.

EMPOWERMENT The expansion of employees' knowledge, tasks, and decision-making responsibilities.

ENCODING Translating a message into understandable symbols or language.

ENTERPRISE RESOURCE PLANNING (ERP) SYSTEMS Multimodule application software packages that coordinate the functional activities necessary to move products from the product design stage to the final customer stage.

ENTREPRENEUR An individual who notices opportunities and decides how to mobilize the resources necessary to produce new and improved goods and services.

ENTREPRENEURSHIP The mobilization of resources to take advantage of an opportunity to provide customers with new or improved goods and services.

EQUAL EMPLOYMENT OPPORTUNITY (EEO) The equal right of all citizens to the opportunity to obtain employment regardless of their gender, age, race, country of origin, religion, or disabilities.

EQUITY The justice, impartiality, and fairness to which all organizational members are entitled.

EQUITY THEORY A theory of motivation that focuses on people's perceptions of the fairness of their work outcomes relative to their work inputs.

ETHICAL DILEMMA The quandary people find themselves in when they have to decide if they should act in a way that might help another person or group even though doing so might go against their own self-interest.

ETHICS The inner guiding moral principles, values, and beliefs that people use to analyze or interpret a situation and then decide what is the "right" or appropriate way to behave.

ETHICS OMBUDSMAN A manager responsible for communicating and teaching ethical standards to all employees and monitoring their conformity to those standards.

EXECUTIVE SUPPORT SYSTEM A sophisticated version of a decision support system that is designed to meet the needs of top managers.

EXPECTANCY In expectancy theory, a perception about the extent to which effort results in a certain level of performance.

EXPECTANCY THEORY The theory that motivation will be high when workers believe that high levels of effort lead to high performance and high performance leads to the attainment of desired outcomes.

EXPERT POWER Power that is based on the special knowledge, skills, and expertise that a leader possesses.

EXPERT SYSTEM A management information system that employs human knowledge, embedded in a computer, to solve problems that ordinarily require human expertise.

EXPORTING Making products at home and selling them abroad.

EXTERNAL LOCUS OF CONTROL The tendency to locate responsibility for one's fate in outside forces and to believe that one's own behavior has little impact on outcomes.

EXTINCTION Curtailing the performance of dysfunctional behaviors by eliminating whatever is reinforcing them.

EXTRAVERSION The tendency to experience positive emotions and moods and to feel good about oneself and the rest of the world.

EXTRINSICALLY MOTIVATED BEHAVIOR Behavior that is performed to acquire material or social rewards or to avoid punishment.

F

FACILITIES LAYOUT The strategy of designing the machine–worker interface to increase operating system efficiency.

FEEDBACK CONTROL Control that gives managers information about customers' reactions to goods and services so that corrective action can be taken if necessary.

FEEDFORWARD CONTROL Control that allows managers to anticipate problems before they arise.

FILTERING Withholding part of a message because of the mistaken belief that the receiver does not need or will not want the information.

FIRST-LINE MANAGER A manager who is responsible for the daily supervision of non-managerial employees.

FLEXIBLE MANUFACTURING The set of techniques that attempt to reduce the costs associated with the product assembly process or the way services are delivered to customers.

FOCUSED DIFFERENTIATION STRATEGY Serving only one segment of the overall market and trying to be the most differentiated organization serving that segment.

FOCUSED LOW-COST STRATEGY Serving only one segment of the overall market and trying to be the lowest-cost organization serving that segment.

FOLKWAYS The routine social conventions of everyday life.

FORMAL APPRAISAL An appraisal conducted at a set time during the year and based on performance dimensions and measures that were specified in advance.

FORMAL GROUP A group that managers establish to achieve organizational goals.

FRANCHISING Selling to a foreign organization the rights to use a brand name and operating know-how in return for a lump-sum payment and a share of the profits.

FREE-TRADE DOCTRINE The idea that if each country specializes in the production of the goods and services that it can produce most efficiently, this will make the best use of global resources.

FRIENDSHIP GROUP An informal group composed of employees who enjoy one another's company and socialize with one another.

FUNCTIONAL STRUCTURE An organizational structure composed of all the departments that an organization requires to produce its goods or services.

FUNCTIONAL-LEVEL PLAN Functional managers' decisions pertaining to the goals that they propose to pursue to help the division attain its business-level goals.

FUNCTIONAL-LEVEL STRATEGY A plan of action to improve the ability of each of an organization's functions to perform its task-specific activities in ways that add value to an organization's goods and services.

G

GATEKEEPING Deciding what information to allow into the organization and what information to keep out.

GENERAL ENVIRONMENT The wide-ranging global, economic, technological, sociocultural, demographic, political, and legal forces that affect an organization and its task environment.

GEOGRAPHIC STRUCTURE An organizational structure in which each region of a country or area of the world is served by a self-contained division.

GLASS CEILING A metaphor alluding to the invisible barriers that prevent minorities and women from being promoted to top corporate positions.

GLOBAL ENVIRONMENT The set of global forces and conditions that operate beyond an organization's boundaries but affect a manager's ability to acquire and utilize resources.

GLOBAL ORGANIZATION An organization that operates and competes in more than one country.

GLOBAL OUTSOURCING The purchase of inputs from overseas suppliers or the production of inputs abroad to lower production costs and improve product quality or design.

GLOBAL STRATEGY Selling the same standardized product and using the same basic marketing approach in each national market.

GLOBALIZATION The set of specific and general forces that work together to integrate and connect economic, political, and social systems *across* countries, cultures, or geographical regions so that nations become increasingly interdependent and similar.

GOAL-SETTING THEORY A theory that focuses on identifying the types of goals that are most effective in producing high levels of motivation and performance and explaining why goals have these effects.

GROUP Two or more people who interact with each other to accomplish certain goals or meet certain needs.

GROUP COHESIVENESS The degree to which members are attracted to or loyal to their group.

GROUP DECISION SUPPORT SYSTEM An executive support system that links top managers so that they can function as a team.

GROUP NORMS Shared guidelines or rules for behavior that most group members follow.

GROUP ROLE A set of behaviors and tasks that a member of a group is expected to perform because of his or her position in the group.

GROUPTHINK A pattern of faulty and biased decision making that occurs in groups whose members strive for agreement among themselves at the expense of accurately assessing information relevant to a decision.

GROUPWARE Computer software that enables members of groups and teams to share information with one another.

H

HAWTHORNE EFFECT The finding that a manager's behavior or leadership approach can affect workers' level of performance.

HERZBERG'S MOTIVATOR-HYGIENE THEORY A need theory that distinguishes between motivator needs (related to the nature of the work itself) and hygiene needs (related to the physical and psychological context in which the work is performed) and proposes that motivator needs must be met for motivation and job satisfaction to be high.

HIERARCHY OF AUTHORITY An organization's chain of command, specifying the relative authority of each manager.

HOSTILE WORK ENVIRONMENT SEXUAL HARASSMENT Telling lewd jokes, displaying pornography, making sexually oriented remarks about someone's personal appearance, and other sex-related actions that make the work environment unpleasant.

HUMAN RELATIONS MOVEMENT A management approach that advocates the idea that supervisors should receive behavioral training to manage subordinates in ways that elicit their cooperation and increase their productivity.

HUMAN RESOURCE MANAGEMENT (HRM) Activities that managers engage in to attract and retain employees and to ensure that they perform at a high level and contribute to the accomplishment of organizational goals.

HUMAN RESOURCE PLANNING Activities that managers engage in to forecast their current and future needs for human resources.

HUMAN SKILLS The ability to understand, alter, lead, and control the behavior of other individuals and groups.

HYBRID STRUCTURE The structure of a large organization that has many divisions and simultaneously uses many different organizational structures.

HYPERCOMPETITION Permanent, ongoing, intense competition brought about in an industry by advancing technology or changing customer tastes.

I

ILLUSION OF CONTROL A source of cognitive bias resulting from the tendency to overestimate one's own ability to control activities and events.

IMPORTING Selling products at home that are made abroad.

INCREMENTAL PRODUCT INNOVATION The gradual improvement and refinement to existing products that occurs over time as existing technologies are perfected.

INDIVIDUAL ETHICS Personal standards and values that determine how people view their responsibilities to others and how they should act in situations when their own self-interests are at stake.

INDIVIDUALISM A worldview that values individual freedom and self-expression and adherence to the principle that people should be judged by their individual achievements rather than by their social background.

INEQUITY Lack of fairness.

INFORMAL APPRAISAL An unscheduled appraisal of ongoing progress and areas for improvement.

INFORMAL GROUP A group that managers or nonmanagerial employees form to help achieve their own goals or meet their own needs.

INFORMAL ORGANIZATION The system of behavioral rules and norms that emerge in a group.

INFORMATION Data that are organized in a meaningful fashion.

INFORMATION DISTORTION Changes in the meaning of a message as the message passes through a series of senders and receivers.

INFORMATION OVERLOAD The potential for important information to be ignored or overlooked while tangential information receives attention.

INFORMATION RICHNESS The amount of information that a communication medium can carry and the extent to which the medium enables the sender and receiver to reach a common understanding.

INFORMATION SYSTEM A system for acquiring, organizing, storing, manipulating, and transmitting information.

INFORMATION TECHNOLOGY The set of methods or techniques for acquiring, organizing, storing, manipulating, and transmitting information.

INITIATING STRUCTURE Behavior that managers engage in to ensure that work gets done, subordinates perform their jobs acceptably, and the organization is efficient and effective.

INITIATIVE The ability to act on one's own, without direction from a superior.

INNOVATION The process of creating new or improved goods and services or developing better ways to produce or provide them.

INPUT Anything a person contributes to his or her job or organization.

INSTRUMENTAL VALUE A mode of conduct that an individual seeks to follow.

INSTRUMENTALITY In expectancy theory, a perception about the extent to which performance results in the attainment of outcomes.

INTEGRATING MECHANISMS Organizing tools that managers can use to increase communication and coordination among functions and divisions.

INTELLECTUAL STIMULATION   Behavior a leader engages in to make followers aware of problems and view these problems in new ways, consistent with the leader's vision.

INTEREST GROUP   An informal group composed of employees seeking to achieve a common goal related to their membership in an organization.

INTERNAL LOCUS OF CONTROL   The tendency to locate responsibility for one's fate within oneself.

INTERNET   A global system of computer networks.

INTRANET   A companywide system of computer networks.

INTRAPRENEUR   A manager, scientist, or researcher who works inside an organization and notices opportunities to develop new or improved products and better ways to make them.

INTRINSICALLY MOTIVATED BEHAVIOR   Behavior that is performed for its own sake.

INTUITION   Feelings, beliefs, and hunches that come readily to mind, require little effort and information gathering, and result in on-the-spot decisions.

INVENTORY   The stock of raw materials, inputs, and component parts that an organization has on hand at a particular time.

J

JARGON   Specialized language that members of an occupation, group, or organization develop to facilitate communication among themselves.

JOB ANALYSIS   Identifying the tasks, duties, and responsibilities that make up a job and the knowledge, skills, and abilities needed to perform the job.

JOB DESIGN   The process by which managers decide how to divide tasks into specific jobs.

JOB ENLARGEMENT   Increasing the number of different tasks in a given job by changing the division of labor.

JOB ENRICHMENT   Increasing the degree of responsibility a worker has over his or her job.

JOB SATISFACTION   The collection of feelings and beliefs that managers have about their current jobs.

JOB SIMPLIFICATION   The process of reducing the number of tasks that each worker performs.

JOB SPECIALIZATION   The process by which a division of labor occurs as different workers specialize in different tasks over time.

JOINT VENTURE   A strategic alliance among two or more companies that agree to jointly establish and share the ownership of a new business.

JUST-IN-TIME (JIT) INVENTORY SYSTEM   A system in which parts or supplies arrive at an organization when they are needed, not before.

JUSTICE RULE   An ethical decision is a decision that distributes benefits and harms among people and groups in a fair, equitable, or impartial way.

K

KNOWLEDGE MANAGEMENT SYSTEM   A company-specific virtual information system that systematizes the knowledge of its employees and facilitates the sharing and integrating of their expertise.

L

LABOR RELATIONS   The activities that managers engage in to ensure that they have effective working relationships with the labor unions that represent their employees' interests.

LATERAL MOVE   A job change that entails no major changes in responsibility or authority levels.

LEADER   An individual who is able to exert influence over other people to help achieve group or organizational goals.

LEADER–MEMBER RELATIONS   The extent to which followers like, trust, and are loyal to their leader; a determinant of how favorable a situation is for leading.

LEADERSHIP   The process by which an individual exerts influence over other people and inspires, motivates, and directs their activities to help achieve group or organizational goals.

LEADERSHIP SUBSTITUTE   A characteristic of a subordinate or of a situation or context that acts in place of the influence of a leader and makes leadership unnecessary.

LEADING   Articulating a clear vision and energizing and enabling organizational members so that they understand the part they play in achieving organizational goals; one of the four principal tasks of management.

LEARNING   A relatively permanent change in knowledge or behavior that results from practice or experience.

LEARNING ORGANIZATION   An organization in which managers try to maximize the ability of individuals and groups to think

and behave creatively and thus maximize the potential for organizational learning to take place.

LEARNING THEORIES   Theories that focus on increasing employee motivation and performance by linking the outcomes that employees receive to the performance of desired behaviors and the attainment of goals.

LEGITIMATE POWER   The authority that a manager has by virtue of his or her position in an organization's hierarchy.

LICENSING   Allowing a foreign organization to take charge of manufacturing and distributing a product in its country or world region in return for a negotiated fee.

LINEAR CAREER   A career consisting of a sequence of jobs in which each new job entails additional responsibility, a greater impact on an organization, new skills, and upward movement in an organization's hierarchy.

LINE MANAGER   Someone in the direct line or chain of command who has formal authority over people and resources at lower levels.

LINE OF AUTHORITY   The chain of command extending from the top to the bottom of an organization.

LONG-TERM ORIENTATION   A worldview that values thrift and persistence in achieving goals.

LOW-COST STRATEGY   Driving the organization's costs down below the costs of its rivals.

M

MANAGEMENT   The planning, organizing, leading, and controlling of human and other resources to achieve organizational goals efficiently and effectively.

MANAGEMENT BY OBJECTIVES (MBO)   A goal-setting process in which a manager and each of his or her subordinates negotiate specific goals and objectives for the subordinate to achieve and then periodically evaluate the extent to which the subordinate is achieving those goals.

MANAGEMENT BY WANDERING AROUND   A face-to-face communication technique in which a manager walks around a work area and talks informally with employees about issues and concerns.

MANAGEMENT INFORMATION SYSTEM (MIS)   A specific form of IT that managers utilize to generate the specific, detailed information they need to perform their roles effectively.

MARKET STRUCTURE An organizational structure in which each kind of customer is served by a self-contained division; also called *customer structure.*

MASLOW'S HIERARCHY OF NEEDS An arrangement of five basic needs that, according to Maslow, motivate behavior. Maslow proposed that the lowest level of unmet needs is the prime motivator and that only one level of needs is motivational at a time.

MATRIX STRUCTURE An organizational structure that simultaneously groups people and resources by function and by product.

MECHANISTIC STRUCTURE An organizational structure in which authority is centralized, tasks and rules are clearly specified, and employees are closely supervised.

MEDIUM The pathway through which an encoded message is transmitted to a receiver.

MENTORING A process by which an experienced member of an organization (the mentor) provides advice and guidance to a less experienced member (the protégé) and helps the less experienced member learn how to advance in the organization and in his or her career.

MERIT PAY PLAN A compensation plan that bases pay on performance.

MESSAGE The information that a sender wants to share.

MIDDLE MANAGER A manager who supervises first-line managers and is responsible for finding the best way to use resources to achieve organizational goals.

MISSION STATEMENT A broad declaration of an organization's purpose that identifies the organization's products and customers and distinguishes the organization from its competitors.

MOOD A feeling or state of mind.

MORAL RIGHTS RULE An ethical decision is one that best maintains and protects the fundamental or inalienable rights and privileges of the people affected by it.

MORES Norms that are considered to be central to the functioning of society and to social life.

MOTIVATION Psychological forces that determine the direction of a person's behavior in an organization, a person's level of effort, and a person's level of persistence.

MULTIDOMESTIC STRATEGY Customizing products and marketing strategies to specific national conditions.

N

NATIONAL CULTURE The set of values that a society considers important and the norms of behavior that are approved or sanctioned in that society.

NEED A requirement or necessity for survival and well-being.

NEED FOR ACHIEVEMENT The extent to which an individual has a strong desire to perform challenging tasks well and to meet personal standards for excellence.

NEED FOR AFFILIATION The extent to which an individual is concerned about establishing and maintaining good interpersonal relations, being liked, and having other people get along.

NEED FOR POWER The extent to which an individual desires to control or influence others.

NEED THEORIES Theories of motivation that focus on what needs people are trying to satisfy at work and what outcomes will satisfy those needs.

NEEDS ASSESSMENT An assessment of which employees need training or development and what type of skills or knowledge they need to acquire.

NEGATIVE AFFECTIVITY The tendency to experience negative emotions and moods, to feel distressed, and to be critical of oneself and others.

NEGATIVE REINFORCEMENT Eliminating or removing undesired outcomes when people perform organizationally functional behaviors.

NETWORKING The exchange of information through a group or network of interlinked computers.

NETWORK STRUCTURE A series of strategic alliances that an organization creates with suppliers, manufacturers, and distributors to produce and market a product.

NOISE Anything that hampers any stage of the communication process.

NOMINAL GROUP TECHNIQUE A decision-making technique in which group members write down ideas and solutions, read their suggestions to the whole group, and discuss and then rank the alternatives.

NONPROGRAMMED DECISION MAKING Nonroutine decision making that occurs in response to unusual, unpredictable opportunities and threats.

NONVERBAL COMMUNICATION The encoding of messages by means of facial expressions, body language, and styles of dress.

NORMS Unwritten, informal codes of conduct that prescribe how people should act in particular situations and are considered important by most members of a group or organization.

NURTURING ORIENTATION A worldview that values the quality of life, warm personal friendships, and services and care for the weak.

O

OBJECTIVE APPRAISAL An appraisal that is based on facts and is likely to be numerical.

OCCUPATIONAL ETHICS Standards that govern how members of a profession, trade, or craft should conduct themselves when performing work-related activities.

ON-THE-JOB TRAINING Training that takes place in the work setting as employees perform their job tasks.

OPENNESS TO EXPERIENCE The tendency to be original, have broad interests, be open to a wide range of stimuli, be daring, and take risks.

OPERANT CONDITIONING THEORY The theory that people learn to perform behaviors that lead to desired consequences and learn not to perform behaviors that lead to undesired consequences.

OPERATING BUDGET A budget that states how managers intend to use organizational resources to achieve organizational goals.

OPERATING SYSTEM SOFTWARE Software that tells computer hardware how to run.

OPERATIONS INFORMATION SYSTEM A management information system that gathers, organizes, and summarizes comprehensive data in a form that managers can use in their nonroutine coordinating, controlling, and decision-making tasks.

OPERATIONS MANAGEMENT The management of any aspect of the production system that transforms inputs into finished goods and services.

OPERATIONS MANAGER A manager who is responsible for managing an organization's production system and for determining where operating improvements might be made.

OPTIMUM DECISION The most appropriate decision in light of what managers believe to be the most desirable future consequences for the organization.

ORDER The methodical arrangement of positions to provide the organization with the greatest benefit and to provide employees with career opportunities.

ORGANIC STRUCTURE   An organizational structure in which authority is decentralized to middle and first-line managers and tasks and roles are left ambiguous to encourage employees to cooperate and respond quickly to the unexpected.

ORGANIZATION   A collection of people who work together and coordinate their actions to achieve a wide variety of goals or desired future outcomes.

ORGANIZATION CHANGE   The movement of an organization away from its present state and toward some desired future state to increase its efficiency and effectiveness.

ORGANIZATIONAL BEHAVIOR   The study of factors that affect how individuals and groups respond to and act in organizations.

ORGANIZATIONAL BEHAVIOR MODIFICA-TION (OB MOD)   The systematic application of operant conditioning techniques to promote the performance of organizationally functional behaviors and discourage the performance of dysfunctional behaviors.

ORGANIZATIONAL CITIZENSHIP BEHAV-IORS (OCBs)   Behaviors that are not required of organizational members but that contribute to and are necessary for organizational efficiency, effectiveness, and competitive advantage.

ORGANIZATIONAL COMMITMENT   The collection of feelings and beliefs that managers have about their organization as a whole.

ORGANIZATIONAL CULTURE   The shared set of beliefs, expectations, values, norms, and work routines that influence the ways in which individuals, groups, and teams interact with one another and cooperate to achieve organizational goals.

ORGANIZATIONAL DESIGN   The process by which managers make specific organizing choices that result in a particular kind of organizational structure.

ORGANIZATIONAL ENVIRONMENT   The set of forces and conditions that operate beyond an organization's boundaries but affect a manager's ability to acquire and utilize resources.

ORGANIZATIONAL ETHICS   The guiding practices and beliefs through which a particular company and its managers view their responsibility toward their stakeholders.

ORGANIZATIONAL LEARNING   The process through which managers seek to improve employees' desire and ability to understand and manage the organization and its task environment.

ORGANIZATIONAL PERFORMANCE   A measure of how efficiently and effectively a manager uses resources to satisfy customers and achieve organizational goals.

ORGANIZATIONAL SOCIALIZATION   The process by which newcomers learn an organization's values and norms and acquire the work behaviors necessary to perform jobs effectively.

ORGANIZATIONAL STRUCTURE   A formal system of task and reporting relationships that coordinates and motivates organizational members so that they work together to achieve organizational goals.

ORGANIZING   Structuring working relationships in a way that allows organizational members to work together to achieve organizational goals; one of the four principal tasks of management.

OUTCOME   Anything a person gets from a job or organization.

OUTSOURCE   To use outside suppliers and manufacturers to produce goods and services.

OUTSOURCING   Contracting with another company, usually abroad, to have it perform an activity the organization previously performed itself.

OVERPAYMENT INEQUITY   The inequity that exists when a person perceives that his or her own outcome–input ratio is greater than the ratio of a referent.

P

PATH–GOAL THEORY   A contingency model of leadership proposing that leaders can motivate subordinates by identifying their desired outcomes, rewarding them for high performance and the attainment of work goals with these desired outcomes, and clarifying for them the paths leading to the attainment of work goals.

PAY LEVEL   The relative position of an organization's pay incentives in comparison with those of other organizations in the same industry employing similar kinds of workers.

PAY STRUCTURE   The arrangement of jobs into categories reflecting their relative importance to the organization and its goals, levels of skill required, and other characteristics.

PERCEPTION   The process through which people select, organize, and interpret what they see, hear, touch, smell, and taste to give meaning and order to the world around them.

PERFORMANCE APPRAISAL   The evaluation of employees' job performance and contributions to their organization.

PERFORMANCE FEEDBACK   The process through which managers share performance appraisal information with subordinates, give subordinates an opportunity to reflect on

their own performance, and develop, with subordinates, plans for the future.

PERSONALITY TRAITS   Enduring tendencies to feel, think, and act in certain ways.

PLANNING   Identifying and selecting appropriate goals and courses of action; one of the four principal tasks of management.

POLITICAL AND LEGAL FORCES   Outcomes of changes in laws and regulations, such as the deregulation of industries, the privatization of organizations, and the increased emphasis on environmental protection.

POOLED TASK INTERDEPENDENCE   The task interdependence that exists when group members make separate and independent contributions to group performance.

POSITION POWER   The amount of legitimate, reward, and coercive power that a leader has by virtue of his or her position in an organization; a determinant of how favorable a situation is for leading.

POSITIVE REINFORCEMENT   Giving people outcomes they desire when they perform organizationally functional behaviors.

POTENTIAL COMPETITORS   Organizations that presently are not in a task environment but could enter if they so choose.

POWER DISTANCE   The degree to which societies accept the idea that inequalities in the power and well-being of their citizens are due to differences in individuals' physical and intellectual capabilities and heritage.

PRACTICAL RULE   An ethical decision is one that a manager has no reluctance about communicating to people outside the company because the typical person in a society would think it is acceptable.

PROACTIVE APPROACH   Companies and their managers actively embrace socially responsible behavior, going out of their way to learn about the needs of different stakeholder groups and utilizing organizational resources to promote the interests of all stakeholders.

PROCEDURAL JUSTICE   A moral principle calling for the use of fair procedures to determine how to distribute outcomes to organizational members.

PROCESS REENGINEERING   The fundamental rethinking and radical redesign of business processes to achieve dramatic improvement in critical measures of performance such as cost, quality, service, and speed.

PRODUCT CHAMPION   A manager who takes "ownership" of a project and provides the leadership and vision that take a product from the idea stage to the final customer.

PRODUCT DEVELOPMENT The management of the value chain activities involved in bringing new or improved goods and services to the market.

PRODUCT LIFE CYCLE The way demand for a product changes in a predictable pattern over time.

PRODUCT STRUCTURE An organizational structure in which each product line or business is handled by a self-contained division.

PRODUCT TEAM STRUCTURE An organizational structure in which employees are permanently assigned to a cross-functional team and report only to the product team manager or to one of his or her direct subordinates.

PRODUCTION BLOCKING A loss of productivity in brainstorming sessions due to the unstructured nature of brainstorming.

PRODUCTION SYSTEM The system that an organization uses to acquire inputs, convert the inputs into outputs, and dispose of the outputs.

PROFESSIONAL ETHICS Standards that govern how members of a profession are to make decisions when the way they should behave is not clear-cut.

PROGRAMMED DECISION MAKING Routine, virtually automatic decision making that follows established rules or guidelines.

PROSOCIALLY MOTIVATED BEHAVIOR Behavior that is performed to benefit or help others.

PUNISHMENT Administering an undesired or negative consequence when dysfunctional behavior occurs.

Q

QUID PRO QUO SEXUAL HARASSMENT Asking for or forcing an employee to perform sexual favors in exchange for receiving some reward or avoiding negative consequences.

R

REAL-TIME INFORMATION Frequently updated information that reflects current conditions.

REALISTIC JOB PREVIEW (RJP) An honest assessment of the advantages and disadvantages of a job and organization.

REASONED JUDGMENT A decision that takes time and effort to make and results from careful information gathering, generation of alternatives, and evaluation of alternatives.

RECEIVER The person or group for which a message is intended.

RECIPROCAL TASK INTERDEPENDENCE The task interdependence that exists when the work performed by each group member is fully dependent on the work performed by other group members.

RECRUITMENT Activities that managers engage in to develop a pool of qualified candidates for open positions.

REFERENT POWER Power that comes from subordinates' and coworkers' respect, admiration, and loyalty.

RELATED DIVERSIFICATION Entering a new business or industry to create a competitive advantage in one or more of an organization's existing divisions or businesses.

RELATIONSHIP-ORIENTED LEADERS Leaders whose primary concern is to develop good relationships with their subordinates and to be liked by them

RELIABILITY The degree to which a tool or test measures the same thing each time it is used.

REPUTATION The esteem or high repute that individuals or organizations gain when they behave ethically.

RESEARCH AND DEVELOPMENT TEAM A team whose members have the expertise and experience needed to develop new products.

RESTRUCTURING Downsizing an organization by eliminating the jobs of large numbers of top, middle, and first-line managers and nonmanagerial employees.

REWARD POWER The ability of a manager to give or withhold tangible and intangible rewards.

RISK The degree of probability that the possible outcomes of a particular course of action will occur.

ROLE MAKING Taking the initiative to modify an assigned role by assuming additional responsibilities.

RULES Formal written instructions that specify actions to be taken under different circumstances to achieve specific goals.

S

SATISFICING Searching for and choosing an acceptable, or satisfactory, response to problems and opportunities, rather than trying to make the best decision.

SCIENTIFIC MANAGEMENT The systematic study of relationships between people and tasks for the purpose of redesigning the work process to increase efficiency.

SELECTION The process that managers use to determine the relative qualifications of job applicants and their potential for performing well in a particular job.

SELF-EFFICACY A person's belief about his or her ability to perform a behavior successfully.

SELF-ESTEEM The degree to which individuals feel good about themselves and their capabilities.

SELF-MANAGED TEAM A group of employees who assume responsibility for organizing, controlling, and supervising their own activities and monitoring the quality of the goods and services they provide.

SELF-MANAGED WORK TEAM A group of employees who supervise their own activities and monitor the quality of the goods and services they provide.

SELF-REINFORCER Any desired or attractive outcome or reward that a person gives to himself or herself for good performance.

SENDER The person or group wishing to share information.

SEQUENTIAL TASK INTERDEPENDENCE The task interdependence that exists when group members must perform specific tasks in a predetermined order.

SERVANT LEADER A leader who has a strong desire to serve and work for the benefit of others.

SHORT-TERM ORIENTATION A worldview that values personal stability or happiness and living for the present.

SKUNKWORKS A group of intrapreneurs who are deliberately separated from the normal operation of an organization to encourage them to devote all their attention to developing new products.

SOCIAL ENTREPRENEUR An individual who pursues initiatives and opportunities and mobilizes resources to address social problems and needs in order to improve society and well-being through creative solutions.

SOCIAL LEARNING THEORY A theory that takes into account how learning and motivation are influenced by people's thoughts and beliefs and their observations of other people's behavior.

SOCIAL LOAFING The tendency of individuals to put forth less effort when they work in groups than when they work alone.

SOCIAL RESPONSIBILITY The way a company's managers and employees view their duty or obligation to make decisions that protect, enhance, and promote the welfare and well-being of stakeholders and society as a whole.

SOCIAL STRUCTURE   The arrangement of relationships between individuals and groups in a society.

SOCIETAL ETHICS   Standards that govern how members of a society should deal with one another in matters involving issues such as fairness, justice, poverty, and the rights of the individual.

SOCIOCULTURAL FORCES   Pressures emanating from the social structure of a country or society or from the national culture.

SPAN OF CONTROL   The number of subordinates who report directly to a manager.

SPIRAL CAREER   A career consisting of a series of jobs that build on each other but tend to be fundamentally different.

STAFF MANAGER   Someone responsible for managing a specialist function, such as finance or marketing.

STAKEHOLDERS   The people and groups that supply a company with its productive resources and so have a claim on and stake in the company.

STANDARD OPERATING PROCEDURES (SOPs)   Specific sets of written instructions about how to perform a certain aspect of a task.

STEADY-STATE CAREER   A career consisting of the same kind of job during a large part of an individual's work life.

STEREOTYPE   Simplistic and often inaccurate beliefs about the typical characteristics of particular groups of people.

STRATEGIC ALLIANCE   An agreement in which managers pool or share their organization's resources and know-how with a foreign company, and the two organizations share the rewards and risks of starting a new venture.

STRATEGIC HUMAN RESOURCE MANAGEMENT   The process by which managers design the components of an HRM system to be consistent with each other, with other elements of organizational architecture, and with the organization's strategy and goals.

STRATEGIC LEADERSHIP   The ability of the CEO and top managers to convey a compelling vision of what they want the organization to achieve to their subordinates.

STRATEGY   A cluster of decisions about what goals to pursue, what actions to take, and how to use resources to achieve goals.

STRATEGY FORMULATION   The development of a set of corporate-, business-, and functional-level strategies that allow an organization to accomplish its mission and achieve its goals.

SUBJECTIVE APPRAISAL   An appraisal that is based on perceptions of traits, behaviors, or results.

SUPPLIERS   Individuals and organizations that provide an organization with the input resources that it needs to produce goods and services.

SWOT ANALYSIS   A planning exercise in which managers identify organizational strengths (S) and weaknesses (W) and environmental opportunities (O) and threats (T).

SYNERGY   Performance gains that result when individuals and departments coordinate their actions.

T

TARIFF   A tax that a government imposes on imported or, occasionally, exported goods.

TASK ENVIRONMENT   The set of forces and conditions that originate with suppliers, distributors, customers, and competitors and affect an organization's ability to obtain inputs and dispose of its outputs because they influence managers on a daily basis.

TASK FORCE   A committee of managers or nonmanagerial employees from various departments or divisions who meet to solve a specific, mutual problem; also called *ad hoc committee*.

TASK INTERDEPENDENCE   The degree to which the work performed by one member of a group influences the work performed by other members.

TASK STRUCTURE   The extent to which the work to be performed is clear-cut so that a leader's subordinates know what needs to be accomplished and how to go about doing it; a determinant of how favorable a situation is for leading.

TASK-ORIENTED LEADERS   Leaders whose primary concern is to ensure that subordinates perform at a high level.

TEAM   A group whose members work intensely with one another to achieve a specific common goal or objective.

TECHNICAL SKILLS   The job-specific knowledge and techniques required to perform an organizational role.

TECHNOLOGICAL FORCES   Outcomes of changes in the technology that managers use to design, produce, or distribute goods and services.

TECHNOLOGY   The combination of skills and equipment that managers use in the design, production, and distribution of goods and services.

TERMINAL VALUE   A lifelong goal or objective that an individual seeks to achieve.

THEORY X   A set of negative assumptions about workers that lead to the conclusion that a manager's task is to supervise workers closely and control their behavior.

THEORY Y   A set of positive assumptions about workers that lead to the conclusion that a manager's task is to create a work setting that encourages commitment to organizational goals and provides opportunities for workers to be imaginative and to exercise initiative and self-direction.

360-DEGREE APPRAISAL   A performance appraisal by peers, subordinates, superiors, and sometimes clients who are in a position to evaluate a manager's performance.

TIME HORIZON   The intended duration of a plan.

TOP MANAGER   A manager who establishes organizational goals, decides how departments should interact, and monitors the performance of middle managers.

TOP-DOWN CHANGE   A fast, revolutionary approach to change in which top managers identify what needs to be changed and then move quickly to implement the changes throughout the organization.

TOP-MANAGEMENT TEAM   A group composed of the CEO, the COO, the president, and the heads of the most important departments.

TRAINING   Teaching organizational members how to perform their current jobs and helping them acquire the knowledge and skills they need to be effective performers.

TRANSACTION-PROCESSING SYSTEM   A management information system designed to handle large volumes of routine, recurring transactions.

TRANSACTIONAL LEADERSHIP   Leadership that motivates subordinates by rewarding them for high performance and reprimanding them for low performance.

TRANSFORMATIONAL LEADERSHIP   Leadership that makes subordinates aware of the importance of their jobs and performance to the organization and aware of their own needs for personal growth and that motivates subordinates to work for the good of the organization.

TRANSITORY CAREER   A career in which a person changes jobs frequently and in which each job is different from the one that precedes it.

TRUST   The willingness of one person or group to have faith or confidence in the goodwill of another person, even though this puts them at risk.

TURNAROUND MANAGEMENT   The creation of a new vision for a struggling company based on a new approach to planning and organizing to make better use of a company's resources to allow it to survive and prosper.

U

UNCERTAINTY   Unpredictability.

UNCERTAINTY AVOIDANCE   The degree to which societies are willing to tolerate uncertainty and risk.

UNDERPAYMENT INEQUITY   The inequity that exists when a person perceives that his or her own outcome–input ratio is less than the ratio of a referent.

UNRELATED DIVERSIFICATION   Entering a new industry or buying a company in a new industry that is not related in any way to an organization's current businesses or industries.

UTILITARIAN RULE   An ethical decision is a decision that produces the greatest good for the greatest number of people.

V

VALENCE   In expectancy theory, how desirable each of the outcomes available from a job or organization is to a person.

VALIDITY   The degree to which a tool or test measures what it purports to measure.

VALUE CHAIN   The coordinated series or sequence of functional activities necessary to transform inputs such as new product concepts, raw materials, component parts, or professional skills into the finished goods or services customers value and want to buy.

VALUE SYSTEM   The terminal and instrumental values that are guiding principles in an individual's life.

VALUES   Ideas about what a society believes to be good, right, desirable, or beautiful.

VERBAL COMMUNICATION   The encoding of messages into words, either written or spoken.

VERTICAL INTEGRATION   Expanding a company's operations either backward into an industry that produces inputs for its products or forward into an industry that uses, distributes, or sells its products.

VICARIOUS LEARNING   Learning that occurs when the learner becomes motivated to perform a behavior by watching another person perform it and be reinforced for doing so; also called *observational learning.*

VIRTUAL TEAM   A team whose members rarely or never meet face-to-face but, rather, interact by using various forms of information technology such as e-mail, computer networks, telephone, fax, and videoconferences.

W

WHOLLY OWNED FOREIGN SUBSIDIARY   Production operations established in a foreign country independent of any local direct involvement.

CREDITS

Notes

Chapter 1

1. H. Dalton, "Apple Chief Tim Cook Opts Out of $75 Million Dividend," www.guardian.co.uk, May 25, 2012.

2. www.apple.com, 2012.

3. G. R. Jones, *Organizational Theory, Design, and Change* (Upper Saddle River, NJ: Pearson, 2008).

4. J. P. Campbell, "On the Nature of Organizational Effectiveness," in P. S. Goodman, J. M. Pennings, et al., *New Perspectives on Organizational Effectiveness* (San Francisco: Jossey-Bass, 1977).

5. M. J. Provitera, "What Management Is: How It Works and Why It's Everyone's Business," *Academy of Management Executive* 17 (August 2003), 152–54.

6. J. McGuire and E. Matta, "CEO Stock Options: The Silent Dimension of Ownership," *Academy of Management Journal* 46 (April 2003), 255–66.

7. www.apple.com, press releases, 2000, 2001, 2003, 2006, 2008, 2009, 2010.

8. www2.goldmansachs.com, 2010; www.jpmorganchase.com, 2010.

9. J. G. Combs and M. S. Skill, "Managerialist and Human Capital Explanations for Key Executive Pay Premium: A Contingency Perspective," *Academy of Management Journal* 46 (February 2003), 63–74.

10. H. Fayol, *General and Industrial Management* (New York: IEEE Press, 1984). Fayol actually identified five different managerial tasks, but most scholars today believe these four capture the essence of Fayol's ideas.

11. P. F. Drucker, *Management Tasks, Responsibilities, and Practices* (New York: Harper & Row, 1974).

12. www.apple.com, press release, 2003.

13. G. McWilliams, "Lean Machine—How Dell Fine-Tunes Its PC Pricing to Gain Edge in a Slow Market," *The Wall Street Journal*, June 8, 2001, A1.

14. C. P. Hales, "What Do Managers Do? A Critical Review of the Evidence," *Journal of Management Studies,* January 1986, 88–115; A. I. Kraul, P. R.

Pedigo, D. D. McKenna, and M. D. Dunnette, "The Role of the Manager: What's Really Important in Different Management Jobs," *Academy of Management Executive,* November 1989, 286–93.

15. A. K. Gupta, "Contingency Perspectives on Strategic Leadership," in D. C. Hambrick, ed., *The Executive Effect: Concepts and Methods for Studying Top Managers* (Greenwich, CT: JAI Press, 1988), 147–78.

16. D. G. Ancona, "Top Management Teams: Preparing for the Revolution," in J. S. Carroll, ed., *Applied Social Psychology and Organizational Settings* (Hillsdale, NJ: Erlbaum, 1990); D. C. Hambrick and P. A. Mason, "Upper Echelons: The Organization as a Reflection of Its Top Managers," *Academy of Management Journal* 9 (1984), 193–206.

17. T. A. Mahony, T. H. Jerdee, and S. J. Carroll, "The Jobs of Management," *Industrial Relations* 4 (1965), 97–110; L. Gomez-Mejia, J. McCann, and R. C. Page, "The Structure of Managerial Behaviors and Rewards," *Industrial Relations* 24 (1985), 147–54.

18. W. R. Nord and M. J. Waller, "The Human Organization of Time: Temporal Realities and Experiences," *Academy of Management Review* 29 (January 2004), 137–40.

19. R. L. Katz, "Skills of an Effective Administrator," *Harvard Business Review,* September–October 1974, 90–102.

20. Ibid.

21. P. Tharenou, "Going Up? Do Traits and Informal Social Processes Predict Advancing in Management," *Academy of Management Journal* 44 (October 2001), 1005–18.

22. C. J. Collins and K. D. Clark, "Strategic Human Resource Practices, Top Management Team Social Networks, and Firm Performance: The Role of Human Resource Practices in Creating Organizational Competitive Advantage," *Academy of Management Journal* 46 (December 2003), 740–52.

23. R. Stewart, "Middle Managers: Their Jobs and Behaviors," in J. W.

Lorsch, ed., *Handbook of Organizational Behavior* (Englewood Cliffs, NJ: Prentice-Hall, 1987), 385–91.

24. S. C. de Janasz, S. E. Sullivan, and V. Whiting, "Mentor Networks and Career Success: Lessons for Turbulent Times," *Academy of Management Executive* 17 (November 2003), 78–92.

25. K. Labich, "Making Over Middle Managers," *Fortune*, May 8, 1989, 58–64.

26. B. Wysocki, "Some Companies Cut Costs Too Far, Suffer from Corporate Anorexia," *The Wall Street Journal*, July 5, 1995, A1.

27. Ibid.

28. www.dell.com, 2008, 2010, 2012.

29. K. Peterson, "Boeing 787 Delays Cast Hard Light on Outsourcing," www.reuters.com, April 11, 2011.

30. www.boeing.com, press release, 2011, 2012.

31. K. Maher and B. Tita, "Caterpillar Joins 'Onshoring' Trend," www.yahoo.com, March 12, 2010.

32. S. R. Parker, T. D. Wall, and P. R. Jackson, "That's Not My Job: Developing Flexible Work Orientations," *Academy of Management Journal* 40 (1997), 899–929.

33. B. Dumaine, "The New Non-Manager," *Fortune*, February 22, 1993, 80–84.

34. H. G. Baum, A. C. Joel, and E. A. Mannix, "Management Challenges in a New Time," *Academy of Management Journal* 45 (October 2002), 916–31.

35. A. Shama, "Management under Fire: The Transformation of Management in the Soviet Union and Eastern Europe," *Academy of Management Executive* 10 (1993), 22–35.

36. www.apple.com, 2010; www.nike.com, 2010.

37. K. Seiders and L. L. Berry, "Service Fairness: What It Is and Why It Matters," *Academy of Management Executive* 12 (1998), 8–20.

37. K. Seiders and L. L. Berry, "Service Fairness: What It Is and Why It Matters," *Academy of Management Executive* 12 (1998), 8–20.

495

38. Ibid.

39. C. Anderson, "Values-Based Management," *Academy of Management Executive* 11 (1997), 25–46.

40. W. H. Shaw and V. Barry, *Moral Issues in Business,* 6th ed. (Belmont, CA: Wadsworth, 1995); T. Donaldson, *Corporations and Morality* (Englewood Cliffs, NJ: Prentice-Hall, 1982).

41. www.apple.com, press release, 2010.

42. www.sec.gov, 2010.

43. D. Janoski, "Conohan, Ciavarella Face New Charges," www.thetimestribune.com, September 10, 2009.

44. D. Janoski, "Conohan, Ciavarella Deny New Charges," www.thetimestribune.com, September 15, 2009.

45. S. Jackson et al., *Diversity in the Workplace: Human Resource Initiatives* (New York: Guilford Press, 1992).

46. G. Robinson and C. S. Daus, "Building a Case for Diversity," *Academy of Management Executive* 3 (1997), 21–31; S. J. Bunderson and K. M. Sutcliffe, "Comparing Alternative Conceptualizations of Functional Diversity in Management Teams: Process and Performance Effects," *Academy of Management Journal* 45 (October 2002), 875–94.

47. D. Jamieson and J. O'Mara, *Managing Workforce 2000: Gaining a Diversity Advantage* (San Francisco: Jossey-Bass, 1991).

48. http://digital.virtualmarketing partners.com/vmp/accenture/diversity-inclusion/index.php, 2010.

49. Press release, "Dell CEO Kevin Rollins Cites Workforce Diversity as Key to Gaining Competitive Advantages in Business," www.dell.com, March 6, 2006.

50. "Union Bank of California Honored by U.S. Labor Department for Employment Practices," press release, September 11, 2000.

Appendix A

1. F. W. Taylor, *Shop Management* (New York: Harper, 1903); F. W. Taylor, *The Principles of Scientific Management* (New York: Harper, 1911).

2. L. W. Fry, "The Maligned F. W. Taylor: A Reply to His Many Critics," *Academy of Management Review* 1 (1976), 124–29.

3. J. A. Litterer, *The Emergence of Systematic Management as Shown by the Literature from 1870–1900* (New York: Garland, 1986).

4. D. Wren, *The Evolution of Management Thought* (New York: Wiley, 1994), 134.

5. C. Perrow, *Complex Organizations,* 2nd ed. (Glenview, IL: Scott, Foresman, 1979).

6. M. Weber, *From Max Weber: Essays in Sociology,* ed. H. H. Gerth and C. W. Mills (New York: Oxford University Press, 1946), 331.

7. See Perrow, *Complex Organizations,* Ch. 1, for a detailed discussion of these issues.

8. L. D. Parker, "Control in Organizational Life: The Contribution of Mary Parker Follett," *Academy of Management Review* 9 (1984), 736–45.

9. P. Graham, *M. P. Follett—Prophet of Management: A Celebration of Writings from the 1920s* (Boston: Harvard Business School Press, 1995).

10. M. P. Follett, *Creative Experience* (London: Longmans, 1924).

11. E. Mayo, *The Human Problems of Industrial Civilization* (New York: Macmillan, 1933); F. J. Roethlisberger and W. J. Dickson, *Management and the Worker* (Cambridge, MA: Harvard University Press, 1947).

12. D. W. Organ, "Review of *Management and the Worker,* by F. J. Roethlisberger and W. J. Dickson," *Academy of Management Review* 13 (1986), 460–64.

13. D. Roy, "Banana Time: Job Satisfaction and Informal Interaction," *Human Organization* 18 (1960), 158–61.

14. For an analysis of the problems in distinguishing cause from effect in the Hawthorne studies and in social settings in general, see A. Carey, "The Hawthorne Studies: A Radical Criticism," *American Sociological Review* 33 (1967), 403–16.

15. D. McGregor, *The Human Side of Enterprise* (New York: McGraw-Hill, 1960).

16. Ibid., 48.

Chapter 2

1. D. Roberts, "Under Armour Gets Serious," *Fortune,* November 7, 2011, 152–62; K. Plank, As told to Mark Hyman, "How I Did It: Kevin Plank: For the Founder of Apparel-Maker Under Armour, Entrepreneurship Is 99% Perspiration and 1% Polyester," *Inc.,* http://www.inc.com/magazine/20031201/howididit_Printer_Friendly.html, March 26, 2012.

2. Roberts, "Under Armour Gets Serious"; Plank, As told to Mark Hyman, "How I Did It" ; "Under Armour's Kevin Plank: Creating the Biggest, Baddest Brand on the Planet," Knowledge@Wharton, January 5, 2011, http://knowledge.wharton.upenn.edu/printer_friendly.cfm?articleid=2665, March 26, 2012; "2011 Under Armour Annual Report," Under Armour, Inc.—Annual Report & Proxy, http://investor.underarmour.com/annuals.cfm?sh_print=yes&, March 30, 2012.

3. Roberts, "Under Armour Gets Serious."

4. "2011 Under Armour Annual Report"; "Under Armour Reports Fourth Quarter Net Growth of 25% and Fourth Quarter EPS Growth of 51%," http://investor.underarmour.com/releasedetail.cfm?ReleaseID=736945, March 12, 2013.

5. Roberts, "Under Armour Gets Serious"; "Creating the Biggest, Baddest Brand on the Planet."

6. Roberts, "Under Armour Gets Serious."

7. Ibid.

8. "2011 Under Armour Annual Report."

9. "2011 Under Armour Annual Report."

10. "Under Armour-Inc-Board of Directors," http://investor.underarmour.com/directors.cfm?sh_print=yes&, March 12, 2013.

11. Roberts, "Under Armour Gets Serious."

12. Ibid.

13. "2011 Under Armour Annual Report."

14. Roberts, "Under Armour Gets Serious."

15. Roberts, "Under Armour Gets Serious"; "Creating the Biggest, Baddest Brand on the Planet."

16. Roberts, "Under Armour Gets Serious."

17. S. Carpenter, "Different Dispositions, Different Brains," *Monitor on Psychology,* February 2001, 66-68.

18. J. M. Digman, "Personality Structure: Emergence of the Five-Factor Model," *Annual Review of Psychology* 41 (1990), 417–40; R. R. McCrae and P. T. Costa, "Validation of the Five-Factor Model of Personality across Instruments and Observers," *Journal of Personality and Social Psychology* 52 (1987), 81–90; R. R. McCrae and P. T. Costa, "Discriminant Validity of NEO-PIR Facet Scales," *Educational and Psychological Measurement* 52 (1992), 229–37.

19. Digman, "Personality Structure"; McCrae and Costa, "Validation of the Five-Factor Model"; McCrae and Costa, "Discriminant Validity"; R. P. Tett and D. D. Burnett, "A Personality Trait-Based Interactionist Model of Job Performance," *Journal of Applied Psychology* 88, no. 3 (2003), 500–17; J. M. George, "Personality, Five-Factor Model," in S. Clegg and J. R. Bailey, eds., *International Encyclopedia of Organization Studies* (Thousand Oaks, CA: Sage, 2007).

20. L. A. Witt and G. R. Ferris, "Social Skills as Moderator of Conscientiousness–Performance Relationship: Convergent Results across Four Studies," *Journal of Applied Psychology* 88, no. 5 (2003), 809–20; M. J. Simmering, J. A. Colquitte, R. A. Noe, and C. O. L. H. Porter, "Conscientiousness, Autonomy Fit, and Development: A Longitudinal Study," *Journal of Applied Psychology* 88, no. 5 (2003), 954–63.

21. M. R. Barrick and M. K. Mount, "The Big Five Personality Dimensions and Job Performance: A Meta-Analysis," *Personnel Psychology* 44 (1991), 1–26; S. Komar, D. J. Brown, J. A. Komar, and C. Robie, "Faking and the Validity of Conscientiousness: A Monte Carlo Investigation," *Journal of Applied Psychology* 93 (2008), 140–54.

22. Digman, "Personality Structure"; McCrae and Costa, "Validation of the Five-Factor Model"; McCrae and Costa, "Discriminant Validity."

23. J. B. Rotter, "Generalized Expectancies for Internal versus External Control of Reinforcement," *Psychological Monographs* 80 (1966), 1–28; P. Spector, "Behaviors in Organizations as a Function of Employees' Locus of Control," *Psychological Bulletin* 91 (1982), 482–97; "Dirty Jobs: Season 1 DVD Set— Discovery Channel Store—754317," http://shopping.discovery.com/product-60948.

html?jzid=40588004-66-0, March 30, 2012.

24. J. Brockner, *Self-Esteem at Work* (Lexington, MA: Lexington Books, 1988).

25. D. C. McClelland, *Human Motivation* (Glenview, IL: Scott, Foresman, 1985); D. C. McClelland, "How Motives, Skills, and Values Determine What People Do," *American Psychologist* 40 (1985), 812–25; D. C. McClelland, "Managing Motivation to Expand Human Freedom," *American Psychologist* 33 (1978), 201–10.

26. D. G. Winter, *The Power Motive* (New York: Free Press 1973).

27. M. J. Stahl, "Achievement, Power, and Managerial Motivation: Selecting Managerial Talent with the Job Choice Exercise," *Personnel Psychology* 36 (1983), 775–89; D. C. McClelland and D. H. Burnham, "Power Is the Great Motivator," *Harvard Business Review* 54 (1976), 100–10.

28. R. J. House, W. D. Spangler, and J. Woycke, "Personality and Charisma in the U.S. Presidency: A Psychological Theory of Leader Effectiveness," *Administrative Science Quarterly* 36 (1991), 364–96.

29. G. H. Hines, "Achievement, Motivation, Occupations and Labor Turnover in New Zealand," *Journal of Applied Psychology* 58 (1973), 313–17; P. S. Hundal, "A Study of Entrepreneurial Motivation: Comparison of Fast- and Slow-Progressing Small Scale Industrial Entrepreneurs in Punjab, India," *Journal of Applied Psychology* 55 (1971), 317–23.

30. M. Rokeach, *The Nature of Human Values* (New York: Free Press 1973).

31. Ibid.

32. Ibid.

33. A. P. Brief, *Attitudes In and Around Organizations* (Thousand Oaks, CA: Sage, 1998).

34. P. S. Goodman, "U.S. Job Losses in December Dim Hopes for Quick Upswing," *The New York Times*, http://www.nytimes.com/2010/01/09/business/economy/09jobs.html?pagewanted=print, February 3, 2010; U.S. Bureau of Labor Statistics, Economic News Release Employment Situations Summary, http://data.bls.gov/cgi-bin/print.pl/news.release/empsit.nr0.htm, February 3, 2010; B. Steverman, "Layoffs: Short-Term Profits, Long-Term Problems,"

BusinessWeek, http://www.businessweek.com/print/investor/content/jan2010/pi20100113_133780.htm, February 3, 2010.

35. J. Aversa, "Americans' Job Satisfaction Falls to Record Low," http://news.yahoo.com/s/ap/20100105/ap_on_bi_ge/us_unhappy_workers/print, February 3, 2010.

36. The Conference Board, Press Release/News, "U.S. Job Satisfaction at Lowest Level in Two Decades," January 5, 2010, http://www.conference-board.org/utilities/pressPrinterFriendly.cfm?press_ID=3820, February 3, 2010.

37. Aversa, "Americans' Job Satisfaction"; Conference Board, Press Release/News, "U.S. Job Satisfaction."

38. Ibid.

39. Ibid.

40. "Subaru of Indiana Automotive Welcomes New President," Press Release, March 26, 2012, Subaru of Indiana Automotive, Inc., (SIA), http://www.subaru-sia.com/news/release/okawaraPR.pdf, April 2, 2012; "Outline of Production Facility," March 1, 2011, Subaru of Indiana Automotive, Inc., (SIA), http://www.subaru-sia.com/company/sia.outline.english.pdf, April 12, 2012; "SIA Presented with Governor's Service Award," http://www.subaru-sia.com/news/release/20121002.pdf, March 12, 2013.

41. R. Farzad, "The Scrappiest Car Manufacturer in America," *Bloomberg Businessweek,* June 6, 12, 2011, 68–74.

42. Ibid.

43. Ibid.

44. Ibid.

45. Ibid.

46. Farzad, "Scrappiest Car Manufacturer"; "SIA and Wellfit Reward Weight-Loss Winners," Press Release, November 29, 2011, Subaru of Indiana Automotive, Inc., (SIA), http://www.subaru-sia.com/news/release/20111129.pdf, April 1, 2012.

47. Farzad, "Scrappiest Car Manufacturer."

48. Ibid.

49. Ibid.

50. D. W. Organ, *Organizational Citizenship Behavior: The Good Soldier Syndrome* (Lexington, MA: Lexington Books, 1988).

51. J. M. George and A. P. Brief, "Feeling Good—Doing Good: A Conceptual Analysis of the Mood at Work—Organizational Spontaneity Relationship," *Psychological Bulletin* 112 (1992), 310–29.

52. W. H. Mobley, "Intermediate Linkages in the Relationship between Job Satisfaction and Employee Turnover," *Journal of Applied Psychology* 62 (1977), 237–40.

53. C. Hymowitz, "Though Now Routine, Bosses Still Stumble during Layoff Process," *The Wall Street Journal,* June 25, 2007, B1; J. Brockner, "The Effects of Work Layoffs on Survivors: Research, Theory and Practice," in B. M. Staw and L. L. Cummings, eds., *Research in Organizational Behavior,* vol. 10 (Greenwich, CT: JAI Press, 1988), 213–55.

54. Hymowitz, "Though Now Routine."

55. Ibid.

56. Ibid.

57. Goodman, "U.S. Job Losses in December Dim Hopes for Quick Upswing."

58. M. Luo, "For Small Employers, Rounds of Shedding Workers and Tears," *The New York Times,* May 7, 2009, A1, A3.

59. Luo, "Rounds of Shedding Workers and Tears."

60. Ibid.

61. N. Solinger, W. van Olffen, and R. A. Roe, "Beyond the Three-Component Model of Organizational Commitment," *Journal of Applied Psychology* 93 (2008), 70–83.

62. J. E. Mathieu and D. M. Zajac, "A Review and Meta-Analysis of the Antecedents, Correlates, and Consequences of Organizational Commitment," *Psychological Bulletin* 108 (1990), 171–94.

63. D. Watson and A. Tellegen, "Toward a Consensual Structure of Mood," *Psychological Bulletin* 98 (1985), 219–35.

64. Watson and Tellegen, "Toward a Consensual Structure of Mood."

65. J. M. George, "The Role of Personality in Organizational Life: Issues and Evidence," *Journal of Management* 18 (1992), 185–213.

66. H. A. Elfenbein, "Emotion in Organizations: A Review and Theoretical Integration," in J. P. Walsh and A. P. Brief, eds., *The Academy of Management Annals,* vol. 1 (New York: Lawrence Erlbaum Associates, 2008), 315–86.

67. J. P. Forgas, "Affect in Social Judgments and Decisions: A Multi-Process Model," in M. Zanna, ed., *Advances in Experimental and Social Psychology,* vol. 25 (San Diego, CA: Academic Press, 1992), 227–75; J. P. Forgas and J. M. George, "Affective Influences on Judgments and Behavior in Organizations: An Information Processing Perspective," *Organizational Behavior and Human Decision Processes* 86 (2001), 3–34; J. M. George, "Emotions and Leadership: The Role of Emotional Intelligence," *Human Relations* 53 (2000), 1027–55; W. N. Morris, *Mood: The Frame of Mind* (New York: Springer-Verlag, 1989).

68. George, "Emotions and Leadership."

69. J. M. George and K. Bettenhausen, "Understanding Prosocial Behavior, Sales Performance, and Turnover: A Group Level Analysis in a Service Context," *Journal of Applied Psychology* 75 (1990), 698–709.

70. George and Brief, "Feeling Good—Doing Good"; J. M. George and J. Zhou, "Understanding When Bad Moods Foster Creativity and Good Ones Don't: The Role of Context and Clarity of Feelings," Journal of Applied Psychology 87(2002), 687–697; A. M. Isen and R. A. Baron, "Positive Affect as a Factor in Organizational Behavior," in B. M. Staw and L. L. Cummings, eds., *Research in Organizational Behavior,* vol. 13 (Greenwich, CT: JAI Press, 1991), 1–53.

71. J. M. George and J. Zhou, "Dual Tuning in a Supportive Context: Joint Contributions of Positive Mood, Negative Mood, and Supervisory Behaviors to Employee Creativity," *Academy of Management Journal* 50 (2007), 605–22; J. M. George, "Creativity in Organizations," in J. P. Walsh and A. P. Brief, eds., *The Academy of Management Annals,* vol. 1 (New York: Lawrence Erlbaum Associates, 2008), 439–77.

72. J. D. Greene, R. B. Sommerville, L. E. Nystrom, J. M. Darley, and J. D. Cohen, "An FMRI Investigation of Emotional Engagement in Moral Judgment," *Science,* September 14, 2001, 2105–08; L. Neergaard, "Brain Scans Show Emotions Key to Resolving Ethical Dilemmas," *Houston Chronicle,* September 14, 2001, 13A.

73. George and Zhou, "Dual Tuning in a Supportive Context."

74. George and Zhou, "Dual Tuning in a Supportive Context;" J. M. George, "Dual Tuning: A Minimum Condition for Understanding Affect in Organizations?" *Organizational Psychology Review,* no. 2 (2011), 147–64.

75. R. C. Sinclair, "Mood, Categorization Breadth, and Performance Appraisal: The Effects of Order of Information Acquisition and Affective State on Halo, Accuracy, Informational Retrieval, and Evaluations," *Organizational Behavior and Human Decision Processes* 42 (1988), 22–46.

76 D. Heath and C. Heath, "Passion Provokes Action," *Fast Company,* February 2011, 28–30; "Our Management Team," Our Management Team—North American Tool Corporation, North American Tool, http://www.natool.com/staff/our-management-team, April 3, 2012; March 12, 2013.

77. Heath and Heath, "Passion Provokes Action."

78. Ibid.

79. Heath and Heath, "Passion Provokes Action"; "About Us," About Us, http://cedars-sinai.edu/About-Us/, April 3, 2012.

80. Heath and Heath, "Passion Provokes Action."

81. Ibid.

82. Ibid.

83. Ibid.

84. D. Goleman, *Emotional Intelligence* (New York: Bantam Books, 1994); J. D. Mayer and P. Salovey, "The Intelligence of Emotional Intelligence," *Intelligence* 17 (1993), 433–42; J. D. Mayer and P. Salovey, "What Is Emotional Intelligence?" in P. Salovey and D. Sluyter, eds., *Emotional Development and Emotional Intelligence: Implications for Education* (New York: Basic Books, 1997); P. Salovey and J. D. Mayer, "Emotional Intelligence," *Imagination, Cognition, and Personality* 9 (1989–1990), 185–211.

85. S. Epstein, *Constructive Thinking* (Westport, CT: Praeger, 1998).

86. "Leading by Feel," *Inside the Mind of the Leader,* January 2004, 27–37.

87. P. C. Early and R. S. Peterson, "The Elusive Cultural Chameleon: Cultural Intelligence as a New Approach to Intercultural Training for the Global Manager," *Academy of Management Learning and Education* 3, no. 1 (2004), 100–15.

88. George, "Emotions and Leadership"; S. Begley, "The Boss Feels Your Pain," *Newsweek,* October 12, 1998, 74; D. Goleman, *Working with Emotional Intelligence* (New York: Bantam Books, 1998).

89. "Leading by Feel," *Inside the Mind of the Leader,* January 2004, 27–37.

90. George, "Emotions and Leadership."

91. J. Zhou and J. M. George, "Awakening Employee Creativity: The Role of Leader Emotional Intelligence," *Leadership Quarterly* 14 (2003), 545–68.

92. H. M. Trice and J. M. Beyer, *The Cultures of Work Organizations* (Englewood Cliffs, NJ: Prentice-Hall, 1993).

93. J. B. Sørensen, "The Strength of Corporate Culture and the Reliability of Firm Performance," *Administrative Science Quarterly* 47 (2002), 70–91.

94. "Personality and Organizational Culture," in B. Schneider and D. B. Smith, eds., *Personality and Organizations* (Mahwah, NJ: Lawrence Erlbaum, 2004), 347–69; J. E. Slaughter, M. J. Zickar, S. Highhouse, and D. C. Mohr, "Personality Trait Inferences about Organizations: Development of a Measure and Assessment of Construct Validity," *Journal of Applied Psychology* 89, no. 1 (2004), 85–103.

95. T. Kelley, *The Art of Innovation: Lessons in Creativity from IDEO, America's Leading Design Firm* (New York: Random House, 2001).

96. "Personality and Organizational Culture."

97. B. Schneider, "The People Make the Place," *Personnel Psychology* 40 (1987), 437–53.

98. "Personality and Organizational Culture."

99. Ibid.

100. B. Schneider, H. B. Goldstein, and D. B. Smith, "The ASA Framework: An Update," *Personnel Psychology* 48 (1995), 747–73; J. Schaubroeck, D. C. Ganster, and J. R. Jones, "Organizational and Occupational Influences in the Attraction–Selection– Attrition

Process," *Journal of Applied Psychology* 83 (1998), 869–91.

101. Kelley, *The Art of Innovation.*

102. www.ideo.com, February 5, 2008.

103. Kelley, *The Art of Innovation.*

104. "Personality and Organizational Culture."

105. Kelley, *The Art of Innovation.*

106. George, "Emotions and Leadership."

107. Kelley, *The Art of Innovation.*

108. Ibid.

109. D. C. Feldman, "The Development and Enforcement of Group Norms," *Academy of Management Review* 9 (1984), 47–53.

110. G. R. Jones, *Organizational Theory, Design, and Change* (Upper Saddle River, NJ: Prentice-Hall, 2003).

111. H. Schein, "The Role of the Founder in Creating Organizational Culture," *Organizational Dynamics* 12 (1983), 13–28.

112. J. M. George, "Personality, Affect, and Behavior in Groups," *Journal of Applied Psychology* 75 (1990), 107-116.

113. J. Van Maanen, "Police Socialization: A Longitudinal Examination of Job Attitudes in an Urban Police Department," *Administrative Science Quarterly* 20 (1975), 207–28.

114. www.intercotwest.com/Disney; M. N. Martinez, "Disney Training Works Magic," *HRMagazine*, May 1992, 53–57.

115. P. L. Berger and T. Luckman, *The Social Construction of Reality* (Garden City, NY: Anchor Books, 1967).

116. H. M. Trice and J. M. Beyer, "Studying Organizational Culture through Rites and Ceremonials," *Academy of Management Review* 9 (1984), 653–69.

117. Kelley, *The Art of Innovation.*

118. H. M. Trice and J. M. Beyer, *The Cultures of Work Organizations* (Englewood Cliffs, NJ: Prentice-Hall, 1993).

119. B. Ortega, "Wal-Mart's Meeting Is a Reason to Party," *The Wall Street Journal,* June 3, 1994, A1.

120. H. M. Trice and J. M. Beyer, "Studying Organizational Culture through Rites and Ceremonies," *Academy of Management Review* 9 (1984), 653-69.

121. Kelley, *The Art of Innovation.*

122. www.ibm.com; IBM Investor Relations—Corporate Governance, Executive Officers, "Executive Officers," http://www.ibm.com/investor/governance/executive-

officers.wss, February 5, 2010; "Board of Directors," IBM Annual Report 2011—Board of Directors and Senior Leadership, http://www.ibm.com/annualreport/2011/board-of-directors.html, April 4, 2012.

123. K. E. Weick, *The Social Psychology of Organization* (Reading, MA: Addison Wesley, 1979).

124. B. McLean and P. Elkind, *The Smartest Guys in the Room: The Amazing Rise and Scandalous Fall of Enron* (New York: Penguin Books, 2003); R. Smith and J. R. Emshwiller, *24 Days: How Two Wall Street Journal Reporters Uncovered the Lies That Destroyed Faith in Corporate America* (New York: HarperCollins, 2003); M. Swartz and S. Watkins, *Power Failure: The Inside Story of the Collapse of ENRON* (New York: Doubleday, 2003).

Chapter 3

1. "Whole Foods Market History," http://www.wholefoodsmarket.com/company-info/whole-foods-market-history, March 13, 2013.

2. www.wholefoodsmarket.com, 2012.

3. "The Green Machine," *Newsweek,* March 21, 2005, E8–E10.

4. www.wholefoodsmarket.com, 2012.

5. "Whole Foods Market Reports First Quarter Results," http://www.wholefoodsmarket.com/sites/default/files/media/global/company%20info/pdf, March 13, 2013.

6. "John Mackey's Blog: 20 Questions with Sunni's Salon," www.wholefoodsmarket.com, 2006.

7. Ibid.

8. "Fortune 100 Rankings/whole Foods Market," http://www.wholefoodsmarket.com/career/fortune-100-rankings, March 13, 2013.

9. "Declaration of Interdependence/whole Foods Market," http://www.wholefoodsmarket.com/mission-values/core-values/declaration-interdependence, March 13, 2013.

10. A. E. Tenbrunsel, "Misrepresentation and Expectations of Misrepresentation in an Ethical Dilemma: The Role of Incentives and Temptation," Academy of Management Journal 41 (June 1998), 330–340.

11. D. Kravets, "Supreme Court to Hear Case on Medical Pot," www.yahoo.com, June 29, 2004; C. Lane, "A Defeat for Users of Medical Marihuana," www.washingtonpost.com, June 7, 2005.

12. www.yahoo.com, 2003; www.mci.com, 2004.

13. J. Child, "The International Crisis of Confidence in Corporations," *Academy of Management Executive* 16 (August 2002), 145–48.

14. T. Donaldson, "Editor's Comments: Taking Ethics Seriously—A Mission Now More Possible," *Academy of Management Review* 28 (July 2003), 463–67.

15. R. E. Freeman, *Strategic Management: A Stakeholder Approach* (Marshfield, MA: Pitman, 1984).

16. J. A. Pearce, "The Company Mission as a Strategic Tool," *Sloan Management Review,* Spring 1982, 15–24.

17. C. I. Barnard, *The Functions of the Executive* (Cambridge, MA: Harvard University Press, 1948).

18. Freeman, *Strategic Management.*

19. P. S. Adler, "Corporate Scandals: It's Time for Reflection in Business Schools," *Academy of Management Executive* 16 (August 2002), 148–50.

20. W. G. Sanders and D. C. Hambrick, "Swinging for the Fences: The Effects of CEO Stock Options on Company Risk Taking and Performance," *Academy of Management Journal* 53, no. 5 (2007), 1055–78.

21. T. L. Beauchamp and N. E. Bowie, eds., *Ethical Theory and Business* (Englewood Cliffs, NJ: Prentice-Hall, 1979); A. MacIntyre, *After Virtue* (South Bend, IN: University of Notre Dame Press, 1981).

22. R. E. Goodin, "How to Determine Who Should Get What," *Ethics,* July 1975, 310–21.

23. E. P. Kelly, "A Better Way to Think about Business" (book review), *Academy of Management Executive* 14 (May 2000), 127–29.

24. T. M. Jones, "Ethical Decision Making by Individuals in Organizations: An Issue Contingent Model," *Academy of Management Journal* 16 (1991), 366–95; G. F. Cavanaugh, D. J. Moberg, and M. Velasquez, "The Ethics of Organizational Politics," *Academy of Management Review* 6 (1981), 363–74.

25. L. K. Trevino, "Ethical Decision Making in Organizations: A Person–Situation Interactionist Model," *Academy of Management Review* 11 (1986), 601–17; W. H. Shaw and V. Barry, *Moral Issues in Business,* 6th ed. (Belmont, CA: Wadsworth, 1995).

26. T. M. Jones, "Instrumental Stakeholder Theory: A Synthesis of Ethics and Economics," *Academy of Management Review* 20 (1995), 404–37.

27. B. Victor and J. B. Cullen, "The Organizational Bases of Ethical Work Climates," *Administrative Science Quarterly* 33 (1988), 101–25.

28. D. Collins, "Organizational Harm, Legal Consequences and Stakeholder Retaliation," *Journal of Business Ethics* 8 (1988), 1–13.

29. R. C. Soloman, *Ethics and Excellence* (New York: Oxford University Press, 1992).

30. T. E. Becker, "Integrity in Organizations: Beyond Honesty and Conscientiousness," *Academy of Management Review* 23 (January 1998), 154–62.

31. S. W. Gellerman, "Why Good Managers Make Bad Decisions," in K. R. Andrews, ed , *Ethics in Practice: Managing the Moral Corporation* (Boston: Harvard Business School Press, 1989).

32. J. Dobson, "Corporate Reputation: A Free Market Solution to Unethical Behavior," *Business and Society* 28 (1989), 1–5.

33. M. S. Baucus and J. P. Near, "Can Illegal Corporate Behavior Be Predicted? An Event History Analysis," *Academy of Management Journal* 34 (1991), 9–36.

34. Trevino, "Ethical Decision Making."

35. A. S. Waterman, "On the Uses of Psychological Theory and Research in the Process of Ethical Inquiry," *Psychological Bulletin* 103, no. 3 (1988): 283–98.

36. M. S. Frankel, "Professional Codes: Why, How, and with What Impact?" *Ethics* 8 (1989): 109–15.

37. J. Van Maanen and S. R. Barley, "Occupational Communities: Culture and Control in Organizations," in B. Staw and L. Cummings, eds., *Research in Organizational Behavior,* vol. 6 (Greenwich, CT: JAI Press, 1984), 287–365.

38. Jones, "Ethical Decision Making by Individuals in Organizations."

39. M. Conlin, "Where Layoffs Are a Last Resort," *BusinessWeek,* October 8, 2001, *BusinessWeek* Archives; *Southwest Airlines Fact Sheet,* June 19, 2001, www.swabiz.com.

40. G. R. Jones, *Organizational Theory: Text and Cases* (Reading, MA: Addison-Wesley, 1997).

41. P. E. Murphy, "Creating Ethical Corporate Structure," *Sloan Management Review* (Winter 1989), 81–87.

42. W. B. Swann, Jr., J. T. Polzer, D. C. Seyle, and S. J. Ko, "Finding Value in Diversity: Verification of Personal and Social Self-Views in Diverse Groups," *Academy of Management Review* 29, no. 1 (2004), 9–27.

43. "Usual Weekly Earnings Summary," *News: Bureau of Labor Statistics,* April 16, 2004 (www.bls.gov/news.release/whyeng.nr0.htm); "Facts on Affirmative Action in Employment and Contracting," *Americans for a Fair Chance,* January, 28, 2004 (fairchance.civilrights.org/research_center/details.cfm?id=18076); "Household Data Annual Averages," www.bls.gov, April 28, 2004.

44. "Prejudice: Still on the Menu," *BusinessWeek,* April 3, 1995, 42.

45. "She's a Woman, Offer Her Less," *BusinessWeek,* May 7, 2001, 34.

46. "Glass Ceiling Is a Heavy Barrier for Minorities, Blocking Them from Top Jobs," *The Wall Street Journal,* March 14, 1995, A1.

47. "Catalyst Report Outlines Unique Challenges Faced by African-American Women in Business," *Catalyst news release,* February 18, 2004.

48. C. Gibson, "Nation's Median Age Highest Ever, but 65-and-Over Population's Growth Lags, Census 2000 Shows," *U.S. Census Bureau News,* May 30, 2001 (www.census.gov); "U.S. Census Press Releases: Nation's Population One-Third Minority," *U.S. Census Bureau News,* May 10, 2006 (www.census.gov/Press-Release/www/releases/archives/population/006808.html); "The World Factbook," *Central Intelligence Agency,* https://www.cia.gov/library/publications/the-world-factbook/fields/2177.html, April 5, 2012.

49. "Table 2: United States Population Projections by Age and Sex: 2000–2050," *U.S. Census Board, International Data Base, 94,* April 28, 2004 (www.census.gov/ipc/www.idbprint.html); "An Older and More Diverse Nation by Midcentury," August 14, 2008, Newsroom: Population, http://www.census.gov/newsroom/releases/archives/population/cb08-123.html, April 5, 2012.

50. U.S. Equal Employment Opportunity Commission, "Federal

Laws Prohibiting Job Discrimination—Questions and Answers," www.eeoc.gov, June 20, 2001.

51. "Sex by Industry by Class of Worker for the Employed Civilian Population 16 Years and Over," *American FactFinder*, October 15, 2001 (factfinder.census.gov); "2002 Catalyst Census of Women Corporate Officers and Top Earners in the *Fortune* 500," www.catalystwomen.org, August 17, 2004; WB—Statistics & Data, http://www.dol.gov/wb/stats/main.htm?PrinterFriendly=true&, February 9, 2010; "Statistical Overview of Women in the Workplace," *Catalyst*, December 2011, http://www.catalyst.org/publication/219/statistical-overview-of-women-in-the-workplace, April 4, 2012.

52. "Profile of Selected Economic Characteristics: 2000," *American FactFinder*, October 15, 2001 (factfinder.census.gov); "Usual Weekly Earnings Summary," www.bls.gov/news.release, August 17, 2004; WB—Statistics & Data, http://www.dol.gov/wb/stats/main.htm?PrinterFriendly=true&, February 9, 2010; "Usual Weekly Earnings of Wage and Salary Workers Fourth Quarter 2011," January 24, 2012, *Bureau of Labor Statistics, U.S. Department of Labor (BLS)*, http://www.bls.gov/news.release/pdf/wkyeng.pdf, April 5, 2012.

53. "Women in Management in the United States, 1960–Present," July 2011, *Catalyst*, http://www.catalyst.org/publication/207/women-in-management-in-the-united-states-1960-p, April 5, 2012.

54. "2000 Catalyst Census of Women Corporate Officers and Top Earners of the *Fortune* 500," www.catalystwomen.org, October 21, 2001; S. Wellington, M. Brumit Kropf, and P. R. Gerkovich, "What's Holding Women Back?" *Harvard Business Review*, June 2003, 18–19; D. Jones, "The Gender Factor," *USA Today.com*, December 30, 2003; "2002 Catalyst Census of Women Corporate Officers and Top Earners in the *Fortune* 500," www.catalystwomen.org, August 17, 2004; "2007 Catalyst Census of Women Corporate Officers and Top Earners of the *Fortune* 500," www.catalyst.org/knowledge/titles/title.php?page=cen_COTE_07, February 8, 2008; "No News Is Bad News: Women's Leadership Still Stalled in Corporate America," December 14, 2011, *Catalyst*, http://www.catalyst.org/press-release/199/no-news-is-bad-news-womens-leadership-still-sta . . . , April 5, 2012.

55. T. Gutner, "Wanted: More Diverse Directors," *BusinessWeek*, April 30, 2001, 134; "2003 Catalyst Census of Women Board Directors," www.catalystwomen.org, August 17, 2004; "2007 Catalyst Census of Women Board Directors of the *Fortune* 500," www.catalyst.org/knowledge/titles/title.php?page+cen_WBD_07, February 8, 2008; "Statistical Overview of Women in the Workplace," *Catalyst*, December 2011, http://www.catalyst.org/publication/219/statistical-overview-of-women-in-the-workplace, April 4, 2012.

56. Günter, "Wanted: More Diverse Directors"; "2003 Catalyst Census of Women Board Directors."

57. R. Sharpe, "As Leaders, Women Rule," *BusinessWeek*, November 20, 2000, 75–84.

58. Ibid.

59. "New Catalyst Study Reveals Financial Performance Is Higher for Companies with More Women at the Top," *Catalyst news release*, January 26, 2004.

60. P. Sellers, "Women on Boards (NOT!)," *Fortune*, October 15, 2007, 105.

61. United States Census 2010, U.S. Department of Commerce, U.S. Census Bureau; K. R. Hums, N. A. Jones, and R. R. Ramirez, "Overview of Race and Hispanic Original: 2010," *2010 Census Briefs*, March 2011, *United States Census Bureau*, http://www.census.gov/prod/cen2010/briefs/c2010br-02.pdf, April 5, 2012.

62. United States Census 2010.

63. B. Guzman, "The Hispanic Population," U.S. Census Bureau, May 2001; U.S. Census Bureau, "Profiles of General Demographic Characteristics," May 2001; U.S. Census Bureau, "Revisions to the Standards for the Classification of Federal Data on Race and Ethnicity," November 2, 2000, 1–19.

64. L. Chavez, "Just Another Ethnic Group," *The Wall Street Journal*, May 14, 2001, A22.

65. Bureau of Labor Statistics, "Civilian Labor Force 16 and Older by Sex, Age, Race, and Hispanic Origin, 1978, 1988, 1998, and Projected 2008," stats.bls.gov/emp, October 16, 2001.

66. "An Older and More Diverse Nation by Midcentury," August 14, 2008, http://www.census.gov/newsroom/releases/archives/population/cb08-123.html, April 5, 2012; Humes, Jones, and Ramirez, "Overview of Race and Hispanic Original: 2010."

67. Humes, Jones, and Ramirez, "Overview of Race and Hispanic Original: 2010."

68. "U.S. Census Bureau, Profile of General Demographic Characteristics: 2000," *Census 2000*, www.census.gov; "U.S. Census Press Releases: Nation's Population One-Third Minority," *U.S. Census Bureau News*, May 10, 2006 (www.census.gov/Press-Release/www/releases/archives/population/006808.html); Humes, Jones, and Ramirez, "Overview of Race and Hispanic Original: 2010."

69. "An Older and More Diverse Nation by Midcentury," August 14, 2008, http://www.census.gov/newsroom/releases/archives/population/cb08-123.html, April 5, 2012.

70. "Usual Weekly Earnings of Wage and Salary Workers Fourth Quarter 2011," January 24, 2012, Bureau of Labor Statistics U.S. Department of Labor (BLS), http://www.bls.gov/news.release/pdf/wkyeng.pdf, April 5, 2012.

71. J. Flint, "NBC to Hire More Minorities on TV shows," *The Wall Street Journal*, January 6, 2000, B13.

72. J. Poniewozik, "What's Wrong with This Picture?" *Time*, June 1, 2001 (www.Time.com).

73. Ibid.

74. National Association of Realtors, "Real Estate Industry Adapting to Increasing Cultural Diversity," *PR Newswire*, May 16, 2001.

75. "Toyota Apologizes to African Americans over Controversial Ad," *Kyodo News Service*, Japan, May 23, 2001.

76. J. H. Coplan, "Putting a Little Faith in Diversity," *BusinessWeek Online*, December 21, 2000.

77. Ibid.

78. Ibid.

79. K. Holland, "When Religious Needs Test Company," *The New York Times*, February 25, 2007, BU17.

80. J. N. Cleveland, J. Barnes-Farrell, and J. M. Ratz, "Accommodation in the Workplace," *Human Resource Management Review* 7 (1997), 77–108; A. Colella, "Coworker Distributive Fairness Judgments of the Workplace Accommodations of Employees with Disabilities," *Academy of Management Review* 26 (2001), 100–16.

81. Colella, "Coworker Distributive Fairness"; D. Stamps, "Just How Scary Is the ADA," *Training* 32 (1995), 93–101; M. S. West and R. L. Cardy, "Accommodating Claims of Disability: The Potential Impact of Abuses," *Human Resource Management Review* 7 (1997), 233–46.

82. G. Koretz, "How to Enable the Disabled," *BusinessWeek*, November 6, 2000 (*BusinessWeek* Archives).

83. Colella, "Coworker Distributive Fairness."

84. "Notre Dame Disability Awareness Week 2004 Events," www.nd.edu/~bbuddies/daw.html, April 30, 2004.

85. P. Hewitt, "UH Highlights Abilities, Issues of the Disabled," *Houston Chronicle*, October 22, 2001, 24A.

86. "Notre Dame Disability Awareness"; Hewitt, "UH Highlights Abilities, Issues of the Disabled."

87. Astein Wellner, "The Disability Advantage," Inc., October 2005, 29–31.

88. A. Merrick, "Erasing 'Un' From 'Unemployable,'" *The Wall Street Journal*, August 2, 2007, B6; "2012 Spirit of Social Work Awards Luncheon – Public Citizen of the Year Award / Online. . . , http://www.event.com/events/2012-spirit-of-social-work-awards-luncheon/custom-19-a3be. . . , April 11, 2012.

89. Merrick, "Erasing 'Un' From 'Unemployable.'"

90. Ibid.

91. "Habitat International: Our Products," www.habitatint.com/products.htm, April 6, 2006; "Habitat International, Inc. Home Page," www.habitatint.com, April 6, 2006; "Habitat International, Inc. Home Page," http://www.habitatint.com/, April 11, 2012.

92. Wellner, "The Disability Advantage."

93. "Habitat International: Our People," Habitat International—Our People, http://www.habitatint.com/people.htm, February 10, 2010.

94. Wellner, "The Disability Advantage."

95. "Habitat International: Our People"; Wellner, "The Disability Advantage."

96. Ibid; http://habitatint.com, March 14, 2013.

97. Ibid.

98. Ibid.

99. J. M. George, "AIDS/AIDS-Related Complex," in L. H. Peters, C. R. Greer, and S. A. Youngblood, eds., *The Blackwell Encyclopedic Dictionary of Human Resource Management* (Oxford, UK: Blackwell, 1997), 6–7.

100. J. M. George, "AIDS Awareness Training," 6.

101. S. Armour, "Firms Juggle Stigma, Needs of More Workers with HIV," *USA Today*, September 7, 2000, B1.

102. Armour, "Firms Juggle Stigma."

103. Armour, "Firms Juggle Stigma"; S. Vaughn, "Career Challenge; Companies' Work Not Over in HIV and AIDS Education," *Los Angeles Times*, July 8, 2001.

104. R. Brownstein, "Honoring Work Is Key to Ending Poverty," *Detroit News*, October 2, 2001, 9; G. Koretz, "How Welfare to Work Worked," *BusinessWeek*, September 24, 2001 (*BusinessWeek* Archives).

105. "As Ex-Welfare Recipients Lose Jobs, Offer Safety Net," *The Atlanta Constitution*, October 10, 2001, A18.

106. C. S. Rugaber, "Job Openings in a Squeeze," *Houston Chronicle*, February 10, 2010, D1.

107. Press Releases, U.S. Census Bureau, "Income, Poverty and Health Insurance Coverage in the United States: 2008," http://www.census.gov/Press-Release/www/releases/archives/income_wealth/014227.html, February 8, 2010; "The 2009 HHS Poverty Guidelines," http://aspe.hhs.gov/poverty/09poverty.shtml, February 8, 2010; "Income, Poverty and Health Insurance Coverage in the United States: 2010," September 13, 2011, http://www.census.gov/newsroom/releases/archives/income_wealth/cb11-157.html, April 5, 2012.

108. U.S. Census Bureau, "Poverty—How the Census Bureau Measures Poverty," *Census 2000*, September 25, 2001.

109. Press Releases, U.S. Census Bureau, "Income, Poverty and Health Insurance Coverage in the United States: 2008," http://www.census.gov/Press-Release/www/releases/archives/income_wealth/014227.html, February 8, 2010; "The 2009 HHS Poverty Guidelines," http://aspe.hhs.gov/poverty/09poverty.html, February 8, 2010; "Income, Poverty and Health Insurance Coverage in the United States: 2010," September 13, 2011,

http://www.census.gov/newsroom/releases/archives/income_wealth/cb11-157.html, April 5, 2012.

110. I. Lelchuk, "Families Fear Hard Times Getting Worse/$30,000 in the Bay Area Won't Buy Necessities, Survey Says," *San Francisco Chronicle*, September 26, 2001, A13; S. R. Wheeler, "Activists: Welfare-to-Work Changes Needed," *Denver Post*, October 10, 2001, B6.

111. B. Carton, "Bedtime Stories: In 24-Hour Workplace, Day Care Is Moving to the Night Shift," *The Wall Street Journal*, July 6, 2001, A1, A4.

112. Carton, "Bedtime Stories"; Mission, Core Values, and Philosophy, *Children's Choice Features*, http://childrenschoice.com/AboutUs/MissionCoreValuesand Philosophy/tabid/59/Default.aspx, February 9, 2010.

113. Carton, "Bedtime Stories."

114. Ibid.

115. G. J. Gates, "How many people are lesbian, gay, bisexual, and transgender?" April 2011, *The William Institute*, http://williamsinstitute.law.ucla.edu/wp-content/uploads/Gates-How-Many-People-LGBT-Apr-2011.pdf, April 5, 2012.

116. S. E. Needleman, "More Programs Move to Halt Bias against Gays," *The Wall Street Journal*, November 26, 2007, B3.

117. K. Fahim, "United Parcel Service Agrees to Benefits in Civil Unions," *The New York Times*, July 31, 2007, A19.

118. J. Hempel, "Coming Out in Corporate America," *BusinessWeek*, December 15, 2003, 64–72; "LGBT Equality at the Fortune 500," *Human Rights Campaign*, http://www.hrc.org/resources/entry/lgbt-equality-at-the-fortune-500, April 5, 2012.

119. Hempel, "Coming Out in Corporate America."

120. J. Files, "Study Says Discharges Continue under 'Don't Ask, Don't Tell,'" *The New York Times*, March 24, 2004, A14; J. Files, "Gay Ex-Officers Say 'Don't Ask' Doesn't Work," *The New York Times*, December 10, 2003, A14.

121. Hempel, "Coming Out in Corporate America"; "DreamWorks Animation SKG Company History," www.dreamworksanimation.com/dwa/opencms/company/history/index.html, May 29, 2006; J. Chng, "Allan Gilmour: Former Vice-Chairman

of Ford Speaks on Diversity," www.
harbus.org/media/storage/paper343/
news/2006/04/18/News/Allan.
Gilmour.Former.ViceChairman.
Of.Ford.Speaks.On.Diversity-1859600.
html?nore write200606021800&sourced
omain=www.harbus.org, April 18, 2006;
"Allan D. Gilmour Profile," Forbes.com,
http://people.forbes.com/profile/
print/allan-d-gilmour/27441, April 11,
2012.

122. Needleman, "More Programs
Move to Halt Bias."

123. Hempel, "Coming Out in
Corporate America."

124. D. Kopecki, "JPMorgan, Goldman
Rank Among Best Workplaces for Gays,
Lesbians," December 9, 2011, *Bloomberg
BusinessWeek,* http://www.businessweek.
com/news/2011-12-09/jpmorgan-
goldman-rank-among-best-work. . . ,
April 5, 2012; "Best Places to Work
2012," http://www.hrc.org/resources/
entry/best-places-to-work-2012, April
5, 2012; "Award for Workplace Equality
Innovation," *Human Right Campaign,*
http://www.hrc.org/resources/
entry/award-for-workplace-equality-
innovation, April 5, 2012.

125. Needleman, "More Programs
Move to Halt Bias"; www.chubb.com,
March 13, 2013.

126. Ibid.

127. "Best Places to Work 2012."

128. "For Women, Weight May Affect
Pay," *Houston Chronicle,* March 4, 2004,
12A.

129. V. Valian, *Why So Slow? The
Advancement of Women* (Cambridge, MA:
MIT Press, 2000).

130. S. T. Fiske and S. E. Taylor, *Social
Cognition,* 2d ed. (New York: McGraw-
Hill, 1991); Valian, *Why So Slow?*

131. Valian, *Why So Slow?*

132. S. Rynes and B. Rosen, "A
Field Survey of Factors Affecting the
Adoption and Perceived Success of
Diversity Training," *Personnel Psychology*
48 (1995), 247–70; Valian, *Why So Slow?*

133. V. Brown and F. L. Geis, "Turning
Lead into Gold: Leadership by Men
and Women and the Alchemy of Social
Consensus," *Journal of Personality and
Social Psychology* 46 (1984), 811–24;
Valian, *Why So Slow?*

134. Valian, *Why So Slow?*

135. J. Cole and B. Singer, "A Theory
of Limited Differences: Explaining the
Productivity Puzzle in Science," in H.
Zuckerman, J. R. Cole, and J. T. Bruer,

eds., *The Outer Circle: Women in the
Scientific Community* (New York: Norton,
1991), 277–310; M. F. Fox, "Sex, Salary,
and Achievement: Reward Dualism
in Academia," *Sociology of Education*
54 (1981), 71–84; J. S. Long, "The
Origins of Sex Differences in Science,"
Social Forces 68 (1990), 1297–1315; R.
F. Martell, D. M. Lane, and C. Emrich,
"Male–Female Differences: A Computer
Simulation," *American Psychologist* 51
(1996), 157–58; Valian, *Why So Slow?*

136. Cole and Singer, "A Theory of
Limited Differences"; Fox, "Sex, Salary,
and Achievement"; Long, "The Origins
of Sex Differences"; Martell, Lane, and
Emrich, "Male–Female Differences: A
Computer Simulation"; Valian, *Why So
Slow?*

137. G. Robinson and K. Dechant,
"Building a Case for Business Diversity,"
Academy of Management Executive 3
(1997), 32–47.

138. A. Patterson, "Target
'Micromarkets' Its Way to Success; No 2
Stores Are Alike," *The Wall Street Journal,*
May 31, 1995, A1, A9.

139. "The Business Case for Diversity:
Experts Tell What Counts, What Works,"
DiversityInc.com, October 23, 2001.

140. B. Hetzer, "Find a Niche—and Start
Scratching," *BusinessWeek,* September 14,
1998 (*BusinessWeek* Archives). B. Hetzer,
"Find a Niche—and Start Scratching,"
BusinessWeek, September 14, 1998
(*BusinessWeek* Archives).

141. K. Aaron, "Woman Laments
Lack of Diversity on Boards of Major
Companies," *The Times Union,* May 16,
2001 (www.timesunion.com).

142. "The Business Case for Diversity."

143. B. Frankel, "Measuring Diversity Is
One Sure Way of Convincing CEOs of
Its Value," DiversityInc.com, October 5,
2001.

144. A. Stevens, "Lawyers and Clients,"
The Wall Street Journal, June 19, 1995, B7.

145. J. Kahn, "Diversity Trumps the
Downturn," *Fortune,* July 9, 2001, 114–16.

146. "Chevron Settles Claims of 4
Women at Unit as Part of Sex Bias Suit,"
The Wall Street Journal, January 22, 1995,
B12.

147. D. K. Berman, "TWA Settles
Harassment Claims at JFK Airport for
$2.6 Million," *The Wall Street Journal,*
June 25, 2001, B6.

148. A. Lambert, "Insurers Help
Clients Take Steps to Reduce Sexual

Harassment," *Houston Business Journal,*
March 19, 2004 (Houston.bizjournals.
com/Houston/stories/2004/03/22/
focus4.html).

149. L. M. Holson, "Chief of American
Apparel Faces Second Harassment
Suit," *New York Times,* March 24,
2011, B2.

150. T. Segal, "Getting Serious about
Sexual Harassment," *BusinessWeek,*
November 9, 1992, 78–82.

151. J. Green, "The Silencing of Sexual
Harassment," *Bloomberg BusinessWeek,*
November 21–27, 2011, 27–28.

152. U.S. Equal Employment
Opportunity Commission, "Facts about
Sexual Harassment," www.eeoc.gov/
facts/fs-sex.html, May 1, 2004.

153. B. Carton, "Muscled Out? At Jenny
Craig, Men Are Ones Who Claim Sex
Discrimination," *The Wall Street Journal,*
November 29, 1994, A1, A7.

154. R. L. Paetzold and A. M. O'Leary-
Kelly, "Organizational Communication
and the Legal Dimensions of Hostile
Work Environment Sexual Harassment,"
in G. L. Kreps, ed., *Sexual Harassment:
Communication Implications* (Cresskill,
NJ: Hampton Press, 1993).

155. M. Galen, J. Weber, and A. Z.
Cuneo, "Sexual Harassment: Out of the
Shadows," *Fortune,* October 28, 1991,
30–31.

156. A. M. O'Leary-Kelly, R. L. Paetzold,
and R. W. Griffin, "Sexual Harassment
as Aggressive Action: A Framework for
Understanding Sexual Harassment,"
paper presented at the annual meeting
of the Academy of Management,
Vancouver, August 1995.

157. B. S. Roberts and R. A. Mann,
"Sexual Harassment in the Workplace:
A Primer," www3.uakron.edu/lawrev/
robert1.html, May 1, 2004.

158. "Former FedEx Driver Wins EEOC
Lawsuit," *Houston Chronicle,* February 26,
2004, 9B.

159. Ibid.

160. J. Robertson, "California Jury
Awards $61M for Harassment," http://
news.Yahoo.com, June 4, 2006.

161. S. J. Bresler and R. Thacker, "Four-
Point Plan Helps Solve Harassment
Problems," *HR Magazine,* May 1993,
117–24.

162. "Du Pont's Solution," *Training,*
March 1992, 29.

163. Ibid.

164. Ibid.

Chapter 4

1. www.nokia.com, 2011.

2. L. J. Bourgeois, "Strategy and Environment: A Conceptual Integration," *Academy of Management Review* 5 (1985), 25–39.

3. M. E. Porter, *Competitive Strategy* (New York: Free Press, 1980).

4. "Coca-Cola versus Pepsi-Cola and the Soft Drink Industry," Harvard Business School Case 9-391–179.

5. www.splenda.com, 2010.

6. A. K. Gupta and V. Govindarajan, "Cultivating a Global Mind-Set," *Academy of Management Executive* 16 (February 2002), 116–27.

7. "Boeing's Worldwide Supplier Network," *Seattle Post-Intelligencer,* April 9, 1994, 13.

8. I. Metthee, "Playing a Large Part," *Seattle Post-Intelligencer,* April 9, 1994, 13.

9. "Business: Link in the Global Chain," *The Economist,* June 2, 2001, 62–63.

10. www.hbi.com, 2012.

11. M. E. Porter, *Competitive Advantage* (New York: Free Press, 1985).

12. www.walmart.com, 2012.

13. www.amazon.com, 2010.

14. T. Levitt, "The Globalization of Markets," *Harvard Business Review,* May–June 1983, 92–102.

15. "Dell CEO Would Like 40 Percent PC Market Share," www.dailynews.yahoo.com, June 20, 2001.

16. For views on barriers to entry from an economics perspective, see Porter, *Competitive Strategy;* (New York: Free Press, 1980). For the sociological perspective, see J. Pfeffer and G. R. Salancik, *The External Control of Organization: A Resource Dependence Perspective* (New York: Harper & Row, 1978).

17. Porter, *Competitive Strategy;* J. E. Bain, *Barriers to New Competition* (Cambridge, MA: Harvard University Press, 1956); R. J. Gilbert, "Mobility Barriers and the Value of Incumbency," in R. Schmalensee and R. D. Willig, eds., *Handbook of Industrial Organization,* vol. 1 (Amsterdam: North Holland, 1989).

18. Press release, www.amazon.com, May 2001.

19. C. W. L. Hill, "The Computer Industry: The New Industry of Industries," in Hill and Jones, *Strategic Management: An Integrated Approach* (Boston: Houghton Mifflin, 2010).

20. J. Schumpeter, *Capitalism, Socialism and Democracy* (London: Macmillan, 1950), 68. Also see R. R. Winter and S. G. Winter, *An Evolutionary Theory of Economic Change* (Cambridge, MA: Harvard University Press, 1982).

21. N. Goodman, *An Introduction to Sociology* (New York: HarperCollins, 1991); C. Nakane, *Japanese Society* (Berkeley: University of California Press, 1970).

22. For a detailed discussion of the importance of the structure of law as a factor explaining economic change and growth, see D. C. North, *Institutions, Institutional Change, and Economic Performance* (Cambridge: Cambridge University Press, 1990).

23. R. B. Reich, *The Work of Nations* (New York: Knopf, 1991).

24. J. Bhagwati, *Protectionism* (Cambridge, MA: MIT Press, 1988).

25. M. A. Carpenter and J. W. Fredrickson, "Top Management Teams, Global Strategic Posture, and the Moderating Role of Uncertainty," *Academy of Management Journal* 44 (June 2001), 533–46.

26. www.ikea.com, 2012.

27. Bhagwati, *Protectionism.*

28. For a summary of these theories, see P. Krugman and M. Obstfeld, *International Economics: Theory and Policy* (New York: HarperCollins, 1991). Also see C. W. L. Hill, *International Business* (New York: McGraw-Hill, 1997), chap. 4.

29. A. M. Rugman, "The Quest for Global Dominance," *Academy of Management Executive* 16 (August 2002), 157–60.

30. www.wto.org.com, 2004.

31. www.wto.org.com, 2012.

32. C. A. Bartlett and S. Ghoshal, *Managing across Borders* (Boston: Harvard Business School Press, 1989).

33. C. Arnst and G. Edmondson, "The Global Free-for-All," *BusinessWeek,* September 26, 1994, 118–26.

34. W. Konrads, "Why Leslie Wexner Shops Overseas," *BusinessWeek,* February 3, 1992, 30.

35. E. B. Tylor, *Primitive Culture* (London: Murray, 1971).

36. For details on the forces that shape culture, see Hill, *International Business,* chap. 2.

37. G. Hofstede, B. Neuijen, D. D. Ohayv, and G. Sanders, "Measuring Organizational Cultures: A Qualitative and Quantitative Study across Twenty Cases," *Administrative Science Quarterly* 35 (1990), 286–316.

38. M. H. Hoppe, "Introduction: Geert Hofstede's Culture's Consequences: International Differences in Work-Related Values," *Academy of Management Executive* 18 (February 2004), 73–75.

39. R. Bellah, *Habits of the Heart: Individualism and Commitment in American Life* (Berkeley: University of California Press, 1985).

40. R. Bellah, *The Tokugawa Religion* (New York: Free Press, 1957).

41. C. Nakane, *Japanese Society* (Berkeley: University of California Press, 1970).

42. Ibid.

43. G. Hofstede, "The Cultural Relativity of Organizational Practices and Theories," *Journal of International Business Studies,* Fall 1983, 75–89.

44. Hofstede et al., "Measuring Organizational Cultures."

45. J. Perlez, "GE Finds Tough Going in Hungary," *The New York Times,* July 25, 1994, C1, C3.

46. www.ge.com, 2004, 2010, 2012.

47. J. P. Fernandez and M. Barr, *The Diversity Advantage* (New York: Lexington Books, 1994).

48. www.ibm.com, 2012.

49. www.sony.com, press release, 2010, 2011.

50. www.sony.com, press release, 2012.

Chapter 5

1. S. Clifford, "Marc Shuman Was Determined to Expand Fast," *Inc.,* March, 2006, 44–50; D. Kocieniewski, "After $12,000, There's Even Room to Park the Car," *The New York Times,* February 20, 2006; "The World's Cleanest Garage," www.garagetek.com, May 30, 2006 (www.garagetek.com/nav.asp); "What Is Garagetek?" www.garagetek.com, May 30, 2006 (www.garagetek.com/content_CNBC.asp); L. Christie, "7 Franchises: Riding the Housing Boom," CNNMoney.

com, March 7, 2006 (http://money.cnn.com/2006/03/07/smbusiness/homefranchises/index.htm); "745 Businesses to Start Now!" *Entrepreneur,* January 2005, 88, 192, 193; "Franchise Opportunities Available," http://www.garagetek.com/FranchiseOpportunities/February 16, 2010; GarageTek Inc.: Private Company Information—*BusinessWeek,* http://investing.businessweek.com/research/stocks/private/snapshot.asp?privcapId=126174. . . , February 15, 2010; "Garage Makeover," *Inc.,* July 2007, p. 53; "GarageTek—About Us," http://www.garagetek.com/AboutUs, April 9, 2013.

2.   "About Us," April 17, 2012.

3.   Clifford, "Marc Shuman Was Determined to Expand Fast."

4.   Ibid.

5.   Ibid.; "Franchise Opportunities," *Garage Tek,* www.garagetek.com/FranchiseOpportunities/GarageTek-Opportunities.aspx, February 14, 2008.

6.   Clifford, "Marc Shuman Was Determined to Expand Fast."

7.   Ibid.

8.   "Franchise Opportunities Available," *Garagetek,* http://www.garagetek.com/Franchise Opportunities/, April 17, 2012.

9.   Clifford, "Marc Shuman Was Determined to Expand Fast."

10.   "About Us," April 9, 2013.

11.   Clifford, "Marc Shuman Was Determined to Expand Fast."

12.   G. P. Huber, *Managerial Decision Making* (Glenview, IL: Scott, Foresman, 1993).

13.   Clifford, "Marc Shuman Was Determined to Expand Fast."

14.   Martin Cooper—History of Cell Phone and Martin Cooper, http://inventors.about.com/cs/inventorsalphabet/a/martin_cooper.htm?p=1, February 16, 2010; "Motorola Demonstrates Portable Telephone to Be Available for Public Use by 1976," April 3, 1973, www.motorola.com, February 17, 2009; "The Cellular Telephone Concept—An Overview," September 10, 1984, www.motorola.com, February 17, 2009; "iPad," http://www.apple.com/, February 16, 2010.

15.   H. A. Simon, *The New Science of Management* (Englewood Cliffs, NJ: Prentice-Hall, 1977).

16.   D. Kahneman, "Maps of Bounded Rationality: A Perspective on Intuitive Judgment and Choice," Prize Lecture, December 8, 2002; E. Jaffe, "What Was I Thinking? Kahneman Explains How Intuition Leads Us Astray," *American Psychological Society* 17, no. 5 (May 2004), 23–26; E. Dane and M. Pratt, "Exploring Intuition and Its Role in Managerial Decision Making," *Academy of Management Review* 32 (2007), 33–54.

17.   One should be careful not to generalize too much here, however; for as Peter Senge has shown, programmed decisions rely on the implicit assumption that the environment is in a steady state. If environmental conditions change, sticking to a routine decision rule can produce disastrous results. See P. Senge, *The Fifth Discipline: The Art and Practice of the Learning Organization* (New York: Doubleday, 1990).

18.   Kahneman, "Maps of Bounded Rationality"; Jaffe, "What Was I Thinking?"

19.   Kahneman, "Maps of Bounded Rationality"; Jaffe, "What Was I Thinking?"

20.   J. Lehrer, "The Science of Irrationality," *The Wall Street Journal,* October 15, 2011, C18.

21.   J. Smutniak, "Freud, Finance and Folly: Human Intuition Is a Bad Guide to Handling Risk," *The Economist* 24 (January 2004), 5–6.

22.   Kahneman, "Maps of Bounded Rationality"; Jaffe, "What Was I Thinking?"

23.   Kahneman, "Maps of Bounded Rationality"; Jaffe, "What Was I Thinking?"

24.   J. Pfeffer, "Curbing the Urge to Merge," *Business 2.0,* July 2003, 58; Smutniak, "Freud, Finance and Folly."

25.   Kahneman, "Maps of Bounded Rationality"; Jaffe, "What Was I Thinking?"

26.   Pfeffer, "Curbing the Urge to Merge"; Smutniak, "Freud, Finance and Folly."

27.   M. Landler, "New Austerity for German Car Industry," *The New York Times,* September 29, 2005, C3; E. Taylor and C. Rauwald, "DaimlerChrysler to Cut 8,500 Jobs at Mercedes," *The Wall Street Journal,* September 29, 2005, A6; G. Edmondson, "On the Hot Seat at Daimler," *BusinessWeek Online,*

February 17, 2006 (www.businessweek.com/autos/content/feb2006/bw20060217_187348.htm?campaign_id=search); Daimler AG News—*The New York Times,* http://topics.nytimes.com/topics/news/business/companies/daimler_ag/index.html., February 19, 2010.

28.   "Hiring Freeze and Cost Cuts at Time Inc.," *The New York Times,* August 2005, B13.

29.   Pfeffer, "Curbing the Urge to Merge."

30.   J. Lehrer, "The Science of Irrationality," *The Wall Street Journal,* October 15, 2011, C18.

31.   Pfeffer, "Curbing the Urge to Merge."

32.   H. A. Simon, *Administrative Behavior* (New York: Macmillan, 1947), 79.

33.   H. A. Simon, *Models of Man* (New York: Wiley, 1957).

34.   K. J. Arrow, *Aspects of the Theory of Risk Bearing* (Helsinki: Yrjo Johnssonis Saatio, 1965).

35.   Ibid.

36.   R. L. Daft and R. H. Lengel, "Organizational Information Requirements, Media Richness and Structural Design," *Management Science* 32 (1986), 554–71.

37.   R. Cyert and J. March, *Behavioral Theory of the Firm* (Englewood Cliffs, NJ: Prentice-Hall, 1963).

38.   J. G. March and H. A. Simon, *Organizations* (New York: Wiley, 1958).

39.   H. A. Simon, "Making Management Decisions: The Role of Intuition and Emotion," *Academy of Management Executive* 1 (1987), 57–64.

40.   M. H. Bazerman, *Judgment in Managerial Decision Making* (New York: Wiley, 1986). Also see Simon, *Administrative Behavior.*

41.   Scott G. McNealy Profile—Forbes.com, http://people.forbes.com/profile/scott-g-mcnealy/75347, February 16, 2010; Sun Oracle, "Overview and Frequently Asked Questions," www.oracle.com, February 16, 2010.

42.   "Sun Microsystems—Investor Relations: Officers and Directors," www.sun.com/aboutsun/investor/sun_facts/officers_directors.html, June 1, 2004; "How Sun Delivers Value to Customers," *Sun Microsystems—Investor Relations: Support & Training,* June 1, 2004

(www.sun.com/aboutsun/investor/sun_facts/core_strategies.html); "Sun at a Glance," *Sun Microsystems—Investor Relations: Sun Facts,* June 1, 2004 (www.sun.com/aboutsun/investor/sun_facts/index.html); "Plug in the System, and Everything Just Works," *Sun Microsystems—Investor Relations: Product Portfolio,* June 1, 2004 (www.sun.com/aboutsun/investor/sun_facts/portfolio/html).

43.   N. J. Langowitz and S. C. Wheelright, "Sun Microsystems, Inc. (A)," Harvard Business School Case 686–133.

44.   R. D. Hof, "How to Kick the Mainframe Habit," *BusinessWeek,* June 26, 1995, 102–104.

45.   Bazerman, *Judgment in Managerial Decision Making;* Huber, *Managerial Decision Making;* J. E. Russo and P. J. Schoemaker, *Decision Traps* (New York: Simon & Schuster, 1989).

46.   M. D. Cohen, J. G. March, and J. P. Olsen, "A Garbage Can Model of Organizational Choice," *Administrative Science Quarterly* 17 (1972), 1–25.

47.   Cohen, March, and Olsen, "A Garbage Can Model."

48.   Bazerman, *Judgment in Managerial Decision Making.*

49.   Senge, *The Fifth Discipline.*

50.   E. de Bono, *Lateral Thinking* (London: Penguin, 1968); Senge, *The Fifth Discipline.*

51.   Russo and Schoemaker, *Decision Traps.*

52.   Bazerman, *Judgment in Managerial Decision Making.*

53.   B. Berger, "NASA: One Year after *Columbia*—Bush's New Vision Changes Agency's Course Midstream," *Space News Business Report,* January 26, 2004 (www.space.com/spacenews/businessmonday_040126.html).

54.   J. Glanz and J. Schwartz, "Dogged Engineer's Effort to Assess Shuttle Damage," *The New York Times,* September 26, 2003, A1.

55.   M. L. Wald and J. Schwartz, "NASA Chief Promises a Shift in Attitude," *The New York Times,* August 28, 2003, A23.

56.   J. Light, "Sustainability Jobs Get Green Light at Large Firms," *The Wall Street Journal,* July 11, 2011, B5.

57.   Ibid. "Scott Wicker—UPS Pressroom," http://www.pressroom.ups.com/Biography/Scott+Wicker, April 18, 2012, April 9, 2013.

58.   "Scott Wicker—UPS Pressroom."

59.   L. J. Fisher, DuPont.com: Meet the Executives, http://www2.dupont.com/Our_Company/en_US/executives/fisher.html, April 18, 2012; "Bio Linda J. Fisher, VP, DuPont SHE, Chief Sustainability Officer," http://www.2.dupont.com/corp/en-us/our-company/leadership/exec-leadership/fisher.html, April 9, 2013.

60.   "An Interview with Linda Fisher Chief Sustainability Officer, DuPont," February 13, 2012, http://www.globe.net.com/articles/2012/february/9/an-interview-with-linda-fisher-chief-su. . . , April 18, 2012.

61.   Coca-Cola–Press Center–Press Kits—Beatriz Perez Named Chief Sustainability Officer, May 19, 2011, http://www.thecoca-colacompany.com/dynamic/press_center/2011/05/new-chief-sustainab. . . , April 18, 2012; "Beatriz Perez: Executive Profile & Biography *Businessweek,*" http://investing.businessweek.com/research/stocks/people/person.asp?personID=346510798-111, April 9, 2013

62.   M. Albanese, "How She Leads: Coca-Cola's Beatriz Perez," October 3, 2011, http://www.greenbiz.com/print/44395, April 18, 2012.

63.   Ibid.

64.   Russo and Schoemaker, *Decision Traps.*

65.   I. L. Janis, *Groupthink: Psychological Studies of Policy Decisions and Disasters,* 2nd ed. (Boston: Houghton Mifflin, 1982).

66.   C. R. Schwenk, *The Essence of Strategic Decision Making* (Lexington, MA: Lexington Books, 1988).

67.   See R. O. Mason, "A Dialectic Approach to Strategic Planning," *Management Science* 13 (1969) 403–14; R. A. Cosier and J. C. Aplin, 'A Critical View of Dialectic Inquiry in Strategic Planning," *Strategic Management Journal* 1 (1980), 343–56; I. I. Mitroff and R. O. Mason, "Structuring III—Structured Policy Issues: Further Explorations in a Methodology for Messy Problems," *Strategic Management Journal* 1 (1980), 331–42.

68.   Mary C. Gentile, *Differences That Work: Organizational Excellence through Diversity* (Boston: Harvard Business School Press, 1994); F. Rice, "How to Make Diversity Pay," *Fortune,* August 8, 1994, 78–86.

69.   B. Hedberg, "How Organizations Learn and Unlearn," in W. H. Starbuck and P. C. Nystrom, eds., *Handbook of Organizational Design,* vol. 1 (New York: Oxford University Press, 1981), 1–27.

70.   Senge, *The Fifth Discipline.*

71.   Ibid.

72.   P. M. Senge, "The Leader's New Work: Building Learning Organizations," *Sloan Management Review,* Fall 1990, 7–23.

73.   W. Zellner, K. A. Schmidt, M. Ihlwan, and H. Dawley, "How Well Does Wal-Mart Travel?" *BusinessWeek,* September 3, 2001, 82–84.

74.   J. M. George, "Creativity in Organizations," in J. P. Walsh and A. P. Brief, eds., *The Academy of Management Annals,* Vol. 1 (New York: Erlbaum, 2008), 439–77.

75.   Walsh and Brief, "Creativity in Organizations."

76.   C. Saltr, "FAST 50: The World's Most Innovative Companies," *Fast Company,* March 2008, 73–117.

77.   R. W. Woodman, J. E. Sawyer, and R. W. Griffin, "Towards a Theory of Organizational Creativity," *Academy of Management Review* 18 (1993), 293–321.

78.   T. Evans, "Entrepreneurs Seek to Elicit Workers' Ideas," *The Wall Street Journal,* December 22, 2009, B7; D. Dahl, "Rounding Up Staff Ideas," Inc.com, February 1, 2010, http://www.inc.com/magazine/20100201/rounding-up-staff-ideas_Printer_Friendly.html, February 12, 2010; "About Borrego Solar," http://www.borregosolar.com/solar-energy-company/solar-contractor.php, February 15, 2010.

79.   T. J. Bouchard Jr., J. Barsaloux, and G. Drauden, "Brainstorming Procedure, Group Size, and Sex as Determinants of Problem Solving Effectiveness of Individuals and Groups," *Journal of Applied Psychology* 59 (1974), 135–38.

80.   M. Diehl and W. Stroebe, "Productivity Loss in Brainstorming Groups: Towards the Solution of a Riddle," *Journal of Personality and Social Psychology* 53 (1987), 497–509.

81.   D. H. Gustafson, R. K. Shulka, A. Delbecq, and W. G. Walster, "A Comparative Study of Differences in Subjective Likelihood Estimates Made by Individuals, Interacting Groups, Delphi Groups, and Nominal Groups," *Organizational Behavior and Human Performance* 9 (1973), 280–91.

82.   N. Dalkey, *The Delphi Method: An Experimental Study of Group Decision Making* (Santa Monica, CA: Rand Corp., 1989).

83. T. Lonier, "Some Insights and Statistics on Working Solo," www.workingsolo.com.

84. I. N. Katsikis and L. P. Kyrgidou, "The Concept of Sustainable Entrepreneurship: A Conceptual Framework and Empirical Analysis," *Academy of Management Proceedings,* 2007, 1–6, web.ebscohost.com/ehost/delivery?vid=7&hid=102&sid=434afdf5-5ed9-45d4-993b-, January 24, 2008; "What Is a Social Entrepreneur?" http://ashoka.org/social_entrepreneur, February 20, 2008; C. Hsu, "Entrepreneur for Social Change," *U.S.News.com,* October 31, 2005, www.usnews.com/usnews/news/articles/051031/31drayton.htm; D. M. Sullivan, "Stimulating Social Entrepreneurship: Can Support from Cities Make a Difference?" *Academy of Management Perspectives,* February 2007, 78.

85. Katsikis and Kyrgidou, "The Concept of Sustainable Entrepreneurship"; "What Is a Social Entrepreneur?"; Hsu, "Entrepreneur for Social Change"; Sullivan, "Stimulating Social Entrepreneurship."

Chapter 6

1. www.cott.com, 2010, 2012.

2. www.cocacola.com, 2010; www.pepsico.com, 2010.

3. A. Chandler, *Strategy and Structure: Chapters in the History of the American Enterprise* (Cambridge, MA: MIT Press, 1962).

4. Ibid.

5. H. Fayol, *General and Industrial Management* (1884; New York: IEEE Press, 1984).

6. Ibid., 18.

7. F. J. Aguilar, "General Electric: Reg Jones and Jack Welch," in *General Managers in Action* (Oxford: Oxford University Press, 1992).

8. Aguilar, "General Electric."

9. www.ge.com, 2010.

10. C. W. Hofer and D. Schendel, *Strategy Formulation: Analytical Concepts* (St. Paul, MN: West, 1978).

11. J. A. Pearce, "The Company Mission as a Strategic Tool," *Sloan Management Review,* Spring 1992, 15–24.

12. D. F. Abell, *Defining the Business: The Starting Point of Strategic Planning* (Englewood Cliffs, NJ: Prentice-Hall, 1980).

13. G. Hamel and C. K. Prahalad, "Strategic Intent," *Harvard Business Review,* May–June 1989, 63–73.

14. D. I. Jung and B. J. Avolio, "Opening the Black Box: An Experimental Investigation of the Mediating Effects of Trust and Value Congruence on Transformational and Transactional Leadership," *Journal of Organizational Behavior,* December 2000, 949–64; B. M. Bass and B. J. Avolio, "Transformational and Transactional Leadership: 1992 and Beyond," *Journal of European Industrial Training,* January 1990, 20–35.

15. J. Porras and J. Collins, *Built to Last: Successful Habits of Visionary Companies* (New York: HarperCollins, 1994).

16. E. A. Locke, G. P. Latham, and M. Erez, "The Determinants of Goal Commitment," *Academy of Management Review* 13 (1988), 23–39.

17. K. R. Andrews, *The Concept of Corporate Strategy* (Homewood, IL: Irwin, 1971).

18. www.campbellsoup.com, 2001.

19. G. Mulvihill, "Campbell Is Really Cooking," SanDiegoTribune.com, August 5, 2004.

20. W. D. Crotty, "Campbell Soup Is Not So Hot," www.MotleyFool.com, May 24, 2004.

21. A. Halperin, "Chicken Soup for the Investor's Soul," *BusinessWeek Online,* May 25, 2006 (www.businessweek.com).

22. A. Carter, "Lighting a Fire under Campbell," www.businessweek.com, *December* 4, 2006.

23. www.campbellsoupcompany.com, 2012.

24. "Campbell Completes $850M Godiva Sale," www.yahoo.com, March 18, 2008.

25. R. D. Aveni, *Hypercompetition* (New York: Free Press, 1994).

26. M. E. Porter, *Competitive Strategy* (New York: Free Press, 1980).

27. C. W. L. Hill, "Differentiation versus Low Cost or Differentiation and Low Cost: A Contingency Framework," *Academy of Management Review* 13 (1988), 401–12.

28. For details, see J. P. Womack, D. T. Jones, and D. Roos, *The Machine That Changed the World* (New York: Rawson Associates, 1990).

29. Porter, *Competitive Strategy.*

30. www.zara.com, 2010.

31. C. Vitzthum, "Just-in-Time-Fashion," *The Wall Street Journal,* May 18, 2001, B1, B4.

32. www.zara.com, 2010.

33. M. K. Perry, "Vertical Integration: Determinants and Effects," in R. Schmalensee and R. D. Willig, *Handbook of Industrial Organization,* vol. 1 (New York: Elsevier Science, 1989).

34. "Matsushita Electric Industrial (MEI) in 1987," Harvard Business School Case 388–144.

35. www.dell.com, 2012.

36. www.ibm.com, 2010.

37. E. Penrose, *The Theory of the Growth of the Firm* (Oxford: Oxford University Press, 1959).

38. M. E. Porter, "From Competitive Advantage to Corporate Strategy," *Harvard Business Review* 65 (1987), 43–59.

39. D. J. Teece, "Economies of Scope and the Scope of the Enterprise," *Journal of Economic Behavior and Organization* 3 (1980), 223–47.

40. M. E. Porter, *Competitive Advantage: Creating and Sustaining Superior Performance* (New York: Free Press, 1985).

41. www.3M.com, 2005, 2010, 2012.

42. www.3M.com, 2012.

43. C. Wyant, "Minnesota Companies Make *BusinessWeek*'s 'Most Innovative' List," *Minneapolis/St. Paul Business Journal,* April 18, 2008.

44. www.vfc.com, 2012.

45. Ibid.

46. www.timberland.com, 2012.

47. Ibid.

48. For a review of the evidence, see C.W.L. Hill and G. R. Jones, *Strategic Management: An Integrated Approach,* 5th ed. (Boston: Houghton Mifflin, 2011), chap. 10.

49. C. R. Christensen et al., *Business Policy Text and Cases* (Homewood, IL: Irwin, 1987), 778.

50. C. W. L. Hill, "Conglomerate Performance over the Economic Cycle," *Journal of Industrial Economics* 32 (1983), 197–213.

51. V. Ramanujam and P. Varadarajan, "Research on Corporate Diversification: A Synthesis," *Strategic Management Journal* 10 (1989), 523–51. Also see A. Shleifer and R. W. Vishny, "Takeovers in the 1960s and 1980s: Evidence and Implications," in R. P. Rumelt, D. E. Schendel, and D. J. Teece, eds., *Fundamental Issues in Strategy* (Boston: Harvard Business School Press, 1994).

52. J. R. Williams, B. L. Paez, and L. Sanders, "Conglomerates Revisited," *Strategic Management Journal* 9 (1988), 403–14.

53. G. Marcial, "As Tyco Splits into Three," www.businessweek.com, March 12, 2007.

54. www.tyco.com, 2008.

55. C. A. Bartlett and S. Ghoshal, *Managing across Borders* (Boston: Harvard Business School Press, 1989).

56. C. K. Prahalad and Y. L. Doz, *The Multinational Mission* (New York: Free Press, 1987).

57. "Gillette Co.9s New $40 Million Razor Blade Factory in St. Petersburg, Russia," *Boston Globe, June* 7, 2000, *C*6.

58. D. Sewell, "P&G Replaces Ex-Gillette CEO at Operations," www.yahoo.com, May 24, 2006.

59. www.pg.com, 2005, 2008, 2010.

60. R. E. Caves, *Multinational Enterprise and Economic Analysis* (Cambridge: Cambridge University Press, 1982).

61. B. Kogut, "Joint Ventures: Theoretical and Empirical Perspectives," *Strategic Management Journal* 9 (1988), 319–33.

62. "Venture with Nestlé SA Is Slated for Expansion," *The Wall Street Journal,* April 15, 2001, B2.

63. B. Bahree, "BP Amoco, Italy's ENI Plan $2.5 Billion Gas Plant," *The Wall Street Journal,* March 6, 2001, A16.

64. N. Hood and S. Young, *The Economics of the Multinational Enterprise* (London: Longman, 1979).

Chapter 7

1. www.avon.com, 2012.

2. N. Byrnes, "Avon: More Than Just Cosmetic Changes," www.businessweek.com, March 12, 2007.

3. www.avon.com, 2012.

4. G. R. Jones, *Organizational Theory, Design and Change: Text and Cases* (Upper Saddle River: Prentice Hall, 2003).

5. J. Child, *Organization: A Guide for Managers and Administrators* (New York: Harper & Row, 1977).

6. P. R. Lawrence and J. W. Lorsch, *Organization and Environment* (Boston: Graduate School of Business Administration, Harvard University, 1967).

7. R. Duncan, "What Is the Right Organizational Design?" *Organizational Dynamics,* Winter 1979, 59–80.

8. T. Burns and G. R. Stalker, *The Management of Innovation* (London: Tavistock, 1966).

9. D. Miller, "Strategy Making and Structure: Analysis and Implications for Performance," *Academy of Management Journal* 30 (1987), 7–32.

10. A. D. Chandler, *Strategy and Structure* (Cambridge, MA: MIT Press, 1962).

11. J. Stopford and L. Wells, *Managing the Multinational Enterprise* (London: Longman, 1972).

12. C. Perrow, *Organizational Analysis: A Sociological View* (Belmont, CA: Wadsworth, 1970).

13. F. W. Taylor, *The Principles of Scientific Management* (New York: Harper, 1911).

14. R. W. Griffin, *Task Design: An Integrative Approach* (Glenview, IL: Scott, Foresman, 1982).

15. Ibid.

16. www.ddir.com, 2012.

17. http://seattletimes.nwsource.com/html/obituaries/2001211576_dicks23m.html.

18. Ibid.

19. J. R. Hackman and G. R. Oldham, *Work Redesign* (Reading, MA: Addison-Wesley, 1980).

20. J. R. Galbraith and R. K. Kazanjian, *Strategy Implementation: Structure, System, and Process,* 2d ed. (St. Paul, MN: West, 1986).

21. Lawrence and Lorsch, *Organization and Environment.*

22. Jones, *Organizational Theory.*

23. Lawrence and Lorsch, *Organization and Environment.*

24. R. H. Hall, *Organizations: Structure and Process* (Englewood Cliffs, NJ: Prentice Hall, 1972); R. Miles, *Macro Organizational Behavior* (Santa Monica, CA: Goodyear, 1980).

25. Chandler, *Strategy and Structure.*

26. G. R. Jones and C. W. L. Hill, "Transaction Cost Analysis of Strategy-Structure Choice," *Strategic Management Journal* 9 (1988), 159–72.

27. www.gsk.com, 2006.

28. Ibid.

29. S. M. Davis and P. R. Lawrence, *Matrix* (Reading, MA: Addison-Wesley, 1977); J. R. Galbraith, "Matrix Organization Designs: How to Combine Functional and Project Forms," *Business Horizons* 14 (1971), 29–40.

30. L. R. Burns, "Matrix Management in Hospitals: Testing Theories of Matrix Structure and Development," *Administrative Science Quarterly* 34 (1989), 349–68.

31. C. W. L. Hill, *International Business* (Homewood, IL: Irwin, 2003).

32. Jones, *Organizational Theory.*

33. A. Farnham, "America's Most Admired Company," *Fortune,* February 7, 1994, 50–54.

34. P. Blau, "A Formal Theory of Differentiation in Organizations," *American Sociological Review* 35 (1970), 684–95.

35. S. Grey, "McDonald's CEO Announces Shifts of Top Executives," *The Wall Street Journal,* July 16, 2004, A11.

36. www.mcdonalds.com, 2010.

37. Child, *Organization.*

38. S. McCartney, "Airline Industry's Top-Ranked Woman Keeps Southwest's Small-Fry Spirit Alive," *The Wall Street Journal,* November 30, 1995, B1; www.swamedia.com, 2010.

39. P. M. Blau and R. A. Schoenherr, *The Structure of Organizations* (New York: Basic Books, 1971).

40. Jones, *Organizational Theory.*

41. Lawrence and Lorsch, *Organization and Environment,* 50–55; www.dell.com, 2012.

42. J. R. Galbraith, *Designing Complex Organizations* (Reading, MA: Addison-Wesley, 1977), chap. 1; Galbraith and Kazanjian, *Strategy Implementation,* chap. 7.

43. Lawrence and Lorsch, *Organization and Environment,* 55.

44. B. Kogut, "Joint Ventures: Theoretical and Empirical Perspectives," *Strategic Management Journal* 9 (1988), 319–32.

45. G. S. Capowski, "Designing a Corporate Identity," *Management Review,* June 1993, 37–38.

46. J. Marcia, "Just Doing It," *Distribution,* January 1995, 36–40.

47. "Nike Battles Backlash from Overseas Sweatshops," *Marketing News,* November 9, 1998, 14.

48. J. Laabs, "Nike Gives Indonesian Workers a Raise," *Workforce,* December 1998, 15–16.

49. W. Echikson, "It's Europe's Turn to Sweat about Sweatshops," *BusinessWeek,* July 19, 1999, 96.

50. Copyright © 2006, Gareth R. Jones.

Chapter 8

1. www.ford.com, 2012.

2. D. Kiley, "The New Heat on Ford," www.businessweek.com, June 4, 2007.

3. Ibid.

4. W. G. Ouchi, "Markets, Bureaucracies, and Clans," *Administrative Science Quarterly* 25 (1980), 129–41.

5. P. Lorange, M. Morton, and S. Ghoshal, *Strategic Control* (St. Paul, MN: West, 1986).

6. H. Koontz and R. W. Bradspies, "Managing through Feedforward Control," *Business Horizons,* June 1972, 25–36.

7. E. E. Lawler III and J. G. Rhode, *Information and Control in Organizations* (Pacific Palisades, CA: Goodyear, 1976).

8. C.W.L. Hill and G. R. Jones, *Strategic Management: An Integrated Approach,* 6th ed. (Boston: Houghton Mifflin, 2003).

9. E. Flamholtz, "Organizational Control Systems as a Management Tool," *California Management Review,* Winter 1979, 50–58.

10. W. G. Ouchi, "The Transmission of Control through Organizational Hierarchy," *Academy of Management Journal* 21 (1978), 173–92.

11. W. G. Ouchi, "The Relationship between Organizational Structure and Organizational Control," *Administrative Science Quarterly* 22 (1977), 95–113.

12. Ouchi, "Markets, Bureaucracies, and Clans."

13. W. H. Newman, *Constructive Control* (Englewood Cliffs, NJ: Prentice-Hall, 1975).

14. J. D. Thompson, *Organizations in Action* (New York: McGraw-Hill, 1967).

15. R. N. Anthony, *The Management Control Function* (Boston: Harvard Business School Press, 1988).

16. eBay.com, 2010, 2012.

17. Ouchi, "Markets, Bureaucracies, and Clans."

18. Hill and Jones, *Strategic Management.*

19. R. Simons, "Strategic Orientation and Top Management Attention to Control Systems," *Strategic Management Journal* 12 (1991), 49–62.

20. G. Schreyogg and H. Steinmann, "Strategic Control: A New Perspective," *Academy of Management Review* 12 (1987), 91–103.

21. B. Woolridge and S. W. Floyd, "The Strategy Process, Middle Management Involvement, and Organizational Performance," *Strategic Management Journal* 11 (1990), 231–41.

22. J. A. Alexander, "Adaptive Changes in Corporate Control Practices," *Academy of Management Journal* 34 (1991), 162–93.

23. Hill and Jones, *Strategic Management.*

24. G.H.B. Ross, "Revolution in Management Control," *Management Accounting* 72 (1992), 23–27.

25. P. F. Drucker, *The Practice of Management* (New York: Harper & Row, 1954).

26. S. J. Carroll and H. L. Tosi, *Management by Objectives: Applications and Research* (New York: Macmillan, 1973).

27. R. Rodgers and J. E. Hunter, "Impact of Management by Objectives on Organizational Productivity," *Journal of Applied Psychology* 76 (1991), 322–26.

28. M. B. Gavin, S. G. Green, and G. T. Fairhurst, "Managerial Control—Strategies for Poor Performance over Time and the Impact on Subordinate Reactions," *Organizational Behavior and Human Decision Processes* 63 (1995), 207–21.

29. www.cypress.com, 2001, 2005, 2010.

30. B. Dumaine, "The Bureaucracy Busters," *Fortune,* June 17, 1991, 46.

31. D. S. Pugh, D. J. Hickson, C. R. Hinings, and C. Turner, "Dimensions of Organizational Structure," *Administrative Science Quarterly* 13 (1968), 65–91.

32. B. Elgin, "Running the Tightest Ships on the Net," *BusinessWeek,* January 29, 2001, 125–26.

33. P. M. Blau, *The Dynamics of Bureaucracy* (Chicago: University of Chicago Press, 1955).

34. www.ups.com, 2012.

35. walmart.com, 2012.

36. L. Brown, "Research Action: Organizational Feedback, Understanding and Change," *Journal of Applied Behavioral Research* 8 (1972), 697–711; P. A. Clark, *Action Research and Organizational Change* (New York: Harper & Row, 1972); N. Margulies and A. P. Raia, eds., *Conceptual Foundations of Organizational Development* (New York: McGraw-Hill, 1978).

37. W. L. French and C. H. Bell, *Organizational Development* (Englewood Cliffs, NJ: Prentice-Hall, 1990).

38. J. McGregor, "The World's Most Innovative Companies," www.businessweek.com, May 4, 2007.

39. R. Nakashima, "Iger: Disney to Reap $1 Billion Online," www.yahoo.com, March 11, 2008.

40. W. L. French, "A Checklist for Organizing and Implementing an OD Effort," in W. L. French, C. H. Bell, and R. A. Zawacki, eds., *Organizational Development and Transformation* (Homewood, IL: Irwin, 1994), 484–95.

Chapter 9

1. C. J. Loomis, "The Big Surprise Is Enterprise," *Fortune,* July 14, 2006, http://cnnmoney.printthis.clickability.com/pt/cpt?action=cpt&title=Fortune%3A+The+big . . . , March 31, 2008.

2. "Overview," *Enterprise Rent-A-Car Careers—Overview,* http://www.erac.com/recruit/about_enterprise.asp?navID=overview, March 27, 2008; "Enterprise Rent-A-Car Looks to Hire Student-Athletes, Partners with Career Athletes," April 25, 2012, http://www.enterpriseholdings.com/press-room/enterprise-rent-a-car-looks-to-hire-student- . . . , April 30, 2012; "About Enterprise—Customer service is our way of Life," http://aboutus.enterprise.com, April 19, 2013; "Enterprise Holdings—Alamo, Enterprise, National, Wecar," http://www.enterpriseholdings.com, April 9, 2013.

3. A. Fisher, "Who's Hiring New College Grads Now," *CNNMoney.com,* http://cnnmoney.printthis.clickability.com/pt/cpt?action=cpt&title=Who%27s+hiring+coll . . . , March 31, 2008; Francesca Di Meglio, "A Transcript for Soft Skills, Wisconsin Is Considering a Dual Transcript—One for Grades and One to Assess Critical Areas Such as Leadership and Communication," http://www.businessweek.com/print/bschools/content/feb2008/bs20080221_706663.htm, March 28, 2008; "Enterprise Rent-A-Car Career Site," http://www.erac.com/opportunities/default.aspx, May 1, 2012.

4. "Enterprise Ranked in Top 10 of Business Week's 'Customer Service Champs,'" Thursday, February 22, 2007, *Enterprise Rent-A-Car Careers*—Enterprise in the News, http://www.erac.com/recruit/news_detail.asp?navID=frontpage&RID=211, March 27, 2008; L. Gerdes, "The Best Places to Launch a Career, *Business Week,* September 24, 2007, 49–60; P. Lehman, "A Clear Road

to the Top," *Business Week,* September 18, 2006, 72–82.

5. Loomis, "The Big Surprise Is Enterprise"; "About Us," *Enterprise,* http://www.erac.com/pdf/ERAC_Fact_Sheet_2011_20110407120634.pdf, May 1, 2012; "Executive Bios," *Enterprise Holdings,* Press Room, http://www.enterpriseholdings.com/press-room/executive-bios, May 1, 2012, April 9, 2013.

6. "Enterprise Rent-A-Car's Pam Nicholson Named to FORTUNE's 50 Most Powerful Women in Business 2007," Monday, October 1, 2007, http://www.erac.com/recruit/news_details.asp?navID=frontpage&RID=234, March 27, 2008.

7. "Enterprise Ranked in Top 10"; L. Gerdes, "The Best Places to Launch a Career."

8. "It's Running a Business . . . Not Doing a Job," *Enterprise Rent-A-Car Careers— Opportunities,* http://www.erac.com/recruit/opportunities.asp, March 27, 2008.

9. Loomis, "The Big Surprise Is Enterprise"; Lehman, "A Clear Road to the Top."

10. Loomis, "The Big Surprise Is Enterprise"; Lehman, "A Clear Road to the Top."

11. Lehman, "A Clear Road to the Top."

12. Loomis, "The Big Surprise Is Enterprise."

13. Loomis, "The Big Surprise Is Enterprise"; Lehman, "A Clear Road to the Top."

14. J. A. Taylor Kindle, "Enterprise: Why We Give Where We Give," http://www.businessweek.com/print/investor/content/jun2007/pi20070628_339711.htm, March 28, 2008.

15. "Arbor Day Foundation, U.S. Forest Service to Plant 1 Million Trees with Gift from Enterprise Rent-A-Car Foundation," April 26, 2012, http://www.enterpriseholdings.com/press-room/arbor-day-foundation-us-forest-service-to- . . . , April 30, 2012.

16. Kindle, "Enterprise: Why We Give Where We Give."

17. M. Gunther, "Renting 'Green'? Not So Easy," Enterprise *CNNMoney.com,* "Enterprise-Rent-A-Car Goes Green, with Limits," January 17, 2008, http://cnnmoney.printthis.clickability.com/pt/cpt?action=cpt&title=Enterprise-Rent-A-Car . . . , March 3, 2008;

"Enterprise Rent-A-Car Announces Most Comprehensive Environmental Platform in Its Industry," Wednesday, June 06, 2007, *Enterprise Rent-A-Car Careers—Enterprise in the News,* http://www.erac.com/recruit/news_detail.asp?navID=frontpage&RID=221, March 27, 2008; "New Clean Technology: Hybrids," *Enterprise,* http://drivingfutures.com/innovation/, May 1, 2012; "Most Fuel-Efficient Fleet," *Enterprise,* http://drivingfutures.com/innovation/, May 1, 2012.

18. Gunther, "Renting 'Green'? Not So Easy."

19. Loomis, "The Big Surprise Is Enterprise"; Lehman, "A Clear Road to the Top."

20. R. Kanfer, "Motivation Theory and Industrial and Organizational Psychology," in M. D. Dunnette and L. M. Hough, eds., *Handbook of Industrial and Organizational Psychology,* 2nd ed., vol. 1 (Palo Alto, CA: Consulting Psychologists Press, 1990), 75–170.

21. G. P. Latham & M. H. Budworth, "The Study of Work Motivation in the 20th Century," in L. L. Koppes, ed., *Historical Perspectives in Industrial and Organizational Psychology* (Hillsdale, NJ: Laurence Erlbaum, 2006).

22. S. Clark, "Finding Daring Jobs for Bored Bankers," *Bloomberg Businessweek,* June 6–June 12, 2011.

23. Clark, "Finding Daring Jobs for Bored Bankers"; S. Clark, "Ex-Banker Wants You to Trade Wall Street 'Misery' for Mongolia," *Bloomberg,* May 26, 2011, http://www.bloomberg.com/news/print/2011-05-26/ex-banker-wants-you-to-trade-wall-stree. . . , May 1, 2012; S. Clark, "Finding Adventurous Jobs for Bored Bankers," *Businessweek,* June 2, 2011, http://www.businessweek.com/print/magazine/content/11_24/b4232053145331.htm, May 1, 2012; "Escape the City—Do something Different," http://www.escapethecity.org, April 9, 2013.

24. Team Esc, "How to Use Escape the City," November 24, 2011, http://blog.escapethecity.org/categories/how-to-use-escape-the-city/, May 1, 2012.

25. Clark, "Finding Daring Jobs for Bored Bankers."

26. Clark, "Finding Daring Jobs for Bored Bankers"; "The Team—Escape the City," http://escapethecity.org/pages/team, May 1, 2012.

27. Clark, "Finding Daring Jobs for Bored Bankers."

28. Ibid.

29. N. Nicholson, "How to Motivate Your Problem People," *Harvard Business Review,* January 2003, 57–65.

30. A. M. Grant, "Does Intrinsic Motivation Fuel the Prosocial Fire? Motivational Synergy in Predicting Persistence, Performance, and Productivity," *Journal of Applied Psychology* 93, no. 1 (2008), 48–58.

31. Grant, "Does Intrinsic Motivation Fuel the Prosocial Fire?"; C. D. Batson, "Prosocial Motiviation: Is It Ever Truly Altruistic?" in L. Berkowitz, ed., *Advances in Experimental Social Psychology,* vol. 20 (New York: Academic Press, 1987), 65–122.

32. Ibid.

33. J. P. Campbell and R. D. Pritchard, "Motivation Theory in Industrial and Organizational Psychology," in M. D. Dunnette, ed., *Handbook of Industrial and Organizational Psychology* (Chicago: Rand McNally, 1976), 63–130; T. R. Mitchell, "Expectancy Value Models in Organizational Psychology," in N. T. Feather, ed., *Expectations and Actions: Expectancy Value Models in Psychology* (Hillsdale, NJ: Erlbaum, 1982), 293–312; V. H. Vroom, *Work and Motivation* (New York: Wiley, 1964).

34. N. Shope Griffin, "Personalize Your Management Development," *Harvard Business Review* 8, no. 10 (2003), 113–119.

35. T. A. Stewart, "Just Think: No Permission Needed," *Fortune,* January 8, 2001 (www.fortune.com, June 26, 2001).

36. M. Copeland, "Best Buy's Selling Machine," *Business 2.0,* July 2004, 91–102; L. Heller, "Best Buy Still Turning on the Fun," *DSN Retailing Today* 43, no. 13 (July 5, 2004), 3; S. Pounds, "Big-Box Retailers Cash In on South Florida Demand for Home Computer Repair," *Knight Ridder Tribune Business News,* July 5, 2004 (gateway.proquest.com); J. Bloom, "Best Buy Reaps the Rewards of Risking Marketing Failure," *Advertising Age* 75, no. 25 (June 21, 2004), 16; L. Heller, "Discount Turns Up the Volume: PC Comeback, iPod Popularity Add Edge," *DSN Retailing Today* 43, no. 13 (July 5, 2004), 45; www.bestbuy.com, June 8, 2006.

37. T. J. Maurer, E. M. Weiss, and F. G. Barbeite, "A Model of Involvement in Work-Related Learning and Development Activity: The Effects of Individual, Situational, Motivational,

and Age Variables," *Journal of Applied Psychology* 88, no. 4 (2003), 707–24.

38. A. H. Maslow, *Motivation and Personality* (New York: Harper & Row, 1954); Campbell and Pritchard, "Motivation Theory in Industrial and Organizational Psychology."

39. Kanfer, "Motivation Theory and Industrial and Organizational Psychology."

40. S. Ronen, "An Underlying Structure of Motivational Need Taxonomies: A Cross-Cultural Confirmation," in H. C. Triandis, M. D. Dunnette, and L. M. Hough, eds., *Handbook of Industrial and Organizational Psychology,* vol. 4 (Palo Alto, CA: Consulting Psychologists Press, 1994), 241–69.

41. N. J. Adler, *International Dimensions of Organizational Behavior,* 2nd ed. (Boston: P.W.S. Kent, 1991); G. Hofstede, "Motivation, Leadership, and Organization: Do American Theories Apply Abroad?" *Organizational Dynamics,* Summer 1980, 42–63.

42. F. Herzberg, *Work and the Nature of Man* (Cleveland: World, 1966).

43. N. King, "Clarification and Evaluation of the Two-Factor Theory of Job Satisfaction," *Psychological Bulletin* 74 (1970), 18–31; E. A. Locke, "The Nature and Causes of Job Satisfaction," in Dunnette, *Handbook of Industrial and Organizational Psychology,* 1297–1349.

44. D. C. McClelland, *Human Motivation* (Glenview, IL: Scott, Foresman, 1985); D. C. McClelland, "How Motives, Skills, and Values Determine What People Do," *American Psychologist* 40 (1985), 812–25; D. C. McClelland, "Managing Motivation to Expand Human Freedom," *American Psychologist* 33 (1978), 201–10.

45. D. G. Winter, *The Power Motive* (New York: Free Press, 1973).

46. M. J. Stahl, "Achievement, Power, and Managerial Motivation: Selecting Managerial Talent with the Job Choice Exercise," *Personnel Psychology* 36 (1983), 775–89; D. C. McClelland and D. H. Burnham, "Power Is the Great Motivator," *Harvard Business Review* 54 (1976), 100–10.

47. R. J. House, W. D. Spangler, and J. Woycke, "Personality and Charisma in the U.S. Presidency: A Psychological Theory of Leader Effectiveness," *Administrative Science Quarterly* 36 (1991), 364–96.

48. G. H. Hines, "Achievement, Motivation, Occupations, and Labor Turnover in New Zealand," *Journal of Applied Psychology* 58 (1973), 313–17; P. S. Hundal, "A Study of Entrepreneurial Motivation: Comparison of Fast- and Slow-Progressing Small Scale Industrial Entrepreneurs in Punjab, India," *Journal of Applied Psychology* 55 (1971), 317–23.

49. R. A. Clay, "Green Is Good for You," *Monitor on Psychology,* April 2001, 40–42.

50. J. S. Adams, "Toward an Understanding of Inequity," *Journal of Abnormal and Social Psychology* 67 (1963), 422–36.

51. Adams, "Toward an Understanding of Inequity"; J. Greenberg, "Approaching Equity and Avoiding Inequity in Groups and Organizations," in J. Greenberg and R. L. Cohen, eds., *Equity and Justice in Social Behavior* (New York: Academic Press, 1982), 389–435; J. Greenberg, "Equity and Workplace Status: A Field Experiment," *Journal of Applied Psychology* 73 (1988), 606–13; R. T. Mowday, "Equity Theory Predictions of Behavior in Organizations," in R. M. Steers and L. W. Porter, eds., *Motivation and Work Behavior* (New York: McGraw-Hill, 1987), 89–110.

52. A. Goldwasser, "Inhuman Resources," *Ecompany.com,* March 2001, 154–55.

53. E. A. Locke and G. P. Latham, *A Theory of Goal Setting and Task Performance* (Englewood Cliffs, NJ: Prentice-Hall, 1990).

54. Locke and Latham, *A Theory of Goal Setting and Task Performance*; J. J. Donovan and D. J. Radosevich, "The Moderating Role of Goal Commitment on the Goal Difficulty–Performance Relationship: A Meta-Analytic Review and Critical Analysis," *Journal of Applied Psychology* 83 (1998), 308–15; M. E. Tubbs, "Goal Setting: A Meta Analytic Examination of the Empirical Evidence," *Journal of Applied Psychology* 71 (1986), 474–83.

55. E. A. Locke, K. N. Shaw, L. M. Saari, and G. P. Latham, "Goal Setting and Task Performance: 1969–1980," *Psychological Bulletin* 90 (1981), 125–52.

56. P. C. Earley, T. Connolly, and G. Ekegren, "Goals, Strategy Development, and Task Performance: Some Limits on the Efficacy of Goal Setting," *Journal of Applied Psychology* 74 (1989), 24–33; R. Kanfer and P. L. Ackerman, "Motivation

and Cognitive Abilities: An Integrative/ Aptitude–Treatment Interaction Approach to Skill Acquisition," *Journal of Applied Psychology* 74 (1989), 657–90.

57. W. C. Hamner, "Reinforcement Theory and Contingency Management in Organizational Settings," in H. Tosi and W. C. Hamner, eds., *Organizational Behavior and Management: A Contingency Approach* (Chicago: St. Clair Press, 1974).

58. "Our Story / Stella & Dot," http://www.stelladot.com/about, May 2, 2012, April 9, 2013; "Our History / Stella & Dot," http://www.stelladot.com/about/our-history, May 2, 2012.

59. B. Kowitt, "Full-Time Motivation for Part-Time Employees," *Fortune,* October 17, 2011: 58.

60. "Learn How to be a Jewelry+Accessories Stylist/Stella & Dot," "Training Program," http://www.stelladot.com/stylist/training-program, May 2, 2012.

61. Kowitt, "Full-Time Motivation for Part-Time Employees."

62. Ibid.

63. "How to be a Jewelry+Accessories Stylist ."

64. Kowitt, "Full-Time Motivation for Part-Time Employees."

65. B. F. Skinner, *Contingencies of Reinforcement* (New York: Appleton-Century-Crofts, 1969).

66. H. W. Weiss, "Learning Theory and Industrial and Organizational Psychology," in Dunnette and Hough, *Handbook of Industrial and Organizational Psychology,* 171–221.

67. Hamner, "Reinforcement Theory and Contingency Management."

68. A. Bandura, *Principles of Behavior Modification* (New York: Holt, Rinehart and Winston, 1969); A. Bandura, *Social Learning Theory* (Englewood Cliffs, NJ: Prentice-Hall, 1977); T.R.V. Davis and F. Luthans, "A Social Learning Approach to Organizational Behavior," *Academy of Management Review* 5 (1980), 281–90.

69. A. P. Goldstein and M. Sorcher, *Changing Supervisor Behaviors* (New York: Pergamon Press, 1974); F. Luthans and R. Kreitner, *Organizational Behavior Modification and Beyond* (Glenview, IL: Scott, Foresman, 1985).

70. Bandura, *Social Learning Theory;* Davis and Luthans, "A Social Learning Approach to Organizational Behavior";

Luthans and Kreitner, *Organizational Behavior Modification and Beyond.*

71. A. Bandura, "Self-Reinforcement: Theoretical and Methodological Considerations," *Behaviorism* 4 (1976), 135–55.

72. K. H. Hammonds, "Growth Search," *Fast Company,* April, 2003, 74–81.

73. B. Elgin, "Managing Google's Idea Factory," *BusinessWeek,* October 3, 2005, 88–90.

74. A. Bandura, *Self-Efficacy: The Exercise of Control* (New York: W.H. Freeman, 1997); J. B. Vancouver, K. M. More, and R. J. Yoder, "Self-Efficacy and Resource Allocation: Support for a Nonmonotonic, Discontinuous Model," *Journal of Applied Psychology* 93, no. 1 (2008), 35–47.

75. A. Bandura, "Self-Efficacy Mechanism in Human Agency," *American Psychologist* 37 (1982), 122–27; M. E. Gist and T. R. Mitchell, "Self-Efficacy: A Theoretical Analysis of Its Determinants and Malleability," *Academy of Management Review* 17 (1992), 183–211.

76. E. E. Lawler III, *Pay and Organization Development* (Reading, MA: Addison-Wesley, 1981).

77. P. Dvorak and S. Thurm, "Slump Prods Firms to Seek New Compact with Workers," *The Wall Street Journal,* October 19, 2009, A1, A18.

78. D. Mattioli, "Rewards for Extra Work Come Cheap in Lean Times," *The Wall Street Journal,* January 4, 2010, B7.

79. Mattioli, "Rewards for Extra Work Come Cheap"; http://www.rockwellcollins.com/, March 3, 2010.

80. Mattioli, "Rewards for Extra Work Come Cheap."

81. Ibid.

82. Lawler, *Pay and Organization Development.*

83. Ibid.

84. J. F. Lincoln, *Incentive Management* (Cleveland: Lincoln Electric Company, 1951); R. Zager, "Managing Guaranteed Employment," *Harvard Business Review* 56 (1978), 103–15.

85. Lawler, *Pay and Organization Development.*

86. M. Gendron, "Gradient Named 'Small Business of Year,' " *Boston Herald,* May 11, 1994, 35; Gradient—Environmental Consulting, http://www.gradientcorp.com/index.php, March 3, 2010.

87. W. Zeller, R. D. Hof, R. Brandt, S. Baker, and D. Greising, "Go-Go Goliaths," *BusinessWeek,* February 13, 1995, 64–70.

88. N. Byrnes, "A Steely Resolve" *BusinessWeek,* April 6, 2009, 54.

89. "Stock Option," *Encarta World English Dictionary,* June 28, 2001 (www.dictionary.msn.com); personal interview with Professor Bala Dharan, Jones Graduate School of Business, Rice University, June 28, 2001.

90. Personal interview with Professor Bala Dharan.

91. Ibid.

92. C. D. Fisher, L. F. Schoenfeldt, and J. B. Shaw, *Human Resource Management* (Boston: Houghton Mifflin, 1990); B. E. Graham-Moore and T. L. Ross, *Productivity Gainsharing* (Englewood Cliffs, NJ: Prentice-Hall, 1983); A. J. Geare, "Productivity from Scanlon Type Plans," *Academy of Management Review* 1 (1976), 99–108.

93. K. Belson, "Japan's Net Generation," *BusinessWeek,* March 19, 2001 (*BusinessWeek* Archives, June 27, 2001).

94. K. Belson, "Taking a Hint from the Upstarts," *BusinessWeek,* March 19, 2001 (*BusinessWeek* Archives, June 27, 2001); "Going for the Gold," *BusinessWeek,* March 19, 2001 (*BusinessWeek* Archives, June 27, 2001); "What the Government Can Do to Promote a Flexible Workforce," *BusinessWeek,* March 19, 2001 (*BusinessWeek* Archives, June 27, 2001).

Chapter 10

1. "Management Team," *Aricent Group,* http://www.aricent.com/about/management-team.html, May 14, 2012; "Management," *Frog,* http://www.frogdesign.com/about/management.html, May 14, 2012, April 11, 2013.

2. A. Bryant, "What's the Mission? Your Troops Want to Hear It From You," *The New York Times,* http://www.nytimes.com/2011/03/27/business/27corner.html?_r=1&pagewanted=print, May 14, 2012.

3. Ibid.

4. "Creative Change-Makers Invited to 'Reinvent Business' at Hackathon in San Francisco," May 9, 2012, http://www.frogdesign.com/archive/press-release/creative-change-makers-invited-reinvent . . . , May 14, 2012.

5. J. K. Glei, "Doreen Lorenzo: Clients Don't Deserve Surprises,"

http://the99percent.com/articles/6983/Doreen-Lorenzo-Clients-Dont-Deserve-Surprises/print, May 14, 2012; "Work," *frog,* http://frogdesign.com/work/, May 14, 2012.

6. Bryant, "What's the Mission?"; "About frog," *frog,* http://www.frogdesign.com/about, May 14, 2012; "Creative Change-Makers Invited to 'Reinvent Business.' "; Glei, "Clients Don't Deserve Surprises"; D. Lorenzo, "Why Conviction Drives Innovation More Than Creativity, *CNNMoney,* October 17, 2011, http://tech.fortune.cnn.com/2011/10/17/innovation-creativity/, May 14, 2012; "Work."

7. Bryant, "What's the Mission?".

8. Lorenzo, "Why Conviction Drives Innovation."

9. Ibid.

10 Bryant, "What's the Mission?"

11. Glei, "Doreen Lorenzo."

12. Ibid.

13. Bryant, "What's the Mission?"

14. Ibid.

15. Ibid.

16. Ibid.

17. G. Yukl, *Leadership in Organizations,* 2nd ed. (New York: Academic Press, 1989); R. M. Stogdill, *Handbook of Leadership: A Survey of the Literature* (New York: Free Press, 1974).

18. W. D. Spangler, R. J. House, and R. Palrecha, "Personality and Leadership," in B. Schneider and D. B. Smith, eds., *Personality and Organizations* (Mahwah, NJ: Lawrence Erlbaum, 2004), 251–90.

19. Spangler, et al., "Personality and Leadership"; "Leaders vs. Managers: Leaders Master the Context of Their Mission, Managers Surrender to It," www.msue.msu.edu/msue/imp/modtd/visuals/tsld029.htm, July 28, 2004; "Leadership," Leadership Center at Washington State University; M. Maccoby, "Understanding the Difference between Management and Leadership," *Research Technology Management* 43, no. 1 (January–February 2000), 57–59, www.maccoby.com/articles/UtDBMaL.html; P. Coutts, "Leadership vs. Management," www.telusplanet.net/public/pdcoutts/leadership/LdrVsMgnt.htm, October 1, 2000; S. Robbins, "The Difference between Managing and Leading," www.Entrepreneur.com/article/0,4621,304743,00.html, November 18, 2002; W. Bennis, "The

Leadership Advantage," *Leader to Leader* 12 (Spring 1999), www.pfdf.org/leaderbooks/121/spring99/bennis/html.

20. Spangler et al., "Personality and Leadership"; "Leaders vs. Managers"; "Leadership"; Maccoby, "Understanding the Difference between Management and Leadership"; Coutts, "Leadership vs. Management"; Robbins, "The Difference between Managing and Leading"; Bennis, "The Leadership Advantage."

21. "Greenleaf: Center for Servant Leadership: History," *Greenleaf Center for Servant Leadership,* www.greenleaf.org/aboutus/history.html, April 7, 2008.

22. "What Is Servant Leadership?" *Greenleaf: Center for Servant Leadership,* http://www.greenleaf.org/whatissl/index.html, April 2, 2008.

23. "What Is Servant Leadership?"; Review by F. Hamilton of L. Spears and M. Lawrence, *Practicing Servant Leadership: Succeeding through Trust, Bravery, and Forgiveness* (San Francisco: Jossey-Bass, 2004), in *Academy of Management Review* 30 (October 2005), 875–87; R. R. Washington, "Empirical Relationships between Theories of Servant, Transformational, and Transactional Leadership," *Academy of Management,* Best Paper Proceedings, 2007, 1–6.

24. "Greenleaf: Center for Servant Leadership: History"; "What Is Servant Leadership?"; "Greenleaf: Center for Servant Leadership: Our Mission," *Greenleaf Center for Servant Leadership,* www.greenleaf.org/aboutus/mission.html, April 7, 2008.

25. B. Burlingham, "The Coolest Small Company in America," *Inc.,* January 2003, www.inc.com/magazine/20030101/25036_Printer_Friendly.html, April 7, 2008; A. Weinzweig, "Step into the Future," *Inc.,* February 2011: 85–91.

26. Burlingham, "The Coolest Small Company in America"; "Zingerman's Community of Businesses," *About Us,* www.zingermans.com/AboutUs.aspx, April 7, 2008; L. Buchanan, "In Praise of Selflessness," *Inc.,* May 2007, 33–35; Zingerman's Community of Businesses, http://www.zingermanscommunity.com, March 3, 2010, April 11, 2013; D. Walsh, "No secrets: Businesses find it pays to open books to employees," *Crain's Detroit Business,* January 28, 2010, http://www.crainsdetroit.com/

article/20100117/FREE/301179994/no-secrets-businesses-fi. . . , May 17, 2012.

27. Burlingham, "The Coolest Small Company in America"; "Zingerman's Community of Businesses"; Buchanan, "In Praise of Selflessness."

28. Buchanan, "In Praise of Selflessness."

29. Ibid.

30. Burlingham, "The Coolest Small Company in America"; Food Gatherers, "In a Nutshell," http://www.foodgatherers.org/about.htm, April 7, 2008, March 3, 2010, May 17, 2012.

31. "In a Nutshell."

32. Buchanan, "In Praise of Selflessness."

33. R. Calori and B. Dufour, "Management European Style," *Academy of Management Executive* 9, no. 3 (1995), 61–70.

34. Calori and Dufour, "Management European Style."

35. H. Mintzberg, *Power in and around Organizations* (Englewood Cliffs, NJ: Prentice-Hall, 1983); J. Pfeffer, *Power in Organizations* (Marshfield, MA: Pitman, 1981).

36. R. P. French, Jr., and B. Raven, "The Bases of Social Power," in D. Cartwright and A. F. Zander, eds., *Group Dynamics* (Evanston, IL: Row, Peterson, 1960), 607–23.

37. C. Frey, "Nordstrom Salesman's Million-Dollar Secret Is in His Treasured Client List," *Seattle Post-Intelligencer,* Saturday, March 27, 2004, http://www.seattlepi.com/business/166571_retail27.html, March 5, 2010; "Macy's Herald Square, New York, NY: Retail Commission Sales Associate—Women's Shoes," http://jobview.monster.com/Macy's-Herald-Square-New-York-NY-Retail-Commission-Sale . . . , March 5, 2010.

38. R. L. Rose, "After Turning Around Giddings and Lewis, Fife Is Turned Out Himself," *The Wall Street Journal,* June 22, 1993, A1.

39. "Company Overview," *Liberty Media,* http://www.libertymedia.com/company-overview.aspx, May 17, 2012; "Management," *Liberty Media Corporation,* http://ir.libertymedia.com/management.cfm, May 17, 2012, April 12, 2013 "Gregory B. Maffei Profile," Forbes.com, http://people.forbes.com/profile/print/gregory-b-maffei/28822, May 17, 2012.

40. "Company Overview"; "Management" *Liberty;* "Gregory B. Maffei Profile."

41. "Management"; "Gregory B. Maffei Profile"

42. A. Bryant, "Take Me On, You Might Get a Promotion," *The New York Times,* January 9, 2011: BU2.

43. "Management"; "Gregory B. Maffei Profile."

44. Bryant, "Take Me On."

45. Ibid.

46. Ibid.

47. Ibid.

48. A. Grove, "How Intel Makes Spending Pay Off," *Fortune,* February 22, 1993, 56–61; "Craig R. Barrett, Chief Executive Officer: Intel Corporation," *Intel,* July 28, 2004, www.intel.com/pressroom/kits/bios/barrett/bio.htm; "Craig R. Barrett Bio," http://www.intel.com/pressroom/kits/bios/barrett.htm, March 3, 2010.

49. "Craig R. Barrett Bio," April 8, 2008; Microsoft Press Pass—Microsoft Board of Directors, www.microsoft.com/presspass/bod/default.mspx, April 8, 2008; "Tachi Yamada Selected to Lead Gates Foundation's Global Health Program," Announcements—Bill & Melinda Gates Foundation, February 6, 2006, www.gatesfoundation.org/GlobalHealth/Announcements/Announce-060106.htm, April 8, 2008; Microsoft PressPass—Microsoft Executives and Images, "Microsoft Board of Directors," http://www.microsoft.com/presspass/bod/bod.aspx, March 3, 2010; Tachi Yamada—Bill & Melinda Gates Foundation, http://www.gatesfoundation.org/leadership/Pages/tachi-yamada.aspx, March 3, 2010; "Microsoft PressPass—Microsoft Executives and Images," http://www.microsoft.com/en-us/news/exec/bod.aspx, May 17, 2012; L. Timmerman, "Tachi Yamada, Former Gates Foundation Leader, Joins Frazier for New VC Gig," http://www.xconomy.com/seattle/2011/06/27/tachi-yamada-former-gates-foundation-leade. . . , May 17, 2012.

50. M. Loeb, "Jack Welch Lets Fly on Budgets, Bonuses, and Buddy Boards," *Fortune,* May 29, 1995, 146.

51. T. M. Burton, "Visionary's Reward: Combine 'Simple Ideas' and Some Failures; Result: Sweet Revenge," *The Wall Street Journal,* February 3, 1995, A1, A5.

52. L. Nakarmi, "A Flying Leap toward the 21st Century? Pressure from Competitors and Seoul May Transform the Chaebol," *BusinessWeek,* March 20, 1995, 78–80.

53. B. M. Bass, *Bass and Stogdill's Handbook of Leadership: Theory, Research, and Managerial Applications,* 3rd ed. (New York: Free Press, 1990); R. J. House and M. L. Baetz, "Leadership: Some Empirical Generalizations and New Research Directions," in B. M. Staw and L. L. Cummings, eds., *Research in Organizational Behavior,* vol. 1 (Greenwich, CT: JAI Press, 1979), 341–423; S. A. Kirpatrick and E. A. Locke, "Leadership: Do Traits Matter?" *Academy of Management Executive* 5, no. 2 (1991), 48–60; Yukl, *Leadership in Organizations;* G. Yukl and D. D. Van Fleet, "Theory and Research on Leadership in Organizations," in M. D. Dunnette and L. M. Hough, eds., *Handbook of Industrial and Organizational Psychology,* 2nd ed., vol. 3 (Palo Alto, CA: Consulting Psychologists Press, 1992), 147–97.

54. E. A. Fleishman, "Performance Assessment Based on an Empirically Derived Task Taxonomy," *Human Factors* 9 (1967), 349–66; E. A. Fleishman, "The Description of Supervisory Behavior," *Personnel Psychology* 37 (1953), 1–6; A. W. Halpin and B. J. Winer, "A Factorial Study of the Leader Behavior Descriptions," in R. M. Stogdill and A. I. Coons, eds., *Leader Behavior: Its Description and Measurement* (Columbus Bureau of Business Research, Ohio State University, 1957); D. Tscheulin, "Leader Behavior Measurement in German Industry," *Journal of Applied Psychology* 56 (1971), 28–31.

55. E. A. Fleishman and E. F. Harris, "Patterns of Leadership Behavior Related to Employee Grievances and Turnover," *Personnel Psychology* 15 (1962), 43–56.

56. F. E. Fiedler, *A Theory of Leadership Effectiveness* (New York: McGraw-Hill, 1967); F. E. Fiedler, "The Contingency Model and the Dynamics of the Leadership Process," in L. Berkowitz, ed., *Advances in Experimental Social Psychology* (New York: Academic Press, 1978).

57. J. Fierman, "Winning Ideas from Maverick Managers," *Fortune,* February 6, 1995, 66–80; "Laybourne, Geraldine, U.S. Media Executive," *Laybourne, Geraldine,* http://museum.tv/ archives/etv/L/htmlL/laybournege/laybournege.htm, April 8, 2008.

58. M. Schuman, "Free to Be," *Forbes,* May 8, 1995, 78–80; "Profile—Herman Mashaba," *SAIE—Herman Mashaba,* www.entrepreneurship.co.za/page/herman_mashaba, April 8, 2008.

59. House and Baetz, "Leadership"; L. H. Peters, D. D. Hartke, and J. T. Pohlmann, "Fiedler's Contingency Theory of Leadership: An Application of the Meta-Analysis Procedures of Schmidt and Hunter," *Psychological Bulletin* 97 (1985), 274–85; C. A. Schriesheim, B. J. Tepper, and L. A. Tetrault, "Least Preferred Co-Worker Score, Situational Control, and Leadership Effectiveness: A Meta-Analysis of Contingency Model Performance Predictions," *Journal of Applied Psychology* 79 (1994), 561–73.

60. M. G. Evans, "The Effects of Supervisory Behavior on the Path–Goal Relationship," *Organizational Behavior and Human Performance* 5 (1970), 277–98; R. J. House, "A Path–Goal Theory of Leader Effectiveness," *Administrative Science Quarterly* 16 (1971), 321–38; J. C. Wofford and L. Z. Liska, "Path–Goal Theories of Leadership: A Meta-Analysis," *Journal of Management* 19 (1993), 857–76.

61. S. Kerr and J. M. Jermier, "Substitutes for Leadership: Their Meaning and Measurement," *Organizational Behavior and Human Performance* 22 (1978), 375–403; P. M. Podsakoff, B. P. Niehoff, S. B. MacKenzie, and M. L. Williams, "Do Substitutes for Leadership Really Substitute for Leadership? An Empirical Examination of Kerr and Jermier's Situational Leadership Model," *Organizational Behavior and Human Decision Processes* 54 (1993), 1–44.

62. Kerr and Jermier, "Substitutes for Leadership"; Podsakoff et al., "Do Substitutes for Leadership Really Substitute for Leadership?"

63. J. Reingold, "You Got Served," *Fortune,* October 1, 2007, 55–58; "News on Women," *News on Women: Sue Nokes SVP at T-Mobile,* http://newsonwomen.typepad.com/news_on_women/2007/09/sue-nokes-svp-a.html, April 8, 2008.

64. "Company Information," "T-Mobile Cell Phone Carrier Quick Facts," http://www.t-mobile/Company/CompanyInfo.aspx?tp=Abt_Tab_CompanyOverview, April 8, 2008; "T-Mobile Cell Phone Carrier Quick Facts," http://www.t-mobile.com/Company/CompanyInfo.aspx?tp=Abt_Tab_CompanyOverview, March 5, 2010; "T-Mobile Company Information / Quick Facts," http://www.t-mobile.com/Company/CompanyInfo.aspx?tp=Abt_Tab_CompanyOverview, May 17, 2012.

65. Reingold, "You Got Served."

66. Reingold, "You Got Served"; "Company Information," "Highest Customer Satisfaction & Wireless Call Quality—J.D. Power Awards," http://www.t-mobile.com/Company/CompanyInfo.aspx?tp=Abt_Tab_Awards, April 8, 2008.

67. Reingold, "You Got Served."

68. Ibid.

69. B. M. Bass, *Leadership and Performance beyond Expectations* (New York: Free Press, 1985); Bass, *Bass and Stogdill's Handbook of Leadership;* Yukl and Van Fleet, "Theory and Research on Leadership."

70. Reingold, "You Got Served."

71. Ibid.

72. Ibid.

73. Ibid.

74. Ibid.

75. Ibid.

76. J. A. Conger and R. N. Kanungo, "Behavioral Dimensions of Charismatic Leadership," in J. A. Conger, R. N. Kanungo, and Associates, *Charismatic Leadership* (San Francisco: Jossey-Bass, 1988).

77. Bass, *Leadership and Performance beyond Expectations;* Bass, *Bass and Stogdill's Handbook of Leadership;* Yukl and Van Fleet, "Theory and Research on Leadership;" Reingold, "You Got Served."

78. Ibid.

79. Reingold, "You Got Served."

80. Bass, *Leadership and Performance beyond Expectations.*

81. Bass, *Bass and Stogdill's Handbook of Leadership;* B. M. Bass and B. J. Avolio, "Transformational Leadership: A Response to Critiques," in M. M. Chemers and R. Ayman, eds., *Leadership Theory and Research: Perspectives and Directions* (San Diego: Academic Press, 1993), 49–80; B. M. Bass, B. J. Avolio, and L. Goodheim, "Biography and the Assessment of Transformational Leadership at the World Class Level," *Journal of Management* 13 (1987), 7–20;

J. J. Hater and B. M. Bass, "Supervisors' Evaluations and Subordinates' Perceptions of Transformational and Transactional Leadership," *Journal of Applied Psychology* 73 (1988), 695–702; R. Pillai, "Crisis and Emergence of Charismatic Leadership in Groups: An Experimental Investigation," *Journal of Applied Psychology* 26 (1996), 543–62; J. Seltzer and B. M. Bass, "Transformational Leadership: Beyond Initiation and Consideration," *Journal of Management* 16 (1990), 693–703; D. A. Waldman, B. M. Bass, and W. O. Einstein, "Effort, Performance, Transformational Leadership in Industrial and Military Service," *Journal of Occupation Psychology* 60 (1987), 1–10.

82. R. Pillai, C. A. Schriesheim, and E. S. Williams, "Fairness Perceptions and Trust as Mediators of Transformational and Transactional Leadership: A Two-Sample Study," *Journal of Management* 25 (1999), 897–933; "About us," HP, http://www8.hp.com/us/en/hp-information/about-hp/index.html, May 14, 2012.

83. "2000 Catalyst Census of Women Corporate Officers and Top Earners of the *Fortune* 500," www.catalyst women.org, October 21, 2001; S. Wellington, M. Brumit Kropf, and P. R. Gerkovich, "What's Holding Women Back?" *Harvard Business Review*, June 2003, 18–19; D. Jones, "The Gender Factor," USA *Today.com*, December 30, 2003; "2002 Catalyst Census of Women Corporate Officers and Top Earners in the *Fortune* 500," www.catalystwomen.org, August 17, 2004; "2007 Catalyst Census of Women Corporate Officers and Top Earners of the *Fortune* 500," www.catalyst.org/knowledge/titles/title/php?page=cen_COTE_07, February 8, 2008; "No News Is Bad News: Women's Leadership Still Stalled in Corporate America," December 14, 2011, *Catalyst,* http://www.catalyst.org/press-release/199/no-news-is-bad-news-womens-leadership-still-sta. . . , April 5, 2012.

84. "50 Most Powerful Women—1. Indra Nooyi (1)—*Fortune*," http://money.cnn.com/galleries/2009/fortune/0909/gallery.most_powerful_women.fortune/i . . . , March 5, 2010.

85. L. Tischler, "Where Are the Women?" *Fast Company*, February 2004, 52–60.

86. A. H. Eagly and B. T. Johnson, "Gender and Leadership Style: A Meta-Analysis," *Psychological Bulletin* 108 (1990), 233–56.

87. Eagly and Johnson, "Gender and Leadership Style: A Meta-Analysis."

88. The Economist, "Workers Resent Scoldings from Female Bosses," *Houston Chronicle*, August 19, 2000, 1C.

89. Ibid.

90. Ibid.

91. Ibid.

92. A. H. Eagly, S. J. Karau, and M. G. Makhijani, "Gender and the Effectiveness of Leaders: A Meta-Analysis," *Psychological Bulletin* 117 (1995), 125–45.

93. Ibid.

94. J. M. George and K. Bettenhausen, "Understanding Prosocial Behavior, Sales Performance, and Turnover: A Group-Level Analysis in a Service Context," *Journal of Applied Psychology* 75 (1990), 698–709.

95. T. Sy, S. Cote, and R. Saavedra, "The Contagious Leader: Impact of the Leader's Mood on the Mood of Group Members, Group Affective Tone, and Group Processes," *Journal of Applied Psychology* 90(2), (2005), 295–305.

96. J. M. George, "Emotions and Leadership: The Role of Emotional Intelligence," *Human Relations* 53 (2000), 1027–55.

97. George, "Emotions and Leadership."

98. J. Zhou and J. M. George, "Awakening Employee Creativity: The Role of Leader Emotional Intelligence," *The Leadership Quarterly* 14, no. 45 (August–October 2003), 545–68.

99. Ibid.

100. Ibid.

Chapter 11

1. D. Kesmodel, "Boeing Teams Speed Up 737 Output," *The Wall Street Journal*, February 7, 2012: B10; D. Gates, "Boeing Fetes Renton Workers for Higher 737 Output, *Seattle Times*, http://o.seattletimes.nwsource.com/html/businesstechnology/2017205845_boeing11.html, May 22, 2012.

2. Kesmodel, "Boeing Teams Speed Up 737 Output."

3. Ibid.

4. Ibid.

5. Ibid.

6. Ibid.

7. Ibid.

8. Ibid.

9. Gates, "Boeing Fetes Renton Workers"; S. Ray, "Boeing to Build MAX Next to Current 737 with Efficiency Push," *Bloomberg,* January 10, 2012, http://www.bloomberg.com/news/print/2012-01-10/being-will-build-max-model-alongside. . . , May 22, 2012; E. Olson, "Lucky Number 38!" http://www.boeing.com/feautures/2013/04/bca_rate-increase_04_16_13.html, April 17, 2013.

10. Kesmodel, "Boeing Teams Speed Up 737 Output"; C. Drew, "Boeing Lifts Forecast after a Strong Quarter," *The New York Times,* April 25, 2012, http://www.nytimes.com/2012/04/26/business/boeing-lifts-forecast-after-a-srong-quarter.h. . . , May 22, 2012.

11. T. M. Mills, *The Sociology of Small Groups* (Englewood Cliffs, NJ: Prentice-Hall, 1967); M. E. Shaw, *Group Dynamics* (New York: McGraw-Hill, 1981).

12. R. S. Buday, "Reengineering One Firm's Product Development and Another's Service Delivery," *Planning Review,* March–April 1993, 14–19; J. M. Burcke, "Hallmark's Quest for Quality Is a Job Never Done," *Business Insurance,* April 26, 1993, 122; M. Hammer and J. Champy, *Reengineering the Corporation* (New York: HarperBusiness, 1993); T. A. Stewart, "The Search for the Organization of Tomorrow," *Fortune,* May 18, 1992, 92–98; "Hallmark Corporate Information/About Hallmark," http://corporate.hallmark.com/Company, March 15, 2010; "Hallmark Corporate Information / Hallmark Facts," http://corporate.hallmark.com/Company/Hallmark-Facts, May 24, 2012.

13. "Amazon.com Investor Relations: Officers & Directors," http://phx.corporate-ir.net/phoenix.zhtml?c=97664&p=irol-govManage, June 19, 2006, April 18, 2013; "Amazon.com Investor Relations: Press Release," http://phx.corporate-ir.net/phoenix.zhtml?c=97664&p=irol-newsArticle&ID=1102342&hi. . . , April 17, 2008; "Amazon.com Investor Relations: Officers & Directors," http://phx.corporate-ir.net/phoenix.zhtml?c=97664&p=irol-govmanage_pf, March 14, 2010; "Amazon.com Investor Relations: Officers & Directors," http://phx.corporate-ir.net/phoenix.zhtml?c=97664&p=irol.govmanage, May 24, 2012.

14. R. L. Brandt, "Birth of a Salesman," *The Wall Street Journal*, October 15, 2011: C1-2.

15. A. Deutschman, "Inside the Mind of Jeff Bezos," *Fast Company*, August 2004, 50–58.

16. Deutschman, "Inside the Mind of Jeff Bezos"; "Amazon.com Digital Media Technology," http://media-server. amazon.com/jobs/jobs.html, June 19, 2006.

17. "Amazon.com: Kindle: Amazon's New Wireless Reading Device: Kindle Store," www.amazon.com/gp/product/B000F173MA/ref=amb_link_6369712_2?pf_rd_m=A. . . , April 17, 2008; "Amazon.com: Kindle Wireless Reading Device (6" Display, U.S. Wireless): Kindle Store," http://www.amazon.com/Kindle-Wireless-Reading-Device-Display/dp/B00154JDAI, March 15, 2010; "Kindle Touch 3G: Touchscreen e-Reader with Free 3G + Wi-Fi, 6" E Ink Display, 3G Wo. . . , http://www.amazon.com/gp/product/B005890G8O/ref=famstripe_kt3g, May 24, 2012.

18. Deutschman, "Inside the Mind of Jeff Bezos."

19. "Online Extra: Jeff Bezos on Word-of-Mouth Power," *BusinessWeek Online*, August 2, 2004, www.businessweek.com; R. D. Hof, "Reprogramming Amazon," *BusinessWeek Online*, December 22, 2003, www.businessweek.com; "About Amazon.com: Company Information," www.amazon.com/exec/obidos/tg/browsw/-/574562/104-0138839-3693547, June 19, 2006; "Amazon.com Investor Relations: Press Release."

20. "RockBottom Restaurants," www.rockbottom.com/RockBottomWeb/RBR/index.aspx?PageName=/RockBottom. . . , April 15, 2008; "Craft Works Restaurants & Breweries Inc.," http://www.craftworksrestaurants.com/executive.html, May 24, 2012.

21. S. Dallas, "Rock Bottom Restaurants: Brewing Up Solid Profits," *BusinessWeek*, May 22, 1995, 74.

22. J. A. Pearce II and E. C. Ravlin, "The Design and Activation of Self-Regulating Work Groups," *Human Relations* 11 (1987), 751–82.

23. B. Dumaine, "Who Needs a Boss?" *Fortune*, May 7, 1990, 52–60; Pearce and Ravlin, "The Design and Activation of Self-Regulating Work Groups."

24. Dumaine, "Who Needs a Boss?"; A. R. Montebello and V. R. Buzzotta, "Work Teams That Work," *Training and Development*, March 1993, 59–64.

25. C. Matlack, R. Tiplady, D. Brady, R. Berner, and H. Tashiro, "The Vuitton Machine," *BusinessWeek*, March 22, 2004, 98–102; "America's Most Admired Companies," *Fortune.com*, August 18, 2004, www.fortune.com/fortune/mostadmired/snapshot/0,15020,383,00.html; "Art Samberg's Ode to Steel," *Big Money Weekly*, June 29, 2004, http://trading.sina/com/trading/rightside/bigmoney_weekly_040629.b5.shtml; "Nucor Reports Record Results for First Quarter of 2004," www.nucor.com/financials.asp?finpage=newsreleases, August 18, 2004; "Nucor Reports Results for First Half and Second Quarter of 2004," www.nucor.com/financials.asp?finpage=newsreleases; J. C. Cooper, "The Price of Efficiency," *BusinessWeek Online*, March 22, 2004, www.businessweek.com/magazine/content/04_12/b3875603.htm; "LVHM—Fashion & Leather Goods," www.lvmh.com, June 18, 2006; C. Matlack, "Rich Times for the Luxury Sector," *BusinessWeek Online*, March 6, 2006, www.businessweek.com/globalbiz/content/mar2006/gb20060306_296309.htm?campaign_id=search; N. Byrnes, "The Art of Motivation," *BusinessWeek*, May 1, 2006, 56–62; "Nucor Steel," http://www.nucor.com/indexinner.aspx?finpage=aboutus, April 16, 2008, April 18, 2013; "Annual General Meetings—Group Investor Relations—Corporate Governance," http://www.lvmh.com/comfi/pg_home.asp?rub=6&srub=0, March 16, 2008; B. Sowray, "Louis Vuitton: the world's most valuable luxury brand," *Telegraph*, May 24, 2012, http://fashion.telegraph.co.uk/news-features/TMG9287478/Louis-Vuitton-the-world-most. . . , May 24, 2012; "Nucor Corporation / Our Story / Chapter 1: Corporate Overview," http://www.nucor.com/story/chapter1/, May 24, 2012; "Louis Vaitton, New, Now," http://www.louisvaitton.com/front, April 18, 2013.

26. Matlack et al., "The Vuitton Machine."

27. M. Arndt, "Out of the Forge and into the Fire," *BusinessWeek*, June 18, 2001, *BusinessWeek* Archives; Byrnes, "The Art of Motivation."

28. S. Baker, "The Minimill That Acts Like a Biggie," *BusinessWeek*, September 30, 1996, 101–104; S. Baker, "Nucor," *BusinessWeek*, February 13, 1995, 70; S. Overman, "No-Frills at Nucor," *HRMagazine*, July 1994, 56–60.

29. www.nucor.com, November 21, 2001; "Nucor: About Us."

30. Baker, "The Minimill That Acts Like a Biggie"; Baker, "Nucor"; Overman, "No-Frills at Nucor"; www.nucor.com; Byrnes, "The Art of Motivation"; "Nucor: About Us."

31. N. Byrnes, "A Steely Resolve," *BusinessWeek*, April 6, 2009, 54.

32. Matlack et al., "The Vuitton Machine"; "About Nucor"; "America's Most Admired Companies"; "Art Samberg's Ode to Steel"; "Nucor Reports Record Results for First Quarter of 2004"; "Nucor Reports Results for First Half and Second Quarter of 2004"; Byrnes, "The Art of Motivation."

33. T. D. Wall, N. J. Kemp, P. R. Jackson, and C. W. Clegg, "Outcomes of Autonomous Work Groups: A Long-Term Field Experiment," *Academy of Management Journal* 29 (1986), 280–304.

34. A. Markels, "A Power Producer Is Intent on Giving Power to Its People," *The Wall Street Journal*, July 3, 1995, A1, A12; "AES Corporation/The Power of Being Global," www.aes.com/aes/index?page=home, April 15, 2008.

35. W. R. Pape, "Group Insurance," *Inc.* (Technology Supplement), June 17, 1997, 29–31; A. M. Townsend, S. M. DeMarie, and A. R. Hendrickson, "Are You Ready for Virtual Teams?" *HR Magazine*, September 1996, 122–126; A. M. Townsend, S. M. DeMarie, and A. M. Hendrickson, "Virtual Teams: Technology and the Workplace of the Future," *Academy of Management Executive* 12, no. 3 (1998), 17–29.

36. Townsend et al., "Virtual Teams."

37. Pape, "Group Insurance"; Townsend et al., "Are You Ready for Virtual Teams?"; L. Gratton, "Working Together . . . When Apart," *The Wall Street Journal*, June 16–17, 2007, R4.

38. D. L. Duarte and N. T. Snyder, *Mastering Virtual Teams* (San Francisco: Jossey-Bass, 1999); K. A. Karl, "Book Reviews: *Mastering Virtual Teams*," *Academy of Management Executive*, August 1999, 118–19.

39. B. Geber, "Virtual Teams," *Training* 32, no. 4 (August 1995), 36–40; T. Finholt and L. S. Sproull, "Electronic Groups at Work," *Organization Science* 1 (1990), 41–64.

40. Geber, "Virtual Teams."

41. E. J. Hill, B. C. Miller, S. P. Weiner, and J. Colihan, "Influences of the Virtual Office on Aspects of Work and Work/Life Balance," *Personnel Psychology* 31 (1998), 667–83; S. G. Strauss, "Technology, Group Process, and Group Outcomes: Testing the Connections in Computer-Mediated and Face-to-Face Groups," *Human Computer Interaction,* 12 (1997), 227–66; M. E. Warkentin, L. Sayeed, and R. Hightower, "Virtual Teams versus Face-to-Face Teams: An Exploratory Study of a Web-Based Conference System," *Decision Sciences* 28, no. 4 (Fall 1997), 975–96.

42. S. A. Furst, M. Reeves, B. Rosen, and R. S. Blackburn, "Managing the Life Cycle of Virtual Teams," *Academy of Management Executive* 18, no. 2 (May 2004), 6–20.

43. Furst et al., "Managing the Life Cycle of Virtual Teams."

44. Gratton, "Working Together . . . When Apart."

45. Ibid.

46. Ibid.

47. Ibid.

48. A. Deutschman, "The Managing Wisdom of High-Tech Superstars," *Fortune,* October 17, 1994, 197–206.

49. J. S. Lublin, "My Colleague, My Boss," *The Wall Street Journal,* April 12, 1995, R4, R12.

50. R. G. LeFauve and A. C. Hax, "Managerial and Technological Innovations at Saturn Corporation," *MIT Management,* Spring 1992, 8–19.

51. B. W. Tuckman, "Developmental Sequences in Small Groups," *Psychological Bulletin* 63 (1965), 384–99; B. W. Tuckman and M. C. Jensen, "Stages of Small Group Development," *Group and Organizational Studies* 2 (1977), 419–27.

52. C. J. G. Gersick, "Time and Transition in Work Teams: Toward a New Model of Group Development," *Academy of Management Journal* 31 (1988), 9–41; C. J. G. Gersick, "Marking Time: Predictable Transitions in Task Groups," *Academy of Management Journal* 32 (1989), 274–309.

53. J. R. Hackman, "Group Influences on Individuals in Organizations," in M. D. Dunnette and L. M. Hough, eds., *Handbook of Industrial and Organizational Psychology,* 2nd ed., vol. 3 (Palo Alto, CA: Consulting Psychologists Press, 1992), 199–267.

54. Hackman, "Group Influences on Individuals."

55. Ibid.

56. L. Festinger, "Informal Social Communication," *Psychological Review* 57 (1950), 271–82; Shaw, *Group Dynamics.*

57. Hackman, "Group Influences on Individuals in Organizations"; Shaw, *Group Dynamics.*

58. D. Cartwright, "The Nature of Group Cohesiveness," in D. Cartwright and A. Zander, eds., *Group Dynamics,* 3rd ed. (New York: Harper & Row, 1968); L. Festinger, S. Schacter, and K. Black, *Social Pressures in Informal Groups* (New York: Harper & Row, 1950); Shaw, *Group Dynamics.*

59. T. F. O'Boyle, "A Manufacturer Grows Efficient by Soliciting Ideas from Employees," *The Wall Street Journal,* June 5, 1992, A1, A5.

60. Lublin, "My Colleague, My Boss."

61. T. Kelley and J. Littman, *The Art of Innovation* (New York: Doubleday, 2001)

62. Ibid.

63. "Shared Commitment," www. valero.com/Work/SharedCommitment. htm, April 18, 2008.

64. R. Levering and M. Moskowitz, "100 Best Companies to Work For: The Rankings," *Fortune,* February 4, 2008, 75–94.

65. J. Guyon, "The Soul of a Moneymaking Machine," *Fortune,* October 3, 2005, 113–20.

66. Ibid.

67. Ibid.

68. Ibid.

69. P. C. Earley, "Social Loafing and Collectivism: A Comparison of the United States and the People's Republic of China," *Administrative Science Quarterly* 34 (1989), 565–81; J. M. George, "Extrinsic and Intrinsic Origins of Perceived Social Loafing in Organizations," *Academy of Management Journal* 35 (1992), 191–202; S. G. Harkins, B. Latane, and K. Williams, "Social Loafing: Allocating Effort or Taking It Easy," *Journal of Experimental Social Psychology* 16 (1980), 457–65; B. Latane, K. D. Williams, and S. Harkins, "Many Hands Make Light the Work: The Causes and Consequences of Social Loafing," *Journal of Personality and Social Psychology* 37 (1979), 822–32; J. A. Shepperd, "Productivity Loss in Performance Groups: A Motivation Analysis," *Psychological Bulletin* 113 (1993), 67–81.

70. George, "Extrinsic and Intrinsic Origins"; G. R. Jones, "Task Visibility, Free Riding, and Shirking: Explaining the Effect of Structure and Technology on Employee Behavior," *Academy of Management Review* 9 (1984), 684–95; K. Williams, S. Harkins, and B. Latane, "Identifiability as a Deterrent to Social Loafing: Two Cheering Experiments," *Journal of Personality and Social Psychology* 40 (1981), 303–11.

71. S. Harkins and J. Jackson, "The Role of Evaluation in Eliminating Social Loafing," *Personality and Social Psychology Bulletin* 11 (1985), 457–65; N. L. Kerr and S. E. Bruun, "Ringelman Revisited: Alternative Explanations for the Social Loafing Effect," *Personality and Social Psychology Bulletin* 7 (1981), 224–31; Williams et al., "Identifiability as a Deterrent to Social Loafing"; Harkins and Jackson, "The Role of Evaluation in Eliminating Social Loafing"; Kerr and Bruun, "Ringelman Revisited."

72. M. A. Brickner, S. G. Harkins, and T. M. Ostrom, "Effects of Personal Involvement: Thought-Provoking Implications for Social Loafing," *Journal of Personality and Social Psychology* 51 (1986), 763–69; S. G. Harkins and R. E. Petty, "The Effects of Task Difficulty and Task Uniqueness on Social Loafing," *Journal of Personality and Social Psychology* 43 (1982), 1214–29.

73. B. Latane, "Responsibility and Effort in Organizations," in P. S. Goodman, ed., *Designing Effective Work Groups* (San Francisco: Jossey-Bass, 1986); Latane et al., "Many Hands Make Light the Work"; I. D. Steiner, *Group Process and Productivity* (New York: Academic Press, 1972).

Chapter 12

1. "Looking for Ideas in Shared Workspaces. Established Companies Hope Interaction with Others Will Spark Collaboration," *The Wall Street Journal* (http://www.zappos.com/ streetwear), March 20, 2012, http:// about.zappos.com/press-center/ media-coverage/looking-ideas-shared-workspaces-est . . ., April 23, 2012.

2. D. Garnick, "CEO Takes a Walk on the Whimsical Side," *Boston Herald,* Wednesday, May 20, 2009, http:// about.zappos.com/press-center/ media-coverage/ceo-takes-walk-whimsical-side, February 22, 2010; C. Palmeri, "Zappos Retails Its

Culture," *BusinessWeek,* December 30, 2009, http://www.businessweek.com/print/magazine/content/10_02/b4162057120453.htm, February 22, 2010; "On a Scale of 1 to 10, How Weird Are You?" *The New York Times,* January 10, 2010, http://www.nytimes.com/2010/01/10/business/10corner.html?pagewanted=print, February 22, 2010; M. Chafkin, "Get Happy," *Inc.,* May 2009, 66–73; "Keeper of the Flame," *The Economist,* April 18, 2009, 75; M. Rich, "Why Is This Man Smiling," *The New York Times,* April 8, 2011.

3. 100 Best Companies to Work For 2010: Zappos.com—AMZN—from FORTUNE, "15. Zappos.com," http://money.cnn.com/magazines/fortune/bestcompanies/2010/snapshots/15.html, February 22, 2010; "Zappos.com, Best Companies to Work For 2012," *Fortune,* http://money.cnn.com/magazines/fortune/best-companies/2012/snapshots/11.html, April 23, 2012; "Fortune 100 Best Companies to work For," http://money.cnn.com/magazines/fortune/best-companies/2013/list, April 19, 2013.

4. R. Wauters, "Amazon Closes Zappos Deal, Ends Up Paying $1.2 Billion," TechCrunch, November 2, 2009, http://techcrunch.com/2009/11/02/amazon-closes-zappos-deal-ends-up-paying-1-2-billion/, February 22, 2010.

5. J. McGregor, "Zappo's Secret: It's an Open Book," *BusinessWeek,* March 23 & 30, 2009, 62; "About.zappos.com," Tony Hsieh—CEO, http://about.zappos.com/meet-our-monkeys/tony-hsieh-ceo, February 22, 2010; Chafkin, "Get Happy."

6. Chafkin, "Get Happy"; "Keeper of the Flame."

7. "On a Scale of 1 to 10, How Weird Are You?"; Chafkin, "Get Happy."

8. Chafkin, "Get Happy."

9. Chafkin, "Get Happy"; "Keeper of the Flame."

10. In The Beginning—Let There Be Shoes/about.zappos.com, http://about.zappos.com/zappos-story/in-the-beginning-let-there-be-shoes, February 22, 2010; Looking Ahead—Let There Be Anything and Everything/about.zappos.com, http://about.zappos.com/zappos-story/looking-ahead-let-there-be-anything-and-everything, February 22, 2010; J. B. Darin, "Curing Customer Service," *Fortune,* May 20, 2009, http://about.zappos.com/press-center/media-coverage/curing-customer-service, February 22, 2010.

11. "Happy Feet—Inside the Online Shoe Utopia," *The New Yorker,* September 14, 2009, http://about.zappos.com/press-center/media-coverage/happy-feet-inside-online-shoe-utopia, February 22, 2010.

12. "Happy Feet—Inside the Online Shoe Utopia."

13. Chafkin, "Get Happy"; "Keeper of the Flame."

14. "After Zappos Hack, Some Online Shopping Safety Tips to Consider, January 17, 2012, http://news.consumerreports.org/electronics/2012/01/after-zappos-hack-some-online-shopp . . ., April 23, 2012; M.C. White, "Zappos Hacked: Expert Says You Need a Better Password," January 18, 2012, http://moneyland.time.com/2012/01/18/zappos-hacked-expert-says-you-need-a-better-pass . . ., April 23, 2012; T. Bradley, "Zappos Hacked: What You Need to Know," *PCWorld,* January 16, 2012, http://www.pcworld.com/printable/article/id,248244/printable.html, April 23, 2012; D. Goldman, "Zappos Hacked, 24 million Accounts Accessed," *CNNMoneyTech,* January 16, 2012, http://money.cnn.com/2012/01/16/technology/zappos_hack/index.htm, April 23, 2012; "Security Email," *Zappos.com,* http://blogs.zappos.com/securityemail, April 23, 2012; "Password Change," *Zappos.com,* http://www.zappos.com/passwordchange, April 23, 2012.

15. "Security Email," *Zappos.com,* http://blogs.zappos.com/securityemail, April 23, 2012.

16. Chafkin, "Get Happy"; "Keeper of the Flame."

17. "From Upstart to $1 Billion Behemoth, Zappos Marks 10 Years," *Las Vegas Sun,* Tuesday, June 16, 2009, http://about.zappos.com/press-center/media-coverage/upstart-1-billion-behemoth-zappos- . . ., February 22, 2010; Chafkin, "Get Happy"; "Keeper of the Flame."

18. Chafkin, "Keeper of the Flame"; "Get Happy."

19. Chafkin, "Get Happy."

20. 100 Best Companies to Work For 2010: Zappos.com; Chafkin, "Get Happy."

21. Chafkin, "Get Happy"; "Keeper of the Flame"; 100 Best Companies to Work For 2010: Zappos.com; "Zappos.com, Best Companies to Work for 2012," *Fortune,* http://money.cnn.com/magazines/fortune/best-companies/2012/snapshots/11.html, April 23, 2012; "Fortune 100 Best Companies to work For," April 19, 2013.

22. J. E. Butler, G. R. Ferris, and N. K. Napier, *Strategy and Human Resource Management* (Cincinnati: Southwestern Publishing, 1991); P. M. Wright and G. C. McMahan, "Theoretical Perspectives for Strategic Human Resource Management," *Journal of Management* 18 (1992), 295–320.

23. L. Clifford, "Why You Can Safely Ignore Six Sigma," *Fortune,* January 22, 2001, 140.

24. J. B. Quinn, P. Anderson, and S. Finkelstein, "Managing Professional Intellect: Making the Most of the Best," *Harvard Business Review,* March–April 1996, 71–80.

25. Quinn et al., "Managing Professional Intellect."

26. C. D. Fisher, L. F. Schoenfeldt, and J. B. Shaw, *Human Resource Management* (Boston: Houghton Mifflin, 1990).

27. Wright and McMahan, "Theoretical Perspectives."

28. L. Baird and I. Meshoulam, "Managing Two Fits for Strategic Human Resource Management," *Academy of Management Review* 14, 116–28; J. Milliman, M. Von Glinow, and M. Nathan, "Organizational Life Cycles and Strategic International Human Resource Management in Multinational Companies: Implications for Congruence Theory," *Academy of Management Review* 16 (1991), 318–39; R. S. Schuler and S. E. Jackson, "Linking Competitive Strategies with Human Resource Management Practices," *Academy of Management Executive* 1 (1987), 207–19; P. M. Wright and S. A. Snell, "Toward an Integrative View of Strategic Human Resource Management," *Human Resource Management Review* 1 (1991), 203–225.

29. Equal Employment Opportunity Commission, "Uniform Guidelines on Employee Selection Procedures," *Federal Register* 43 (1978), 38290–315.

30. R. Stogdill II, R. Mitchell, K. Thurston, and C. Del Valle, "Why AIDS Policy Must Be a Special Policy," *BusinessWeek,* February 1, 1993, 53–54.

31. J. M. George, "AIDS/AIDS-Related Complex," in L. Peters, B. Greer, and S. Youngblood, eds., *The Blackwell Encyclopedic Dictionary of Human Resource Management* (Oxford, England: Blackwell Publishers, 1997).

32. George, "AIDS/AIDS-Related Complex."

33. George, "AIDS/AIDS-Related Complex"; Stogdill et al., "Why AIDS Policy Must Be a Special Policy"; K. Holland, "Out of Retirement and into Uncertainty," *The New York Times,* May 27, 2007, BU17.

34. S. L. Rynes, "Recruitment, Job Choice, and Post-Hire Consequences: A Call for New Research Directions," in M. D. Dunnette and L. M. Hough, eds., *Handbook of Industrial and Organizational Psychology,* vol. 2 (Palo Alto, CA: Consulting Psychologists Press, 1991), 399–444.

35. "Kelly Services—Background," http://www.kellyservices.com/web/global/services/en/pages/background.html, April 24, 2012.

36. R. L. Sullivan, "Lawyers a la Carte," *Forbes,* September 11, 1995, 44.

37. E. Porter, "Send Jobs to India? U.S. Companies Say It's Not Always Best," *The New York Times,* April 28, 2004, A1, A7.

38. D. Wessel, "The Future of Jobs: New Ones Arise; Wage Gap Widens," *The Wall Street Journal,* April 2, 2004, A1, A5; "Relocating the Back Office," *The Economist,* December 13, 2003, 67–69.

39. The Conference Board, "Offshoring Evolving at a Rapid Pace, Report Duke University and The Conference Board," August 3, 2009, http://www.conference-board.org/utilities/pressPrinterFriendly.cfm?press_ID=3709, February 24, 2010; S. Minter, "Offshoring by U.S. Companies Doubles," *Industry Week,* August 19, 2009, http://www.industryweek.com/Print Article.aspx?ArticleID=19772&Section ID=3, February 24, 2010; AFP, "Offshoring by U.S. Companies Surges: Survey," August 3, 2009, http://www.google.com/hostednews/afp/article/ALeqM5iDaq1D2KZU16YfbKrM PdborD7 . . ., February 24, 2010; V. Wadhwa, "The Global Innovation Migration," *BusinessWeek,* November 9, 2009, http://www.businessweek.com/print/technology/content/nov2009/tc2009119_331698.htm, February 24, 2010; T. Heijmen, A. Y. Lewin, S. Manning, N. Perm-Ajchariyawong, and J. W. Russell, "Offshoring

Research the C-Suite," 2007–2008 ORN Survey Report, *The Conference Board,* in collaboration with Duke University Offshoring Research Network.

40. The Conference Board, "Offshoring Evolving at a Rapid Pace"; Minter, "Offshoring by U.S. Companies Doubles"; AFP, "Offshoring by U.S. Companies Surges"; V. Wadhwa, "The Global Innovation Migration"; Heijmen et al., "Offshoring Research the C-Suite."

41. V. Wadhwa, "The Global Innovation Migration."

42. The Conference Board, "Offshoring Evolving at a Rapid Pace."

43. The Conference Board, "Offshoring Evolving at a Rapid Pace"; Minter, "Offshoring by U.S. Companies Doubles"; AFP, "Offshoring by U.S. Companies Surges"; Heijmen et al., "Offshoring Research the C-Suite."

44. "Outsourcing: A Passage Out of India," *Bloomberg Businessweek,* March 19–March 25, 2012.

45. "Outsourcing: A Passage Out of India"; "IBM Research—Brazil," http://www.research.ibm.com/brazil/, April 25, 2012; "BRASSCOM Brazil Association of information Technology and Communication Companies," http://brasscomglobalitforum.com. April 19, 2013.

46. "Outsourcing: A Passage Out of India."

47. Ibid.

48. "Outsourcing: A Passage Out of India"; "Senior Management—Copal Partners," http://www.copalpartners.com/Senior%20Management, April 25, 2012.

49. "Outsourcing: A Passage Out of India."

50. Ibid.

51. Ibid.

52. R. J. Harvey, "Job Analysis," in Dunnette and Hough, *Handbook of Industrial and Organizational Psychology,* 71–163.

53. E. L. Levine, *Everything You Always Wanted to Know about Job Analysis: A Job Analysis Primer* (Tampa, FL: Mariner Publishing, 1983).

54. R. L. Mathis and J. H. Jackson, *Human Resource Management,* 7th ed. (Minneapolis: West, 1994).

55. Rynes, "Recruitment, Job Choice, and Post-Hire Consequences."

56. R. Sharpe, "The Life of the Party? Can Jeff Taylor Keep the Good Times Rolling at Monster.com?" *BusinessWeek,* June 4, 2001 (*BusinessWeek* Archives); D. H. Freedman, "The Monster Dilemma," *Inc.,* May 2007, 77–78; P. Korkki, "So Easy to Apply, So Hard to Be Noticed," *The New York Times,* July 1, 2007, BU16.

57. Jobline International—Resume Vacancy Posting, Employment Resources, Job Searches, http://www.jobline.net, February 25, 2010.

58. www.jobline.org, Jobline press releases, May 8, 2001, accessed June 20, 2001.

59. J. Spolsky, "There Is a Better Way to Find and Hire the Very Best Employees," *Inc.,* May 2007, 81–82; "About the Company," www.fogcreek.com, March 5, 2008; "Fog Creek Software," www.fogcreek.com, March 5, 2008; Fog Creek Software—About the company, http://fogcreek.com/About.html, February 25, 2010, April 19, 2013.

60. Spolsky, "Better Way to Find and Hire"; "Fog Creek Software."

61. Ibid.

62. Ibid.

63. Spolsky, "Better Way to Find and Hire"; "Intern in Software Development," http://www.fogcreek.com/jobs/summerintern.html, April 25, 2012.

64. Spolsky, "Better Way to Find and Hire."

65. Ibid.

66. Spolsky, "Better Way to Find and Hire"; "About the Company"; "Fog Creek Software."

67. Spolsky, "Better Way to Find and Hire."

68. R. M. Guion, "Personnel Assessment, Selection, and Placement," in Dunnette and Hough, *Handbook of Industrial and Organizational Psychology,* 327–97.

69. T. Joyner, "Job Background Checks Surge," *Houston Chronicle,* May 2, 2005, D6.

70. Joyner, "Job Background Checks Surge"; "ADP News Releases: Employer Services: ADP Hiring Index Reveals Background Checks Performed More Than Tripled since 1997," *Automatic Data Processing, Inc.,* June 3, 2006 (www.investquest.com/iq/a/aud/ne/news/adp042505background.htm); "Employee Benefits Administration," *ADP,* http://www.adp.com/, April 25, 2012.

71. "Background Checks and Employment Screening from ADP," http://www.adp-es.co.uk/employment-screening/?printpreview=1, April 25, 2012.

72. "ADP News Releases."

73. Noe et al., *Human Resource Management;* J. A. Wheeler and J. A. Gier, "Reliability and Validity of the Situational Interview for a Sales Position," *Journal of Applied Psychology* 2 (1987), 484–87.

74. J. Flint, "Can You Tell Applesauce from Pickles?" *Forbes,* October 9, 1995, 106–8.

75. Ibid.

76. "Wanted: Middle Managers, Audition Required," *The Wall Street Journal,* December 28, 1995, A1.

77. I. L. Goldstein, "Training in Work Organizations," in Dunnette and Hough, *Handbook of Industrial and Organizational Psychology,* 507–619.

78. "Disney Workplaces: Training & Development," *The Walt Disney Company,* 2010 Corporate Citizenship Report, http://corporate.disney.go.com/citizenship2010/disneyworkplaces/overview/trainingandde . . ., April 25, 2012.

79. N. Banerjee, "For Mary Kay Sales Reps in Russia, Hottest Shade Is the Color of Money," *The Wall Street Journal,* August 30, 1995, A8.

80. T. D. Allen, L. T. Eby, M. L. Poteet, E. Lentz, and L. Lima, "Career Benefits Associated with Mentoring for Protégés: A Meta-Analysis," *Journal of Applied Psychology* 89, no. 1 (2004), 127–36.

81. P. Garfinkel, "Putting a Formal Stamp on Mentoring," *The New York Times,* January 18, 2004, BU10.

82. Ibid.

83. Allen et al., "Career Benefits Associated with Mentoring"; L. Levin, "Lesson Learned: Know Your Limits. Get Outside Help Sooner Rather Than Later," *BusinessWeek Online,* July 5, 2004 (www.businessweek.com); "Family, Inc.," *BusinessWeek Online,* November 10, 2003 (www.businessweek.com); J. Salamon, "A Year with a Mentor. Now Comes the Test," *The New York Times,* September 30, 2003, B1, B5; E. White, "Making Mentorships Work," *The Wall Street Journal,* October 23, 2007, B11.

84. Garfinkel, "Putting a Formal Stamp on Mentoring."

85. J. A. Byrne, "Virtual B-Schools," *BusinessWeek,* October 23, 1995, 64–68;

Michigan Executive Education Locations around the Globe, http://exceed.bus.umich.edu/InternationalFacilities/default.aspx, February 25, 2010.

86. Fisher et al., *Human Resource Management.*

87. Fisher et al., *Human Resource Management;* G. P. Latham and K. N. Wexley, *Increasing Productivity through Performance Appraisal* (Reading, MA: Addison-Wesley, 1982).

88. J. S. Lublin, "It's Shape-Up Time for Performance Reviews," *The Wall Street Journal,* October 3, 1994, B1, B2.

89. J. S. Lublin, "Turning the Tables: Underlings Evaluate Bosses," *The Wall Street Journal,* October 4, 1994, B1, B14; S. Shellenbarger, "Reviews from Peers Instruct—and Sting," *The Wall Street Journal,* October 4, 1994, B1, B4.

90. C. Borman and D. W. Bracken, "360 Degree Appraisals," in C. L. Cooper and C. Argyris, eds., *The Concise Blackwell Encyclopedia of Management* (Oxford, England: Blackwell Publishers, 1998), 17; D. W. Bracken, "Straight Talk about Multi-Rater Feedback," *Training and Development* 48 (1994), 44–51; M. R. Edwards, W. C. Borman, and J. R. Sproul, "Solving the Double Bind in Performance Appraisal: A Saga of Solves, Sloths, and Eagles," *Business Horizons* 85 (1985), 59–68.

91. M. A. Peiperl, "Getting 360 Degree Feedback Right," *Harvard Business Review,* January 2001, 142–47.

92. A. Harrington, "Workers of the World, Rate Your Boss!" *Fortune,* September 18, 2000, 340, 342; www.ImproveNow.com, June 2001.

93. Lublin, "It's Shape-Up Time for Performance Reviews."

94. S. E. Moss and J. I. Sanchez, "Are Your Employees Avoiding You? Managerial Strategies for Closing the Feedback Gap," *Academy of Management Executive* 18, no. 1 (2004), 32–46.

95. J. Flynn and F. Nayeri, "Continental Divide over Executive Pay," *BusinessWeek,* July 3, 1995, 40–41.

96. J. A. Byrne, "How High Can CEO Pay Go?" *BusinessWeek,* April 22, 1996, 100–106.

97. A. Borrus, "A Battle Royal against Regal Paychecks," *BusinessWeek,* February 24, 2003, 127; "Too Many Turkeys," *The Economist,* November 26, 2005, 75–76; G. Morgenson, "How

to Slow Runaway Executive Pay," *The New York Times,* October 23, 2005, 1, 4; S. Greenhouse, *The Big Squeeze: Tough Times for the American Worker* (New York: Alfred A. Knopf, 2008); "Trends in CEO Pay," *AFL-CIO,* http://www.aflcio.org/Corporate-Watch/CEO-Pay-and-the-99/Trends-in-CEO-Pay, April 26, 2012.

98. "Executive Pay," *BusinessWeek,* April 19, 2004, 106–110.

99. "Home Depot Chief's Pay in 2007 Could Reach $8.9m," *The New York Times,* Bloomberg News, January 25, 2007, C7; E. Carr, "The Stockpot," *The Economist, A Special Report on Executive Pay,* January 20, 2007, 6–10; E. Porter, "More Than Ever, It Pays to Be the Top Executive," *The New York Times,* May 25, 2007, A1, C7.

100. K. Garber, "What Is (and Isn't) in the Healthcare Bill," *U.S. News & World Report,* March 22, 2010, http://www.usnews.com/articles/news/politics/2010/02/22/what-is-and-isnt-in-the-healthca . . ., March 29, 2010; S. Condon, "Health Care Bill Signed by Obama," Political Hotsheet-CBS News, http://www.cbsnews.com/8301-503544_162-20000981-503544.html, March 29, 2010; T. S. Bernard, "For Consumers, Clarity on Health Care Changes," *The New York Times,* March 21, 2010, http://www.nytimes.com/2010/03/22/your-money/health-insurance/22consumer.html?sq=h . . ., March 29, 2010; CBSNews.com, "Health Care Reform Bill Summary: A Look At What's in the Bill," March 23, 2009, http://www.cbsnews.com/8301-503544_162-20000846-503544.html, March 29, 2010; Reuters, "Factbox: Details of final healthcare bill", March 21, 2010, http://www.reuters.com/article/idUSTRE62K11V20100321, March 29, 2010.

101. E. Tahmincioglu, "Paths to Better Health (On the Boss's Nickel)," *The New York Times,* May 23, 2004, BU7.

102. Ibid.

103. S. Shellenbarger, "Amid Gay Marriage Debate, Companies Offer More Benefits to Same-Sex Couples," *The Wall Street Journal,* March 18, 2004, D1.

104. S. Premack and J. E. Hunter, "Individual Unionization Decisions," *Psychological Bulletin* 103 (1988), 223–34.

105. M. B. Regan, "Shattering the AFL-CIO's Glass Ceiling," *BusinessWeek,* November 13, 1995, 46; S. Greenhouse, "The Hard Work of Reviving Labor," *The New York Times,* September 16, 2009, pp. B1, B7.

106. S. Greenhouse, "Survey Finds Deep Shift in the Makeup of Unions," *The New York Times,* November 11, 2009, p. B5; "Union Members Summary," http://www.bls.gov/news.release/union2.nr0.htm, January 27, 2012, April 26, 2012, April 22, 2013.

107. www.aflcio.org, June 2001; About Us, AFL-CIO, http://www.aflcio.org/aboutus/, February 25, 2010, April 22, 2013.; S. Greenhouse, "Most U.S. Union Members Are Working for the Government, New Data Shows," *The New York Times,* January 23, 2010, http://www.nytimes.com/2010/01/23/business/23labor.html?pagewanted=print, February 25, 2010; "About the AFL-CIO," http://www.aflcio.org/About, April 27, 2012.

108. Greenhouse, "Most U.S. Union Members Are Working for the Government"; "Union Members Summary."

109. Greenhouse, "Survey Finds Deep Shift in the Makeup of Unions"; "Union Members Summary."

110. Greenhouse, "Most U.S. Union Members Are Working for the Government; "Union Members Summary."

111. G. P. Zachary, "Some Unions Step Up Organizing Campaigns and Get New Members," *The Wall Street Journal,* September 1, 1995, A1, A2.

Chapter 13

1. D. A. Kaplan, "Salesforce's Happy Workforce," *Fortune,* February 6, 2012: 101–12; "Salesforce Software: Welcome to the Social Enterprise," 2012 Annual Report, http://www2.sfdcstatic.com/assets/pdf/investors/AnnualReport.pdf.

2. Kaplan, "Salesforce's Happy Workforce"; "Salesforce Software"; "Trusted Clouds Apps and Platform for the Social Enterprise," http://www.salesforce.com/products/, May 30, 2012.

3. Kaplan, "Salesforce's Happy Workforce"; "Salesforce Service Cloud and Customers Take Home Four 2012 CRM Magazine Service Awards," http://www.salesforce.com/company/news-press/press-releases/2012/03/120319.jsp, May 30, 2012; "Salesforce Software: Welcome to the Social Enterprise," 2012 Annual Report, http://www2.sfdcstatic.com/assets/pdf/investors/AnnualReport.pdf.

4. "Salesforce Software."

5. "Salesforce.com Announces Fiscal 2013 First Quarter Results," http://www2.sfdcstatic.com/assets/pdf/investors/Q113_Earnings_Press_Release_w_financials.pdf, June 1, 2012.

6. Kaplan, "Salesforce's Happy Workforce"; "Careers #dreamjob," *Salesforce.com,* http://www.salesforce.com/careers/main/, June 5, 2012.

7. "What Does APP mean?"—APP Definition—Meaning of APP—InternetSlang.com, http://www.internetslang.com/APP-meaning-definition.asp, June 1, 2012.

8. Kaplan, "Salesforce's Happy Workforce."

9. Ibid.

10. Ibid.

11. Ibid.

12. Ibid.

13. Ibid.

14. Kaplan, "Salesforce's Happy Workforce"; "Salesforce Software."

15. N. B. Macintosh, *The Social Software of Accounting Information Systems* (New York: Wiley, 1995).

16. C. A. O'Reilly, "Variations in Decision Makers' Use of Information: The Impact of Quality and Accessibility," *Academy of Management Journal* 25 (1982), 756–71.

17. G. Stalk and T. H. Hout, *Competing against Time* (New York: Free Press, 1990).

18. R. Cyert and J. March, *Behavioral Theory of the Firm* (Englewood Cliffs, NJ: Prentice-Hall, 1963).

19. E. Turban, *Decision Support and Expert Systems* (New York: Macmillan, 1988).

20. W. H. Davidson and M. S. Malone, *The Virtual Corporation* (New York: Harper Business, 1992); M. E. Porter, *Competitive Advantage* (New York: Free Press, 1984).

21. S. M. Dornbusch and W. R. Scott, *Evaluation and the Exercise of Authority* (San Francisco: Jossey-Bass, 1975).

22. J. Child, *Organization: A Guide to Problems and Practice* (London: Harper & Row, 1984).

23. www.ups.com, 2010.

24. Macintosh, *The Social Software of Accounting Information Systems.*

25. www.cypress.com, 2010.

26. www.hermanmiller.com, 2010.

27. www.fortune.com, 2010.

28. www.boeing.com, 2010.

29. C. A. O'Reilly and L. R. Pondy, "Organizational Communication," in S. Kerr, ed., *Organizational Behavior* (Columbus, OH: Grid, 1979).

30. M. Totty, "The Path to Better Teamwork," *The Wall Street Journal,* May 20, 2004, R4; "Collaborative Software," *Wikipedia,* August 25, 2004, en.wikipedia.org/wiki/Collaborative_software; "Collaborative Groupware Software," www.svpal.org/grantbow/groupware.html, August 25, 2004.

31. Totty, "The Path to Better Teamwork"; "Collaborative Software."

32. Ibid.; "Collaborative Groupware Software."

33. Totty, "The Path to Better Teamwork"; "Collaborative Software."

34. Ibid.

35. Ibid.

36. E. M. Rogers and R. Agarwala-Rogers, *Communication in Organizations* (New York: Free Press, 1976).

37. W. Nabers, "The New Corporate Uniforms," *Fortune,* November 13, 1995, 132–56.

38. R. B. Schmitt, "Judges Try Curbing Lawyers' Body-Language Antics," *The Wall Street Journal,* September 11, 1997, B1, B7.

39. D. A. Adams, P. A. Todd, and R. R. Nelson, "A Comparative Evaluation of the Impact of Electronic and Voice Mail on Organizational Communication," *Information and Management* 24 (1993), 9–21.

40. R. Winslow, "Hospitals' Weak Systems Hurt Patients, Study Says," *The Wall Street Journal,* July 5, 1995, B1, B6.

41. C. Hymowitz, "Sometimes, Moving Up Makes It Harder to See What Goes On Below," *The Wall Street Journal,* October 15, 2007, B1.

42. Ibid.; J. Sandberg, "Shooting Messengers Makes Us Feel Better but Work Dumber," *The Wall Street Journal,* September 11, 2007, B1.

43. Hymowitz, "Sometimes, Moving Up Makes It Harder to See What Goes On Below"; "FatWire Software Appoints Former CA Executive Yogesh Gupta President and CEO," http://news.manta.com/press/description/200708070500230_66132700_1-0304, April 23, 2008.

44. "Management," *FatWire US: Company—Management,* www.fatwire.com/cs/Satellite/ManagementPage_US.html, April 23, 2008; "Company

Overview," *Company Overview—CA,* www. ca.com/us/ca.aspx, April 24, 2008.

45. Hymowitz, "Sometimes, Moving Up Makes It Harder to See What Goes On Below."

46. Ibid.

47. Ibid.

48. K. Holland, "The Silent May Have Something to Say," *The New York Times,* November 5, 2006, http://www. nytimes.com/2006/11/05/business/ yourmoney/05mgmt.html, June 29, 2008.

49. Ibid.

50. Ibid.

51. Ibid.

52. R. L. Daft, R. H. Lengel, and L. K. Trevino, "Message Equivocality, Media Selection, and Manager Performance: Implications for Information Systems," *MIS Quarterly* 11 (1987), 355–66; R. L. Daft and R. H. Lengel, "Information Richness: A New Approach to Managerial Behavior and Organization Design," in B. M. Staw and L. L. Cummings, eds., *Research in Organizational Behavior* (Greenwich, CT: JAI Press, 1984).

53. R. L. Daft, *Organization Theory and Design* (St. Paul, MN: West, 1992).

54. "Lights, Camera, Meeting: Teleconferencing Becomes a Time-Saving Tool," *The Wall Street Journal,* February 21, 1995, A1.

55. Daft, *Organization Theory and Design.*

56. T. J. Peters and R. H. Waterman Jr., *In Search of Excellence* (New York: Harper and Row, 1982); T. Peters and N. Austin, *A Passion for Excellence: The Leadership Difference* (New York: Random House, 1985).

57. "Lights, Camera, Meeting."

58. R. Kirkland, "Cisco's Display of Strength," *Fortune,* November 12, 2007, 90–100; "Cisco TelePresence Overview," Overview *(TelePresence)—Cisco Systems,* www.cisco.com/en/US/solutions/ ns669/networking_solutions_products_ genericcont. . ., April 25, 2008.

59. R. Kirkland, "Cisco's Display of Strength."

60. Ibid.; "Cisco TelePresence Overview."

61. "E-Mail Etiquette Starts to Take Shape for Business Messaging," *The Wall Street Journal,* October 12, 1995, A1.

62. E. Baig, "Taking Care of Business—Without Leaving the House," *BusinessWeek,* April 17, 1995, 106–7.

63. "Life Is Good for Telecommuters, but Some Problems Persist," *The Wall Street Journal,* August 3, 1995, A1.

64. "E-Mail Abuse: Workers Discover High-Tech Ways to Cause Trouble in the Office," *The Wall Street Journal,* November 22, 1994, A1; "E-Mail Alert: Companies Lag in Devising Policies on How It Should Be Used," *The Wall Street Journal,* December 29, 1994, A1.

65. "Employee-Newsletter Names Include the Good, the Bad, and the Boring," *The Wall Street Journal,* July 18, 1995, A1.

66. A. Overholt, "Intel's Got [Too Much] Mail," *Fast Company,* March 2001, 56–58.

67. Ibid.

68. Ibid.

69. See M. M. J. Berry and J. H. Taggart, "Managing Technology and Innovation: A Review," *R & D Management* 24 (1994), 341–53; K. B. Clark and S. C. Wheelwright, *Managing New Product and Process Development* (New York: Free Press, 1993).

70. V. P. Buell, *Marketing Management* (New York: McGraw-Hill, 1985).

71. See Berry and Taggart, "Managing Technology and Innovation."

72. M. Gort and J. Klepper, "Time Paths in the Diffusion of Product Innovations," *Economic Journal,* September 1982, 630–53. Looking at the history of 46 products, Gort and Klepper found that the length of time before other companies entered the markets created by a few inventive companies declined from an average of 14.4 years for products introduced before 1930 to 4.9 years for those introduced after 1949—implying that product life cycles were being compressed. Also see A. Griffin, "Metrics for Measuring Product Development Cycle Time," *Journal of Production and Innovation Management* 10 (1993), 112–25.

73. www.sgi.com, 2012.

74. A. D. Chandler, *The Visible Hand* (Cambridge, MA: Harvard University Press, 1977).

75. C. W. L. Hill and J. F. Pickering, "Divisionalization, Decentralization, and Performance of Large United Kingdom Companies," *Journal of Management Studies* 23 (1986), 26–50.

76. O. E. Williamson, *Markets and Hierarchies: Analysis and Anti-Trust Implications* (New York: Free Press, 1975).

77. www.fedex.com, 2009.

78. Turban, *Decision Support and Expert Systems.*

79. Ibid., 346.

80. Rich, *Artificial Intelligence.*

81. P. P. Bonisson and H. E. Johnson, "Expert Systems for Diesel Electric Locomotive Repair," *Human Systems Management* 4 (1985), 1–25.

Chapter 14

1. www.zynga.com, 2011, 2012.

2. The view of quality as including reliability goes back to the work of W. Edwards Deming and Joseph Juran. See A. Gabor, *The Man Who Discovered Quality* (New York: Times Books, 1990).

3. D. F. Abell, *Defining the Business: The Starting Point of Strategic Planning* (Englewood Cliffs, NJ: Prentice Hall, 1980).

4. M. E. Porter, *Competitive Advantage* (New York: Free Press, 1985).

5. This is a central insight of the modern manufacturing literature. See R. H. Hayes and S. C. Wheelwright, "Link Manufacturing Process and Product Life Cycles," *Harvard Business Review* (January–February 1979), 127–36; R. H. Hayes and S. C. Wheelwright, "Competing through Manufacturing," *Harvard Business Review* (January–February 1985), 99–109.

6. B. O'Brian, "Flying on the Cheap," *The Wall Street Journal,* October 26, 1992, A1; B. O'Reilly, "Where Service Flies Right," *Fortune,* August 24, 1992, 116–17; A. Salpukas, "Hurt in Expansion, Airlines Cut Back and May Sell Hubs," *The Wall Street Journal,* April 1, 1993, A1, C8.

7. www.fgx.com, 2010.

8. www.crm.com, 2012.

9. www.crm.com, 2006.

10. The view of quality as reliability goes back to the work of Deming and Juran; see Gabor, *The Man Who Discovered Quality.*

11. See also D. Garvin, "What Does Product Quality Really Mean?" *Sloan Management Review* 26 (Fall 1984),

25–44; P. B. Crosby, *Quality Is Free* (New York: Mentor Books, 1980); Gabor, *The Man Who Discovered Quality.*

12. www.jdpa.com, 2013.

13. www.starwood.com, 2012.

14. S.E. Ante, "Six Sigma Kick-Starts Starwood," www.businessweek.com, August 30, 2007.

15. Ibid.

16. J. Griffiths, "Europe's Manufacturing Quality and Productivity Still Lag Far behind Japan's," *Financial Times,* November 4, 1994, 11.

17. S. McCartney, "Compaq Borrows Wal-Mart's Idea to Boost Production," *The Wall Street Journal,* June 17, 1994, B4.

18. R. Gourlay, "Back to Basics on the Factory Floor," *Financial Times,* January 4, 1994, 12.

19. P. Nemetz and L. Fry, "Flexible Manufacturing Organizations: Implications for Strategy Formulation," *Academy of Management Review* 13 (1988), 627–38; N. Greenwood, *Implementing Flexible Manufacturing Systems* (New York: Halstead Press, 1986).

20. M. Williams, "Back to the Past," *The Wall Street Journal,* October 24, 1994, A1.

21. C. Salter, "This Is One Fast Factory," *Fast Company,* August 2001, 32–33.

22. G. Stalk and T. M. Hout, *Competing Against Time* (New York: Free Press, 1990).

23. For an interesting discussion of some other drawbacks of JIT and other "Japanese" manufacturing techniques, see S. M. Young, "A Framework for Successful Adoption and Performance of Japanese Manufacturing Practices in the United States," *Academy of Management Review* 17 (1992), 677–701.

24. T. Stundza, "Massachusetts Switch Maker Switches to Kanban," *Purchasing,* November 16, 2000, 103.

25. B. Dumaine, "The Trouble with Teams," *Fortune,* September 5, 1994, 86–92.

26. See C. W. L. Hill, "Transaction Cost Economizing, National Institutional Structures, and Competitive Advantage: The Case of Japan," *Organization Science* (1995),

119–31; M. Aoki, *Information, Incentives, and Bargaining in the Japanese Economy* (Cambridge: Cambridge University Press, 1989).

27. J. Hoerr, "The Payoff from Teamwork," *BusinessWeek,* July 10, 1989, 56–62.

28. M. Hammer and J. Champy, *Reengineering the Corporation* (New York: Harper Business, 1993), 35.

29. Ibid., 46.

30. Ibid.

31. For example, see V. Houlder, "Two Steps Forward, One Step Back," *Financial Times,* October 31, 1994, 8; Amal Kumar Naj, "Shifting Gears," *The Wall Street Journal,* May 7, 1993, A1; D. Greising, "Quality: How to Make It Pay," *BusinessWeek,* August 8, 1994, 54–59.

32. L. Helm and M. Edid, "Life on the Line: Two Auto Workers Who Are Worlds Apart," *BusinessWeek,* September 30, 1994, 76–78.

33. Dumaine, "The Trouble with Teams."

Photo Credits

Chapter 1

Opener: Kimihiro Hoshino/AFP/ Getty Images; 9: AP Photo; 10: Michael Nagle/ Getty Images; 12: Mark Peterson/Redux Pictures, NYC; 20: ©Dan Lamont/ Alamy; 21: Scott Olson/Getty Images; 27: AP Photo/Mark Moran/The Citizen's Voice; 28: Courtesy Accenture; 29: Photo by James Berglie/ZUMA Press (©) Copyright 2006 by James Berglie; 37: Bettmann/Corbis; 39: The Granger Collection, New York; 40: With permission from Henley Management College; 41: Fox Photos/Getty Images.

Chapter 2

Opener:© David Yellen/Corbis; 52: © Digital Vision; 56: Motor Trend - http://www.trucktrend.com/features/ travel/163_1107_touring_subaru_of_ indiana_automotive_inc/photo_03. html; 58: © Jon Feingersh/Blend Images LLC; 61: OJO Images/Getty Images; 65: Courtesy IDEO; 69: © Orjan F. Ellingvag/Dagbladet/Corbis.

Chapter 3

Opener: AP Photo; 82: The Granger Collection, New York; 85: Spencer Platt/ Getty Images; 98: Cultura Limited/ Getty Images; 99: © Color Blind Images/Blend Images LLC; 102: Tannis Toohey/TorontoStar/ZUMA Press/ Newscom; 104: Yellow Dog Productions/ Getty Images; 106: © Mikkel Baekhoj Christensen/De/Demotix/Corbis.

Chapter 4

Opener: Copyright © Nokia 2010; 124: AP Photo/The News Tribune, Lui Kit Wong; 125: Simon Dawson/Bloomberg via Getty Images; 129: AP Photo/Itsuo Inouye; 132: Getty Images; 137: AP Photo/Matt Houston; 145: Comstock/Getty Images; 147: David Becker/Getty Images.

Chapter 5

Opener: Courtesy GarageTek, Inc.; 157: AP Photo/Nati Harnik; 158:

AP Photo; 167: Chip East/Reuters/ Corbis; 169: © Digital Vision/ PunchStock; 172: Morgan Lane Photography/Alamy; 176: Radius Images/Getty Images.

Chapter 6

Opener: Courtesy of Cott Corporation; 188: Ryan McVay/Getty Images; 196: AP Photo/Mel Evans; 202: Bloomberg via Getty Images; 207: Bill Varie/Corbis; 208: Art Directors & TRIP/Alamy; 211(left): AP Photo/Kasumi Kasahara; 211(right): Pablo Bartholomew/Getty News/Liaison.

Chapter 7

Opener: Courtesy of Avon; 228: Jeffery Allan Salter/Corbis; 229: Seattlepi.com; 234: Tim Boyle/Getty Images; 236: Kim Steele/Photodisc/Green/Getty Images; 241: AP Photo/Orlin Wagner; 250: AP Photo.

Chapter 8

Opener: Fabrizio Costantini/The New York Times/Redux Pictures; 262: © Vario Images GmbH & Company/ Alamy; 267: Tony Avelar/Bloomberg via Getty Images; 271: AP Photo/Harry Cabluck; 280: ZUMA Press/Newscom; 285: Felix Clay/Financial Times-REA/ Redux Pictures.

Chapter 9

Opener: AP Photo/Carlos Osorio; 300: Simon Dawson/Bloomberg via Getty Images; 301: © LWA/Dan Tardiff/Blend Images/Corbis; 306: Jim Esposito/Blend Images; 311: Stockbyte/ PunchStock; 313: Courtesy Stella & Dot; 316: © Vario Images GmbH & Company/Alamy.

Chapter 10

Opener: Benjamin Sklar/The New York Times/Redux Pictures; 331: Courtesy Zingerman's; 334: Matthew Staver/The New York Times/Redux Pictures; 336:

Yun Suk Bong/Reuters/Corbis; 342: © Stockbyte/Getty Images; 345: D. Clarke Evans/NBAE via Getty Images.

Chapter 11

Opener: © Stephen Brashear/Getty Images; 360: image100/Alamy; 361: Brand X Pictures/PunchStock; 364: Comstock Images/Picture Quest; 366: AP Photo/Alexandra Boulet VII; 368: David P. Hall/Corbis; 376: hana/ Datacraft/Getty Images.

Chapter 12

Opener: Ronda Churchill/Bloomberg via Getty Images; 395: © David Pearson/ Alamy; 396: Amy Etra/PhotoEdit, Inc.; 397: Courtesy Fog Creek Software; 399: Cabruken/Taxi/Getty Images; 400: © Corbis Bridge/Alamy; 402: Fuse/Getty Images; 403: Reza Estakhrian/Getty Images/Photographers Choice; 408: Helen Ashford/Workbook Stock/Getty Images.

Chapter 13

Opener: © David Paul Morris/ Bloomberg via Getty Images; 425: Bill Freeman/PhotoEdit, Inc.; 427: Courtesy Herman Miller, Inc.; 431: Christopher Robbins/Digital Vision/Getty Images; 435: Digital Vision/Getty Images; 437: Copyright 2008 NBAE., Photo by Jennifer Pottheiser/NBAE via Getty Images; 441: Lourens Smak/Alamy; 443: Courtesy of Sun Microsystems.

Chapter 14

Opener: John Lee/Aurora Photos/ Corbis; 458: AP Photo; 460: Andy Sotiriou/Photodisc/Getty Images; 463: Corbis; 469: Courtesy Dell Computer; 472: Justin Sullivan/Getty Images; 480: Gail Albert Halaban/Corbis.

Index

Names

Subject

Company